Corporate Liability:
Work Related Deaths
and Criminal Prosecutions

Corporate Liability:
Work Related Deaths
and Criminal Prosecutions

General editor

Gerard Forlin

Editor

Michael Appleby

With specialist contributors

 LexisNexis™ UK

Members of the LexisNexis Group worldwide

United Kingdom	LexisNexis UK, a Division of Reed Elsevier (UK) Ltd, Halsbury House, 35 Chancery Lane, LONDON, WC2A 1EL, and 4 Hill Street, EDINBURGH EH2 3JZ
Argentina	LexisNexis Argentina, BUENOS AIRES
Australia	LexisNexis Butterworths, CHATSWOOD, New South Wales
Austria	LexisNexis Verlag ARD Orac GmbH & Co KG, VIENNA
Canada	LexisNexis Butterworths, MARKHAM, Ontario
Chile	LexisNexis Chile Ltda, SANTIAGO DE CHILE
Czech Republic	Nakladatelství Orac sro, PRAGUE
France	Editions du Juris-Classeur SA, PARIS
Germany	LexisNexis Deutschland GmbH, FRANKFURT, MUNSTER
Hong Kong	LexisNexis Butterworths, HONG KONG
Hungary	HVG-Orac, BUDAPEST
India	LexisNexis Butterworths, NEW DELHI
Ireland	LexisNexis, DUBLIN
Italy	Giuffrè Editore, MILAN
Malaysia	Malayan Law Journal Sdn Bhd, KUALA LUMPUR
New Zealand	LexisNexis Butterworths, WELLINGTON
Poland	Wydawnictwo Prawnicze LexisNexis, WARSAW
Singapore	LexisNexis Butterworths, SINGAPORE
South Africa	LexisNexis Butterworths, DURBAN
Switzerland	Stämpfli Verlag AG, BERNE
USA	LexisNexis, DAYTON, Ohio

© Reed Elsevier (UK) Ltd 2003

A CIP Catalogue record for this book is available from the British Library.

ISBN 0 406 93176 3

Typeset by Doyle & Co, Colchester
Printed and bound in Great Britain by Hobbs the Printers Ltd, Totton, Hampshire

Visit LexisNexis UK at www.lexisnexis.co.uk

Foreword by
the Rt Hon The Lord Cullen of Whitekirk

Over the last thirty years increasing emphasis has been placed on the legal responsibility of companies for managing the safety of their employees and of those who may be affected by their activities. Under the statutory regime which was introduced by the Health and Safety at Work etc Act 1974 this has been given positive expression in the introduction of regulations which set general safety goals for companies rather than prescribing particular safety precautions for them to take. Thus companies have to demonstrate that they have assessed the relevant risks and decided how they are to be dealt with, and on a continuing basis. All this is to put the responsibility clearly on the shoulders of those by whom the risks are created.

At the same time it is clear that there are matters in regard to which legal regulation has to be prescriptive in its demands, and it is unthinkable that it would be otherwise. Furthermore, the law has to provide sanctions for clear failures in the management of safety. In this respect the law has perhaps not been fully effective – or is perceived not to have been. Failures in the management of safety can have serious and even disastrous consequences, and it is right that they should be the concern of the criminal law. There has been an evident growth in public expectations. The scale of penalties for statutory offences, and the use which is made of them by the courts, need to be adequate to maintain public confidence. Owing to the courts' adherence to the principle of identification (*Attorney-General's Reference (No 2 of 1999)* [2000] QB 796) the scope for establishing guilt of corporate manslaughter is limited. The position in Scotland in regard to culpable homicide is essentially the same. It remains to be seen whether the recent legislative proposals for a crime of corporate manslaughter will lead to a workable, suitable and sufficient means of filling what many perceive to be a regrettable gap in the law.

It is a privilege and a pleasure for me to welcome this comprehensive and thorough guide to an important and topical area of the law which has undergone, and is undergoing, significant change. Readers will find in this book a wealth of information and a valuable resource.

Preface

The idea for this book came about some seven years ago in early 1997, just after the acquittal of my client Peter Afford, the train driver charged with manslaughter over the Watford train crash in 1996.

Since then I have been fortunate enough to be involved in many of the highest profile Manslaughter, Heath and Safety and Disaster Inquires and cases both in the UK and abroad.

In approximately 2000 after I went to LexisNexis with the idea, I was commissioned to write the book and I set about assembling a number of contributors from various industry sectors.

It is true to say that the whole process has taken much longer than I initially thought and so in August 2002 I asked Mike Appleby whether he would help me in this extremely time-consuming task.

Since 1997, despite many promises and desk banging by the government to honour their 1997 Manifesto commitment to introduce corporate killing, it still remains but a promise.

From a personal legal point of view, I sincerely hope that the government will not introduce any personal liability provisions, as the current law of gross negligence manslaughter (and ss 7 and 37 of the Health and Safety at Work etc Act 1974) is more than sufficient. Where I think change is needed to step around the current perceived difficulties of aggregation and identification in big companies is to introduce the concept of management failure which should only be prosecuted in clear instances where profit has been put before safety.

Although the corporate killing bill was not in the Queen's Speech 2003, it would appear clear that there will be a draft bill in late December 2003 or early 2004 which sources tell me will culminate in legislation before the next election in 2005.

The reason why the bill is being put out again for consultation is allegedly to iron out certain outstanding issues including Crown immunity and Unincorporated Associations being able to be prosecuted. We will just have to wait and see!

In the meantime, more individuals and companies are being prosecuted by the CPS and HSE than ever before and I predict that this trend will increase and accelerate over the coming years.

Given the whole issue of Corporate Governance has become generally much higher profile, including the recent mention in the Queen's Speech of new laws to tighten auditing rules and strengthen powers to investigate companies, the issues of workplace deaths and criminal prosecutions will not go away.

I thank Lord Cullen for agreeing to provide the foreword. Anyone who has appeared before him, which I was lucky enough to do at the Paddington Train Crash Public Inquiry, cannot be anything but greatly impressed by both his clarity of thought and great politeness. I am very grateful!

I thank all the staff at LexisNexis UK, who throughout the germination of this book have been fantastic.

I would also like to thank all the many contributors to this book. They managed to find time in their already extremely busy schedules, and great credit should go to them for their excellent contributions.

I thank my family, friends and colleagues who have encouraged me to keep going when things have been extremely busy at the Bar.

Finally, last but by no means least, I thank Mike Appleby for all his enthusiasm, care, time and great skill. Not only was he one of the first solicitors to give me a chance when I came back to the Bar in 1996 from practising and lecturing abroad, but he has become a greatly trusted and valued personal friend. I owe him much!

The law is to the best of all our ability up to date as of 1 December 2003. There will be many changes to it in the coming months and years, of that I am certain!

Gerard Forlin
2–3 Gray's Inn Square
Gray's Inn
London
WC1R 5JH
1 December 2003

The contributors

General Editor

Gerard Forlin, Barrister, 2-3 Gray's Inn Square, is a leading barrister specialising in manslaughter, health and safety, disaster litigation, aviation, regulatory and disciplinary offences, human rights, inquests and public inquiries. Described in the 2004 *Chambers Directory* as 'exuberant' and an 'excellent orator and natural advocate', he has also been named 'the manslaughter guy' since over half of his practice is in this area. He writes and lectures extensively and is co-author with Michael Appleby (below) in many publications including the legal chapter in *Tolley's Handbook of Disaster and Emergency Management: Principles and Practice* (2002) and a chapter in *Licensed Premises: Law & Practice* (2004).

Editor

Michael Appleby, Solicitor, joined Fisher Scoggins LLP in 2003 to concentrate on acting for companies and individuals in relation to manslaughter prosecutions and health and safety. Michael defended the two train drivers involved in the Watford and Southall train crashes. He represented the train drivers' union ASLEF at the public inquiries that followed the Southall and Ladbroke Grove crashes. He frequently writes and lectures on health and safety issues and writes a regular column for *Safety and Health Practitioner*.

Contributors

John Abramson is a solicitor and regional counsel for a global insurance group. While in private practice in London, he specialised in aviation insurance and corporate liability matters. He has been a regular speaker at industry seminars and conferences and has written numerous articles on aspects of these subjects. The views expressed in his chapter are his own.

Kiran Bhogal was a partner at Wansbroughs Willey Hargrave and then following a merger with Beachcroft Stanleys 1999 became a partner in healthcare law. Qualified as an Advocate (Kenya), Kiran has extensive knowledge and experience in dealing with medico-legal issues, eg coroner's inquests, children and Mental Health Acts, child protection matters, risk management, untoward incidents, clinical and corporate governance, patient care issues (including consent, confidentiality, complaints handling, declarations of treatment), judicial review, Human Rights Act, Data Protection Act as well as advising on a wide range of other health and public sector issues such as care in the community and primary care services including the management of practitioners. Kiran was assisted in the preparation of the Healthcare chapter by **Andrew Stokes**.

Dr John Bond is a Chartered Chemist and Chartered Engineer, Fellow of the Royal Society of Chemistry and Fellow of the Institution of Chemical Engineers. He spent 45 years in development, operation and auditing for safety in the chemical industry, and worked for BP Chemicals Ltd before he retired. He is author of two books: *Sources of Ignition* and *Hazard of Life and all that.*

Michael Elliker LLB(Lond) 1971 was articled with Booth and Co, Leeds before being admitted as a solicitor in 1974. He is a Legal Director with Addleshaw Goddard and is a solicitor-advocate (with higher rights of audience – criminal). He now deals exclusively with 'white collar' crime – being manslaughter, health and safety, trading standards and environmental matters. He is on the approved panel to prosecute for the Health and Safety Executive in this area. The views expressed in his chapter are his own.

Robert Elvin is a partner at the international law firm Hammonds. He is a Health, Safety and Environmental lawyer with particular expertise in defending corporations and individuals in prosecutions brought by the HSE and the CPS following workplace fatal accidents. He has considerable experience in the chemical industry having advised companies such as BASF Plc, Bayer Plc, and FMC Lithium.

Jeremy Farr joined Ince & Co in 1985 as a trainee solicitor and became a partner in 1994. Having started on the dry shipping side of the firm, his practice today is split between oil and gas, dry shipping/international trade, aviation and insurance related disputes with a particular affinity for cases involving complex engineering/technical issues. As a Russian speaker for over 20 years, he has developed particular knowledge and experience of handling disputes arising from casualties in and concerning Eastern Europe and this experience stands him in good stead in matters concerning other developing economies. He has a particular interest in civil emergency management issues as they relate to major marine, aviation and energy disasters and advises regularly in this area. He is the author of the shipping section of a book on corporate killing.

Helen Grice joined Masons in 1996, and concentrated full time on health and safety law in 1999, in which she is greatly assisted by having worked at Sellafield as a health and safety co-ordinator for British Nuclear Fuels plc. During seven years at Sellafield, she was responsible for setting policy, reviewing working practices and investigating accidents and incidents, including taking witness statements and preparing formal reports. She currently provides a wide range of health and safety services to public and private sector clients. She also regularly writes articles, lectures and advises clients on all aspects of health and safety law. Helen is a corporate member of the Institution of Occupational Safety and Health (IOSH) and the Society for Radiological Protection.

Victoria Howes MEd (Manchester), MA (Salford), Barrister, is Lecturer in Law in the University of Salford and has served as Deputy Director, European Occupational Health and Safety Law Research Centre from 2000–2002. Her research interests and publications lie in the fields of human rights at work, environmental law and EU labour law and comparative labour regulation, especially in relation to the transition countries of Central and Eastern Europe.

Jonathan Lawton is a Solicitor-Advocate with Hill Dickinson, specialising in road transport and health and safety law. He is the co-author of two books on commercial vehicle law, and author of numerous articles on both road transport on health and safety. He has appeared in the Divisonal Court of Appeal and in the House of Lords and is a well-known speaker at seminars and other presentations. He has also appeared both on radio and television.

David Leckie is a partner at Maclay Murray & Spens. He was formerly Legal Counsel for Schlumberger. He is a contributor to *Tolley's Health and Safety, Green's Employment Law* and has co-authored *The Human Rights Act 1998, Explained.* He lectures in the Diploma in Health and Safety at Heriot Watt University.

Caroline May is a partner at Hammonds and heads the Safety, Health & Environment Group. She has been a specialist environmental lawyer for the past 14 years and is recognised as a leading expert in her field in *Legal 500*, the *Chambers Directory* and the *Guide to the World's Leading Environmental Lawyers.* She has extensive experience of both contentious and non-contentious environmental law and has been involved in two of the largest toxic tort pieces of litigation in the UK involving dioxin emissions and methane escape from a landfill waste site. She has experience in statutory nuisance and emissions control, brownfield site regeneration and redevelopment and corporate acquisitions and divestitures. She has developed a specialism in environmental impairment and environmental indemnity insurance and related environmental professional indemnity issues. She has experience in all aspects of related health and safety law and has extensive contacts and clients throughout the environmental community in the UK and Europe and an increasing network of contacts and clients in the US.

Paul Rice is head of the Environment and Health & Safety unit at the City law firm, Lawrence Graham. He has a Masters degree in Environmental Laws from King's College London, is a member of UKELA and the Chartered Institution of Waste Management. He advises on all aspects of UK and EU environmental and health and safety law and policy.

Malcolm Ross spent 30 years in West Midlands Police before retiring as a Detective Superintendent. As Head of the Murder Investigation Unit, he was seconded to the Hillsborough Disaster with West Midlands Police. He holds an MSc (with commendation) in Emergency Management and Disaster Planning. He has been engaged as a national and international lecturer in criminal investigation, child protection matters and continuity planning matters. He is a lecturer at the National Police Colleges of Centrex and NSLEC and also lecturers at a number of British universities. He is also engaged in reviewing cases (in both criminal and child protection matters) for various police forces in the UK.

Professor Frank B Wright, LLB, (Leeds), LLM, (Leicester), PhD (Leicester), FRIPH, FRSA is Director of the European Law Research Centre, an Associate Dean of Faculty and Professor of Law at the University of Salford. He is a member of the IUCN Commission on Environmental Law, the International Council of Environmental Law and a Fellow of the Royal Institute of Public Health and Hygiene and the Royal Society of Arts. His publications include *Law of Health and Safety at Work* (1997) and contributions to jointly authored and edited books in health and safety law and environmental law including: *ILO Encyclopedia of Health and Safety* (4th edn, 1998), *Clays Handbook of Environmental Health* (17th, 18th and 19th edns), *Occupational Health & Safety Law in the UK and Ireland* (1998), EuroOSH (1995), *Noise at Work*

Regulations 1990 (2nd edn, 1994), *Tolley's Environmental Law Handbook* (1994), *European Communities Health and Safety Legislation* (1992), *The Protection of Workers from Harmful Physical and Biological Agents at Work* (1989), and *Law of Health and Safety at Work: The New Approach* (1983). Professor Wright has made contributions to more than one hundred papers and casenotes in the following journals: *International Journal of Comparative Labour Law and Industrial Relations, Environmental Law & Management, Environmental Policy and Law, New Law Journal, Justice of the Peace, Local Government Review, Health and Social Service Journal, Journal of Occupational Safety and Health* and *Health and Safety at Work and Environmental Health.* He has worked on a large number of projects funded by the European Commission, the International Labour Organisation and the Health and Safety Executive.

Contents

Table of statutes

Table of statutory instruments

Table of EU legislation

Table of foreign legislation

Table of cases

D

E

F

R

CHAPTER 1

Criminal responsibility for work related accidents

Gerard Forlin, Barrister, 2–3 Grays Inn Square, London

Michael Appleby, Solicitor, Fisher Scoggins LLP, London

Introduction

1.1   Corporate governance is a subject that has rarely been out of the news in recent years, steadily moving up the government's agenda. Much of the activity has been in relation to financial matters, particularly in the wake of the Enron and World.Com scandals.

1.2   In April 2001 Sir Howard Davies, Chairman of the Financial Services Authority, told a Munich audience:

> 'When things go wrong, we shall we shall look directly to senior management, whom we shall hold accountable. In the case of Barings or the pensions mis-selling, senior management have not been held directly accountable. Now we have a system of personal registration, where specified individuals at the top of the company have clearly set out responsibilities for risk management compliance for which we hold them accountable.'[1]

1   R Baldwin and R Anderson *Rethinking regulatory risk* (2002). Commissioned by the Regulatory Group of the law firm DLA, available at www.dla.com/rrr/introduction.html.

1.3   A look at competition law shows the hard line the government is taking. The Enterprise Act 2002 has a strong deterrent effect. Guilty individuals can be imprisoned for up to five years for participation in certain types of cartel. It also provides for directors to be disqualified for up to 15 years if their conduct contributed to a company's breach of competition law (or they suspected the company was breaking competition law but did not do anything to prevent it).

1.4   A tough stance is being taken in the USA as well. In July 2002 George W Bush signed the Sarbanes-Oxley Act, which introduced fines of up to $5 million and prison sentences of up to 25 years for chief executive officers and chief financial officers who sign misleading accounts.

1.5   But concern about corporate conduct is not just restricted to financial matters. All aspects of the running of a company are under scrutiny, including responsibility for injury and death that occurs in the course of its business. A number of public inquiries in the past into disasters have criticised the management of safety.

1.6   After the Piper Alpha disaster, Lord Cullen found that Occidental Petroleum had 'significant flaws in the quality of [its] management of safety'.[1] In the Inquiry into the Clapham Junction train crash Mr Justice Hidden QC criticised British Rail for letting its working practices 'slip to unacceptable and dangerous standards'.[2] Mr Justice Fennell QC in his Inquiry into the Kings Cross fire criticised London Underground for 'collective failure from the most senior management level downward over many years to minimise the outbreak of fire'.[3] Lord Cullen in his report concerning the Ladbroke Grove train crash wrote of the 'incompetent management and inadequate procedures' of Railtrack, the then infrastructure controller.[4]

1   The Hon Lord WD Cullen *The Public Inquiry into the Piper Alpha Disaster* (Cm 1310, 1990).
2   A Hidden QC *Investigation into the Clapham Junction Railway accident* (Cm 820, 1989).
3   D Fennel QC *Investigation into the King's Cross Underground Fire* (Cm 499, 1988).
4   The Rt Hon Lord WD Cullen PC *The Ladbroke Grove Rail Inquiry, part 1 report* (2001), available at www.pixunlimited.co.uk/pdf/news/transport/ladbrokegrove.pdf.

1.7   As a consequence there has been a growing desire for companies and their directors to be held criminally liable if incidents result from management failings. Although health and safety prosecutions might follow, in the public's eyes any resulting convictions do not treat the 'wrong doing' as truly criminal: there is not the stigma nor the chance of custodial sentences (as the vast majority of breaches of health and safety law only carry a financial penalty).

1.8   Whilst it is possible to prosecute a company for corporate manslaughter, there have only been a few successful cases, all against small companies. Plcs and other large companies have appeared immune from prosecution. This has been blamed on the legal technicalities of proving the offence.

1.9   The government in its election manifesto of 1997 and in Queen's Speeches promised a new offence of 'corporate killing', the purpose of which is to make it easier to prosecute companies. The Home Office issued a consultation paper in 2000 on the proposals[1] based on the Law Commission's recommendations of 1996.[2]

1   The Rt Hon J Straw MP *Reforming the law on involuntary manslaughter: the government's proposals* (2000).
2   Law Commission *Legislating the criminal code: involuntary manslaughter. Item 11 of the sixth programme of law reform: criminal law* (Law Com no 237, 1996).

1.10   In a statement released in May 2003 reaffirming the government's commitment to introduce the corporate killing legislation (following pressure from Labour backbenchers), Home Secretary David Blunkett said: 'There is great public concern at the criminal law's lack of success in convicting companies of manslaughter where death has occurred due to gross negligence by the organisation as a whole.'[1] He added that the new law needed to: 'bite properly on large corporations whose failure to set or maintain standards causes death.' However, he said it would not target individual directors. A timetable for the introduction of corporate killing is due for issue by the end of 2003.

1   Home Office press release 142/2003 'Government to tighten laws on corporate killing', 20 May 2003.

Health and safety regulation

1.11   The Robens Report of 1972[1] was the first comprehensive review of health and safety law in the UK. The report recommended that in place of what it described as the 'haphazard mass of ill assorted and intricate detail' of the existing legislation, there should be a 'comprehensive and orderly' set of revised provisions under a new enabling Act. This Act would contain a clear statement of the basic principles of safety responsibilities and be supported by regulations and by non-statutory codes of practice.

1   Lord Robens's report on *Safety and Health at Work* was published in June 1972 (Cmnd 5034, 1972).

1.12   As a consequence of this recommendation the Health and Safety at Work etc Act 1974 (HSWA 1974) was born. This sets out a number of general duties upon employers. It also set up the Health and Safety Commission (HSC) and its operating arm, the Health and Safety Executive (HSE). However, despite the Act much of the previous law remained in place which it had been intended it should replace.

1.13   However, the original aim of a single set of regulations did not come about until some two decades later when a number of European Health and Safety Directives were enacted into UK law as regulations through HSWA 1974. The bulk of these regulations appeared in 1992. They are often referred to as the 'six-pack'. The regulations are: the Management of Health and Safety at Work Regulations, now the Management of Health and Safety at Work Regulations 1999 (MHSWR),[1] the Workplace (Health, Safety and Welfare) Regulations 1992,[2] the Personal Protective Equipment at Work Regulations 1992,[3] the Provision and Use of Work Equipment Regulations, now the Provision and Use of Work Equipment Regulations 1998,[4] the Manual Handling Operations Regulations 1992[5] and the Health and Safety (Display Screen Equipment) Regulations 1992.[6] Most of these regulations are supplemented by Approved Codes of Practice that place meat on the bones of the law in the regulations.

1   SI 1999/3242.
2   SI 1992/3004.
3   SI 1992/2966.
4   SI 1998/2306.
5   SI 1992/2793.
6   SI 1992/2792.

1.14   The 'framework' regulations of the six-pack are the MHSWR,[1] which enacted the Framework Directive, Council Directive 89/391/EEC. The MHSWR has as its bedrock the principle of *risk assessment*. In the last three decades there has been a change in the way safety legislation is framed in a number of industrialised counties. There has been a move away from laws that specify the way in which safe working should be achieved, to laws that set out the attainment of safety goals.

1   SI 1999/3242.

1.15   The focus of regulatory supervision has shifted towards an examination of the way health and safety is managed and standards are set, implemented and monitored. The traditional approach was strong on where the ultimate responsibility lay but did not seek to establish what kind of continuing external monitoring was necessary.

1.16   It is said that a scheme of monitoring and auditing by a safety regulator, which examines an organisation's management, control and design arrangements (and looks at the criteria on which decisions are made), can exert a positive influence to reduce risk without supplanting or diminishing the prime responsibility on the company.

1.17   With risk assessment-based legislation, rather than prescriptive legislation which sets out what action needs to be taken, companies are required to carry out risk assessments to set out their own goals in reducing risk. The emphasis is upon reducing the probability of accident occurrence and if an accident does occur, reducing the harmful consequences of the accident.

The Health and Safety at Work etc Act 1974

1.18   The essential purpose of HSWA 1974 is to secure the health, safety and welfare of employees at work and to protect the public from the activities of a company's business (see HSWA 1974, s 1). HSWA 1974 sets out a number of general duties upon employers and their employees. If one of these duties is breached, this may amount to a criminal offence.

1.19   The main duties upon employers are set out in HSWA 1974, ss 2 and 3. A breach of one or both of these duties normally form the basis of most prosecutions of employers pursuant to HSWA 1974.

1.20   HSWA 1974, s 2(1) states:

'It shall be the duty of every employer to ensure so far as is reasonably practicable, the health and safety and welfare at work of all its employees.'

1.21   HSWA 1974, s 3(1) states:

'It shall be the duty of every employer to conduct his undertaking in such a way as to ensure, so far as is reasonably practicable, that persons not in his employment who may be effected thereby are not thereby exposed to risks to their health and safety.'

1.22   The other general duties under HSWA 1974 are s 4, concerning duties of employers to people not in their employment in relation to premises in their control, and s 6 in relation to manufacturers as regards articles and substances for use at work.

1.23   The main duty upon an employee is contained in HSWA 1974, s 7(a), which states:

> 'It shall be the duty of every employee while at work … to take reasonable care for the health and safety of himself and of other persons who may be affected by his acts or omissions at work …'

1.24   The important words in HSWA 1974, s 2(1) and s 3(1) are: 'so far as is reasonably practicable' (often referred to as SFAIRP). The test as to what is reasonably practicable was set out in the case of *Edwards v National Coal Board.*[1] This case established the risk must be balanced against the 'sacrifice', whether in money, time or trouble, needed to avert or mitigate the risk. By carrying out this exercise the employer can determine what measures are reasonable to take. This is effectively an implied requirement for a risk assessment.

1   [1949] 1 KB704. Lord Atkin stated: '"reasonably practicable" is a narrower term than "physically possible" and seems to me to imply that a computation must be made by the owner, in which the quantum of risk is placed on one scale and the sacrifice in the measures necessary for averting the risk (whether in money, time or trouble) is placed on the other; and if it be shown that there is a gross disproportion between them the risk being insignificant in relation to the sacrifice the [person on whom the duty is placed] discharges the onus on them [of proving that compliance was not reasonably practicable].'

Risk assessment

The requirement for risk assessment

1.25   The main requirement for risk assessment is contained in the MHSWR.[1] The Regulations require the company to assess the risks and, in effect, to act to neutralise them. Failure to carry out an adequate risk assessment may amount to a criminal offence.

1   SI 1999/3242.

1.26   MHSWR, reg 3[1] states:

> '(1) Every employer shall make a suitable and sufficient assessment of—
> (a) the risks to the health and safety of his employees to which they are exposed whilst they are at work; and
> (b) the risks to the health and safety of persons not in his employment arising out of or in connection with the conduct by him of his undertaking
> for the purpose of identifying the measures he needs to take to comply with the requirement and prohibitions imposed upon him, by or under the relevant statutory provision and by Part II of the Fire Precautions (Workplace) Regulations 1997.'[2]

1   SI 1999/3242, reg 3.
2   SI 1997/1840, Pt II.

1.27   MHSWR, reg 4[1] sets out the way in which the risk should be approached:

> 'Where an employer implements any preventative and protective measures he shall do so on the basis of the principal specified in Schedule 1[2] of these Regulations.'

1   SI 1999/3242, reg 4.
2   SI 1999/3242, Sch 1.

1.28   MHSWR, Sch 1[1] details the following:

'(a) Avoid Risks;
(b) Evaluate the risks which cannot be avoided;
(c) Combat the risks at source;
(d) Adapt the work to the individual, especially as regards the design of workplaces, the choice of work, equipment and the choice of working and production method, with a view, in particular, to alleviating monotonous work and work at predetermined work rate and to reducing their effect on health;
(e) Adapt to technical process;
(f) Replace the dangerous by the non-dangerous or the less dangerous;
(g) Develop a coherent overall prevention policy which covers technology, organisation of work, working conditions, social relationships and the influence of factors relating to the working environment;
(h) Give collective protective measures priority over individual protective measures; and
(i) Give appropriate instructions to employees.'

1   SI 1999/3242, Sch 1.

1.29   Note the hierarchy of requirements. Thus, for example, it would not be appropriate for an employer to give instructions to an employee on how to deal with the risk, as a control measure, if it was reasonably practicable to avoid the risk altogether.

1.30   Risk assessment appears in three ways in the health and safety legislation. The first way is as a general risk assessment that is to assess the risks from hazards in a workplace. A general risk assessment is required by MHSWR, reg 3.[1]

1   SI 1999/3242, reg 3.

1.31   Another way a risk assessment can be used is by supporting another piece of legislation which sets out a safety goal. For example, the Provision and Use of Work Equipment Regulations 1998, reg 11[1] (PUWER) requires employers to ensure that measures are taken which are effective to prevent access to any dangerous part of machinery, for example, providing a guard on the machine. In order to assess the possible control measure a risk assessment under MHSWR, reg 3[2] will need to be carried out.

1   SI 1998/2306, reg 11.
2   SI 1999/3242, reg 3.

1.32   A third way a risk assessment can be carried out is as a specific risk assessment. For example, a general risk assessment under MHSWR, reg 3[1] may highlight the fact that in the workplace there are a number of manual operations (ie lifting) hazards. These are covered by the Manual Handling Operations Regulations 1992 (MHOR). MHOR, reg 4[2] requires manual handling operations be avoided so far as is reasonably practicable. If they cannot be avoided then reg 4 requires a specific risk assessment to be carried out of the manual handling operation in order to ensure that the risk is to reduced to the lowest level as far as is reasonably practicable.

1   SI 1999/3242, reg 3.
2   SI 1992/2793, reg 4.

What is a suitable and sufficient risk assessment?

1.33 The Approved Code of Practice (ACOP) for the MHSWR[1] is the 'bible' of risk assessment.[2] When considering whether there should have been a risk assessment or, if one exists, whether it is suitable and sufficient, reference should be made to this and also to any industry literature, ACOP of other relevant legislation and other HSE documentation relevant to the industry or operation (see generally para 31 of the ACOP to the MHSWR).

1   SI 1999/3242.
2   ACOP L21.

1.34 ACOP L21 deals with the following:

• General principles of risk assessment – paras 9 to 12.
• What is a suitable and sufficient risk assessment – paras 13 and 14.
• Risk assessment in practice – paras 15 to 18.
• Identifying the hazards, who might be harmed and evaluating the risks – paras 19 to 25.
• Recording risk assessments – pars 23 to 26.
• Review and revision of risk assessments – para 27.
• Assessments under other regulations – paras 27 and 28.

1.35 There is also a general guide published by the HSE that deals with the process of risk assessment entitled *5 Steps to Risk Assessment*.[1] This gives the basic approach as:

1   Look for the hazard.
2   Decide who might be harmed.
3   Evaluate the risks from the hazards and decide whether existing precautions are adequate or more should be done.
4   Record the findings.
5   Review the assessment from time to time and review it.

1   IND(G)163 (1998), available at. www.hse.gov.uk/pubns163.pdf and from HSE Books, ISBN 0717615804.

1.36 Risk assessment essentially considers the question: 'What if ?' It is not sufficient to base a risk assessment solely on an employers own accident experience. In the case of *Walker v Bletchley Fletons Ltd*[1] the court found the employer liable in negligence. It was said in the judgment the fact that an accident had never happened did not necessarily diminish the chances of one happening. Thus a company is not entitled to wait for a near miss or accident before it considers a potential risk.

1   [1937] 1 All ER 170.

1.37 As to the meaning of risk, in *R v Board of Trustees of the Science Museum*[1] the Court of Appeal said that risk means the *possibility* of danger and not *actual* danger.

1   [1993] 3 All ER 853, CA.

1.38 It should be noted that risk assessment should consider not only the frequency that the hazard will occur, but also the severity of harm if the hazard materialises (see para 11 of the ACOP). Essentially if the risk of the hazard occurring is small but the severity of the consequence is great, there must be control measures put in place (if the hazard cannot be avoided).

1.39   This was highlighted in the sentencing remarks of Mr Justice Clarke following health and safety prosecutions in relation to the collapse of a walkway onto a ferry at Ramsgate Port in 1994 which killed six passengers (*R v Fartygsentreprenader AB, Fartygskonstructioner AB, Port Ramsgate Ltd and Lloyd's Register of Shipping*[1]). He said:

> '... if thought had been given to its responsibilities especially having regard to the provision of the 1974 Act [HSWA 1974], Port Ramsgate could have appreciated that there were potential risks, albeit, perhaps very small risks ... Further, once it was appreciated that there were potential risks, it would have been appreciated that such risks should have been guarded against because of the catastrophic consequences if anything went wrong.'

1   (28 February 1997, unreported).

1.40   There are two types of risk assessment: qualitative and quantitative. The former is an assessment that is judgment-based to determine contributory factors or potential outcomes. The latter assessment produces numerical values of the risk involved and evaluates the results against specific risk criteria. The appropriate type of risk assessment will be determined by the nature of the hazards being assessed.

1.41   Particularly where risk reduction or elimination involves high costs, companies may carry out cost benefit analysis (CBA). A CBA should clearly present its assumptions and finding so that decision-makers understand the results and uncertainties. There is an interesting discussion on the use of CBA in the *Report of the Joint Inquiry into Train Protection* chaired by Lord Cullen and Professor Uff.[1]

1   Professor John Uff QC and the Rt Mon Lord Cullen PC *The Joint Inquiry into Train Protection* (2001).

Responsibility for risk assessment

1.42   MHSWR, reg 7[1] imposes the duty upon the employer to have someone within his or her own organisation carry out the necessary risk assessments. This person must have the appropriate expertise and training and be provided with the appropriate information. For many companies advice from outside consultants will be the exception rather than the rule, but in complex industries consultants are more likely to be used. However, it will still be for the companies to ensure these are the appropriate experts and that they are provided with all the relevant information to carry out the task.

1   SI 1999/3242, reg 7.

1.43   MHSWR, reg 7(1)[1] states:

> 'Every employer shall ... appoint one or more competent persons to assist him in undertaking the measures he needs to take to comply with the requirements and prohibitions imposed upon him by or under the relevant statutory provisions ...'

1   SI 1999/3242, reg 7(1).

1.44   MHSWR, reg 7(8)[1] states:

'Where there is a competent person in the employer's employment, that person shall be appointed for the purposes of paragraph (1) in preference to a competent person not in his employment.'

1   SI 1999/3242, reg 7(8).

1.45   MHSWR, reg 7(4)[1] states:

'The employer shall ensure that—
(a)   Any person appointed by him in accordance with paragraph (1) who is not in his employment—
    (i)   is informed of the factors known to him to affect, or suspected by him of effecting, the health and safety of any person working in his undertaking and
    (ii)   has access to the information referred to in Regulation 10;[2] and
(b)   Any person appointed by him in accordance with paragraph (1) is given such information about any person working in his undertaking who is—
    (i)   employed by him under a fixed term contract of employment, or
    (ii)   employed in an employment business,
as is necessary to enable that person properly to carry out the function specified in that paragraph.'

1   SI 1999/3242, reg 7(4).
2   SI 1999/3242, reg 10.

1.46   MHSWR, reg 7[1] makes it clear (if there was ever any doubt) that it does not matter who carries out the risk assessment, the company is responsible and liable for that risk assessment. Further MHSWR, reg 21[2] says that a company cannot defend criminal proceeding because a person appointed to do risk assessment has failed to carry out that risk assessment adequately.

1   SI 1999/3242, reg 7.
2   SI 1999/3242, reg 21.

Risk management

1.47   Risk assessment and risk management are distinct. Risk management addresses the *appraisal* of assessed risk and the *making of decisions* concerning risks, in particular safety measures and their subsequent implementation. The carrying out of risk assessment does not remove from managers the responsibility for safety decisions, but forms an important part of making decisions about health and safety.

1.48   MHSWR, reg 5[1] states:

'Every employer shall make and give effect to such arrangements as are appropriate, having regard to the nature of his activities and the size of his undertaking, for the effective planning, organisation, control, monitoring and review of the preventative and proactive measures.'

1   SI 1999/3242, reg 5.

1.49   Risk management is a continual process, which includes:

- *Policy*: aims and objectives to be achieved, informed by risk profile or other risk assessment outputs and defining measures for success of failure.
- *Planning*: the steps to be taken to manage the identified risks.
- *Implementation*: rolling out and executing the plan.
- *Monitoring*: checking on progress against objectives through audit, performance measurements, incident/accident investigation and management review.

1.50 This approach is amplified in the HSE's guide *Successful health and safety management*[1] and applies risk assessment as a basis for good management by ordinary good practice.

1 HS(G)65 (2nd edn, 1997).

1.51 In the Ladbroke Grove Rail Inquiry no 2,[1] before Lord Cullen, concerning safety on the railways, Counsel to the Inquiry, described HS(G)65 as a 'seminal' work. At that Inquiry, David Eves, the then Deputy Director General of the HSE, said in evidence:

'When HSE first published HSG65, it wanted to describe a framework for managing health and safety effectively. There now seems to be an emerging international consensus on the essential elements of a health and safety management system. The debate is moving on from the models of health and safety management towards the more challenging issues of health and safety culture and human factors.'

1 The Rt Hon Lord WD Cullen PC *The Ladbroke Grove Rail Inquiry, part 2 report* (2001).

Reporting of Injuries, Diseases and Dangerous Occurrences Regulations 1995

1.52 The Reporting of Injuries, Diseases and Dangerous Occurrences Regulations 1995[1] (RIDDOR) impose a duty on employers to report to the enforcing authority, usually the HSE, certain types of accidents. These include the following:

- fatal accidents;
- major injury accidents; and
- dangerous occurrences.

1 SI 1995/3163.

1.53 All of the above must be reported immediately (normally by telephone) to the enforcing authority. This is then followed by a written report on form F2508 within ten days.

Human factors

1.54 The HSE's view is that accidents, ill health and adverse incidents are seldom random events. The immediate cause may be human or technical failure, but these in turn usually stem from organisational failures which are the responsibility of management.[1]

1 HS(G)65 *Successful health and safety management* (2nd edn, 1997) p 9 states:
'Accidents, ill health and incidents are seldom random events. They generally arise from failures of control and involve multiple contributory elements. The immediate cause may be

a human or technical failure, but they usually arise from organisational failings which are the responsibility of management. Successful policies aim to exploit the strengths of employees. They aim to minimise the contribution of human limitations and fallibilities by examining how the organisation is structured and how jobs and systems are designed.

Organisations need to understand how human factors affect health and safety performance. These are explained in more detail in the HSE publication HSG48 [*Reducing error and influencing behaviour*] which also contains guidance on how to develop suitable control strategies in a systematic way ...'

1.55   Mr J Kooger, Senior Consultant at DuPont Safety Resources, when giving evidence to Lord Cullen's Rail Inquiry no 2,[1] said that people behaviour was one of the most important factors in safety management. In his opinion 90% of all accidents in any company were likely to be due to deviations in behaviour rather than to functional failures, such as failures in systems or equipment.

1   The Rt Hon Lord WD Cullen PC *The Ladbroke Grove Rail Inquiry, part 2 report* (2001).

1.56   Lord Cullen concluded:[1]

'The clear conclusion is that a high proportion of accidents, incidents and near misses on the railways follow unsafe acts by people, whether front line workers or managers. I do not seek here to imply, by any means, that all such people are performing their duties below the standard which should reasonably be expected of them. They may very well be dedicated employees, working to the best of their abilities. Rather, their unsafe acts should be seen as the result of underlying deficiencies in the management of safety, and tackled accordingly.'

1   The Rt Hon Lord WD Cullen PC *The Ladbroke Grove Rail Inquiry, part 2 report* (2001) para 5.4.

1.57   The HSE definition of human factors, given in its publication *Reducing error and influencing behaviour*,[1] is that it refers to environment, organisational and job factors as well as human and individual characteristics which influence behaviour at work in a way that can affect health and safety.

1   HS(G)48 (2nd edn, 1999), available at www.hse.gov.uk/hid/land/comah/level3/5C72542.htm.

1.58   Human factors in the consideration of safety management arguably came to the fore with the publication of Sir Frank Layfield QC's report following the Public Inquiry concerning the nuclear power station Sizewell B.[1]

1   Sir Frank Layfield *Sizewell B Public Inquiry, Report for the Secretary of State* (1987).

1.59   Chapter 25 of the report[1] discusses human factors and sates in the introduction:

'One of the most widely held reasons for anxiety about the safety of Sizewell B was the possibility that accidents might be caused or aggravated by human error. Human error can occur at many stages in the design, manufacture, construction, operation and maintenance of the station.'

1   Sir Frank Layfield *Sizewell B Public Inquiry, Report for the Secretary of State* (1987).

1.60   Sir Frank Layfield QC concluded:[1]

'I regard human factors as of outstanding significance in assessing the safety of Sizewell B, since they impinge on all stages from design to manufacture, construction, operation and maintenance. The accident at Three Mile Island[3] raised public awareness of the potential for human error, and focussed attention in particular on the role of the operator. But it should be recognised that human actions may avoid or mitigate accidents, as well as cause or exacerbate them ...

I draw the following more general conclusion on human factors:

(a) The most meticulous and exhaustive attention must be paid to minimising the occurrence and effects of human error ... the risk from human error might otherwise exceed other risks from Sizewell B.

(b) The CEGB has the commitment and resources to enable it to deal adequately with human factors aspects of the station.'

1   Sir Frank Layfield *Sizewell B Public Inquiry, Report for the Secretary of State* (1987).

1.61   HS(G)48 makes it clear it is no longer acceptable to blame accidents on 'human error':[1]

'Over the last 20 years we have learnt much more about the origins of human failure. We can now challenge the commonly held belief that incidents and accidents are the result of a 'human error' by a worker in the 'front line'. Attributing incidents to 'human error' has often been seen as a sufficient explanation in itself and something which is beyond the control of managers. This view is no longer acceptable to society as a whole. Organisations must recognise that they need to consider human factors as a distinct element which must be recognised, assessed and managed effectively in order to control risks.'

1   *Reducing error and influencing behaviour* (2nd edn, 1999) p 7.

1.62   Earlier HS(G)48 states:[1]

'Many accidents are blamed on the actions or omissions of an individual who was directly involved in operational or maintenance work. This typical but short-sighted response ignores the fundamental failures which led to the accident. These are typically rooted deeper in the organisation's design, management and decision-making functions.'

1   *Reducing error and influencing behaviour* (2nd edn, 1999) p 4.

1.63   The key message of HS(G)48 is that human factors are something that should be controlled like any other risk by management.

1.64   According to HS(G)48 the consequences of human failures can be immediate or delayed. It divides this into active failures and latent failures.

1.65   An active failure has an immediate consequence and is usually made by front line employees such as a driver, control room staff member or machine operator. In a situation where there is no room for error these active failures have an immediate impact on health and safety.

1.66   Latent failures are made by people whose tasks are removed in time and space from operational activities, for example, designers, decision-makers and managers. Examples of latent failures given are:

- poor design of plant and equipment;
- ineffective training;
- inadequate supervision;
- ineffective communications; and
- uncertainties in roles and responsibilities.

1.67   Of latent failures HS(G)48 says that these can:

'Provide as great, if not greater potential danger to health and safety as active failures. Latent failures are usually hidden within our organisation until they are triggered by an event likely to have serious consequences.'

1   *Reducing error and influencing behaviour* (2nd edn, 1999) p 11.

1.68   HS(G)48 stresses that the scale of the human contributions towards accidents is not surprising since people are involved throughout the life cycle of an organisation. It advises employers to address human factors in four ways:

- during risk assessments;
- when analysing incidents, accidents and omissions;
- in design and procurement; and
- in aspects of day-to-day health and safety management – such as communications and culture.

1.69   Professor James Reason in his book *Managing the Risks of Organizational Accidents* states:[1]

'The evidence from a large number of accident inquiries indicates that bad events are more often the result of error prone situations and error prone activities than they are of error prone people.'

1   (1997) p 29.

Directors' responsibilities for health and safety

1.70   The conclusions to a report by Angela O'Dea and Rhona Flin of the University of Aberdeen for the HSE entitled *The role of managerial leadership in determining workplace safety outcomes* state:

'The realisation of management as an important source of stability and reliability (or otherwise) within industrial organisations does not reflect a sudden increase in management failures, rather it reflects a development in our thinking about accidents, their causes and their consequences. It also reflects a change in regulation, which places responsibility for the management squarely on the shoulders of management.'

1   Research report 044 (2003).

1.71   In recent years there has been guidance (which is not legally binding) regarding what is expected of companies and their directors: this is contained in a specific guidance for directors on health and safety and in what has become known as the *'Turnbull' Guidelines*. However, as Lord Cullen wrote in his report following the *Public Inquiry into the Piper Alpha Disaster* concerning the offshore gas explosion in 1988:[1]

'There is, of course, nothing new in the idea that safety requires to be managed.'

1   The Hon Lord WD Cullen *The Public Inquiry into the Piper Alpha Disaster* (Cm 1310, 1990).

Guidance upon directors' responsibilities for health and safety

1.72   In 2001 the Health and Safety Commission (HSC) issued guidance for board members of all types of organisations in both the public and private sectors entitled *Directors' responsibilities for health and safety*.[1] This was published following a consultation exercise earlier in that year. Originally it was intended there should be a Code, however, the resulting document has guidance status only.

1   IND(G)343, available at www.hse.gov.uk/pubns/indg343.

1.73   The guidance sets out five action points:

1   The board needs to accept formally and publicly its collective role in providing health and safety leadership in its organisation.
2   Each member of the board needs to accept his or her individual role in providing health and safety leadership for their organisation.
3   The board needs to ensure that all board decisions reflect its health and safety intentions, as articulated in the organisation's health and safety policy statement.
4   The board needs to recognise its role in engaging the active participation of workers in improving health and safety.
5   The board needs to ensure that it is kept informed of, and alert to, relevant health and safety risk management issues. The guide recommends that one of the Board members be appointed as the 'Health & Safety Director'.

1.74   The guide states that by appointing a health and safety director the company will have a board member who can ensure health and safety risk management issues are properly addressed. During the consultation employers' organisations and trade associations failed to persuade the HSC not to have reference to a named health and safety director. The Confederation of British Industry, Construction Confederation, Engineering Employers' Federation and Institute of Directors all opposed the appointment of a health and safety director arguing that it would promote a 'blame culture and detract from collective responsibility'. The fear is that if an incident occurs the named director would become a 'scapegoat'.

1.75   On publication of the guidance, the HSC chairman, Bill Callaghan, said:

'Health and safety is a boardroom issue. Good health and safety reflects strong leadership from the top.'

The 'Turnbull' Guidelines

1.76   In 1999 the Institute of Chartered Accountants for England and Wales published the *Turnbull Report*[1] that provides complementary guidance to the London Stock

Exchange's *Combined Code on Corporate Governance (1998). Turnbull* requires listed UK companies to have a system of internal control (IC) so that the board can identify and control its exposure to significant risks to the business. Although it is aimed at stock market listed companies, its relevance is far wider.

1 N Turnball (chair) Institute of Chartered Accountants for England and Wales *Internal control: guidance for directors on the combined code* (1999).

1.77 The *Turnbull Guidelines* require an IC to help safeguard shareholders' investments against all risks to the business, which includes health and safety risks as well as financial risks.

1.78 The health and safety risks include: operational risk, catastrophic accident, multiple health claims and legal risk. Where the risks are substantial, *Turnbull* requires the board to assess, control and if necessary, report on them. These risks can occur from human error (particularly of front line workers), staff not adhering to control measures, poor decision-making by management and the occurrence of unforeseeable circumstances.

1.79 The board of a company has responsibility for the IC. When considering the risks, the board will rely upon information and assurances provided by its senior and other management.

1.80 The board is required to carryout an annual assessment of the IC and make a statement in its annual report and accounts. The assessment should include any incidents where there were significant failings in control measures or weaknesses as well as whether these have resulted in unforeseen outcomes.

1.81 Angela O'Dea and Rhona Flin in *The role of managerial leadership in determining workplace safety*[1] say of the *Turnbull Guidelines*:

'[The Guidelines] argue that it makes sound business sense to manage risk effectively and to embed internal control in the business process by which the company pursues its objectives. Thus, risk management and internal control are firmly linked with the ability of a company to fulfil its business objectives. Such benefits are achievable through a reduction in time spent fire fighting, identifying a better basis for strategy setting and the resultant achievement of competitive advantage.'

1 University of Aberdeen research report 044 (for the HSE) (2003).

Health and safety prosecutions

The HSC's enforcement policy statement

1.82 The HSC issued a new enforcement policy statement in January 2002[1] outlining when and how the HSE and other health and safety enforcing authorities (for example, local authorities) will take action to investigate and prosecute companies and individuals for breaches of health and safety law.

1 HSC15 *Enforcement policy statement* (2002), available at www.hse.gov.uk/pubns/hsc15.pdf.

1.83   The publication revises the previous enforcement statement policy issued in 1995. It came after the House of Commons' Environment, Transport and Regional Affairs Select Committee published a report in February 2000 that was scathing about the HSE's performance.[1] It concluded that the HSE was failing to investigate a sufficient number of workplace accidents and was not bringing enough prosecutions against companies that flouted health and safety legislation.

1   *The Work of the Health and Safety Executive Report and Proceedings of the Committee.*

1.84   In response, the government and the HSC in the summer of 2000 announced plans to increase the number of investigations by the HSE into workplace accidents. Later in the autumn of 2000 the HSC launched a public consultation on proposed changes to the enforcement policy statement.

1.85   The policy applies to all Britain's enforcing authorities, including the HSE and all local authorities in England, Scotland and Wales.

1.86   It makes clear to inspectors, employers, workers and the public, what standards they should expect when it comes to enforcing health and safety in the workplace.

1.87   The policy determines when enforcing authorities should take action. The enforcing authorities have a range of options at their disposal to enable them to secure compliance with the law and to ensure a proportionate response to criminal offences committed by companies. These options include writing warning letters to companies, serving improvement and prohibition notices, withdrawing approvals, varying licence conditions, the issue of formal cautions and the ultimate deterrent, prosecution.

1.88   Decisions on whether to investigate a workplace incident must take into account a number of factors including:

- the severity and scale of potential or actual harm;
- the seriousness of any potential breach of health and safety law;
- the offending company's previous health and safety record; and
- the wider relevance of the incident, including the public concern caused by it.

1.89   The policy sets out when a prosecution should normally take place in the public interest. This includes any one of a number of circumstances, such as:

- where a death has occurred as a result of a breach of health and safety legislation;
- when the gravity of the offence, taken together with the seriousness of any actual or potential harm, or the general record and approach of the offending company warrants it;
- if there has been a reckless disregard of health and safety requirements by the offending company;
- if there have been repeated breaches by the offending company of health and safety law which give rise to significant risk, or persistent and significant poor compliance; or
- when a company's standard of managing health and safety is far below what is required by health and safety law and gives rise to a significant risk.

1.90   In the past there have been very few prosecutions of directors and senior managers when there have been serious health and safety breaches. But, the policy makes it clear that the conduct of management should be considered. In particular enforcing authorities should consider the management chain and the role played by individual directors and managers. It says action should be taken against them where the inspection or investigation reveals that the offence was committed with their consent or connivance or to have been attributable to neglect on their part.[1] The policy statement also says, where appropriate, enforcing authorities should seek to have directors disqualified under the Company Directors Disqualification Act 1986.

1   The HSE has also issued instructions entitled *Prosecuting individuals* which came into effect on 1 July 2003.

1.91   When the policy statement was published, Bill Callaghan, Chairman of the HSC, commented:

'Inspectors must consider carefully the role of individual managers and directors when serious failures do occur – and ensure that appropriate action is taken against them if the evidence justifies it ...

Now, more than ever, there is no excuse for those at the top to be ignorant of their responsibilities or to fail to take effective action. If you cannot manage health and safety, then you cannot manage.'[1]

1   Press release 28 January 2002.

1.92   However, it would appear that the number of HSE investigations might fall. There are a number of proposed changes set out in the HSE document *Improving Health & Safety: Some developments and new approaches to incident investigation management and a revision of the incident criteria*[1] that are designed to reduce the duration and number of incident investigations carried out by the HSE Field Operation Division (FOD).

1   (2003), available on the Centre for Corporate Accountability website at www.corporateaccountability.org.

Reducing risks, protecting people

1.93   Another important document which details the HSC/HSE's approach is *Reducing risks, protecting people – HSE's decision-making process* (often referred to as R2P2).[1] This evolved from a discussion document published by the HSE in May 1999 also entitled *Reducing risks, protecting people*. The main aim of that document was to set out an overall framework for HSE decision-taking within the scope of HSWA 1974. The framework was based on the method applied by the HSE to the control of risk at nuclear power stations set out in *The tolerability of risks from nuclear power stations*.[2]

1   HSE (2001).
2   HSE (1992).

1.94   The centrepiece of the document is the concept of the 'tolerability of risk' (TOR). This refers to a willingness to live with a risk so as to secure certain benefits in the confidence that the risk is one that is worth taking and that it is being properly controlled. Thus a 'tolerable' risk is not necessarily one that will be judged as 'acceptable' by those taking it.

1.95   In relation to tolerable risk control, measures must be introduced to drive the residual risk towards being broadly acceptable. If the residual risk remains in the tolerable region (and society desires the benefit of the activity) the residual risk is tolerable only if further risk reduction is impracticable or requires action that is 'grossly disproportionate' in time, trouble and effort to the reduction in risk achieved.

1.96   R2P2 emphasises the role of risk assessment in the decision-making process and expands on the role of 'good practice' in determining control measures that employers must put in place for addressing hazards.

1.97   The document says its aim is to explain the decision-making process in the HSE rather than to provide guidance to individual duty-holders on what they need to do in order to comply with the law.

Improvement and prohibition notices

Improvement notice

1.98   Pursuant to HSWA 1974, s 21, inspectors can issue an improvement notice when they consider health and safety legislation is being contravened. The notice can be issued whether the legislation being breached is HSWA 1974 or some other health and safety statutory provision.

1.99   The notice must specify the legal requirements that the inspector thinks are being broken and give reasons. The time allowed to put matters right cannot be less than 21 days (as this is the time limit to submit an appeal to the Employment Tribunal). How long is allowed is in the discretion of the inspector. It will depend on factors such as the seriousness of the matters involved and the ease with which action necessary to comply with the notice can be taken. In the notice the inspector can also set out what he or she needs to be done to put matters in order.

Prohibition notice

1.100   An inspector may issue a prohibition notice pursuant to HSWA 1974, s 22 when he or she thinks that there is a risk of *serious personal injury*. The notice prohibits the carrying on of the work activity that the inspector believes is creating the risk of injury. If the inspector considers the risk is of imminent danger, the notice must take immediate effect and the work activity stopped at once. If not, the notice can be deferred, stating that the work activity must be stopped within a certain time. There does not have to be immanent danger for a notice to be issued (see *Tesco v Kippax COIT* [1]).

1 No 7605, HSIB 180, p 8.

1.101   The case of *Railtrack v Smallwood* [1] concerned railway signal SN109 that was passed at danger on 5 October 1999 resulting in the Ladbroke Grove railway crash. On 8 October 1999 a prohibition notice was served prohibiting the use of the signal and the section of track on which it was situated. Railtrack, who controlled the infrastructure at the time, appealed the notice on the basis that when it was issued the track was not in use. It was held that even though work activities were suspended at the time, 'activities' were still carried on for the purpose of HSWA 1974, s 2?

1 [2001] ICR 714.

1.102 The prohibition notice can be issued for any activities to which the relevant statutory provisions apply. There does not have to be an actual breach of a legal duty although if it is thought the law is being broken, the notice must state this and detail any breach. The notice must also state the matters which in the inspectors view are creating the risk of serious personal injury and may include directions on what steps should be taken to rectify matters.

Power to deal with cause of immanent danger

1.103 Where there is an article or substance that the inspector thinks creates an immanent risk of injury, then by HSWA 1974, s 25 he or she can seize the article or substance or 'cause it to be rendered harmless (whether by destruction or otherwise)'.

Service of notices

1.104 An improvement notice is served on the person responsible for the breach of legal requirements. Thus, if the legal requirement being breached imposes duties on employers, the improvement notice is served on the employer, even if employees or other people have been involved in the events that led to the issue of the notice.

1.105 A prohibition notice is served on the person carrying on or in control of the activities concerned, whether or not that person would also be responsible for any breach of legal requirements. Therefore, for example, a prohibition notice could be served on a site manager, even though the legal duty is upon his or her employers. However, a copy of the notice would also be sent to the employers as well.

1.106 The inspector usually serves the notice personally. Notices can, however, also be served by post. In the case of a corporate body (for example, a limited company or local authority) or of a partnership it will be sent to the principal office or registered address. However, the person to be served can specify the address where the notice should be sent.

Withdrawal of notices

1.107 Once the remedial action has been taken to comply with the notice, the notice ceases to have effect and so does not have to be withdrawn. However, there are certain circumstances where the notice can be withdrawn, for example, if the situation that gave rise to the notice changes.

Extension of time limits

1.108   Inspectors can extend the time limit specified in the notice providing there is no appeal pending.

Appeals

1.109   Someone served with a notice may appeal to an employment tribunal (HSWA 1974, s 24). The appeal may challenge the inspector's views about whether the law has been broken or about the risk of serious personal injury, the time limit in the notice or, if applicable, the measures specified for remedying matters.

1.110   An appeal should be made in writing to an employment tribunal within 21 days (unless extended) of the service of the notice. The procedure for appeals is contained in the Employment Tribunals (Constitution and Rules of Procedure) Regulations 2001, Sch 5.[1]

1   SI 2001/1171, Sch 5.

1.111   An appeal automatically suspends the operation of an improvement notice until the outcome of the hearing. However, it does not mean the time specified in the notice is automatically extended.

1.112   A prohibition notice is not automatically suspended on appeal. However, an application can be made to the tribunal for suspension and, if the tribunal agrees, it is suspended from the time the tribunal directs this.

1.113   After the hearing the employment tribunal can cancel the notice or affirm it as it stands or affirm it with certain amendments, for example, it can rephrase a notice (see *Chrysler (UK) Ltd v McCarthy*[1]) or can extend time limits for remedying the breach (see *Campion v Hughes (HM Inspector)*[2]).

1   [1978] ICR 939.
2   [1975] IRLR 291.

Offences under HSWA 1974

1.114   HSWA 1974, s 33 sets out a number of offences that can be prosecuted under the Act. These include:

*   Failing to comply with general duties imposed on employers, the self-employed, people in control of premises, manufacturers etc (ie general duties contained in HSWA 1974, ss 2–7) or failing to comply with any requirement imposed by regulations made under the Act, for example, failing to carry out a suitable and sufficient risk assessment pursuant to MHSWR, reg 3.[1]
*   Obstructing or failing to comply with any requirements imposed by inspectors in the exercise of their powers.
*   Failing to comply with an improvement or prohibition notice.
*   Failing to supply information as required by a notice issued by the HSC.
*   Failing to comply with a court order to remedy the cause of an offence.

1   SI 1999/3242, reg 3.

1.115   Individuals and corporate bodies such as limited companies and local authorities can commit offences. If an offence is committed by a corporate body was committed 'with the consent or connivance of, or to have been attributable to any neglect on the part of any director, manager, or secretary or other similar officer' then he or she is also guilty of the offence and may be prosecuted as well as the corporate body (HSWA 1974, s 37).

1.116   If someone commits an offence under HSWA 1974 because of an 'act or default' of someone else, then that person will also be guilty of an offence pursuant to HSWA 1974, whether the other person is prosecuted or not (HSWA 1974, s 36).

Prosecutions of employers following work related incidents

1.117   The majority of prosecutions of employers following work related incidents are on the basis of breaches of the general duties of HSWA 1974, s 2(1) and HSWA 1974, s 3(1), ie a failures by the employers to conduct their business so as to ensure the health and safety of employees and non-employees (including members of the public) respectively, 'so far as is reasonably practicable'.

1.118   Because of the correlation between these duties and the requirement to manage risk, it is now becoming more common for employers also to be charges with a failure to carryout a suitable and sufficient risk assessment pursuant to MHSWR, reg 3.[1]

1   SI 1999/3242, reg 3.

1.119   Further the employers can in certain circumstances be prosecuted with other breaches of health and safety law. For example, if an employee was injured or killed because of a failure to have a guard on a machine, then the employer could also be expected to be prosecuted for a breach of PUWER, reg 11.1

1   SI 1998/2306, reg 3.

How bad does the failure have to be?

1.120   British Rail was prosecuted for breaches of HSWA 1974, ss 2 and 3 following the Clapham train crash of 1988. Thirty-five people died. BR pleaded guilty. The case came before Mr Justice Wright at the Old Bailey for sentencing on 14 June 1991, two-and-a-half years after the incident. He observed that the underlying causes of the tragedy were:[1]

'... a failure of any proper systems of preparation for work, supervision of work, inspection of work, testing and checking of work of the re-signalling work that was being carried out ... Standing instructions were not properly distributed; individual personnel were not fully trained or instructed in their responsibilities; there was no proper co-ordination of instructions or system for ensuring that those instructions were complied with.'

1   (14 June 1991, unreported).

1.121   The judge's comments upon the level of failure required for an employer to be guilty of HSWA 1974 offence. He said:[1]

'... the charges that British Rail face today do not involve any connotation or allegation of recklessness. The allegation is no more than that; a failure to maintain and observe the high standards required by the Health and Safety at Work legislation ...'

1   (14 June 1991, unreported.

Level of exposure to risk

1.122   The level of exposure to risk required for an employer to have breached HSWA 1974, s 3(1) was an issue in dispute in the case of *R v Board of Trustees of the Science Museum*.[1] This case concerned an inspection of the museum which found a bacteria that caused legionnaires' disease existed in the air cooling system. There was no evidence that anyone had been infected but it was common ground between the parties that escape of the bacteria could infect people.

1   [1993] 3 All ER 853, CA.

1.123   Counsel for the prosecution gave an example of different levels of risk. Imagine, he said, a loose object on a roof near a pavement. In case A the loose object is in a position in which it might fall off and hit a pedestrian. He referred to that as a 'mere' risk. In case B the object in fact falls and exposes pedestrians to actual danger. In case C the object falls and causes injury. Whilst there was no doubt that cases B and C came within HSWA 1974, the prosecution argued that case A also came within the Act.

1.124   The Court of Appeal agreed and (as stated earlier) said that risk meant the possibility of danger and not just actual danger.

1.125   However, will 'any' risk, no matter how remote, be sufficient for the prosecution to have the basis of a case? The answer is perhaps not.

1.126   In *Koonjul v Thameslink Healthcare Services*,[1] a civil claim for compensation for personal injuries the Court of Appeal considered the issue of risk for the purposes of MHOR, reg 4,[1] which requires a specific risk assessment to be carried out by employers in relation to manual handling operations performed by employees. Lady Justice Hale (at P126) in considering the level of risk which is required to bring a case within reg 4, said: '... there must be a real risk, a foreseeable possibility of injury; certainly nothing approaching a probability.' In the roof example given in *R v The Board of Trustees of the Science Museum*[3] (see **para 1.123** above), case A, described by prosecuting counsel as a 'mere' risk, arguably, nonetheless presents not just 'any' risk but a 'real' risk.

1   [2000] PIQR P123.
2   SI 1992/2793, reg 4.
3   [1993] 3 All ER 853, CA.

Causation

1.127   It follows that it is not necessary for the prosecution to prove a causal link between any injury or death that may have occurred. The prosecution only has to prove that there was a risk of exposure to harm, so that proof of actual harm is unnecessary. However, in *Davies v Health and Safety Executive*,[1] which concerned a breach of HSWA 1974, s 3(1), the Court of Appeal made the following observation:

> 'There may be real issues about whether the defendant owes the relevant duty or whether in fact the safety standard has been breached, for example where the cause of an accident is unknown or debatable.'

1 [2002] EWCA Crim 2949 (Dec).

Defence under HSWA 1974, s 40

1.128 HWSA 1974, s 40 states:

> 'In any proceedings for an offence under any relevant statutory provisions consisting of a failure to comply with a duty or requirement to do something so far as is practicable or so far as is reasonably practicable, or to use the best means to do something, it shall be for the accused to prove (as the case may be) that it was not practicable or not reasonably practicable to do more than was in fact done to satisfy the duty or requirement, or that there was no better practicable means than was in fact used to satisfy the duty or requirement.'

1.129 In other words, if the prosecution proves (beyond reasonable doubt) that there has been a criminal breach of a duty, the onus then falls upon the employer to prove (on the lower standard of proof, a balance of probabilities – see *R v Carr-Briant*[1] and *R v Dunbar*[2]) that all that was reasonably practicable to do was done.

1 [1943] 2 All ER 156, CCA.
2 [1958] 1 QB 1, CCA.

1.130 The question is when does the defence come into play?

1.131 In *R v British Steel PLC*,[1] the Court of Appeal said that a breach of HSWA 1974, s 3(1) (and thus HSWA 1974, s 2(1) as well) imposed absolute criminal liability on an employer subject only to the defence of reasonable practicability. In the House of Lords case of *R v Associated Octel Co Ltd*[2] it was said that s 3(1) requires the employer to conduct his undertaking in a way which, subject to reasonable practicability, does not create risks to people's health and safety.

1 [1995] 1 WLR 1356.
2 [1996] 4 All ER 846.

1.132 In *Lockhart v Kevin Oliphant*[1] it was said that once there is a 'prima facie' case against the employer that the health, safety and welfare of employees was not ensured then the onus under HSWA 1974, s 40 is on the defendant. According to *Redgrave's Health and Safety*,[2] the prosecution 'does not have to prove that it was reasonably practicable to comply' with HSWA 1974.

1 1992 SCCR 774.
2 (4th edn, 2002) p 99.

1.133 In *Davies v Health and Safety Executive*[1] there was an issue as what the prosecution had to prove before the defendant was required to rely on the defence of

HSWA 1974, s 40. The prosecution argued that once it had proved an exposure to risk, then the offence (under HSWA 1974, s 3(1)) was proved unless the defendant establishes the s 40 defence. As the Court of Appeal put it: 'In other words reasonable practicability is not an essential ingredient of the offence.'

1   [2002] EWCA Crim 2949 (Dec).

1.134   The Court of Appeal rejected that submission.[1] They went on to say:

> 'The duty cast on the defendant is a "duty ... to ensure as far as is reasonably practicable". It is a breach of a qualified duty which gives rise to the offence. [Prosecuting counsel] had to concede that but for section 40 [HSWA 1974, s 40] it would be for the [prosecution] to negative reasonable practicability.'

1   *Davies v Health and Safety Executive* [2002] EWCA Crim 2949 (Dec).

1.135   Despite what is said in *Davies v Health and Safety Executive*[1] it is suggested that once the prosecution has proved there was a risk that personal injury could be caused, it is then for the defendant to rely upon HSWA 1974, s 40.

1   [2002] EWCA Crim 2949 (Dec).

Is HSWA 1974, s 40 compatible with the Human Rights Act 1998?

1.136   The main issue before the Court of Appeal in *Davies v Health and Safety Executive*[1] was whether HSWA 1974, s 40 is compatible with the Human Rights Act 1998. This Act incorporates into English law significant provisions of the European Convention on Human Rights (ECHR).

1   [2002] EWCA Crim 2949 (Dec).

1.137   The HSE has always interpreted HSWA 1974, s 40 as meaning it is for an employer to prove, on a balance of probabilities, he or she could not do more than was reasonably practicable. Davies appealed his conviction on the basis that this interpretation breached the ECHR, art 6(2). This says that everyone charged with a criminal offence 'shall be presumed innocent until proved guilty according to law'.

1.138   It was argued on behalf of Davies that a defendant should not have to prove he did all that was reasonable practicable to be able to rely on the HSWA 1974, s 40 defence, but merely had to give sufficient evidence to raise the issue.

1.139   The Court of Appeal rejected this argument. It accepted that HSWA 1974, s 40 made 'some in road into the presumption of innocence' but said this was 'justified, necessary and proportionate'. The court observed:

- HSWA 1974 is regulatory and its purpose is to protect people's health and safety.
- The reversal of the burden of proof takes into account that employers have chosen to engage in work or commercial activity (probably for gain) and are in charge of it.
- Before a defendant has to rely on HSWA 1974, s 40, the prosecution has to prove that the defendant owes a duty and that the safety standard has been breached.

- The facts relied upon for an HSWA 1974, s 40 defence should not be difficult to prove because they will be within the defendant's knowledge. Whether the defendant should have done more will be judged objectively.
- In complex cases, if the defendant only had to put forward evidence that reasonably practicable steps were taken, then enforcement could be virtually impossible where the only relevant expertise was that of the defendant
- Finally, for the offence where HSWA 1974, s 40 applies the defendants do not face imprisonment.

Directors and senior managers

1.140   In the case of a corporate body, to prove a breach, for example, of HSWA 1974, s 2(1) or HSWA 1974, s 3(1), it is not necessary to show that the directors or senior managers of the employers have personally failed not to expose people to the risk of harm only that the company has failed. Further it is no defence for the directors and senior managers to argue that they had personally done all that was reasonably practicable .[1]

1   See *R v British Steel PLC* [1995] 1 WLR 1356.

1.141   However, as stated earlier, if the directors or senior manages had some involvement personally in the company's breach then they can be prosecuted individually as well, pursuant to HSWA, s 37. In a work related incident this is most likely to be on the basis it was 'attributable' the director's or senior manager's 'neglect'.

1.142   The meaning of 'attributable' in relation to neglect for the purposes of HSWA, s 47, was considered in *Wotherspoon v HM Advocate*.[1] It was said that:

'... any degree of attributability will suffice and in that sense it is evident that the commission of a relevant offence by a body corporate may well be found to be attributable to the failure on the part of each of a number of directors, managers or other officers to take certain steps which he could or should have taken in the discharge of the particular functions of his particular office.'

1   [1978] JC 74 at 78.

1.143   In the same case[1] the meaning of 'neglect' was also considered. It was said that neglect:

'... in its natural meaning pre-supposes the existence of some obligation or duty on the part of the person charged with neglect.'

1   *Wotherspoon v HM Advocate* [1978] JC 74 at 78.

1.144   Further it was said:[1]

'... in considering in a given case whether there has been neglect ... on the part of a particular director or other particular officer charged, the search must be to discover whether the accused has failed to take some steps to prevent the commission of an offence by the corporation to which he belongs if the taking of those steps either expressly falls within or should be held to fall within the scope of the functions of the office which he holds.'

1   *Wotherspoon v HM Advocate* [1978] JC 74 at 78.

1.145   In relation to the definition of 'manager' this is likely be viewed as only those responsible for deciding corporate policy and strategy (see *R v Boal (Francis)*[1] which was a prosecution in relation to the Fire Precautions Act 1971).

1   [1992] 3 All ER 177, CA.

Health and safety duties cannot be delegated

1.146   Employers cannot delegate their health and safety duties or 'contract out' of them. When a certain activity has given rise to a risk or exposure to harm, the issue is whether that activity came within the defendant's undertaking, for example, its business.

1.147   In the case of *R v Associated Octel Co Ltd*,[1] which came before the House of Lords, a specialist independent contractor using its own workers was engaged by the defendant company to repair the lining of a tank on the defendants' chlorine plant. While carrying out the maintenance an employee of the contractors was badly burnt when a bucket of highly inflammable acetone used for cleaning ignited.

1   [1996] 4 All ER 846.

1.148   The House of Lords said it was a matter of fact whether an activity came within the defendants' undertaking. In this case they found that any reasonable jury would find on the facts of these case that the activities did amount to the conduct of a defendant's undertaking. The facts were: the tank was part of the defendant's' chemical plant; the contractor's employees worked on more or less a permanent basis; the defendants authorised the work to be carried out by these employees, which enabled them to impose conditions upon the way the work was carried out; and the defendants provided them with the safety equipment.

Failures by employees which cause employer's breach of duty

1.149   In *R v Nelson Group (Maintenance) Ltd*[1] the defendant company installed, serviced and maintained gas appliances nationally. It appealed a conviction relating to a breach of HSWA 1974, s 3(1).

1   [1998] 4 All ER 331.

1.150   One of the company's fitters had removed a defective and dangerous gas fire in a private house. The trial judge directed the jury that if it found the fitter had been negligent by not capping the gas pipe, the company was in breach of HSWA 1974, s 3 and guilty. The jury found the fitter had been negligent in this way. The fitter was also prosecuted and convicted under HSWA 1974.

1.151   The Court of Appeal considered the distinction between the duties of employers and the duties of their employees. It said it was not necessary for the adequate protection of the public for the company to be held criminally liable as well as the employee. It was open to the company to show it had done everything reasonably practicable to avoid the risk. The court accepted the company had because there was a good system of training and instruction. The conviction was quashed.

1.152   MHSWR, reg 21 is designed to reverse the effect of this case. The regulation states an employer will not have a defence to a health and safety prosecution because of any act or default by an employee. Thus the defence in the *Nelson* case[2] should not succeed in the future.

1   SI 1999/3242, reg 21.
2   *R v Nelson Group (Maintenance) Ltd* [1998] 4 All ER 331.

Prosecutions of employees following work related incidents

1.153   As to when an employee breaches their duty under HSWA 1974, s 7(a) (ie to take reasonable care for the health and safety of him or herself and of other persons who may be affected by his or her acts or omissions at work) is somewhat of a grey area of law. The reason for this is that the vast majority of cases are dealt with in the magistrates' courts. As a consequence there are very few reported cases.

1.154   There are two types of prosecutions: those of employees that can be described as 'front line' workers and those of employees that are at management level (normally lower or middle management).

1.155   For a 'front line' employee to be prosecuted his or her actions normally have to be bordering on the reckless. An example is the case of *R v Holland*[1] where the defendant exposed a 17-year-old colleague to hydrochloric acid as a 'practical joke'.

1   (1997, unreported), Bridgnorth Magistrates' Court.

1.156   For a manager to be prosecuted the negligence does not have to be so bad. A manager can be prosecuted if he or she has failed to carry out their job (or has violated procedures) so that health and safety standards are as a consequence significantly lowered. An example is the case of *R v Helmrich*.[1] The defendant was the health and safety manager of a national restaurant chain. At one of its restaurants a fatal accident occurred when an employee was electrocuted. The defendant was not prosecuted in relation to this incident. The defendant was prosecuted on the basis that he failed to implement an adequate heath and safety system for his employers.

1   (2003, unreported), Lincoln Magistrates' Court.

Manslaughter

1.157   Negligence can form the basis of criminal liability in involuntary manslaughter; however, the negligence has to be *gross*. In work related death cases, recent history suggests that gross negligence manslaughter is the most appropriate form to prosecute an individual whose conduct it is alleged has materially contributed to the death.

1.158   The law relating to gross negligence manslaughter was radically altered by the House of Lords judgment in *R v Adomako*.[1] The case concerned an anaesthetist in charge during an eye operation. He failed to notice that an endotracheal tube (to allow the patient to breathe normally) had become disconnected for a period of about six minutes. As a consequence, the patient died. The defence conceded at trial the doctor had been negligent but denied this negligence was so bad that it should be deemed a criminal offence.

1   [1995] 1 AC 171.

1.159   The only speech was given by the then Lord Chancellor, Lord Mackay of Clashfern, who said:[1]

> '... in my opinion the ordinary principles of the law of negligence apply to ascertain whether or not the defendant has been in breach of a duty of care towards the victim who has died. If such breach of duty is established the next question is whether that breach of duty caused the death of a victim. If so the jury must go onto consider whether that breach of duty should be characterised as gross negligence and therefore as a crime. This will depend on the seriousness of the breach of duty committed by the defendant in all the circumstances in which the defendant was placed when it occurred. The jury will have to consider whether the extent to which the defendant's conduct parted from the proper standard of care incumbent upon him, involving as it must have done, a risk of death [to the deceased], was such that it should be judged criminal.'

1   *R v Adomako* [1995] 1 AC 171 at 187.

1.160   *Adomako*[1] establishes that to convict someone of gross negligence manslaughter the jury must be satisfied that:

1   the defendant owed a duty of care to the deceased;
2   he or she was in breach of that duty;
3   the breach of duty was a *substantial* cause of death; and
4   the breach was so grossly negligent that the defendant can be deemed to have had such disregard for life of the deceased that it should be seen as criminal and deserving of punishment by the state.

1   *R v Adomako* [1995] 1 AC 171.

1.161   Note that evidence as to the defendant's state of mind is not a prerequisite of a conviction (see *Attorney-General's Reference (No 2 of 1999)* which related to the Southall train crash of 1997).

1.162   In many ways this is a civil case in a criminal arena. It has to be proved that the defendant's negligence was one of the causes of the death as in a civil case. The differences are:

•   The standard of proof (ie beyond reasonable doubt in a criminal case as opposed to on the balance of probabilities in a civil case).
•   The negligence must be a *substantial* cause in a criminal case.
•   The negligence must be *gross*.

Duty of care

1.163   The ordinary principles of the law of negligence apply to determine whether the defendant owed a duty of care and was in breach of that duty. In *R v Khan and Khan*[1] it was said that it is for the trial judge to decide whether the facts of the case are capable of giving rise to a duty of care and to direct the jury accordingly. If such a direction is given, then the jury goes onto decide whether there was a duty.

1   [1998] Crim LR 830, CA.

Substantial cause

1.164   In *Adomako*[1] causation was not an issue. However, in work related deaths there are often a number of causes. Therefore the issue will be whether the individual's conduct was a substantial cause of death.

1   *R v Adomako* [1995] 1 AC 171.

1.165   The prosecution for gross negligence manslaughter in the case *R v O' Connor*[1] concerned the sinking of a fishing vessel, the *Pescado*, where all six crew members died. The prosecution's case against Mr O'Connor, who was a managing agent, was that he was grossly negligent in allowing the vessel to go to sea in an unseaworthy condition. This was compounded by the absence of specific life-saving equipment which it was argued led to the loss of life. There was no direct evidence on the cause of the sinking or when exactly the boat sank.

1   [1997] Crim LR 516, CA.

1.166   The case centred on whether the vessel had capsized as a result of inherent instability or, as was suggested by the defence, as a result of a collision with another ship.

1.167   There had been a number of breaches of the Fishing Vessels (Safety Provisions) Rules 1975.[1] This included a breach that only one life raft had been provided instead of the prescribed two. The prosecution was able to prove that Mr O'Connor's gross negligence had been a substantial cause of the deaths. The Court of Appeal approved the trial judges ruling that proving a substantial cause was sufficient.

1   SI 1975/330.

1.168   There is old authority for saying that liability for manslaughter does not arise where the defendant's conduct is not a direct and immediate cause of death. However, given the terms of *Adomako*[1] and the modern-day understanding of the causes of workplace accidents (see, for example, the HSE's *Successful health and safety management*[2]) this is likely not to be accepted as a limitation on determining whether a defendant's conduct was a substantial cause.

1   *R v Adomako* [1995] 1 AC 171.
2   HS(G)65 (1997).

1.169   If the deceased's own negligence contributed to his or her death this will not necessarily defeat a prosecution. The issue is whether the defendant's negligence was a substantial cause.

Gross negligence

1.170   As to what constitutes gross negligence, Lord Mackay said in *Adomako*[1]

'It is true that to a certain point extent this involves an element of circularity, but in this branch of the law I do not believe that is fatal to its being correct as a test of how far conduct must depart from accepted standards to be characterised as criminal. This is necessarily a question of degree and an attempt to specify that degree more closely is I think likely to achieve only spurious precision. The essence of the matter, which is supremely a jury question, is whether, having regard to the risk of death involved, the conduct of the defendant was so bad in all the circumstances as to amount in their judgement to a criminal act or omission.'

1   *R v Adomako* [1995] 1 AC 171 at 187.

1.171   To set this test in context it is worth looking at the direction given by the trial judge in *R v Litchfield*,[1] which was approved by the Court of Appeal. Mr Litchfield was both master and owner of a square-rigged schooner that foundered off the north Cornish coast. Consequently the schooner was blown onto rocks at Rump Point, just outside Padstow Bay, causing it to break up. Three of the 14 crew died.

1   [1998] Crim LR 507, CA.

1.172   The prosecution argued that Mr Litchfield had steered an unsafe course, too close to a notoriously dangerous shoreline and had plotted the course relying on engines that he knew, or should have known, were liable fail through fuel contamination.

1.173   The direction given was as follows:[1]

'Before you could convict this defendant of manslaughter, the negligence established must go way beyond the mere matter of compensation between parties. It must be more than just some degree of fault, or mistake, or error of judgement, or careless even though that led to death. It must be such as to demonstrate a reckless disregard for the lives of others of such a nature, and to such an extent, that in your judgement the negligence is so bad that it can properly amount to a criminal act.'

1   *R v Litchfield* [1998] Crim LR 507, CA.

1.174   The test is very high. It is entirely a matter for the jury to say whether the conduct is so negligent (using the ordinary meaning of the word) that penal sanction should follow.

Omission manslaughter

1.175   Most work related deaths occur due to negligent omissions rather than negligent acts. As Lord Mackay says in relation to gross negligence the offence includes omissions as well as acts. The case of *R v Khan and Khan*[1] confirms that manslaughter by omission is not a separate entity but is part of gross negligence manslaughter.

1   [1998] Crim LR 830, CA.

Reckless manslaughter

1.176 In *Adomako*[1] Lord Mackay said the trial judge is free to use the word 'reckless' in his direction 'as Lord Atkin put it "in the ordinary connotation of that word ..."' He said it was not necessary to refer to the definition of recklessness set out in *R v Lawrence*.[2]

1 *R v Adomako* [1995] 1 AC 171.
2 [1982] AS 510, HL, a case relating to the Criminal Damage Act 1971. Definition of recklessness was given as follows:
　'Recklessness on the part of the doer of an act presupposes that there is something in the circumstances that would have drawn the attention of an ordinary prudent [and sober] individual to the possibility that his act was capable of causing the kind of serious harmful consequences that the section that created the offence was intended to prevent, and that the risk of those harmful consequences occurring was not so slight that an ordinary prudent individual would feel justified in treating them as negligible. It is only when this is so that the doer of the act is acting "recklessly" if, before doing the act, he either fails to give any thought to the possibility of there being such a risk or having recognised that there was such a risk, he nevertheless goes on to do it.'

1.177 Lord Mackay said[1] the ordinary connotation of 'reckless' had been set out accurately in *R v Stone and Dobinson*[2] and *R v West London Coroner, ex p Gray*.[3] In the latter case it was said:[4]

'It should be explained that to act recklessly means that there was an obvious and serious risk to the health and welfare of M to which that police officer, having regard to his duty, was indifferent or that, recognising that risk to be present, he deliberately chose to run the risk by doing nothing about it. It should be emphasised, however, that a failure to appreciate that there was such a risk would not by itself be sufficient to amount to recklessness.'

1 *R v Adomako* [1995] 1 AC 171.
2 [1977] QB 354, 64 Cr App R 186, CA.
3 [1988] QB 467, DC.
4 [1988] QB 467, DC.

1.178 It is possible to bring a manslaughter prosecution in relation to a work related death on the basis of recklessness and not gross negligence. However, given the nature of most work related deaths it is difficult to see when reckless manslaughter is going to be more appropriate. Particularly as recklessness requires an 'act' on the part of the defendant, and as stated earlier, most work related deaths occur due to omissions.

Corporate manslaughter

1.179 The prosecution of P & O Ferries after the capsizing of the *Herald of Free Enterprise* ferry in 1987,[1] killing 192 people, confirmed it was possible to charge a company with corporate manslaughter. In this case not only was the company charged but also seven directors were charged with manslaughter.

1 *R v P&O European Ferries (Dover) Ltd* [1991] 93 Cr App R 72.

The 'directing mind'

1.180 In *Tesco Supermarkets Ltd v Nattrass*[1] which concerned a prosecution pursuant to the Trades Descriptions Act 1968, the House of Lords held that a company can only be held criminally liable for the acts of only:

'... the Board of Directors, the Managing Director and perhaps other superior officers of the company ... [who] ... carry out the functions of management and speak and act as the company.'

1   [1972] AC 153.

1.181   In *R v Her Majesty's Coroner for East Kent, ex p Spooner*,[1] which was a judicial review of a decision of the coroner at the inquest into the deaths following the sinking of the *Herald of Free Enterprise*, Bingham LJ said:

'It is important to bear in mind an important distinction. A company may be vicariously liable for the negligent acts and omissions of its servants and agents but for a company to be criminally liable for manslaughter ... it is required that the mens rea [the mental element of the crime] and the actus reus [the act/omission of the crime] should be established not against those who acted for or in the name of the company but against those who were to be identified as the embodiment of the company itself.'

1   [1989] 88 Cr App R 10.

1.182   The prosecution of P & O followed after the inquest failed.[1] The trial collapsed in 1990 when Turner J directed the jury that, as a matter of law, there was no evidence upon which they could properly convict the company of manslaughter. The mains reason for his decision was that in order to convict of manslaughter one of the individual defendants who could be 'identified' within the company would have to himself be guilty of manslaughter and since there was insufficient evidence on which to convict any of the individual defendants, the case against the company had to fail. During the course of his judgment, Turner J said:[2]

'Since the 19th century there has been a huge increase in numbers and activities of corporations whether nationalised, municipal or commercial which enter the private lives of all or most of 'men and subjects' in a diversity of ways. A clear case can be made for imputing to such corporations social duties including duty not to offend all relevant parts of the criminal law. By tracing the history of the cases decided by the English courts over the period of the last 150 years, it can be seen how first tentatively and finally confidently the courts have been able to ascribe to corporations a "mind" which is generally one of the essential ingredients of common law and statutory offences. Indeed, it can be seen that in many acts of Parliament the same concept has been embraced ... once a state of mind could be effectively attributed to a corporation, all that remained was to determine the means by which that state of mind could be ascribed and imputed to a non natural person. That done, the obstacle to the acceptance of general criminal liability of a corporation was overcome ... there is nothing essentially incongruous in the notion that a corporation, through the controlling mind of one of its agents, does an act which fulfils the pre-requisites of the crime of manslaughter, it is properly indictable for the crime of manslaughter.'

1   *R v P & O European Ferries (Dover) Ltd* [1991] 93 Cr App R72.
2   [1991] 93 Cr App R 72.

1.183   Turner J emphasised the need to prove that the person prosecuted as the 'directing mind' (or 'controlling mind' as it is also referred to) had sufficient responsibility for safety to establish guilt. It was not permissible to 'aggregate' the faults of a number different individuals, none of whose faults on their own would merit individual prosecution.

1.184   The charge of manslaughter in the *P&O* case[1] was brought on the basis of recklessness. However, as said earlier, the appropriate form in work related deaths is gross negligence manslaughter.

1   *R v P & O European Ferries (Dover) Ltd* [1991] 93 Cr App R72.

1.185   Great Western Trains were prosecuted for corporate manslaughter, based on gross negligence, in relation to the Southall train crash of 1997 where a safety device on the train was inoperative which it is likely would have prevented it. Counsel for the prosecution argued that as the test in *Adomako*[1] is objective, and so does not require a mental element to prove the crime (ie mens rea does not have to be proved) then it was not necessary to prosecute a director of the company as a 'directing mind'. The trial judge, Mr Justice Scott-Baker, rejected this argument saying:[2]

> 'In my judgement it is still necessary to look for ... a directing mind and identify where gross negligence is that fixes the company with criminal responsibility ... Accordingly I conclude that the doctrine of identification which is both clear, certain and established is the relevant doctrine by which a corporation may be fixed for manslaughter by gross negligence ...'

1   *R v Adomako* [1995] 1 AC 171.
2   Transcript of the hearing at the Central Criminal Court on 30 June 1999, pp 26 and 27.

1.186   The Court of Appeal agreed that this was the correct position – see the Attorney-General's appeal to the Court of Appeal on 15 February 2000.[1]

1   *Attorney-General's Reference (No 2 of 1999).*

1.187   Therefore to have a successful corporate manslaughter prosecution a director or senior manager must be convicted of manslaughter (most likely on the basis of gross negligence manslaughter).

Duty of care of directors

1.188   The fact that an individual is a director of a company does not, of itself, give rise to a duty of care on that person's part to someone who is injured or killed by the company's activity. This point was highlighted by Mr Justice Scott Baker in his ruling on the corporate manslaughter charges against Great Western Trains.[1] He said:

> 'The requirements of foreseeability, proximity, fairness, justice and reasonableness must be satisfied in order to satisfy such a duty. The law is careful as to the circumstances in which a director acting in his capacity as such is personally liable. It would ordinarily require that he procured, directed authorised a commission of the tort in question.'

1   Transcript of the hearing at the Central Criminal Court on 30 June 1999, p 27.

1.189   It is probably overstating the position to say that there has to necessarily be some positive action on the part of a director for a duty to arise. It is suggested that in practice the question is more likely to be not whether there is a duty of care, but the extent of that duty.

Successful prosecutions

1.190   There have been very few successful corporate manslaughter prosecutions and all have been against small companies.

1.191   In December1989 the CPS prosecuted two directors of David Holt Plastic Ltd.[1] A workman at the company had been dragged into a machine devised to 'crumble' plastic. He was sliced by a 20–50 inch blade revolving at 1,200 revolutions per second. The machine should have been only able to operate with its lid down. However, the police investigation revealed that someone had removed the lid bolt allowing the machine to operate with its lid up.

1   (1989) unreported.

1.192   One of the directors was present at the time of the incident. He pleaded guilty to manslaughter. No evidence was offered against the other director on the basis that although he knew as much as his fellow director about the machine, he was not physically present at the time of the incident.

1.193   In November 1994 OLL Ltd became the first company in English legal history to be convicted of manslaughter.[1] Peter Kite also became the first director to be given an immediate custodial sentence arising out of the operation of a business. This case concerned a canoeing accident in 1993 in which four students died.

1   (1994) unreported.

1.194   A teacher, a group of eight students and two instructors from OLL Ltd tried to canoe across the sea from Lyme Regis to Charmouth, a distance of about one-and-a-half miles. The teacher got into difficulties and one of the instructors went over to assist. The other instructor proceeded with the students. The group drifted out to sea where the students drowned.

1.195   Mr Kite was one of two directors of the company. He had the primary responsibility for devising, instituting, enforcing and maintaining an appropriate safety policy. The jury found he failed in his responsibility and this was a substantial cause of the deaths.

1.196   In September 1996 Jackson Transport (Ossett) Ltd and its managing director, Alan Jackson, were convicted for the manslaughter of James Hodgson (21) who died in May 1994 after cleaning chemical residues at the rear of a road of a road tanker.[1] He died when he used steam pressure to clean a valve in a tanker blocked with highly toxic chemicals. When the incident happened he was wearing ordinary overalls and a baseball cap. He was not provided with the appropriate personal protective equipment nor supervision or adequate training.

1   (1996) unreported.

1.197   In October 1999 Stephen Bowles and his sister Julie Bowles, both directors of Roy Bowles Transport Ltd were convicted of gross negligence manslaughter.[1] This related to the death of two people in October 1997 in a seven-vehicle pile up on the M25 after a lorry driver working for the company fell asleep at the wheel. The Old Bailey heard the lorry driver and other colleague drivers worked long hours with the knowledge of the directors. The driver pleaded guilty to the offence of death by dangerous driving.

1   (1999) unreported.

1.198   In August 2001, English Brothers Ltd, a Wisbech based construction company pleaded guilty to the manslaughter of Bill Larkman, a gang foreman, who died in June 1999 when he fell over eight metres through a fragile roof to his death. The prosecution had earlier accepted a plea of 'not guilty' from Melvyn Hubbard, a director of the company. The court heard that in 1997 inspectors from the HSE had seen Bill Larkman working at another English Brothers site without using correct safety equipment, and had spoken to the company about its safety failings.

1   (2001) unreported.

1.199   In February 2003 Teglgaard Hardwood (UK) and John Horner, Managing Director, pleaded guilty to gross negligence manslaughter in relation to the death of an 18-year-old labourer. The company imported timber. The deceased was crushed to death when a pile of poorly stacked hardwood packs toppled over on top of him. The underlying cause of the incident was the failure to carryout a suitable risk assessment covering the storage of the hardwood packs. The timber packs were frequently off-set and protruding from the pile, making them unstable. Further the steel binding on some of the packs, used to keep the packs together, were damaged resulting in reduced stability.

1   (2003) unreported.

Risk

1.200   With the HSE's guidance entitled *Directors' responsibilities for health and safety*[1] and the *Turnbull Report*[2] major health and safety risks are something that are expected to be dealt with at board level. Thus, the issue of how a company and its board deal with risk is likely to become more relevant to corporate manslaughter cases. An illustration of this is the prosecution of Euromin and its director Mr Martell following the death of Simon Jones in April 1998.[3]

1   IND(G)343 (2001), available at www.hse.gov.uk/pubns/indg343.pdf.
2   N Turnbull (chair) Institute of Chartered Accountants for England and Wales *Internal control: guidance for directors on the combined code* (the *Turnbull Report*) (1999).
3   (2001) unreported.

1.201   Simon Jones, aged 24, died on his first day at work at Shoreham Docks while unloading cargo from a ship when the jaws of a grab closed around his neck. It transpired that the crane operator could not see inside the ship's hold and the person responsible for communication between the crane driver and the hold was a Polish seaman and could not speak English.

1.202   Ultimately the case was unsuccessful with the company and its director being acquitted of manslaughter at the Old Bailey in November 2001. It should be noted that the manslaughter investigation did not start until six weeks after the incident, which as a consequence, meant there were evidential problems. Further the trial judge seemed to have concerns that the error of the crane driver broke the chain of causation.

1 (2001) unreported.

1.203   However, the case is significant for the judicial review by the deceased's family of the original decision by the CPS not to prosecute (*R v DPP, ex p Jones*[1]). At the judicial review the Director of Public Prosecutions argued that there was no evidence the managing director had been warned of the dangers of the system of work being operated. The judge said:

> 'The point can be put in this way. A clear and potential ... major criticism [of the managing director and the company] is that they set up the unsafe system ... it was unsafe because, *inter alia*, it arguably presented a danger of death – the danger that in fact had eventuated. Such a system requires detailed precautions to be taken to ensure the incipient dangers did not in fact eventuate.'

1 [2000] IRLR 373.

1.204   Another way of looking at this is to say the company should have carried out a risk assessment and that failure to do so was a cause of the death. It would be for the jury to consider whether that was a substantial cause and if the failure amounted to gross negligence.

Causation

1.205   Most work related deaths occur when there is a human error by a front line worker. The traditional approach of the police has been to view the error as breaking the 'chain of causation' to any failure on the part of a director of a company. This approach to causation does not sit comfortably with the HSE's view of the root causes of such incidents. As stated at **para 1.54 n 1** above, *Successful health and safety management*[1] says accidents, ill health and incidents are seldom random events and generally arise from management and organisational failures.

1 HS(G)65 (2nd edn, 1997).

1.206   In the Southall train crash, the judge when sentencing Great Western Trains on 27 July 1999 for the health and safety offence which it had pleaded guilty to, did not view the driver in its employment passing a red signal as breaking the chain of causation. He stated:[1]

> '... But a substantial contributory cause was the fact that the defendant company permitted the train to run from Swansea to Paddington at speeds of up to 125 m.p.h. with the Automatic Warning System (AWS) isolated ...
>   The company should have applied its mind to the risk created by allowing a high speed train to travel a journey of this length and this speed without the AWS operating. It maybe that the likelihood of a driver passing a red signal was relatively small. But if the event occurred the consequences were going to be, as in the event they were, appalling.'

1 (1999) unreported.

1.207 Difficulties with causation occur in other areas of law. In 2002 the House of Lords heard appeals in cases concerning personal injury claims relating to the contraction of mesothelioma – *Fairchild v Glenhaven Funeral Services Ltd*.[1] The main issue before the court was causation.

1 [2002] 3 All ER 305.

1.208 Mesothelioma is a fatal lung disease that is caused by exposure to asbestos. It is thought that only one asbestos fibre in the lung is needed to develop the disease which can lay dormant for 20 years.

1.209 The claimants in these cases had worked for more than one employer who had negligently exposed them to asbestos. Because it was medically impossible to prove in which employment the fatal fibre had been received, the Court of Appeal ruled that on a strict interpretation of the law of causation the claims failed. This was overturned by the House of Lords.

1.210 Lord Bingham said a traditional approach 'denies recovery where our instinctive sense of justice ... tells us the victim should obtain compensation'. In his judgment[1] he referred to the environmental prosecution case *Empress Car Co (Abertillery) Ltd v National Rivers Authority*.[2] Here there was an argument whether the act of an unknown person broke the chain of causation.

1 *Fairchild v Glenhaven Funeral Services Ltd* [2002] 3 All ER 305.
2 [1998] 1 All ER 481.

1.211 The company was prosecuted for polluting a river contrary to the Water Resources Act 1991, s 65(1). The House of Lords said what had to be determined was whether the event, the act of the unknown person, was ordinary (if so the company was guilty and the chain of causation was not broken) or extraordinary (if so the company was not guilty).

1.212 Lord Hoffmann in this case said:[1]

'Questions of causation often arise for the purpose of attributing responsibility to someone, for example, so as to blame him for something which has happened or to make him guilty of an offence or liable in damages. On such cases, the answer will depend on the rule by which responsibility is being attributed.'

1 *Empress Car Co (Abertillery) Ltd v National Rivers Authority* [1998] 1 All ER 481.

1.213 In 2000 Lord Cullen chaired the Public Inquiry into the causes of the Ladbroke train crash of October 1999 that killed 29 passengers and the drivers of both trains involved in the collision. The driver of the Thames Turbo train, Michael Hodder passed signal SN109 at red. This signal had been passed on eight previous occasions in just over five years and each time the incident was recorded as 'driver error'. Three days after the crash, the Her Majesty's Railway Inspectorate (part of the HSE) served a prohibition notice on Railtrack, the then operators of the railway infrastructure.

1.214 Prior to the start of the Inquiry the police announced there would be no manslaughter prosecutions. Lord Cullen in his Report[1] declined to blame Mr Hodder for the crash. He concluded Mr Hodder passed the signal because of poor 'sighting' of the signal, both in itself and with other signals on the gantry on which it was situated.

1   The Rt Hon Lord WD Cullen PC *The Ladbroke Grove Rail Inquiry, Part 1 Report* (2001), available at www.pixunlimited.co.uk/pdf/news/transport/ladbrokegrove.pdf.

1.215   Lord Cullen found that there was a 'lamentable failure on the part of Railtrack' to respond to recommendations of inquiries into two serious incidents in the Paddington area involving signals passed at danger (SPADs). However, the recognition by Railtrack of a SPAD problem in the area led to the formation of a number of groups to deal with the problem. But Lord Cullen said little was achieved because they were so 'disjointed and ineffective'. He accused Railtrack of not dealing with the problem in a 'prompt, proactive and effective manner'. Lord Cullen quoted the comments of the Zone Director of Railtrack who said: 'The culture of the place had gone seriously adrift over many years.'

1.216   After publication of the report, lawyers for the bereaved and injured campaigned for a reconsideration of corporate manslaughter charges. Following the Crown Prosecution Service obtaining advice concerning in part causation from a leading academic in this field of law, in May 2002 it was announced that the police investigation would be re-opened to reconsider the case against Railtrack. One of the main reasons given by the Crown Prosecution Service for the original decision not to proceed against Railtrack and any of its senior people was that any fault on the part of Railtrack could not be linked to the collision.[1]

1   It should be noted that in October 2003 the HSE announced that it would be prosecuting Thames Trains, the employer of Mr Hodder, for health and safety breaches. However, a decision was still awaited from the CPS as to whether there would be corporate manslaughter charges against Railtrack.

1.217   On 17 October 2000 there was a train derailment at Hatfield which killed four people. It has been established that a broken rail was the cause of the accident. In July 2003 Balfour Beatty, the company that maintained the track at the time of the accident, and Network Rail, who took over from Railtrack as owners of the infrastructure, were summonsed for corporate manslaughter. Senior people from both companies have been charged with manslaughter in their own right and have been identified as directing minds. No front line workers have been charged with manslaughter.

1.218   Whether any convictions result from the Ladbroke Grove and Hatfield cases remains to be seen. However, whatever happens, the significance is that it shows the prosecuting authorities are starting to take a broader approach to the issue of causation which is more in line with the HSE's approach to the underlying causes of work related incidents.

Reforming involuntary manslaughter law

1.219   As stated earlier, the Home Office in its consultation paper entitled *Reforming the Law on Involuntary Manslaughter: The Government's Proposals* published in May 2000 set out its proposals for a new offence of corporate killing.[1]

1   The Rt Hon J Straw MP (2000), available at www.homeoffice.gov.uk/docs/invmans.html.

1.220   The paper states the need for reform is because there have been a number of disasters in recent years which have evoked demands for the use of the law of manslaughter and failures to successfully prosecute have led to an 'apparent perception among the public' that the current law does not work. It says this is heightened because inquiries into disasters have found companies at fault which has merited severe criticism.

1.221   It is interesting to note that the four disasters highlighted in the paper involved 'human factors'.

- *Herald of Free Enterprise* (1987). Immediate cause was the failure to close the bow doors of the ferry before leaving port. There was no effective reporting system to check the bow doors.
- *The Kings Cross fire* (1987). A discarded cigarette probably set fire to grease and rubbish underneath one of the escalators. Organisational changes had resulted in poor escalator cleaning. The fire took hold because of the wooden escalator, the failure of water fog equipment and inadequate fire and emergency training of staff. There was a culture which viewed fire as inevitable.
- *The Clapham train crash* (1988). Immediate cause was a signal failure caused by a technician failing to isolate and remove a wire. Contributory causes included degradation of working practices, problems with training, testing quality and communication standards, poor supervision. No effective system for monitoring or limiting excessive hours.
  The Southall train crash (1997). The immediate cause as stated at **para 1.206** above was the driver of the high speed train passing a red signal. Underlying causes were the failure to have an operative AWS (automatic warning system – designed to help prevent signals being passed at danger) on the train and confusion over the industry rules regarding what action should be taken when there was an AWS failure.

1.222   Apart from the proposal for the offence of corporate killing the paper also sets out new offences against individuals for involuntary manslaughter.

1.223   The current manslaughter offences based on gross negligence for individuals and companies would be replaced by *killing by gross carelessness* for an individual and *corporate killing* for a company.

Killing by gross carelessness

1.224   A person commits killing by gross carelessness if:

- His or her conduct causes the death of another.
- A risk that his or her conduct will cause death or serious injury would be obvious to a reasonable person in his or her position.
- He or she is capable of appreciating that risk at this material time (but did not in fact do so).

And either:

- his or her conduct falls far below what can reasonably be expected in the circumstances; *or*
- he or she intends by his or her conduct to cause some injury, or is aware of, and unreasonably takes, the risk that it may do so, *and* the conduct causing (or intended to cause) the injury constitutes an offence.

1.225   In a work related death involving an individual's negligence it is likely to be the first limb of the offence (conduct falling below what can be reasonably be expected) that will be used.

1.226   In gross negligence manslaughter it has to be shown that the defendant's negligence was a *substantial cause*. This offence makes no use of the word 'substantial' and so it would appear that the prosecution would only have to show the defendant's conduct (negligence) was a *cause*, which is obviously much easier to prove.

1.227   In a sense, the term 'gross carelessness' appears a contradiction in terms, particularly when compared with the definition of 'gross negligence'. It suggests the level of negligent conduct does not have to be as bad for gross carelessness as it does for gross negligence and so will be easier to prove.

Reckless killing

1.228   This offence against an individual is proved if:

- the defendant's conduct caused death;
- the defendant was aware of the risk the conduct might cause death or serious injury; and
- the defendant unreasonably took the risk having regard to the known circumstances.

1.229   In a work related death, it is suggested that this offence is unlikely to be used.

Corporate killing

1.230   The offence of corporate killing mirrors that of the offence for gross carelessness. However, the main difference between the corporate offence and the individual one is that the risk does not have to be obvious to the company nor does the company have to be capable of appreciating that risk for there to be a conviction.

1.231   A company will be guilty of the offence if:

- A 'management failure' by the company is the cause or one of the causes of a person's death.
- The management failure fell 'far below what can reasonably be expected' of the company in the circumstances.

1.232   Unlike corporate manslaughter, the prosecution does not have to prove a 'directing mind'. Like the offence for the individual of gross carelessness, it does not appear to require the cause to be a substantial nor that the failure be as bad as in gross negligence. It also says that the failure can be a cause, even if the 'immediate cause is the act or omission of an individual'.

1.233   The question is: what is a management failure? The proposed offence states that there is a management failure by a company if 'the way in which its activities are managed or organised fails to ensure the health and safety of persons employed in or affected by those activities'.

1.234 Further, how far does a company's management failure need to fall below what can reasonably be expected? In the prosecution of Stephen Bowles and his sister Julie Bowles, both directors of Roy Bowles Transport Ltd mentioned at **PARA 1.197** above,[1] evidence was given to the court that the hours worked by the company's drivers were in line with the haulage industry as a whole. Despite this the directors were still found to be grossly negligent. Thus pointing to what is common practice in the type of business the company is in, may not amount to a defence.

1 (1999) unreported.

Directors

1.235 The government originally proposed that individuals (directors or officers) who could be shown to have had some influence on, or responsibility for, the circumstances in which a management failure falling far below what could be reasonably expected was a cause of someone's death, should be disqualified from acting in a management role in Great Britain. This proposal has now been dropped. However, such an individual might still be disqualifies under the Company Directors' Disqualification Act 1986 where appropriate.

1.236 Directors and senior managers could also be prosecuted under the individual offence of killing by gross carelessness. However, these prosecutions would still face the same problems of proving causation as discussed at **paras 1.205-1.218** above.

Criticisms of corporate killing?

1.237 Louise Christian, the solicitor who represented the bereaved and injured at the recent rail inquiries, has pointed out that the distinction between the new law and the existing health and safety law 'could purely be a semantic one, in the absence of someone in the dock'.[1]

1 L Christian 'Rail crash litigation – Southall and Ladbroke' (2001) J Personal Injury Law, December.

1.238 Corporate killing could be a disincentive to the police to investigate the conduct of individual directors, because it would be easier just to investigate the company. There is no indication that the level of fines imposed on a company would be significantly greater than under health and safety law (although there would be the added stigma of a corporate-killing prosecution). The law may not result in a significant increase in convictions as it will always be much easier to prove the management failure created a risk of harm (the requirement for health and safety offences) rather than prove it caused death.

1.239 David Grimley, Technical Claims Manager at the insurance company St Pauls, warns that there may be increased premiums for employer's liability (EL) insurance as a result of a change in the law. At present, companies often plead guilty to health and safety offences where death has occurred. Grimley predicts companies would rely upon provisions in their EL insurance to defend corporate killing prosecutions. He also fears the impact of private prosecutions for the offence if it can be brought without the consent of the Director of Public Prosecutions.[1]

1 Personal communication with Michael Appleby.

1.240   An editorial in the *Financial Times*[1] – which said that Home Secretary David Blunkett's proposal 'is unlikely to please anyone' – argued that the new law could delay payments of compensation to the families of victims because companies would want to avoid any possible admission of guilt. Further it would encourage 'cover-ups and buck passing – a blame culture that does little to reduce accidents' (although any director involved in a cover-up runs the risk of being prosecuted for perverting the course of justice).

1   'Corporate killing: Blunkett's late conversion is unlikely to please anyone' (editorial) *Financial Times*, 21 May 2003, p 22.

Conclusion

1.241   In law, a company is a separate legal entity. It appears ludicrous, on the face of it, to need to prove that one of its directors or senior managers has been grossly negligent in order to prove the same against the company. But the reality is, you cannot send a company to jail; only fine it. So, in practical terms, there would be no difference between a health and safety conviction and one for corporate killing.

1.242   No doubt, the lawyers will have a field-day arguing what exactly a management failure is. When the prosecution has established a management failure, it still has to go on to prove causation. These problems are not inherent in a health and safety prosecution.

1.243   As the proposals are likely to be drafted, a conviction for corporate killing will not result in a director being sent to prison. A director could be convicted of the individual offence of killing by gross carelessness – where the health and safety risk would need to be obvious to the director and he or she must be capable of appreciating it – if his or her conduct warranted it. In reality, this would mean that the problems involved in proving a 'directing mind' in corporate manslaughter are still there – ie the director's management failure has to be linked to the incident.

1.244   The government says targeting individual directors or managers 'would just create scapegoats and that would not be in the interests of justice'.[1] But the families of victims will want to see someone in the dock held personally responsible. Arguably, the offence of killing by gross carelessness is easier to prove against front line workers and lower management than is gross-negligence manslaughter. The problems of causation would not exist against them and a judge is likely to direct that their conduct had an obvious risk. The danger might be that these people will become the actual scapegoats of the proposed changes.

1   'Directors will escape liability in corporate killing cases' *Financial Times*, 21 May 2003, p 3.

1.245   The government could just bring in the offence of corporate killing, and leave the law of involuntary manslaughter alone. It is difficult to see what this would achieve, apart from the added stigma of such a conviction on the company's reputation.

1.246   Despite the government's reaffirming in May 2003 of its intention to legislate, the Queen's Speech on 26 November 2003 made no mention of corporate killing. According to the Centre for Corporate Accountability the Home Office has confirmed to them that the government is still committed to publish a Bill by the end of 2003.[1]

Even if eventual legislation is still a remote possibility, this does not mean that companies and their directors have reason to be complacent

1. www.corporateaccountability.org/Updates/manslaughter.htm, updated 27 November 2003.

1.247   In the case of *Davies v Health and Safety Executive*[1] the Court of Appeal said that health and safety offences were not truly criminal. If the sanctions of HSWA 1974 were comparable with the Enterprise Act 2002, including the provision for imposing custodial sentences, then perhaps the perception would be different. This is not beyond the realms of possibility given the proposed changes to sanctions set out in the government and HSC's strategic document *Revitalising health and safety*.[2] Further, as shown in the HSC enforcement policy statement, there is a greater willingness to look at the chain of management and the individuals at management involvesd[3]

1   [2002] EWCA Crim 2949.
2   HSC *Revitalising Health and Safety strategy statement* (2000).
2   HSC *Enforcement policy statement* HSC15 (2002), available at www.hse.gov.uk/pubns/hsc15.pdf.

1.248   There is no reason either to suspect that the authorities have given up on the law of corporate manslaughter as it currently stands. This is evidenced by the prosecutions in relation to Hatfield and the police's and HSE's greater readiness in recent years to investigate companies and their directors for manslaughter when there is a work related death.

1.249   Even if there is no manslaughter prosecution, the HSE in recent years have appeared more ready to prosecute where there has been a fatality. Some believe the HSE have become to willing to prosecute and is seen as unreasonable. This is highlighted by Mr Alan Osborne, the former Director of Rail Safety at the HSE, in his resignation statement in October 2003. He refered to the prosecution earlier this year of the Commissioner of the Metropolitan Police and his predecessor for a lax safety culture after the death of an officer who fell through a fragile roof.[1] He said: 'The prosecution of the Metropolitan police demonstrated just how out of touch the [HSE] has become.'[2]

1   At the trial at the Central Criminal Court, Sir John Stevens, the Commissioner of the Metropolitan police was cleared of two of the three health and safety charges brought against him and Lord Condon of two of the four health and safety charges brought against. On the outstanding counts the HSE decided not to proceed to a retrial. See HSE press release E116:03-27 June 2003.
2   *Guardian*, Friday 28 November 2003.

1.250   However the media's perception, which has become the public's reality, is that companies have been getting away with 'murder'. The pressure is there for action to be taken.

1.251   Whether corporate killing becomes law or not, what can be said for certain is that when things go wrong, companies can expect their health and safety procedures to be scrutinised and for there to be a prosecution of some form if they are deemed to be lacking.

CHAPTER 2

Sentencing

Gerard Forlin, Barrister, 2-3 Grays Inn Square, London and

Michael Appleby, Solicitor, Fisher Scoggins LLP, London

Introduction

2.1   This chapter looks at the sentencing powers of the courts in health and safety prosecutions and manslaughter prosecutions and gives examples of past cases for guidance. It also sets out the sentencing powers contained in the corporate killing proposals.

Health and safety offences – employers

Sentencing powers of the courts

2.2   The courts can only impose a fine upon an employer guilty of a breach of one of the general duties under the Health and Safety at Work etc Act 1974 (HSWA 1974) (ie the duties pursuant to HSWA 1974, ss 2–6) and related regulations. In the magistrates' court the maximum fine that can be imposed is £20,000. In the Crown Court there is no limit upon the amount the employer can be fined.

Guidance on imposing fines

2.3   The leading case on the levels of fines to be imposed upon employers for breaches of health and safety law is *R v F Howe & Son (Engineers) Ltd.*[1] The Court of Appeal in this case responded to the public's disquiet that the level of fine for health and safety offences was too low.

1   [1999] 2 All ER 249.

2.4   The Court of Appeal acknowledged there was increasing recognition of the seriousness of such offences and that judges and magistrates who rarely deal with these cases had found it difficult to know how to approach sentencing. It therefore took the opportunity to set out some sentencing guidelines while emphasising each case would turn on its own particular circumstances. The Court of Appeal said it was not possible to set any tariff or to set any specific relationship between the fine and the employer's turnover or profits.

2.5   Mr Justice Scott Baker said the law requires employers to do 'what good management and common sense requires them to do anyway ie look at what the risks are and take sensible measures to tackle them'. He pointed out that failure to fulfil these general duties under HSWA 1974 is particularly serious as they are the 'foundations for protecting health and safety'. He went on to say:[1]

'The objective for health and safety offences in the workplace is to achieve a safe environment for those who work there and for other members of the public who may be affected. A fine need to be large enough to bring that message home where the defendant is a company not only to those who manage it but also to its shareholders.'

1   *R v F Howe & Son (Engineers) Ltd* [1999] 2 All ER 249 at 255.

2.6   Although it was accepted in general a fine should not be so large as to imperil the earnings of employees or create a risk of bankruptcy, there may be cases where the offences are so serious that the defendant ought not to be in business.

2.7   Mr Justice Scott Baker also made it clear that the standard of care imposed by the health and safety legislation is the same regardless of the size of the defendant company.

2.8   The Court of Appeal said the following factors should be taken into account.

General factors

2.9

1   The gravity of the offence – how far short of the appropriate standard the defendant fell in failing to take reasonably practicable steps to ensure health and safety.
2   The degree of risk and the extent of the danger created by the offence.
3   The extent of the breach or breaches, for example, whether it was an isolated incident or continued over a period.
4   An important factor is the defendant's resources and the effect of the fine on its business.

Aggravating features

2.10

1   A failure to heed warnings.
2   Deliberately profiting financially from failure to take necessary health and safety steps or specifically running the risk to save money. It was said: 'A deliberate breach of health and safety legislation with a view to profit seriously aggravates the offence.'
3   The breach has resulted in death. The penalty 'should reflect the public disquiet at the unnecessary loss of life'.

Mitigating factors

2.11

1   Prompt admission of responsibility and a timely plea of guilty.
2   Steps to remedy deficiencies after they are drawn to the defendant's attention.
3   A good safety record.

2.12   The Court of Appeal said that any fine should reflect not only on the gravity of the offence but also the means of the offender, and that this applies just as much as to corporate defendants as any other. It went on to say:[1]

> 'Difficulty is sometime found in obtaining timely and accurate information about a corporate defendant's means. The starting point is its annual accounts. If a defendant company wishes to make a submission to the court about its ability to pay a fine it should supply copies of its accounts and any other financial information on which it intends to rely in good time before the hearing both to the court and to the prosecution.
> This will give the prosecution the opportunity to assist the court should the court wish it. Usually accounts need to be considered with some care to avoid reaching a superficial and perhaps erroneous conclusion. Where accounts or other financial information are deliberately not supplied the court will be entitled to conclude that the company is in a position to pay any financial penalty it is minded to impose. Where the relevant information is provided late it may be desirable for sentence to be adjourned, if necessary at the defendant's expense, so as to avoid the risk of the court taking what it is told at face value and imposing an inadequate penalty.'

1   *R v F Howe & Son (Engineers) Ltd* [1999] 2 All ER 249 at 254.

2.13   It should be noted, as was pointed out by counsel for the defendant in this case, neither the fines nor the costs imposed upon an employer are deductible against tax and therefore the full burden falls upon the company.

2.14   The Court of Appeal also stated that in its judgement magistrates should always think carefully before accepting jurisdiction in health and safety at work cases where it is arguable that the fine may exceed the limit of their jurisdiction or where death or serious injury has resulted from the offence. The trend now appears for more cases to be heard in the Crown Court.

2.15 In the case of *R v Friskies Petcare Ltd*[1] the Court of Appeal recommended that where there is a plea of guilty, the prosecution and defence should set out in advance the aggravating and mitigating features in the case. In practice the prosecution is required to serve a schedule setting out the aggravating and mitigating features of the case for agreement. This has become known as a 'friskies schedule'. The Court of Appeal said in this case if it is possible to place an agreed basis of plea before the court that should be done. If there is a 'disagreement of substance', the presiding judge can determine whether a Newton hearing is required.[2]

1 [2000] Cr App R (S) 401.
2 A Newton hearing is where the defendant admits his guilt but does not accept the facts presented by the prosecution as the basis of his guilt: *R v Newton* [1983] Crim LR 198. Evidence is then called at the hearing in order to determine the facts.

2.16 In this case[1] the Court of Appeal also commented that fines in excess of £500,000 tend to be reserved for cases of major public disasters. This led to defence arguments in subsequent cases that effectively there should be a ceiling on fines of £500,000 for incidents that were not major public disasters.

1 *R v Friskies Petcare Ltd* [2000] Cr App R (S) 401.

2.17 However the Court of Appeal in the case of *R v Colthrop Board Mill* made it clear this was not the position:[1]

'It appears from the authorities that financial penalties of up to around half a million pounds are appropriate for case which result in the death even of a single employee, and perhaps of the serious injury of such a single employee. We would not wish the sum of £500,000 to appear to be set in stone or to provide and sort of maximum limit for such cases. On the contrary, we anticipate that as time goes on and awareness of the importance of safety increases, that courts will uphold sums of that amount and even in excess of them in serious cases, whether or not they involve what could be described as major public disasters.'

1 [2002] 2 Cr App R (S) 80.

2.18 Finally in *R v Rollco Screw and Rivet Co*[1] the Court of Appeal said the question was not only the level of penalty merited by the offence, but also the level the defendants could reasonably be expected to meet. In relation to the later it was relevant to consider the issue of time over which the penalty should be payable.

1 [1999] IRLR 439.

Examples of fines imposed

2.19 The following are examples of fines imposed upon employers for breaches of health and safety duties. Although some predate the *Howe* case,[1] they are still useful as a guide.

1 *R v F Howe & Son (Engineers) Ltd* [1999] 2 All ER 249.

2.20 There are few reported cases on sentencing in health and safety cases. Details of cases can be found on the HSE website[1] or reported in health and safety magazines such as Safety Management and Safety and Health Practitioner.

1 At www.hse.gov.uk.

2.21   The figures given are for fines only and do not include costs of prosecution or defence.

2.22   British Railways Board was fined £250,000 on 14 June 1991 at the Old Bailey in relation to the Clapham Junction train crash of 1988 in which 35 people died.[1] British Railways Board pleaded guilty to breaches of HSWA 1974, ss 2 and 3. Immediate cause was a signal failure caused by a technician failing to isolate and remove a wire. Contributory causes included degradation of working practices, problems with training, testing quality and communication standards, poor supervision.

1   (14 June 1991, unreported), Central Criminal Court.

2.23   Mersey Docks and Harbour Company pleaded guilty to a breach of HSWA 1974, s 3. The matter went before the Court of Appeal on sentence.[1] The company had failed to ascertain whether there were any 'dangerous spaces' where flammable cases could be found after discharging the cargo of the vessel in port. Two workmen died and others were injured when a torch conflagrated gases remaining in the holds. The company was fined £250,000. Hobhouse LJ stated:

> '… nothing that we say … detracts from the duty of the Master of the vessel, or indeed those responsible for the operation of a vessel. But the duty imposed by statute upon persons in the position of the … company is that they themselves have the duty. It is a non delegable duty and they must carry out that duty. It is not mitigation for them to say that they just leave it to other people. If that is their attitude to the discharge of their statutory duty, then it is important the Courts when there has been a breach of the duty, should impose fines which leave people such as this Harbour Company in no doubt that it is their duty and that they have to discharge it. Anything less than a substantial fine will fail to bring the matter home to them.'

1   *R v Mersey Docks and Harbour Company* [1995] 6 Cr App R (S) 806.

2.24   British Railways Board was fined £200,000 at Snaresbrook Crown Court on 7 October 1996 in relation to a train collision at Wood Street in North East London in 1995. There were no casualties. British Railways Board pleaded guilty to breaches of HSWA 1974, ss 2 and 3. The immediate cause was a signal failure cause by human error when carrying out maintenance to a section of track. Underlying causes were that the work had not been properly planned and the maintenance staff had not been properly trained.

2.25   Fartygsentreprenader AB, Fartygskonstruction AB, Port Ramsgate Ltd and Lloyd's Register of Shipping had fines imposed upon them at the Central Criminal Court on 28 February 1997 totalling £1.7 million and ordered to pay £600,00 towards the HSE investigation costs and pay the trial costs of £115,000.[1] The case concerned the collapse in 1994 of a walkway suspended 30 feet above the ground killing six people and injuring seven others. The companies were prosecuted under HSWA 1974, s 3 and Port Ramsgate was also prosecuted for a breach of the Docks Regulations 1988, reg 7.[2]

1   28 February 1997, unreported.
2   SI 1998/1655, reg 7.

2.26   South East Infrastructure Maintenance Company Ltd, Railtrack PLC and Southern Track Renewals Company received a global fine of £150,000 on 8 February 1998 following an incident at Bexley Kent in February 1997. Seven freight trains derailed at a bridge over Bexley High Street. Four members of the public who were near the bridge were injured. Each company pleaded guilty to a breach of HSWA 1974, s 3.

2.27   Sainsbury's was fined 450,000in November 1998 at Winchester Crown Court after pleading guilty to six breaches of HSWA 1974 and other associated legislation. A warehouse worker died after a forklift truck toppled over and crushed him while he was inspecting it. The safety-cut-off-switch had been deliberately disconnected. Mr Justice Kay said when sentencing:

'… The story is a picture of working procedures that date back to the dark ages.'

2.28   Milford Havern Port Authority was prosecuted by the Environmental Agency in relation to pollution resulting from an oil spillage of 72,000 tonnes of crude oil from the *Sea Empress*, a Russian ship that ran aground in 1996 because of an inexperienced pilot. Although this is not a health and safety case as such, it is important to note from a sentencing point of view.

2.29   At Cardiff Crown Court on 16 January 1999, Mr Justice Steel imposed a fine of £4 million on the Port Authority. He said: 'The accident occurred because of the "careless" navigation of a pilot who had never attempted this manoeuvre with a ship of this size at low tide.' The judge went on to say: 'The pilot was put in a position by the Port Authority where he could make an error of navigation.'

2.30   In relation to the fine the judge said this was required 'to reflect the genuine and justified public concerns'. The clean up operation cost £60 million. The judge recognised that the Port Authority did not have the '… vast reserves of a major oil company or manufacturing company'.

2.31   F Howe & Son (Engineers) Ltd[1] (the case mentioned at **paras 2.3–2.14** above where sentencing guidelines were set out by the Court of Appeal) pleaded guilty to a breaches of HSWA 1974, s 2, the Electricity at Work Regulations 1989, reg 4[2] and the Management of Health and Safety at Work Regulations 1992, regs 3 and 11. The prosecution resulted from a fatal accident in August 1996 when a 20-year-old employee was electrocuted. The company was small with limited resources. The electrical equipment in question was in a bad state. The Court of Appeal ruled the appropriate fine in this case was £15,000.

1   *R v F Howe & Son (Engineers) Ltd* [1999] 2 All ER 249.
2   SI 1989/635, reg 4.
1   SI 1992/2051, reg 3 and SI 1992/2051, reg 11.

2.32   Balfour Beatty Civil Engineering Ltd on 15 February 1999 at the Central Criminal Court was fined £1.2 million following the collapse of three tunnels during the construction of the Heathrow Express railway link at Heathrow Airport on 21 October 1994. No one was injured in the collapse that occurred at 1 am. Balfour Beatty was the main contractor, using the New Australian Tunnelling Method (NATM) on which Geoconsult ZT GmbH were consultants

2.33   Balfour Beatty pleaded guilty to breaches of HSWA 1974, ss 2 and 3. Geoconsult were also prosecuted for breaches of HSWA 1974, ss 2 and 3 but pleaded not guilty. The company was convicted and fined £500,000.

2.34   Great Western Trains wad fined £1.5 million at the Central Criminal Court on 27 July 1999 in relation to the Southall train crash of 1997 in which seven people died.[1] The driver of the GWT train passed a signal at danger (SPAD). The automatic warning system (AWS) that was designed to help prevent SPADs and would have given the driver an audible warning of the cautionary signals was isolated, ie inoperative. The judge when passing sentence said that the risk of the driver passing a danger signal was small but that if this did happen the consequences were likely to be 'appalling' and so took the view that the company should have ensured that the train was not running in that condition. Great Western Trains pleaded guilty to a breach of HSWA 1974, s 3.

1   (27 May 1999, unreported), Central Criminal Court.

2.35   London Underground Limited were fined £300,000 at the Central Criminal Court on 27 July 1999 having pleaded guilty to a breach of HSWA 1974, s 3 and the Railways (Safety Case) Regulations 1994, reg 7(1).[2] This related to an incident at Eastcote Station on 31 December 1996. An elderly passenger fell between a train and the platform when alighting at the station. Apparently she had become caught in the doors. The train moved off, killing the passenger. The driver was originally investigated for manslaughter but this eventually did not proceed. At the inquest evidence was given that there was a 50-yard blind spot and so the driver would not have been able to see the passenger.

1   SI 1994/237, reg 7(1).

2.36   Keltbray Ltd was fined £200,000 at Southwark Crown Court on 7 September 1999[1] having pleaded guilty to a breach of the Construction (Health, Safety and Welfare) Regulations 1996, reg 6.[2] *R v F Howe & Son (Engineers) Ltd*[3] was followed. The fine was upheld on appeal. The case related to the death of two men after the floor they were working on collapsed.

1   The defendants appealed the sentence which was upheld by the Court of Appeal: *R v Ketbray Ltd* [2001] 1 Cr App Rep (S) 132.
2   SI 1996/1592, reg 6.
3   [1999] 2 All ER 249.

2.37   BG Exploration & Production Ltd was fined £300,000 at Kingston-upon-Hull Crown Court on 10 February 2000. This followed an incident in February 1998 when a large volume of natural gas was released from a leak in a pipework joint on the company's Rough 47/3B offshore gas platform. The gas did not ignite and there were no injuries. The company pleaded guilty to breaches of HSWA 1974, the Offshore Installations (Prevention of Fire and Explosion, and Emergency Response) Regulations 1995[1] and the Reporting of Injuries, Diseases and Dangerous Occurrences Regulations 1995.[2]

1   SI 1995/743.
2   SI 1995/3163.

2.38   Friskies Petcare (UK) Ltd (mentioned at **para 2.15**ff above) had its fine reduced by the Court of Appeal in March 2000 to £250,000.[1] This related to the electrocution of an employee. He was repairing a metal ribbon stirrer at the bottom of a silo. He was arc welding in a confined, damp, conductive environment in the silo when he was electrocuted while changing welding electrodes. The company pleaded guilty to a breach of HSWA 1974, s 2 and a breach of the Management of Health and Safety at Work Regulations 1999, reg 3.[2]

1 [2000] Cr App R (S) 401.
2 SI 1999/3242, reg 3.

2.39 Colthrop Board Mills Limited were fined £350,000 in 2001 at Reading Crown Court in relation to an accident in February 2000 in which one of its employees lost the use of his right hand.[1] The company pleaded guilty to breaches of HSWA 1974, s 2 and the Provision and Use of Work Equipment Regulations 1998, reg 11.[2] The accident occurred when the employee was checking to see if a roller on the mill's paper production needed cleaning by running his hand along the roller and as a consequence his hand become caught between two rollers, dragging him into the machine. The company was aware of this unsafe practice and a month before the accident the company carried out a risk assessment that identified there was a high risk of a fatality and that guarding should be provided. At the time of the accident the guarding had not been installed.

1 [2002] 2 Cr App R (S) 80.
2 SI 1998/2306, reg 11.

2.40 Doncaster Metropolitan Borough Council was fined £400,000 on 20 February 2001 at Doncaster Crown Court following the electrocution of an electrician who had been called to repair a heating unit in a false ceiling. He came into contact with exposed wires. There was evidence that council managers had been aware of the danger for some time but failed to take action or notify the electrician.

2.41 On sentencing His Honour Judge Crabtree said:

'The Council's performance was dismal and disgraceful. This was a death waiting to happen and nobody was bothered … they ignored the most elementary safety precautions … If the Council had been a profit-making company with £10 million annual profits I would have fined them £10 million.'

2.42 Smurfit UK Ltd was fined £100,000 in June 2001 at Burnley Crown Court after pleading guilty to a breach of HSWA 1974, s 2. This followed the death of a worker who was killed while attempting to clean a paper machine at its Burnley paper and board mill in Lancashire in January 2000. The presiding judge said the incident was 'a very serious breach of duty indeed'.

2.43 Fresha Bakeries and its owners Harvestime Ltd were fined £250,000 and £100,000 respectively for breaches of HSWA 1974, ss 2 and 3 on 18 July 2001 at Leicester Crown Court. This related to the deaths of two men who had been sent into giant oven to retrieve a broken part and died as a result of the 100°C temperature. There were also prosecutions of individuals in relation to HSWA 1974, s 7 and HSWA 1974, s 37 (see **para 2.87** below).

2.44 Costain Ltd was fined £200,000 at Cardiff Crown Court in August 2001 after a 31-year-old labourer died when he became trapped between the end of a wall and a 13 tonne hydraulic excavator in October 1999. The labourer was employed by Abedare Construction which had been contracted by Costain Ltd to work on the Lynfi Valley combined sewer overflow scheme in Bridgend, Wales, where the accident happened. The company pleaded guilty to a breach of HSWA 1974, s 3.

2.45   Birse Construction was fined £80,000 with £20,000 costs at Croydon Crown Court in September 2001. The company pleaded guilty to a breach of HSWA 1974, s 3. The accident happened when an employee of S&J Chatteris, who had been contracted by Birse, slipped and fell beneath the guard-rail on the roof he was working on. The gap between the rail and the roof was too big. HSE inspectors who visited the site two weeks before the incident had warned of the dangers of this gap.

2.46   Sentencing, the judge said he took into account the company's early plea of guilty and the fact it had taken significant steps in improving its safety management. However he went on to say:

> 'But I have also taken into account the tragic loss of life which resulted and the fact that the company failed to act on the warning given by HSE two weeks before the incident occurred. The fines imposed should reflect the gravity of the accident and should bring home the message to Directors and Shareholders that the health and safety of its staff needs to be top priority.'

2.47   Mayer Parry (Recycling) Ltd was fined £200,000 at Blackfriars Crown Court on 27 September 2001 following the death of a fitter at one of its scrap metal processing plants. The deceased was killed during the annual overhaul of the fragmentising machine at the plant. He was lifting a 130 kg steel plate using a two-leg chain sling when one of the legs caught on part of the machine and then released violently, striking the deceased on the head. The company pleaded guilty to a breach of HSWA 1974, s 2.

2.48   Railtrack Plc and English, Scottish and Welsh Railways were fined £50,000 and £70,000 respectively at Nottingham Crown Court on 31 October 2001 following the death of a 12-year-old boy at railway sidings. Both companies pleaded guilty to a breach of HSWA 1974, s 3. This case was the first time the HSE had prosecuted a company with respect to a failure to prevent a trespass on railway lines. However the judge in sentencing emphasised there was no causal link between the death of the boy and the offences.

2.49   Corus UK Ltd was fined £300,000 plus costs of £11,591.38 at Cardiff Crown Court in November 2001 after pleading guilty to breaches of HSWA 1974, ss 2 and 3. The prosecution was taken following an explosion at its Basic Oxygen Steel plant at a site near Newport, South Wales, in September 2000, when slag spilled on to a floor area and came into contact with water. As a result of the incident an employee fell from a ladder he was working on and fractured his spine.

2.50   Judge Hickbottom when sentencing said:

> 'This was a most serious incident and was caused by Corus's failure to meet statutory safety requirements. Steel making is dangerous, but there is a regulatory scheme designed to ensure that employees are given every reasonable protection from risks and failures to comply. The objective of prosecution cases is to achieve a safe environment for workers and members of the public.
>
> Any fine need to be large enough to bring home the message about health and safety to both management and shareholders. A very substantial fine is necessary. Life was not lost, but Mr Bagnall suffered catastrophic injuries and this was such an incident which could have led to more injuries and possible deaths.

Corus were aware of the risks of such an explosion. Repair would have cost little in direct terms. There was a gross failure by Corus to heed warnings from both employees and contractors. Advice from the HSE, contained in a letter written in 1995, also went unheeded. This is very serious breach of the regulatory scheme.'

2.51 Costain Ltd and Yarm Road Ltd on 30 November 2001 at Bristol Crown Court were fined a total of £500,000 for breaches of HSWA 1974, ss 2 and 3. This related to an incident at Avonmouth Bridge. Four men were working on a gantry suspended beneath the road bridge. They were removing and replacing old runway beams from the bridge. To do this they were moving the gantry along the bridge. The gantry ran along runway beams underneath the bridge and was only restrained by rope pulling machines, called tirfors, and beam clamps.

2.52 The wind moved the gantry off the ends of the runway beams. When this happened the gantry swung down vertically. All four men working on the gantry then plunged over 25 metres to their deaths.

2.53 Judge Owen said when sentencing:

'This is a case of great gravity. Perhaps the most tragic feature of this case is that the accident could and should have been prevented by a number of simple measures.

The failures on the part of the defendants were of a very serious nature. This is not a case of a single and isolated fault.'

2.54 The London Borough of Hammersmith and Fulham were fined £350,000 at Blackfriars Crown Court on 7 December 2001 after pleading guilty to breaches of the Management of Health and Safety Regulations 1992, reg 4[1] (the provision is now reg 5 of the 1999 Regulations of the same name[2]) and HSWA 1974, s 3. The prosecution related to the death of two council tenants from carbon monoxide poisoning as a result of a faulty boiler that was overdue its annual safety check.

1   SI 1992/2051, reg 4.
2   SI 1999/3242, reg 5.

2.55 Sentencing, Judge Timothy Pontius condemned the Council for 'prolonged dereliction of duty to its tenants' and said:

'… the lamentable history of failure fully to accept its responsibility dates back a considerable number of years …

It is all the more regrettable that an earlier tragic death arose in precisely the same circumstances only five years before the two deaths in this case. That earlier tragedy provided the plainest salutary lesson imaginable, which should fully have been learned. Regrettably, it was not.'

2.56 Avon Lippiatt Hobbs (Contracting) Ltd was fined £250,000, comprising a fine of £175,000 for a breach of HSWA 1974, s 3 and £75,000 for a breach of HSWA 1974, s 2. The company pleaded guilty to the offences at Merthyr Crown Court on 13 December 2001. The prosecution related to a gas explosion that injured an employee, demolished a house and seriously damaged two others.

2.57   Sentencing the company, the JudgeJohn Curren said:

> 'The firm was responsible for a series of failures on the day of the explosion, and inadequate steps were taken to find out whether there was a gas pipe underneath the pavement on Abercynon Road, where the incident took place.
>   This could have very easily been a fatal accident, and firms must understand that, when dealing with gas, it is necessary to follow the most rigorous of safety standards.
>   I believe that a penalty should be imposed to properly reflect the concerns of the public.'

2.58   BP was fined a total of £1 million at Falkirk Sheriff Court, Scotland, on 18 January 2002 following two incidents at the company's Grangemouth refinery in June 2000, one where a catalytic converter caught fire and the other where there was a steam rupture.The company pleaded guilty to breaches of HSWA 1974, ss 2 and 3. It was noted at court that only good fortune avoided fatalities and serious injuries.

2.59   London Underground Ltd (LUL) pleaded guilty to six offences for breaches of HSWA 1974, s 3 and was fined £225,000 at Blackfriars Crown Court on 10 January 2002. The court was told that between April 1998 and January 2000 track maintenance workers were forced to carry out repairs using metal tools beside live rails on the Central Line in Loughton, Essex. The workers had been working in dark, rainy conditions, which exposed them to a risk of electrocution.

2.60   Mr Judge Samuuels said that safety was 'sacrificed' to keep trains running. He added:

> 'LUL, despite the lip service it paid to health and safety issues, fell lamentably short of the proper safety standards. A pattern of protracted disregard for basic safety procedures by senior management for so long must be marked by a heavy penalty.'

2.61   SDC Builders Ltd was fined £100,000 on 12 March 2002 for breaches of HSWA 1974, ss 2 and 3, at Cambridge Crown Court, after a contested trial. The prosecution related to the death of a sub-contractor who was knocked down and killed by a reversing delivery van on the site access road.

2.62   Sentencing, Judge Haworth said:

> 'The company, in my view, fell short of proper standards in relation to the use of the access road and neither installed nor maintained proper measures to the use of that road in relation to their work. Proper segregation was justified but no risk assessment was ever taken. Quite clear measures were necessary in regard to the access road.'

2.63   The driver of the deliver van pleaded guilty to a breach of HSWA 1974, s 7(a) (see **para 2.88** below).

2.64   RMD Kwikforum Ltd was fined £180,000 for three breaches of the Construction (Health, Safety and Welfare) Regulations 1996[1] and £60,000 for a breach of HSWA 1974, s 3 at Cardiff Crown Court in December 2002. In relation to the same matter

Taylor Woodrow was fined £80,000 for a breach of HSWA 1974, s 3. The prosecutions arose when poorly assembled scaffolding attached onto a 12-storey office building collapsed in high winds. Although no one was injured the court heard how this could have been a major catastrophe if the collapse had happened in the daytime.

1   SI 1996/1592.

2.65   Klargester Environmental was fined £250,000 for two breaches of the Provision and Use of Work Equipment Regulations 1998[1] and a breach of HSWA 1974, s 2 at Aylesbury Crown Court on 22 March 2003 following the death of an employee whose head was crushed while he was setting a Hanwood vacuum-forming machine.

1   SI 1998/2306.

2.66   Passing sentence, Judge Morton Jack said:

'... that there were multiple failings, some of which must have been present for a long period, some for many years ...
    ... the defendant was unable to demonstrate a proper system for inspection and maintenance, necessary to prevent accidents ...
    ... the situation at the factory was serious and horrifying.'

2.67   William Hare Ltd was fined £75,000 at the Old Bailey on 8 May 2003 after pleading guilty to a breach of HSWA 1974, s 2. The prosecution related to the fall of two workers who fell from height, resulting in the death of one of them, while doing construction work at the Imperial War Museum in London.

2.68   Nestle UK Ltd and Monotronic Ltd were fined £220,000 for a breach of HSWA 1974, s 3 and £25,000 for a breach of HSWA 1974, s 2 respectively at Isleworth Crown Court on 30 May 2003, having both pleaded guilty. This was in relation to the death of an employee of Monotronic who was electrocuted undertaking work at one of Nestle's factories. The incident occurred while he was pulling out redundant cables from trunking in the coffee plant of the factory.

2.69   Ford Motor Company was fined a total £300,000 for breaches of HSWA 1974, ss 2 and 3, to which it pleaded guilty, at Winchester Crown Court on 16 June 2003. An employee was killed when he fell into an emulsion paint over-spray capture tank used to collect excess paint from spray booths on a transit van production line.

2.70   Earls Court Ltd and Unusual Rigging Ltd were fined £80,000 and £20,000 respectively at the Old Bailey on 3 October 2003, having both pleaded guilty to breaches of HSWA 1974, s 3. The prosecution followed the death of a worker who fell 35 metres to his death. He fell through fragile, false ceiling tiles while dismantling mobile platforms as part of a refurbishment project. Six months earlier another worker had been killed in a similar incident for which Earls Court Ltd was fined £70,000.

Name and shame

2.71   The HSE website[1] has a public record of HSE convictions. The site gives details of all prosecution cases by the HSE which has resulted in convictions. This has become known as the 'name and shame' list. There is a similar list on the website for enforcement notices.

1   At www.hse.gov.uk.

2.72   It would appear that the name and shame list is something that insurers are starting to look at when considering employers' liability insurance and public liability insurance. Links are being made between insurance premiums and health and safety performance. This is evidenced by an initiative by the Association of British Insurers (ABI) which aims to benefit businesses with good health and safety practices by giving them 'greater access' to the employers' liability market.[1]

1   At marketwork@abi.org.uk.

2.73   There is also anecdotal evidence that some companies are consulting the name and shame list before awarding commercial contracts.

Health and safety offences – individuals

HSWA 1974, s 37

2.74   On summary conviction the maximum fine is £ £20,000 ut if convicted in the Crown Court, the court has the power to impose an unlimited fine. A custodial sentence cannot be imposed by the court. The average fine is a little under £3,000.[1]

1   HSE *Health and Safety Offences and Penalties 2002/2003 – A report by the Health and Safety Executive* (2003).

2.75   Under the Company Director's Disqualification Act 1986, the courts may also disqualify directors who have been found guilty of health and safety offences. A total of eight directors have been disqualified since the act came into force.[1] However, the trend is now that if a director is convicted, the HSE is requesting the court to consider making a disqualification order. The maximum a director can be disqualified in the magistrates' court is five years, but in the Crown Court the maximum is 15 years. An example is the managing director of Waste Recycling Ltd in Essex who was disqualified in August 1999 having been prosecuted under HSWA 1974, s 37 for breaching the Provision and Use of Work Equipment Regulations 1992, reg 11.[2]

1   HSE *Health and Safety Offences and Penalties 2002/2003 – A report by the Health and Safety Executive* (2003).
2   SI 1992/2932, reg 11.

Examples of fines imposed

2.76   Roger Folkes, managing director of Folkes (Great Yarmouth) Ltd, pleaded guilty of a breach of HSWA 1974, s 37 at Norwich Crown Court in June 1999 and was fined £10,000, following the death of a driver of a poorly maintained digger who drowned when his machine rolled into a lake. Both the brakes and the handbrake of the digger were not working. The company was fined £15,000.

2.77   John Bridston, the managing director of Fresha Bakeries and of Harvestime Ltd, was fined £10,000 for each company's breach of health and safety (see the HSE report at PARA **2.74 N 1** above with respect to the fines for each company), making a total fine of £20,000, on 18 July 2001, for two offences pursuant to HSWA 1974, s 37.

2.78   Christopher Allot, director of Triplex Components Group, was fined £6,000 for a breach of HSWA 1974, s 37 at Cardiff Magistrates' Court in May 2002. This was in relation to an incident where an employee suffered serious injuries to his wrists while carrying out maintenance work. The company was also fined £6,000 for a breach of HSWA 1974, s 2.

2.79   Bipin Bhagani, a director of Whitefields Care Homes Ltd, was fined £7,500 after pleading guilty to a breach of HSWA 1974, s 37 at Reading Crown Court on 29 April 2003. This followed an incident at the company's care home where an 85-year-old resident sustained serious burns to her legs while asleep in her bed. Her legs had come into contact with a hot radiator and pipes. The company pleaded guilty to a breach of HSWA 1974, s 3 and was fined £10,000.

2.80   Keith Stait, managing director, and Nicholas Martin, technical director, of Mays (Pressure Diecastings) Ltd were each fined £3,000 at Southwark Crown Court in April 2003. This was in relation to employees and members of the public being exposed to the risk of legionella bacteria because the company had failed adequately to maintain cooling towers at its site. Martin had received a report from a consultant stating the company needed to establish a regular cleaning and water treatment programme for the towers. The managing director was made aware of the report but both he and the technical director failed to take action. The company was fined £30,000.

2.81   Mark Foley and Daniel O'Brian, directors of Wessex Stone Ltd, were each fined £10,000 for breaches of HSWA 1974, s 37 at Bristol Crown Court. This was as a consequence of a worker's arm being severed when it became trapped in an unguarded conveyor belt. The company was fined £15,000.

2.82   Paul Mackenzie, director of Philip Services Ltd (Europe) Ltd, and Peter Preston, service manager of the same company, were each fined £5,000 for a breach of HSWA 1974, s 37 on 16 June 2003 resulting from the death of an employee who was killed at a Ford factory when he fell into an emulsion paint over-spray capture tank (see report of prosecution of Fords at **para 2.69** above). The prosecution of Philip Services (Europe) Ltd for a breach of HSWA 1974, s 2 was dropped as the company no longer existed in the UK.

Breaches of HSWA 1974, s 7

2.83   In the magistrates' court the maximum fine for a breach of HSWA 1974, s 7 is £5,000 and in the Crown Court it is unlimited. The court is unable to impose a custodial sentence.

Examples of fines imposed

2.84   Mark Holland was fined £159 for breach of HSWA 1974, s 7(a) at Bridgnorth Magistrates' Court in October 1997. He poured a small amount of floor-cleaning material, which he found in a cupboard, underneath a toilet door. A 17-year-old part-time worker was locked in the toilet. This was done as a practical joke. The liquid contained hydrochloric acid which reacted with dirt on the floor to produce toxic fumes. The 17-year-old suffered from the effects of the fumes.

2.85   Brian Watkins was fined £250 for a breach of HSWA 1974, s 7(a) at Newport Magistrates' Court in April 1999. Watkins, a school teacher, was prosecuted after pupils were splashed with molten metal when a class-room experiment went wrong.

2.86   David Alexander, a London Underground Ltd (LUL) manager, was fined £2,400 in relation to four counts of HSWA 1974, s 7(a) at Blackfriars Crown Court on 16 July 2001 because he forced track workers to carry out repairs using metal tool beside live rails, risking electrocution. LUL was later fined £225,000 in relation to the same matters in January 2003 (see **para 2.59** above).

2.87   Denis Masters, the Chief Engineer of Fresha Bakeries, and Brian Jones, an employee of Fresha Bakeries, were fined £2,000 and £1,000 respectively on 18 July 2001 for breaches of HSWA 1974, s 7(a). See the report at **para 2.43** above with respect to the prosecution of Fresha Bakeries.

2.88   Paul Jones was fined £3,000 on 12 March 2002 at Cambridge Crown Court after pleading guilty to a breach of HSWA 1974, s 7(a). He was the driver of a delivery van reversing into an access road, which killed a sub-contracted employee to SDC Builders Ltd. The company were fined for breaches of HSWA 1974, ss 2 and 3 (see **para 2.63** above).

2.89   Paul Dove, a schoolteacher, was fined £2,000 at Portsmouth Crown Court in November 2002 after a nine-year-old child drowned whilst on a school sailing trip. The child was part of the group of which he was in charge. The school was also fined £25,000.

2.90   John Cullen, a site foreman employed by O'Rouke Civil and Structural Engineering Ltd, was fined £1,500 at the City of London Magistrates' Court on 26 June 2003 after pleading guilty to a breach of HSWA 1974, s 7(a).He was given the task of establishing the site, which included the erection of a site hoarding around the perimeter. Several large billboards were in place which prevented the hoarding being erected. Although it was not Cullen's job to get them removed he came to make arrangements to have them lifted by an excavator. The project manager told him to stop, but he continued. As the result one of the employees suffered severe injuries to his legs.

2.91   Paul Ellis, a teacher from Fleetwood High School, pleaded guilty in September 2003 to manslaughter at Manchester Crown Court. The prosecution, brought by the Crown Prosecution Service, followed the death of Max Palmer, a ten-year-old boy, in May 2002. Max was with his mother, who was helping with a trip from the school to the Lake District organised by Paul Ellis. Mr Ellis led an activity which was to jump into a natural rock pool in Glenridding Beck. Max got into difficulties in cold and turbulent water, and was swept out of the pool and down the beck. Mr Ellis was sentenced to 12 months' imprisonment in relation to the manslaughter. However, he also pleaded guilty to a breach of HSWA 1974, s 7(a) for which, according to the HSE website,[1] he was sentenced to six months' imprisonment to run concurrently. As explained at **para 2.83** above, the court does not have the power to impose such a sentence.

1 At www.hse.gov.uk.

Contravention of an Improvement or Prohibition Notice

2.92 For the breach of the terms of an improvement or prohibition notice the maximum penalty in the magistrates' court is £20,000 fine and/or six months imprisonment. In the Crown Court, the maximum penalty is an unlimited fine and/or two years imprisonment.

Manslaughter

2.93 If an individual is convicted of manslaughter in relation to a work related incident, then he or she is likely to receive a custodial sentence in the region of 18 months to two years. Obviously, however, each case will turn upon its own facts. In certain circumstances the court might be prepared to suspend the sentence.

2.94 Where corporate manslaughter is proved, then the company will also be fined.

Examples of sentencing

R v Adomako

2.95 In *R v Adomako*,[1] the leading case on gross negligence manslaughter, the defendant was sentenced to six months' imprisonment suspended for 12 months. In this case the defendant was an anaesthetist in charge during an eye operation and failed to notice that an endotracheal tube (to allow the patient to breathe normally) had become disconnected for approximately six minutes.

1 [1995] 1 AC 171.

R v OLL Ltd and Kite

2.96 In this case OLL ltd and Mr Kite, the managing director, was convicted of the manslaughter in November 1994 of four students who died during a canoeing trip in Lyme Regis. The group of students was accompanied by a schoolteacher and two unqualified instructors. The group was swept out to sea and the four students died. The company had not provided distress flares and not advised the coastguard of the expedition.

2.97 Mr Kite was originally sentenced to three years' imprisonment, which was reduced to two years' on appeal. The company was fined £60,000.

2.98 When the trial judge sentenced Mr Kite, he said:

'... beyond doubt, these matters are so serious as to demand a sentence of immediate custody and of some substance.'

2.99   At his appeal the Court of Appeal agreed with the trial judge's view but reduced the sentence. The court observed:

> 'Mr Kite is now aged 46 and he is a man of previous impeccable character. Any prison sentence imposed on a man in these circumstances is, of course devastating to him. Nonetheless as we have said, the facts quite clearly demand a substantial sentence.'

R v Jackson Transport (Ossett) Ltd and Jackson

2.100   Alan Jackson was the sole director of the company. An employee died after cleaning chemical residues at the rear of a road tanker. The company had not provided preventative equipment, supervision or adequate training. Alan Jackson was sentenced to 12 months' imprisonment and the company was fined £15,000.

R v Litchfield

2.101   In *R v Litchfield*[1] Mr Litchfield was both master and owner of a square-rigged schooner which foundered off the north Cornish coast. He was sentenced to 18 months' imprisonment concurrently on three counts of manslaughter.

1   [1998] Crim LR 507.

2.102   He did not appeal against sentence, but did appeal against conviction, which was unsuccessful. At that appeal Simon Brown LJ stated:

> 'We add only this. We do not pretend to have found this an altogether easy case. Manslaughter convictions based on findings of gross negligence are always troubling. Defendants – very often, as here, of previously unblemished character – are being prosecuted for consequences they never for an instant intended or desired. It is to juries, however, that these difficult decisions are entrusted. Fidelity to the Jury system requires that [Mr Litchfield's] conviction stands.'

R v Roy Bowles Transport Ltd, Stephen Bowles and Julie Bowles

2.103   In October 1999 brother and sister Stephen and Julie Bowles were directors of the company. They were convicted of manslaughter in relation to a seven-vehicle pile-up on the M25 after a lorry driver working for them fell asleep at the wheel. The drivers at the company had been working excessive hours in the knowledge of both directors. Stephen Bowles and Julie Bowles were sentenced to 15 months' and 12 months' imprisonment respectively, suspended for two years.

R v Edward Crow and Alistair Crow

2.104   In July 2001 the two defendants, farmers, were found guilty of the manslaughter of a 16-year-old trainee. He was crushed by a seven tonne JCB potato loader that he was operating. As a 16-year-old with limited experience he should not have been operating the machine. Mr Alistair Crow was jailed for 15 months and his father received a one-year suspended sentence.

R v Brian Dean[1]

2.105   In April 2002 Brian Dean, former owner of Brian Dean Demolition and Civil Engineers, was convicted of the manslaughter of two employees who died when a kiln collapsed on top of them. His conviction was quashed on appeal. However, at first instance when he was sentenced he received a custodial sentence of 18 months.

1   [2002] EWCA Crim 2410.

R v Teglgaard (UK) Ltd and John Horner

2.106   Mr Horner was the managing director of the company. A worker was crushed to death when a pile of poorly stacked hardwood packs toppled over on top of him. Mr Horner and the company were convicted of manslaughter in March 2003. Mr Horner was sentenced to 15 months' imprisonment suspended for two years and the company was fined £25,000.

R v Ian Morris

2.107   In August 2003 Ian Morris, the owner of a factory, was convicted of gross negligence manslaughter of two employees who died when they inhaled toxic fumes during an unsafe paint-stripping operation. He was sentenced to nine months' imprisonment.

Corporate killing

2.108   It is proposed that the offence of corporate killing will be indictable only, ie only tried in the Crown Court.[1] This is unlike a prosecution of a company for breach of HSWA 1974, s 2 or 3 which is triable either way (ie can be tried in the magistrates' court or the Crown Court). However, like a conviction under HSWA 1974 (if in the Crown Court) the court has the power to impose an unlimited fine.

1   The Rt Hon J Straw MP (2000) *Reforming the law on involuntary manslaughter, the government's proposals.*

2.109   It is also proposed that the court should have the power to impose a remedial order against a company convicted of corporate killing[1]. The court would order the company to take steps within a certain period to remedy the failure which has been the subject of the prosecution or any other matter which it appears to the court to have resulted from the management failure.

1   The Rt Hon J Straw MP (2000) *Reforming the law on involuntary manslaughter, the government's proposals*

2.110   If the company fails to comply with the remedial order it can be fined a maximum of £20,000 in the magistrates' court and an unlimited fine in the Crown Court.

2.111   Originally the proposals had provision that individuals (directors and officers) influencing or with responsibility for management failure resulting in death could be subject to disqualification from acting in a management role. The government has now dropped that proposal.[1] However they would still be subject to the Company Directors' Disqualification Act 1986.

1   Letter sent by the Home Office, dated 10 September 2002, to private industry as part of the Regulatory Impact Assessment on proposed changes to the law on corporate manslaughter.

2.112   In relation to the individual offences, for a person guilty of killing by gross carelessness it is proposed the maximum sentence should be ten years and for reckless killing, life imprisonment.

Costs

2.113   The power to award costs against a defendant is contained in the Prosecution of Offences Act 1985, s 18(1). In relation to the level of costs the defendant is ordered to pay:

- They should be just and reasonable.
- They will include the cost of the prosecuting authority carrying out investigations with a view to prosecuting.[1]
- The defendant can be ordered to pay the whole of the prosecution costs in addition to any fine imposed.

1   See *R v Associated Octel Co Ltd* [1996] 4 All ER 846.

2.114   While costs of defending a prosecution may be covered by insurance (directors and officers policy, employers liability policy or public liability policy), the prosecution's costs, like any fine imposed by the court, will not be covered by insurance.

Conclusions

2.115   What can be seen from the examples given above of fines following breaches of HSWA 1974 is that since the guidance was handed down in *R v F Howe & Son (Engineers) Ltd*,[1] is that the courts have on occasions been prepared to impose substantial fines. However Timothy Walker, Director General of the HSE, argues that fines are still too low.[2]

1   [1999] 2 All ER 249.
2   Foreword to *Heath and Safety Offences and Penalties 2002/2003 – A report by the Health and Safety Executive* (2003).

2.116   It should be remembered that fines and prosecution (and investigation) costs are not covered by insurance (and is not tax deductible). Thus companies have to consider how much turnover they need to generate to meet the order for fine and costs.

2.117 However, it is not only the cost in terms of money, but also in terms of reputation, which can have an indirect impact upon the financial well-being of the company.

2.118 It is not clear whether, if a company is convicted of corporate killing, the fines will be greater than in a health and safety conviction. The guidance in *Howe*[1] already sets out death caused by the exposure to risk as being an aggravating factor. Some argue that if corporate killing does become law, then the over all fines in health and safety convictions might start to reduce.

1 *R v F Howe & Son (Engineers) Ltd* [1999] 2 All ER 249.

2.119 Very few offences under HSWA 1974 can attract a custodial sentence. In the government's and HSC's strategy document *Revitalising Health and Safety*[1] one of the proposals is to give the courts powers to impose custodial sentences for most HSWA 1974 offences. There has been an unsuccessful private members' Bill which proposed amendments to HSWA 1974 to achieve this recommendation included in the strategy document.

1 Health and Safety Commission *Revitalising Health and Safety Strategy Statement* (2000).

2.120 It may well be that if the government stalls in introducing corporate killing legislation it may find itself forced to amend the sanctions of HSWA 1974 to make them tougher.

CHAPTER 3

Practical issues

Gerard Forlin, Barrister, 2–3 Grays Inn Square, London

Michael Appleby, Solicitor, Fisher Scoggins LLP, London

Introduction

3.1   Professor James Reason writes:[1]

> 'The mind is prone to match like with like. It is therefore natural for us to believe that disastrous accidents must be due to equally monstrous blunders. But the close investigation of organizational catastrophes has a way of turning conventional wisdom on its head. Defences [designed to prevent accidents] can be dangerous. The best people can make mistakes. The greatest calamities can happen to conscientious and well run organizations. Most accident sequences, like the road to hell, are paved with good intentions – or with what seemed like good ideas at the time.'

1   Professor J Reason *Managing the Risks of Organizational Accidents* (1997) p 21.

3.2   When a criminal investigation is instigated it should not be assumed that those investigating have the necessary expertise to understand the mechanics and causes of the incident. It can be difficult, particularly in a police investigation, to explain the circumstances as a whole and why the incident may have occurred. There can be a tendency for the investigators to concentrate, to the exclusion of other factors, upon what they believe the individual or company has done wrong.

3.3 As Professor Reason warns, the 'mind is prone to match like with like'.[1] Thus it is easy for an investigation to be swayed by the consequences of a failure or series of failures, rather than to put the incident in context in relation to each failing.

1 Reason, **para 3.1 n 1** above.

3.4 When an incident happens and an investigation begins, it is easy for panic to set in and for confusion to reign. Trying to decide the best way to proceed, at that stage, can place the company or individuals under investigation in an invidious position. Often senior people within a company believe that they simply have to explain what has happened to those investigating and that will be an end to the matter. This can be dangerous and foolhardy. It is also fair to say that what happens in the first 48 hours after the incident will have important ramifications upon the way the investigation proceeds and the direction of it. Planning, organisation and consideration of tactics are essential at an early stage.

3.5 The role of the media should not be underestimated. The way the incident is reported can have a dramatic effect upon a company's reputation. The media will be interested in a 'good' story.

3.6 This chapter looks at issues that will face companies, individuals and their lawyers if a criminal investigation and/or prosecution results from a work related incident. The issues covered are by no means an exhaustive list.

Progress of a prosecution

3.7 It is beyond the scope of this book to set out in detail how a work related incident prosecution progresses through the courts. What follows is merely an outline.

3.8 If companies are prosecuted for manslaughter or health and safety offences, they will be summonsed. If an individual is prosecuted for manslaughter he or she will be charged with the offence. If an individual is prosecuted for breach of the Health and Safety at Work etc Act 1974, s 7 (HSWA 1974) or HSWA, s 37, he or she will be summonsed to appear at court.

3.9 Health and safety offences are 'either way' offences, ie can be heard in the magistrates' court (if it accepts jurisdiction) or in the Crown Court. Manslaughter is an indictable offence so can only be tried in the Crown Court. If a company or individual is prosecuted for manslaughter and health and safety offences relating to the same incident, then the trial of these will all be heard in the Crown Court.

3.10 If the prosecution is for health and safety offences only then there will be a hearing where a plea will be entered and then it will be determined if the matter is going to be heard before the magistrates or to go to the Crown Court (this is known as the mode of trial). The magistrates may decline jurisdiction (because of the serious nature of the case) or the defendant may elect for the case to be committed to the Crown Court.

3.11 In manslaughter cases the first hearing will be in the magistrates' court, which will send the case direct to the Crown Court pursuant to the Crime and Disorder Act 1998, s 51. At the first appearance in the Crown Court, a timetable will be set for the case. The prosecution will then serve the evidence upon which it relies. The defence will then have to consider whether it wishes to make an application for the case to be dismissed. If no application is made, or it is unsuccessful, there will be a plea and directions hearing (PDH). After that hearing, the matter will either proceed to trial or, if a guilty plea is entered, for sentencing.

Funding

3.12 It is the professional duty of a lawyer to advise his or her client of the availability of public funding. Public funding is available to individuals in relation to criminal matters for:

• advice and assistance;
• advocacy assistance; and
• representation.

3.13 Public funding can only be provided where the solicitors hold a general criminal contract with the Legal Services Commission. If the client decides not to proceed with public funding it is prudent to ask him or her to confirm that decision in writing.

3.14 With a private client (ie one not in receipt of public funding) it is important to send a client care letter, not only setting out who will be dealing with the case and the complaints procedure of the firm, as required by the Solicitors' Practice Rules, r 15, but also providing details in respect of costs, as required by the Solicitors' Costs Information and Client Care Code.

3.15 In the vast majority of cases, the cost of the defence in work related incidents will be covered by insurance.

3.16 Directors' and officers' liability and company reimbursement policies (often referred to as 'D&O Policies') provide insurance for senior executives against legal bills arising from their corporate responsibilities. It is not possible to obtain insurance to pay fines and penalties. D&O policies are not compulsory.

3.17 These policies are on a 'claims made' basis. That is to say, not when the incident happens but when the executive needs to rely upon the policy, for example, when first interviewed by the police, which may be some time after the incident. The limit of indemnity is aggregate and costs are inclusive in the limit of indemnity. Thus if there is more than one director being prosecuted covered by the policy, once their costs added together have reached the limit of the policy, there will be no further cover (and so they may need to rely upon public funding for further representation).

3.18 As for the costs of companies in corporate manslaughter/health and safety prosecutions, these may be covered by employers' liability insurance or public liability insurance (depending upon the nature of the matter). It is important to check the terms of the policy. Some policies may state that they only cover a breach of statutory duty (which therefore will not include corporate manslaughter proceedings) and others may say they only cover proceedings in the magistrates' court.

Conflicts of interest

3.19   When a work related death or serious incident occurs it is understandable that there is a desire on the part of the employer, their insurers and legal representatives to want to investigate the matter as soon as possible. There will be a wish to interview 'front line' workers involved and no doubt also managers. However, care needs to be taken as to how this is done and when this is done.

3.20   If there is a possibility of any criminal investigation of an individual, the first issue a legal representative of a company needs to consider is whether there is any conflict of interest between the company and the individual. The possibility of a conflict might be more obvious if a criminal investigation (either by the police or the Health and Safety Executive (HSE)) is being dealt with in the immediate aftermath. However, a conflict might be a possibility if dealing initially with civil issues (for example, personal injury claims) or the preparation for an inquest (note that the coroner can refer the papers to the police if he or she believes there should be a criminal investigation).

3.21   The difficulty will arise if the company and an employee have the potential to be come become co-defendants. The result may be that the solicitor would have to decline to act for any party. Before the solicitor could agree to continue to act for one party, for example, the company, the solicitor would need to consider carefully whether there is any information in his or her possession relating to the other 'clients' which may be relevant to the retained client.[1]

1   See *R v Ataou* [1988] QB 789.

3.22   It should also be borne in mind that conflicts of interests can arise between the company and its directors if both are being investigated.

Interviews under caution

3.23   An interview under caution and a suspect's detention at a police station are governed by the provisions of the Police and Criminal Evidence Act 1984 (PACE). The tactics of how an interview under caution by the police is dealt with can have a significant bearing upon the progression of the case. It is important that any solicitor representing a suspect in this type of interview in relation to a work related incident has experience of representing clients in this position, is familiar with the Codes of Practice to PACE and understands the legal and evidential issues involved in this type of matter.

3.24   Before the interview commences, the suspect will be cautioned. The caution is:

'You do not have to say anything, but it may harm your defence if you fail to mention something that you later rely on in Court. Anything you say may be used in evidence.'

3.25   The Criminal Justice and Public Order Act 1994, s 34 permits adverse inferences to be drawn from a defendant's failure, when interviewed by the police, to mention facts that he or she later relies on in defence at trial.

3.26   An interview with the police will usually be by prior arrangement. Often the interview will take place on a voluntary basis, ie the client will not be arrested and just interviewed. He or she will of course still be cautioned at the start of the interview and informed of the offences he or she is being investigated for.

3.27   However, it is becoming more common for the police to insist on arresting the client when he or she attends the police station. If this happens, then at the end of the interview, the client will normally be bailed to return to the police station at a future date. Failure to surrender to bail is a criminal offence.

3.28   It is prudent to discuss with the officer who will be carrying out the interview how he or she intends to conduct matters.

3.29   Interviews will be tape-recorded. It is now be coming common for interviews concerning manslaughter investigations carried out pursuant to the work related deaths protocol[1] to have an HSE officer present in the interview as well.

1   HSE *Work-related deaths: a protocol for liaison* (2003). The full text is also available at www.hse.gov.uk/pubns/misc491.pdf.

3.30   Before the interview takes place, the officer will normally provide disclosure of relevant documents, which set out the case against the suspect. Sometimes this can be sent to the solicitor in advance of the interview date. The disclosure may include a case summary that the officer may be prepared to allow the legal representative to have a copy of in order to assist in taking instructions.

3.31   The decision to be taken after disclosure is how to deal with the interview. There are three options:

1   to make no comment;
2   to give a full interview; or
3   for the suspect to read out a prepared statement.

3.32   Some situations where it might be appropriate for suspects to make no comment are as follows:

•   The greater the complexity of the case, the more likely that a court will consider it appropriate for a suspect to give a no comment interview.[1]
•   Where the police have not given sufficient prior to disclosure to enable the suspect properly to comment.
•   The police have little or evidence against the suspect.

1   See *R v Roble* [1997] Crim LR 449.

3.33   Often in work related incidents the police, as lay people, have difficulty understanding the mechanics and the circumstances of the incident. The danger is that misunderstandings can arise simply because the police do not understand the explanation being given, which can lead in some cases to charges.

3.34   One way of overcoming this is for a prepared statement to be read out and then for no comment to be made in response to further questions. In the case of *R v Knight*[1] the defendant was accused of two offences of indecent assault. A prepared statement was read out at interview. At trial the judge directed that they might draw adverse inferences from this. The defendant was convicted. His appeal against conviction was allowed. The Court of Appeal held that no adverse inference could be drawn under the Criminal Justice and Public Order Act 1994, s 34 if the statement contained the matters upon which he relied on in his defence at trial (which it did). The court said the purpose of the provision was to procure the early disclosure of a suspect's account and not the scrutiny and testing of it by the police. However, the defendant may face difficulties if something significant, which is relied upon at trial, was omitted from the prepared statement.[2]

1 (29 July 2003, unreported), CA.
2 (6 November 2003, unreported), CA.

3.35 An HSE officer can interview a suspect under caution subject to PACE. However, the important thing to remember is that an HSE officer does not have the power of arrest (therefore if the suspect refuses to be interviewed, the HSE officer cannot force the suspect to be interviewed, unlike a police officer who can simply arrest the suspect and interview him or her).

Disclosure

3.36 Under the Criminal Procedure and Investigations Act 1996, on a case being committed to the Crown Court, the prosecutor is required to disclose to the accused previously undisclosed material which in the opinion of the prosecutor might undermine the prosecution case (this is known as primary disclosure), or else to give the accused a written statement that there is no such material (pursuant to the Criminal Procedure and Investigations Act 1996, s 3). Once a defence statement is served, the position with respect to disclosure is considered again. If further documents are considered relevant in the light of the defence statement, secondary disclosure will be given.

3.37 In work related incident cases, because of their complex nature, the police usually give full disclosure of documentation as there is a fear of withholding evidence which might be later found to be relevant, but the police failed to realise this.

Defence statement

3.38 Once the case has been sent to the Crown Court, the defendant has 14 days to file a defence statement or risk an adverse inference being drawn at trial. Care should be taken in drafting these statements and, because of the complexities of these types of cases, drafting will take time. It is therefore important to apply for an extension of time for the filing of the statement. It is also important to remember that a defendant can not only be cross examined upon what he or she said in their police interview, but also upon what is contained in the defence statement.

Prosecution case summary

3.39 In complex work related death cases it is usual for the prosecution to serve a full case summary setting out in detail the case against the defendants fully cross-referencing to the evidence relied upon. It is essential that this document is obtained before a defence statement is served.

3.40   In health and safety prosecutions it is said by the court that the prosecution should always be required to set out precisely what its case is. The obligation upon them to do so was emphasised in *R (on the application of Bernard) v Dudley Metropolitan Borough Council*:[1]

> 'When Informations are laid and proceedings commenced, it is manifest that there is a clear obligation upon the prosecuting authority to make it plain just what the allegation is, and upon what evidence they seek to rely to substantiate that allegation … It is not sufficient for a prosecuting authority in a Health and Safety at Work Act [HSWA 1974] case merely to serve the summonses and the statements.'

1   [2003] EWHC 147 (Admin).

Experts

3.41   In prosecutions concerning work related incidents, so often it is not the facts of what happened that are in dispute, but the interpretation of those facts. Because of this experts usually play a vital role. It is vital that consideration is given to instructing experts at an early stage. So often finding appropriate experts can be a time consuming exercise.

3.42   It is important that experts give evidence within their own expertise. Those instructing should ensure that the experts are provided with the appropriate evidence and material, understand their duties to the court (note the Practice Direction to the Civil Procedure Rules Part 35 sets out an expert's duties to the court) and understand what the case is (from a legal point of view as well as a factual point of view) that the prosecution is seeking to prove. In relation to any expert report, as the law currently stands in criminal cases, litigation privilege attaches to that report (see *R (Morgan Grenfell) v Special Comr of Income Tax*[1]).

1   [2002] UKHL 21, [2002] 3 All ER 1.

Other non-criminal proceedings

3.43   Criminal investigations and prosecutions can be lengthy. In the meantime it is likely that claims for compensation will be made. For example, under the pre-action protocols in personal injury claims the insurance company has three months to investigate a claim upon receipt of full details. It is required to give views on liability and to provide certain accident documentation if liability is denied. A company will need to ensure that this procedure does not prejudice its position in respect of the criminal proceedings. There must be liaison between the company's lawyers, the insurance company and the lawyers dealing with the civil claims (if different).

Company documentation

3.44   When an investigation takes place there will be a great deal of interest in the company's documentation. Companies are well advised to have a good document management system in place so that management know what documents there are. The Civil Procedure Rules define a document as 'anything in which information of any description is recorded' (see CPR 31).

3.45 There is sanctity in the existence of documents following the commencement of an inquiry or legal proceedings. A company may have a policy for the destruction of documents. This may have to be halted, in order to fulfil the duty of preservation of relevant documents. Certain aspects of this policy may have to be specifically identified and dealt with, such as: automatic destruction of files after a period of time has elapsed; scanning of documents and destruction of originals; destruction of duplicates; and destruction of manuscript notes and inter-office memos. The destruction of documents could amount to perverting the course of justice. In the case of *R v Selvage and Morgan*[1] It was held that the offence is made out by acts which did and were intended to interfere with pending or imminent proceedings or with investigations which might end with criminal proceedings being brought. Further, the Companies Act 1985, s 450 provides that a company officer who destroys, mutilates, or falsifies a document affecting the company's property or affairs may be liable to prosecution unless the officer can prove that no intent to conceal or defeat the law. There is a responsibility upon a solicitor to ensure his/her client understands this. It was said in *Rockwell Machine Tool Co v EP Barrus (Concessionaires)*:[2]

> '... It seems to me necessary for solicitors to take positive steps to ensure that their clients appreciate at an early stage of the litigation, ... not only the duty of discovery and its worth but also the importance of not destroying documents which might by possibility have to be disclosed. This burden extends, in my judgment, to taking steps to ensure that in any corporate organisation knowledge of this burden is passed on to any who may be affected by it.'

1 [1982] 1 All ER 96.
2 [1968] 1 WLR 693 at 694.

3.46 Emails are often written in a rush, not fully considered and can be ambiguous. However, these can become evidence. It is therefore important for companies to have an email policy.

3.47 This is illustrated by the case of *United States v Microsoft*.[1] The Justice Department alleged that Microsoft used its Windows monopoly unfairly to crush the Netscape Navigator Web Browser. The prosecutors produced emails going back to 1993 to attack the credibility of Microsoft executives. In February 1999, the chief lawyer for the government produced a 1996 email message from Bill Gates to the chairman of another software manufacturer, seemingly offering a bribe if the manufacturer used Microsoft Internet Explorer rather than Netscape Navigator.

1 US case (1999) .

3.48 Note that more so than paper documents, emails are stored. It is often assumed that deleting a record or file removes it from the hard drive. In fact, the only thing that is removed is the file name and protection overwrite, leaving data on the drive. Even using disk erasing utilities, fragments of the file remain which can be pieced together.

Inquests

3.49   Only a small proportion of deaths reported to the coroner require a public inquest. The Coroners Act 1988, s 8 requires an inquest to be held where there is reasonable cause for the coroner to suspect that the deceased died:

- a violent or an unnatural death;
- a sudden death and cause unknown; or
- in prison.

3.50   Not all inquests have a jury. Two circumstances when a jury is required are where the coroner has reason to suspect that:

- the death was caused by accident, poisoning or disease notice of which is required to be given to the HSE under HSWA 1974; or
- the death occurred in circumstances prejudicial to public health.

3.51   The purpose of the inquest is to determine who the deceased was, where and when the deceased died, and how they died. The means by which the deceased came by his or her death is a limited question.[1]

1   See *R v HM Coroner for North Humberside and Scunthorpe, ex p Jamieson* [1995] QB 1.

3.52   The verdicts of an inquest in a work related death that might be given are:

- accidental death (misadventure);
- unlawful killing; or
- open verdict.

3.53   It is important to note that there is no statutory requirement that the verdict of the inquest be in any particular form. However, there is a prohibition on a verdict being framed in such a way as to appear to determine any question of criminal or civil liability.

3.54   Any interested party to the inquest can be represented at the inquest. This includes any person whose act or omission or that of his or her agent or servant in the opinion of the coroner may have caused, or contributed to, the death of the deceased.

3.55   At the conclusion of the evidence the legal representatives cannot make an address to the jury. The coroner cannot be addressed on the facts, but can be on the law in relation each possible verdict.

3.56   An inquest will not take place until the police have confirmed that there are to be no prosecutions. However, if evidence arises in the inquest then the coroner is able to refer the matter back to the police to reconsider the matter. If there is an unlawful killing verdict then the matter automatically is referred back to the police. In relation to health and safety prosecutions these normally, but not always, are brought after the inquest has been concluded.

3.57   It is now becoming more common for representatives of the family of the deceased to take a proactive role in these proceedings with a view to raising issues in cross examination that are relevant to criminal liability. It is therefore important that any witness who might be criticised has explained to them the rule against self incrimination in respect of a criminal offence.

Judicial review

3.58 The families of deceased who have died in a work related incident are more likely to make submissions to the police/CPS/HSE about who should be prosecuted and why. It should be noted that para 6.7 of the Code for Crown Prosecutors states:

'The Crown Prosecution Service prosecutes cases on behalf of the public at large and not just in the interests of any particular individual. However, when considering the public interest test Crown Prosecutors should always take into account the consequences for the victim of the decision whether or not to prosecute, and any views expressed by the victim or the victim's family.'

3.59 If a decision not to prosecute is taken, then it is open to the family to judicially review that decision. This is a means by which public law disputes are resolved by brining the matter before the High Court. This form of action was described as 'a remedy invented by the judge to restrain the excess or abuse of power'.[1] The procedure for bringing a judicial review is set out in statute: the Supreme Court Act 1981, s 31, on which CPR 54 elaborates.

1 Lord Templeman in *R v Secretary of State for the Home Department, ex p Bond* [1991] AC 696, HL.

3.60 There is a pre-action protocol that covers judicial reviews. A judicial review must be brought promptly and within three months of the decision or action which gives rise to the action. The defendant will be the body that has taken the decision not to prosecute. The proceedings must also be served on any interested party, which includes any likely defendant in relation to the criminal proceedings which are the subject of the judicial review.

3.61 The decision-makers subject to judicial review must not act in a way that no reasonable decision-maker would consider justifiable. The benchmark decision on this principle was made in the *Wednesbury* case,[1] which said:

'If a decision on a competent matter is so unreasonable that no reasonable authority could ever come to it, then the courts can interfere … but to prove a case of that kind would require something overwhelming …'

1 *Associated Provincial Picture Houses Ltd v Wednesbury Corpn Ltd* [1948] 1 KB 223, HL.

3.62 In the judicial review that considered the CPS's decision not to bring manslaughter charges in relation to the death of Simon Jones in a work related incident, the court said the relevant issues were:[1]

'1. has the decision maker properly understood and applied the law?
2. has he explained the reasons for his conclusions in terms that the court can understand and act upon? And
3. has he taken into [account] an irrelevant matter or is there a danger that he may have done so?'

1 *R v DPP, ex p Jones* [2000] IRLR 373.

3.63 If the matter has been fully considered by the CPS, then it is usually difficult for the judicial review to succeed. In *R v Director of Public Prosecutions, ex p Manning* it was said:[1]

> 'The primary decision to prosecute or not is entrusted by Parliament to the Director [of Public Prosecutions] as head of an independent, professional prosecuting service answerable to the Attorney-General in his role as guardian of the public interest and to no-one else. It makes no difference that in practice the decision will ordinarily be taken by a senior member of the Crown Prosecution Service ... In any borderline case the decision may be one of acute difficulty, since while a defendant whom a jury would be likely to convict should properly be brought to justice and tried, a defendant whom a jury would be likely to acquit should not be subjected to the trauma inherent in a criminal trial. The Director and his officials ... will bring to their task of deciding whether to prosecute an experience and an expertise which most courts called upon to review their decisions could not match. In most cases the decision will turn not on an analysis of the relevant legal principles but on the exercise of an informed judgement of how a case against a particular defendant, if brought, would be likely to fare in the context of a criminal trial before ... a jury. The exercise of judgement involves an assessment of the strength by the end of the trial, of evidence against the defendant and of the likely defences. It will often be impossible to stigmatise a judgement on such matters as wrong even if one disagrees with it. So the courts will not easily find that a decision not to prosecute is bad in law, on which basis alone the court is entitled to interfere. At the same time the standard of review should not be set too high, since judicial review is the only means by which a citizen can seek redress against a decision not to prosecute and if the test were too exacting an effective remedy would be denied.'

1 [2000] 3 WLR 463.

3.64 The order that will be sought in a judicial review is that the decision not to prosecute be quashed and that there be a mandatory order that the decision be reconsidered afresh.

Public inquiries

3.65 After a disaster or major accident has occurred a public inquiry might be set up to look at its causes, what lessons can be learnt from the incident and to make recommendations as to how matters might be improved.

3.66 Nowadays a public inquiry is likely to be conducted pursuant to HSWA 1974, s 14(2)(b). Examples of such inquiries are those that followed the Southall and Ladbroke Grove train crashes. This enables the HSC with the consent of the Secretary of State to direct an inquiry be held. The procedures for inquiries under this provision are regulated by the Health and Safety Inquiries (Procedure) Regulations 1975.[1]

1 SI 1975/335.

3.67 A person will be appointed to chair the inquiry and is usually a senior lawyer (although this is not always the case). The Chair can appoint assessors, who will be experts in particular fields relevant to the nature of the incident, to assist him or her with understanding technical issues and evidence.

3.68 A counsel to the inquiry will be appointed, an experienced advocate and, normally Queen's Counsel. Counsel to the inquiry will be supported by a team of lawyers. His or her role is to advise the Chair on legal issues, to arrange the evidence to be placed before the inquiry and usually to take the witnesses called to the inquiry through their evidence. A secretary to the inquiry will also be appointed and along with his or her team will deal with the administration of the inquiry.

3.69 Public inquiries can be delayed because of criminal proceedings. The reason being is that if the inquiry was to take place before these are concluded, then any trial might be prejudiced. The Southall train crash Inquiry was delayed for two years while criminal proceedings were taken against one of the train drivers involved and his employers, Great Western Trains.

3.70 Public inquiries are meant to be inquisitorial and not adversarial like normal legal proceedings. However, because so much is at stake as the outcome can influence civil and criminal liability, this is not so easy to achieve in practice.

3.71 Professor HWR Wade and CF Forsyth comment in relation to inquiries (authorised under the Tribunals of Inquiry (Evidence) Act 1921):[1]

'Experience of Tribunals of Inquiry has revealed the dangers to which a procedure of this kind is naturally prone. The Inquiry is inquisitorial in character, and usually takes place in a blaze of publicity. Very damaging allegations may be made against persons who may have little opportunity to defend themselves and against whom no legal charge is preferred.'

[1] Professor HWR Wade and CF Forsyth *Administrative Law* (7th edn) p 1008.

3.72 Thus any person giving evidence to an inquiry where there is the possibility he or she may be criticised should consider strongly having legal representation and, if employed by a party involved in the inquiry, separate legal representation from them in case there is a possibility of a conflict of interests.

3.73 Since the Access to Justice Act 1999, s 17 came into effect, any inquests will normally be adjourned until after the public inquiry as effectively the inquiry will determine the cause of the incident and thus how the deceased came to die.

Human Rights Act 1998

3.74 The Human Rights Act 1998 (HRA) came into force on 2 October 2000. The Act 'gives further effect to' the European Convention for the protection of Human Rights and Fundamental Freedoms (ECHR) in domestic law:

3.75 The Human Rights Act 1998 has been given partial effect since 22 May 1999, in Scotland, by virtue of the Scotland Act 1998. As a result of the Human Rights Act 1998, ECHR rights can now be directly relied upon, argued and enforced in the UK courts and tribunals at all levels. The acts or omissions of 'public authorities' can be challenged as part of any legal proceedings, by judicial review or as an entirely new course of action under the Act.

3.76 It should be remembered that once all domestic remedies have been exhausted in the domestic courts, an appeal still lies to the European Court of Human Rights in Strasbourg. Decisions of the European Court of Human Rights are final and binding on member states.

3.77 The articles of the ECHR that are most relevant to criminal proceedings in relation to work related incidents are art 2, the 'Right to Life' and art 6, the 'Right to a Fair Trial'.

3.78 An offshore disaster such as Piper Alpha would undoubtedly trigger a challenge under the ECHR, art 2. Remember 'life' includes 'physical integrity'. There is a clear obligation on the state to investigate deaths fully.

3.79 Although questions of causation will always arise, public authorities such as the Health and Safety Executive, local authorities, health authorities, etc may be under a duty to protect the public (and their employees) from health risks such as AIDS, BSE, E-coli and from environmental danger and life threatening hazards such as radiation, explosions, asbestos etc – eg Bhopal gas leak, Chernobyl etc (See *Indian Council for Enviro-Legal Action v Union of India*[1]).

1 [1996] 2 LRC 226.

3.80 In *Guerra v Italy*[1] illegal toxic emissions caused arsenic poisoning and possibly cancer. There was a claim under the ECHR, art 2. The court awarded £3,000 to the applicants to compensate them for the fact that the authorities had not provided them with sufficient information about a pesticide factory to enable them to assess the risks of living in its vicinity.

1 (1998) 26 EHRR 357.

3.81 It is clear that the HRA will have an ever increasing importance in the area of Health and Safety and Corporate Manslaughter. In order to properly advise and represent clients, lawyers need to be fully familiar with the provisions of the HRA and ancillary legislation, and the relevant procedures in this expanding body of ECHR law.

Media

3.82 A company should have procedures in place for dealing with the media. Simply trying to hide from the media may well make matters worse. If any one in the company is going to speak to the media, then they should have the appropriate training. Obviously care shpuld be taken as to what is said, particularly once charges have been brought

3.83 A company should make sure that there are systems in place to deal appropriately and sensitively with the relatives of those killed or injured as a result of an incident. A jury will give much weight to these sorts of matters. At the Southall Rail Inquiry a great deal of criticism was made by the passengers and families of those killed and injured of how they were treated following the accident. To act decently in such circumstances does not amount to an admission of guilt and provides good evidence of the attitude of the company.

Conclusions

3.84 It has only been possible to touch the tip of the iceberg of the practical issues that may arise in a manslaughter and/or health and safety investigation and prosecution. Many of these issues often arise from the very nature of the case and the industry in which the incident occurred. What is also clear is that this is an area which is rapidly developing bring forth new challenges for the lawyers involved.

CHAPTER 4

Investigations by the police and HSE

Malcolm Ross, MSc, former Detective Superintendent, West Midlands Police

Michael Elliker, Partner, Addleshaw Goddard, Leeds

Introduction

4.1   For many years the investigation into deaths, especially those occurring in the workplace, were seen by the police as a matter for the Health and Safety Executive (HSE) and the coroner to determine whether any offences had been committed. If any offences were proved they would usually be offences contrary to health and safety legislation and not involve the police in the prosecution.

4.2   However, things changed with the publication in 1998 of *The protocol for liaison: work related deaths*, which set out the mechanism for a workplace manslaughter investigation. For the first time the police were required to consider whether work related death had been caused by a serious criminal offence (for example, manslaughter). The Protocol envisages a joint investigation by the police and the HSE into any workplace death. The Protocol was updated in March 2003.[1]

1 HSE *Work-related deaths: a protocol for liaison* (2003). The full text is available at www.hse.gov.uk/pubns/misc491.pdf.

4.3   This chapter considers how a police and HSE investigation proceeds into a work related death.

Protocols and guidance

Work-related deaths- a protocol for liaison

4.4   The protocol *Work-related deaths – a protocol for liaison*,[1] was created by agreement between the Association of Chief Police Officers (ACPO) the Health and

Safety Executive (HSE), the Crown Prosecution Service (CPS), British Transport Police (BTP) and the Local Government Association (LGA) in March 2003. This document superseded an earlier version introduced in 1998.[2]

1   (2003), available at www.hse.gov.uk/pubns/misc491.pdf.
2   *The protocol for liaison: work related deaths.*

4.5   The Protocol is an agreement that establishes working practices for the investigation of deaths in the workplace. It is this document that should concentrate the actions of the police and it instils in the service the need for a more assertive approach to such investigations. The Protocol establishes the need for a police officer to attend the scene of a work related death or injury so serious it is likely to result in death and to determine if there is sufficient evidence to justify a manslaughter investigation or indeed an investigation into any criminal offence, including HSE offences arising out of, or in connection with, work.

4.6   The Protocol calls for the attendance of a supervisor to ensure the correct actions have been taken and that the police are dealing with the death in accordance with the local procedures for the respective force, which will inevitably include the early notification of the Criminal Investigation Department (CID). The supervisor should also ensure consultation between the police and the HSE at the earliest opportunity.

4.7   The police will conduct their investigation with technical support from the HSE, until such time as it is clear that there is no evidence of manslaughter or other serious criminal offences. In such cases the police will pass the inquiry to the HSE for the HSE to pursue relevant offences, but the police will continue to give local support to the HSE if requested to do so.

4.8   If new evidence arises after the police have passed the investigation back to the HSE, the case should be referred back to the police for them to assess whether the new evidence would constitute or further progress towards a manslaughter charge. Any investigation conducted under the provisions of this Protocol is designed to be a joint investigation between the police, the HSE and other agencies and it is envisaged that police officers, HSE officers and other agencies will work together in teams in order to afford the investigation the best knowledge base possible in the inquiry.

4.9   The Protocol states that its underlying principles are:[1]

*   an appropriate decision concerning prosecution is made based on sound investigation of the circumstances surrounding work related deaths;
*   the police will conduct an investigation where there is an indication of the commission of a serious offence (other than a health and safety offence) and the HSE (or local authority or other enforcing authority) will investigate health and safety offences;
*   the decision to prosecute will be co-ordinated and made without due delay;
*   the bereaved and witnesses will be kept suitably informed; and
*   the parties to the Protocol will maintain effective mechanisms for liaison.

1   HSE *Work-related deaths: a protocol for liaison* (2003).

Murder Investigation Manual

4.10   The *Murder Investigation Manual*[1] was introduced by ACPO in November 2000. The document, initially introduced in 1999 and issued nationally to all senior investigating officers (SIOs), offers guidance in cases of murder, rape and abduction, but the principles of investigation pertain to all criminal investigations to a more or lesser degree. For many years SIOs investigated murders and serious offences relying on their own experience and the experience and working practices of others who had gone before them. There had been a lack of measurement as to whether these working practices were effective, correct or indeed within the guidance and mandate of the law. It was realised that there was a need to introduce a formal structure to such investigations and to look behind the rationale of the decision-making processes adopted by SIOs in order that the decisions could be justified years hence. This was particularly important when one considers the introduction of disclosure legislation in the Criminal Procedure and Investigations Act 1996, the Human Rights Act 1998 and the increasingly popular decisions by the government to call for public inquiries.

1   Association of Chief Police Officers *Murder Investigation Manual* (2000).

4.11   The SIOs' training course now consists of a generic course dealing with the management of serious crime investigations, followed by a series of modules touching on law, procedure, forensic awareness and intelligence. Other modules to be included in the training course in the very near future will deal exclusively with child abuse, organised crime and in particular the role of the SIO in major incidents and disasters. It will be in this module that particular reference will be made to the role of the SIO in cases involving the proposed legislation. The next reprint of the *Murder Investigation Manual* will include details of the additional modules.

4.12   The *Manual* breaks down the investigative processes into logical, manageable and sequential 'blocks' and is designed so it can be used as an aid memoire by all SIOs. It is particularly useful for those SIOs whose knowledge and experience in the CID is somewhat limited. Not all SIOs have had a career path in the CID and for some there is a steep learning curve when dealing with suspicious death investigations, especially work related deaths.

Major Incident Room Standardised Administrative Procedures

4.13   The manual *Major Incident Room Standardised Administrative Procedures* (MIRSAP)[1] is used with the police's computerised system for investigation called HOLMES (Home Office Large Major Inquiry System). This stipulates the rules and conventions for HOLMES. MIRSAP is designed to ensure a common practice across the country when using the HOLMES computerised system for major inquiries. More importantly, MIRSAP ensures a structured audited process of information and paper management throughout the investigation. MIRSAP brings with it its own rules and conventions, which, if complied with, will result in a credible accurate system, designed to withstand any scrutiny.

1   Association of Chief Police Officers *Major Incident Room Standard Administrative Procedures* (2001).

Process of the police investigation

The Murder Investigation Manual[1]

4.14   The police investigation will follow the outline of an investigation as determined by the *Murder Investigation Manual* but in cases where corporate manslaughter is being pursued, the SIO will find that there are additional issues to consider.

1   Association of Chief Police Officers *Murder Investigation Manual* (2000).

4.15   In order to illustrate the differences it is requisite that the process of such an investigation is explained and the role of the police in corporate manslaughter cases is examined in detail, taking into account the guidance set out in the three documents mentioned above.[1]

1   Association of Chief Police Officers *Murder Investigation Manual* (2000); Association of Chief Police Officers *Major Incident Room Standard Administrative Procedures* (2001); HSE *Work-related deaths: a protocol for liaison* (2003).

The action of the police at the initial scene

4.16   Following the notification of a death to the police, it is the usual practice to dispatch a uniformed officer for the initial response and to give the police control an overview of the occurrence and what is required from both the police and the other emergency services. It has to be appreciated that in the context of corporate manslaughter, the scene may be a house, home, institution, part of a factory or the site of a major disaster. It may also be a road where a serious or fatal accident has occurred. Whatever the 'scene' the first officer attending would be required to act as the forward control point and be responsible for the communication of information to and from the scene. The officer would also be required to act in a co-ordinating role on the arrival of other resources until relieved by another officer.

4.17   To assist officers to communicate relevant information, officers are taught to use the mnemonic 'CHALETS':

C – *Casualties* – number of dead and injured

H – *Hazards* – present and potential

A – *Access* – routes for emergency vehicles and rendezvous points

L – *Location* – exact location including map reference if known

E – *Emergency* – emergency services required

T – *Type* – type of incident

S – *Start log* – commence a comprehensive log of activities

4.18   This method of communication conveys the necessary information for the police control to assess the required response and, if necessary, inform senior officers to take charge. In the cases involving death or life threatening injury the CID would be informed.

4.19 This method of communicating information is contained in the ACPO *Emergency Procedures Manual* (1999), designed to assist forces to plan and prepare for a major emergency of any kind.

4.20 Once initial information has been communicated the next step is for the implementation of 'building blocks' as described in the *Murder Investigation Manual*.

4.21 There are five 'building blocks':

• preservation of life;
• preservation of the scene;
• securing evidence;
• identifying victims;
• identifying suspects,

which can be further explained as follows.

Preservation of life

4.22 This is the primary responsibility of the first officers at the scene, together with the other emergency personnel. Whilst carrying out this task however, it should be possible for the officer to 'think evidence' and take steps to preserve the scene and recover evidence.

4.23 It is important that a record is made when bodies are removed. The coroner and the investigation will require precise details of the exact location. This is difficult to achieve at the scene of a major incident, as the priority of other rescue services will be to extricate the victims and treat the living casualties. Fire fighters and ambulance personnel are not readily concerned with the position of a body at a time when immediate action is required, but with their assistance and co-operation a relatively accurate picture of the events at the scene can be achieved with some care being taken.

Preservation of the scene

4.24 This can only be achieved by the speedy deployment of sufficient officers to the scene with the aim of preventing the loss or contamination of valuable evidence. Officers should ensure that there is no unauthorised access to the scene thereby preventing any person touching or removing potential evidence or exhibits. It is at this stage that police personnel must adopt a high profile and a professional approach to their duties.

4.25 It is requisite that a cordon be placed around the scene – a physical cordon involving either officers, barriers or tape – to prevent unauthorised access. Taking advice from the other emergency services present, the first officer on the scene should ensure that a cordon exists and that an officer is nominated to be responsible for the integrity of that cordon. It is necessary therefore for entry and exit points to be identified and movement through these points by any emergency service personnel to be noted and monitored by an officer on a crime scene log. This will ensure that any later investigation into who had access to the scene will be possible with a high degree of accuracy. Very often forensic evidence is a consideration at this stage of the incident and the crime scene log itself is precious evidence.

4.26   Cordons and crime scene logs are possible when the scene is manageable. The scene of the Lockerbie incident spread over some 280 square miles and cordons around the whole scene were clearly impossible. In these cases, each significant locus should be treated as its own scene and requires its own crime scene log.

4.27   It goes without saying that cordons and crime scene logs place a great burden on the resources of any police force, but they are an essential first step in the investigation of an offence or possible offence.

4.28   It could well be the case that victims have been taken to hospital by ambulance and it is necessary for their clothing to be taken as exhibits for forensic examination. The hospital and perhaps even the ambulances are considered a scene and each area will be dealt with accordingly.

Securing the evidence

4.29   In addition to securing physical evidence from the scene, officers are in a position to secure evidence by speaking to people who are present at the scene. This is especially important when dealing with a death or deaths, where issues may arise concerning the accountability of others, ie when attempting to establish a causation chain. (Those in an organisation who are responsible for making decisions that may have had a bearing on the death.) Initial inquiries at scenes may determine the identity of the victim and the identity of potential witnesses.

4.30   This will be the start of the 'hands on' role of the CID, although all of the above should have been completed with the supervising detective's approval.

Identifying the victim

4.31   It is crucial that any victim is identified as quickly as possible. From that identification there will arise many 'fast track actions' that officers will need to complete. Actions such as the identification of a family liaison officer, arranging a post-mortem examination, in the case of a suspicious death, by a Home Office-appointed forensic pathologist, obtaining formal identification of the dead and informing relatives. All of these issues will be dealt with in more detail below.

Identifying suspects

4.32   When a death occurs in the workplace, or indeed elsewhere, which is deemed to be suspicious, the identification of possible suspects must be at the forefront of the mind of the officer attending the scene. Inquires by the police to establish if there is a continued threat to others by the suspect must be made.

4.33   Whilst the 'building blocks' described at PARA **4.20**ff above are issues for the first officers at the scene to consider, they are ongoing issues for the detective who will be continuing with the investigation. The fundamental principle for the first officer at the scene to remember is that if he or she does not secure, preserve and cordon the scene properly the integrity of the investigation is flawed from the start. Historical reviews of serious cases, especially murder cases, indicate that the police service as a whole has not been very professional where crime scene management is concerned. Issues around the continuity of the scene and the integrity of the cordon have often been pursued by the defence at court, which, not infrequently, has created some doubt about crime scene management. More latterly, however, a more focused training strategy, the appointment of duly trained and qualified crime scene managers and a greater awareness of the requirements of scene preservation across the service in general have improved this area of investigation substantially.

The investigation

4.34   Once the scene has been properly secured, it is time for the investigation to commence. Usually headed by an SIO of the rank of Detective Inspector, Detective Chief Inspector or Detective Superintendent according to the complexity of the incident, the case will take the form of a manslaughter investigation. In many cases the SIO will need to comply with the guidelines set out in the tri-partite agreement, *Work related deaths – a protocol for liaison.*[1]

1   HSE (2003). The full text is available at www.hse.gov.uk/pubns/misc491.pdf.

4.35   The Protocol places the emphasis on the CID to take control of such an incident by mandating that a detective of supervisory rank, ie at least a Detective Sergeant, attends the scene of a death in the workplace and makes an initial assessment as to whether the circumstances might justify a charge of manslaughter or any other serious criminal offence. As a general rule the police will investigate where there is evidence or a suspicion of deliberate intent or gross negligence or recklessness on the part of an individual or company, rather than human error of carelessness. It may take some time before the police are sure that there have been no serious criminal offences committed, so the investigation needs to commence and continue with manslaughter in mind from the beginning.

4.36   The Protocol further states that the investigation will be a joint investigation with the police and the HSE working closely together throughout. If the police reach a stage where they are satisfied that no serious criminal offences have been committed, the case will be passed wholly to the HSE for the HSE to continue in the prosecution of any HSE offences. Clearly this indicates that the preservation of the scene and the initial actions of the police must be correct and professional as failure in this respect may affect or compromise subsequent HSE prosecutions.

4.37   With the Protocol and the *Murder Investigation Manual* in mind, the SIO commences the investigation. If the incident is of sufficient size in terms of casualties, deaths, the number of witnesses and potential defendants, or due to its complexity, the SIO may well consider opening a major incident room. This is a computer-driven process for handling information and creating actions, lines of inquiries and parameters of the investigation in order to assemble all of the information and evidence available.

4.38   Officers will be deputed to take charge of exhibits, read statements, create actions for other officers to make inquiries, deal with disclosure of evidence and, perhaps one of the most important issues, to be responsible for the family liaison officers. The Protocol determines that this issue should be a joint venture between the police and the HSE. So too will be the media strategy, which will be discussed below.

4.39   Working to the structure outlined in the *Murder Investigation Manual*, the SIO will commence 'fast track actions' or those tasks the SIO needs to consider at a very early stage of the investigation.

Interviewing suspects and witnesses

4.40   It is not unusual for HSE inspectors and police officers to interview witnesses jointly, although separate statements may be obtained by each investigating body. As and when potential responsibility has been considered, it may be necessary for 'PACE interviews' (ie interviews to which the Police and Criminal Evidence Act 1984 applies) to be conducted and, again, it is increasingly common for those interviews to be conducted by police and HSE inspectors jointly. On a practical basis, it is similarly not uncommon for inspectors to listen in to the interviews from a separate room, with the consent of all concerned, and provide technical guidance and assistance to the officers conducting the questioning.

Post-mortems

4.41   In the case of deaths which are deemed to be suspicious, the usual practice is for the local coroner to be informed and a decision made as to whether a post-mortem examination is required. The general rule is that if a person has died suddenly and unexpectedly from an unknown cause, the coroner will order a post-mortem examination of the person to ascertain the cause of death. Provisions under the Coroners Act 1988 and the Coroners Rules 1984[1] deal with post-mortems.

1   SI 1984/522.

4.42   If, however, the death is deemed suspicious, ie the supervising detective considers that there is sufficient evidence to commence a manslaughter investigation, the coroner may order a forensically qualified pathologist to perform the post-mortem examination, as would be the case for a murder or manslaughter arising from any other cause.

4.43   From the post-mortem examination the SIO would hope to establish the cause of death and recover any evidence or indication to support charges against an individual or a corporation. It would be determined whether the deceased had had a natural illness that contributed to his or her death, or whether the death was caused as direct result of the incident under investigation. It may be the case that the death had been caused as a result of an industrial disease, which is something the SIO would expect the pathologist to determine during the post-mortem and from evidence gained during subsequent tests.

4.44   The coroner would open an inquest, and would hear evidence of identification, the time of death, the place of death and the cause of death, if known at that stage.

The inquest would normally be adjourned to a date to be arranged, when the coroner would hear additional evidence regarding the reasons for the death and whether any individual or corporation is to be charged in connection with the death. In the event of a prosecution the coroner's role would usually be finalised by a formal paper inquest, where no additional evidence is heard. In the event of there not being a prosecution, the coroner will hold a full inquest, where evidence would be heard covering all of the facts.

Victim identification

4.45   This brings the SIO to the first major line of inquiry he or she would have to consider, that of the formal positive identification of the deceased person(s).

4.46   It is for the coroner to be satisfied that the police provide sufficient evidence of identification to warrant positive identification. There are numerous methods of identification, which the police are able to use, for instance:

- visual;
- DNA;
- circumstantial;
- jewellery;
- documentation,

and the coroner will determine which one of the above, or which permutation of the above he or she will accept as positive evidence.

4.47   The identification of deceased persons in recent years has proved problematical and many lessons have been learned, especially from the spate of fatal disasters in the period from the 1980s to the present day. There have been numerous incidents of misidentification and the SIO has to be particularly careful that the evidence with regard to identification is correct.

4.48   One major lesson learned in recent years is that, contrary to belief, visual identification may not always be the most reliable method of identifying a deceased person. It is usually a close relative who is responsible for the visual identification and research has shown that many relatives pass through various stages of expectation and emotions when they are requested visually to identify a relative.

4.49   Their emotions and expectations range from disbelief that such a thing could happen to their relative and the police must be wrong in their information, to the belief that the police must be correct because they could not possibly make a mistake of this magnitude.

4.50   Careful training of the family liaison officers within all police forces now ensures that relatives are properly prepared for the viewing of the body so as to avoid emotional trauma and the expectation that the body will look as it did the last time the witness saw the person before death. This is a common feeling among witnesses and many have suffered psychological illnesses following such a viewing.

4.51   Research has shown that there are five common results in a visual viewing scenario:

- the correct body is identified;
- the wrong body is identified;
- no body is identified;
- the correct body is not identified; or
- the witness identifies a body and then changes their mind.

4.52 Clearly the first option is the preferred choice but the chance of a correct, reliable identification is by no means certain.

4.53 It is often the case that the coroner will instruct the SIO to include another identification option in order to be certain.

Family liaison

4.54 This issue has developed in recent years and is seen as a vital part of the major incident room (MIR) and something for which the SIO has to be responsible. The contact with the families of the victims, whether deceased or injured, is crucial and working together with them can provide essential evidence for the investigation as well as fulfilling a duty the SIO has to keep the family informed and, indeed, involve them with every part and development of the investigation.

4.55 Police forces are investing a great deal of human and financial resources into training officers in the role of family liaison officers and a nationally agreed structured course has been designed and developed based on many instances in the past from which lessons have been learned.

4.56 As stated above, in cases of deaths where the Protocol[1] is involved, a joint family liaison strategy between the police and HSE is essential in order to keep the families of those involved informed with up-to-date information.

1 HSE *Work-related deaths: a protocol for liaison* (2003).

4.57 It is now recognised by police forces that relatives of victims of major disasters, or even work related deaths, form themselves into large, well-organised, well-financed and legally well-briefed pressure groups: Disaster Action, SAMM (Support after Murder and Manslaughter) and other groups that relate directly to their particular incident, Hillsborough Families etc. These groups will want answers to questions at once and the SIO will need to prepare responses to them, perhaps with the HSE, at a very early stage. To keep the families on the side of the investigation is a skill the SIO should possess and it is very important that regular contact with the SIO is maintained.

Lines of inquiry

4.58 In any major investigation the SIO will determine 'lines of inquiry' or those inquiries that will achieve the overall aim of the investigation. Lines of inquiry are an essential element in the investigation, as they will assist in prioritising the actions raised for officers to follow.

4.59 The fundamental purpose of the investigation would be to:

- determine how and why the person died or was seriously injured;
- prove or disprove that a criminal offence has been committed (including any Health and Safety at Work etc Act 1974 offences);
- determine who is responsible if a criminal offence has been committed; and
- determine whether there is sufficient evidence to prosecute any individual or organisation for any criminal offence (including Health and Safety at Work etc Act 1974 offences).

4.60   The SIO has to appreciate the fundamental differences between investigating a corporate killing and a traditional suspicious death, but not forget that the principle of securing evidence to assist with a prosecution will remain the same.

4.61   There may be human and corporate offenders. Many SIOs will not have much experience in dealing with corporations or businesses as defendants, other than perhaps road traffic offences. Issues will arise regarding the 'causation chain' within a business and difficulties may arise in proving that all important 'directing mind' essential in proving manslaughter charges against a corporation. More will be said about the 'causation chain' below.

4.62   The incident may involve multiple victims; far more victims, either dead or injured, than the SIO has had experience of before. When large numbers are involved issues of identification are raised. The incident may involve persons from different countries, religions and cultures and the SIO will need to be aware of this. The onus will be on the SIO to appreciate the differing wishes and demands from relatives. Multiple victims demand numerous family liaison officers and police force contingency plans should cater for this eventuality.

4.63   Many police forces have major contingency plans, which in the event of a major incident are put into operation. Many of the plans include the facility of a 'body identification commission', which, when effected, provides trained officers whose duty it is to recover bodies from the scene, deal with identification and prepare reports for the coroner as a set out above. It is essential that forces consider this structure, because without it, delay, confusion and mistakes can occur. Some of the major events of the 1980s mentioned above attracted criticism of the police in their handling of the dead and the identification issues. A properly trained team of officers can alleviate the potential problems.

4.64   The SIO may be faced with a unique crime scene such as the oilrig *Piper Alpha* or the 280+ square miles of scene from the Lockerbie incident. Equally, the scene can be the small factory or office and may well include the management offices of such premises, from where evidence may be obtained. This part of any such business must be considered a scene and treated accordingly. The scene may be as simple as a house with a blocked boiler flue.

4.65   Another difference between these incidents and the 'normal' death investigation is the likelihood of a judicial or public inquiry being announced by the government, which may take place at the same time as the investigation. This begs the question – 'Who has primacy over the evidence?'

4.66   If a judicial or public inquiry commences during the time the investigation is live, there may well arise problems for the SIO, in that the judicial inquiry may be hearing evidence before the manslaughter investigation is in possession of it. Whilst that process is a matter for the Chair of the judicial inquiry and the government, experience indicates that it causes problems with the investigation tracing witnesses and subsequently taking statements from them, especially if the witness has already given verbal evidence to the inquiry. Previous similar situations have arisen and the witness is often reluctant to provide the police with statements, on the understanding that they have already given evidence before the inquiry and decline to repeat the process.

4.67 Other 'fast track actions' the SIO will consider involve tracing significant witnesses and arranging to interview them. Significant witnesses are:

- those witnesses who may have been, or claim to have been, an eye witness or witness to the immediate event in some other way; or
- those witnesses having a particular relationship to the deceased or someone having a central position in the investigation.

4.68 The SIO will obtain 'best evidence' from the first group upon which the court may be able to rely. It is important for the SIO to record this evidence as soon as possible, usually on video.

4.69 The second group may provide the SIO will obtain background information about the deceased and/or the company involved. It is important that the officers deputed to interview significant witnesses are in possession of as much information as possible about the scene, the events and if possible the history of the circumstances that caused the incident. It has to be remembered that the interviewing officers may be both police and HSE officers. It should be the case that interviewing officers are duly trained and qualified. Significant witnesses may be suffering from a degree of shock and trauma and will need special handling. Trained officers are able to cope with this eventuality but the SIO needs to remember that there may well be a need for some sort of counselling to be arranged for the witness. It is recommended that the witness is seen and the statement taken before any counselling is administered. This will remove that argument that the evidence from the witness has been coached and rehearsed.

4.70 The SIO will give early consideration to obtaining technical expert assistance, usually from the HSE, but also from other areas of industry and universities both in this country and abroad. It is essential that leading experts assist the investigating team and the SIO must be aware of the possibility of the defence obtaining their assistance and advice if the investigation team do not. This process requires a degree of knowledge by the SIO as to which expert witnesses could assist him or her in the investigation. Once decided, the SIO has to determine where those witnesses can be contacted and, more importantly for the police service, who is going to pay for them to assist and possibly give evidence for the prosecution. It may be that such experts demand high costs, something the police force involved needs to manage.

4.71 An immediate consideration by the SIO at the scene of a death in the workplace is preventing the company concealing or destroying evidence that may be relevant to the investigation. It cannot be denied that some unscrupulous companies may attempt to frustrate the investigation by destroying incriminating documents, minutes from meetings and policies, once the company is under suspicion. Swift deployment of officers to take possession of such documents may prevent this occurring. It necessarily follows that the officers will have to be briefed by the SIO and perhaps the HSE as to what they are being asked to seize. This task rests with the SIO or deputy SIO and it will form part of the SIOs policy document, reference to which will be made in more detail at below.

4.72   The SIO will need to establish a 'causation chain' This is the process of determining who in the organisation is responsible for making decisions, finance, training, safety etc. There will be a need to establish if any one person was responsible for making the decision that results directly in the incident occurring. This will be particularly difficult in large organisations such as city councils, or large national and international corporations. The SIO may need to recruit assistance from experts in this field to prevent the investigation being side-tracked by bureaucracy. There should be a determined effort to establish the roles and responsibilities of management within an organisation so that those who made the decisions are held accountable This is especially so if the decisions are proved to be cause of an incident and thereby in breach of the law. To assist in this area, the SIO will need to consider information and intelligence from other non-police sources, such as HM Customs & Excise VAT Department, the government's Public Health Department and the Inland Revenue to name a few. Any of these non-police sources may provide information that will corroborate evidence obtained by the investigation team. It may be that the company has previously been prosecuted under health and safety legislation, which may be of relevance in the investigation.

Dealing with the media

4.73   It is the responsibility of the SIO to deal with the media at the scene. Previous major incidents have demonstrated the effect the media can have within minutes of incidents occurring. To prevent loss of evidence and to ensure the release of crucial information pertinent to the investigation, it is important that the media are managed correctly. The SIO will also be aware of the value of using the media to communicate messages to the public, relatives etc. An important part of the SIO's training involves media management. There is a recognition that the media will be at the scene of a large scale or unusual death before the SIO and it is vital that officers at the scene awaiting the arrival of the SIO are briefed as to what they can and cannot tell the media.

4.74   The media will hunt for a story and will very often trace witnesses before the police are able to trace them. Some less responsible media personnel will take advantage of the situation and transmit facts of the event, often during a live broadcast. This practice very often has the effect that witnesses give wrong, mistaken or misleading information to the world at large, which may be prejudicial to the investigation or may prematurely inform relatives of a person's death. Quite often the facts given out by 'live' witnesses with the assistance of the media are incorrect and cause problems for the SIO in managing the release of information. It is essential that this is not allowed to happen and it is the responsibility of the SIO to ensure steps are taken to manage and use the media correctly.

4.75   The investigation then moves to another phase, referred to in the *Murder Investigation Manual* as the 'theoretical process'. This involves the use of various experts to give the police every chance of professional advice during the inquiry. These experts include victimologists and offender profilers, not forgetting the professional interpretation of the information obtained from the post-mortem examination by the pathologist. As well as the lines of inquiry under this heading, the SIO should consider examining the company's safety strategy and performance. It would be essential for the SIO to determine if the company had a robust strategy on safety, which would include training for staff, a comprehensive reporting and recording policy regarding accidents and injuries within the company, and duly qualified personnel to undertake the training. These issues may provide evidence to support a charge against a company or an organisation and will portray an image of the company's attitude towards such issues.

4.76   The investigation will then move to another phase called the 'planned method of investigation'. Issues under this heading relate to the policy the SIO will adopt throughout the investigation regarding the prioritisation of actions and lines of inquiry. Some lines of inquiry will be considered more important than others, preventing the company destroying evidence, for example, and the prioritisation process will assist the SIO to adopt a structure, understood by the remainder of the officers involved in the investigation and justified in the SIO's policy book.

4.77   Also under this heading are issues around the creation of a forensic strategy or those means by which exhibits are to be examined. It may be the case that the exhibit to be examined is so unusual or unique, an aircraft engine, for example, that the Forensic Science Service is not considered the correct authority to carry out the examination. In these cases the SIO may well turn to the HSE for assistance and use their expertise and facilities to carry out such tests, as well as relying upon experts from industry. It is important for the SIO to record in his or her strategy – by what method, and by which 'body', the examination of such exhibits was carried out so as to prove the integrity of the exhibit. Equal care must be taken over the integrity and safety of an engine as a piece of paper recovered from an office. Every movement of the exhibit must be logged and statements are usually taken from everyone who handles the exhibit. The same rule applies to all exhibits, no matter how large or complex they are.

4.78   It is under this heading, 'The planned method of investigation', that the SIO will record the policy around working together with other agencies, such as the HSE, and the logistical arrangements and structure of the investigation under the Protocol.[1] Details of working patterns for the investigation team must be recorded so as to later justify any decision made should questions be raised at a future tribunal.

1   HSE *Work-related deaths: a protocol for liaison* (2003).

4.79   Actions should be raised for officers to examine and, if necessary, take possession of records detailing meetings and briefings the company has had. Management meeting records could have dealt with issues relative to the incident, for example, maintenance procedures, response to concerns expressed by the workforce and comments made by union or safety representatives.

4.80   Once completed, the SIO moves from the planned method of investigation onto another part of the murder investigation model – 'suspect inquiries'. It is under this heading that the SIO concentrates on the 'suspect', who in these cases may be a company, an organisation or an individual.

The company profile

4.81   The SIO will quickly commission officers to create a profile of the company, concentrating on the management and structure of the company. This will assist in the aforementioned 'fast track action' and 'theoretical process' aspects of the investigation structure. The investigation will need to determine who are the management and whether have they come to the notice of the police, the HSE or any other investigative body before, either within this company/corporation or another. The SIO will be mindful of the fact that directors of companies can, with relative ease, move from one company to another, especially following liquidations etc. Therefore there is a possibility that a person who has previous convictions for either criminal or HSE offences at a previous company is the senior member of another company. Research may show that similar facts may exist with the company under investigation, which will add to the modus operandi and the 'guilty knowledge' the SIO will be wishing to prove.

4.82   It will be necessary to establish the training philosophy of the company and determine who are the trainers and what relevant qualifications they possess. A similar situation exists in relation to the safety structure and those responsible for ensuring the workforce are aware of the requirements of the safety regulations. The SIO may well instruct the seizure of the accident recording book held at the premises, which may indicate similar incidents with less serious consequences occurring previously. As to the possible seizure of the documents by HSE inspectors, see **para 4.97** below.

4.83   The SIO will be interested in whether training is a 'stand-alone' issue within the company or whether those responsible have other duties within the organisation with the result that training or safety is a task rarely performed. This will give an indication as to where training sits within the organisation and the priority training is given. Another measure would be to assess the cost of training and safety against the gross profit of the company. In a successful company the SIO would determine if the training and safety budgets were reasonable compared to the overall worth of the company, taking into account the type of incident that has occurred.

The financial profile of the company

4.84   This brings the lines of inquiry onto the financial situation of the company. Detectives will be required to acquire a financial profile of the organisation to determine whether spending on safety was appropriate given the amount of gross profit. The object of this line of inquiry would be to ascertain if the company took training and safety seriously thereby providing a safe environment in which the workforce can operate. The SIO would be able to manage this profile in the case of a small 'single-handed ' company. There would be officers in force with sufficient accountancy knowledge to perform this role. It would be a different story if the company were a large corporation or an international organisation. In the event of this scenario arising, the SIO would need to recruit experts in financial matters – a large company of auditors, for example. This in itself would prove costly, so the SIO would have to justify the expenditure to his or her senior officers at ACPO level. The fact remains, however, that if the SIO wishes to prove negligence against a company, a financial profile will be essential.

4.85 The decision-making process within an organisation will be of great interest to the SIO. Senior management will be asked to justify decisions made regarding training, safety and processes. With the need to determine the 'directing mind' being foremost in the SIOs mind, the SIO will be looking for documentation which relates to these decisions in the form of policies, memoranda and structures etc.

4.86 The SIO will appreciate that the investigation will have a multi agency approach in line with the Protocol.[1] It may also be that other investigative organisations are involved with the investigation – the Air Accident Investigation Board, the Marine Investigation Authority and so on. With this in mind the SIO will be expected to keep a policy book. This is a written record of all of the decisions made relating to the process of the investigation, as opposed to actions required to be completed. The policy book will conform to nationally agreed guidelines, created by ACPO and used in all police forces. In that document the SIO will record the various strategies he or she decides upon and the form that they will take. For instance, detailed entries regarding the forensic strategy, the media strategy and the search strategy will be made, so the rationale behind those decisions will be recalled in years to come.

1 HSE *Work-related deaths: a protocol for liaison* (2003).

The documentation search strategy

4.87 The documentation search strategy is something with which the SIO may well require expert assistance. There may be occasions where a large organisation will need to be examined for various documents, for example, the policies mentioned above. Working on the basis that the company/organisation itself will offer no assistance, the SIO has to have a contingency plan to cover this eventuality.

4.88 Most forces will have officers deployed within a fraud department, who being properly trained are used to dealing with large amounts of paper and documents. It may very well be different for those officers when faced with a large corporation or international business with numerous sites, massive administrative systems and computerised records. The SIO may need to 'buy in' the services of an expert company who would perform that task on behalf of the police and the HSE.

Disclosure and the legal strategy

4.89 One of the most important strategies upon which the SIO and the HSE will have to decide will be the legal strategy. It will be essential for the SIO to have constant legal advice regarding the progress of the investigation, and consultation with counsel at an early stage will assist with the lines of inquiry in particular and the investigation in general. Alongside this strategy will be the disclosure strategy. The SIO will have to consider obtaining legal assistance to determine the disclosure policy for the investigation, with consideration being given to any future discovery in civil cases and the possibility of a public inquiry being held, perhaps years later. It is thought best practice for the police, via the CPS, to engage the most suitable legal advice in the field of corporate killing. It is suggested that if this means providing finance for those eminent in this field to present the prosecution case rather than to defend, then the police service needs to facilitate that process

4.90   With this in mind the police and the HSE in any such investigation will need to consider early contact with legal advice, the CPS or other suitable representation, in order to ensure that the investigation is 'on the right tracks' and that there is sufficient evidence to comply with the legislation.

The HSE

Who investigates health and safety offences?

4.91   The Health and Safety (Enforcing Authority) Regulations 1989[1] allocate investigation and enforcement responsibilities between the HSE and local authorities. By and large, the HSE investigates activities carried on in factories, construction sites and agricultural locations. Local authorities, by and large, investigate activities in wholesale and retail premises, offices and catering premises. Reference will need to be made to the detailed regulations if the question of jurisdiction needs to be considered.

1   SI 1989/1903.

The role of the HSE inspector

4.92   The role of the HSE inspector is to gather the facts relating to the incident and prepare a report for those who need to consider what action should be taken. Inspectors will initially interview witnesses alongside police officers, their role being to assist the police and provide technical expertise which may be lacking on the part of officers who, although well used to handling crime scenes, will not possess the technical skills required to analyse the immediate aftermath of an industrial accident, which might have been caused as a result of the failure of complex equipment *or* procedures.

4.93   The inspector will have in mind the possibility that if manslaughter charges are not pursued by the CPS, it is almost inevitable, in view of the fact that a death has occurred, that a prosecution will be brought under the provisions of the Health and Safety at Work etc Act 1974. The inspector will from the outset be considering the matters which need to be investigated to establish whether such charges should be brought.

4.94   One immediate consideration will be whether it is appropriate to prosecute an individual, either as well as or in substitution for the organisation which was operating the business. Individuals will be interviewed in their capacity as managers of the organisation in order to gather information as to how the company was managing its business. However, if evidence begins to emerge of a possible serious breach of duty on the part of an individual it will then be necessary to consider whether that person should be interviewed under caution in his or her personal capacity. It should be remembered, however, that an HSE inspector does not have the powers of arrest given to a police officer. The statutory basis for the prosecution of an individual is set out in the Health and Safety at Work etc Act 1974, s 37.

4.95   The inspector is required to gather the facts and prepare a report with a view to possible prosecution. Guidelines exist within HSE for the assessment as to whether it is appropriate to bring a prosecution.

4.96   The factors to be considered in deciding whether a prosecution should be brought are:

1   Has a death occurred or has there been serious injury?
2   Has the company ignored previous warnings or guidance relating to health and safety issues?
3   Has the company sought to obstruct the investigation?
4   Can it be said that there is no culture within the organisation of taking health and safety issues seriously?
5   Could it be said that corners have been cut?

Powers of an HSE inspector

4.97   In carrying out the investigation the inspector is armed with a substantial array of powers provided by the Health and Safety at Work etc Act 1974, s 20. These powers include:

1   the power to enter premises;
2   the power to examine equipment;
3   the power to take photographs;
4   the power to seize items of plant and equipment;
5   the power to copy documentation;
6   the power to require those who have information relating to the incident to provide that information to the inspector and then sign a written statement setting out such information; and
7   any other power required to give effect to the preceding powers.

4.98   It can be seen that the powers are more extensive and wide ranging than those possessed by police officers who, in order to carry out such an investigation, would require a search warrant. The power to require individuals to provide information is clearly one which is not possessed police officers. It is an offence punishable by a fine to refuse to provide information or to obstruct an inspector carrying out an investigation.

4.99   The safeguard which exists in the legislation, however, is that if any individual is compelled pursuant to the Health and Safety at Work etc Act 1974, s 20 to provide information, the information so provided cannot be used in the course of any prosecution of that individual. In practical terms it means therefore that employees can be required to give any information which is required relating to the employer's business and the circumstances leading up to and relating to the actual death. It also follows that if there is any suggestion that the individual concerned might have personal responsibility for what has occurred, the powers under s 20 cannot be used, the individual must be cautioned and an interview conducted in accordance with the requirements of the Police and Criminal Evidence Act 1984.

Closing thoughts

4.100   The Protocol *Work-related deaths: a protocol for liaison* [1] has had a big impact upon the way in which work related deaths are investigated. Although the Protocol has been in place since 1998,[2] it is only in recent years that those involved have been aware of and relied upon its provisions.

1   HSE (2003). The full text is available at www.hse.gov.uk/pubns/misc491.pdf.
2   *The protocol for liaison: work related deaths* (1988).

4.101   While the Protocol is a significant improvement upon what went before, there are those *who* argue that the issue of training and the provision of investigation manuals for the police and the HSE in relation to work related deaths needs to be addressed. However, one thing is for certain, that both the police and the HSE continue to gain more experience of working together and how to approach these investigations.

4.102   It is also worth noting that one direct consequence of the Protocol is an increase in the number of prosecutions now commenced against individuals together with the organisations which employ them.

CHAPTER 5

Construction industry

Helen Grice, Solicitor, Masons, Manchester

(with additional material by Michael Appleby, Solicitor, Fisher Scoggins LLP, London)

Introduction

5.1   The most appropriate starting point for this chapter must surely be what is meant by the phrase 'the construction industry'. The word 'construction' is quite often used loosely, to describe various industries including engineering, power, water, utilities and so on. However, given that most of those industries are dealt with elsewhere in this text, 'construction' in this chapter, will be used in the narrower sense.

5.2   The term 'construction work' also covers a wide variety of operations, from routine maintenance and redecoration to multi-million pound projects. One definition, contained in the Construction (Health, Safety and Welfare) Regulations 1996[1] (CHSWR) defines construction as: the carrying out of any building, civil engineering or engineering construction work.[2] This includes alteration, conversion, fitting out, commissioning, renovation, repair, upkeep, redecoration and other maintenance.[3] Where cleaning involves the use of water or other abrasives at high pressure or the use of substances classified as corrosive or toxic[4] this also comes within the meaning of construction under the CHSWR, as does decommissioning, demolition or dismantling of a structure. The Regulations also allow for the preparation of a site for construction (except for site survey),[5] assembly and disassembly of prefabricated elements,[6] removal of waste,[7] and installation and maintenance of services.[8]

1   SI 1996/1592.

2 SI 1996/1592, reg 2(1)(a).
3 SI 1996/1592, reg 2(1).
4 For the purpose of the Carriage of Dangerous Goods by Road and Rail (Classification, Packaging and Labelling) Regulations 1994, SI 1994/669.
5 SI 1996/1592, reg 2(1)(b).
6 SI 1996/1592, reg 2(1)(c).
7 SI 1996/1592, reg 2(1)(d).
8 SI 1996/1592, reg 2(1)(e).

5.3   Under the CHSWR, the term 'structure' also has a wide definition and includes almost any manmade feature. A construction site is any place where the principal work activity being carried out is construction work.

5.4   There are other statutory definitions of 'construction', including that contained in the Housing Grants, Construction and Regeneration Act 1996. The Housing Grants Construction and Regeneration Act 1996, s 105(1) defines 'construction operations' as building, alterations, demolition, installation of fittings like heating and ventilation systems and painting and decorating internal and external surfaces. It specifically excludes work under contracts with a residential occupier, agreements under the Private Finance Initiative and development agreements.

5.5   This chapter will discuss construction as defined in the CHSWR, ie it will cover all such types of construction work carried out on sites and in premises where the principal activity is that of construction work. The chapter will remain of interest to other industries to the extent that they carry out construction works (for example, maintenance, refurbishment, redecoration and repairs).

The construction industry

5.6   The construction industry has a number of key features which set it apart from other industries:

- the widespread use of standard form contracts and frequent amendment of those forms to create bespoke contracts for particular projects;
- the large number of players involved in any one contract, including client, architect/designer, planning supervisor, main contractor, trade/sub-contractors, quantity surveyor, suppliers, manufacturers etc, and the complexities created by the interaction of those parties;
- the fact that most projects are one-offs, with no standardisation of design, materials or construction methods;
- the wide ranging variety and values of construction projects;
- the fact that most of the parties will not have worked together before commencing the particular project (although the emerging popularity of partnering may change this);
- the cut throat nature of market competition, which often gives rise to relatively low profit margins;
- the fact that most of the work is carried out outdoors, leaving contractors at the mercy of the elements;
- the widespread use of heavy plant and equipment requiring operation by skilled workmen; and
- the employment of temporary, and sometimes unskilled, workers.

Health and safety in the construction industry

5.7 All the above factors contribute to there being a higher risk of injury and death on a construction site than in most other workplaces. Indeed, recent statistics[1] show that the construction industry is still one of the most hazardous industries to work in. Whilst the construction industry employs approximately 6% of the UK working population, in 2002–03 it accounted for over 30% of work related deaths.

1 Health and Safety Executive Statistics of Fatal Injuries 2002/2003, available at www.hse.gov.uk/statistics/overal/fat10203.pdf

5.8 Back in 1988, the Health and Safety Executive (HSE) published *Blackspot Construction*, a report on its five-year study (1981–85) into fatal accidents in the construction industry. *Blackspot* stated that:[1]

'A recurring theme throughout [the report] is that people are killed during simple, routine work. In many cases, a clear lack of planning contributed to the tragedy. Experience is no safeguard and experienced workers are just as likely to be killed as trainees.'

1 HSE *Blackspot Construction: a study of five years fatal accidents in the building and civil engineering industries* (1988).

5.9 In *Blackspot*, the HSE cited the construction industry as 'amongst the most dangerous of all industries'. During the study period, 739 people died on construction sites, or in construction related works. Of these deaths, 720 (97%) were due to just five causes.

5.10 By 2002–03, the number of fatalities in the construction industry had dropped to 71, but, as can be seen below, the causes of these deaths remained almost the same.

	1981–85	2002–03 (3 December)
Falls from height	52%	47%
Falling objects and materials	19%	15%
Transport and mobile plant	18%	7%
Electricity	5%	10%
Asphyxiation/drowning	3%	0%

5.11 Various governments (both in the UK and in Europe) recognised the lack of planning and communication as being at the root of the high accident rates in the construction industry. This has resulted in the increase in industry-specific health and safety legislation imposing statutory duties on all parties to plan and co-ordinate construction work.

5.12 After a steady decrease in accident rates throughout the 1990s, the industry was disappointed in 2001 to find it had gone back to the rates of the early 1990s. In 2000–01, the number of fatalities rose sharply to 114 deaths,[1] of which 106 were workers (including employees and self-employed). This triggered further initiatives, such as the Health and Safety Summit[2] which the government, in conjunction with the HSE, aimed to encourage industry players to improve working practices.

1   HSE Statistics Bulletin 2000/2001.
2   Held on 27 February 2001, jointly chaired by the HSE and the Department of the Environment, Transport and the Regions, at which the construction industry was challenged to reverse the upward trend in worker fatalities.

5.13   All parties to a construction project now have responsibilities for health and safety – from the client through designers to contractors and individual workers. Although the main construction contractor is still responsible for all onsite operations, all those working on the site have a duty to co-operate with each other and the main contractor.

5.14   This means that a death on a construction site is likely to have a number of causes and, consequently, a number of potential defendants to charges of breaches of health and safety legislation and/or manslaughter.

5.15   To date (2003) there has only been one successful prosecution of a construction company for corporate manslaughter,[1] which involved a small company. Although the fatality rate in the construction industry is high, there are many reasons for the low prosecution rate, which include the facts that:

•   most construction sites are remote from the company's head office (particularly in the case of large construction companies) meaning that anyone who is high enough up the chain of command to be considered the 'directing mind and will' is unlikely to have had any active involvement in events leading up to the accident; and
•   construction industry accidents do not generally receive significant media attention, since they tend to involve workers rather than members of the public, and even the worst accidents generally result in small numbers of casualties.

1   English Brothers Ltd, a Cambridgeshire construction company pleaded guilty to corporate manslaughter in August 2001.

Origins of corporate responsibility for construction safety

The history of health and safety legislation in construction

5.16   This chapter next traces the origins of corporate responsibility for safety from the earliest days through to current and prospective legislation and guidance.

5.17   UK health and safety law as we know it dates back to 1802, when a law was passed to improve the conditions for child labour. The next health and safety law was passed in 1819 and many statutes and subordinate regulations followed. As large numbers of people left the agricultural and handicraft industries to work in factories, workshops and construction it was recognised that some form of statutory protection for them was necessary.

5.18   The laws introduced were, however, fragmented (in that each Act only affected one specific industry or risk) and imposed prescriptive requirements on employers. There was no coherence to these rules until a review by a Royal Commission resulted in the Factory and Workshop Act 1878. Between 1878 and 1974 legislation to protect people at work and those affected by work activities proliferated.

5.19 The first law in relation to the construction industry was contained in the Factories Act 1937. This Act provided a comprehensive code for safety, health and welfare requirements and was applicable to all factories. Included in its provisions were requirements for building activities.

5.20 The Factories Act 1961 was, however, the first statute of key importance to the construction industry. Various regulations stemmed from it including the Construction (General Provisions) Regulations 1961,[1] the Construction (Lifting Operations) Regulations 1961,[2] the Construction (Health and Welfare) Regulations 1966[3] and the Construction (Working Places) Regulations 1966.[4] These addressed the technicalities of health and safety in the construction industry.

1 SI 1961/1580.
2 SI 1961/1581.
3 SI 1966/95.
4 SI 1966/94.

The Health and Safety at Work etc Act 1974

5.21 In 1970, the Robens committee was set up to review the provision made for the health and safety of persons in the course of their employment. By that time, although there were numerous Acts containing safety requirements, over 5 million employees still had no statutory protection. Where protection was provided, it was uneven. Administration of the law was diverse and the enforcement powers were inadequate. The wording and intent of the legislation was not directed towards the personal involvement of the worker and, in parts, it was obsolete.

5.22 Following the Robens Report, the Health and Safety at Work etc Act 1974 (HSWA 1974) was passed to correct many of these defects. It presented a new approach to health and safety legislation: it emphasised the individual and his or her duties and applied to all work activities.

5.23 The aim of HSWA 1974 was to provide an all-encompassing framework of general duties in relation to health and safety at work. HSWA 1974 made provision for specific regulations to be passed easily by the Secretary of State, without the need to return to Parliament, thus ensuring that health and safety law remains 'in date'.

European law

5.24 The European Communities Act 1972 incorporated the Treaties constituting the EU into UK legislation. EU law becomes law in the UK by various means. For health and safety legislation, it is usually implemented by statutory instrument.

5.25 The Treaty of Rome, as amended, emphasises the importance of the health and safety of workers.[1] Various directives on health and safety have now been incorporated into UK law, including:

• the Temporary and Mobile Construction Sites Directive,[2] implemented by the Construction (Design and Management) Regulations 1994;[3] and
• the Workplace Directive[4] implemented for construction sites by the Construction (Health, Safety and Welfare) Regulations 1996.[5]

1 Art 118A states that member states are to 'pay particular attention to encouraging improvements, especially in the working environment, as regards the health and safety of workers'.
2 Council Directive 92/57/EEC of 24 June 1992.
3 SI 1994/3140.
4 Council Directive 89/654/EEC of 16 March 1998.
5 SI 1996/1592.

Current law and practice

5.26   Employers carry the main responsibility for ensuring the health and safety of employees and for reducing risks to others, including members of the public, affected by work activities. Under the requirements of HSWA 1974, ss 2 and 3:

'2(1) It shall be the duty of every employer to ensure, so far as is reasonably practicable, the health, safety and welfare at work of all his employees.'

'3(1) It shall be the duty of every employer to conduct his undertaking in such a way as to ensure, so far as is reasonably practicable, that persons not in his employment who may be affected thereby are not thereby exposed to risks to their health or safety.'

5.27   These general duties are expanded by a number of regulations. HSWA 1974 is worded such that it is up to the defendant employer to prove that it did everything reasonably practicable in the circumstances. This is difficult to establish, particularly in hindsight, making it the main reason why most employers plead guilty to health and safety charges. A breach of health and safety legislation can result in a criminal prosecution by the HSE through the magistrates' courts and Crown Courts. The sanctions for health and safety offences are fines and imprisonment.

Management of Health and Safety at Work Regulations 1999

5.28   The Management of Health and Safety at Work Regulations 1999[1] (MHSWR) implemented most of Council Directive 89/391/EEC of May 1990, the 'Framework Directive', and also Council Directive 91/383/EEC dealing with the health and safety of those who are employed on a fixed-term or other temporary basis. The Regulations are in addition to the requirements of HSWA 1974.

1 SI 1999/3242.

5.29   The Framework Directive[1] created a framework for further directives. It imposed broad and general duties on employers, employees and the self-employed. Subsequent Directives addressed specific hazards and work situations.

1 Council Directive 89/391/EEC.

5.30   The MHSWR requires employers to:

- assess the work-related risks to employees and others who may be affected;
- have effective arrangements in place for planning, organising, controlling, monitoring and reviewing preventive and protective measures;

- appoint one or more competent persons to help in undertaking the measures needed to comply with health and safety law; and
- provide employees with comprehensible and relevant information on the risks they face and the preventive and protective measures that control those risks.

5.31 Employers need to consult their employees in good time about any issues that may affect employees' health and safety. Recognised trade unions have the right to appoint health and safety representatives who carry out functions such as workplace inspections.

Construction (Design and Management) Regulations 1994

5.32 The Construction (Design and Management) Regulations 1994[1] (CDMR) give effect to Council Directive 92/57/EEC regarding the implementation of minimum health and safety requirements at temporary or mobile construction sites. The aim of the Directive was to attempt to stem the increase in construction fatalities throughout the EU by apportioning responsibility to everyone involved in the construction process. The intention was to co-ordinate the management of health and safety from conception and design through to actual construction and to increase the client's influence on health and safety.

1 SI 1994/3140.

5.33 CDMR[1] came into force on 31 March 1995 and applies to all 'construction work'. The definition of such work is very wide but effectively mirrors the definition in the CHSWR[2] (see **para 5.2ff** above) and means the carrying out of any building, civil engineering or engineering construction work.

1 SI 1994/3140.
2 SI 1996/1592.

5.34 To prevent the full requirements of the CDMR[1] applying to every construction work activity, however minor, there are a number of exemptions when either all or some of the provisions do not apply, for example, for minor works. Note, however, that the HSE considers the demolition and dismantling of any structure to be so hazardous that the CDMR always applies, whatever the duration or number of people working on the project.

1 SI 1994/3140.

5.35 Under the CDMR,[1] duties are placed on those responsible for all stages of a construction project, from initial conception right through to eventual demolition. The key requirements are to identify hazards and risks and to eliminate, reduce or control them. To be effective, this requires significant planning, co-operation and communication by all parties in the supply chain.

1 SI 1994/3140.

5.36 The CDMR[1] focuses on the co-ordination and co-operation of all parties concerned with construction work, by placing obligations on five different duty holders:

- client (see **para 5.165ff** below);
- designer (see **para 5.187ff** below);

- planning supervisor (see **para 5.210**ff below);
- principal contractor (see **para 5.220**ff below); and
- other contractors (see **para 5.220**ff below).

1 SI 1994/3140.

5.37 Two sets of formal documentation are also required:

- the health and safety plan; and
- the health and safety file.

5.38 It is expected that the HSC will publish a Consultative Document in the spring of 2004 on proposed changes to the CDMR.[1] This is in response to the construction industry's concerns over issues such as the bureaucracy associated with the regulations. The likely proposals will seek to simplify the regulations by focussing attention more on safety management issues and discouraging unnecessary paperwork.

1 SI 1994/3140.

Construction (Health, Safety and Welfare) Regulations 1996

5.39 The Construction (Health, Safety and Welfare) Regulations 1996[1] (CHSWR) replaced the Construction (General Provisions) Regulations 1961,[2] the Construction (Health and Welfare) Regulations 1966[3] and the Construction (Working Places) Regulations 1966,[4] which have all been revoked.

1 SI 1996/1592.
2 SI 1961/1580.
3 SI 1966/95.
4 SI 1966/94.

5.40 The requirements of the CHSWR,[1] which came into force on 2 September 1996, are designed to mirror the health, safety and welfare requirements on construction sites afforded to others by the Workplace (Health, Safety and Welfare) Regulations 1992[2] and implement the EU Workplace Directive.[3]

1 SI 1996/1592.
2 SI 1992/3004.
3 Council Directive 89/654/EEC.

5.41 The CHSWR imposes duties on employers, the self-employed and those who have control over construction work[1] in so far as the CHSWR affects them or persons under their control or relates to matters under their control.

1 As defined in CHSWR, SI 1996/1592, reg 4(1) and (2).

5.42 Every person at work also has a duty, under CHWSR, reg 4(4),[1] to co-operate with any person upon whom a duty or requirement is imposed by the CHWSR and to report to that person anything which he or she is aware may endanger the health or safety of him or herself or another person.

1 SI 1996/1592, reg 4(4).

5.43 The primary duties under the CHWSR[1] relate to:

* the provision of a safe place of work;
* prevention of falls;
* stability of structures;
* safe demolition;
* safe excavations;
* safety when working on or near water;
* vehicle safety/traffic management;
* fire and emergency provisions;
* welfare provisions;
* inspections by competent people; and
* training of employees.

1 SI 1996/1592.

5.44 The CHSWR[1] is less prescriptive than the Regulations it replaced.[2] Words such as 'sufficient' and 'adequate' are often used and detailed specifications are generally absent. However, some duties are worded to impose strict liability, such as the duty to take steps to prevent falls from height. This has been held to impose a strict liability to take *some* measures.[3]

1 SI 1996/1592.
2 See **para 5.39** above.
3 *R v Keltbray Ltd* [2001] 1 Cr App Rep (S) 132.

Approved Codes of Practice and Statutory Guidance

5.45 The Health and Safety Commission (HSC) is empowered by the Secretary of State to approve and issue Approved Codes of Practice (ACOP) to certain Regulations (for example, CDMR[1]). ACOPs prove guidance on how to comply with the duties contained in the health and safety regulations.

1 SI 1994/3140.

5.46 An ACOP can be drawn up by the HSE or HSC. In every case, however, the relevant government department must be consulted beforehand and the approval of the Secretary of State obtained for publication.

5.47 An ACOP enjoys a special status under HSWA 1974. Although compliance with the provision of an ACOP is not a legal requirement, non-compliance shifts the burden of proof on to a defendant to show that its procedures were at least as good as the ACOP.

Codes of Practice

5.48 A Code of Practice is issued in the same manner as an ACOP but without the approval of the relevant minister or Secretary of State. As such, it does not carry the same weight in law. Unlike the ACOP, compliance with a Code of Practice does not in itself infer compliance with the Regulations. It cannot therefore be used as a defence in criminal proceedings in the same way as an ACOP. Non-compliance can, however, be referred to by the prosecution as evidence of a failure to comply with good practice.

HSE Guidance Notes

5.49   The Guidance Notes issued by the HSE have no legal status. They are issued on a purely advisory basis to provide guidance on good health and safety practice, on specific hazards or on compliance with regulations. However, they can be referred to by the prosecution as evidence of a failure to comply with good practice. There are six series of Guidance Notes:

- legal (L);
- chemical safety (CS);
- plant and machinery (PM);
- medical series (MS);
- environmental hygiene (EH); and
- general series (GS).

European standards

5.50   European standards are harmonised standards within the member states of the EU. Produced by National Standards Agencies (in the UK by the British Standards Institute (BSI)), they provide sound guidance on numerous issues. EU Standards are frequently referred to by enforcement officers as the correct way of complying with a legal duty.

Manufacturers' information and instructions

5.51   HSWA 1974, s 6, as amended by the Consumer Protection Act 1987, requires manufacturers, designers, importers and installers of 'articles and substances used at work' to provide information relating to the safe use, storage etc of their products. Such information may include operating instructions for machinery or hazard data sheets for dangerous substances. Information provided should be sufficiently comprehensive and understandable to enable a judgment to be made on their safe use at work.

Common law

5.52   With regard to common law, case law on health and safety did not appear until the nineteenth century. Employees were often unsuccessful in their legal actions and there were various restrictions on entitlement to compensation.

5.53   There are now various provisions from case law relating to health and safety. An employer must take reasonable care to protect its employees from the risk of foreseeable injury, disease or death at work. Reasonable care includes providing a safe system of work, satisfactory training, a safe place of work, safe plant and equipment, competent fellow workers etc and as such mirror the duties imposed by HSWA 1974, s 2(1).

5.54   Case law in relation to clients, designers and contractors is discussed at **para 5.57**ff below. General trends include an increasing amount of responsibility being placed on clients. Even where experts are employed and the client does not have construction knowledge, the client still has a responsibility to ensure that people (workers and members of the public) are not exposed to health and safety risks.[1]

1   See *HSE v Port of Ramsgate Ltd* (1997, unreported), Central Criminal Court, and **paras 5.179–5.186** below.

5.55   The HSE and courts are trying to change the whole cultural mindset of companies by encouraging them to give safety as high a priority as economics. An important aspect of this is to ensure that all those involved in a project co-operate and focus on health and safety matters, from client to bricklayer. Above all, an effective risk management strategy must be in place.

5.56   However, in practice, the onus is still very much on the contractor. The courts have held that if a contractor becomes aware of an unsafe situation it should object until someone takes notice and, if that fails, refuse to continue to work.[1]

1   See *Plant Construction plc v Clive Adams Associates and JMH Construction Services Ltd* TLR 01/03/2000.

Case law

R v Keltbray Ltd[1]

5.57   Keltbray Limited was fined £200,000 after two employees were killed falling from the eighth storey of a building. The employees had been cutting out holes in the concrete floors to act as debris wells. Although the method statement indicated that the workers should start at the top of the building and work down (thus minimising the possible fall height), work on the top floor was delayed because services were still present. The employees therefore worked from the seventh floor down and returned to the top, eighth, floor to complete the well shaft.

1   [2001] 1 Cr App Rep (S) 132.

5.58   The employees, for reasons known only to themselves, were standing on the cut away section when, whilst cutting the fourth side, the slab gave way, plunging the men to their deaths.

5.59   The company was prosecuted under CHSWR, reg 6:[1]

'suitable and sufficient steps shall be taken to prevent, so far as is reasonably practicable, any person falling.'

1   SI 1996/1592, reg 6.

5.60   Keltbray changed its plea to guilty after hearing that the judge intended to direct the jury that this duty was one of strict liability and that, since Keltbray had taken no steps to prevent falls (no guard rails, harnesses or even anchor points for harnesses), it would be found guilty.

5.61   It appealed against the £200,000 fine imposed, on the basis that it was disproportionately high for a company of its size. The Court of Appeal took into consideration the guilty plea of the company, its good safety record and the steps taken since the accident to improve further its approach to safety of demolition work, but decided to uphold the fine.

R v English Bros[1]

5.62 This case concerns the death of Bill Larkman, a 40 year old sub-contractor. Mr Larkman fell eight metres through fragile insulation material whilst in the process of erecting an onion store on a farm in Wisbech on 29 June 1999. English Brothers, his employer, pleaded guilty to his manslaughter and breach of HSWA 1974, s 3(1) in that it failed to conduct its undertaking in such a way as to ensure that people not in its employ were not exposed to risks to their safety. As with all previous corporate manslaughter convictions, English Brothers is a small company with hands-on directors. Despite the conviction, it is unlikely to secure good law since, due to the circumstances of the case, the company pleaded guilty on the basis that the charges of manslaughter against the directors were dropped.

1   (30 July 2001, unreported).

5.63 The company was fined £30,000 plus £12,500 costs, which represented over a year's profits. Courts are increasingly looking to 'hurt' companies in an attempt to make them take health and safety seriously. Being fined a year's profit appears to be an effective way of doing this.

R v Dean[1]

5.64 Dean employed two men to demolish a tunnel kiln. The men died when the kiln collapsed upon them. It collapsed because the men had cut a steel skeleton of buck stays and tie bars which held the structure together before the brickwork was demolished. Both prosecution and defence experts agreed that the only safe way to demolish the kiln was to remove the brickwork and only then to remove the buck stays and the tie bars. It was accepted that once the buck stays were removed, vast areas of unsupported brickwork were likely to lead to an uncontrolled collapse, as in fact happened. Dean was convicted of gross negligence manslaughter at Stafford Crown Court in April 2002 on the basis that he had failed to warn the men of the danger of removing the buck stays first. He was sentenced to 18 months' imprisonment.

1   [2002] EWCA Crim 2410.

5.65 The defendant appealed his conviction which was quashed on 2 October 2002.[1] The Court of Appeal found that there were defects in the trial judge's summing up which made the conviction unsafe. The Court of Appeal substitutes a conviction pursuant to HSWA, s 33 for a breach of HSWA, s 2.

1   *R v Dean* [2002] EWCA Crim 2410.

Minimising the risk of prosecution

5.66 To minimise the risk of a corporate manslaughter or corporate killing prosecution, it is suggested a company should ensure that:

- Its health and safety policy and safety management systems are drafted and operated by well-trained and competent personnel and reviewed regularly to ensure that they are working. Regular monitoring needs to be undertaken of all safety systems. All accidents and near misses must be investigated and the lessons learned and implemented.
- It performs regular, robust checks to ensure that contractors are competent to carry out work safely, before they are appointed. Once in place, contractors must be monitored and supervised to ensure that they comply with all health and safety requirements.
- It benchmarks its own and its contractors' health and safety performance.
- It retains the contractual ability to remove contractors for poor health and safety performance, preferably without financial implications.
- It keeps accurate records. For example, safety committee meetings must be properly minuted and taken by one person only as duplicate sets often give a different view of a meeting.
- It regularly reviews accident records to ensure that efforts and resources are being concentrated where there is the highest risk and where safety critical work is undertaken.
- It can justify the delegation of responsibilities and knows what each delegate is doing. A key time is following recruitment of temporary or agency staff, for example, as holiday relief or covering sickness absence.
- All individuals understand the health and safety implication of their job. Managers must also ensure that their teams are adequately supervised and that any deficiencies identified by their teams are reported back to them.

5.67 If a fatal accident does occur, the company should:

- Strongly consider legal advice before, and representation during, any interviews with the police/HSE. Individuals should be careful not to be drawn into answering questions about documents which are not in front of them.
- Be cautious in the conclusions of accident investigation reports and similar documents, meeting minutes and emails. In general, such documents do not attract privilege (as they are not prepared in contemplation of litigation), and will probably have to be disclosed to the police/HSE.
- Urgently review the relevant documentation. It is important to find out as soon as possible where strengths and weaknesses are.
- Deal kindly with the relatives and dependants of the deceased. It is not an admission of guilt to behave decently towards the injured and bereaved. The company should keep them informed of any investigation progress and do what it can do help out with their immediate practical problems. Public pressure can also affect the decision of the HSE or CPS over whether or not to prosecute and if so on what charges.

Recent developments

Increase in deaths in the construction industry

5.68 There is much talk of the poor safety record of the construction industry. This is unfortunately true and is best revealed by considering bald facts and statistics available from the HSE:

- Of the entire working population of the UK, approximately 6% work in construction. However, construction workers account for more than 30% of fatal accidents reported each year.
- Construction workers are five times more likely to be killed at work than the average British worker in all other industries.
- Around 700 construction workers die every year from previous exposure to asbestos.

5.69   One obvious explanation for this poor record is the very nature of construction work. Another is the financial pressure on the industry.

5.70   At the Health and Safety Summit called by the DETR and HSE in February 2001, all the speakers from the construction industry cited financial pressures on the industry as being a major factor in its poor record in health and safety. Many construction companies bid on a lowest cost basis which results in safety being compromised to complete a project on time and close to budget.

5.71   However, the industry has taken positive steps to improve health and safety through a number of initiatives. These include:

- Revitalising Health and Safety – joint HSC and DETR initiative affecting all industries;
- Client Charter – aimed at those procuring construction work;
- MCG Charter – aimed at the UK's largest construction contractors;
- M4I – aimed at promoting best practice on construction projects; and
- Safety Summit – aimed at challenging the entire 'construction' industry to improve health and safety.

Revitalising health and safety

5.72   The 'Revitalising Health and Safety' initiative was jointly launched in June 2000 by John Prescott, the Deputy Prime Minister, and Bill Callaghan, the Chair of the HSC. It was designed to achieve a 'step change' in health and safety performance in all workplaces over the next decade. It is intended to reform HSWA 1974 and take safety legislation into the current century.

5.73   In this campaign, the government set out its targets for improving health and safety performance over the next ten years. These targets include reducing the incidence rate of fatalities and major injuries by 10% by 2010. This move complements the reforms on corporate killing and demonstrates the government's determination to tackle health and safety issues from all angles.

5.74   To achieve the targets, the initiative sets out a number of key measures including:

- tougher penalties, for example, increasing magistrates' court fines to £20,000 for all offences, and making prison sentences of up to two years available for most offences;
- new innovative penalties, for example, prohibition on bonuses, suspension without pay and community service orders;

- education programmes in schools and the key professions (such as architects and engineers);
- grant programmes and help for small businesses; and
- making directors more accountable for health and safety.

5.75 The initiative targets the sectors with the poorest health and safety records, ie the construction industry and small to medium-sized businesses. To achieve the targets and implement the measures, the initiative highlights 44 'action points' contained in an Action Plan. Public procurement is scrutinised, with future projects requiring health and safety issues to be a top priority, in particular in relation to the content of construction contracts.

5.76 In September 2002 the HSE published *Revitalising Health and Safety in Construction Discussion Document*, based on discussions with the HSC's Construction Advisory Committee (CONIAC), to stimulate discussion about the best ways to improve health and safety standards in construction. There were almost 300 responses. Some of the key areas identified were:

- The industry culture topped the list of the greatest barriers to change with inertia and complacency the most frequently cited characteristics.
- High importance was attached to education, training and competence based assessment.
- The role of clients and the need for realistic timescales and greater emphasis on 'best value' rather than 'cheapest and quickest'.
- Effective involvement of the workforce.

5.77 In 2002 the HSE formed the Construction Division. This was to provide a new focus of HSE resources and effort on working with industry to improve health and safety. The Division has produced a plan for its work for 2003–04.[1] A priority of the Division is to reduce the toll of deaths and serious accidents caused by poor transport and falls.

1 See HSE press release, 24 April 2003.

5.78 The HSE since 2002 has had a programme of rolling inspection blitzes of construction sites around the country. This is where an area of the country is selected and then a team of inspectors is sent to inspect construction sites in that area.

5.79 The first blitz was in London and took place between 29 April and 3 May 2002. Thirty-one inspectors from the HSE, including 12 from outside London, took part in the blitz, arriving unannounced at both small and large sites across the capital. They were organised into three teams which covered the London Boroughs of Camden; Islington; Hackney; Tower Hamlets; Southwark; Lambeth; Lewisham; Greenwich; Westminster, Kensington and Chelsea; and Hammersmith and Fulham. During the blitz 110 prohibition notices were served.

Client's Charter

5.80 The Confederation of Construction Clients (CCC) was formed in November 2000 to represent the interests of everyone who purchases construction services. It is a condition of membership that members sign up to the Client's Charter

5.81   The Client's Charter was born from an acknowledgement by clients that they would improve both the industry's and their own performance by giving public evidence of their determination to do so. It commits clients to identifying and implementing programmes of continuous improvement in the way they manage their construction activities. An important aspect of this is developing a culture which promotes health and safety.

5.82   The Client's Charter commits clients to adopting a policy of respect for all people including their health and safety, staff training, clear briefing, assessing performance in use and clearly identifying risk. Emphasis is placed on addressing health and safety aspects at the earliest stages of a project – clients must involve their integrated supply teams from the outset.

5.83   The Client's Charter recognises the need for a nationally accepted single point occupational registration scheme for construction workers, in collaboration with the Construction Industry Training Board (CITB).

5.84   By registering for the Charter, CCC members have committed to take into account suppliers' commitment to health and safety when assessing suitability for invitations to tender.

Movement for Innovation and Key Performance Indicators

5.85   The Movement for Innovation (M4I) works with the Housing Forum, the Local Government Taskforce and the Central Government Taskforce/Government Construction Clients Panel to achieve radical improvement in performance within the construction industry, under the banner of *Rethinking Construction*.[1]

1   (1998) This was the report of Sir John Egan's Construction Taskforce. It set the national agenda and framework for improving the performance of the industry.

5.86   Changes are measured by the use of Key Performance Indicators (KPIs). There is a three-tier hierarchy:

- a headline indicator is critical to the overall success of the firm;
- an operational indicator is designed to enable management to identify and focus on specific aspects of the firm's activities for improvement; and
- a diagnostic measure provides information on why certain changes may have occurred in the headline or operation indicator and helps to analyse areas for improvement in more detail.

5.87   The M4I has split the health and safety aspects of work in the construction industry. In its November 2000 report, it identified the fact that far more construction workers die as a result of poor occupational health risk management than are killed or injured in accidents. It acknowledged that a radical step change was needed in the way occupational health risks were managed throughout all stages of the project and within firms and stated that all levels of management and individuals should take responsibility for avoiding and controlling such risks. Three tool kits are now available to help construction firms identify, manage and control occupational health risks. The M4I proposes that 'Tool Box Talks', with accompanying guidance, be delivered to site workers who may be exposed to occupational health risks.

5.88 A Health Map has been composed to enhance understanding and management of occupational health. The M4I is trying to effect a change in attitudes with regard to safety in the industry. It has emphasised the costs of accidents for the industry as a whole and stresses that an improvement in health and safety will only come about if all the parties make it a fundamental issue from the beginning of every project.

5.89 With regard to safety, two checklists have been developed which address safety at all stages of the project. The first checklist covers health and safety in the procurement and design stages of the project and is aimed at clients, consultants, those engaged in design and other members of the project team. The second is aimed at site operations and can be used by all parties to ensure safety is adequately managed during construction.

5.90 The M4I has demonstration projects which have consistently proved that the application of Egan's *Rethinking Construction* principles[1] delivers significantly enhanced performance in terms of site safety. In 2001, M4I demonstration projects were nearly twice as safe as their industry counterparts, for example, the M4I major accident rate was 619 in 2000 compared with the industry average of 2,088 per 100,000 workers.

1 Sir John Egan *Rethinking Construction* (1998).

5.91 The HSE invited its Industry Advisory Committees to set targets for their industries. The Construction Industry Advisory Committee's (CONIAC) targets include:

- reducing the incidence rate of fatal and major injuries by 40% by 2004–05 and 66% by 2009–10;
- reducing work relating ill-health; and
- reducing the number of working days lost from work related injury and ill-health.

Safety summit

5.92 In February 2001, construction industry leaders attended a health and safety summit called by the DETR and HSE. The aim of the summit was to set targets to reduce deaths, injuries and illness on construction sites.

5.93 John Prescott, the Deputy Prime Minister, said:

'In the 25 years since the HSWA there has been a 75% reduction in fatalities but the construction industry is bucking the trend and is still six times more dangerous that the average industry. It is totally unacceptable that, for much of last year, two construction workers were killed each week and that in the space of nine days, five people died.'

5.94 Outside the conference venue, leaders from the TGWU, victims of building site accidents and bereaved relatives displayed a pyramid of safety helmets representing each of the workers killed on site in the year 2000.

5.95 Michael Meecher, Minister of State for the Environment, expressed the view that the industry's culture was to blame.

'Macho attitudes, unrealistic timescales and costs, inadequate training, unacceptable hours, stress, poor supervision and lack of management. But it's a cop out simply to say that construction work is dangerous. Site safety should be given importance by the cost of a safety supervisor being included in tender figures. Construction trade organisation leaders here concluded that safety should be "designed in" to projects, that education be given a higher priority and that health and safety be an integral subject of University and College courses.'

The MCG Charter

5.96   In an attempt to change attitudes, the Main Contractors Group (MCG) has set out a Health and Safety Charter. The MCG consists of the 23 largest construction contractors in the UK. In its Health and Safety Charter, the MCG sets out its commitment to operating construction sites that are safe and free from health hazards for everybody in the construction industry and for members of the public. Each MCG member has a commitment to:

- a target reduction of 10% year-on-year in the incidence rate of all reportable injuries and dangerous occurrences until 2010;
- a fully qualified workforce by the end of 2003;
- a site specific induction process before anyone is allowed to work on a site;
- all workers being consulted on health and safety matters in a three-tier system based on project, work gang and individual workers;
- holding best practice workshops on health and safety practices and setting up a system to disseminate lessons learnt from health and safety incidents;
- publishing an annual report of members' safety performance as a group, highlighting the positive achievements of the year and the accident statistics of the whole group; and
- supporting the Construction Confederation's aim of reducing the incidence rate of work related ill-health in the construction industry by 10% year-on-year.

The health strategy involves each individual member implementing its own health strategy with the specified target of no detrimental impact on construction workers' health from work activities.

5.97   The MCG Charter is perhaps the biggest revolution in safety practices and attitudes for more than 20 years.

The Turnbull,[1] Egan[2] and Latham[3] Reports

5.98   The Latham and Egan Reports gave the construction industry a new set of principles to improve working practices and, indirectly, health and safety. Sir John Egan stated that: 'if the industry is to achieve its full potential, substantial changes in its culture and structure are also required to support improvement. The industry must provide decent and safe working conditions and improve management and supervisory skills at all levels.' There was therefore a recognition that improving health and safety will reap economic benefits as well.

1 N Turnbull *Internal Control: Guidance for Directors on the Combined Code* (the Turnbull Report) (1999).
2 Sir John Egan *Rethinking Construction* (1998).
3 M Latham *Constructing The Team, Final Report of the Government/Industry Review of Procurement and Contractual Arrangements In The UK Construction Industry* (1994).

5.99 Sir John Egan headed the Construction Task Force and produced a report entitled *Rethinking Construction* on 16 July 1998.[1] The report expressed the view that whilst the UK construction industry at its best was excellent, as a whole it was under-achieving.

1 Sir John Egan *Rethinking Construction* (1998).

5.100 Five key drivers of change were suggested to set the agenda for the construction industry at large. These were:

- committed leadership;
- focus on the customer;
- integrated processes and teams;
- a quality driven agenda; and
- commitment to people.

5.101 In relation to health and safety, the HSE advised the Task Force that to motivate change, the industry should not just act on the purely welfare consequences of a poor health and safety record but should consider its cost in terms of lost working days, potential prosecutions and, in extreme cases, the enforced closure of construction sites.

5.102 The Turnbull report was entitled *The Internal Control Guidance for Directors on the Combined Code*. It was the report of the Institute of Chartered Accountants in England and Wales on Corporate Governance.[1] It advised that directors should at least annually review systems of control including final operational and controls and risk management that are key to the fulfilment of a company's business objectives.

1 N Turnbull *Internal Control: Guidance for Directors on the Combined Code* (the Turnbull Report) (1999).

5.103 The principles of internal control recommended in the report have an application to health and safety. A key risk area is the health and safety of a company's employees, its customers and members of the public. This risk must be managed. The HSC have issued guidance on this topic.[1]

1 'Managing Health and Safety: First Steps to Success' (1998) – free leaflet.

Risk analysis and minimisation specific to the industry

5.104 Some hazards create such a high risk to health and safety that there is specific legislation in place to minimise the risk. The general legislation such as HSWA 1974 discussed above still applies to these hazards and specific legislation is an additional measure, usually intended to clarify and define what steps must be taken to avoid the risk. Such legislation will generally be in the form of regulations, although Guidance Notes and Approved Codes of Practice will often give greater detail as to what is expected

5.105   The activities discussed below are those which are considered to give the highest risk of fatalities in the construction industry.

Asbestos

5.106   Asbestos related diseases (mainly cancers of the chest and lungs) kill an estimated 3,000 in the UK each year. The figure is expected to grow and the HSE predict it will peak at 10,000 deaths in the year 2020.

5.107   Many of the victims worked in construction, and were exposed to asbestos dust by working with asbestos-containing materials. A big problem for the industry is that often a thorough risk assessment cannot be made because information on asbestos in the area is not available. .

5.108   The Control of Asbestos at Work Regulations 2002 (CAWR) came into effect on 21 November 2002.[1] These revoked the 1987 regulations of the same name.[2] The new regulation extend the duty to manage and control asbestos from employers to employers, owners and controllers of non-domestic premises.

1   SI 2002/2675.
2   SI 1987/2115.

5.109   The 1987 Regulations[1] place a duty on employers to:

*   identify through survey the presence of asbestos, its type and condition and whether it presents a risk to their employees or others;
*   carry out risk assessments of exposure to asbestos containing materials and produce a plan of work;
*   notify the HSE if work involving asbestos takes place;
*   provide information, instruction and training for employees who may be exposed to asbestos-containing materials and also to keep records;
*   prevent and control exposure to asbestos containing materials through removal or safeguarding against disturbance;
*   monitor control measures and the condition of the asbestos; and
*   keep records of employees who may be exposed.

1   Control of Asbestos at Work Regulations 1987, SI 1987/2115.

5.110   The new Regulations[1] retain the existing duties. However, on 21 May 2003 they introduced a duty to manage asbestos in non-domestic premises which extends the duty of care to owners and controllers of non-domestic premises as well as employers.

1   CAWR, SI 2002/2675.

5.111   A 1998 case[1] reminded builders that breach of the CAWR[2] can lead to jail.

1   *R v Rollco Screw & Rivet Co Ltd* [1999] 2 Cr App R (S) 436.
2   This was taken under the 1987 Regulations, SI 1987/2115.

5.112   A company called Rollco took over some factory premises, where the roof needed repairing. It obtained quotes from two builders. One thought that the brown insulation might contain asbestos and gave Rollco the name of an analyst. Rollco did not investigate the matter. It asked the other builder, M & M, to confirm in writing that the roof work would be done in accordance with the CAWR.[1] M & M confirmed that it would.

1 SI 1987/2115.

5.113 Mr Paul Evans contracted with M & M to organise the labour and strip the installation. He worked for an asbestos removal contractor and so should have known that the insulation contained amosite (brown) asbestos.

5.114 Evans ignored both the risks and the CAWR.[1] In its investigation, the HSE discovered amosite spread all over the factory. Where Evans had disposed of it in uncovered skips, children were seen playing with it. Evans was sentenced to nine months in prison. The Crown Court judge said that he had lied steadily, was manifestly dishonest and had displayed criminal irresponsibility.[2]

1 SI 1987/2115.
2 *R v Rollco Screw & Rivet Co Ltd* [1999] 2 Cr App R (S) 436.

5.115 Rollco was fined £70,000, including costs. The company later paid a further £68,000 to get the work done to the proper standard and also lost six weeks' production.

5.116 Obviously, it will not be known for some time whether the exposure to amosite will lead to any deaths.

Confined spaces

5.117 The foremost risks to workers when working in confined spaces is the potential lack of breathable air and explosion. The proximity to other workers and a restricted ability to manoeuvre compound these pre-existing dangers. Fatalities are commonly due to asphyxiation, from either gas, fumes or free flowing solids (which leads to drowning).

5.118 The Confined Spaces Regulations 1997[1] govern this work. A 'confined space' means any chamber, tank, vat, silo, pit, trench, pipe, sewer flue, well or similar space which due to its enclosed nature has a reasonably foreseeable risk.

1 SI 1997/1713.

5.119 Confined spaces should not be entered into unless it is not reasonably practicable to work from outside the space.[1] If entry is necessary, work should be performed in accordance with a system rendering the work safe.

1 Confined Spaces Regulations 1997, SI 1997/1713, reg 4(1).

5.120 Employers must ensure compliance with the provisions of the Regulations in respect of employees[1] and ensure, as far as is reasonably practicable, that this applies to persons other than employees insofar as the provisions relate to matters within their control.

1 Confined Spaces Regulations 1997, SI 1997/1713, reg 3(1)(a).

5.121 The case of *R v Associated Octel Co Ltd*[1] concerned a specialist contractor cleaning a chlorine tank, whose employees were injured by a flash fire ignited by an unsafe lamp. The House of Lords held that an employer had to take all reasonably practicable steps to avoid risk to a contractor's employees arising from inadequate arrangements between employer and contractor.

1   [1996] 4 All ER 846.

Dangerous substances

5.122   It is easy for members of the construction industry to focus on the more obvious causes of death, such as falls from height, and forget about the insidious risks involved with various substances.

5.123   Many of the requirements in the management of dangerous substances are common to all substances and include good personal hygiene, good housekeeping practices, provision of personal protective equipment and training. The Control of Substances Hazardous to Health Regulations 2002 (COSHH) must also be complied with. Some hazards are excluded from COSHH, for example, lead[2] and asbestos,[3] since these are governed by their own statutory framework.

1   SI 2002/2677.
2   Governed by the Control of Lead at Work Regulations 2002, SI 2002/2676.
3   Governed by the CAWR, SI 2002/2675.

5.124   Employers must not carry out any work which is liable to expose any employees, or any other persons, to any substances hazardous to health unless he or she has made a suitable and sufficient assessment of the risks created by that work and taken preventative measures.[1] The assessment must also be reviewed regularly and if the review identifies that any changes in the assessment are required, those changes must be made.[2]

1   COSHH, SI, 2002/2677, reg 6(1).
2   COSHH, SI 2002/2677, reg 6(2).

5.125   Every employer must prevent the exposure of its employees to substances hazardous to health so far as is reasonably practicable. Where this is not reasonably practicable then the exposure must be controlled.[1] COSHH imposes a hierarchy of control measures starting with elimination then substitution with a less hazardous substance, with personal protective equipment being used as last resort.

1   COSHH, SI 2002/2677, reg 7(1).

5.126   Exposure should be monitored in accordance with a suitable procedure[1] and records kept and be made available for a period of 40 years in the case of monitoring of personal exposure of identifiable employees and for five years in all other cases.[2] Workers who are liable to be exposed to a hazardous substance should be kept under health surveillance.[3]

1   COSHH, SI 2002/2677, reg 10(1).
2   COSHH, SI 2002/2677, reg 10(2).
3   COSHH, SI 2002/2677, reg 11.

5.127   Employers must provide employees who may be exposed to hazardous substances with suitable and sufficient information, instruction and training. Employees should be made aware of the risks to health created by such exposure and the precautions which should be taken.

5.128 In addition to COSHH[1] regulations, those who specify construction materials have a duty under the CDMR[2] to eliminate hazardous materials from their design and, where this is not possible, to specify the least hazardous product which will perform to an acceptable standard.

1 SI 2002/2677.
2 SI 1994/3140.

5.129 Substances likely to be encountered in construction include:

- lead (generally in paint);
- arsenics;
- blue billy (containing cyanides);
- solvents; and
- wood dusts.

Demolition

5.130 The demolition or dismantling of a structure or part of a structure carries a high risk to workers. Workers and passers-by can be injured by the premature and uncontrolled collapse of structures and flying debris. Risks from high levels of dust, noise and other site contamination are also present. CHSWR, reg 10[1] provides that the action should be planned and performed in such a way as to prevent such danger.[2] Work must only be carried out under the supervision of a competent person[3] with sufficient and suitable steps to be taken to prevent danger, as far as is practicable.

1 SI 1996/1592, reg 10.
2 SI 1996/1592, reg 10(1).
3 SI 1996/1592, reg 10(2).

5.131 To minimise risk and manage the demolition process, there should be a pre-demolition survey, an agreement as to action prior to and during demolition and a procedure to ensure close supervision of demolition sites.

5.132 Risks to be considered are, for example, people being too near the demolition, the work making the structure itself or nearby buildings unstable, the remaining parts of the structure being able to take the weight of removed materials or machinery, live services such as gas or electricity and contamination by hazardous materials from previous use of the site.

Electrical hazards

5.133 Each year about 1,000 accidents at work involving electric shock or burns are reported to the HSE. Around 30 of these are fatal, with most of the fatalities arising out of contact with overhead or underground power cables. Even a non-fatal shock can cause serious injury and may lead to falls from scaffolding or ladders that result in death.

5.134 The major hazards in working with electricity are:

- contact with live parts causing shock and burns;
- faults which could cause fires; and

- fire or explosion where electricity may be the source of ignition in a potentially flammable or explosive atmosphere.

Emergency procedures

5.135   The quality of emergency procedures can mean the difference between life and death. General requirements for emergency procedures are governed by CHSWR, reg 20.[1] Where it is necessary to do so in the interests of health and safety, there must be prepared, and where necessary implemented, suitable and sufficient arrangements for dealing with any foreseeable emergency. Every person to whom the arrangements extend must be familiar with those arrangements and the arrangements should be tested by being put into effect at suitable intervals.[2]

1   SI 1996/1592, reg 20.
2   SI 1996/1592, reg 20(3)(c).

5.136   The requirements for emergency routes and exits are contained within CHSWR, reg 19.[1]

1   SI 1996/1592, reg 19.

Excavations

5.137   Excavation work presents great danger to construction workers. It must be properly planned in order to avoid the primary risks such as collapse of the sides or people and vehicles falling into the excavation. It is essential to ensure that all the necessary equipment needed such as trench sheets, props and baulks is available on site before work starts. CHSWR, reg 12[1] provides detailed rules to ensure the safety of workers engaged in excavation work and guidance.

1   SI 1996/1592, reg 12.

5.138   Other risks associated with excavation works include striking cables and other buried services, and contact with earth containing dangerous substances or biological hazards.

Explosives and explosive atmospheres

5.139   There are relatively few deaths caused by explosives, no doubt due to the fact that the risk is more obvious and carefully controlled, but explosives are included in the 'high risk' category due to the potentially devastating effects. The CHSWR[1] impose a general duty to prevent, as far as is reasonably practicable, the risk of injury during construction work to any person from fire or explosion. They also impose a strict duty in relation to the actual use of explosives. Suitable steps should be taken to ensure that no person is at risk from the explosion or from material projecting from it.

1   SI 1996/1592.

5.140   Specific legislative duties concerning explosives are found in CHSWR, regs 11 and 18,[1] the Control of Explosives Regulations 1991[2] and the Carriage of Explosives by Road Regulations 1996.[3]

1 SI 1996/1592, reg 11 and SI 1996/1592, reg 18.
2 SI 1991/1531.
3 SI 1996/2093.

Falls

5.141 Working at height characterises many areas of construction work, for example, scaffolding, roofing, lifts installation and servicing, heating and air conditioning maintenance and window cleaning. The risk of a fall is a common hazard in such activities and falls from height are the largest cause of death and serious injury on construction sites. The hazard has been highlighted as one of the target areas in the government's 'Revitalising Health and Safety' initiative. It is also proposed to issue new regulations regarding falls from height which will be known as the Work at Height Regulations.[1]

1 Intended to implement the Temporary Work at Height Directive, Council Directive 2001/45/EC.

5.142 The main regulations governing the prevention of this hazard are to be found in the CHSWR. CHSWR, reg 6(1)[1] states that suitable and sufficient steps should be taken to prevent, *so far as is reasonably practicable*, any person falling. There are obvious areas in which workers will be at risk. Preventative action should be taken where *anyone* is exposed to a fall of over two metres, including at the edges of excavations and access to any place of work via a place at height. See the case of *Keltbray*[2] at **paras 5.57–5.61** above. Employers have a strict duty to take at least some steps to prevent falls.

1 SI 1996/1592, reg 6(1).
2 *R v Keltbray Ltd* [2001] 1 Cr App Rep (S) 132.

5.143 The Workplace (Health, Safety and Welfare) Regulations 1992[1] (WHSWR) apply less stringent requirements upon employers to prevent injury from falls or falling objects but nonetheless will apply in some situations which fall outside the parameters of the CHSWR,[2] for example, window cleaning.

1 SI 1992/3004.
2 SI 1996/1592.

5.144 The greatest danger of falls from height is where ladders and scaffolding are used. The CHSWR provides that ladders should not be used as, or as a means of access to, a place of work unless it is reasonable to do so and where used, should comply with the provisions of CHSWR, Sch 5.[1]

1 SI 1996/1592, Sch 5.

5.145 There are specific rules concerning falls through fragile material when a person would be liable to fall a distance of two metres or more. These are contained within CHSWR, reg 7[1] and include preventing persons passing across or working from fragile materials without adequate supports. The supports must be able to support the weight of that person and guardrails, coverings and warning notices must also be in place. The duty to prevent a fall through fragile material is one of strict liability and there is no defence to a breach of reg 7 on the grounds that the measures necessary were not reasonably practicable.

1 SI 1996/1592, reg 7.

5.146   There are a number of deaths and injuries each year from falls through fragile roofs. As a consequence the HSE asks very tough questions of any client or designer who proposes the installation of fragile materials.

5.147   Where, during the course of construction work, there is a risk that any person is liable to fall into water or any other liquid with a risk of drowning, the CHSWR dictates that suitable and sufficient steps must be taken to prevent the fall as far as reasonably practicable. The risk of drowning in the event of such a fall must be minimised and suitable rescue equipment provided, maintained and, where necessary, used.[1]

1   SI 1996/1592, reg 14(1).

Fire

5.148   The CHSWR place a general duty to prevent, so far as reasonably practicable, the risk of injury to any person during the carrying out of construction work arising from fire or explosion.[1] CHSWR, reg 21[2] applies only to work on construction sites.

1   SI 1996/1592, reg 18.
2   SI 1996/1592, reg 21.

5.149   There must be suitable and sufficient fire fighting equipment, fire detectors and alarm systems which must be suitably located[1] and properly maintained.[2] Any fire fighting equipment which is not designed to come into use automatically should be easily accessible[3] and indicated by suitable signs.[4] In assessing what is suitable and sufficient, various factors should be considered,[5] including the type of work being carried out on the construction site and the plant and equipment being used.

1   CHSWR, SI 1996/1592, reg 21(1).
2   SI 1996/1592, reg 21(3).
3   SI 1996/1592, reg 21(4).
4   SI 1996/1592, reg 21(7).
5   SI 1996/1592, reg 21(2) and SI 1996/1592, reg 19(4).

5.150   The main causes of fire on construction sites include hot works such as welding, use of bitumen in roof works and liquid propane gas storage.

Head injuries

5.151   Construction is the most dangerous work activity for head injuries. CHSWR, reg 8[1] provides that the fall of any material or object should be prevented so far as is reasonably practicable. Where it is not reasonably practicable to do so, steps should be taken to protect persons from being struck by falling objects. This regulation imposes a strict liability, not on preventing objects falling per se, but on the prevention of a falling object striking and injuring a person. Throwing or tipping items from a height in circumstances that are liable to cause injury is strictly prohibited.[2] Contractors should use debris chutes instead.

1   SI 1996/1592, reg 8.
2   SI 1996/1592, reg 8(4).

5.152 The Construction (Head Protection) Regulations 1989[1] impose requirements upon employers and employees in relation to the provision and wearing of head protection and apply to building operations and works of engineering construction.[2]

1 SI 1989/2209.
2 In either case within the meaning of the Factories Act 1961.

Lead

5.153 A person will be at risk from exposure to lead in a variety of operations including hot cutting in demolition and dismantling operations and some painting of buildings. Refurbishment of old buildings where lead was used in paints is a particular risk to workers in the construction industry. Continued uncontrolled exposure can lead to kidney, nerve and brain damage. Exposure to lead is governed by the Control of Lead at Work Regulations 2002.[1]

1 SI 2002/2676.

Legionellosis

5.154 The majority of cases of legionnaires' disease are caused by the bacteria legionella pneumophila which is found in natural water supplies, soil and many recirculating water supply systems. The risks must be dealt with under HSWA 1974 and COSHH.[1] Risk assessments must be carried out and method statements prepared to prevent/control exposure.

1 SI 2002/2677.

Silica

5.155 Silica occurs as a natural component of many materials used or encountered in construction activities such as stone masonry, blast cleaning of buildings especially using sand, demolition processes, concrete scabbling cutting or drilling and tunnelling. Crystalline silica is present in substantial quantities in sand, sandstone and granite and can also be found in many other naturally occurring building products such as clay and slate as well as man-made products such as concrete and mortar. Breathing in the fine dust of crystalline silica can lead to the development of silicosis which can, in extreme circumstances, lead to death within a few months of onset, although it is more common that the disease is more progressive.

5.156 The uncontrolled use of power tools to cut or dress stone may lead to high exposures and other activities will lead to varying levels of exposure depending upon how confined the working space is and how near the worker's breathing zone is to the source of the dust.

5.157 Activities which may expose workers to silica are subject to COSHH[1] which require the health risks to be assessed and prevented or controlled including considering the need for atmospheric sampling.

1 SI 2002/2677.

Ultraviolet light

5.158   Many construction workers spend long periods of time working outdoors and should be aware of the risks of exposure to ultraviolet light. In the short term, exposure is likely only to cause discomfort such as reddening of the skin and blistering. However, prolonged exposure can increase the chances of developing skin cancer. Contact with some chemicals used in the construction industry such as wood preservatives, coal tar and pitch products can make skin more sensitive to sunlight.

5.159   There is currently no precedent for suggesting that an employer may be liable for a death due to skin cancer following prolonged exposure to ultraviolet light at work. However, as regulations become more stringent, it is possible that employers may have a duty at least to warn employees of the dangers and, possibly, provide protective equipment in the form of hats and sunscreens.

Traffic

5.160   Traffic includes the movement of people and vehicles. Risks exist to pedestrians and those in control of or on board vehicles. Generally, construction sites should be organised in such a way that, so far as is reasonably practicable, pedestrians and vehicles can move safely and without risk to health.[1] Obvious risks arise due to the large plant, restricted spaces and noise found on construction sites.

1   CHSWR, SI 1996/1592, reg 15(1).

5.161   Various rules contained in the CHSWR seek to prevent accidents relating to traffic. Traffic routes should be suitable in terms of number, position and size for the persons or vehicles using them.[1] No vehicle should be driven on a traffic route unless the route is free from obstruction and permits sufficient clearance, so far as this is reasonably practicable.[2] If it is not reasonably practicable to ensure that traffic routes are free from obstruction, suitable and sufficient steps must be taken to warn the driver of the vehicle and any passenger of any approaching obstruction or lack of clearance.[3] Where it is necessary for reasons of health and safety, all traffic routes must be indicated by suitable signs.[4]

1   SI 1996/1592, reg 15(2).
2   SI 1996/1592, reg 15(4).
3   SI 1996/1592, reg 15(5).
4   SI 1996/1592, reg 15(6).

5.162   Ensuring that traffic on construction sites is regulated in a safe manner is a relatively easy way of preventing death in the construction industry.

Unstable structures

5.163   Under CHSWR, reg 9 where any new or existing structure (or part of structure) may become unstable or temporarily weak, all practicable steps (whether reasonable or not) must be taken to ensure such structures do not collapse accidentally.[1] This is not a strict liability duty but is a more onerous burden than that required to satisfy a 'reasonably practicable' requirement.

1   SI 1996/1592, reg 9(1).

5.164   Any temporary support used to prevent such a collapse must be carried out only under the supervision of a competent person and structures should not be loaded in a way which may make them unsafe.[1]

1   CHSWR, SI 1996/1592, reg 9(1) and (3).

Issues concerning clients

5.165   The *client* is any individual or organisation for whom a construction project is carried out, whether by external workers/contractors or 'in-house'. This definition comes from the Construction (Design and Management) Regulations 1994[1] (CDMR), which imposes the main obligations on clients of construction projects.

1   SI 1994/3140.

5.166   The term includes anyone who is engaged in a trade, business or other undertaking. Only domestic clients are exempt from the CDMR.[1] Commercial developers (including most house builders) who sell homes before construction work is complete, and flat maintenance companies formed by leaseholders, are clients for the purposes of the CDMR.

1   SI 1994/3140.

Multiple clients/client's agent

5.167   The CDMR[1] provides for the situation where there are either multiple clients or the client is unfamiliar with construction work, by permitting the appointment of either:

- one individual client to act as sole client; or
- an agent to act on behalf of the client(s).

1   SI 1994/3140.

5.168   This is effected by the designated client or agent completing and sending a declaration form to the HSE. Once this form is received by the HSE, the appointee is responsible for carrying out the respective duties under the CDMR.[1] Note that the appointment does not relieve any liabilities for action taken before appointment or any duties under other health and safety legislation.

1   SI 1994/3140.

5.169   The client's (or agent's) duties under the CDMR[1] are to:

- appoint competent individuals/organisations for each phase of the project, ie designer(s), planning supervisor and principal contractor;
- provide relevant information to the planning supervisor on existing hazards and the condition of premises;
- ensure that construction work does not start before a health and safety plan has been completed; and
- retain the health and safety file for future inspection.

1   SI 1994/3140.

Appointees

5.170   The key to the CDMR,[1] and its aim of improving safety, is to ensure that all those appointed are competent and can allocate sufficient resources to the project. Where the client is unfamiliar with construction, it should obtain advice from either consultants or the designer before appointments are made. The appointments needed are:

- *Designer* – when checking competency, clients should ensure that the designer is able to identify and then eliminate or minimise safety hazards. Where one or more designers are appointed (for example, architects, engineers etc), they must be appointed in good time to allow design work to be co-ordinated. Note that overseas designers have no duties under the CDMR, so, if appointed, it is up to the client to ensure that health and safety issues will be properly considered (for example, by including this as a contractual requirement).

- *Planning supervisor* – the CDMR permits flexibility as to who should be appointed as the planning supervisor. It could be the client, the lead member of the design team, a contractor or an organisation set up to act as specialist planning supervisors. This appointment should be made as soon as possible, preferably at the feasibility/concept stage, since this is the time when risks can be designed out of the project.

- *Principal contractor* – means any contracting organisation that carries out or manages construction work.

1   SI 1994/3140.

5.171   Although both the planning supervisor and the principal contractor must be appointed as soon as it is practicable, this should only take place once the client is satisfied as to their competence and ability to adequately resource the works.

Competence

5.172   Before making the appointments, the client must be *reasonably satisfied* that the person or organisation to be appointed is both sufficiently competent to fulfil the responsibilities placed upon them and has allocated adequate resources to enable them to comply with their respective statutory duties. This requirement also extends to where the client (or indeed others) engages a designer, whether an external organisation or internal department, to prepare a design.

5.173   The smaller and less complicated a project is, the less extensive the enquiries need to be. Decisions of competence should be based on the individual's or organisation's knowledge and understanding of:

- the specific work involved;
- the nature of the project;
- assessment and management of risks; and
- the relevant health and safety standards.

5.174   Competence is not merely a matter of technical qualifications or training achievement. It should be a wider assessment of abilities and experience relevant to the work to be carried out.

5.175 Pre-qualification procedures and the use of the pre-tender health and safety plan are the key means by which clients can seek to satisfy themselves that adequate provision has been made for health and safety. Factors to consider when determining whether adequate resources have been allocated include the time, plant and equipment, materials and personnel available to the person or organisation.

Providing information

5.176 Clients must take reasonable steps to find out about pre-existing hazards and pass this information on to the planning supervisor.

Health and safety plan

5.177 An easily overlooked requirement is for the client to ensure that the health and safety plan has been sufficiently well developed by the principal contractor before construction work starts. Many of the prosecutions of clients have been for failing to perform this duty. Further, a breach of this obligation provides an automatic right of civil action for anyone who is injured or suffers damage as a consequence.

5.178 One key message for clients is to allow sufficient time between awarding the contract and the programmed start date to allow the principal contractor to develop the plan. Time spent at this planning stage is often essential to successful safety management during construction work, and may not affect the eventual project completion date.

Case law

HSE v Port of Ramsgate Ltd[1]

5.179 At midnight on 14 September 1994, passengers were boarding a ferry at Ramsgate in Kent when the walkway they were standing on collapsed. The passengers fell 32 feet onto a pontoon. Six died and a further seven were injured. The walkway had been installed just four months earlier.

1 (28 February 1997, unreported), Central Criminal Court.

5.180 The HSE investigated and established that the immediate cause of the collapse was the failure of a weld in a safety critical support element of the structure. Further investigation revealed gross deficiencies in the design which would have ensured failure of safety critical elements within a fairly short period of the structure's lifespan. The HSE concluded that the technical deficiencies arose from the failure of various parties involved in the procurement, design and installation of the walkway to manage the project effectively and in particular to carry out any reasonable risk assessment of the project.[1]

1 See HSE *Walkway collapse at Port Ramsgate: a report on the investigation into the walkway collapse at Port Ramsgate on 14 September 1994.*

5.181 The HSE prosecuted the two Swedish firms who designed and constructed the walkway, Port Ramsgate Ltd who employed them to do the work and Lloyd's

Register of Shipping who certified that the walkway was safe. All were prosecuted under HSWA 1974, s 3(1) for failing to ensure that persons not in their employment (ie the passengers) were not exposed to risks to their health and safety. All were convicted.

5.182   The two Swedish firms were held responsible for gross design defects and were fined a total of £1 million (as yet unpaid). Lloyd's Register of Shipping was found guilty of gross negligence and fined £500,000 – after accepting that it had failed to check the safety of the design, construction and installation under its own rules. The Port of Ramsgate authority was fined £200,000.

5.183   The HSE argued that HSWA 1974, s 3 placed a duty on employers that could not be delegated or avoided by employing third parties to design and construct the walkway. Mr Justice Clark said that the Port of Ramsgate should be judged against two facts. First, it had employed contractors and designers of the highest reputation and competence: the Swedish firms had many years experience building pontoons and marine walkways for heavy goods. Secondly, it had insisted that the walkway be checked by Lloyd's, which had an international reputation for safety.

5.184   However, whilst acknowledging that Port of Ramsgate was far less culpable than the other defendants, the judge believed it should still be convicted. It had not shown that it was not reasonably practicable to install a failsafe system, such as chains, to the walkway and had not ensured that proper quality assurance provisions were included in the contract with the Swedish companies. He held that Port of Ramsgate had indeed failed to give any thought to its responsibilities under HSWA 1974, s 3. If it had it would have realised that there were risks that should be guarded against.[1]

> 'Someone at Port Ramsgate should have sat down and given detailed thought to what parts were capable of moving and what lubrication [of the axle] was required, especially in circumstances where it knew that no maintenance manual or other detailed instructions had been provided.'

1   (28 February 1997, unreported), Central Criminal Court,

5.185   This decision has naturally caused concern to clients. What should Port of Ramsgate have done? How far can a client now rely on an expert? It is arguably impossible for a non-expert client to judge the health and safety risks of a project. However, Port of Ramsgate's argument that it was innocent as it had no engineering knowledge or experience was not accepted by the jury or the HSE.

5.186   Clients would be advised to ensure that the duties of experts are clearly laid out in the contract and that the provisions of the CDMR[1] are followed. However, they should remember that they themselves will remain responsible for health and safety and risk criminal convictions if the requirements of HSWA 1974 are not met. As explained by Mr Justice Clark, the safety of the public is paramount.[2]

1   SI 1994/3140.
2   *HSE v Port of Ramsgate Ltd* (28 February 1997, unreported), Central Criminal Court.

Issues concerning designers

5.187   Designers play a crucial part in the way CDMR[1] is applied to a project. According to the HSE, research shows that designers are failing to exploit the potential they have to eliminate and reduce risks on site.[2] Decisions made at the very earliest stages of a project determine whether safety risks are designed out or designed in. Only where hazards cannot be eliminated should measures be put in place to control and minimise them.

1 SI 1994/3140.
2 See www. hse.gov.uk/construction/designers/index.htm.

5.188 The CDMR[1] definition of a designer came under court scrutiny in early 2000, in the case of *R v Paul Wurth SA*,[2] and resulted in the amendment of CDMR.

1 SI 1994/3140.
2 (2000) ICR 860.

Who is a designer?

5.189 CDMR, reg 13(2)(a)[1] required: a *designer* to 'ensure that any construction design *he prepares* ... shows adequate regard to the need to avoid predictable risks to the health and safety of any person carrying out or affected by the construction work'.

1 SI 1994/3140, reg 13(2)(a).

5.190 The Court of Appeal thought it 'difficult to extract a coherent scheme' from the way CDMR was drafted.[1] CDMR defined the word 'designer' in reg 2,[1] as being anyone (in business) who either prepares a design or arranges for a person under his control to prepare a design.

1 *R v Paul Wurth SA* (2000) ICR 860.
2 SI 1994/3140, reg 2.

5.191 CDMR, reg 2(2)(a)[1] tries to help by explaining when 'arranging' occurs, as being:

* when the work is to be done by a specified person (for example, a nominated sub-contractor); or
* when the work is done in-house by an employee.

1 SI 1994/3140, reg 2(2)(a).

5.192 CDMR, reg 2(2)(b)[1] also tries to explain when 'arranging' does *not* occur:

* when the work is done by a self-employed person or another partner in a firm (including within a Scottish partnership);
* when the work is done by an employee otherwise than in-house; or
* when a person, having arranged for one person to do the work, does not object to the work being done by a third party.

1 SI 1994/3140, reg 2(2)(b).

R v Paul Wurth SA[1]

5.193 In September 1997, Cambrian Stone Ltd commissioned a slag granulation plant for the Port Talbot Steel Works. The plant converts a steel making waste product into granulated sand, which can then be used by the construction industry. Cambrian Stone placed a contract with Paul Wurth SA to design, manufacture, supply, and install the plant. Paul Wurth then contracted with Fairport Engineering Ltd to convert its design into manufacturing and construction drawings. Fairport sub-contracted the manufacture of the conveyor element to Universal Conveyor Co Ltd.

1   (2000) ICR 860.

5.194   In accordance with the contracts, Universal prepared and submitted its detailed manufacturing drawings to Fairport for approval, which in turn passed them on to Paul Wurth. Paul Wurth, as main contractor obtained copyright in the drawings.

5.195   Unfortunately, the design drawing for the conveyor's two latching posts was flawed, in that no locking or securing pin was included. The drawings were approved, without anyone noticing the omission. When a Mr Harrison came to install the conveyor, the lack of securing pins caused it to fall, fatally injuring him.

5.196   Following the accident, the HSE prosecuted all three companies, and Universal and Fairport pleaded guilty. Paul Wurth changed its plea to guilty after the judge indicated how he would advise the jury on the interpretation of CDMR, reg 13.[1] Paul Wurth, after being fined £60,000 and ordered to pay £50,000 in costs, appealed the judge's interpretation of the CDMR.

1   SI 1994/3140, reg 13.

5.197   The Court of Appeal looked at the definition of designer and held that, in the context of this case:[1]

- Universal 'prepared the design';
- Paul Wurth 'arranged' for Fairport, who in turn 'arranged' for Universal to prepare the design; and
- Paul Wurth did not object to Universal doing the work.

1   *R v Paul Wurth SA* (2000) ICR 860.

5.198   The Court of Appeal held that Paul Wurth did not prepare the design, nor did it arrange for another to prepare the design, since it simply did not object to the work being sub-contracted to Universal. In addition, the court held that 'preparing' does not include approving drawings. Paul Wurth therefore won its appeal and the court quashed its conviction.[1]

1   *R v Paul Wurth SA* (2000) ICR 860.

5.199   However, the court went on to state that CDMR, reg 13(2)[1] only applied to a designer who *prepares* the design.[2] This meant that there was a loophole in the CDMR. Someone who arranges for the design to be prepared, for example, in-house by his employees or by a nominated sub-contractor, would not be a 'designer' for the purposes of CDMR.

1   SI 1994/3140, reg 13(2).
2   *R v Paul Wurth SA* (2000) ICR 860.

5.200   The HSE acted swiftly to block this loophole, by amending the definition of a designer in the CDMR, to become:[1]

'2(1) 'designer' means any person who carries on a trade, business or other undertaking in connection with which he prepares a design; and

…

(3A) Any reference in [CDMR] to a person preparing a design shall include a reference to his employee or other person at work under his control preparing it for him, but nothing in this paragraph shall be taken to affect the application of paragraph (2).'

1 SI 1994/3140, reg 2.

5.201 The loophole closed when the new Construction (Design and Management) (Amendment) Regulations 2000[1] came into force on 2 October 2000.

1 SI 2000/2380.

5.202 The amendment restores the position to that first intended – ie anyone who prepares design details, specifications, bills of quantities and other such documents is considered a designer. This definition includes architects, engineers, quantity surveyors and project managers to the extent that they are involved in the *design*. Note that individuals who simply produce construction products are not considered designers under CDMR,[1] but have other obligations under HSWA 1974.

1 SI 1994/3140.

Duties of designers

5.203 Whenever the CDMR[1] applies to a project, and whenever the designer *prepares* a design, whether or not a client exists or other appointments are made, the designer must:

- make the client aware of its duties under CDMR and their implications;
- prepare designs with adequate regard to safety;
- provide adequate information to others about the design; and
- co-operate with the planning supervisor and other designers.

1 SI 1994/3140.

Adequate regard to safety

5.204 The designer must understand the concepts of a *hazard* (something with the potential to cause harm) and a *risk* (the likelihood of that harm being realised). Once hazards and risks are identified, then designers must tackle them by first eliminating hazards wherever possible. Any hazards which cannot be eliminated must be tackled at source by designs to reduce the risk to those constructing and maintaining the structure as far as possible. The design should protect the whole workforce rather than relying on other measures (for example, protective clothing or equipment) to protect individual workers. For example, edge protection should be designed in, rather than relying on workers wearing harnesses.

5.205 Designers must balance the risks to health and safety presented by a feature of the design as against the costs of excluding that feature. Cost in this context is counted not just in financial terms but also those of fitness for purpose, buildability, aesthetics and environmental impact.

Adequate Information

5.206   Designers must provide adequate health and safety information about any *hazard* which has not been eliminated or minimised in the design process. In particular, designers must make it clear to planning supervisors, and anyone else working with the pre-tender health and safety plan, the assumptions they have made about working methods and precautions.

5.207   Only *significant hazards* need to be pointed out, ie those which would not be obvious to other designers or a competent contractor, and those which are likely to be difficult to control.

5.208   The information should be provided through:

- annotations on drawings;
- suggested working methods or sequences;
- contract documents; and
- a risk register showing hazards with suggested control measures.

5.209   Information should also be included in the health and safety plan (by the planning supervisor) and, if relevant, the health and safety file.

Issues concerning planning supervisors

5.210   The planning supervisor can be a company, a partnership or an individual. Given the nature and extent of the planning supervisor's duties under the CDMR,[1] and the range of competencies necessary to fulfil such a role, it is unlikely, except perhaps in smaller and more straightforward projects, that the planning supervisor will be a single individual.

1   SI 1994/3140.

5.211   The planning supervisor's role is one of co-ordination and gathering information. The main duties are to:

- notify the HSE of the project (using Form 10) as soon as possible after appointment – details of additional appointment and changes must also be notified to the HSE;
- advise the client (and, where appropriate, any contractor) if requested on the competency of designers and contractors and the adequacy of their resources, and on whether the health and safety plan has been sufficiently developed by the principal contractor;
- ensure that a pre-tender health and safety plan is prepared in good time;
- ensure that the design has eliminated or reduced hazards where possible and that adequate information is provided; and
- prepare the health and safety file.

Planning supervisors and the design

5.212 Where there is only one designer, the planning supervisor must simply ensure that the designer has complied with its CDMR[1] duties in relation to designing out risks and providing information.

1   SI 1994/3140.

5.213 Where a number of designers are involved, the planning supervisor must ensure co-operation so that the health and safety aspects of the design are properly considered and co-ordinated, particularly where the work of different designers overlaps and for temporary works. This may be done by maintaining a free flow of information (for example, drawings) between the different designers, and resolving any conflicts which could affect health and safety.

Pre-tender health and safety plan

5.214 The planning supervisor must ensure that a health and safety plan is prepared *before* any contractor is appointed. That plan should include arrangements for the management of the works and monitoring compliance. It should also identify the main hazards to health and safety likely to be encountered during construction.

5.215 This *pre-tender* health and safety plan should form part of the tender documentation passed to prospective principal contractors, allowing them to demonstrate their competence for that specific project. It should include information on:

- *significant hazards*, which the designer has not been able to eliminate or sufficiently reduce in the design;
- *non-obvious hazards* and constraints relating to the site itself, for example, contaminated land; and
- *significant assumptions* made about working methods and consequent precautions.

Health and safety file

5.216 The planning supervisor must also prepare a health and safety file containing information which it is reasonably foreseeable will be necessary for the health and safety of any person maintaining, cleaning or demolishing the structure at any stage in its life. The file should include information on design aspects which must be amended such that it describes the 'as built' design.

5.217 Once construction is complete, the planning supervisor should carry out a final check that the file is complete before sending it to the client. If the building is subsequently sold, the file should be passed on to the new owner.

5.218 Preparing the file requires the co-operation of all duty holders, which makes it important to identify early on the type of information required, so that the file can be prepared during the course of the project, and handed over to the client as soon as possible after completion.

5.219   Note that the aim of the file is to assist anyone carrying out future construction work or cleaning, and as such it does *not* need to contain information on:

- construction phase risk assessments or method statements;
- accident statistics; or
- operation or emergency procedures.

Issues concerning contractors

Principal contractor

5.220   Despite the aims of the CDMR,[1] to impose health and safety duties on everyone involved in a project, the principal contractor still bears the most responsibility for health and safety on site.

1   SI 1994/3140.

5.221   The principal contractor must be a person or firm carrying out or managing the construction work, ie a contractor. Its role is to manage and ensure an integrated approach to safety on site. The key risk management issues should be set out in the construction phase health and safety plan together with the arrangements for co-ordinating all workers on site and training requirements.

5.222   In general, there should only be one principal contractor for the site. However, on very large projects, the client may let unrelated packages of work separately, resulting in more than one principal contractor either working on adjacent sites or on independent systems. For example, bridge work may be let to a different principal contractor to the road works, resulting in adjacent working. The principles of the CDMR[1] and the MHSWR[2] require such contractors to co-operate with each other and co-ordinate their work to maximise safety.

1   SI 1994/3140.
2   SI 1999/3242.

5.223   As might be expected, principal contractors have a number of duties. They must:

- satisfy themselves that any designers (for example, in design and build contracts) and contractors they appoint are competent and have adequate resources;
- prepare an adequate construction phase health and safety plan before construction work starts;
- display the project notification on the site;
- ensure only authorised persons can gain access to the site;
- promote co-operation between contractors and provide suitable information;
- enforce the site rules;
- promptly provide the planning supervisor with relevant information for the health and safety file;
- encourage workers (or their representatives) to provide health and safety advice; and
- ensure that workers receive adequate information and training on safety.

Develop the health and safety plan

5.224 The principal contractor must develop the pre-tender health and safety plan to identify the hazards and assess the risks at each of the main stages throughout the construction phase.

5.225 The level of detail should be proportionate to the size and nature of the project. It should include:

- a description of the project;
- information on restrictions affecting the work or site (for example, services, traffic flows etc);
- site layout;
- management structure of the project team;
- arrangements for passing information and directions to contractors, including requirements for management meetings;
- method statements;
- site rules;
- health and safety standards for the project;
- selection procedures for designers, contractors and suppliers;
- arrangements for hazardous activities;
- exclusion of unauthorised persons;
- public protection;
- emergency procedures;
- incident reporting arrangements;
- provision of welfare facilities;
- arrangements for induction training and task/toolbox talks;
- arrangements for monitoring compliance with legislation, safety standards and site rules; and
- project review – to ensure improvements are identified and applied to future projects.

5.226 The construction phase health and safety plan must be regularly reviewed and updated to reflect any changes to the design or working methods.

Preventing unauthorised access

5.227 Access to the site should be restricted to explicitly authorised persons who must have relevant induction training and understand the site rules. Some persons, for example, HSE inspectors, have a statutory right to enter all sites and are therefore automatically authorised persons.

5.228 Unusually for health and safety legislation, a breach of this requirement of the CDMR[1] confers an automatic right of civil action for anyone injured or suffering damage as a result, making it particularly important to ensure compliance with this duty. Arrangements must be made to secure the site to prevent access by members of the public, especially children.

1 SI 1994/3140.

Other contractors

5.229 Everyone working on a construction site, including contractors and the self-employed, have a part to play in ensuring that the site is a safe place to work. Communication and co-operation between all those involved is therefore crucial. The key duties are to:

- co operate with the principal contractor, and comply with its directions and site rules;
- provide the principal contractor with information about *risks* from their work, and any accidents or dangerous occurrences;
- ensure that projects for domestic clients are notified to the HSE (where the CDMR[1] applies but no planning supervisor has been appointed); and
- provide employees with information and training.

1   SI 1994/3140.

Case law

R v Balfour Beatty Civil Engineering Ltd and Geoconsult ZT GMBH[1]

5.230 The collapse of the Heathrow Express railway tunnels has been described as one of the worst civil engineering disasters ever in the UK. It took place during the night of 20–21 October 1994. No one was killed or even injured, but it merits inclusion in this chapter as large numbers of both workers and members of the public were at great risk. It is easy to imagine the horror that would have occurred had the tunnels collapsed during the daytime.

1   (15 February 1999, unreported), Central Criminal Court.

5.231 The tunnels were in the course of construction beneath the central terminal area at Heathrow Airport. They were being constructed using the New Austrian Tunnelling Method.

5.232 Balfour Beatty was the principal contractor; Geoconsult was the expert tunnelling advisor engaged to design the tunnels and to provide onsite technical assistance. Both were prosecuted for breaches of HSWA 1974. Balfour Beatty pleaded guilty to breaching HSWA 1974, ss 2(1) and 3(1), and was fined £1.2 million.

5.233 Geoconsult was found guilty and fined £500,000 for a breach of two similar charges. Balfour Beatty was judged to be more culpable than Geoconsult since it was in overall charge of the project.

5.234 The judge, Mr Justice Cresswell, said: 'This engineering disaster is a disgrace in that employees and those not employed were exposed to very serious risks to their safety … It occurred under the world's busiest airport and close to the Piccadilly Line – 75 metres away… There can be no compromise on public safety.'[1]

1   *R v Balfour Beatty Civil Engineering Ltd and Geoconsult ZT GMBH* (15 February 1999, unreported), Central Criminal Court.

5.235 A report by the HSE was published in 2001.[1] The HSE's investigation found that the direct cause of the collapse was a chain of events involving:

- substandard construction in the initial length of the concourse tunnel over a period of three months;
- grout jacking that damaged the same length of tunnel plus inadequate repairs to it two months before the collapse;
- the construction of a parallel tunnel in failing ground; and
- major structural failure in the tunnels, progressive failure in the adjacent ground, and further badly executed repairs during October 1994.

1   K Myers *The collapse of NATM tunnels at Heathrow Airport* (2001), published on 4 July 2001 by the HSE.

5.236 The HSE's report recommended practices for workplace managers to adopt which were to

- recognise and address the potential for major accidents, particularly in projects with potentially aggravating factors such as those involving new or unfamiliar technologies or close proximity to the public;
- secure a culture in which health and safety is paramount;
- put effective risk management at the core of robust health and safety systems; and
- ensure that clients, designers, contractors and workers co-operate.

Plant Construction PLC v Clive Adams Associates and JMH Construction Services Ltd[1]

5.237 This is a civil case based on a claim for contractual damages which could have a far-reaching effect on contractors.

1   TLR 03/01/2000.

5.238 JMH was Plant's sub-contractor. It was employed to carry out the temporary support of the roof of a factory. The factory had been designed by the client. Under the original terms of the subcontract, JMH was responsible for the design of the temporary support. However, one of the client's in-house engineers dictated the design of the support to JMH and in doing so the court held that he, in effect, varied the terms of the sub-contract such that JMH was no longer responsible for the design of the support.

5.239 In the event, the support, as designed and instructed by the client, was inadequate and the roof collapsed. JMH had realised that there were dangers in the design and had communicated its concerns to Plant who conveyed them on to the client. The client rejected them, telling JMH they should be reassured by the existence of an adjacent steel stanchion which was to support half the weight of the roof. JMH allowed itself to be persuaded and the work proceeded until the roof collapsed. No one was injured since the collapse happened at night but very significant collateral damage was caused. Plant and the client settled their dispute at about £1.3 million and Plant sought to recover the remedial costs element of this from JMH.

5.240 The issues for the court were, first, whether JMH was under any *contractual* duty to warn Plant of the risks inherent in the design instructed by the client, and, secondly, if there were such a duty, whether JMH had discharged that duty. Finally, the court had to decide that if JMH had indeed caused Plant's loss, whether the client would have listened to JMH in any event. In other words, if JMH was in breach of its duty, would compliance with that duty have made any difference to what happened? The case was decided at first instance by His Honour Judge Hicks QC and was then appealed to the Court of Appeal who referred the issue of causation back to Judge Hicks.[1]

1   *Plant Construction plc v Clive Adams Associates and JMH Construction Services Ltd* TLR 03/01/2000.

5.241   The existence of a duty to warn is a relatively new concept for the courts. The source of such a duty is likely to be from the term normally implied into a building contract, that the contractor will perform its contract with the skill and care of an ordinarily competent contractor in the circumstances of the actual contractor. However, there may be express terms of the contract that mean such a term cannot be implied – for example the contract may expressly impose a higher standard of care on a contractor.

5.242   In this case,[1] the Court of Appeal had no difficulty with the implication of a general duty of care. The judges then went on to consider the duty to warn specifically. In this case it was considered that two circumstances were critical. First, JMH knew the works were dangerous and, secondly, the obviousness of that danger. The Court of Appeal decided that these circumstances provided an overwhelming case for the duty to warn of such danger forming part of JMH's general duty of ordinary competence and care.

1   *Plant Construction plc v Clive Adams Associates and JMH Construction Services Ltd* TLR 03/01/2000.

5.243   The court was then required to consider whether JMH had breached that duty.[1] The court decided that, even though JMH had warned Plant of the dangers, it should have done so more vigorously. The court considered that the assurance given by the client as to the metal stanchion was manifestly irresponsible and JMH should have recognised it as such. JMH's engineers should not have simply swallowed their misgivings and allowed themselves to be persuaded. They should have protested more vigorously.

1   *Plant Construction plc v Clive Adams Associates and JMH Construction Services Ltd* TLR 03/01/2000.

5.244   To add to JMH's misery, Judge Hicks, when he took the case back from the Court of Appeal on the issue of causation, ruled that a complaint from JMH with a proper degree of fortitude or vociferousness would have played sufficient enough part in preventing the collapse that JMH could be said to have caused Plant's loss. Judge Hicks also went further than the Court of Appeal in considering what else JMH should have done to comply with their duty to warn in this case. He said:[1]

'[the objections] could and should have been progressively more formal and insistent if not met – for example by being put in writing if oral representations were ignored, by going to successively higher levels of management in Plant and the [client] if lower levels did not respond – and they could have been accompanied by the threat or actuality of report to regulatory authorities. The crucial question is whether JMH could and should, in the last resort, have refused to continue to work if the safety of workmen was at risk ... I am clear that it could and should have done so.'

1 *Plant Construction plc v Clive Adams Associates and JMH Construction Services Ltd* TLR 03/ 01/2000.

5.245 The safety implications of a roof in danger of collapse played a significant part in the decision of the courts in this case. As we have seen, Judge Hicks particularly thought that on safety grounds alone, JMH should have pressed its objections and as a last resort should have refused to continue to work if the safety of the workmen was at risk.[1]

1 *Plant Construction plc v Clive Adams Associates and JMH Construction Services Ltd* TLR 03/ 01/2000.

5.246 The message is clear – safety should not be knowingly compromised. If a contractor becomes aware of a situation where this is so then it must object until someone takes notice and if that fails then down tools. Half-hearted complaints which are too easily capable of dismissal will not release a contractor from its duty to warn.

5.247 How this works in practice would necessarily depend on how immediate the danger was. In this case[1] the courts accepted that JMH could not justifiably have threatened to down tools immediately, although in certain circumstances this may be appropriate.

1 *Plant Construction plc v Clive Adams Associates and JMH Construction Services Ltd* TLR 03/ 01/2000.

5.248 There have been subsequent cases which have narrowed the duty to warn to things which the contractor has *actual* knowledge about *and* are part of his remit. For example, a roofing contractor will have no duty to warn about groundworks.

Conclusions

5.249 There are many features of the construction industry that contribute to it being one of the most hazardous industries to work in. This has been recognised by both the government, the HSE and the industry itself, leading to an increase in industry-specific health and safety legislation and industry bodies themselves initiating health and safety measures. One of the most significant changes in recent years is the placing of responsibilities for health and safety on all the parties involved in a construction project.

5.250 However, given the high number of deaths per year of employees in construction and given that the industry is one those that is targeted by the HSE, it is clear that the industry will remain under the spotlight for the foreseeable future in respect of health and safety as well manslaughter investigations.

CHAPTER 6

Railways

Gerard Forlin, Barrister, 2-3 Grays Inn Square, London

Michael Appleby, Solicitor, Fisher Scoggins LLP, London

Introduction

6.1   A look at both health and safety prosecutions and those for manslaughter related to railway incidents shows that these often reflect trends in the way safety and culpability is viewed more generally.

6.2   The prosecution of British Rail under the Health and Safety at Work etc Act 1974 (HSWA 1974) in relation to the Clapham Junction train crash was a defining moment for the Act in setting out the level of negligent conduct required to prosecute an employer.[1] The failed prosecution of Great Western Trains in 1999 for corporate manslaughter concerning the Southall train crash[2] renewed the call for the 'corporate killing' legislation, which had been a Labour party manifesto pledge in the 1997 election. The announcement of the prosecution of Network Rail and Balfour Beatty Rail Infrastructure Services Ltd, along with senior mangers from those companies, for manslaughter in July 2003 following the Hatfield train crash, shows that the prosecuting authorities have not get given up on convicting large companies under the present corporate manslaughter law.

1   (14 June 1991, unreported), Central Criminal Court.
2   *A-G's Reference (No 2 of 1999)* [2000] QB 796.

6.3   In addition to coping with a number of high-profile disasters in the last decade, the industry has also undergone a major organisational transformation with the privatisation of British Rail.

6.4   This chapter considers the structure of the UK railway system, the relevant specific safety legislation to the industry and the way in which railway incidents over the years have been treated in terms of criminal culpability. It does not consider the structure of the underground railways or incidents upon them.

The structure of the railways

6.5 Following privatisation, British Rail was broken up and sold off in a large number of separate organisations. The main ones were:

1   A company to own the infrastructure (ie track, signalling, bridges, tunnels, stations, depots, electrification systems etc). This was originally called Railtrack Plc, which took over the infrastructure on the 1 April 1994. In October 2001, the company was placed into railway administration by the then Secretary of State for Transport, Local Government and the Regions, Stephen Byers. Network Rail Ltd, a not-for-profit company, took over the operation of the network on 3 October 2002.
2   Contractors took over the maintenance and renewals of the track with contracts being awarded and administered by the infrastructure owner. However, in October 2003 it was announced that by the summer of 2004, maintenance (but not renewals) would be taken 'in-house' by Network Rail.
3   Twenty-six train operating companies (TOCs) took over the running of the passenger train services.
4   Two companies took over the operation of freight (known as freight operating companies – FOCs).
5   Rolling stock was allocated to three train leasing companies (known as rolling stock companies – ROSCOs).

6.6 The government, through the Department of Transport, sets the overall railway policy within the wider context, including road, rail and water. There are three bodies that govern the regulation of the industry:

1   The *Strategic Rail Authority* (SRA) which operates under the direction and guidance issued by the government. It is the strategic, planning and co-ordinating body for the rail industry and the 'guardian' of the rail passengers' interests. It is responsible for awarding the franchises for the train operating services and encouraging private investment in the industry.

2   *Her Majesty's Railway Inspectorate* (HMRI) is the regulatory authority for health and safety on the railways. It enforces HSWA 1974 and other related safety legislation. It is part of the Health and Safety Executive. It was previously headed by the Chief Inspector of Railways, which position has now been replaced by the Director of Rail Safety.

3   The *Rail Regulator* is independent of government and the regulator's function, in basic terms, is to provide economic regulation of the monopoly and dominant elements of the rail industry. This includes determining the level. Structure and charges levied by Network Rail and regulation the company's stewardship of the rail network. With the passing of the Railways and Transport Safety Act 2003 a Regulatory Board will come to replace the Rail Regulator, in line with standard practice for the regulation of utilities

6.7 The British Transport Police (BTP) is the national police force for the rail transport system. It is responsible for providing a police service for the train operators, their staff and the passengers. When a railway incident occurs and there is a possibility that a criminal offence has been committed, then an investigation will be initiated. BTP will investigate offences, like manslaughter, jointly with the HMRI, who will consider breaches of health and safety law.

6.8   The Railways and Transport Safety Act 2003 creates a police authority for the BTP, transferring responsibility for it from the SRA and existing BTP Committee to the new police authority. It gives the BTP a wholly statutory, rather than part-statutory and part-contractual, jurisdiction over the railways.

6.9   Lord Cullen in his second report into Ladbroke Grove concerning the safety of the railways in general[1] recommended that an independent rail accident investigation body be established on similar lines to the air (AAIB) and marine (MAIB) accident investigation branches. The sole focus of this body known as the Rail Accident Investigation Branch (RAIB) will be to establish the cause of accidents and promulgate safety lessons, without apportioning blame or liability. It will be responsible for investigating serious incidents. The legislation setting up this body is the Railways and Transport Safety Act 2003.

1   The Rt Hon Lord WD Cullen PC *The Ladbroke Grove Rail Inquiry, part 2 report* (2001).

6.10   Announcing the appointment of the Chief of the RAIB on 16 April 2003, Transport Secretary Alistair Darling said:

'Too often the focus following a rail accident is finding who is to blame and litigation. The questions that need answering most urgently are: "what went wrong" and "how do we avoid this happening again". The RAIB is being set up to ensure that these questions are addressed with the right priority and as quickly as possible; and to carry out investigations into the prevention of accidents in a broader sense.'[1].

1   Department of Transport press release, 16 April 2003.

6.11   The work of the RAIB will not prevent or curtail criminal investigations by the BTP or HMRI. However, any evidence gathered by the RAIB will not be able to be used in subsequent criminal proceedings by the prosecution.

6.12   Many of the detailed rules and technical standards that relate to the railway are not contained in legislation but in what are called 'Railway Group Standards'. The Railway Group are those companies operating on the railway that have a safety case (see **para 6.17** below). Originally when the industry was privatised, the Safety and Standards Directorate (S&SD) was a section of Railtrack Plc, which wrote and issued Railway Group Standards.

6.13   After the Ladbroke Grove Crash in 1999, the functions of S&SD were taken over by Railway Safety Ltd (RSL), a wholly owned subsidiary of Railtrack. On 1 April 2003, the Rail Safety and Standards Board (RSSB) took over the functions of RSL another of Lord Cullen's recommendations[1]. RSSB, like Network Rail Ltd, is a not-for-profit company.

1   The Rt Hon Lord WD Cullen PC *The Ladbroke Grove Rail Inquiry, part 2 report* (2001).

6.14   In addition to producing and maintaining Railway Group Standards, part of the role of the RSSB is to:

1   Develop and publish the Railway Group Safety Plan.
2   Lead the development of an existing long-term safety strategy for the industry.
3   Be an agent for change and improved safety performance through facilitation of the research and development programme, education and awareness of safety issues.

4   Represent the UK rail industry in the development of European legislation and standards that impact on the safe interworking of trains and infrastructure.
5   Measure, report and inform on safety performance and provide safety intelligence, data and risk information.
6   Lead UK rail industry formal inquiries to ensure safety lessons are learned and acted on.
7   Audit the compliance of Railway Group members with their safety cases and with Railway Group Standards.

Relevant railway legislation

6.15   The Railways Act 1993, passed on 5 November 1993, empowered the Conservative government of the day to put in effect the privatisation of rail. New regulations were then introduced to provide the legal framework for the new safety regime. The principal Regulations are:

1   The Railways (Safety Case) Regulations 2000[1] (formerly the 1994 Regulations[2]).
2   The Railways (Safety Critical Work) Regulations 1994.[3]
3   The Carriage of Dangerous Goods by Rail Regulations 1994.[4]
4   The Railway Safety (Miscellaneous Provisions) Regulations 1997.[5]

1   SI 2000/2688.
2   Railways (Safety Case) Regulations 1994, SI 1994/237.
3   SI 1994/299.
4   SI 1994/670.
5   SI 1997/553.

6.16   These regulations are outlined below.

Railways (Safety Case) Regulations 2000[1]

6.17   Under the safety regime of the Railways (Safety Case) Regulations 2000, each railway operator is required to produce a safety case setting out its safety policy, risk assessment, management, maintenance and operational arrangements. The safety case therefore adopts a similar risk-based approach to the Management of Health and Safety at Work Regulations 1999.[2] The safety case must demonstrate that the management system is adequate to ensure that the operator's safety duties are met.

1   SI 2000/2688.
2   SI 1999/3242.

6.18   Under the 1994 Regulations,[1] HMRI were given the duty of validating the safety case of the infrastructure controller, with the infrastructure controller in turn validating the safety cases of operators under the 'cascade' principle and carry out audits of their performance. However, under the Railways (Safety Case) Regulations 2000[2] this responsibility was removed from the infrastructure controller to be accepted by HMRI.

1   Railways (Safety Case) Regulations 1994, SI 1994/237.
2   SI 2000/2688.

Railways (Safety Critical Work) Regulations 1994[1]

6.19 The Railways (Safety Critical Work) Regulations 1994 require that employers should not permit employees to perform 'safety critical work', unless they are competent and fit, ensure records of any assessments of the workers are kept and that the employee has a means of identification. Safety critical workers include: train drivers, guards, conductors, signalmen and maintenance staff. Lord Cullen in his second Ladbroke Grove Report[2] recommended that a national licensing system be developed for train drivers and signallers.

1   SI 1994/299.
2   The Rt Hon Lord WD Cullen PC *The Ladbroke Grove Rail Inquiry, part 2 report* (2001).

Carriage of Dangerous Goods by Rail Regulations 1994[1]

6.20 The Carriage of Dangerous Goods by Rail Regulations 1994, as the name implies, concern the carriage of dangerous goods and bring into UK law the EU Directive on this matter.[2]

1   SI 1994/670.
2   Council Directive 97/49/EC.

Railway Safety (Miscellaneous Provisions) Regulations 1997[1]

6.21 The main provisions of these regulations are as follows:

1   Regulation 3[2] requires a person in control of a transport system infrastructure to ensure, so far as is reasonably practicable and so far as is necessary for safety, that unauthorised access to the infrastructure is prevented.
2   Regulation 5[3] requires that an infrastructure controller must ensure, so far as is reasonably practicable, that appropriate procedures and equipment are in place to prevent collisions between vehicles or with buffer stops and derailments caused by excessive speed or incorrectly placed points.
3   Regulation 6[4] requires vehicle operators to ensure that suitable and sufficient brakes are provided and maintained.
4   Regulation 7[5] requires infrastructure controllers, vehicle operators, employers of those working on transport systems and self-employed people working on transport systems to ensure, so far as is reasonably practicable, that appropriate procedures and equipment are in place, provided and maintained so as to prevent people working on the transport systems from being struck by or falling from a vehicle.

1   SI 1997/553.
2   SI 1997/553, reg 3.
3   SI 1997/553, reg 5.
4   SI 1997/553, reg 6.
5   SI 1997/553, reg 7.

Other legislation

Railways and Transport Safety Act 2003

6.22   As mentioned at **paras 6.8–6.9** above, The Railways and Transport Safety Act 2003, amongst other things, brings into existence the RAIB, provides for a Regulatory Board to replace the Rail Regulator and creates a police authority for the British Transport Police Force.

Railways and Other Transport Systems (Approval of Works, Plant and Equipment) Regulations 1994[1]

6.23   The Railways and Other Transport Systems (Approval of Works, Plant and Equipment) Regulations 1994 require the approval of the Secretary of State before new works, plant or equipment is brought into use for the purpose of a relevant transport system. This approval will be given through the HMRI.

1   SI 1994/157.

Railway Safety Regulations 1999[1]

6.24   The Railway Safety Regulations 1999 relate to the introduction of train protection systems to prevent or mitigate the effects of signals passed at danger (SPADs).

1   SI 1999/2244.

Transport and Works Act 1992

6.25   This makes it an offence for a person to work on a railway system (for example, a train driver) while unfit to carry out that work through drink or drugs. If convicted a person can be imprisoned for up to six months in the magistrates' court and two years in the Crown Court.

Offences Against the Person Act 1861, s 34

6.26   This provides that any unlawful act or wilful omission or neglect which endangers the safety of persons conveyed or otherwise on the railways shall be a 'misdemeanour' punishable by imprisonment for a maximum of two years. In modern day language, wilful omission or neglect means acting in a reckless manner. Given that the trend is now to prosecute work related incidents by looking at negligence and gross negligence (which does not fit comfortably with a charge based on recklessness), it is unlikely that this provision will be relied upon in the future.

Prosecutions

6.27   Below are detailed the main prosecutions that have followed major railway accidents since the end of the Second World War that have resulted in fatalities.

Nearly all of them involve the prosecution of train drivers. Also included are incidents where at the time of writing criminal investigations or prosecutions are ongoing.

Lewisham (St Johns' Wood) train crash 1957

6.28   A train driver of an express steam passenger train running in dense fog passed a red signal and collided with another train, killing 90 passengers. The driver was charged with gross negligence manslaughter. The jury were unable to reach a verdict and a retrial was ordered. At the retrial it was stated that further proceedings would prove a serious danger to the mental condition of the accused. In the circumstances the Crown offered no evidence and the driver was acquitted.[1]

1   Unreported. Tried in the Central Criminal Court between 21 and 23 April 1958. The retrial took place on 7 May 1958.

Eastbourne train crash 1958

6.29   A train driver passed a red signal in poor weather conditions and collided with a train, killing four people. He was tried for manslaughter and acquitted.[1]

1   Unreported. Acquitted on 19 December 1958 at Sussex Assizes in Lewes.

6.30   Mr Justice Slade (as he was then) was the trial judge. He said that it was possible for the 'grossest' negligence to cause no damage at all, while a slight degree of negligence might cause the 'gravest damage'. He went on to say that it would not be right 'to visit the consequences of this misfortune' upon someone who made a mistake, merely because people died as a result.[1]

1   *The Times* 11 December 1958.

The Kidsgrove train crash 1973

6.31   In this accident a goods train collided with a stationary newspaper train in good visibility. The goods train passed a red signal. The train was being driven by the 'second man', ie a trainee driver, subject to the supervision of the train driver. The train driver advised the second man to turn off the Automatic Warning System (AWS), a system designed to help drivers from passing signals at danger (known as a SPAD – Signal Passed at Danger), as it was making too much noise.

6.32   To understand how the AWS works it is first necessary to understand the four colour light system used on the railways.

6.33   It takes quite a distance to bring a train to a stand. As a rough rule of thumb it takes a mile to stop a train travelling at 100 mph. It is not like driving a car. For this reason the driver needs information further up the line to tell him or her that they might have to stop.

6.34   Railway track is divided into sections. If a section is occupied by a train, then the signal behind it will be red (stop), the signal behind that yellow (caution) and the signal behind that, double yellow (be prepared to stop). It does not always follow that if, for example, a driver has a double yellow, the next signal will be a yellow. There could be another double yellow or a green: it depends upon what is happening ahead.

6.35   Before each signal is an AWS magnet. It is usually 200 yards before the signal. If the signal is green the driver will hear a bell in the cab when the train goes over the magnet. He or she does not have to do anything in response to this. If the signal is yellow, double yellow or red, the driver will hear a horn when the train goes over the magnet. If he or she does not press a button on the control panel in three seconds to cancel the horn, the brakes are automatically applied.

6.36   The second man was killed in the crash, but the train driver survived. The train driver was tried on charges of gross negligence manslaughter and endangering the safety of persons on the railways (pursuant to the Offences Against the Person Act 1861, s 34).[1] He was found not guilty of the manslaughter charge. He pleaded guilty to the lesser charge of endangering lives.

1   Unreported. Stafford Crown Court, 16 December 1973.

Nuneaton train derailment 1975

6.37   In this case a train driver failed to respond to a speed restriction indicated by a railway warning board and, as a consequence, the train derailed causing the death of six passengers. The Department of Transport considered that the driver without the positive reminder of the illuminated warning board (because the gas lighting had gone out) had momentarily forgotten the speed restriction.

6.38   The driver was charged with gross negligence manslaughter, but was acquitted.[1] Following this incident British Railways commenced a programme of fitting AWS magnets (which are placed in the track and cause the AWS to sound) to warning board of temporary speed restrictions so that drivers could have an audible warning of the presence of the speed restriction.

1   Unreported. See *Depertment of Transport Report*, dated 27 September 1976.

Clapham Junction train crash 1988

6.39   At 8.10 am on 12 December 1988, a northbound commuter train ran into the back of a stationary train in a cutting just south of Clapham Junction station. A third train, going south, ran into the wreckage of the first train. Thirty-five people died.

6.40   The immediate cause of the crash was a signal that failed because it was showing a green light instead of a red one, thus concealing the presence of a stationary train from the driver of the northbound commuter train. By the time the driver observed the stationary train, because of the speed he was travelling (as he believed he had a clear track), there was insufficient time and distance to stop the train.

6.41   The signal failure was directly due to the working practices of a technician engaged in rewiring the signal on the previous day. Rather than cutting off or tying back the old wires, he merely pushed them aside. It was also his practice to re-use old insulating tape, though on this occasion no tape at all was wrapped around the bare ends of the wire. As a result, the wire came into contact with nearby equipment causing a 'wrongside' signal failure.

6.42   At the Public Inquiry chaired by Mr Anthony Hidden QC made the following comments in relation to the way British Rail managed safety:[1]

> '[British Rail] is responsible for an industry where concern for safety should be at the forefront of the minds of everyone, from the Board itself at the top to the newest beginner at the bottom. The concept of absolute safety must be a gospel spread across the whole workforce and paramount in the minds of management. The vital importance of this concept of absolute safety was acknowledged time and time again in the evidence which the Court heard. This was perfectly understandable because it is so self-evident.
>
> The problem with such concern for safety was that the remainder of the evidence demonstrated beyond dispute two things:
> 1.   there was total sincerity on the part of all who spoke of safety in this way but nevertheless
> 2.   there was failure to carry those beliefs through from thought into deed.
> The appearance was not the reality. The concern for safety was permitted to co-exist with working practices ... Were positively dangerous. This unhappy co-existence was never detected by management and so the bad practices were never eradicated. The best of intentions regarding safe working practices was permitted to go hand in hand with the worst of inaction in ensuring that such practices were put into effect.
>
> The evidence therefore showed the sincerity of the concern for safety. Sadly, however, it also showed the reality of the failure to carry that concern through into action. It has to be said that a concern for safety which is sincerely held and repeatedly expressed but, nevertheless, is not carried through into action, is as much protection from danger as no concern at all.'

1   A Hidden QC *Investigation into the Clapham Junction Railway accident* (Cm 820, 1989).

6.43   No individual was prosecuted for manslaughter or health and safety offences. British Rail pleaded guilty to breaches of HSWA 1974, ss 2 and 3.[1] Mr Justice Wright when sentencing made it clear there was no question of recklessness on the part of British Rail. He said the case against BR was 'a failure to maintain and observe the high standards required by the Health and Safety at Work legislation ...'

1   (14 June 1991, unreported), Central Criminal Court.

Purley train crash 1989

6.44   On Saturday 4 March 1989 the 12.50 pm Electrical Multiple Unit (EMU) from Horsham to London Victoria made its usual stop on the slow line platform in the direction of London at Purley. On departure it crossed from the slow line to the fast line in the direction of London. A non-stopping train was closely approaching Purley on the fast line heading for London driven by Mr Robert Morgan. Mr Morgan failed to stop at signal T168 which was showing red. As a consequence his train collided with the rear of the Horsham to London train, killing five people.

6.45 The AWS was working on the train. Mr Morgan saw signal T168 at red and made an emergency brake application but was going too fast to stop. He could not recollect the previous cautionary yellow signals but must have cancelled the horn of the AWS or otherwise the train would have been automatically stopped.

6.46 Two of the criticisms of the AWS are that from the audible point of view it does not distinguish between the different types of cautionary signals and when a driver is driving on a series of cautionary signals there is a danger of him or her automatically cancelling the horn without comprehending the status of the signal.

6.47 On 3 September 1990 at the Old Bailey Robert Morgan pleaded guilty to an indictment charging him with two specimen counts of manslaughter.[1] He was sentenced by Mr Justice Ian Kenedy to 18 months' imprisonment of which 12 months were suspended, one on each count, to run concurrently. This was later reduced on Appeal before the then Lord Chief Justice of England, Lord Lane, Mr Justice Roch and Mr Justice Auld on 30 October 1990 to a sentence of four months' imprisonment.[2]

1   (3 September 1990, unreported), Central Criminal Court.
2   (30 October 1990, unreported), CA.

6.48 Prior to the Purley crash there had been four SPADs at T168 in as many years, but none of these resulted in a collision. After the crash a 'banner' repeater signal was fitted. This is effectively a reminder signal to the driver. Despite this on 6 June 1991 another SPAD occurred at signal T168 (the sixth), and an almost identical accident to the one involving Mr Morgan was narrowly avoided. Following this the Regional Signal and Telecommunications Engineer of the Southern Region of British Rail applied 'double blocking' immediately to signal T168. This is where if a signal is red, the one prior to it is also red (instead of yellow). Since this modification there have been no further SPADs at signal T168

The Watford train crash 1996

6.49 Just south of Watford Junction there are four lines: two 'up' and two 'down'. Facing in the Watford direction from Euston, and taking the line on the far left as the first and going across to the right, the lines are arranged as follows: 1, Down Fast – the fast line in the direction from Euston to Watford; 2, Up Fast – the fast line in the direction Watford to Euston; 3, Down Slow – the slow line in the direction of Euston to Watford; and 4, Up Slow – the slow line in the direction of Watford to Euston.

6.50 On 8 August 1996, the 5.04 pm from Euston to Milton Keynes, driven by Driver Afford, called at Harrow and Wealdstone and it was approaching its next stop at Watford Junction. It was running on the Down Slow line. The Down Slow line signal at Watford Junction WJ759 protects a crossover. The signal was at red because an empty passenger train was routed across Driver Afford's path from the Up Slow to the Up Fast line. This was not usual. Driver Afford had a SPAD at signal WJ759. He applied the brake as soon as he saw the red signal but stopped just on the points of the crossover. There was a glancing collision between the two trains. One passenger died.

6.51 Approximately three years before the crash the track and signalling had been altered. The 20 mph crossovers were changed to 50 mph crossovers, which required the tracks of the crossovers to be lengthened (to accommodate the increase in speed) and signals to be moved. The overlap between WJ759 and the points on the Down Slow at the crossover was 162 yards instead of the normal 200 yards.

6.52   Just before signal WJ759 was about to be commissioned the BR Railway Operations Manager noticed the short overlap and required the signal to be moved or the situation to be mitigated. He said the only way it could be mitigated was by double blocking. This is where when the signal is at red the signal behind it is also held at red. A cheaper solution considered was applying a speed restriction. This was thought possible because a signalling standard was misinterpreted. Instead of applying the speed restriction all the way up to WJ759, it was only applied up to the single yellow signal. The drivers were never told of the reason for the speed restriction.

6.53   Like signal T168 at Purley, signal WJ759 had previously been passed at red. Between the beginning of 1994 and August 1996 there were four SPADs, the last in July 1996. The Watford train crash was the fifth SPAD. Interestingly on the Down Fast, where the corresponding signals had exactly the sane spacing as on the Down Slow, there had only been one SPAD, and this was due to a brake failure on a high speed train. It was found that in the 3,000 yards to WJ759 there were 11 pieces of information for the driver to assimilate. It was also calculated if Driver Afford had been travelling at 2 mph slower when he applied the brakes the accident would have been avoided.

6.54   Railtrack, the infrastructure owners at the time of the crash, had not carried out any form of risk assessment following the SPADs nor had it convened a signal sighting committee, pursuant to its Group Standard, following the third SPAD. A signal sighting committee had been arranged for the fourth SPAD to be held on 18 August 1996, which turned out to be ten days after the crash.

6.55   Driver Afford was charged with manslaughter based on his gross negligence. The prosecution alleged that Driver Afford had failed to brake after passing the single yellow signal and that he had anticipated that the red signal would change to a proceed aspect.[1]

1   Unreported. Trial took place at Luton Crown Court between 24 February and 11 March 1998.

6.56   The defence admitted that Driver Afford had passed WJ759 at danger but put forward the following factors in the defence: this was a multi-SPAD signal, so this pointed towards there being something being wrong with the infrastructure, there was an overload of information to the driver and if the overlap had been the correct length the accident would not have occurred (ie a control measure was inadequate). Effectively the defence was saying that the signal was a hazard and should have been adequately assessed. The defence called a number of experts, including a human factors expert. The jury took two hours to acquit Driver Afford in this difficult and complex manslaughter.[1]

1   Unreported. Acquitted on 11 March 1998 at Luton Crown Court.

6.57   Immediately after the accident signal WJ759 was taken out of action, thus preventing the crossing movement which happened on the day. In October 1997, the HMRI allowed Railtrack to use the signal with the interim solution of a speed restriction that went all the way up to WJ759.

6.58   During the course of the trial in February 1998,[1] Railtrack issued a new Group Standard clarifying the signalling standard used to mitigate the short overlap. In April 1998, two days before the HMRI published its report into the crash,[2] Railtrack applied double blocking to WJ759, the solution that had been suggested five years earlier.

1   Group Standard GK/RT 0078.
2   *Railway Accident At Watford* (1998), published by HSE Books, ISBN 9 780717 615100.

6.59   The HMRI report[1] highlighted management deficiencies as underlying causes, in particular in relation to the pacing of the speed restriction to mitigate the overlap. There were no prosecutions of Railtrack, British Rail or any other party under HSWA 1974.

1   *Railway Accident At Watford* (1998), published by HSE Books, ISBN 9 780717 615100.

Southall train crash 1997

6.60   At approximately 1.15 pm on 19 September 1997, the 10.32 am Swansea to Paddington, a high speed train (HST) driven by Driver Harrison, passed a red signal and collided with a goods train routed across its path. Driver Harrison applied the brakes upon seeing the red signal when his train was travelling at line speed of 125 mph, but this was too late to be able to stop the train and avoid the collision. Miraculously he survived. Seven passengers lost their lives. At the signal in question, SN254, there had never previously been a SPAD.

6.61   Within minutes of the crash, in a state of shock, Driver Harrison telephoned the signalman from a lineside telephone. He told him that he remembered packing his bag and that his AWS was not working. The conversation was overheard by a policeman. Driver Harrison was later arrested and taken to the police station where he was interviewed that evening on suspicion of manslaughter. He was released on bail.

6.62   The next day reports emerged that not only was the AWS not working but also the automatic train protection (ATP) was not switched on. Unlike AWS, which is an advisory safety system, ATP is supervisory, ie cannot be overridden by the driver. If the ATP had been working the crash would not have happened.

6.63   Driver Harrison took over control of the train at Cardiff. Since a fault that had occurred earlier that day the AWS had been switched off when the train left Swansea. As the previous driver had not been trained on ATP, he had not switched the device on at Swansea. As the rules stood at the time, the system could not be turned on mid journey. Driver Harrison had never driven an HST without AWS.

6.64   Because of concerns about train operating companies (TOCs) operating trains with the AWS isolated Mr Vic Coleman (at the time the Deputy Chief Inspector) of HMRI sent a circular to all TOCs, 11 days after the crash on 30 October 1997, saying:

'HMRI regard the AWS as an extremely important safety system and we expect all trains companies to ensure that it is available for use to the maximum extent.'[1]

1   Professor John Uff QC *The Southall Rail Accident Inquiry Report* (2000) p 107.

6.65   Six months before the crash the CIRAS (confidential incident reporting and analysis system) Journal had raised concerns about trains operating without AWS. It said that the rules were ambiguous about taking a train out of service with defective AWS. It further said:

> '... in our opinion, the absence of functioning AWS poses a risk which is increased as the journey gets longer. Furthermore, a driver accustomed to work with AWS may well be at greater risk when it fails than a driver who has never had the benefit of this safety aid.'

6.66   In addition to a criminal investigation of the driver, an investigation also started against his employers, Great Western Trains (GWT) for corporate manslaughter on the basis of the safety systems being inoperative. The day after the crash the Deputy Prime Minister announced a public inquiry. This opened on 24 February 1998 and then adjourned until after the criminal proceedings were complete.

6.67   Mr Harrison was charged with manslaughter on 17 April 1998. On that day he was interviewed again. He was unable to give an explanation as to why he had missed the two cautionary signals before the red. He explained that the items he had packed in his bag were three pieces of paperwork. He estimated that this would have taken him a matter of seconds.

6.68   On 1 December 1998 a further charge was brought against Driver Harrison for a breach of HSWA 1974, s 7. On the same day the GWT was charged with corporate manslaughter and an offence for breach of HSWA 1974, s 3. No director was charged.

6.69   At a preliminary hearing the judge, Mr Justice Scott Baker, ruled that as no director had been charged with manslaughter, the case against GWT for corporate manslaughter could not continue.

6.70   On 2 July 1999, GWT pleaded guilty to an HSWA 1974 offence. Because of the Inquiry the prosecution decided not to appeal within the case the decision on corporate manslaughter but to deal with this by way of an Attorney-General's Reference (a sort of technical appeal to sort out the law – in this case the decision of the judge was supported by the Court of Appeal). The company was fined a record £1.5 million.

6.71   No evidence was offered by the prosecution against Driver Harrison and not guilty verdicts were entered on all charges.

6.72   The Public Inquiry started on 20 September 1999. During the course of the Inquiry the Ladbroke Grove Crash occurred (killing 31 people) and another public inquiry was ordered.

6.73   Driver Harrison told the Inquiry that he could not recall what had happened at the cautionary signals. He was in the witness box for over three hours. He was cross-examined on why he had missed the signals on numerous occasions whilst giving evidence. He was asked by Professor Uff, the Chairman of the Inquiry, whether he thought he had been inattentive on one occasion which caused him to miss both cautionary signals or on two separate occasions which had happened to coincide with the two cautionary signals. Driver Harrison said he did not know why he missed the signals and did not want to speculate. Driver Harrison confirmed that he had placed his weekly notices, late notice and diagram (all of which amounted to a small booklet and a few pieces of paper) in his bag, but estimated that this would have taken no more than five seconds

6.74 Professor Uff put the same question to Dr Debbie Lucas called on behalf of the HSE as its human factors expert. She said:

'I would have thought two periods would be more likely, and I would have thought we would perhaps also ought to consider the fact that, at the second [cautionary signal], the yellow one, there are a few things for him to look at, that may have distracted him, so it could be a different reason for him missing the second signal than the first ... There is always perhaps a desire to think of one explanation that covers the whole situation but what we may have here is a combination of situations that influenced his performance.'

6.75 Questions were raised that Driver Harrison could not remember what happened in the immediate lead up to the crash. Professor Groeger (a human factors expert instructed on behalf of Driver Harrison and his union, ASLEF), an expert on memory explained that in a traumatic situation the human mind concentrates on the trauma, as this is the unusual event. In this case the trauma is the red signal and impending crash. Dr Lucas stated:

'I think I would agree with the evidence [of Professor Groeger], amnesia after the accident. I probably would not have expected him to remember a great deal.'

6.76 The central issue for the defence of Driver Harrison in the criminal proceedings had been the absence of the AWS. There was interesting evidence given by the human factors experts.

6.77 Professor Groeger told the Inquiry:

'Especially driving high speed trains, several signals may be encountered every minute ... experience has shown, that it is unreasonable to expect a driver to have to solely on his own eyesight for obtaining all the information he need to drive the train.'

6.78 Professor Moray (another human factors expert instructed on behalf of Driver Harrison and his union ASLEF) said:

'Auditory warning is extremely important. One of the great characteristics of auditory warnings, is that ultimately we do not have ear balls and ear lids, so even if our eyes are looking in one direction, an auditory warning will attract your attention, indeed, and catch your attention even though your attention is not directed to it. It is a very potent attention catcher.'

6.79 Dr Lucas in her report to the Inquiry wrote:

'Detection of signals by observers is rarely 100% accurate ...
I agree with ... Professor Groeger ... about the increased risk when driving without AWS.'

6.80   Dr Lucas told the inquiry that she did not think that a train driver should drive a train without AWS for more than 30 minutes, at most 40 minutes. At the time of the crash, Driver Harrison had been driving the train without AWS for more than an hour and three-quarters.

6.81   Driver Harrison told the Inquiry that he did not realise how dangerous it was to drive a train without AWS. At the criminal proceedings GWT admitted that it too did not realise the risks of running a train without AWS and confirmed that prior to the crash no risk assessment had been carried out in respect of AWS isolation.

6.82   Mr Muttram, the then Head of the Safety and Standards Directorate told the Inquiry:

> 'On the day of the Southall Accident, the operational safety system was AWS and, had it been working, I do not believe the accident would have occurred.'

6.83   'The AWS fault on the train had been reported the day before the crash. The train went to the Old Oak Common depot. The fault was not picked up by the maintenance team.'

6.84   The yellow signal (the one before the red) was so badly aligned that the beams of the signal were pointing at the ground, making the signal more difficult to read. During the course of the Inquiry it was discovered that Railtrack had not re-aligned the signal and this had to be attended to urgently. The double yellow signal could be sighted just under the required time of the relevant Group Standard of seven seconds. Studies in the industry have shown that poorly placed and sighted signals are more likely to result in SPADs.

6.85   Mr Steve Wilkins a signalling engineer called on behalf of the HMRI talked about the issues of 'visibility' and 'readability' of a signal. He said:

> 'Well there is no group standard defining readability. There never has been and I suggest that there will probably never will be in the foreseeable future at least. Readability is dependent on so many issues. Not only is there the question of the visibility of the signal. Readability encompasses a whole range of other factors, many of which are human factors, such as interpretability and other issues regarding the driver's ability to understand and in all respects to make cognisance of the signal. Those are factors that can never be quantified simply and put into a group standard in simple terms.'

6.86   In relation to the cause of the accident, the judge when sentencing GWT said:

> 'The immediate cause of the accident was the passing of a red signal by [Driver Harrison]. But a substantial contributory cause was the fact that [GWT] permitted the train to run from Swansea to Paddington at speeds of up to 125mph with the ... AWS isolated.'

6.87   Prosessor Uff's findings in his report published on 24 February 2000[1] as to causation were as follows:

'The primary cause of the accident was Driver Harrison's failure to respond to the two cautionary signals. Other causes of the accident were the failure of GWT's maintenance system to identify and repair the AWS fault, the failure of GWT to react to the isolation of the AWS, the failure of Railtrack to put in place rules to prevent normal running of an GST with AWS isolated and the failure of GWT to manage the ATP Pilot Scheme such that the ATP equipment was switched on.'

1   Professor John Uff QC *The Southall Rail Accident Inquiry Report* (2000).

6.88   He rejected that the signal sighting of the cautionary signals were causative.

6.89   He rejected the human factors evidence called on behalf of Driver Harrison and his union and the HMRI. He said:

'Having heard the witness' oral evidence I believe that it would be unsafe to apply behavioural theory in the absence of firm evidence as to the actual pattern of drivers' behaviour in the cab, which is substantially lacking.'

1   Professor John Uff QC *The Southall Rail Accident Inquiry Report* (2000) p 16.

6.90   In the Joint Inquiry into Train Protection Systems held in 2000, as part of the Public Inquiries into the Southall crash and the Ladbroke Grove train crash (see below), chaired by Lord Cullen and Professor Uff, the report (published on 28 March 2001) says in relation to signal sighting and SPAD mitigation:[1]

'The issue of signal sighting was regarded by drivers, through their unions and advisers, as being of central importance. We accept and endorse their concern that signal sighting should be carried out with the aid of all the best available practices including expertise on human behaviour, with the objective of maximising the visibility and comprehensibility of signals to the driver.'

1   Prof John Uff QC and the Rt Hon Lord Cullen PC *The Joint Inquiry into Train Protection Systems* (2001) p 92.

6.91   In relation to human factors it says:[1]

'The Joint Inquiry received a substantial body of evidence from a number of experts called on behalf of different parties … The evidence is relevant to a number of topics, particularly to SPAD avoidance.'

1   Prof John Uff QC and the Rt Hon Lord Cullen PC *The Joint Inquiry into Train Protection Systems* (2001) p 98.

6.92   Annexed to the report is a joint report by human factors experts that provided evidence to the Inquiry.[1] In relation to incident investigation it says:

'The investigation of incidents of signals passed at danger should be informed by human factors theories cast in appropriate investigatory tools. The causal analysis of such incidents and accidents should consider possible combinations of human factors relating to individual and system/equipment aspects and to the interface between individuals and systems (Groeger). The information provided by on train monitoring recorders should routinely be investigated following a SPAD. Statistical analysis of data from such accidents and incidents should build on research already published including that on the influence of organisational and managerial factors on incidents (Muir, Lucas). Suitable caution should be exercised when the attributed cause of a serious SPAD is solely dependent on the recollection of those involved. Information reported by traumatised individuals can be unreliable and should be supported by other information sources (Groeger).'

1   Prof John Uff QC and the Rt Hon Lord Cullen PC *The Joint Inquiry into Train Protection Systems* (2001) annex 7.

The Ladbroke Grove train crash 1999

6.93   During the course of the Southall Rail Accident Public Inquiry before Professor Uff, the Ladbroke train crash occurred on 5 October 1999 killing both drivers of the trains involved and 19 passengers.

6.94   A Turbo of Thames Trains, driven by Michael Hodder, left Paddington Station at approximately 8.06 am bound for Bedwyn in Wiltshire. At 8.25 am the Turbo passed signal SN109 on gantry 8 at red. It had passed the previous signal SN87 that was showing a single yellow. Because of the way the points had been set, it meant that if the Thames train failed to stop at SN109 it would be heading for the Up main line. Meanwhile a HST of First Great Western was approaching the Up main line. Both trains collided almost head on as the Thames train entered onto the main line.

6.95   A Public Inquiry was announced by the government which commenced in May 2000 before Lord Cullen. His report into the accident was published in June 2001.[1]

1   The Rt Hon Lord WD Cullen PC *The Ladbroke Grove Rail Inquiry, part 1 report* (2001), available at www.pixunlimited.co.uk/pdf/news/transport/ladbrokegrove.pdf.

6.96   Evidence was given to the Inquiry that there was persistent difficulty in the sighting of signals which formed part o the signalling scheme at Paddington between the station and Ladbroke Grove, and in particular on gantry 8. SN109 (just like the signals at Purley and Watford) had been passed on previous occasions: eight occasions since August 1993.

6.97   Driver Hodder had only recently passed out as a driver. His employers accepted in the Inquiry that there had been shortcomings in his training.

6.98   Lord Cullen was satisfied that Driver Hodder thought he had a proceed signal at gantry 8. He wrote:[1]

'It is more probable than not that the poor sighting of SN109, both in itself and in comparison with the other signals on and at gantry 8, allied to the effect of the bright sunlight at a low angle, were factors which led [Driver Hodder] to believe that he had a proceed aspect and so that it was appropriate for him to accelerate as he did after passing SN87 ... The unusual configuration of SN109 ... not only impaired initial sighting of the red aspect, but also might well have misled an inexperienced driver ... into thing it was not showing a red but a proceed aspect.

1   The Rt Hon Lord WD Cullen PC *The Ladbroke Grove Rail Inquiry, part 1 report* (2001) p 2.

6.99 Prior to the crash, there had been problems with SPADs in the Paddington area. Lord Cullen concluded:[1]

> 'There was a lamentable failure on the part of Railtrack (the then infrastructure owner) to respond to recommendations of inquiries into two serious incidents, namely the accident at Royal Oak on 10 November 1995 and the serious SPAD at SN109 on 4 February 1998. The recognition of the problem of SPADs in the Paddington area led to the formation of a number of groups to consider the problem. However, this activity was so disjointed and ineffective that little was achieved. The problem was not dealt with in a prompt, proactive and effective manner. In 1998 Railtrack dispensed with the services of a significant number of senior Great Western Zone personnel or moved them on to other work. In the course of what was correctly described as a "devastating critique" of their deficiencies and other management failures, the incoming Zone Director said: "The culture of the place had gone seriously adrift over many years."'

1 The Rt Hon Lord WD Cullen PC *The Ladbroke Grove Rail Inquiry, part 1 report* (2001) pp 3 and 4.

6.100 Prior to the start of the Public Inquiry it was announced that there would no manslaughter or corporate manslaughter prosecutions. However, after publication of Lord Cullen's report there was pressure from the bereaved and injured for the police investigation to be reopened. In May 2002 the investigation was indeed reopened but only in respect of Railtrack and its senior managers/directors. As yet there have been no charges and the investigation is ongoing.

6.101 In October 2003, the HSE announced that it was commencing a prosecution under HSWA 1974 against Thames Trains. It has already announced that it intends to prosecute Railtrack as well; however, the HSE is unable to commence those proceedings until the outcome of the police investigation is concluded.

The Hatfield Train derailment 2000

6.102 On 17 October 2000, the Great North Eastern Railway (GNER) Kings Cross to Leeds Intercity 225 express train derailed at 12.23 pm south of Hatfield Station. The derailment occurred between Welham Green and Hatfield, approximately 27 km from Kings Cross station. Four passengers were killed and 70 people suffered injuries, four seriously, including two GNER staff.

6.103 According to the HSE's interim report into the matter dated 23 January 2003[1] all the evidence points to the derailment having been caused by fracture and subsequent fragmentation of a rail between Welham Green and Hatfield on a right-hand curve in the track.

1 Available on the HSE's website, www.hse.gov.uk.

6.104 At the time of the incident the infrastructure was owned by Railtrack and the maintenance was carried out by a company which was part of the Balfour Beatty Group.

6.105 On 9 July 2003 four senior managers who worked for Railtrack at the time of the incident and two who worked for Balfour Beatty were charged with gross negligence manslaughter. Network Rail (the successor of Railtrack) and Balfour Beatty

Rail Infrastructure Services Ltd are also being prosecuted for corporate manslaughter with the respective managers being named as the 'directing minds' of the companies. The defendants were charged with breaches of HSWA 1974 as well: the managers with a breach of HSWA 1974, s 37 and each company with a breach of HSWA 1974, s 3.

6.106   In addition to the six individuals charged with manslaughter, a further six managers, including Gerard Corbett Gerard Corbett, the former chief executive of Railtrack and now chairman of , were summonsed for a breach of HSWA 1974, s 37.

6.107   Mr Corbett,, told the media on the news of the prosecutions:[1]

'I was the chief executive when something went wrong, and that is why I immediately tendered my resignation.

But taking responsibility for one's organisation does not necessarily mean that I accept that the rail breaking was in any sense attributable to neglect on my part.'

1   Channel 4 News, 9 July 2003.

6.108   It is likely that the trial will not start until the end of 2004 at the earliest and it is anticipated that it will last for many months.

The Potters Bar train derailment 2002

6.109   On 10 May 2002 the rear coach of a four-coach commuter train, bound for Kings Lynn from Kings Cross, derailed passing over points 2182A just before Potters Bar station. The coach detached from the others and came to rest on its side wedged under the canopies of the station and bridging adjacent platforms. The other three coaches remained upright, travelled on through the station and were brought to a halt around 400 metres north of it. At the time of the accident the train was travelling just below the speed limit for this class of train, which is 100 mph.

6.110   According to an HSE report:[1]

'A derailment analysis has identified a sequence of events that is consistent with the derailment having been caused by faults in points 2182A that led to their catastrophic failure as the train passed over them, allowing both switch rails to be in contact with their respective stock rails ... This resulted in the wheels of the rear three sets of bogies being "squeezed" – the left hand wheels being directed straight on and the right hand wheels directed to the left – resulting in "flange climb" and subsequent derailment. "Flange climb" is where abnormal forces between the flange of a wheel and the rail are such as to cause the flange to ride up the side of the rail onto the top surface.'

1   HSE *Train derailment at Potters Bar 10 May 2002 – A Progress Report by the HSE Investigation Board* (2003): see Summary, available on the HSE's website at www.hse.gov.uk.

6.111   It was suggested after the crash that the derailment might have been the result of sabotage. The HSE report[1] rules this out.

1   HSE *Train derailment at Potters Bar 10 May 2002 – A Progress Report by the HSE Investigation Board* (2003).

6.112 Following the crash a joint criminal investigation was launched into the incident by BTP and HMRI. It is understood that Network Rail, the infrastructure owners and Jarvis Rail, the then company responsible for maintenance on the line, are being investigated.

The future

6.113 Since 1988 there have been five major public inquiries concerning the railways:

1   The Clapham Junction Railway Accident Inquiry.[1]
2   The Southall Rail accident Inquiry.[2]
3   The Ladbroke Grove Rail Inquiry Part 1.[3]
4   The Ladbroke Grove Rail Inquiry Part 2.[4]
5   The Joint Inquiry into Train Protection.[5]

1   A Hidden QC *Investigation into the Clapham Junction Railway accident* (Cm 820, 1989).
2   Professor John Uff QC *The Southall Rail Accident Inquiry Report* (2000).
3   The Rt Hon Lord WD Cullen PC *The Ladbroke Grove Rail Inquiry, part 1 report* (2001), available at www.pixunlimited.co.uk/pdf/news/transport/ladbrokegrove.pdf.
4   The Rt Hon Lord WD Cullen PC *The Ladbroke Grove Rail Inquiry, part 2 report* (2001).
5   Professor John Uff QC and the Rt Hon Lord WD Cullen PC *The Joint Inquiry into Train Protection Systems* (2001).

6.114 Public inquiries into the Hatfield and Potters Bar Derailments have been ruled out by the government. With the intense scrutiny of the industry in recent times by this process, it is difficult to see what further could be achieved by more public inquiries.

6.115 When there is an incident on the railways, particularly if there is loss of life, it will be front-page news. Given this publicity, it would be easy to gain the impression that the railways are inherently unsafe. However, the fact of the matter is that travelling by rail is the safest form of land transport. When there are fatal incidents on the road, there is rarely the same media coverage and even if there is, it does not attract the same public outcry as when a railway incident occurs. As Mr Kim Howells, miinster for Railways, has said: "We look at every single [rail] accident as if it is the end of civilisation."[1]

1   *Guardian*, 28 November 2003.

6.116 Since privatisation the industry has been dogged by a number of high-profile incidents involving the deaths of passengers. It is too easy to blame these purely on privatisation. Fatal accidents occurred in the nationalised industry, although it was not often these ended in prosecution. The criticisms of management failings in British Rail made in the Clapham Junction Accident Report[1] seem to have a resonance with those made in the Ladbroke Grove Inquiry Report[2] of the companies involved.

1   A Hidden QC *Investigation into the Clapham Junction Railway accident* (Cm 820, 1989).
2   The Rt Hon Lord WD Cullen PC *The Ladbroke Grove Rail Inquiry, part 1 report* (2001); *The Ladbroke Grove Rail Inquiry, part 2 report* (2001).

6.117 The industry is in a state of flux, with the pace of change being relentless since the introduction of the Railway Act 1993. Matters have not been helped by the resignation in October 2003 of the Director of Rail Safety of the HSE, Alan Osborne, complaining of the number of barriers he has encountered at the HSE in trying to implement Lord Cullen's recomendations.[1]

1   *Guardian*, 28 Novenber 2003.

6.118   While it is must be right that breaches of health and safety and work related fatal accidents are investigated fully, it is all too easy to assume when there has been a catastrophic accident on the railways, that this has been due to grossly negligent conduct on the part of individuals and/or companies. It must be self-evident that prosecutions, let alone the happening of the events and the devastation they cause, are damaging to the morale of the industry. Only time will tell whether prosecutions have a positive affect upon the safety of the railways.

CHAPTER 7

Motor vehicle

Jonathan Lawton, Solicitor-Advocate, Hill Dickinson

The haulage industry

7.1   Ever since the first motor cars moved onto the public roads, there has been an awareness of the potential for danger, whether or not that awareness was founded on fact. The early requirement, resulting from pressure by the majority who rode horses, that a vehicle be proceeded by a man carrying a red flag might have been seen not only as a warning that a vehicle was approaching, if indeed it could neither be seen nor heard, but also as a warning of what was to come. In those early, heady, days of mechanically propelled vehicles, however, few foresaw that those first vehicles would be rapidly followed by an ever-increasing variety of vehicles, capable of carrying out a multitude of tasks. Vehicles which, in turn, became bigger and quicker.

7.2   The modern articulated vehicle can operate, in the UK, at a total laden weight of 41 tonnes[1] and that weight can, in certain circumstances, be increased to 44 tonnes.[2] Vehicles and trailers designed to carry particularly heavy loads, so called 'abnormal loads', can operate at weights in excess of 100 tonnes.[3] Additionally, we have a wide range of vehicles designed for special purposes. Vehicles such as mobile concrete pumps, road sweepers, mobile access platforms, mobile cranes and so on. There is no doubt but that, as a new problem arises, a new vehicle will be designed to deal with it.

1   Road Traffic Act 1988, s 41.
2   Road Vehicles (Construction and Use) Regulations 1986, SI 1986/1078, reg 80.
3   Motor Vehicles (Authorisation of Special Types) General Order 1979, SI 1979/1198, art 18

7.3   Whilst we now live in a country in which the majority of people have access to a car there still remains much of the 'red flag' mentality in our attitude to the commercial vehicle. There is a perception amongst those in the transport industry that the public has never considered the way in which goods are transported to, say, a super-market. Plans to ban the larger commercial vehicles from town centres are hugely popular, whatever the cost impact may be on the goods that are to be carried. It is increasingly difficult to find a site that will be considered by planning officers to be suitable for the location of a haulage depot. The increased opportunities given to the public to raise environmental objections to the use of land as a haulage depot[1] have, predictably, been widely welcomed and used. Even those hauliers occupying established sites are not free from certain environmental controls.

1   Goods Vehicles (Licensing of Operators) Act 1995, s 14.

7.4   The modern commercial vehicle is technically sophisticated. Three-line airbrakes, air suspension (the so called 'road friendly suspension'), ABS systems and so on, all increase the administrative requirements imposed on the haulier in relation to the maintenance of the vehicles. Methods of recording 'drivers' hours' become more accurate. The waxed disc currently used in a tachograph is soon to be replaced by a plastic 'credit' card, and the operator will need more electronic equipment to download the stored information. That information has to be analysed to ensure that the driver has not exceeded the permitted hours of driving, that the driver has not exceeded any relevant speed limit and that the driver has not interfered with the recording equipment.

7.5   External pressures arise not only from the increasing severity of enforcement, but also from increased competition from EU-based operators. A European vehicle can fill its tanks with diesel in Calais, cross the channel and travel to the North East of England to deliver a load. It can then collect a load and return to France all on the same tank of fuel. Fuel that, as this is written, may cost £400 less than the English operator would have to pay for the same tank-full.

7.6   None of this information should disguise the fact that, out of some 4,000 deaths on the road each year, about one-third are work related[1] – a total that exceeds the aggregate total of all other work related deaths. A Health and Safety Executive (HSE) Task Group, set up to examine the steps that might be taken to reduce the number of work related road deaths, produced 18 recommendations.[2] One of these recommendations, number 16, suggested 'Police authorities/Chief Constables should pursue employers who fail to meet their responsibilities under road traffic law, prosecuting as appropriate.'

1   HSE *HSE and Work Related Safety* (2000).
2   HSE press release CO53, 1 November 2001.

7.7   Not surprisingly, the haulage industry is in recession. Traditionally the industry was made up by a large number of small operators. Owner-drivers and businesses with no more than five vehicles were normal. Today we see the growth of much larger companies as the smaller operators disappear. At the same time, we see no reduction in the proliferation of legislative controls aimed at those who use commercial vehicles; indeed the number of statutory and regulatory controls is increasing.

7.8   The volume of legislation designed to control those who make use of our public roads, whether on horse, on a bicycle or in a motor vehicle, is greater than that directed to any other activity. Regulatory controls of both the nuclear industry and of the railways are extensive, but are confined to a limited number of activities. It is the wide spectrum of control that distinguishes the haulage industry. Legislation follows changes in vehicle design, new concepts of vehicle and passenger safety, the need to introduce new methods of supervision and control such as laser speed measuring devices and, on occasion, a public demand for intervention. Inevitably, the law lags behind advances in vehicle design and, equally inevitably, the more technical vehicles become, the more difficult it may be for courts to follow a technical argument. Again, the haulage industry feels that it is, to a degree, victimised. Although the Road Traffic Act 1988 provides, in the majority of offences affecting commercial vehicles, for the prosecution of those who 'cause' or 'permit' offences,[1] the absolute offence of 'using' is preferred by the prosecution because of the ease of proof. Many cases of overloading result from the carriage of a sealed container accompanied by documents, maybe the notes required under the provisions of the Convention Relative au Contract de Transport International de Marchandises par Route (CMR) required when goods are carried between states which are signatories to the Convention, confirming the weight of the load. Only too frequently these declared weights are found to be inaccurate, but it is rare to find a prosecuting authority attempting to proceed against the consignor.

1   Road Traffic Act 1988, ss 40A–44.

7.9   The public are largely unaware of the fact that a prosecution for an offence for which the operator of a vehicle, or the driver, is convicted has to be reported to the Traffic Commissioner for the area in which the operator is based. That, in turn, may result in the revocation of the licence required in order to carry on the business of a haulage contractor.

7.10   The controlling legislation is contained in the Goods Vehicles (Licensing of Operators) Act 1995. Under this legislation, vehicles with a gross laden weight of more than 3.5 tonnes must be authorised by the Traffic Commissioner for the area in which the vehicle is to be based.[1] This authorisation requires that the vehicle's base, the 'operating centre', is suitable both in relation to the environmental impact arising from the operation of commercial vehicles, and also in relation to the safety of the premises in the context of the relationship of the access to adjacent public roads.

1   Goods Vehicles (licensing of Operators) Act 1995, s 2 and Goods Vehicles (licensing of Operators) Act 1995, Sch 1, paras 2–4.

7.11   Given a suitable operating centre, the operator must demonstrate that there is a sufficient financial reserve. The intention is to ensure that the operator can afford to maintain the vehicles in a roadworthy condition. The operator must explain how, and by whom, the vehicles are to be maintained. The operator must also confirm to the Traffic Commissioner the intervals at which safety checks will be carried out. These, so-called preventative maintenance inspections (PMIs) are normally carried out at four or six-weekly intervals. Currently most of the major commercial vehicle manufacturers offer maintenance contracts to those who purchase new vehicles.

7.12   There must also be a nominated transport manager, unless the licence held is a 'restricted licence'. The transport manager must hold a Certificate of Professional Competence (CPC). When the requirement to hold a CPC was first introduced the transitional period entitled those with sufficient experience to obtain a CPC under 'Grandfather rights'. Others had to take an examination and, currently, the majority of CPC holders have taken the examination. The standard of the required qualifications in the UK is recognised as not being as high as that in the majority of other European countries. The UK standard tends to reflect the pragmatic ability of the applicant whereas in Europe the emphasis is on academic ability. Perhaps belatedly, steps are being taken to improve the academic standards required for a CPC in the UK.

7.13   It is not unusual for a company to employ more than one CPC holder. The holding of the CPC attracts no particular responsibility unless the holder is nominated on an operator's licence as a transport manager. The nominated transport manager, however, has responsibility for controlling drivers' hours, ensuring that they do not exceed speed limits, and ensuring both that they carry out the daily inspections of the vehicle required of a driver, and also that they do not interfere either with the tachographs or the speed limiter.[1] Additionally the transport manager must ensure that the vehicles are put through a PMI at the intervals that have previously been advised to the Traffic Commissioner.

1   The duties of a transport manager are set out in the Goods Vehicles (Licensing of Operators) Act 1995, s 58. This is the 'definition' section and the definition of transport manager contains the following requirement: 'has continuous and effective responsibility for the management of the transport operations of the business in so far as they relate to the carriage of goods.' On the application of Messrs Bhandal and Deo for a licence in the West Midlands traffic area, the Traffic Commissioner refused the licence on the grounds that a transport manager who was 200 miles from the operating centre, and visited the premises every one to two months, and otherwise kept in touch by telephone, could not satisfy the definition: 28 January 2002.

7.14   The assurances given to the Traffic Commissioner in relation to the maintenance of the authorised vehicles, and to the keeping of drivers' hours, are given by way of undertaking, and a failure in any of these areas is treated as a serious breach of a formal undertaking that has been given to the Traffic Commissioner.

7.15   Any application for a licence that raises environmental, financial or maintenance issues will be considered at a public inquiry, as will any disciplinary hearing called as the result of an alleged breach of the undertakings given by the operator. Perhaps the most common reason for a disciplinary public inquiry is a failure to maintain vehicles in a safe condition. All applications for a new licence, or applications to vary an existing licence, have to be advertised in a paper that is widely read in the locality. This gives local residents the opportunity to register environmental concerns.[1]

1   Goods Vehicles (Licensing of Operators) Act 1995, s 35.

7.16   In environmental cases the Traffic Commissioner may refuse to grant the licence if it is considered that the environmental impact would be excessive. Where the environmental impact can be mitigated, perhaps by restricting the hours during which premises may be used, or the hours between which vehicles may enter and leave the premises, the Traffic Commissioner may grant the licence subject to conditions.[1]

1   Goods Vehicles (Licensing of Operators) Regulations 1995, SI 1995/2869, reg 15.

7.17   Commercial vehicle operators, therefore, not only have to contend with the mass of legislation directed at any road user, but also have to contend with controls specifically directed to them in their capacity as road hauliers. Additionally, since the introduction of the Health and Safety at Work etc Act 1974, they have to comply with a mass of health and safety legislation covering every aspect of their business, including, in many cases, the goods that they are required to carry.

7.18 In every transport undertaking there will be an administrative office which may, for example, require consideration of the Health and Safety (Display Screen Equipment) Regulations 1992,[1] there may well be a workshop which will attract a variety of other regulations, such as the Control of Substances Hazardous to Health Regulations 1988,[2] as amended. The reality is that there is very little health and safety legislation that does not affect the road haulier, particularly as it has been determined that a vehicle is a 'workplace' for the purpose of the legislation. Legislation covers the personal safety of the drivers, the safety of the load, the methods used to secure the load, hazards associated with the goods that are being carried, manual handling, and so on. Recently we have seen a growing awareness of the problems of fatigue underlined by cases such as the rail crash at Selby. The haulier has to remember that compliance with the drivers' hours regulations does not necessarily mean that a driver may not be fatigued. Those companies who employ 'representatives', or others, required to travel about the country in company cars, are beginning to realise that fatigue is a very real problem with which they have to deal. Police officers, investigating a serious road traffic accident, will work with officers from the HSE investigating the background of the driver. Additionally the operator needs to consider the possible effects of alcohol and drug abuse.

1 SI 1992/2792.
2 SI 1988/1657.

7.19 In the context of criminal law the individual responsibility of directors has been recognised for some time. In 1993 the director of a company offering adventure holidays in Faversham was imprisoned following a canoeing tragedy.[1] In October 1999 the directors of Roy Bowles Transport Ltd were given suspended prison sentences for manslaughter following a fatal accident caused by a fatigued driver.[2] The probable reason for the limited number of similar cases is the evidential problem of proving a direct link between the senior officers of a company and the circumstances that led to the accident. In both the Faversham and Bowles cases the company was small and the directors had the 'hands on' control on a day-to-day basis. Although, under the provisions of the Road Traffic Act 1988, and the Transport Act 1968, companies or proprietors operating commercial vehicles are prosecuted, these prosecutions are normally based on the absolute liability of the operator of the vehicle in the capacity of 'user'. Cases involving technical offences, whether to do with the condition of the vehicle or drivers' hours, rarely attract wide public attention. Traffic Commissioners, however, have started considering the collective responsibility of the officers of a company. In the appeal of *Dukes Transport (Craigavon) Ltd and the Vehicle Inspectorate*[3] the question arose as to whether the sanction of 'loss of repute' should be applied to directors who had, apparently, no direct responsibility for the day-to-day operations of the appellant company. A person who is found to have 'lost their repute' may take no part in the control of the operations of a haulage business for so long as the Traffic Commissioner may direct. The Appeal Court supported the findings of the Traffic Commissioner who justified the application of the sanction of 'loss of repute' to all the directors, albeit for different periods, by finding that 'a board has to operate like a cabinet and take joint responsibilities and decisions ... so that all the directors must be satisfied that its road transport undertakings are run responsibly within the law ...'

1 *R v Kite* [1996] 2 Cr App Rep (S) 295.
2 *R v Roy Bowles Transport* (October 1999, unreported).
3 Transport Tribunal 68/2001.

7.20   In the haulage industry, therefore, corporate responsibility appears to be an established fact. A Traffic Commissioner may penalise each company officer as the result of an error by a colleague even if the level of punishment may not reflect the actual degree of culpability. In the *Dukes* case,[1] for example, the periods during which 'repute' would be deemed to be lost, varied from ten years to two years, but no director escaped, whatever might have been their responsibility within the company. The other relevant issue raised in the *Dukes* case turned upon the question as to whether or not the company's responsibility could be delegated. The company had transport managers in place that had the relevant CPC. The company was called to inquiry as the result of an investigation, which found that tachograph records were being falsified. The directors argued that, in the absence of any information that might have put them on notice, they were entitled to rely on the competence of the transport managers. On the hearing of the appeal, the Tribunal referred to the case of *Alison Jones t/a Jones Motors*[2] in which the court said: 'In our view this statutory undertaking requires more than that the operator should set up adequate systems and then leave them to run themselves; what is required is constant supervision and monitoring to ensure that the systems work.' The implication of that decision in the context of corporate responsibility is self-evident.

1   *Dukes Transport (Craigavon) Ltd and the Vehicle Inspectorate* Transport Tribunal 68/2001.
2   Appeal 1999 L56.

7.21   Perhaps curiously, notwithstanding the obvious importance of some of these decisions, public inquiries attract little public attention. Local papers may report cases in which environmental issues have been raised, but that will be the extent of the public reporting. The 'trade press' may well report the case, but few, outside the industry, read the trade papers. Conversely, the industry appears to see these reports as being personal to the company involved and shows little sign of understanding the broader implications.

7.22   Public inquiries may also be called if there are environmental objections to the use of an operating centre.

7.23   There is no doubt but that the call for corporate accountability has resulted from a comparatively small number of high-profile cases, which have attracted the attention of the tabloid press in particular, and in which, in the view of the public, the guilty company has escaped prosecution. In 1993, at Sowerby Bridge in West Yorkshire, a tipping lorry ran into a building at the bottom of a hill, in the process killing six people. An examination of the vehicle established that the brakes were, for all practical purposes, ineffective. The Crown Prosecution Service, however, did not prosecute the company for manslaughter and there was a public outcry. Ultimately, and belatedly, as a result of the public pressure, a prosecution was brought which failed.[1] That public pressure has, of course, continued, as a result of further high-profile cases, such as the Hatfield rail crash, in which employers appear to have escaped prosecution. More recently, however, company directors have been successfully prosecuted under the criminal law. Curiously, however successful those prosecutions may have been, the public remained persuaded that companies, and directors, were not being held accountable, and, no doubt as a result of public pressure, in April 2000 a Bill to crate three new offences, 'reckless killing', 'killing by gross carelessness', and 'corporate killing', was accepted by Parliament.

1   *R v Crown Prosecution Service, ex p Waterworth* [1996] COD 277, QBD.

Legislation

7.24   The current position of criminal law is dealt with elsewhere. Looking specifically at the road transport industry, however, there are three relevant statutes. The Transport Act 1968, the Road Traffic Act 1988, and the Health and Safety at Work etc Act 1974 (HSWA 1974).

7.25   The Transport Act 1968 is relevant only in so far as it deals with the control of drivers' hours. Whether under domestic regulations contained in the Transport Act 1968, Pt VI,[1] or the EC Regulations, Council Regulation 3820/85/EEC and Council Regulation 3821/85/EEC, the amount of time that a driver can spend driving, or working, is strictly controlled, as are the hours of required rest. The purpose of the legislation is to avoid the presence of vehicles on the public road whose driver's capability may be affected by fatigue. Clearly, if the required records show that a driver has driven for longer periods than the law permits, there will be a presumption, in the case of a serious accident, that the driver was fatigued.

1   Transport Act 1968, s 95.

7.26   As the result of pressure from the Traffic Commissioners, operators commonly have the drivers' records checked by independent analysts. These analysts produce computer-generated reports drawing the attention of the operator to any offences that might be disclosed on the records.[1] The operator is then expected to take whatever action may be required, including disciplinary action, against an offending driver. In the context of the transport industry, it is now clear that an operator cannot discharge the duty to check the activities of a driver by delegating the task to an outside consultant or independent analyst despite the fact that, in a large company, the cost of in-house analysis may be prohibitive. The equipment designed to produce these records has become increasingly sophisticated. Already enforcement officers can download information about a driver's hours of driving and speeds by plugging electronic equipment, contained in their own vehicle, into the vehicle being checked. The next generation of recording equipment is likely to require the driver to carry some form of plastic card only, and it said that, in the foreseeable future, enforcement officers will be able to download information as a vehicle drives past.

1   Council Regulations 3820/85/EEC and 3821/85/EEC.

7.27   Clearly, information about the way in which a vehicle has been driven before an accident may be extremely important. Defence advocates in particular are accustomed to using a tachograph record to persuade a court that a driver's standard of driving, prior to an incident, was satisfactory, or that the vehicle was being driven at a legal speed. Recently there has been a substantial change in the approach to the investigation of road traffic accidents (RTAs). Commonly the police and officers of the HSE will treat the investigation as a joint investigation. The factual circumstances will, of course, be carefully examined but additionally there will be an investigation into the background of the driver to determine whether fatigue might have been a contributory factor. In the event that there is any evidence which raises issues about the driver's fitness to drive at the time of the accident, then the company and its officers will also be investigated.

7.28   The tachograph record will not only show the distance the vehicle has travelled, the number of hours that have been occupied by driving, the rest breaks that have been taken, but, and arguably more importantly, it may also allow the manner in which the vehicle has been driven prior to the accident to be established. Erratic variations in speed, or sudden and heavy breaking, may indicate that a driver was affected by fatigue or, in some case, drugs or alcohol.

7.29   The employer must have a system of checking records which will provide informations about the manner of driving, either by ensuring that the analysis reports produced by the external consultants are sufficiently detailed or by periodically checking the reports against the appropriate tachograph record. The one thing that is increasingly clear from recent decisions, such as that in the *Dukes* case,[1] is the fact that the responsibility cannot be delegated. This resistance to the defence of appropriate delegation is underlined by an HSE press release warning 'buyers' and 'sellers' of second-hand industrial machinery that the standard contractual provision 'sold as seen' will not amount to a protection from the liabilities imposed by the health and safety legislation.[2]

1   *Dukes Transport (Craigavon) Ltd and the Vehicle Inspectorate* Transport Tribunal 68/2001. See PARA **7.19** above.
2   HSE press release E124:03, 11 July 2003.

7.30   In practice, where drivers are convicted of offences relating to the keeping of their records of driving, whilst the operator may or may not be prosecuted for related offences, the probability is that the Traffic Commissioner will call the operator to public inquiry which may result in the loss of the operators' licence.

7.31   The Road Traffic Act 1988 is primarily relevant as the authority for laying informations in respect of breaches of the numerous subsidiary regulations. The most important of these are the Road Vehicles (Construction and Use) Regulations 1986.[1]

1   SI 1986/1078.

7.32   It is, for all practical purposes, true to say that every mechanical function of a commercial vehicle is subject to regulatory control. Prosecutions are brought for defective tyres, defective brakes, excess movement in parts such as the track rod ends or bushes and overweight vehicles. The list is as long as the number of parts on a vehicle that are susceptible to breakage, wear and maladjustment. The justification for a prosecution, if one were needed, is the determination to protect the public from badly maintained vehicles, which are inherently extremely dangerous.

7.33   To prevent the failure of any part of a vehicle, the operator is required to have access to a maintenance system, whether in-house or not, that is based on preventative maintenance inspections. These inspections should be at intervals that balance the commercial need to keep the vehicle on the road and the need to keep the vehicle in sound mechanical condition. Normally that interval will be not less than four weeks and not more than six weeks. Trailers, however, may have an inspection interval of eight weeks.

7.34   This maintenance system must be in writing,[1] and recorded in such a way that an enforcement officer, normally a vehicle inspector, can see when the next PMI is due and when the last one took place. The detailed record of the actual checks must be retained for inspection. Additionally the operator must be able to show that the driver checks the vehicle at the start of any period of duty and records, in writing, whether or not any defect has been detected and reported in the course of the day's work; the so-called 'nil defect' system of reporting. In the event that a defect has been reported, the operator must be able to produce a record confirming the rectification of the defect.

1 Transport Act 1968, s 99.

7.35   In an increasing number of cases the maintenance work is contracted out, but that does not relieve the operator of the duty to keep the records, nor does it assist the operator to be able to show delegation to a competent person, or company, in the event of a defect occurring. In the majority of prosecutions under the Road Vehicles (Construction and Use) Regulations 1986,[1] the legal duty is absolute, as the vehicle operator will be prosecuted as the 'user'. Given the increasingly technical nature of these prosecutions, however, a defence may be available if the information is factually inaccurate.

1   SI 1986/1078.

7.36   The more sophisticated vehicles become, the more opportunity there is for the failure of a part. In the course of a working day a leaf in a road spring may break, an air bag on the 'road friendly suspension' may spring a leak, as may one of the air pipes servicing the braking system. Defects of this sort are defects of which the driver will almost certainly be unaware, and which may not become known until the next PMI. Whilst the fact that a driver may reasonably be unaware of a fault may amount to good mitigation, in the case of a prosecution for 'using', that lack of knowledge would never provide a defence. This potential for failure is exacerbated by the possibility that the driver will not carry out the required daily check thereby missing some obvious defect such as loose wheel nuts.

7.37   In the case of an operator who has all the required systems in place, but whose vehicle was involved in a fatal accident, a prosecution for manslaughter might still be brought where the vehicle involved was found to be defective. The decision to prosecute would depend on the prosecution's decision as to whether the fault was the result of an act of commission or omission.[1] It is important to remember, however, that, in the event of any conviction arising out of the operation of a licensed vehicle, the operator must report the matter to the relevant Traffic Commissioner whether or not the conviction arises as the result of the condition of the vehicle or as the result of offences committed by drivers in relation either to their records of driving or their hours of work. The reported conviction of an operator or of the employed drivers may well lead to a public inquiry.

1   *R v Crown Prosecution Service, ex p Waterworth* [1996] COD 277, QBD.

7.38   It can be argued that the sanctions available to a Traffic Commissioner at a public inquiry are potentially far more severe than those presently available in either magistrates' or Crown Courts. Not only can the operators licence be revoked which may cause a business be closed, but the responsible individuals may lose their right to work in the haulage industry.[1] There is a growing practice amongst the Vehicle Inspectorate, as an enforcement authority, to ignore the criminal courts and to recommend that the operator be called to public inquiry. This practice effectively avoids the need to prove the case to the standard that might otherwise be required and, incidentally, largely avoids the possibility of an extended cross-examination.

1   Goods Vehicles (Licensing of Operators) Act 1995, ss 26–29.

7.39   HSWA 1974 had, initially, very little impact on the transport industry. Notwithstanding the extraordinary effect that the legislation was going to have in the future, it was generally felt that there would be a sufficient compliance if the employer had a statement setting out the health and safety policy. Those early health and safety policies were frequently contained on one side of an A4 sheet of paper and were rarely, if ever, seen by anyone other than the employers. The fact that a 'vehicle' was capable of being a 'workplace' for the purpose of the legislation, although noted by some, caused no great concern. In retrospect, it seems likely that there were insufficient enforcement staff, and that those enforcement officers that there were, were unclear as to the extent of their authority. Certain individual cases attracted the attention of the HSE but they tended to be accidents that were unusual, accidents that did not occur in the ordinary course of day-to-day business life. The current position is vastly changed. The transport industry is seen as a 'target' industry by the HSE, and regulatory controls increase at a dramatic rate.

7.40   The key factor in an effective health and safety regime is, of course, the carrying out of appropriate risk assessments. Not only does the operator of a transport company have a wide range of activities that will require assessment, but it will also be necessary to consider the work done by employees in the premises of customers who may well be located at a considerable distance form the main operating centre. This separation becomes extremely important where vehicles are loaded at customers premises. Insecure loads cause many accidents, and, from time to time, such accidents may result in a fatality. In the event of such an accident, not only would the employer be expected to be able to show that steps had been taken to determine the risks, but those who had loaded the vehicle would also be investigated.

7.41   It is clear that an employer might be reluctant to carry out a risk assessment in the case of a customer for whom work is either casual or, at best, very irregular. The duty does exist, however, and the employer must at least consider whether or not the nature of the load makes it possible that there will be unusual risks.

Corporate responsibility in the transport industry

7.42   The *Dukes* case[1] has underlined the fact that, in the transport industry at least, the concept of corporate responsibility is already established. Currently, in the context of the transport industry, this question of corporate responsibility will only become an issue in the course of a disciplinary inquiry. A disciplinary inquiry will be called as a result of either a number of convictions for serious offences or because the operator has received an unsatisfactory number of vehicle defect reports. Offences such as the falsification by drivers of their records, or a series of convictions arising from the use of defective vehicles or a series of convictions following the use of substantially overloaded vehicles. It is clear that, in all these cases, there are issues of public safety. The Traffic Commissioners have determined that the obligation to achieve safety can be delegated neither to external services, such as tachograph analysts, nor to a company's managers. This means that, in appropriate cases, not only may the company lose its licence, but its directors and transport managers may be denied the opportunity to continue to work in the industry. Although judges in criminal cases can exercise sanctions against directors under the Companies Act 1989 it can be argued that the sanctions available to the Traffic Commissioners go far beyond those that are presently available in the criminal courts.

1 *Dukes Transport (Craigavon) Ltd and the Vehicle Inspectorate* Transport Tribunal 68/2001. See PARA **7.19** above.

7.43 Prosecutions for manslaughter have already underlined the potential liability of a director, or senior company officer, of a transport undertaking and, as the creation of a corporate offence seems ever more likely, it is worth remembering that, in the transport industry, the potential for serious accident needs to be seen against a very wide base of opportunity for an accident. The workshop, the warehouse, the vehicle and the road and yard all provided opportunities for disaster. Each of these areas of work may be controlled by a manger who may have individual responsibility for a department or for a number of departments. It is also likely that part of the responsibility for control may have been delegated to a foreman, or to an outside contractor or consultant.

7.44 It is a truism to observe that human error will be a contributory factor in all accidents. The transport industry provides little opportunity for introducing electronic or other controls, which will reduce the opportunity for human involvement. That position has to be seen against an increasing determination by the legislators and courts to refuse to accept that human error can absolve management from responsibility.

Tachographs

7.45 Commercial vehicles with a Gross Vehicle Weight (GVW) of over 3.5 tonnes are required to produce a record of the vehicles' activity. This is normally achieved either by the driver keeping written records (domestic rules), or by using a tachograph. A tachograph is a piece of equipment that looks like, and functions as, a speedometer, but which keeps a record of the speed, distance travelled, and driving time, by marking traces on a waxed disc. The analysis of a tachograph record is a specialised task. Those who carry out this work need not only to be able to 'read' the chart as it comes from the tachograph in the vehicle, but also to understand whether or not there has been any breach of the drivers' hours regulations. They also need to be able to determine whether the speed limiter, if one is fitted, is working and whether or not, in any event, the driver has complied with the relevant speed limits.[1]

1 Council Regulation 3821/85/EEC, art 12ff.

7.46 The equipment needed to analyse a chart varies from a hand-held reader to free-standing, computer-based machines. Where an operator has only a small number of vehicles, a hand-held reader may be sufficient, provided that the person analysing the charts is competent. In a larger fleet, a computer-based machine may be essential, but the cost of the equipment, with the salary of the operator, may be too high. Transport operators may choose to avoid having to bear the cost of the equipment and the salaries of the trained operators by using consultants offering the service of tachograph analysis to any haulier who is prepared to pay the fees. In return, the haulier gets a written report, which highlights any offences that may have been committed by the driver.

7.47 Routinely, in the case of an RTA, the tachograph disc is being retained either by the police or the HSE, and examined, with discs for previous days if necessary, to see if the driver was driving at excessive speeds, or was, possibly, fatigued. In the

Bowles case,[1] it was the tachographs that provided the evidence to the prosecution. Given that, in a particular case, the operator has engaged the service of a tachograph analyst following a fatal RTA, and an examination of the chart discloses that the driver has driven for an excessive period of time, and that, for whatever reason, the offence has been missed by the analyst, where does that leave the company? On the view of the Traffic Commissioners, the delegation of the task affords no defence, and, as that is now the accepted view, the employers are likely to be found guilty and sanctioned on the basis of corporate responsibility. The argument of the Traffic Commissioner being to the effect that, had the company not delegated the task of analysing the charts, it would necessarily have discovered the driver's offence.

1   *R v Roy Bowles Transport* (October 1999, unreported). See **para 7.19** above.

Vehicles

7.48   The more sophisticated commercial vehicles become, the more opportunity there is for things to go wrong. Vehicle manufacturers would maintain, with every justification, that manufacturing standards have improved, but the fact remains that vehicle parts do fail. In certain types of work, perhaps the operation of a tipping vehicle on a landfill site, for example, the stress on the vehicle can be substantial.

7.49   An operator can become aware of a vehicle defect in two ways. In the first instance, the operator is required to have a system in place by which the driver can notify vehicle defects to the employer. Currently drivers are expected to make such a record on a daily basis, recording, if appropriate, the fact that nothing appears to be wrong: a so-called 'nil defect' report. The driver is also expected to carry out a check on the vehicle before it is taken on to the road.

7.50   In the second instance, the vehicle is required to be inspected by qualified mechanic at the declared intervals. These 'preventative maintenance inspections' are intended to pick up faults and also, perhaps more importantly, to identify potential problems. A common example would be wear on a part which does not require immediate attention, but which will require attention later.

7.51   The problem is that, even with a good system in place, a vehicle can fail. A tyre can 'blow out' on a motorway with disastrous results even though, on a routine examination, the tyre appeared to be good. A latent fault in a wheel bearing can have the same result. Periodic maintenance is routinely contracted out; indeed modern commercial vehicles are normally sold with a 'maintenance package' as part of the incentive to buy the vehicle. Clearly some failures can raise issues of 'product liability' and, as the doctrine of absolute management responsibility is extended, it may be that there will be prosecutions of those who have supplied a vehicle in which the failure of a part contributed to a fatal accident.

7.52   Whilst Traffic Commissioners require evidence of these systems, designed to confirm the safety of the vehicle, once again they will not readily accept delegation as a defence if something goes wrong. Unhappily it is not uncommon for drivers to fail to carry out the daily walk-round check. An early morning start in atrocious weather conditions may not be conducive to a full check, but if, as a result of that failure the driver fails to see an obvious fault, the Traffic Commissioner is likely to want to see persuasive evidence that strong disciplinary action was taken, before considering whether the employer has discharged the duty of care.

7.53 Mechanics employed by commercial garages that undertake the maintenance of vehicles can, and do, make mistakes. A mistake in the maintenance of a vehicle can lead to a serious accident but, yet again, the Traffic Commissioner will not accept that the operator can discharge the duty to have an effective maintenance system by contracting the maintenance out, however good the garage may appear to be. Curiously, whilst the practice of contracting out maintenance is increasing, the Vehicle Inspectorate, which is responsible for checking commercial vehicles, has no right to inspect garages who offer to undertake maintenance.

7.54 It follows from this that, if a disciplinary inquiry were to be called as the result of an apparent and serious failure of the maintenance systems put in place by an operator, not only might the licence be removed but, again, the directors and their nominated transport managers might 'lose their repute' for whatever period time the Traffic Commissioner considered to be appropriate.

7.55 Currently, delegation is virtually impossible.

Corporate responsibility

7.56 Under the existing law of manslaughter, it is clear that, whether or not it is appropriate to delegate a task, and whether or not the person to whom the task is delegated is competent, the direct line of causal responsibility will not be broken. Delegation can certainly amount to something approaching gross negligence, but nonetheless the prosecution has to show the direct causal link. This problem, if in fact it is a problem, has been the stumbling block that has frustrated the various recent attempts to prosecute company directors for 'manslaughter' There have been only five successful prosecutions of individuals in their role as a director and, in each of those cases, the direct link between the failure of the director and the accident has been clear. In the case of a large company with a complex management structure it is probably true to say that gross negligence by a controlling mind could never be established.

7.57 In the transport industry the concept of director's liability is already established. The view of the traffic commissioners is that their role, in ultimate terms, is to achieve public safety and, although this view has not been expressed, if delegation were to be capable of affording a defence, given the inevitability of delegation within the industry, it would be difficult, if not impossible to impose effective sanctions. In the face of evidence that a system has failed, the Traffic Commissioners proceed on the basis that the controlling minds of the company must be at fault. To that view has to be added the additional view that there must be corporate responsibility regardless of the actual function of the individual – a view that entirely accords with the intention of the proposed new legislation.

Enforcing bodies

7.58 The four authorities that have a direct control over transport operators are:

1   The police.
2   The Vehicle Inspectorate.
3   The Health and Safety Executive.
4   Trading Standards.

7.59   All of these agencies can prosecute. Additionally, the police and the Vehicle Inspectorate can report matters to the Traffic Commissioner who may decide to call a public inquiry.

Police

7.60   Only the police have the authority to require a moving vehicle to stop. Only the police can prosecute for moving traffic offences such as 'driving without due care and attention', or exceeding a speed limit. Other offences, such a breach of the Road Vehicles (Construction and Use) Regulations 1986,[1] which are prosecuted under the provisions of the Road Traffic Act 1988, may also be prosecuted by the Vehicle Inspectorate and, in the case of overloading offences, the Trading Standards authorities.

1   SI 1986/1078.

7.61   A new dimension has appeared in the way in which the police deal with RTAs, in that they now work with the HSE in appropriate cases. That is to say cases in which driver error may appear to have been the result of his or her working conditions, or cases in which the background systems, such as maintenance programmes, are faulty. The police appeared to see a clear dividing line between those cases that they should properly investigate, and those that were better left to the HSE. That has now changed and, whilst the police will continue to prosecute those cases in which they have traditionally been the prosecuting authority, they will involve the HSE at an early stage and will leave cases involving health and safety issues to the HSE, even if the police analyse the tachograph charts. A recent protocol[1] suggests that the CPS should make the decision as to who should prosecute. It must be remembered that an indictment for manslaughter does not preclude proceedings under HSWA 1974. Offences under HSWA 1974 can be prosecuted at the same time as related criminal offences. Prosecuting authorities are encouraged to consider, particularly in a case of manslaughter, whether it would be appropriate to issue separate proceedings under HSWA 1974, s 2 or 3. In appropriate cases there may well be a joint prosecution of course.

1   HSE *Work Related Deaths – A Protocol* (2002).
2   Goods Vehicles (Licensing of Operators) Act 1995, s 42.

Vehicle inspectorate

7.62   The Vehicle Inspectorate provides the main check on the condition of commercial vehicles and drivers' hours of work. It engages in police-assisted roadside checks, goes to operator's premises to examine both vehicle and drivers' records, and, like Trading Standards officers, weighs vehicles to confirm that they are not overloaded.

7.63   Not only can the Vehicle Inspectorate prosecute if it discovers breaches of the drivers' hours regulations made under the Transport Act 1968, but it can also prosecute under the provisions of the Road Traffic Act 1988[1] for construction and use offences. It has the power to prohibit the movement of a vehicle if, in the course of a roadside check, a serious defect is discovered, and it will check the suitability of an operator and the operator's premises at the direction of the Traffic Commissioner. These latter checks are normally required if there is to be a public inquiry, and will involve a physical inspection of one or more of the transport operator's vehicles, and a check of the maintenance and drivers records.

1 Goods Vehicles (Licensing of Operators) Act 1995, ss 40 and 41.

7.64 Not only can an adverse report from the vehicle inspector influence the Traffic Commissioner's decision, but, were there to be a written, and critical, report on the standards of maintenance, then, in the event of an investigation following a fatal accident, the report would be likely to have a direct bearing on a question of corporate responsibility.

7.65 Although there is an appeal procedure if the operator does not accept the decision of an inspector, in practice it has proved difficult to persuade the Inspectorate to review decisions. It has to be remembered that, in the event of a prosecution for corporate killing following an accident in which there has been a mechanical failure of a vehicle, the evidence of the vehicle inspector may be critical to the prosecution. The inadequacy of the existing appeal procedure may be extremely relevant.

7.66 Certain police officers are now authorised to check vehicles mechanically and they can, as can the Vehicle Inspectorate, prohibit the movement of vehicles if the mechanical defect is sufficiently serious. Additionally the Goods Vehicles (Licensing of Operators) Act 1995 gives them specific powers that match those given to the vehicle inspectors.

Health and Safety Executive

7.67 The health and safety legislation makes no distinction between the transport industry and any other industry. Although there are industry specific publications, such as 'Transport in The Workplace', the role of the HSE is common to all industrial activity. It has an unlimited power of access to premises during working hours, and may stop any activity perceived to be dangerous. It may take away any company records, and, surprisingly, not only is a person being interviewed given no right to legal representation, but the person being interviewed may not refuse to answer questions. In practice the HSE will normally allow a person being interviewed to be represented, but that is a matter of discretion. The HSE also publishes guides to good practice, which, in the event of a prosecution, may be used to demonstrate to the court both that guidance was available and also to underline the alleged breach of the regulations.

7.68 The employer's primary duty of care is to the employee, but also to any person who might be injured as a result of an employee's activity in the course of his or her work.[1]

1 HSWA 1974, ss 2 and 3.

7.69 The HSE has substantial technical resources, and an increasing use of those resources will be seen, as prosecutions become more and more frequent. Clearly some accidents, however serious the consequences, are simple. As the result of a vehicle being carelessly driven in a haulage yard, for instance, a person is injured. The issue of responsibility is likely to turn on questions of the steps taken to separate vehicles and pedestrians, and whether or not there is a policy that employees should wear high-visibility clothing, which is enforced. But where the accident follows mechanical failure, of whatever sort, it is inevitable that the prosecution will look for expert evidence, and that evidence is likely to be provided either by the HSE or the Vehicle Inspectorate.

7.70   One area of potential failure by an employer, which is specifically within the scope of the HSE, arises from the statutory requirement to carry out 'risk assessments' with a related 'safe system of work'.[1]

1   Management of Health and Safety at Work Regulations 1999, SI 1999/3242, reg 3.

7.71   There can be no acceptable excuse for a failure to have risk assessments available covering hazardous activities at employer's premises. Equally, where the assessed risk requires action, there should be the relevant written 'safe system of work'. The transport industry faces a specific problem because much of the work undertaken by a company's employees is carried out elsewhere than at the employer's premises. This problem may be exacerbated by the fact that certain work may be done on an irregular basis; indeed a particular job may be the simple result of a casual request that is not likely to be repeated.

7.72   When a particular trip is regular, then there should be a risk assessment at the customer's premises. Additionally the employer should have obtained copies of the relevant health and safety documentation from the customer. Safety at other premises has to be assessed by the employee, usually a driver, who must either have been trained to carry out a risk assessment or who will have been sufficiently trained to recognise the risk and to seek assistance. The Management of Health and Safety at Work Regulations 1999[1] set out the test for 'competence' in the context of risk assessments. A person will be deemed to be competent if he or she, viewed objectively, would be considered to have sufficient skill, ability, and experience, to justify a description as 'competent'. In some cases the nature of the load to be collected or delivered will put the employer on notice that there is likely to be a particular risk and, in such a case, the employer will be responsible for ensuring that an assessment is carried out by a 'competent person'.

1   SI 1999/3242, reg 3.

7.73   The HSE properly attach a great deal of importance to an employer's ability to produce up-to-date risk assessments. Certainly, in the event of an accident, the written risk assessment is likely to be the first document the employer is required to produce. Again, in the context of the transport industry, this can be a substantial administrative burden, particularly for those companies engaged in general haulage, dealing with a variety of customers and loads. The law is, however, clear and, if there is no risk assessment, an employer is very vulnerable.

7.74   Whenever there is an accident at work, or which arises as a consequence of activity within the scope of a persons employment, the HSE officers will consider whether to not to prosecute in accordance with the Health and Safety Commission's Policy Statement on Enforcement.[1]

1   HSC15 01/02 C250.

Risk analysis

7.75   HSWA 1974 recognised the employer's duty to protect its employees against risk, but did not introduce the concept of risk assessment. 'Risk' was merely one of the potential hazards against which employees were to be protected. 'Risk Assessment' as a defined activity arrived with the 'six pack' in 1992.[1] Since that time the importance of risk assessment has increased to the extent that it has become the 'corner stone' of all safety issues. The problem with all accident investigation is that, with hindsight, any accident could have been avoided. It necessarily follows that, following an accident, it is possible to identify the risk assessment that, had it been made, might have anticipated the circumstances in which the accident occurred.

1   The regulations are: the Management of Health and Safety at Work Regulations, now the Management of Health and Safety at Work Regulations 1999, SI 1999/3242; the Workplace (Health, Safety and Welfare) Regulations 1992, SI 1992/3004; the Personal Protective Equipment at Work Regulations 1992, SI 1992/2966; the Provision and Use of Work Equipment Regulations, now the Provision and Use of Work Equipment Regulations 1998, SI 1998/2306; the Manual Handling Operations Regulations 1992, SI 1992/2793; and the Health and Safety (Display Screen Equipment) Regulations 1992, SI 1992/2792.
2   HSWA 1974, s 1.
3   Management of Health and Safety at Work Regulations 1999, SI 1999/3242. Regulation 3 creates the duty of an employer to 'make a suitable and sufficient assessment of: (a) the risks to the health and safety of his employees to which they are exposed whilst they are at work; and (b) the risk to the health and safety of persons not in his employment arising out of or in connection with the conduct by him of his undertaking'. A similar duty is imposed by reg 3(2) on self-employed people.

7.76   As there is an enforceable duty to carry out a risk assessment, enforcement authorities, many of whom appear to be motivated by performance targets, appear to have seen this primary duty as an opportunity to prosecute, whatever the circumstances of the accident may be. The very fact of the accident suggesting, as it does, that either there had been no assessment, or that the assessment was flawed.

7.77   It has to be remembered that offences prosecuted under HSWA 1974, ss 2 and 3 are deemed to be 'absolute offences'. Although there is a statutory defence if it can be established that it was not 'reasonably practical' to avoid the risk, the defence is extremely difficult to maintain. An argument to the effect that it was not reasonably practical to avoid circumstances that led to a serious or fatal accident is bound to be unattractive. This approach to the duty of an employer colours the whole of the legislation, and, in particular, makes it effectively impossible to justify the absence of a risk assessment however improbable the circumstances may be.

1   *R v British Steel PLC* [1995] ICR 587. The Court of Appeal held that HSWA 1974, s 2(1) imposed absolute criminal liability. They specifically found that delegation of a task would not afford a defence.
2   Where the prosecution allege that a risk assessment is inadequate, they must give details of the inadequacy: *Heeremac VOF v Munro* 1999 SLT 492, HCJ Appeal (Scotland).

7.78   It is the variety of work that a transport operator is likely to undertake that creates the problem. Risk assessments, of course, can be generic. Repeated activity will normally require only one assessment, unless there is some change in the system, or some new information received, which makes a review necessary. In any event an assessment should follow the introduction of any new process and, in the context of this duty to assess, any new customer, load or loading method, will require an assessment.

7.79   This is a substantial administrative responsibility for any employer, but, for the transport operator, the responsibility is huge. It requires an ability to recognise a situation in which an assessment is required, and, of course, the ability to carry out the assessment. It is common practice for companies to seek the assistance of consultants to carry out risk assessments, although delegation in this way may create its own problems. Many employers, however, prefer to use the skill of an expert rather than to rely on their on competence. Where the undertaking is confined to a fixed site or sites, the use of consultants may well be appropriate. Where assessments may be required to be carried out on a random, and possibly a daily, basis, the use of outside agencies may not be effective when considering the necessary speed of response to the new situation.

7.80   The format of a risk assessment is simple. Identify the date and location of the assessment; identify the activity being carried out; determine whether or not there is risk; evaluate the degree of risk; and then confirm the steps that need to be taken to remove or reduce the risk if the degree of risk requires action. Normally, a risk assessment in which a risk is identified will be followed by a written 'safe system of work', or 'method statement', which will set out the manner in which a task or activity may be safely carried out. Put in these terms it might seem that the responsibility for producing an assessment is not great. Most people working in an undertaking would feel able to recognise a hazard. The apparent simplicity of the process is deceptive.

7.81   The key skill needed by those required to carry out a risk assessment is the ability to evaluate the degree of risk being created by the work under review. Only an accurate assessment of the degree of risk will enable an employer to determine what steps should be taken to remove or mitigate the risk. In many cases of accident a risk assessment has been carried out and a 'safe system of work' produced. This should mean that, unless an instruction has not been obeyed, the accident could not occur, but, sometimes, accidents do follow a risk assessment. Faced with the situation in which, notwithstanding an assessment, someone is injured, the enforcement agencies will look for a weakness in the assessment. Given that an accident has occurred, of course, it is likely to be comparatively easy to see where the weakness in the assessment occurred. The primary potential for error, therefore, lies in the need to evaluate the risk.

7.82   In the transport industry particularly, managers are normally drawn from those who have had experience in the industry. Whilst the experience makes for good management, it also means that many decisions are subjective. In the context of risk assessment, however, subjective decisions must be avoided as objectivity is critically important to adequate assessment. Risk assessments, whether carried out in-house or by external consultants, should always be reviewed before they become part of an employer's health and safety regime.

7.83   The need to follow established procedures in respect of activities involving risk will not remove the requirement for transport operators to carry out an assessment. Every time a vehicle goes on a public road, whether a coach or a goods vehicle, there is the potential for, say, a defect in the controlling mechanisms of the vehicle to cause a serious accident. The requirements for a grant of an 'operator's licence' include an ability to demonstrate that adequate steps have been taken to ensure that the mechanical condition is properly supervised and maintained. It might be thought that the existence of an appropriate system of maintenance, with the relevant records, might be a sufficient recognition of the existence of risk with, more importantly, an approved method statement drawn from the requirements of the legislation.

7.84 In practice, however good the maintenance system, it would not avoid the need for a risk assessment. The assessor would be expected to consider the risks that might be associated with the work of the mechanics, and to ensure that a system of work was in place which would avoid the possibility of error – the potential risk being of danger either to the driver, or to any other person who might be affected by the condition of the vehicle, whether another motorist, passenger or pedestrian.

7.85 This problem for the transport industry is exaggerated by the fact that vehicle parts can, and do, break in the course of a journey. The question will then be whether or not the latent defect that led to the accident should have been detected, and, if it was not, whether or not the system of work drawn up after the assessment was adequate.[1] Obviously, if the defect was there for all to see, the assessment would be manifestly inadequate.

1 *R v Crown Prosecution Service, ex p Waterworth* [1996] COD 277, QBD: 'The fundamental question was where the fault lay. Were it to have been some unidentified mechanic who was primarily to blame a jury might be reluctant to convict P and E for their secondary culpability.'

7.86 As has been seen, it is the variety of opportunity for disaster that makes the transport industry so vulnerable. Even compared with the construction and agricultural industries, whose accident rates are high, looking at comparative activities it is arguable that the transport industry is at greater risk. Whatever view may be taken of the legislative burden, it is clear that risk assessment and risk analysis must be given priority.

The EU impact

7.87 The transport industry has clearly, and predictably, been identified as an area in which harmonisation between member states is essential. The majority of goods that are moved within the EU are moved by commercial vehicles, and the intention of the EC would be defeated if transport operators were able to obtain a benefit over their competitors as the result of beneficial domestic legislation. This is particularly true when the control of drivers' hours, and the technical requirements of the vehicles, is concerned, as an operator prepared to take 'short cuts' can make substantial cost savings in these areas.

7.88 As the result of this drive towards harmonisation the European Council has issued a large number of Directives[1] which member states are required to incorporate into their domestic legislation. These Directives deal not only with such things as the hours that a goods or passenger vehicle driver may work and the method of keeping those records, but also with technical standards which deal with a wide variety of matters including such things as sound and exhaust emission levels, spray suppression and light-signalling devices, and rear registration plate lamps for motor vehicles and their trailers.

1 Council Directive 70/220/EEC; Council Directive 91/226/EEC; Commission Directive 97/31/EC.

7.89 The problem for the UK operator arises from the fact that each of these directives sets new standards which have to be met. This, in turn, creates new offences under the Road Vehicles (Construction and Use) Regulations 1986.[1] Each of these offences may not only result in criminal proceedings, but a breach of a regulation may also be material to prosecutions under the health and safety legislation. It is said that, considering the levels of enforcement in the UK compared with those in other EU countries, these directives are 'gold plated' in the UK, but it seems unlikely that the enforcement policy will change.

1   SI 1986/1078

7.90   Whilst this is not the place to explore the cultural differences between the member states of the EU, it is worth observing that there does appear to be a different attitude towards enforcement between states. An element of discretion, exercised by enforcing authorities, goes a long way towards mitigating a regime that may otherwise be seen as being unduly harsh. The perception of the haulage industry in the UK is that there is no discretion, and that the proliferation of legislative control is making the running of a successful business increasingly difficult. This attitude is contrasted with the position in other member states were there appears to be an element of discretion.

7.91   The impact of the EU on the transport industry can properly be described as dramatic. Currently almost every legislative control is founded on an EC Directive. Those responsible for the introduction of these Directives maintain that the justification for the extraordinary number of these Directives is not just the search for harmonisation, it is also the need to improve the safety in operation of commercial vehicles. The consequence of all this is that any conviction for a breach of a regulation may form part of the prosecution case which follows on a serious accident. As the number of potential offences increases, so does the pressure on those who operate commercial vehicles.

Corporate killing and the transport industry

7.92   The underlying public anxiety about the use of commercial vehicles on public roads surfaced in 1993, following an accident at Sowerby Bridge when a lorry, with a 'grossly defective braking system' ran out of control down a steep hill causing the death of six people. The public, encouraged by the tabloid press, were determined that the directors of the company should be called to account as individuals. The fact that the company was prosecuted, and convicted, for the construction and use offence of using a vehicle with defective brakes was no consolation, nor was the fact that two of the directors were disqualified from holding office in the transport industry for periods of three years and one year respectively by the Traffic Commissioner.[1]

1   *R v Crown Prosecution Service, ex p Waterworth* [1996] COD 277, QBD.

7.93   Notwithstanding the substantial public pressure, the Crown Prosecution Service was satisfied that there was insufficient evidence to found a case for involuntary manslaughter against the directors, and declined to prosecute. A private application for a judicial review, was denied by the appeal court on the grounds that 'in order to succeed on a charge of corporate manslaughter the acts or omissions relied upon would need to be coextensive with what could be alleged against (the offender) in a personal capacity'.

7.94   Despite the increasing reference to the offence of 'corporate manslaughter', the term may be new, but the law is not. Manslaughter, which is dealt with elsewhere in this book, is, necessarily, an offence committed by an individual, or by individuals. To obtain a conviction you must be able to show a direct causal link between the act or omission of an individual, whether coextensively with another or not, and the fatality.

1   *R v Crown Prosecution Service, ex p Waterworth* [1996] COD 277, QBD.
2   *R v Great Western Trains Co Ltd* [2000] QB 796. Held: there was no evidence that the courts in their recent decisions had started to move from identification to personal liability as a basis for corporate liability or manslaughter. In relation to the rule of attribution, the courts had considered that the 'directing mind and will' applied, thereby affirming the existence of the identification theory.

7.95   Recent cases have demonstrated that there is no difficulty in obtaining the conviction of a director for manslaughter provided that the required link between that director and the death can be established. The term 'corporate manslaughter' is, at the moment, used to identify the role of the accused in his or her capacity as a director. Despite the increasing use of the term, the fact remains that a 'corporation' has no mind of its own and, therefore, cannot commit a crime which, above all, requires either that a decision is made or is not made. The term is used by the public, and the press, to enable them to articulate their perception that 'directors' are avoiding conviction, but the use is misleading.

1   *R v Roy Bowles Transport Ltd* (October 1999, unreported). In this case the two directors were convicted of manslaughter following an accident which resulted in two deaths as a result of the driver going to sleep whilst driving an articulated vehicle. In the course of the case it was said that: 'The two directors were grossly negligent because they knew, or ought to have known, that Cox [the driver] was in a dangerously defective state because he was working excessive hours.'
2   *R v Jackson's Transport (Ossett) Ltd* (November 1996). The Managing Director of the company was jailed for 12 months following the death of a company employee. The judge, Gerald Coles QC, in the course of his sentence observed that the Managing Director 'was, in every sense, the company'.

7.96   The reality of 'day-to day' commercial life is that company directors will commonly have different responsibilities. A financial director, for instance, may have no input into operational decisions made by a company unless matters of cost are involved. This means that, as the law presently stands, it is entirely probable that following a fatal accident some directors would not be convicted, as the prosecution would be unable to establish the causal link. This is particularly true where a company has intervening layers of management. A workshop foreman, reporting to a transport manager, reporting to the operations director, would be a common management structure in the transport industry. Each of those positions requires that the holder takes decisions and, if that responsibility has been properly delegated to a competent person with the appropriate training, there is, at the moment no reason why an error by, say, the workshop foreman, should be deemed to be the decision of the transport manager or operations director, even if that error results in a fatal accident. Equally, in a case in which a traffic manager sends out a vehicle which is overloaded or carrying too many passengers, and the vehicle is involved in a fatal accident, in circumstances which allow the prosecution to suggest that the overloaded condition of the vehicle contributed to the accident, perhaps because the brakes did not stop the vehicle as they should, the traffic manager may be responsible. His or her decision to allow the vehicle to go out in an overloaded condition might be so careless as to amount to gross negligence but, unless the person at the next stage of management can be shown to have contributed to the decision, either by action or inaction, they would not be prosecuted.

7.97   As a matter of criminal law, therefore, proper delegation may well afford an individual, or a corporation, a defence. A position directly contrary to that which presently appertains in the context of operators' licensing, where delegation is unlikely to afford a defence.

1   *Dukes Transport (Craigavon) Ltd and the Vehicle Inspectorate* Transport Tribunal 68/2001. See PARA **7.19** above.

7.98   The proposed legislation will introduce corporate, as opposed to individual, responsibility. Put another way, one director's error will be treated as if it were the error of each of the individuals who make up the board. The standard of behaviour, against which an individual's error will be measured, will no longer be a test as to whether or not there was 'gross negligence', but will be something less than that. The degree of negligence that will be required before a court will find the offence proved remains to be established by the courts in their decisions.

7.99   It is difficult to find words that are adequate to describe the problems that will have to be faced by the transport industry without sounding either alarmist or paranoid. The truth is, however, that, under the proposed legislation, any fatal accident could lead to prosecution of the board. Given that, with hindsight, the cause of any accident can be determined, and given that such a determination is likely to point to an unsafe system of work, and given that the absence of a written method statement, or the existence of an inadequate method statement, is an offence, it might be seen as an open invitation to the enforcement authorities to prosecute.

7.100   To take but one example. A major risk of accident arises from the need to reverse a vehicle. In warehouses and bus or coach stations, and on construction sites, it is common practice to have a 'banksman'. Someone to watch the rear of the vehicle as the manoeuvre is carried out. The vast majority of commercial vehicles and coaches do not carry a 'second man' as the cost implications would be prohibitive. It is, on the other hand, clearly correct to observe that, if there were to be a 'banksman' available on every occasion that a vehicle reversed, a number of accidents would be avoided. In those circumstances, and in the event of an accident caused by reversing, it may be that a director, with operational responsibility, would be considered to have failed in his or her duty of care by not providing a 'banksman'.

1   Many vehicles are fitted with alarms that operate when a vehicle is reversing. Curiously, whilst the HSE see these alarms as being essential in the contest of safety, the Road Vehicles (Construction and Use) Regulations 1986, SI 1986/1078 do not require them to be fitted. The decision not to make the fitting of an alarm of this sort mandatory apparently reflects concern about the confusion and noise that would be created when many vehicles were reversing at the same time, perhaps, for example, when supermarket deliveries are being made.
2   A case involving the absence of a 'banksman' was considered at Chester Crown before Mr Justice Holland: *R v H J lea Oakes Millers Ltd* T20017049/7051, 24 July 2001, Chester Crown Court. The decision is important for two reasons, first, because it does deal with the need to provide a 'banksman' and, secondly, and more importantly, because the judge reviews the law in relation to corporate manslaughter. The short circumstances are that a driver, B, in the course of a reversing manoeuvre out of premises onto a public road, ran over and killed, a pedestrian. A director, J, and the company, M, were charged with manslaughter. The charge being based on the allegation that J, knowing of the risk involved in the manoeuvre carried out by B, failed to take any or adequate steps to control the risk. Upholding a submission on the part of J that there was no case to answer and referring in passing to part of the judgment in *R v Adomako* [1994] 3 All ER 79 at 86 the judge said:
   '... on what basis are the jury to evaluate J's conduct? I should at least be able in summing up to explain why it is said to be so gross as to be criminal and so as to take it out of the ordinary rut of negligence, and thereby identify the area for their judgement. In the event

there is nothing that has been adduced which begins to suggest that which I have carefully identified in this course of this ruling was criminal and I therefore cannot give that advice. In that way there is a test on the finding that I make thus far. Further I am not satisfied that there is available to the jury evidence upon which they could be sure and satisfied that any negligence on J's part was a substantial cause of [the pedestrian's] death. Manifest negligence which involves 'permitting' does not readily result in 'causing'. The driver may have been permitted to reverse by J's negligence but he was hardly caused to do so ...'

7.101 Taking another example, consider a vehicle being involved in an accident as the apparent result of driver error. Increasingly we see the Vehicle Inspectorate being called out to assist a police investigation into the cause of an accident. In the event of a defect being found in the vehicle they might choose to issue a PG9[1] which, in turn, might lead to the prosecution of the director responsible for the mechanical condition of the vehicle if it could be suggested that the defect had contributed to the accident. The Health and Safety Inspectorate might also investigate the background of the driver to see if there was any evidence of fatigue or drug abuse. Both matters for which an employer has responsibility.

1 A PG9 is a prohibition notice that may be issued either by a vehicle inspector or by certain authorised police officers. The notice will specify the defect that has been found and may either have 'immediate' effect, in which case the vehicle may not be moved until the defect is cured, or it may be 'delayed', requiring the defect to be remedied within a specified period of time.

7.102 In the case of fatigue it is worth noting that a simple compliance with drivers' hours legislation will never be enough. Different types of work are more fatiguing than others, and, on a day-to-day basis, individual employees may be more prone to fatigue than on other days. An examination of the tachograph record might disclose driving conditions that are obviously likely to tire a driver. The employer is required to be aware of the impact of varying types of work, and also to be aware of the daily condition of employees in terms of their fitness for work. Employees must feel able to advise the employer if they feel that their ability to work is affected by fatigue. The point being that if, in the course of an accident investigation, members of staff tell the investigating officers that it was well known that a fellow employee involved in the accident was prone to fatigue, the company directors clearly have problems if they cannot show that steps had been taken to avoid the possible dangers arising from the fatigue of that employee.

7.103 In each of the two examples that have been considered, all the directors would be at risk of prosecution under the proposed legislation if it were to be established that at least one director is at fault. The risk of accident associated with reversing is well known. An investigating officer would want to see the 'risk assessment' dealing with this manoeuvre, and would want to see evidence of training. More importantly the investigating officer would want to see an unbroken chain of responsible action finishing with the director having responsibility for health and safety. In the event of a break in that chain, then the person responsible for the break, with any superior management involved in the health and safety process would be faced with the possibility of prosecution.

7.104 The second example, looking at a defect in a vehicle discovered by a vehicle inspector after an accident, highlights perhaps the most difficult area for a company operating transport, from a health and safety point of view. Clearly a defect found after an accident may have been caused by the accident. That is a question of fact. Where a defect is found that appears to have existed before the accident, the question is whether or not that defect *contributed* to the accident. The defect does not have to have caused the accident. A good example of this type of situation might arise if the brakes were found to have low efficiency; a level of efficiency that was measured at, say, 4% below the required performance. It seems quite clear that the probability is that such a defect will be followed by an investigation into the employer's systems. An investigation which might well be followed by a prosecution.

7.105   The reality is that, in cases of this sort, the operator may well have systems in place that appear to comply with the requirements of the legislation. When those systems are balanced against the incompetence of the reversing driver or the failure of some part of the vehicle it requires no huge flight of fancy to move to a position from which it can be argued that the systems were less than adequate. That inadequacy, of course, if it exists, could derive from the systems themselves, or from an error, whether serious or not, committed by the person to whom the task of driving or repairing, the vehicle had been delegated.

7.106   In those cases in which the fault is the result of human error, it is critically important that an employer should be able to show, by written records, that disciplinary action was taken. The disciplinary action taken must match the actual offence. A court will not be impressed if, for a breach of any health and safety regulation, or of an employers safety rules which, on any test, given the serious nature of the breach, should have resulted in equally serious disciplinary action, including dismissal, the employee is given nothing more than an oral warning.

7.107   All this needs to be seen in the light of the proposed standard of behaviour against which a question of corporate killing is to be measured. The test is intended to be whether or not the failure of either the corporation or an officer 'constitutes conduct falling far below what can reasonably be expected of the (corporation) in the circumstances'. Given the clear drive to establish corporate responsibility, the position of the transport operator, whose vehicle is involved in a serious accident as the result of a parts failure, is not good. The prosecution argument will be to the effect that proper preventative maintenance would have avoided the failure, and, of course, with hindsight that is not an easy argument to gainsay. The position is worsened by the fact that delegation may not afford a defence if the trend in terms of operator's licensing is followed.

1   Corporate Homicide Bill, s 1(1)(b) (April 2000).

7.108   The position of the individual officer is caught by the proposal that any officer will be guilty of the offence of corporate killing if a death is the result of 'management failure'. 'Management failure' is defined in this way: 'there is a management failure by a corporation if the way in which its activities are managed or organised fails to ensure the health and safety of persons employed in or affected by those activities and such a failure may be regarded as the cause of a persons death notwithstanding that the immediate cause is the act or omission of an individual.'[1]

1   Corporate Homicide Bill, s 2(1) and (2).

7.109   There may prove to be a conflict between the evidential requirements of Corporate Homicide Bill, s 2(1)(b) and (2)(a). The phrase 'falling far below what can reasonably be expected ...' and the phrase 'fails to ensure the health and safety of ...' would appear to raise very different standards of care. Doing the best one can with the language is it clear that the proposed standard, against which the decision to prosecute will be taken, falls far below the test of 'gross negligence'. Considering the case of *H J Lea Oakes Miller Ltd*[1] it seems entirely probable that, were J to have been prosecuted for corporate homicide, he would have been convicted. It is arguable that, if as the result of an accident arising either in the course of employment or as the result of the employment of another, a fatality occurs, the employer must have failed in his or her duty to ensure the health and safety of the deceased.

1   *R v H J lea Oakes Millers Ltd* T20017049/7051, 24 July 2001, Chester Crown Court. See **para 7.100 n 2** above.

7.110   The terminology used suggests that the proposed legislation is yet another attempt to create an absolute offence. That, at least, would be consistent with the main sections of HSWA 1974.

7.111   On this analysis of the proposed legislation it would seem that the public demand for action to be taken against individual directors will be met. As the majority of cases that have attracted this type of public response involve commercial vehicles, whether carrying goods or passengers, it may be thought that only an exceptionally brave person would want to be the director of a haulage company. Looking again at the language of the Corporate Homicide Bill in its outline, a director may avoid prosecution. Under the health and safety legislation the ability of a driver to drive safely is a matter for the employer, as is the competence of a mechanic. Under the existing legislation an error by an employee may not attract the quality of guilt by an employer which might be said to amount to gross negligence, but if, with the benefit of hindsight it is possible to see that more training or more or better equipment might have avoided the accident, the director's cause would appear to be lost.

Conclusions

7.112   Despite appearances to the contrary, the transport industry is not alone in having a high accident record. The agricultural and construction industries also have high accident rates. A look at the index of HSE publications clearly shows how much effort is being put into the regulation of accident control in each of these industries. The transport industry, however, suffers from the fact that any serious accident involving a commercial vehicle or coach is likely to receive national coverage in the press. A farm accident or an accident on a construction site, even if fatal, may only be reported in a local newspaper, if at all. As a result of this 'spotlighting' the relationship of the transport industry with the public is not good and is exacerbated by the fact that, as people go about their daily lives, whether as pedestrians, cyclists or drivers, both lorries and buses are always in close proximity giving rise to a constant apprehension of danger.

7.113   This fact has been recognised by the politicians who, in a constant search for votes, are reluctant to be associated with any lobby which appears to support the transport industry, and who, conversely, will give enthusiastic support to schemes which, for instance, control the movement of commercial vehicles in town centres. The coach and bus industries are more fortunate because, of course, they provide both public transport and holiday travel, and, therefore, present a less attractive political target. Those in the industry are aware that standards of maintenance and standards of effective control of drivers' hours are no better in the bus and coach industry than in the commercial vehicle industry, but that is not the public perception. That public perception is echoed by the press, who may continue to run a story involving a commercial vehicle when a story involving a bus or coach would have disappeared from the pages.

7.114   There is no doubt but that the Corporate Homicide Bill was the result of the public outcry that followed the 'Sowerby Bridge' accident.[1] The public were encouraged, primarily by the tabloid press, to believe that the law was flawed in that the directors of the company that operated the vehicle were not to be prosecuted. The public were misled. Had there been any persuasive evidence to link one or more of the directors to the cause of the accident, so as to enable the prosecution to allege conduct that amounted to gross negligence, the directors concerned could, and no doubt would, have been prosecuted. The facts, as they subsequently appeared, made it clear that no director could have been prosecuted for the criminal offence of manslaughter on that basis.

1 *R v Crown Prosecution Service, ex p Waterworth* [1996] COD 277, QBD. See PARA **7.92** above.

7.115   The question that has to be asked is whether or not it is in either the public interest or the interests of justice that the law should be changed to enable a company officer, whose duties are unconnected with daily operations, to be prosecuted. Unhappily, the answer to that question appears to be that, if that is the wish of the public, then so be it.

7.116   In all of this discussion it appears that the sanctions contained in HSWA 1974 have been forgotten. In the 'Sowerby Bridge' case[1] it would appear that the HSE inspectors were not allowed to investigate the circumstances of the accident. Had they been able to investigate it seems possible that charges would have been brought under HSWA 1974 against the company and, perhaps, some individuals. On conviction a Crown Court may impose an unlimited financial penalty, with up to two years' imprisonment – sanctions which are repeated in the Corporate Homicide Bill, save only that, on the indictment of an individual, the term of imprisonment is not defined. It is certainly possible that, had the public seen prosecutions brought under HSWA 1974, there would not have been the outcry that led to the present position.

1 *R v Crown Prosecution Service, ex p Waterworth* [1996] COD 277, QBD. See para **7.92** above.
2 HSWA 1974, s 2 sets out the duty of an employer to employees. HSWA 1974, s 3 deals with the employer's duty to persons not in his or her employment.
3 HSWA 1974, s 33 sets out the various offences that may be committed under the Act with the relevant sanctions.

7.117   There has been, of course, a change in the role of the inspectors working for the HSE. In 1993, when the 'Sowerby Bridge' incident occurred, multi-agency investigations were unknown. Currently the HSE is required to investigate serious road traffic accidents, and the police will initiate requests for assistance with health and safety issues following an accident. The Enforcement Policy Statement published by the HSC requires the investigator to have 'knowledge of the duty holder's past health and safety performance, and also, to consider the 'wider relevance of the event, including serious public concern'.[1] Later, in the same document, those circumstances which might be expected to result in prosecution are set out. The list includes a suggestion that prosecution should follow where 'the gravity of an alleged offence, taken with the seriousness of any actual or potential harm, or the general record and approach if the offender warrants it'.

1 HSC15 01/02 C250, paras 33 and 39.
2 *R v F Howe and Son (Engineers) Ltd* [1999] 2 All ER 249: 'In our judgement magistrates should always think carefully before accepting jurisdiction in health and safety at work cases,

where it is arguable that the fine may exceed the limit of their jurisdiction or where death or serious injury has resulted from the offence.'

7.118 In these circumstances it may well be argued that the decision to put the Corporate Homicide Bill before Parliament cannot be justified unless political expediency justifies legislation that is otherwise unnecessary.

7.119 To the transport industry, in the light of the operational difficulties that have been discussed, the proposed legislation may well prove to be the final straw, if the cliché may be excused. Take an accident in which a commercial vehicle is involved and which results in a fatality, as a starting point. Broadly, there will be one of four possible causes: driver error, vehicle failure, inadequate load security and the fault of a third party, being, of course, someone other than the driver of a commercial vehicle.

7.120 In a case of driver error, and given a determined investigator, it is likely that it will always be possible to suggest that the responsibility is with the management. It may be said that, whether or not the driver held an appropriate licence, there had been insufficient or inadequate training. It may be said that, whether or not the driver had exceeded the permitted driver's hours regulations, the employer should have anticipated that the driver was fatigued. In the event that the driver was found to have excess blood alcohol, or to be under the influence of drugs then the employer must either have failed to have adequate personal checks in place, or, if there were such checks, have failed to operate them correctly.

7.121 In the event of an accident being caused by, or contributed to by, the failure of, say, a tyre or some other vehicle part, then clearly the company's maintenance systems were at fault. Systems which must include the competence of any fitter who was responsible for checking or fitting the part that failed, and any driver who failed adequately to inspect the vehicle at the beginning of the working day.

7.122 In the case of an accident resulting from an insecure load, or the failure of load restraints, then again the finger of suspicion will point to inadequate driver training. When coach or bus passengers are injured because they are not using seatbelts, or because the bus is overloaded, issues of driver training once again come to the fore.

7.123 Even when it is the driving of a third party that is substantially to blame for an accident, questions about the driver's ability are likely to be asked.

7.124 In each of these cases there is the possibility that, with hindsight, an investigator dealing with a fatal accident would be able to say that if there had been better training or better supervision at more frequent intervals, the accident would not have occurred. Is it not, therefore, inevitable that such a failure would be seen as a failure by a corporation to manage or organise its activities to ensure the health and safety of persons employed in, or affected by, those activities. Is it not inevitable that such a failure must amount to conduct falling far below what might reasonably expected of a corporation in the circumstances. In the event that those rhetorical questions attract an affirmative answer then, of course, both the company and the directors, as individuals, would be guilty of corporate killing.

1 Corporate Homicide Bill, ss 1 and 2.

7.125   Given the likelihood of a fatal accident in the course of operating a transport undertaking one might go further and ask whether any lawyer could, in the light of the proposed legislation, justify advising a client either to accept the offer of a directorship in a haulage company or to continue in the post of director. In the latter case the risk would be particularly high if the director in question did not have some degree of operational control. Clearly these comments apply to other risk industries but, looking at the transport industry, it is difficult to see how continuing and profitable management will be maintained.

CHAPTER 8

Corporate liability in the aviation industry

John Abramson, Solicitor[1]

1   I am indebted to Stephen Rosen, aviation partner at London law firm Collyer-Bristow, for reading an early draft of this chapter, and for his comments and encouragement.

Introduction

8.1   In the late 1950s, the fatal accident rate for passenger jet aircraft was more than one per 5 million flights (5×10^{-6}). This reduced to one per one million (1×10^{-6}) in 1980 and is currently below 0.4×10^{-6}. The rate is still reducing. The current average number of accidents worldwide involving large civil aircraft is about 30 per year.

8.2   The international aviation industry has an institutionalised safety culture that is not replicated in any other transport industry sector. Much of this safety culture derives from an intensely developed international legal framework, which mandates co-operation between states, international organisations, national authorities and private companies to achieve global uniformity of standards and practices.

8.3   The UK has an enviable recent safety record with a zero fatal accident rate for fixed-wing passenger aircraft in 2002.[1] It remains the case that no UK aviation organisation has been charged with corporate manslaughter.

1   CAA *Corporate Plan 2003* (2003) Appendix 1.

8.4 The aviation industry as a whole demonstrates an international proactive approach to safety management. This is based on the fundamental principle that detailed investigation into the cause of accidents will ultimately prevent further accidents. There is a strongly held view that the threat of criminal prosecution following accidents may hinder the post-accident learning process.[1]

1 See eg the testimonies to the US House of Representatives Subcommittee on Aviation: Hearing. on the Trend towards Criminalization of Aircraft Accidents, 27 July 2000.

8.5 The civil aviation industry faces challenges posed by growing traffic, new technology, a changing commercial and regulatory framework, awareness of environmental issues and a constant need for investment in infrastructure. In recent years, safety issues have been subjected to public and media scrutiny. There is a resultant public perception that corporations, including aviation organisations, may rationalise expenditure on safety to maximise profitability. The criminalisation of accidents, including aviation accidents, is similarly perceived as a deterrent to further corporate malpractice. This view is countered by a unified response from aviation professionals that the regulatory system of the industry provides sufficient inherent deterrents to unsafe conduct without the added threat of sanction under the general criminal law.

International regulation of aviation safety

Development[1]

8.6 In the early years of aviation an International Air Conference was convened in Paris in 1910, attended by representatives of 18 European states. Although a number of basic principles governing aviation were decided, there was no agreement on a binding code of international air law.

1 For more comprehensive details, see www.icao.int/index.cfm, last visited on 1 May 2003.

8.7 At the end of the First World War, the need for the international regulation of air transport became even more apparent. The war had left Europe with a collection of proven aircraft and trained pilots ready to adapt their skills to peaceful purposes. In 1919, civil air transport enterprises commenced international operations for the carriage of passengers and airmail between Paris and London, and Paris and Brussels. Additionally in June 1919, Alcock and Brown made the first West-East crossing of the North Atlantic from Newfoundland to Ireland and the 'R-34', a British dirigible, made a round trip flight from Scotland to New York.

8.8 The consideration of matters relating to international aviation was a subject at the Paris Peace Conference of 1919. An Aeronautical Commission was convened consistent with the objective of international collaboration in aviation matters in the context of the new peace in Europe.

8.9 The result was the Paris Convention 1919, which was signed by 26 of the 32 allied and associated powers represented at the Paris Peace Conference and ultimately ratified by 38 states. The Paris Convention dealt with all technical, operational and organisational aspects of civil aviation. It also established the International Commission for Air Navigation (ICAN) to monitor developments in civil aviation and to propose measures to States to keep abreast of developments. This Convention adopted all the principles that were formulated by the 1910 International Air Conference in Paris.

8.10 The civil aviation industry developed rapidly, both technically and commercially, in the period between the two World Wars. International air transport was not, at this stage, readily available to all sections of society, and remained an exclusive means of personal transport. It was recognised, however, that the civil aviation industry presented unique legal issues, relating primarily to the movement of passengers and cargo rapidly between and overhead different states and different legal systems. The liability of the air carrier for any damage to passengers or cargo could therefore fall to be determined in the context of one or many legal systems with uncertain and possibly conflicting results. This was dealt with by the Warsaw Convention of 1929,[1] which sets out rules for determining the rights of passengers and cargo owners following an accident in flight, and the liabilities of the air carriers.

1   Convention for the Unification of Certain Rules Relating to International Carriage by Air, signed at Warsaw, 1929. See further **para 8.135** ff below.

8.11 In 1933, further international rules were agreed to deal with the liability for damage caused by aircraft to persons and property on the ground. This Convention also introduced the concept of compulsory insurance for air carriers.[1]

1   Convention on the Unification of Certain Rules related to Damage Caused by Aircraft to Third Parties on the Surface, signed at Rome, 1933. The Rome Convention 1933 was subsequently replaced by the Rome Convention on Damage Caused by Foreign Aircraft to Third Parties on the Surface, signed at Rome in 1952. This Convention has entered into force but has not been widely ratified.

The Chicago Convention

8.12 The utilisation of aviation during the Second World War significantly advanced the technical and operational possibilities of air transport. For the first time, large numbers of people and goods had been transported over long distances and ground facilities had been developed to facilitate this. In 1943, the US initiated studies of post-War civil aviation problems. These studies, once more, concluded that civil aviation should be regulated on an international scale.

8.13 In November 1944, an international convention was convened in Chicago to negotiate and develop a constitution for the international regulation of the civil aviation industry. The result was a suite of conventions including the Convention on International Civil Aviation, which was signed at Chicago on 7 December 1944 by 38 States (the 'Chicago Convention'). A key result of the conference and the resulting conventions was agreement that the civil aviation industry required regulation on an international level. Pending ratification of the Chicago Convention by a further 26 states which would bring it into force, the Chicago Convention established an international regulatory body known as the Provisional International Civil Aviation Organisation (PICAO). This body functioned from 6 June 1945 until March 1947 when the 26th ratification of the Chicago Convention was received. As a result a permanent organisation, the International Civil Aviation Organisation (ICAO), came into being as a specialised agency of the UN.

8.14   The Chicago Convention sets out the purpose of ICAO:

'WHEREAS the future development of international civil aviation can greatly help to create and preserve friendship and understanding among the nations and peoples of the world, yet its abuse can become a threat to the general security; and

WHEREAS it is desirable to avoid friction and to promote that cooperation between nations and peoples upon which the peace of the world depends;

THEREFORE, the undersigned governments having agreed on certain principles and arrangements in order that international civil aviation may be developed in a safe and orderly manner and that international air transport services may be established on the basis of equality of opportunity and operated soundly and economically;

Have accordingly concluded this Convention to that end.'[1]

1   Preamble to the Chicago Convention.

8.15   The aims and objectives of ICAO are to develop the principles and techniques of international air navigation in order, inter alia, to:

* ensure the safe and orderly growth of international civil aviation throughout the world;
* encourage the development of airways, airports and air navigation facilities for international civil aviation;
* meet the needs of the peoples of the world for safe, regular, efficient and economical air transport;
* promote safety of flight in international air navigation;
* promote generally the development of all aspects of international civil aeronautics.

8.16   ICAO has a sovereign body, the Assembly, and a governing body, the Council. The Assembly meets at least once in three years where the work of ICAO in the technical, economic, legal and technical co-operation fields is reviewed.

8.17   The Council is a permanent body responsible to the Assembly and is composed of 33 contracting states elected by the Assembly for a three-year term. The Council may act as an arbiter between contracting states on matters concerning aviation and implementation of the Chicago Convention; it may investigate any situation which presents avoidable obstacles to the development of international air navigation; and, in general, it may take whatever steps are necessary to maintain the safety and regularity of operation of international air transport.

International standards and recommended practices

8.18   To ensure safety, regularity and efficiency of international civil aviation operations, international standardisation is regarded as essential in all matters affecting them. To achieve the highest practicable degree of uniformity worldwide in order to facilitate and improve air safety, efficiency and regularity, the ICAO Council has adopted International Standards and Recommended Practices (SARPs).

8.19 The Council has the responsibility for adoption of these SARPs and approval of these procedures. The principal body concerned with their development is the ICAO Air Navigation Commission. Pursuant to the Chicago Convention, the Commission should be composed of 15 persons who have 'suitable qualifications and experience in the science and practice of aeronautics'.[1] Its members are nominated by contracting states and are appointed by the Council.[2] The Commission reports to the Council and is responsible for the examination, co-ordination and planning of ICAO's technical work programme in the air navigation field. In the advancement of solutions to specialised problems requiring up-to-date and specialised expertise, the Commission is assisted by technical sub-commissions. These are small groups of experts, nominated by contracting states and international organisations and approved by the Commission. The panel members act in their personal expert capacity and not as representatives of their nominators.[3]

1 Chicago Convention, art 56.
2 Chicago Convention, art 56.
3 See the ICAO website at www.icao.int.

8.20 A Standard is a specification with mandatory effect. A Recommended Practice is a specification that is desirable in the interest of the safety, regularity or efficiency of international civil aviation. It is not, therefore, mandatory. The SARPs have been incorporated as Annexes to the Chicago Convention. At present there are 18 Annexes.[1]

1 Annex 1 Personnel licensing.
   Annex 2 Rules of the air.
   Annex 3 Meteorological service for international air navigation.
   Annex 4 Aeronautical charts.
   Annex 5 Units of measurement to be used in air-ground communications.
   Annex 6 Operation of aircraft.
   Annex 7 Aircraft nationality and registration marks.
   Annex 8 Airworthiness of aircraft.
   Annex 9 Facilitation.
   Annex 10 Aeronautical communications.
   Annex 11 Air traffic services.
   Annex 12 Search and rescue.
   Annex 13 Aircraft accident investigation.
   Annex 14 Aerodromes.
   Annex 15 Aeronautical information services.
   Annex 16 Aircraft noise.
   Annex 17 Security.
   Annex 18 Safe transport of dangerous goods by air.

8.21 The SARPS are proactively managed. Proposals to amend or add new SARPs may come from ICAO-sponsored international meetings, deliberative bodies of the Organisation, the Secretariat, the UN and its agencies or interested international organisations.

8.22 Contracting states to the Chicago Convention undertake to collaborate in securing the highest practical degree of uniformity in regulations, standards, procedures and organisation in all matters which will facilitate and improve air navigation.[1] Standards or Recommended Practices are, after consultation with all contracting states and interested international organisations, finalised by the Air Navigation Commission and submitted to the Council for adoption. These Standards and Recommended Practices are considered binding. However, if any contracting state finds it impossible to comply with them, the state is required to inform ICAO of any differences in their own practices.[2] ICAO then publishes these differences in supplements to the Annexes.

1   Chicago Convention, art 37.
2   Chicago Convention, art 38.

Procedures for air navigation services

8.23   In addition to the Standards and Recommended Practices, ICAO also formulates Procedures for Air Navigation Services (PANS). The PANS are developed by the Air Navigation Commission on the basis of proposals from the same sources as for SARPs. Following consultation with all contracting states and interested international organisations, they are approved by the Council and recommended to contracting states for worldwide application. The PANS comprise, for the most part, operating practices, as well as material considered too detailed for SARPs. PANS often amplify the basic principles in the corresponding SARPs to assist in the application of those SARPs. The PANS become applicable on a date set by the Council. Because PANS have a different status from SARPs, contracting states do not have to notify differences in the event of non-implementation.

8.24   In addition to SARPs and PANS, ICAO develops Regional Supplementary Procedures (SUPPs) to meet the needs of specific geographical areas which are not covered by the worldwide provisions. These procedures may indicate modes of implementing procedural provisions in SARPs and PANS, specify detailed procedural options for regional application or promulgate a procedure of justifiable operational significance, additional to, but not in conflict with, existing provisions in the Annexes or PANS.

8.25   To facilitate the implementation by states and to promote the uniform application of SARPs and PANs, ICAO issues technical manuals and guidance material. As the demand for air navigation services and facilities continues to grow, ICAO expects that implementation will continue to be one of the most important questions facing the organisation.[1]

1   See generally, www.icao.org

Safety oversight programme

8.26   ICAO's commitment to international technical standardisation has also been extended to the oversight of safety in air navigation. In 1997, ICAO launched a Strategic Action Plan for the oversight of international safety standards. In its plan, ICAO has set itself up as the international auditor of safety standards for international civil aviation through safety oversight audits. A specialised agency, the Safety Oversight Audit Section of ICAO, has been convened, which was assessed to be ISO 9001 compliant in 2002.

8.27   The role of the Section is to determine the status of implementation of SARPs in the 188 member states of ICAO. It also approves action plans designed to correct identified deficiencies. The partial or non-application of SARPs has been shown to be a factor in many aviation accidents.[1]

1   ICAO press release 'Aviation Safety to Benefit from Compliance with ISO 9001:2000', 20 November 2002.

8.28 A major benefit of the evaluation process leading up to compliance with ISO 9001 has been the refinement and strengthening of the safety audit programme. Once the newly endorsed systems and procedures are in place, ICAO expects it will increase its effectiveness in working with member states to improve their respective safety oversight mechanisms.[1]

1 ICAO press release **para 8.27 n 1** above

8.29 At present the Safety Oversight Audit Programme does not extend to an audit of air traffic services and aerodromes. This is likely to change.

Regulation of aviation safety in the UK

Regulation of civil aviation

8.30 The UK has a comprehensive legislative framework for regulating civil aviation activities which primarily consists of the Civil Aviation Act 1982, the Air Navigation Order 2000,[1] Civil Aviation Publications (CAPs), British Civil Airworthiness Requirements (BCARs), and Joint Aviation Requirements (JARs.) At the regulatory level, the UK is a member of the Joint Aviation Authorities (JAA) and those JARs annexed to Council Regulation 3922/91 have automatic regulatory effect. The Civil Aviation Authority (CAA) also implements in practice a number of JARs not yet adopted under the EU legislation, in addition to having the discretionary power to impose requirements for flight crew licences, certificates of airworthiness and air operator certificates under the CAPs and BCARs. Overall, the framework in place for the regulation of civil aviation activities in the UK mainland is comprehensive and up to date and complies with all international requirements necessary for the control, supervision and enforcement of civil aviation activities.[2]

1 SI 2000/1562.
2 ICAO Universal Safety Oversight Audit Programme *Audit Final Report on the Safety Oversight Audit Mission to the United Kingdom* (2000).

8.31 The Secretary of State for Transport is responsible for the development and regulation of civil aviation in the UK. The CAA is established as a statutory corporation, separate from government, but with general objectives and a corporate plan approved by the Department for Transport (DfT). The Safety Regulation Group of the CAA consists of several divisions including Operating Standards, Design and Production Standards, Medical, and Aerodrome, Air Traffic and Licensing Standards.

8.32 The CAA has established procedures for the issuance of licences and ratings and the issuance of medical certificates. A system for the certification and supervision of commercial air transport operators has been established.

8.33 The ICAO Safety Audit of the UK, carried out in July 2000, concluded inter alia that:

- Aircraft certification and continuing airworthiness activities are adequately organised, effectively implemented and, in most cases, exceed ICAO standards.
- Personnel follow a comprehensive and structured training programme and are appropriately trained in their assigned responsibilities.

- The policies and procedures developed by the CAA to ensure adequate oversight of the aeronautical industry, as well as the control and supervision of the airworthiness system, are well structured and effective.
- With respect to certification and production, procedures manuals are well developed, and certification practices are implemented in a comprehensive manner. Certain airworthiness-related documents do not differentiate between the state of design and the state of manufacturer. [1]

1   ICAO Audit Final Report, **para 8.30 n 1** above.

Aviation legislation

8.34   The primary aviation law in the UK is the Civil Aviation Act 1982 (CAA 1982), which repealed and replaced the Civil Aviation Act 1971. The Act contains 110 sections in five Parts (Administration; Aerodromes and Other Land; Regulation of Civil Aviation; Aircraft; and Miscellaneous and General), and there are 16 Schedules dealing with the application of particular sections. Since 1982, CAA 1982 has been amended once, by the Civil Aviation (Amendment) Act 1996, which expanded the scope of CAA 1982, s 92 to allow for the prosecution of persons committing offences on board foreign aircraft while in flight to the UK.

8.35   CAA 1982[1], provides for the making of an Order, referred to as an Air Navigation Order (ANO), for the purpose of carrying out the provisions of the Chicago Convention and the SARPs of the Annexes to the Chicago Convention. An ANO may regulate, inter alia:

- the registration of aircraft in the UK;
- the requirement for valid certificates of airworthiness to be issued or validated:
- the manner and conditions for the issuance, validation and renewal of certificates and licences; and
- generally, for securing the safety, efficiency and regularity of air navigation and the safety of aircraft. [1]

1   Civil Aviation Act 1982, s 60.

8.36   The Air Navigation Order 2000[1] (ANO 2000) came into force in July 2000. ANO 2000 includes provisions on the certification and supervision of commercial air transport operators, airworthiness and equipment of aircraft, operation of aircraft, fatigue of aircrew and air traffic services (ATS). ANO 2000 replaces the Air Navigation (No 2) Order 1995[2] which had been in force since 29 August 1995. ANO 2000 consolidates six amendments previously made to the 1995 Order and adds new provisions on flying in reduced vertical separation minimum airspace, equipping aeroplanes with a terrain awareness and warning system, and requirements for public transport helicopters flying in instrument conditions or at night.

1   SI 2000/1562.
2   SI 1995/1970.

8.37   CAA 1982, s 61 enables breaches of a provision of the ANO 2000[1] to be made a criminal offence, and ANO 2000, art 122[2] and Sch 12[3] provide for enforcement action and penalties to be imposed on persons who contravene ANO 2000 or regulations made under it. The responsibility for enforcement has been given to the CAA by the

DfT. Offenders are prosecuted in the criminal courts. From January 1995 to July 2000, the CAA conducted a total of 82 investigations into alleged offences of which 18 involved public transport operators, 40 involved shippers/consignors of dangerous goods and 24 involved pilots operating commercial flights.[4]

1 SI 2000/1562.
2 SI 2000/1562, art 122.
3 SI 2000/1562, Sch 12.
4 ICAO *Audit Final Report,* **para 8.30 n 1** above at para 4.1.4.

8.38 Persons authorised by the CAA have the right of access to any aerodrome or any place where an aircraft has landed for the purpose of inspecting the aerodrome, an aircraft or documents or for the purpose of detaining an aircraft under the provisions of the ANO 2000.[1] ANO 2000 grants further access and inspection powers for airworthiness purposes and allows an authorised person to access aerodromes and aircraft factories.[2] Article 78[3] requires the production of documents and records by the operator or commander of an aircraft, and art 79[4] grants an authorised person the power to inspect and copy such documents and records. Authorised persons have the right to detain aircraft for just cause[5] and to provisionally suspend or vary any certificate, licence or document.[6]

1 SI 2000/1562, art 119.
2 SI 2000/1562, art 19.
3 SI 2000/1562, art 78.
4 SI 2000/1562, art 79.
5 SI 2000/1562, art 118.
6 SI 2000/1562, art 81.

8.39 CAA 1982, Sch 1, para 15 enables the CAA to authorise any person to perform functions on its behalf, subject to CAA 1982, s 7(1). SRG Authorisation 1/2000 enables members of the CAA to perform a variety of administrative functions relating to approvals, refusals, suspensions or variations. However, the authorisation document does not extend to maintenance or design organisations.

Civil aviation regulations

8.40 The ANO 2000[1] contains a number of enabling provisions for the development and promulgation of regulations. For example, ANO 2000, art 84[2] empowers the Secretary of State to make regulations regarding rules of the air.[3]

1 SI 2000/1562.
2 SI 2000/1562, art 84.
3 The UK's civil aviation regulations are grouped in CAP 393 and include:
   Rules of the Air Regulations 1996, SI 1996/1393;
   Air Navigation (General) Regulations 1993, SI 1993/1622;
   Air Navigation (Dangerous Goods) Regulations 1994, SI 1994/3187;
   Air Navigation (Restriction of Flying) Regulations 1972, SI 1972/320;
   Civil Aviation Authority Regulations 1991, SI 1991/1672;
   Civil Aviation (Investigation of Air Accidents and Incidents) Regulations 1996, SI 1996/2798;
   Air Navigation (Investigation of Air Accidents involving Civil and Military Aircraft or Installations) Regulations 1986, SI 1986/1953;
   Schemes of Charges made pursuant to CAA 1982, s 11; and
   Air Navigation (Noise Certification) Order 1990, SI 1990/1514.

8.41 The CAA develops and proposes changes to the ANO 2000[1] and regulations but does not have the power actually to amend the legislation. The CAA, however, has been given a great deal of discretionary power under the ANO 2000 to impose requirements. For example, it is entitled to issue flight crew licences,[2] certificates of airworthiness[3] and air transport licences on the basis of being satisfied as to the competence of the applicant.[4] The detailed basis on which it requires to be satisfied is set forth in the CAPs, BCARs or JARs. The CAA is entitled to amend the requirements found in the CAPs and BCARs without reference to Parliament or the DfT, notwithstanding that they contain material which is both regulatory and advisory in nature. These publications are not considered to be criminal law, and failure to comply with a requirement does not constitute a criminal offence. It may, however, form the basis upon which the CAA may grant, refuse, suspend, vary or revoke a licence or certificate.

1   SI 2000/1562.
2   SI 2000/1562, art 22(1).
3   SI 2000/1562, art 8(3) and SI 2000/1562, art 9(1). The CAA's jurisdiction in this regard extends only to aircraft registered in the UK.
4   CAA 1982, s 64(1)(a).

8.42   As a member of the EU and the JAA, the UK is working with other members of the JAA to develop JARs and is committed to adopting JARs as its sole code in the field of design, manufacture, maintenance, operations and flight crew licensing.[1] The key legal instrument for safety regulation in the EU is Council Regulation 3922/91/EEC on the harmonisation of technical requirements and administrative procedures. JARs annexed to this regulation automatically become part of the domestic law of the UK without the need for formal amendment of the ANO 2000[2] and other subsidiary legislation.

1   Shawcross and Beaumont *Air Law* (4th edn, 1996) para 14.1 and n 3.
2   SI 2000/1562.

The Civil Aviation Authority

8.43   The CAA is a statutory corporation created by the Civil Aviation Act 1971, now repealed and replaced by CAA 1982. CAA 1982, s 2 provides for the existence of the CAA and CAA 1982, s 3 sets out its principal functions. The CAA is established separately from government, with the Chairman and board members of the CAA appointed by the Secretary of State for Transport. The Secretary of State sets general objectives for the CAA while the board is responsible for its daily management. The Secretary of State is accountable to Parliament for the proper conduct of the CAA and remains responsible for the development and regulation of civil aviation. Technical regulations, for example, are drafted by the CAA but are routed through the DfT for promulgation by Parliament. Similarly, the government normally leads on any international negotiations but relies on the technical support and expertise within the CAA.[1]

1   ICAO *Audit Final Report* **para 8.30 n 1** above para 4.3.1.1.

8.44   The CAA is now composed of four primary components (groups): the Safety Regulation Group (SRG), the Economic Regulation Group (ERG), the Consumer Protection Group (CPG) and the Directorate of Airspace Policy (DAP). In March 2001, the CAA's responsibility for the provision of air traffic services through National Air Traffic Service (NATS) was transferred to a consortium of airlines together with a 46% share in the ownership of NATS. The state still retains a 49% ownership share of

NATS. In addition, the licensing of air traffic controllers[1] and the regulation of air traffic control services[2] is still the responsibility of the CAA.

1   SI 2000/1562, art 92(1) and SI 2000/1562, art 98(5).
2   Transport Act 2000, s 2(1).

8.45   The ERG regulates airports and airlines and provides advice on aviation policy from an economic standpoint. The ERG acts as expert adviser to the government and collects, analyses and publishes statistical information on airlines and airports. The CPG was formed in 1999 to provide a system of consumer protection for travellers within the scope of the Civil Aviation (Air Travel Organisers' Licensing) Regulations 1995[1] (ATOL) and to ensure that UK air carriers meet applicable licensing requirements on finances, ownership and control and insurance. The DAP is responsible for airspace policy and planning in the UK, including the approval of the design and establishment of controlled airspace, the planning of off-route arrangements and the allocation of radio telephone frequencies and secondary surveillance radar codes.

1   SI 1995/1054.

8.46   The SRG is responsible for the certification and regulatory oversight of UK-registered aircraft and airlines and for the licensing of flight crew, aircraft engineers, air traffic controllers and aerodromes. Its principal areas of activity include type certification, air operator certification, personnel and aerodrome licensing and air traffic services approval.

8.47   In addition, the CAA has established a Safety Intervention Programme to identify significant safety risks to aviation along with safety improvement strategies to reduce the safety risks. Safety interventions are described in a CAA Safety Plan, a document which sets out generic problem statements and detailed action plans.[1]

1   CAA *Corporate Plan 2003* (2003) para 8.

8.48   The UK government, outside the jurisdiction of the CAA, has retained certain aviation responsibilities. For example, responsibility for environmental issues, facilitation, international air agreements and aviation security remains with DfT. Aircraft accident investigation is conducted by an independent branch, the Air Accidents Investigation Branch (AAIB), which reports to the Secretary of State for Transport.

8.49   The budgeted annual expenditure of the CAA for 2002–03 was approximately £159 million.[1] CAA 1982, s 8 requires the CAA fully to recover its costs from those it regulates. Almost all costs are recovered in this way by statutory schemes of charges. There are ten statutory schemes currently in place, seven of which are related to the SRG.

1   CAA *Corporate Plan 2003* (2003) para 4.3.1.

The management of safety

Collection of data

8.50   It is widely believed that the collecting, analysing, and sharing of aviation safety information constitutes a proactive step in enhancing safety management. The US Federal Aviation Administration (FAA) notes that the need to share such information more systematically is reflected by the fact that accident hearings reveal that pilots, mechanics, air traffic controllers and others were often aware of problems that may ultimately have caused or contributed to an accident or incident.[1]

1   See US Federal Aviation Administration, Office of System Safety *Aviation Safety Information: Four Potential Problems; Four Proposed Solutions* (1998).

8.51   In consequence, the FAA proposed the development of a worldwide infrastructure to collect, analyse and disseminate aviation safety information, known as GAIN (Global Analysis and Information Network). GAIN promotes and facilitates the voluntary collection and sharing of safety information by and among users in the international aviation community to improve aviation safety. GAIN states that it does this by:

1   providing information on tools and processes to help safety decision-makers;
2   gathering information on safety management processes from various sources and distributing it to the global aviation community;
3   bringing together diverse groups, and facilitating their co-ordination and co-operation to address general safety issues; and
4   fostering an environment where collection and sharing of safety information can take place.

8.52   GAIN states that it will not collect information about specific safety issues or safety events, nor analyse safety information. GAIN will not endorse specific products or tools.[1]

1   See generally www.gainweb.org.

8.53   In the UK, the CAA manages the CAA Mandatory Occurrence Reporting Scheme (MORS). Under this scheme, all safety hazards or potential hazards involving UK-registered aircraft or aircraft in UK airspace are required to be reported to SRG's Safety Investigation and Data Department. The CAA scheme allows reports to be submitted confidentially, and provides the equivocal assurance that every attempt to maintain confidentiality will be made, on the basis that a confidential report is better than no report.[1] A privately managed organisation, CHIRP (UK Confidential Human Factors Incident Reporting Programme) has operated since 1982 with an impressive record of confidentiality.[2]

1   CAA doc CAP 382 *The Mandatory Occurrence Reporting Scheme: Information and Guidance* (2003).
2   See generally www.chirp.co.uk.

8.54   There are, of course, coherent objections to data collection systems such as GAIN and MORS, primarily from the professional pilot and maintenance communities. The self-evident concern is that, by reporting their own errors and breaches in procedure, pilots and other professionals may risk their jobs. An additional fear is that employers may actively sanction the reporter as a demonstrable form of risk management.

8.55   In the UK, the CAA has encouraged aviation organisations to refrain from taking such action, save in cases of intentional, criminal or grossly negligent behaviour.[1] This was expressly implemented by British Airways in its BASIS (British Airways Safety Information System), which has become a leading proactive aviation safety information programme. In addition, whistleblowers are protected from dismissal by the Public Interest Disclosure Act 1998. In the US, the FAA made a similar commitment in 1995 in relation to its Flight Operations Quality Assurance (FOQA) programme to access flight data recorder information.

1 Statement of the Chairman of the CAA, CAA doc CAP 382 *The Mandatory Occurrence Reporting Scheme: Information and Guidance* (2003) p vii.

8.56 A second issue is that of media access to information that may come into the possession of national or governmental authorities. In the US, for example, most information held by the FAA is subject to public disclosure pursuant to the Freedom of Information Act (FOIA). The fear of public disclosure may present a real deterrent to reporting known aviation safety problems. The FAA has also asked ICAO to urge its member states to review their public disclosure laws and regulations in order to remove this potential barrier to the flow of information that could improve aviation safety.

8.57 Thirdly, the use of reported material in criminal proceedings is a real fear of the pilot community. In New Zealand in 2000, a court hearing criminal proceedings against a pilot allowed the cockpit voice recorder (CVR) tape into evidence, to a vocal objection by the International Federation of Airline Pilots Associations.[1]

1 IFALPA press release, 31 March, 2000.

8.58 A fourth and significant problem, especially in the US, is the concern that attempts may be made to use reported information as evidence in civil proceedings. The best remedy that GAIN has offered is to de-identify its information in order to make sources impossible to discern. Consequently, all information to be used in proceedings will need to be independently verified. The CAA has not commented on this aspect in its guidance notes to MORS.[1]

1 See CAA doc CAP 382, **para 8.53 n 1** above.

8.59 Two US court decisions in civil proceedings have provided conflicting approaches to information originating from aviation safety information programmes. In one case, the judge recognised that American Airlines' confidential information programme (ASAP) would be severely undermined if the litigating parties were given free access to the otherwise confidential information. The court held that it was more important for the airline to have a confidential information programme than it was for the parties in the litigation to have access to it.[1] In an earlier case, however, the court had allowed the parties access to similar information.[2] This issue has not arisen in any significant sense in English aviation accident litigation.

1 *In re Air Crash Near Cali, Columbia, on Dec. 20, 1995,* 959 F Supp 1529 (SD Fla, 1997).
2 *In re Air Crash at Charlotte, North Carolina, on July 2, 1996,* MDL Docket no 1041 (DSC, 1995).

Safety management systems

8.60 Annex 6 to the Chicago Convention sets out the principle that 'an operator shall establish an accident prevention and flight safety programme, which may be integrated with the Quality System, including programmes to achieve and maintain risk awareness by all persons involved in operations'. The ICAO Accident Prevention Manual gives guidance material and describes a safety management system.[1]

1 ICAO Doc 9422

8.61   In the UK, safety management systems have been adopted by the rail, petrochemical and nuclear industries. In early 1998 the CAA, following consultation with the aviation industry, developed certain materials to assist aviation operators in the creation and implementation of a safety management system.[1]

1   CAP 712 *Safety Management Systems for Commercial Air Transport Operations* (2nd edn, 2002).

8.62   The CAA notes that a continuing objective of any operator in the aviation industry must be to monitor and improve safety measures within the operation.[1] The CAA defines safety management as 'the systematic management of the risks associated with flight operations, related ground operations and aircraft engineering or maintenance activities to achieve high levels of safety performance'.[2] One such measure is to encourage individual operators and maintenance organisations to introduce their own safety management system. Such a system is as important to business survival as a financial management system and the implementation of a safety management system should lead to achievement of one of civil aviation's key business objectives, enhanced safety performance aiming at best practice and moving beyond mere compliance with regulatory requirements.[3] A safety management system is defined as an 'explicit element of the corporate management responsibility which sets out a company's safety policy and defines how it intends to manage safety as an integral part of its overall business'.[4]

1   J Done 'Implementation of Safety Management Systems: Challenges and Benefits', 19th Annual FAA/JAA International Conference, 3–7 June 2002.
2   CAP 712, **para 8.60 n 1** above.
3   CAP 712, **para 8.60 n 1** above.
4   CAP 712, **para 8.60 n 1** above.

8.63   Safety culture in an organisation can be described as the way in which it conducts its business and particularly in the way it manages safety. It stems from the communicated principles of top management and results in all staff exhibiting a safety ethos which transcends departmental boundaries. Success in an organisation's safety performance will be greatly strengthened by the existence of a positive safety culture.[1] Safety culture can be measured by informal or formal staff surveys, or by observations conducted in safety related work areas. It is essential that safety must be actively managed from the very top of a company. Safety management must be seen as an integral strategic aspect of business management, recognising the high priority attached by the company to safety.

1   See, particularly, J Reason *Managing the Risk of Organisational Accidents* (2000); R Abeyratne *Emergent Commercial Trends and Aviation Safety* (1999).

8.64   To that end, a demonstrable board level commitment to an effective formal safety management system must exist. The contribution that all staff can make to the effectiveness of an organisation's safety management system cannot be over emphasised.[1]

1   CAP 712, **para 8.60 n 1** above.

Safety management system prerequisites

8.65   The CAA notes in CAP 712 that there are three essential prerequisites for a successful safety management system.

8.66   An effective safety management system will provide a means of achieving enhanced safety performance which meets or exceeds basic compliance with the regulatory requirements associated with safety and quality. Enhanced safety performance is founded upon a proactive safety culture inherent in all safety related activities of the organisation. It is achieved by effective, devolved executive management in association with a means of independent safety oversight, both of which are the ultimate responsibility of the organisation's board and Chief Executive Officer. The board and Chief Executive Officer are then able to demonstrate how safety is managed in the company.

8.67   A corporate approach to safety should be able to meet the following criteria:

- published safety accountabilities of managers and key staff;
- requirements for a safety manager;
- the ability to demonstrate that it generates a positive safety culture throughout the organisation;
- documented business policies, principles and practices in which safety is inherent;
- commitment to a safety oversight process which is independent of line management;
- regularly reviewed safety improvement plans; and
- formal safety review process.

AN EFFECTIVE ORGANISATION FOR DELIVERING SAFETY

8.68   The second essential prerequisite is for an organisation that delivers safe standards by way of:

- effective arrangements for selection, recruitment, development and training of staff;
- safety awareness training for management and staff;
- defined safety standards for, and auditing of, asset purchases and contracted services;
- controls for the early detection of – and action on – deterioration in the performance of safety-significant equipment or systems or services;
- controls for monitoring and recording the overall safety standards of the company;
- the application of appropriate hazard identification, risk assessment and effective management of resources to control those risks;
- change management;
- arrangements enabling staff to communicate significant safety concerns to the appropriate level of management for resolution and feedback of actions taken;
- emergency response planning and simulated exercises to test its effectiveness; and
- assessment of commercial policies with regard to impact on safety.

SYSTEMS TO ACHIEVE SAFETY OVERSIGHT

8.69   The following elements are desirable:

- a system for analysing flight data for the purpose of monitoring flight operations and for detecting unreported safety events;

- a company-wide system for the capture of written safety event issues/reports;
- a planned and comprehensive safety audit review system which has the flexibility to focus on specific safety concerns as they arise;
- a published system for the conduct of internal safety inspections, the implementation of remedial actions and the communication of such information;
- systems for effective use of safety data for performance analysis and for monitoring organisational change as part of the risk management process;
- arrangements for ongoing safety promotion based on the measured internal safety performance and assimilation of experience of other operations;
- periodic review of the continued effectiveness of the safety management system an internal, independent body; and
- line managers' monitoring of work in progress in all safety critical activities to confirm compliance with all regulatory requirements, company standards and local procedures.

The safety management system approach is an attempt to move beyond the traditional reactionary systems to those which try to predict areas of exposure through assessment of any residual risk areas in airworthiness and operations and supplementing them with operational knowledge and professional judgment.

8.70   The CAA has also described the best practice for Flight Data Monitoring (FDM) programmes to assist airlines to identify, quantify, assess and address operational risks. This programme allows the operator to compare its standard operating procedures with those actually achieved in everyday line flights by using data downloaded and analysed from the flight data recorders of the operator's aircraft. The CAA has stated that FDM information has been used to support a range of airworthiness and operational safety tasks to the extent that ICAO has recommended its use for all air transport operators in aircraft over 20 tonnes and will make FDM a standard for all such operations of aircraft over 27 tonnes with effect from 1 January 2005.[1]

1   See CAA doc CAP 739: *Flight Data Monitoring* (29 August 2003).

Accident investigation

Definition of accident

8.71   Before a duty or liability to investigate accidents can be either imposed or inferred, there needs to be an accident. English law has struggled to define the concept and has used various mechanisms to do so. A precise definition of the word 'accident' remains elusive. An early definition, in a case involving workman's compensation, is as follows:

> 'The word "accident" is not a technical legal term with a clearly defined meaning. Speaking generally, but with reference to legal liabilities, an accident means an unintended and unexpected occurrence which produces hurt or loss. But it is often used to denote any unintended or unexpected loss or hurt apart from its cause; and if the cause is not known the loss or hurt itself would certainly be called an accident. The word "accident" is also often used to denote both the cause and the effect, no attempt being made to discriminate between them.'[1]

1   *Fenton v J Thorley & Co Ltd* [1903] AC 443 at 453, per Lord Lindley.

8.72 In this case, Lord Lindley used the word 'occurrence' in order to define 'accident'.[1] It is difficult to find a workable definition of 'occurrence'. In the late nineteenth century, Lord Bowen attempted this in the case of *South Staffordshire Tramways Co Ltd v Sickness and Accident Assurance Association Ltd*.[2] In that case, 40 passengers were injured when a tramcar overturned. According to the court, there were 40 accidents, although only one occurrence.

> 'When we looked to the [insurance] policy, it limits the words of the proposal by adding the words "in respect of accidents". The question is what is the meaning of those words? Is it meant by them to treat as one accident what happens to several persons? I should not think that anyone would suppose … otherwise than that the word "accident" was there used in the sense of injury, accidentally caused to the person … "Accident" meant in the policy the mischief suffered by a person injured to his person or property.'[3]

1 *Fenton v J Thorley & Co Ltd* [1903] AC 443.
2 [1891] 1 QB 402.
3 [1891] 1 QB 402 at 407.

8.73 In international aviation legislation 'accident' receives a similarly broad definition. In Annex 13 to the Chicago Convention[1] the definition of 'accident' is:

> 'An occurrence associated with the operation of an aircraft which takes place between the time any person boards the aircraft with the intention of flight until such time or such persons have disembarked in which:
> (a) a person is slightly or seriously injured …
> (b) the aircraft sustains damage or structural failure …
> (c) the aircraft is missing or is completely inaccessible.'

1 Annex 13 'Aircraft Accident and Incident Investigation' (9th edn, 2001).

8.74 In UK national legislation, CAA 1982, with reference to investigation of accidents, defines 'accident' as 'including any fortuitous or unexpected event by which the safety of an aircraft or any person is threatened'.

8.75 It is clear from these definitions that the term 'accident' is generally associated with the cause of damage rather than to the loss or the injury. A graphic illustration of this is given by the facts and decision of the US Supreme Court in the case of *Air France v Saks*.[1] In this case, the claimant suffered pain in her ears and subsequent deafness following the routine depressurisation of the aircraft cabin during landing. The US Supreme Court found that it is not sufficient that the passenger suffers injury as a result of his or her own internal reaction to the usual, normal and expected operation of the aircraft. Accordingly, the airline was not liable. An 'accident' must be an unexpected or unusual event or happening that is external to the passengers. This definition of 'accident' is considered to be natural and sensible, and 'has passed the test of general acceptance'.[2]

1 (1985) 470 US 392.
2 *Re Deep Vein Thrombosis and Air Travel Group Litigation* [2002] EWHC 2825 (QB), [2003] 1 All ER 935, [2003] 1 All ER (Comm) 418, per Nelson J.

8.76 Shawcross and Beaumont cite illustrative cases of accidents in the aviation context that challenge the definition.[1] The obvious example of an accident is an aircraft crash. That is clearly unexpected and unusual. Less dramatic incidents may also constitute an accident such as a tyre failure on take off or a particularly heavy landing which causes a neck injury. Sufficiently severe turbulence may be classed as to constitute an 'accident' if it results in physical injury.[2]

1   Shawcross and Beaumont, **para 8.42 n 1** above, Section VII.
2   *Weintraub v Capital Intl Airways Inc* 16 Avi Cas 18,058 (NY City Civ Ct, 1980) in which it was held that the defendant had suffered no physical injury and there was, therefore, no accident.

8.77   Incidents with their origin purely within the passenger cabin may also constitute accidents. Decided cases have included the supply of infected food, causing food poisoning, or food contaminated in other ways. The spilling of hot water into a passenger's lap (either as a result of turbulence or inattention on the part of the cabin crew) may be an accident.[1] Similarly, the refusal to move passenger suffering from asthma to a non-smoking section of the aircraft has been held to constitute an accident,[2] as has the refusal to divert an aircraft in the event of a passenger's heart attack following a request to do so.[3]

1   *Fishman v Delta Airlines Inc* (1998) 132 F 3d 138.
2   *Husain v Olympic Airways* (2000) 116 F Supp 2d 1121.
3   *Fulop v Malev Hungarian Airlines* (2001) 175 F Supp 2d 651.

8.78   Another potential source of accidents is the behaviour of other passengers. A sexual assault by one passenger upon another has been held to be an accident in courts both in England and in the US.[1]

1   *Morris v KLM Royal Dutch Airlines* [2002] UKHL 7, [2002] 2 AC 628, HL; *Wallace v Korean Air* (2000) 214 F 3d 293, although in *Morris* it was found that the victim of the assault had suffered no bodily injury. There was, therefore, no liability on the part of the airline.

8.79   Incidents such as hijacking, terrorist attacks and bomb threats have been treated as accidents in cases in France,[1] Israel[2] and in the US.[3] In an extreme case, a court in the US has been prepared to treat as an accident circumstances in which a passenger was forced to remain in a transit lounge for three days while his travel documents were inspected, suffering dehydration and exhaustion as a result.[4]

1   *Haddad v Cie Air France* (1978) 3 Air Law 180.
2   *Daddon v Air France* (1984) 38(3) PD 785.
3   *Husserl v Swiss Air Transport Co Ltd* 485Fd 1240 (2nd Circ, 1973).
4   *Chendrimada v Air India* 802 F Supp 1089 (SDNY, 1992).

8.80   It has conversely been held that some injuries suffered by passenger have not been caused by an accident. *Saks*[1] is the paradigm example. Additional cases have included the injury sustained by an economy class hernia sufferer after the airline refused to allow him to lie flat in a first class seat,[2] and an allergic reaction to the spraying of insecticide in the cabin pursuant to government regulations.[3]

1   *Air France v Saks* (1985) 470 US 392
2   *Abramson v Japan Airlines Co Ltd* (1984) 739 F 2d 130.
3   *Capacchione v Qantas Airways Ltd* (1996) 23 Avi Cas 17,346.

8.81   This definition of 'accident' raises a crucial issue relating to an airline's awareness of risk. Aviation technology is constantly developing; each development invariably produces awareness of new risks. An airline cannot escape liability simply because it carries out each of its flights in the same way and can contend they were usual and that there was therefore no accident. It can be contended that the routine operation of a known unsafe system could be an accident. Further, that the failure of an airline to remove a known risk or to warn its passengers of that risk or failure amounts to an accident.[1]

1 *Husain v Olympic Airlines* (2000) 116 F Supp 2d 1121.

8.82 However, especially in the context of corporate liability, it is important to note that there is no necessary correlation between 'accident' and fault. There may be an 'accident' without fault on the part of the airline, for example, where a passenger assaults another passenger, or an 'act of God' which is clearly beyond human control. Equally there may be fault without an accident, such as a culpable omission which does not cause any unexpected or unusual event to occur. The concept of fault only comes into play to establish legal liability once the passenger has demonstrated loss or damage.

8.83 There appear to be no cases in English law where a pure omission has been found to be an accident. On this basis, the Court of Appeal in England held that airlines bear no liability to passengers who suffer the effects of deep vein thrombosis (DVT). In a test case brought by a group of passengers who had suffered DVT on a variety of different airlines,[1] it was held that their injuries were not caused by an 'accident', due to the absence of an unusual or unexpected event or happening. The court at first instance had found that the airlines had effectively ignored known risks (of DVT) by continuing to provide cramped seating and failing to give warnings of the risks of DVT.[2]

1 *Re Deep Vein Thrombosis and Air Travel Group Litigation* [2003] All ER (D) 69 (Jul), [2003] 3 WLR 956, 3 July 2003
2 *Re Deep Vein Thrombosis and Air Travel Group Litigation* **para 8.75 n 1** above.

8.84 Annex 13 to the Chicago Convention also refers to 'incidents' as 'an occurrence, other than an accident, associated with the operation of an aircraft which affects the safety of operation.'[1] 'A Serious Incident' is defined as 'an incident involving circumstances indicating that an accident nearly happened'. It is noted by ICAO that the difference between an accident and a serious incident lies only in the result.[2] Examples of serious incidents include near collisions requiring an avoidance manoeuvre or an unsafe situation when an avoidance action would have been appropriate; controlled flight into terrain only marginally avoided; aborted take offs on a closed or engaged runway; fires and smoke in the passenger compartment, even if extinguished; and flight crew incapacitation in flight.

1 Annex 13 'Aircraft Accident and Incident Investigation' (9th edn, 2001) p 1. The types of incidents which are of main interest to ICAO for accident prevention studies are listed in the ICAO Accident/Incident Reporting Manual (ICAO Doc 9156).
2 Annex 13, p 2.

International aviation law

8.85 Article 26 of the Chicago Convention deals with investigation of accidents and provides as follows:

'In the event of an accident to an aircraft of a contracting state occurring in the territory of another contracting state, and involving death or serious injury, or indicating serious technical defect in the aircraft or air navigation facilities, the state in which the accident occurs will institute an inquiry into the circumstances of the accident, in accordance, so far as its law permits, with the procedure which may be recommended by the International Civil Aviation Organisation. The state in which the aircraft is registered shall be given the opportunity to appoint observers to be present at the inquiry and the state holding the inquiry shall communicate the report and findings in the matter to that state.'

8.86   The Chicago Convention further provides that international standards and procedures in the investigation of accidents should be adopted. These are set out in Annex 13 on aircraft accident and incident investigation. This annex sets out in detail the international standards and recommended practices to be adopted by contracting states in dealing with an accident or serious incident to an aircraft of a contracting state occurring in the territory of another contracting state, known as the state of occurrence. A further document, the ICAO *Manual of Aircraft Accident Investigation*[1] contains detailed guidance material for the conduct of an investigation.

1   ICAO Doc 6920-AN/855/4.

8.87   Annex 13 of the Chicago Convention states clearly, as an overarching guiding principle, that:

'The sole objective of the investigation of an accident or incident shall be the prevention of accidents and incidents. It is not the purpose of this activity to apportion blame or liability.'

8.88   The responsibility for instituting and conducting the investigation lies with the state in which the occurrence takes place. This state is also responsible for the conduct of the investigation, but it may delegate the whole or any part of the conducting of such investigation to the state of registration of the aircraft or the state of the operator of the aircraft. In any event, the state of occurrence shall use every means to facilitate the investigation.[1]

1   Chicago Convention, Annex 13, ch 5.1.

UK aviation law

8.89   The Civil Aviation Act 1982 grants the power to the Secretary of State for Transport to make regulations for the investigation of accidents.[1] These have been enacted as the Civil Aviation (Investigation of Air Accidents) Regulations 1996[2] (CA(IAA)R). The Civil Aviation Act 1982 echoes the principle of Annex 13 to the Chicago Convention in providing that the main purpose of investigating accidents is to determine the circumstances and causes of the accident with a view to avoiding accidents in the future. Further, that it is not the purpose of such an investigation to apportion blame or liability.[3]

1   Civil Aviation Act 1982, s 75.
2   SI 1996/2798.
3   SI 1996/2798, reg 4.

8.90   The CA(IAA)R[1] provide that the Secretary of State shall appoint persons as Investigators of Air Accident, one of whom shall be appointed as Chief Inspector of Air Accidents. The inspectors form a part of the DfT known as the Air Accidents Investigation Branch (AAIB).[1]

1 SI 1996/2798.
2 SI 1996/2798, reg 8.

8.91   An investigation will carried out by the AAIB into:

- accidents or serious incidents occurring over the UK;
- accidents or serious incidents to UK-registered aircraft occurring outside the territory of a state (for example, over the high seas);
- accidents or serious incidents, occurring to UK-registered aircraft, in or over a country which is not a member of the EU or a contracting state of the Chicago Convention; and
- serious incidents, occurring to aircraft operated by a UK undertaking, in or over a country which is not a member of the EU or a contracting state of the Chicago Convention.[1]

1 SI 1996/2798, reg 8(3).

Air Accidents Investigation Branch

8.92   The Air Accidents Investigation Branch has its origins in the Accidents Investigation Branch (AIB) of the Royal Flying Corps. It was established in 1915 when an 'Inspector of Accidents' was appointed for the Royal Flying Corps, reporting directly to the Director General of Military Aeronautics in the War Office. At the end of the First World War, the AIB became part of the Department of Civil Aviation, to investigate civil and military accidents. Following the Second World War a Ministry of Civil Aviation was created and in 1946 the AIB was transferred to it, but continued to assist the Royal Air Force with accident investigations.

8.93   The AIB passed to the Department of Transport in 1983 and it became the Air Accidents Investigation Branch (AAIB) in 1987. In 1998 the AAIB came under the Department of the Environment, Transport and the Regions (DETR), which in June 2001 became the Department for Transport, Local Government and the Regions (DTLR), and in June 2002 the Department for Transport (DfT). The AAIB is totally independent of the aviation safety regulator, the CAA Safety Regulation Group. Incidents with a potential to affect safety are, however, reported to the CAA under the Mandatory Occurrence Reporting Scheme, and are investigated by the SRG. The Chief Inspector sees summaries of these investigations and can then commission an investigation by the AAIB.

8.94   AAIB inspectors have the right of access to an accident site and are empowered to remove evidence. Inspectors also have immediate access to and use of the contents of the flight recorders and any other recordings.[1] Further powers allow an inspector, by summons, to examine witnesses and require persons to produce any books, papers, documents and articles which the inspector may consider relevant and to retain these.[2]

1 SI 1996/2798, reg 9(1).
2 SI 1996/2798, reg 9(2).

Relationship between AAIB, CAA and HSE

8.96   In April 1998 the CAA's Safety Regulation Group and the Health and Safety Executive (HSE) signed a Memorandum of Understanding to establish a framework for liaison between the SRG and HSE with the aim of ensuring the effective co-ordination of policy issues, enforcement activity, and investigation in terms of SRG and HSE responsibilities for safety in relation to aircraft and the systems in which they operate. Under the Memorandum of Understanding, both the SRG and HSE are committed to close co-operation to minimise duplication of regulatory effort and conflicting demands where both regulatory authorities have an interest.

8.97   The Memorandum further provides that the SRG and HSE will consult, so far as possible, before instituting criminal proceedings in connection with matters of concern to both organisations.[1]

1   *Memorandum of Understanding Between the Civil Aviation Authority Safety Regulation Group and the Health & Safety Executive*, signed on 21 April 1998.

8.98   There is no formal relationship between the HSE and the AAIB.

8.99   Following a fatal accident, a coroner's inquest will be convened to inquire into the cause of the violent or unnatural death of a person.[1] The purpose of the inquest is to determine the cause of death. It is not the purpose of an inquest to apportion any blame for a death, nor determine any question of civil or criminal liability.

1   Coroners Act 1988, s 8.

Use of accident reports in litigation

8.101   Shawcross and Beaumont note that in an investigation there is no properly constituted lis between the parties, and the investigation is not a court of competent authority trying an issue of civil liability. Accordingly the findings of a report are not binding in subsequent litigation.[1] The report, however, may and most likely will be used in evidence.

1   Shawcross and Beaumont, **para 8.42 n 1** above, Section VI, para 63.

8.102   The Singapore Court of Appeal has commented on the value of an accident report on subsequent civil proceedings:

> 'The only plank in the appellants' case was the NTSB report and its sheer vehemence. On a number of previous occasions, the NTSB has been wrong in its assessments of aircraft accidents. We do not think they are yet the last word in aviation accident investigation.'[1]

1   *Clarke v SilkAir (Singapore) PTE Ltd* Civil Appeal no 600146 of 2001, at 66. The National Transportation Safety Board (NTSB) is the agency in the US with primary responsibility for aircraft accident investigation.

8.103   With regard to accident investigation, and partially as a consequence of the SilkAir accident, a decision was taken to begin tests on the benefits of recording the pilot's actions on camera. Resistance from airlines and pilots has prevented the NTSB, despite recommending such action, from moving to enforce this requirement. Similarly, the International Federation of Airline Pilots Associations (IFALPA) has condemned the idea unless legislation is passed to ban the broadcast of such videos.[1]

1   'Pilots Threaten To Strike Over Cockpit Videos' *Observer*, 9 June 2002.

8.104   The NTSB's final report on the crash of EgyptAir 990 raised similar conclusions as their report into the SilkAir crash, that there was strong evidence that the crash was caused by a deliberate act of the pilot. The NTSB concluded that the relief first officer of the EgyptAir flight deliberately input data into the flight control system which caused the aircraft to depart normal cruise flight. The report, however, failed to cite a motive.[1] As in the case of earlier SilkAir accident, the Egyptian civil aviation authorities challenged the NTSB conclusions, and went on record to say:

'It is extraordinary to conclude that the evidence is so strong that it supported determinational probable cause, yet failed to include any explanation for the allegedly intentionally human action.'[2]

1   Aircraft Accident Brief NTSB/AAB-02/01 (PB2002-910401), 13 March 2002.
2   *Aviation Daily*, 22 March 2002.

UK accident investigations

8.105   In the following section, certain accidents that occurred in the UK and the resultant investigations are described. These brief descriptions include two of the most serious fatal aviation accidents to have occurred in the UK. Although the accident investigation reports all made clear safety recommendations, some with far-reaching consequences, no criminal proceedings followed any of these investigations.

British European Airways (BEA) Trident G-ARPI, near Staines on 18 June 1972[1]

8.106   The BEA Trident crashed in a field near Staines on Sunday, 18 June 1972, shortly after taking off from London Heathrow Airport on a scheduled flight to Brussels. All 112 passengers and six crew perished in the accident. The aircraft had a valid Certificate of Airworthiness and a valid Certificate of Maintenance

1   Aircraft Accident Report no 4/73 *Report of the Public Inquiry into the causes and circumstances of the accident near Staines on 18 June 1972* (1973).

8.107   The immediate causes of the accident have never been in any real doubt since the original readout of the flight data recorder was recovered within a few hours of the accident. The AIB (as it was then called), indicated that there was no major mechanical malfunction involved and that movement of the lever in the cockpit retracting the leading edge droop flaps rather than the flaps caused the airliner to stall and crash. A public inquiry was convened in 1982 to determine the underlying causes with a view to preventing so far as possible anything like this accident happening again.

8.108   Early in the inquiry evidence had been given that the commander of the Trident, Captain Stanley Key, was suffering from heart trouble as the Trident took off from Heathrow Airport. Just before the flight, he had been engaged in an argument with a junior colleague.[1] After taking evidence from a BEA flight development manager and other BEA pilots, the inquiry found that the underlying causes of the accident included the abnormal heart condition of Captain Key leading to lack of concentration and impaired judgment sufficient to account for his toleration of the speed errors and to his retraction of, or order to retract, the droops in mistake for the flaps. Despite a finding that the captain was not physically and mentally fit to perform his duties, the operator was not criticised for any failure in this regard. The main recommendation to the carrier was increased training to younger first officers and the possibility of using 'stress test' electrocardiograms should be kept under review. No criminal or regulatory proceedings ensued.

1 'Staines air crash inquiry' Times Newspapers Ltd, 9 January 2001

Boeing 737-236, G-BGJL at Manchester International Airport on 22 August 1985[1]

8.109 British Airtours G-BGJL, carrying 131 passengers and six crew on a charter flight to Corfu, began its take off from runway 24 at Manchester. After about 36 seconds, as the airspeed passed 125 knots, the left engine suffered an uncontained failure, which punctured a wing fuel tank access panel. Fuel leaking from the wing ignited as a large plume of fire trailing directly behind the engine. The crew heard a 'thud', and believing that they had suffered a tyre-burst or bird-strike, abandoned the take off immediately, intending to clear the runway to the right. They had no indication of fire until nine seconds later, when the left engine fire warning occurred. After an exchange with Air Traffic Control, during which the fire was confirmed, the commander warned his crew of an evacuation from the right side of the aircraft, by making a broadcast over the cabin address system, and brought the aircraft to a halt in the entrance to a taxiway off the runway.

1 Aircraft Incident Report no 8/88 *Report on the accident to Boeing 737-236, G-BGJL at Manchester International Airport on 22 August 1985* (1988).

8.110 As the aircraft turned off the runway, the wind carried the fire onto and around the rear fuselage. After the aircraft stopped the fire rapidly penetrated the hull and smoke entered the cabin through the aft right door that had been opened shortly before the aircraft came to a halt. Subsequently fire developed within the cabin. Despite the prompt attendance of the airport fire service, the aircraft was destroyed and 55 persons on board lost their lives.

8.111 The AAIB found that the cause of the accident was an uncontained failure of the left engine, initiated by a failure of a combustion can which had been previously repaired. The resultant fire developed catastrophically, primarily because of effects of the wind, even though the wind was light. The AAIB found further that contributory factors were the vulnerability of the wing tank access panels to impact, a lack of any effective provision for fighting major fires inside the aircraft cabin, the vulnerability of the aircraft hull to external fire and the extremely toxic nature of the emissions from the burning interior materials.

8.112 The major cause of the fatalities on board was rapid incapacitation due to the inhalation of the dense toxic/irritant smoke atmosphere within the cabin, aggravated by evacuation delays caused by a door malfunction and restricted access to the exits.

8.113 The investigators found that the flight crew had responded to the 'thud' in a prompt manner in accordance with their experience and training. Their initial assessment of the problem and their subsequent actions were entirely reasonable based on the cues available to them. A similar conclusion was reached in respect of the cabin crew and the maintenance of the aircraft. No comment was passed on the safety systems of the air carrier.

8.114 Civil proceedings were initiated by the relatives of deceased passengers and by those injured. These proceedings were concluded by settlement and did not proceed to any court hearings. No criminal or regulatory proceedings were initiated.

8.115 This investigation, however, led to several safety recommendations being made. One of these, that passengers are equipped with smoke hoods, has not yet been implemented and remains under debate.

Boeing 737-400 G-OBME near Kegworth, Leicestershire on 8 January 1989[1]

8.116 British Midland G-OBME left Heathrow Airport for Belfast at 7.52 pm with eight crew and 118 passengers on board. As the aircraft was climbing through 28,300 feet a blade in the fan of the no 1 (left) engine detached. This gave rise to a series of stalls in the no 1 engine, which resulted in airframe shuddering, ingress of smoke and fumes to the flight deck and fluctuations of the no 1 engine parameters. Believing, however, that the no 2 engine had suffered damage, the crew throttled that engine back. The shuddering caused by the surging of the no 1 engine ceased as soon as the no 2 engine was throttled back, which persuaded the crew that they had dealt correctly with the emergency. They then shut down the no 2 engine. The no 1 engine operated apparently normally after the initial period of severe vibration and during the subsequent descent.

1 Aircraft Accident Report no 4/90 (EW/C1095) *Report on the accident to Boeing 737-400 G-OBME near Kegworth, Leicestershire on 8 January 1989* (1990).

8.117 The crew initiated a diversion to East Midlands Airport and received a radar direction from air traffic control to position the aircraft for an instrument approach. The approach continued normally, although with a high level of vibration from the no 1 engine, until an abrupt reduction of power, followed by a fire warning, occurred on this engine approx 2.5 miles from the runway. Efforts to restart the no 2 engine were not successful.

8.118 The aircraft initially struck a field adjacent to the eastern embankment of the M1 motorway and then suffered a second severe impact on the sloping western embankment of the motorway. A total of 47 passengers died in the accident.

8.119 The AAIB found that the cause of the accident was that the operating crew shut down the no 2 engine after a fan blade had fractured in the no 1 engine. This engine subsequently suffered a major thrust loss due to secondary fan damage after power had been increased during the final approach to land. The AAIB identified, as a factor that contributed to the incorrect response of the flight crew, their premature and incorrect reaction to the initial engine problem.

8.120 The AAIB did not conclude that any conduct of British Midland was a cause or contributory factor.

BAC 1-11, G-BJRT over Didcot, Oxfordshire on 10 June 1990[1]

8.121   The accident happened when the aircraft was climbing through 17,300 feet on departure from Birmingham International Airport to Malaga, Spain. The left windscreen, which had been replaced prior to the flight, was blown out under effects of the cabin pressure. Most of the 90 securing bolts were of smaller than specified diameter. The commander was sucked halfway out of the windscreen aperture and was restrained by cabin crew whilst the co-pilot flew the aircraft to a safe landing at Southampton Airport.

1   Aircraft Accident Report no 1/92 (EW/C1165) *Report on the accident to BAC One-Eleven, G-BJRT over Didcot, Oxfordshire on 10 June 1990* (1992).

8.122   The AAIB concluded that one of the factors that contributed to the loss of the windscreen was that a safety critical task, not identified as a 'Vital Point', was undertaken by a maintenance person who also carried total responsibility for the quality achieved. The installation was not tested until the aircraft was airborne on a passenger carrying flight.

8.123   Additionally, the shift maintenance manager's potential to achieve quality in the windscreen-fitting process was eroded by his inadequate care, poor trade practices, failure to adhere to company standards and use of unsuitable equipment, which were judged symptomatic of a longer-term failure by him to observe the promulgated procedures.

8.124   The British Airways local management, product samples and quality audits had not detected the existence of inadequate standards employed by the shift maintenance manager because they did not monitor directly the working practices of shift maintenance managers.

8.125   The AAIB concluded that the operator's systems had contributed to cause of this accident. Fortunately, there were no fatalities. No criminal or regulatory prosecutions ensued.

Emerald Airways Ltd HS748 G-OJEM at London Stansted Airport on 30 March 1998[1]

8.126   Immediately after take off from London Stansted Airport, on a night flight with 40 passengers and four crew on board, an uncontained failure of the right engine occurred. This resulted in sudden power loss and a major engine bay fire. The Commander elected to land back on the runway. The aircraft overran the paved surface, and uneven ground in the overrun area caused the nose landing gear to collapse. After the aircraft had come to rest, with the engine bay fire continuing, the crew organised a rapid evacuation and all the occupants escaped, with little or no injury. The Airport Fire Service (AFS) extinguished the engine bay fire, but fuel release continued for some hours.

1   Air Accidents Investigation Branch Aircraft Accident Report no 3/2001 (EW/C98/03/7) (2001).

8.127   The AAIB found that the engine failure was caused by high-cycle fatigue cracking of the disc in the turbine section of the aircraft engine. The sustained fire around the damaged engine bay resulted from fuel system disruption caused by the engine failure. Additionally, electrical wiring damage had rendered a fire extinguisher for the damaged engine bay unserviceable prior to the accident. The crew was unable to deploy the rear door manual chutes to assist the escape from the cabin of the burning aircraft without causing significant delay to the evacuation, and the escape chute system was found to be inadequate.

8.128   Four similar turbine section failures had occurred over the previous 26-year period. The evidence indicated that the CAA had been aware of the previous disc failures, and had been involved with the manufacturer in assessing the continued airworthiness of the engine, judging it to be satisfactory. The manufacturer and the CAA had apparently been satisfied with the continuing airworthiness of the engine type on the basis of failure rate statistics. The predominant factor, in the case of G-OJEM's accident, of the gap between the HP and IP turbine seal rings had apparently not previously been identified or investigated.

8.129   The AAIB recommended that the engine manufacturer and the CAA reassess the susceptibility of the three-stage Dart turbine to a failure of this type, and ensure that effective action aimed at preventing recurrence was taken.[1]

1   Safety Recommendation No 2001-20.

8.130   The reasons for the lack of effective action over a number of years, while failures had continued, could not be fully established. A significant cost would have been associated with a requirement for replacement of the disc with a redesigned version, or for early incorporation of DRS 611 and this was undoubtedly a factor that had militated against such action.

Civil liability for death and serious injury

Introduction

8.131   In very general terms, a civil wrong (known in common law legal systems as a tort, or a delict in legal systems derived from Roman law) is an injury other than a breach of contract, which the law will redress with damages. Distinct from a civil wrong, a crime is an offence against the state, as a representative of the public, which will sanction the offender. The function of a criminal prosecution is not to compensate for an injury resulting from a wrong, but rather to penalise an offender both to protect society and also to deter similar potential offenders. Civil liability exists primarily to compensate the victim by compelling the wrongdoer to pay for the damage.[1] In this text, the treatment of corporate liability for aviation accidents is relevant to an appreciation of how criminal courts may approach this issue in a civil context

1   J Fleming *The Law of Torts* (6th edn, 1983) p 1.

8.132   The essence of establishing liability in tort in English law (as in many other legal systems) is (i) identifying the existence of a duty of care; (ii) identifying a breach of that duty; and (iii) identifying a causal link between the breach and any damages or injury. Once all of this is identified, establishing liability will depend upon evidence that the duty of care has been breached either negligently or recklessly as to the consequences that might result. The amount of compensation payable will be determined according to the rules of quantification of damage. These, and the method of assessment, vary from jurisdiction to jurisdiction, often to a substantial degree.

The Warsaw Convention system

8.133 Given the differences in legal jurisdictions, it became apparent in the early history of commercial air transport that there was a need for the unification of the rules relating to the carriage by air over international boundaries. International air transport had produced a new brand of complicated legal problems, by producing an environment where people were being transported rapidly and potentially dangerously between jurisdictions with different legal systems. Complex legal issues were likely to arise. In particular, there was a need for a unified system of liability whereby passengers could travel with some certainty as to the legal regime governing their relationship with the carrier to whom they had entrusted their safety.

8.134 At the Paris International Conference on private air law in 1925, the principles of this unification were and set out by the Rapporteur of the Commission which was studying the question of liability of carriers as follows:

> 'The Commission asked itself which liability regime to be adopted: risk or fault. The general feeling is that, whilst liability towards third parties must see the application of the risk theory, by contrast, in the matter of the carrier's liability in relation to passengers and goods, one must admit the fault theory.
>
> That being so, one can ask oneself on whom will fall the burden of proof; it has seem fair not to impose that heavy burden on the injured party and a presumption of fault bearing on the carrier has been admitted. But since it is only a presumption, the carrier has obviously the right to adduce contrary evidence and the limit of the fault must be established; where does it start?
>
> What can one require from the air carrier? A normal organisation of his business, a judicious selection of the members of his staff, a constant supervision of his agents and servants, a serious checking of his accessory appliances and materials utilised.
>
> One must admit that anyone using an aircraft does not ignore the risks inherent in a mode of transportation which has not yet reached the point of perfection that one hundred years have given to the railways.
>
> Thus it is just not to impose on the carrier an absolute liability and [it is just] to relieve him from any liability when he has taken the measures which are reasonable and normal in order to avoid the injury; this is the diligence that one can require from a bonus pater familias.'[1]

1 See the text of *Conférence Internationale* (1925), Paris, cited in translation in G Miller *Liability in International Air Transport* (1977) p 63.

The Warsaw Convention

International carriage

8.135 The Paris principles were adopted in an International Convention For The Unification Of Certain Rules Relating To International Carriage By Air, signed at Warsaw on 12 October 1929, known universally as the Warsaw Convention.

8.136   The Warsaw Convention has, for over 70 years, provided a framework for the civil law relationship between airlines and their passengers. Over this time, the Convention has been subject to a variety of amendments and additions, resulting in a collection of international agreements known as the Warsaw Convention System.

8.137   The Warsaw Convention applies only to contracts of international carriage, defined as:

> 'any carriage in which, according to the contract made by the parties, the place of departure and the place of destination ... are situated either within the territories of two High Contracting Parties, or within the territory of a single High Contracting Party, if there is an agreed stopping place within a territory subject to the sovereignty, suzerainty, mandate or authority of another Power ...'[1]

1   Warsaw Convention, art 1.

Liability of the carrier for bodily injury

8.138   The Warsaw Convention aims to set out a clear regime for the liability of air carriers to their passengers for loss or damage suffered:

> 'The carrier is liable for damage sustained in the event of the death or wounding of a passenger or any other bodily injury suffered by a passenger, if the accident which caused the damage so sustained took place on board the aircraft or in a cause of any of the operations of embarking or disembarking.'[1]

1   Warsaw Convention, art 17.

8.139   Article 17 of the Warsaw Convention contains the basis for the carrier's liability, but embodies three major interpretational complexities:

- The carrier is only liable for damage caused by an accident. What constitutes an 'accident' for these purposes?
- The carrier is liable for death or wounding of a passenger or any other bodily injury suffered by a passenger. What constitutes 'bodily injury'?
- What constitutes 'the operations of embarking or disembarking'?

8.140   Article 17 of the Warsaw Convention determines the conditions under which the air carrier shall be liable. Once these conditions are fulfilled, the carrier's liability is engaged.[1] Article 17 does not regulate the question of recoverable damages but only sets out basis of the carrier's liability.

1   Miller, **para 8.134 n 1** above, p 125.

Presumption of liability

8.141   The cornerstone of the Warsaw Convention liability regime is the presumption of the carrier's liability inherent in art 17. This is a presumption of liability, rather than absolute or strict liability.[1] The presumption of liability effectively reverses the burden of proof. In most common law legal systems, the victim of alleged wrong will, in most circumstances, be required to prove that the damage suffered was the result of the negligence of the person being sued. The Warsaw Convention regime turns this around, providing that proof of damage by the passenger is sufficient for the carrier's liability to be assumed.

1   *See* Miller, **para 8.134 n 1** above, who identifies (p 65) the cases where this was unsuccessfully argued.

8.142   The basis of this thinking lies in the relative positions of the passenger and the air carrier, as seen in 1929 by the drafters of the Warsaw Convention. Given the technical sophistication of the aviation industry, and its fledgling nature at that time, airlines accepted a presumption of their liability as a benefit to passengers and consignors of cargo who would not, therefore, have to prove liability in the event of an accident. The decision to institute a regime such as this was also addressed in the light of the availability of insurance coverage for carriers.[1]

1   See comments of the President of the Drafting Committee of the Warsaw Conference, Mr Gianini, quoted in R Abeyratne 'The Spread Of Tuberculosis In The Aircraft Cabin – Issues Of Air Carrier Liability' (2000) 27 Transp LJ 41 at 83.

Defences

8.143   In the Warsaw Convention, the carrier could defeat the presumption of its liability if the carrier was able to establish one of two defences in the Convention. The first defence relieved the carrier from liability if the carrier could prove that it and all its servants and agents had taken all necessary measures to avoid the damage or that it was impossible for them to take such measures.[1]

1   Warsaw Convention, art 20.

8.144   The second defence was afforded to the carrier if it was able to prove that the passenger had been the author of his or her own misfortune and had been contributory negligent in the cause of the damage.[1]

1   Warsaw Convention, art 21.

8.145   Both of these defences have been notoriously difficult to establish.

Limit of liability

8.146   The quid pro quo for the presumption of the carrier's liability, which is of great benefit to the passenger, is the carrier's entitlement to limit its liability. The Warsaw Convention provides that the maximum liability of the carrier following the presumption of liability would be 125,000 gold Francs, which at the time converted to an amount of approximately US$5,000.[1] From the point of view of the passenger or the owner of baggage or cargo, the presumption of the carrier's liability without proof of fault is a very significant advantage. From the point of view of the carrier there are significant advantages in the Convention system. A principal consequence of that system is the exposure of the carrier to liabilities without the freedom to contract out of them. But it defines those situations in which compensation is to be available, and it sets out the limits of liability and the conditions under which claims to establish liability, if disputed, are to be made. A balance has been struck between these competing interests, in the interests of certainty and uniformity.[2]

1   Warsaw Convention, art 22. The limit of the liability has been revised subsequently.
2   *Morris v KLM Royal Dutch Airlines, King v Bristow Helicopters Ltd* [2002] UKHL 7, [2002] 2
     AC 628 at [66], HL, per Lord Hope of Craighead.

Unlimited liability

8.147   The limit of the carrier's liability is not absolute under the Warsaw Convention. The passenger can break the limit of liability on proof that the damage was caused by the wilful misconduct of the carrier.[1]

1   Warsaw Convention, art 25.

Exclusive remedy

8.148   The fundamental principle of the Warsaw Convention was the unification of (at least) certain rules relating to international carriage by air. Accordingly, the Convention provides that it constitutes an exclusive remedy to passengers.[1]

1   Warsaw Convention, art 24.

The Hague Protocol

8.149   By 1938 work had started at an international level to revise some of the terms of the Warsaw Convention that were found to be causing difficulties, primarily in interpretation and application, but also in principle with regard to the liability limit. An international conference was convened by ICAO at The Hague in September 1955 at which the Hague Protocol 1955 was adopted and signed.

8.150   The Hague Protocol amends certain provisions of the Warsaw Convention. The public international law aspects of this Protocol are complex: a state may be a party to the Warsaw Convention without signing the Hague Protocol (for example, the US) or conversely may be a party to the Hague Protocol without having signed the Warsaw Convention (for example, South Korea). Most states, however, have ratified or adhered to the amended Convention (the Warsaw Convention, as amended by the Hague Protocol).

8.151   The Hague Protocol amended the Warsaw Convention in two key areas, for the purposes of this chapter:

- An increase in the liability limit from 125,000 gold Francs to 250,000 gold Francs (approximately US$10,000).
- Review of the concept of wilful misconduct, as the type of conduct to be proved by a passenger in order to breach the carrier's limit of liability. The notion of 'wilful misconduct' was replaced by 'an act or omission of the servant or agent (of the carrier) done with intent to cause damage or recklessly and with knowledge that damage would probably result'.[1]

1   Hague Protocol, art 14(3), amending the Warsaw Convention, art 25.

8.152   An additional amendment to the liability limits provided that they were exclusive of costs and expenses of litigation.

8.153   The Hague Protocol also recognised the fundamental injustice in allowing carriers to limit their liability, while an action might succeed against a servant or agent of the carrier (for example, a pilot or another carrier) without limitation of liability. Accordingly, art 25A of the Hague Protocol extends the availability of the limitation of liability to servants or agents of the carrier, provided that the servant or agent can prove that it was acting within the scope of its employment.

Montreal Inter-Carrier Agreement 1966

8.154   The US has never ratified the Hague Protocol. The view of parts of the US legislature, judicial system and legal profession was that even the revised limits of liability provided by the Hague Protocol (at that time approximately US$16,000) were too low adequately to serve the interests of passengers who might be US citizens. The ICAO convened a special meeting in Montreal in 1966 for a solution to be negotiated. The US delegation to the meeting felt that the aviation industry had matured since 1929, and the economic consequences of an air disaster would be serious enough to justify a higher limit. The opposing view was that an increased limit would benefit only a small proportion of passengers in any event. Not surprisingly, the ICAO special meeting failed to resolve this issue. A solution was ultimately found on the initiative of the member airlines of the International Air Transport Association (IATA) in the form of an Agreement signed in Montreal on 4 May 1966 (known as the Montreal Inter-Carrier Agreement) between several of the airlines which were IATA members at that time.

8.155   The Montreal Inter-Carrier Agreement represented a compromise position, applying a limit of liability for each passenger for death, wounding or other bodily injury in the amount of $75,000 inclusive of legal fees and costs, except where in case of a claim brought in a state where provision is made for a separate award of legal fees and costs, the limit is $58,000 exclusive of legal fees and costs.

8.156   The Montreal Inter-Carrier Agreement was given force of law in the US.[1] It does not, however, have any formal status in international law, and is not part of the Warsaw Convention system of international instruments.

1   Filed with the Civil Aeronautics Board as CAB no 18900, and approved by the CAB under the Federal Aviation Act 1958, s 412.

8.157   The Montreal Inter-Carrier Agreement applies to any international carriage to, from or through the US. The Agreement also provides that the carriers would not use the defence of 'all necessary measures' contained in art 20(1) of the Warsaw Convention. The Montreal Inter-Carrier Agreement effectively changes the basis of liability of the Warsaw Convention system to absolute liability (subject to the defence of contributory negligence).

Developments towards unlimited liability

8.158   Over the last 30 years there has been growing disquiet, mainly within the legal profession, that the provisions of the Warsaw Convention system, even as amended, did not conform to the modern civil aviation industry. In particular, the trend towards separation of airlines from state control allowed the airlines greater flexibility to agree how their passengers would be compensated in the event of an accident. The primary move was towards a regime of unlimited liability for passengers, yet retaining the presumption of liability.

8.159 Following the agreement of the Montreal Inter-Carrier Agreement in 1966, there were several other initiatives to increase or even remove the limits of liability to passengers.

8.160 In 1992, the Japanese carriers amended their conditions of carriage to remove the liability limits in the amended Warsaw Convention. Effectively, therefore, these carriers were providing unlimited liability to their passengers. The presumption of liability remained for claims up to a limit of 100,000 Special Drawing Rights (SDR). For claims in excess of that amount, the passenger would need to prove liability.

8.161 In 1994, the European Civil Aviation Conference (ECAC) recommended that European carriers agree an increase in the limit to at least SDR 250,000. In 1995, an additional IATA Inter-Carrier Agreement on Passenger Liability removed the limits of liability altogether. In 1997, the US Department of Transport approved the IATA Inter-Carrier Agreement but required passengers to prove liability up to SDR 100,000 on flights to, from, or through the US.[1]

1 See P Mendes De Leon, W Eyskens 'The Montreal Convention: Analysis of Some Aspects of the Attempted Modernization and Consolidation of the Warsaw System' 66 J Air L & Com 1155 at n 1.

8.162 In 1997, the European Council enacted Council Regulation 2027/97/EC.[1] This Regulation removed the limit for EU carriers, as well as the defences of contributory negligence and all necessary measures for claims up to SDR 100,000.[2] The regulation also provided for the carrier to make advance payments to the families of victims.[3]

1 Enacted in the UK by the Air Carrier Liability Order 1998, SI 1998/1751. However, note the challenge to its validity in the UK in *R v Secretary of State for Transport, the Environment and the Regions, ex p IATA* [2002] 1 Lloyd's Rep 243 which held that the Regulation conflicted with the Warsaw Convention.
2 This is set out in Council Regulation 2027/97/EC, art 3 which was brought into effect in the UK by way of negative amendment to the Carriage by Air Act 1961, s 1(1) declaring by virtue of new Carriage by Air Act 1961, s 1A that Warsaw Convention, arts 21 and 22(1) and art 20 up to SDR 100,000 'do not have the force of law in the United Kingdom'.
3 Council Regulation 2027/97/EC has been prospectively superseded by Council Regulation 889/2002 which came into force together with the Montreal Convention 1999. See **para 8.163** below.

8.163 Consistent with these developments, the entire Warsaw Convention system has been reviewed.[1] In 1999, a new Convention known as the Montreal Convention 1999 was prepared and opened for signature.[2] It entered into force on 4 November 2003.[3] The principal changes that are brought about by the Montreal Convention, for the purposes of this chapter, are that airlines will face strict liability for claims up to SDR 100,000. For damages above this amount, there is a presumption of liability, but the airline can defend the claim above SDR 100,000 by proving that damage was not due to the negligence or other wrongful act or omission of the carrier or its servants or agents, or such damage is solely due to the negligent act or omission of a third party.[4] Effectively, the limit of liability has been removed, as well as the defence of all necessary measures.

1   'However, for a number of years, the Warsaw Convention has been ailing. Numerous instruments
    in the form of treaties, domestic legislation and regulations, contractual undertakings, have
    grown up since the Second World War to implement, supplement, amend and shore up the
    original Convention, forming in a rather higgledy-piggledy way what is commonly known as
    the Warsaw System': B Cheng *The 1999 Montreal Convention on International Carriage by
    Air Concluded on the Seventieth Anniversary of the 1929 Warsaw Convention (Part 1)* (2000)
    49 ZLW 287.
2   The Convention for the Unification of Certain Rules for International Carriage by Air of May
    28, 1999, ICAO Doc 9740.
3   The convention entered into force on the sixtieth day following the date of deposit of the
    thirtieth instrument of ratification, acceptance, approval or accession. The Convention is
    enacted in the EU by Regulation 889/2002, and in the UK by the Carriage by Air Acts
    (Implementation of the Montreal Convention 1999) Order 2002, SI 2002/263. By February
    2003, 71 states had signed the Convention and 25 states had ratified, accepted, approved or
    acceded to the Convention. On 5 September 2003 the US became the 30th state to ratify the
    Convention.
4   Montreal Convention, art 21.

8.164   The Montreal Convention also provides for the payment of advance payments
to meet immediate economic needs of persons following an aircraft accident.[1]

1   Montreal Convention, art 28.

Wilful misconduct

8.165   Article 25 of the Warsaw Convention provides:

> 'The carrier shall not be entitled to ... exclude or limit his liability, if the damage
> is caused by his wilful misconduct or by such default by his part as, in
> accordance with the law of the Court seised of the case, is considered to be
> equivalent to wilful misconduct.'

8.166   The Warsaw Convention also extended the liability of the carrier to cover
acts or omissions of the carrier's servants or agents to the carrier acting within the
scope of their employment.

8.167   The definition of 'wilful misconduct' in this context has tested courts in both
civil law and common law jurisdictions. The original text of the Warsaw Convention is
in the French language, and uses the words '*dol*' and '*faute equivalente au dol*' in art
25. French Law considers *dol* in the context of an intention to do damage. French
courts, however, have been divided over whether there must be the intention to cause
the precise damage which has resulted, or whether *dol* occurs where there is an
intention only to breach contractual duties, arguably a lesser species of intention.

8.168   Courts in other civil law jurisdictions have avoided this issue by interpreting
dol as 'gross negligence', equating this to the words '*faute lourde*' which are treated
as equivalent based on Roman law.[1] Gross negligence can be defined as 'the intentional
failure to perform a manifest duty in reckless disregard of the consequences as
affecting the life or property of another; such a gross want of care and regard for the
rights of others as to justify the presumption of wilfulness and wantonness'.[2] This
moves the standard of proof further than intentionally doing damage, implying an
intention to commit an act which the actor knows is wrong an adding an element of
knowledge.

1 *Culpa lata dolo aequiparatur* (gross negligence is equivalent to *dol*).
2 *Blacks Law Dictionary* (revised 4th edn), cited in Miller, **para 8.134 n 1** above, p 200.

8.169 Common law courts have struggled to apply a workable definition of 'wilful misconduct'. In the first English case dealing with this point in the unamended Warsaw Convention, the court held that:

> 'To be guilty of wilful misconduct the person concerned must appreciate that he is acting wrongfully, or wrongfully omitting to act and yet persists in so acting or omitting to act regardless of the consequences, or acts or omits to acts with reckless indifference as to what the result may be.'[1]

1 *Horabin v British Overseas Airways Corpn* [1952] 2 All ER 1016 at 1022.

8.170 A US court, at around the same time, held:

> 'There is no dispute as to what constitutes wilful misconduct. The instructions require proof of a "conscious intent to do or omit doing an act from which harm results to another, or an intentional omission of a manifest duty". There must be a realisation of the probability of injury from the conduct, and a disregard of the probable consequences of such conduct.'[1]

1 *Grey v American Airlines Inc* 4 Avi Cas 17,811 (2nd Cir, 1955) at 17,813.

8.171 Accordingly, English and US courts have emphasised the specific character of wilful misconduct as solidly based on an intentional act rather than a negligent one, however gross or culpable the negligence might have been.

Recklessly and with knowledge

8.172 The definition of the conduct to be proved in order to breach the limit of liability was revised in the amended Warsaw Convention as follows:

> 'The limits of liability … shall not apply if it is proved that the damage resulted from an act or omission of the carrier, his servants or agents, done with intent to cause damage or recklessly and with knowledge that damage would probably result; provided that, in the case of such act or omission of a servant or agent, it is also proved that he was acting within the scope of his employment.'[1]

1 Warsaw Convention, art 25A, as amended.

8.173 Article 25A of the amended Warsaw Convention introduced both intention and recklessness. In English law, analysis of these notions is most advanced in the context of criminal law; this analysis must be used with some caution in the very different context of the Carriage by Air Act 1961.[1]

1 Shawcross and Beaumont, **para 8.42 n 1** above, para 445.

8.174 The leading case in English law on the amended article is *Goldman v Thai Airways International Ltd*.[1] In this case the claimant was thrown from his seat during air turbulence and suffered an injury to his spine. He had not fastened his seat belt. The aircraft captain had not illuminated the seat belt sign despite entering an area of forecast moderate clear air turbulence and despite the airline's instructions to pilots to illuminate that sign during all flying in turbulent air and when turbulence could be expected. The trial judge held that in disregarding the instructions the pilot had acted recklessly and with knowledge that damage would probably result. Therefore liability was not limited under the amended Warsaw Convention.

1   [1983] 3 All ER 693, [1983] 1 WLR 1186.

8.175   The Court of Appeal held that to breach the limit under the amended Warsaw Convention, art 25, the act or omission had to have been done both 'recklessly' and 'with knowledge that danger would probably result'. The test was subjective and, therefore, the pilot had only acted recklessly if it was proved that he had omitted to order the passengers to wear seat belts when aware or indifferent to his knowledge of the fact that damage of the kind that did occur would probably result. On the facts it was doubtful whether the pilot had been reckless in interpreting the flight operations manual as giving him discretion to defer switching on the sign for seat belts to be worn until there was an indication of turbulence. Even if he had been reckless in disobeying the manual, the evidence did not disclose that there was a probability of encountering clear air turbulence of a severity that would cause the kind of injury suffered by the claimant. Accordingly, since the pilot could not have had knowledge of the likelihood of the injury, art 25 did not apply and liability remained limited.

8.176   In this case, the Court of Appeal provided an interpretation of the phrase 'recklessly and with knowledge that damage would probably result' based on a subjective analysis.[1] The pilot (in this case) must have knowledge that damage would probably result from his omission, possibly knowledge of the precise type of damage that actually occurred. This is a matter of evidence. This has been called 'subjective awareness' for the purpose of determining liability in an aviation case.[2]

1   *Goldman v Thai Airways International Ltd* [1983] 3 All ER 693, [1983] 1 WLR 1186.
2   *Gurtner v Beaton* [1993] 2 Lloyd's Rep 369.

8.177   An objective analysis, on the other hand, would call for evidence that an independent pilot, with the requisite qualifications and experience, would have that knowledge.[1] This approaches the analysis adopted in criminal cases dealing with the mental state required in order to prove manslaughter. The criminal cases dealing with recklessness in the context of manslaughter have framed the definition of 'recklessness' in terms of appreciating a risk of damage resulting from an act or omission and being indifferent to that risk.[2] In *R v Reid* the court went further and defined the question to be asked as whether 'a reasonable man, in the defendant's position, performing the very act which the defendant intentionally performed, would have realised that he was exposing another or others to an appreciable risk of injury…'[3] Accordingly, the defendant will be criminally reckless if he or she created an obvious and serious risk of death or personal injury and either chose to run the risk or failed to give any thought to the possible existence of the risk.[4]

1   See the judgment of Eveleigh LJ in *Goldman v Thai Airways International Ltd* [1983] 3 All ER 693, [1983] 1 WLR 1186, **para 8.174** above.
2   *R v Caldwell* [1982] AC 341, [1981] 1 All ER 961; *R v Lawrence* [1982] AC 510, [1981] 1 All ER 974.
3   *R v Reid* [1992] 3 All ER 673 at 683.
4   *R v Seymour* [1983] 2 AC 493, [1983] 2 All ER 1058, HL; *R v Adomako* [1995] 1 AC 171, HL.

8.178 The importance of the words in art 25 of the amended Warsaw Convention is that knowledge of the probability of *damage* over and above the *risk* of damage is an integral part of the test for liability. In this respect, in English law at least, the test for unlimited liability in order to breach the limits of liability in the amended Warsaw Convention represents a more stringent evidential burden than the burden on the prosecution in a manslaughter case in the general criminal law. Two consequences follow: first, a company convicted of manslaughter may not necessarily face unlimited liability in a civil action; and, secondly, an airline against whom unlimited damages have been awarded following a successful claim under art 25 may not ipso facto have been liable for manslaughter, because of the difficulties in identifying the controlling mind. It is submitted that under the proposed offence of corporate killing there will be far greater overlap between the evidence used to prosecute a claim under art 25 and the proposed offence of corporate killing.

8.179 However, a useful examination of the concept arose not in a passenger liability case, but in a case involving damage to cargo. So far as the supposed distinction between passenger cases and cargo cases is regarded as one of law, it has absolutely no basis in the language of the Warsaw Convention.[1]

1 Shawcross and Beaumont, **para 8.42 n 1** above, para 447.

8.180 In the case of *SS Pharmaceutical Co Ltd v Qantas Airways Ltd*,[1] the claimants consigned five cartons of pharmaceutical products from Melbourne to Tokyo via Sydney. According to the claimants, the pharmaceutical capsules were first stowed in plastic bags sealed with ties. The plastic bags were then placed in no 3 board cardboard cartons and those cartons were each sealed with 48 mm red PVC adhesive tape. The cartons were then placed in five standard IATA configuration twin cushion, high wet strength, waterproof glue, corrugated cardboard containers. The five containers were fastened with metal staples, strapped with polypropylene banding tape and then each wrapped in a 150 micron plastic bag sealed by shrink-wrapping. The cartons were each marked with a stencilled umbrella to denote that the goods in the carton would be damaged if exposed to water.

1 (1991) 1 Lloyds Rep 288 (Australia CA).

8.181 In Sydney the goods were unloaded and held next to the Qantas Air Cargo Centre. The weather forecast for that day indicated showers with occasional thunderstorms, and there was in fact some rainfall. On arrival at Tokyo it was found that the cartons in the top tier of the pallets were generally in a damp condition while the cartons in the bottom tier were badly wet and in a fragile condition. Qantas did not deny liability but relied on the limit of liability in the amended Warsaw Convention. The claimants alleged that Qantas' conduct was sufficiently reckless to breach the limit.

8.182 The trial judge held that Qantas' conduct was reckless in that there was clear knowledge of the likelihood of damage to especially vulnerable cargo in those weather conditions. The Court of Appeal judges considered the phrase 'recklessly and with knowledge the damage would probably result' as set out in art 25 of the amended Warsaw Convention.[1] They summarised the test as 'a standard of highly reprehensible conduct'. The state of mind involved goes beyond mere carelessness and that actual, as distinct from merely imputed, knowledge that damage would probably result must be shown. They found that this had been made out, based on evidence that servants and agents of the airline had observed the indications on the cargo that it should be stored in a dry environment, observed that it was raining and nevertheless went onto leave the cargo in the open without taking the steps that they knew would protect the cargo. In a subsequent letter to the claimants, a Qantas supervisor had referred to the airline's 'deplorably bad handling'.

1   *SS Pharmaceutical Co Ltd v Qantas Airways Ltd* (1991) 1 Lloyds Rep 288 (Australia CA).

8.183   The third judge in the Court of Appeal[1] dissented from the majority on the basis that the claimants had failed to show, by the subjective standard, that one or more of the servants or agents of Qantas acted recklessly knowing the damage would probably result. They failed to identify the servant or agent to be criticised in such terms, having accepted the subject of standard applies. The dissenting judge noted that the trial judge did not specify the particular act or admission by any servant or agent of Qantas that attracted art 25 of the amended Warsaw Convention. Still less did he demonstrate that any such servant or agent acted recklessly with full knowledge that damage would probably result. The trial judge had treated all of the acts by any Qantas staff (or agents used in the movement of the cargo) as relevant and then to ascribe the knowledge of all such persons to Qantas. The consequence of damage was then noted. The inference was then drawn that the stringent requirements of art 25 had been made out.

1   *SS Pharmaceutical Co Ltd v Qantas Airways Ltd* (1991) 1 Lloyds Rep 288 (Australia CA).

8.184   The dissenting judge in this case[1] has effectively imputed an identification principle into art 25 of the amended Warsaw Convention. This brings the civil standard of recklessness extremely close to the criminal standard. What, therefore, is the difference between the 'stringent' test required by the majority in this case and the requirements of the criminal law under *Adomako*?[2]

1   *SS Pharmaceutical Co Ltd v Qantas Airways Ltd* (1991) 1 Lloyds Rep 288 (Australia CA).
2   *R v Adomako* [1995] 1 AC 171, HL.

8.185   In *Killick and Nugent v Michael Goss Aviation Ltd*[1] the claim arose from the death in 1996 of Mr Matthew Harding in the crash of a helicopter in which he was travelling from Bolton to London as a passenger. The helicopter was piloted by Michael Goss, who was also killed in the crash. The flight was governed by the provisions of the amended Warsaw Convention. The claimants valued the claim at about £59 million and sought to rely on arts 25 and 25A of the amended Convention in order to breach the limit.

1   (2000) 2 Lloyd's Rep 222, per Dyson J.

8.186   The claimants alleged recklessness in a course of conduct coupled with knowledge of probable resultant damage as against the pilot. As to recklessness they contended that the pilot had (i) failed to keep his flying skills up to date; (ii) failed to acquaint himself with navigational aids with which the helicopter was equipped; (iii) failed to plan the flight properly; (iv) flown when he was tired. As to knowledge of probable damage they argued that the probability of damage was within his knowledge in that even if it was not present in his mind at the material time, if he had addressed his mind to the matter, he would have appreciated by reason of his knowledge and skill as an experienced pilot that death or serious injury was probable; alternatively that he had actually known, in the sense appreciated at the time of the contract relied on, that it would probably result in damage.

8.187   The court held that relevant 'knowledge' could be classified as follows:

1   Actual conscious knowledge: actual knowledge in the mind of the pilot at the moment in which the omission occurs.
2   Background knowledge: knowledge that will be present to the mind of a person if he thought about it.
3   Imputed knowledge: knowledge which a person ought to have but does not in fact have.

1   *Killick and Nugent v Michael Goss Aviation Ltd* (2000) 2 Lloyd's Rep 222.

8.188   Only actual conscious knowledge would suffice for the amended Warsaw Convention, art 25 because it is difficult to draw the line between such knowledge and the knowledge in categories in 2 and 3 above. With regards to background knowledge, if a person fails to apply his mind to a fact because he has temporarily forgotten it, he has no more and no less actual knowledge of that fact at the time of his act or omission then a person who fails to apply his mind to it because he has been temporarily distracted. With regards to imputed knowledge, it is not sufficient to show that, by reason of his training and experience, the pilot ought to have known the damage would probably result from his act or omission.

8.189   The Singapore Court of Appeal came to the same conclusion in *Clarke v SilkAir (Singapore) PTE Ltd.*[1] In this case, SilkAir Flight MI 185 left Jakarta for Singapore. Less than an hour after take off, it crashed into the Musi River in daylight and in good weather, killing all on board. The last voice transmission from the crew was shortly before the crash, to Jakarta Air Traffic Control. It was not a distress call.

1   Civil Appeal no 600146 of 2001 (Singapore CA).

8.190   The Indonesian National Transportation Safety Committee (NTSC), which investigated the crash, concluded that the cause of the crash was unascertainable due to a lack of evidence. The US investigators disagreed, citing intentional pilot action as a likely cause. However, an investigation into the personal circumstances of the pilots and crew by the Criminal Investigation Department of Singapore yielded no evidence of motives to crash the aircraft.

8.191   The claimants were the families of six of the deceased. They claimed that the pilots had intended to cause the crash and/or had recklessly caused the crash with knowledge that damage would probably result, based on a theory that one or both of the pilots had deliberately crashed the aircraft in order to commit suicide. Although the claimants could not prove this, they alleged that there was insufficient evidence to show that the pilots had not deliberately caused the crash.

8.192   The Court of Appeal held that the technical evidence did not conclusively reveal the cause of the crash. In particular, there was no evidence of any deliberate action by the pilots that may have caused the accident.[1] In considering whether the airline could limit its liability under the amended Warsaw Convention, the court noted that only subjective, actual conscious knowledge sufficed to establish the test of 'recklessly and with knowledge that damage would probably result' in order to breach the limitation of liability. In this case, the court held there was insufficient available evidence of the pilots' actions and state of mind in order to establish the required level of knowledge. There was no allegation of any failure on the part of the airline. Crucially, the court noted that the claimants had the burden of proving this knowledge.

They could rely on merely disproving the airline's theories, or to show that their explanations were more believable than the airline's. The *standard* of proof is on a balance of probabilities, but a higher degree of probability is required in respect of particularly serious allegations. The claimants here also relied on the legal maxim res ipsa loquitur which would allow an inference to be drawn in the absence of any alternative explanation. The court held that the claimants could not rely on the maxim to establish intent or recklessness with knowledge that damage would probably result.

1   *Clarke v SilkAir (Singapore) PTE Ltd* Civil Appeal no 600146 of 2001 (Singapore CA).

8.193   Note that in this case the Civil Court had the benefit of the outcome of the criminal investigation. The criminal investigation had found that the captain of the aircraft had good relations with his family. He had a high net worth at the time of the crash and his behaviour before the crash was normal. It does not appear that the criminal report investigated the management or actions of the airline, as the employers of the captain, in respect of any causative factors of this accident. The Court of Appeal held that suicide, murder and dangerous stunts would not fall within the scope of employment. No carrier authorises such acts. In any such circumstance, the pilot would be on a frolic of his own. It would not be an act committed in furtherance of the carrier's business.[1]

1   *Clarke v SilkAir (Singapore) PTE Ltd* Civil Appeal no 600146 of 2001 at 33 (Singapore CA), per Yong Pung How CJ.

Civil cases and the identification doctrine

8.194   In English criminal law, the state of mind and required knowledge of damage needs to be imputed to the corporation in order for the criminal liability of the company to be established. This is known as the identification doctrine.

8.195   In the civil law cases, the Warsaw Convention system establishes liability on the company arising out of a relevant acts or omission of an employee acting within the scope of the employee's employment. As can be seen, aviation accidents are often the result of a concatenation of events. This was also referred to in the Sheen Report into the capsize of the ferry *Herald of Free Enterprise*:

> 'All concerned in the management, from the members of the Board of Directors down to the junior superintendents, were guilty of fault in that all must be regarded as sharing responsibility for the failure of management. From the top to the bottom the body corporate was infected with the disease of sloppiness.'[1]

1   Sheen Report *MV Herald of Free Enterprise* Report no 8974, Department of Transport (1987) para 14.

8.196   This line of thinking has been applied in several aviation cases dealing with claims under art 25 of the Warsaw Convention. An Appeal Court in the US has held:

> 'We do not agree with Northwest that the jury should have been prohibited from viewing the airline's individual mistakes together as a "series of actions or inactions" exhibiting reckless disregard for the safety of passengers. No principle of law or logic requires a jury evaluating wilful misconduct to focus exclusively on discrete acts, without regard for the complete chain of events leading to the

accident. This is especially true if those acts, though individual, nevertheless reflect on an overall frame of mind or course of conduct which led to them.'[1]

1 *Polec v Northwest Airlines Inc* 86 F 3d 498 at 545.

8.197 Decided cases under art 25 of the Warsaw Convention generally illustrate that wilful misconduct or reckless acts are based on a series of acts or omissions. Many complex safety systems interact during a flight and an accident may be the product of multiple errors. The line of inquiry to establish liability under art 25 will clearly overlap with the inquiries pursued in the course of a criminal investigation into corporate criminal liability.

Criminal liability for aviation accidents in the UK

The Air Navigation Order 2000

8.198 The Air Navigation Order 2000[1] (ANO 2000) provides a wide-ranging jurisdiction to the CAA to bring criminal prosecutions.

1 SI 2000/1562 (CAP 393). This Order, which came into force on 22 April 2003, revokes and replaces the Air Navigation Order 1980, SI 1980/1965 and the Air Navigation (No 2) Order 1995, SI 1995/1970.

8.199 ANO 2000, art 63[1] provides:

'A person shall not recklessly or negligently act in a manner likely to endanger an aircraft, or any person therein.'

1 SI 2000/1562, art 63.

8.200 ANO 2000, art 64[1] provides:

'A person shall not recklessly or negligently cause or permit an aircraft to endanger any person or property.'

1 SI 2000/1562, art 64.

8.201 These are wide-ranging articles, the scope of which are increased when read together with other provisions of the ANO 2000. For example, these articles apply to all UK registered aircraft anywhere[1] and to all aircraft within the UK.[2] The penalties for breach are a fine, imprisonment for up to two years, or both.[3] In addition, or alternatively, the CAA has the discretion under the ANO 2000 to revoke, suspend or vary a pilot's licence.

1 SI 2000/1562, art 123(1)(a).
2 SI 2000/1562, art 123(1)(b).
3 SI 2000/1562, art 123(6) and SI 2000/1562, Sch 12, Pt B.

8.202 On its wording, ANO 2000, art 63[1] applies to acts which endanger an aircraft on the ground as well as in flight. Similarly, ANO 2000, art 64[2] applies to acts that cause an aircraft to endanger any personal property which could be in the air or on the ground. The wording of these two articles provides some measure of overlap: it is possible, if not likely, that the same reckless or negligent act could fall within the scope of both. For example, an air traffic controller could, by negligently directing a landing aircraft, endanger not only it and persons in it but also property and persons on or within the vicinity of the airport.[3] Accordingly, a prosecution could be brought under one or both of these articles.

1   SI 2000/1562, art 63.
2   SI 2000/1562, art 64
3   Shawcross and Beaumont, **para 8.42 n 1** above, Section IV.

8.203   The scope of these articles is increased even further by the absence of a requirement of actual harm to persons or damage to property in order for an offence under the articles to be made out. Actual harm to persons or damage to property, together with the requisite intent, could additionally lead to a prosecution under the general criminal law. Given the wide scope of these articles, it is noteworthy that there have only been a handful of prosecutions in the UK.

8.204   In order to achieve a prosecution under these articles, the prosecuting authority will need to prove that a person has acted 'recklessly or negligently' and has 'endangered' an aircraft, or any person or property. This will be a criminal prosecution, and it will therefore be put to a jury to decide whether or not an act or omission falls within the scope of the sections. It has proved difficult to define 'recklessly or negligently' in English law in such a way that a jury can apply the terms.

8.205   The interpretation of these words in the context of the ANO 2000 is subject to a possible defence in ANO 2000:[1]

'If it is proved that an act or omission of any person which would otherwise have been a contravention by that person of a provision of this Order or of any regulations made thereunder or of JAR-145 was due to any cause not avoidable by the exercise of reasonable care by that person the act or omission shall be deemed not to be a contravention by that person of that provision.'

1   SI 2000/1562, art 122(2).

8.206   This provision appears to provide a defence of 'reasonable care' to an allegation of reckless or negligent behaviour under the articles.

8.207   In *R v Whitehouse*[1] the court dealt with the interpretation of 'likely' in ANO 2000, art 63.[2] In this case, the defendant was a passenger on a British Airways flight from Madrid to Manchester. One of the cabin crew noticed that he was using a mobile telephone to write a text message. She asked him to turn off the phone and pointed out that using the phone during the flight was not permitted. He refused to comply and eventually did so only after the captain was informed and had asked to be given the mobile phone. On arrival at Manchester, the defendant was arrested and charged under art 63. He was convicted by the jury and sentenced to 12 months' imprisonment.[3] He then appealed on the basis that his actions were not 'likely' to have endangered the aircraft.

1   [2000] Crim LR 172, *Times* 10 December 1999, *Independent* 14 December 1999.
2   SI 2000/1562, art 63.
3   In this case, the appellant was convicted under the Air Navigation (No 2) Order 1995, SI 1995/1970, art 55, which was replaced by the ANO 2000, SI 2000/1562, art 63. The wording is identical.

8.208 As to the meaning of the word 'likely' in ANO 2000, art 63,[1] the Court of Appeal upheld the judge's interpretation of the word:

> 'Let me explain it in this way, members of the jury; if I were to say to you, "it is likely to rain this evening", I would mean by that, there is a real risk of rain, a risk that should not be ignored. That is another meaning to the word "likely" and that is what the Crown contend to be meant by that word. Is there a real risk, a risk that should not be ignored? You will have to decide and consider that.'[2]

It was held that this direction to the jury was in accordance with authority and the appellant's conviction was upheld.[3]

1 SI 2000/1562, art 63.
2 Per Pill LJ.
3 Reported prosecutions against passengers under SI 2000/1562, arts 63 and 64 (and their predecessors) include *R v Ryan* [2001] EWCA Crim 824, [2001] 2 Cr App R(S) 550, CA (lighting fire in toilet); *R v Ayodeji* Transcript ref 2000/3386/Y4 (21 August 2000) (being drunk on board).

Prosecution of a private pilot

8.210 In *R v Warburton-Pitt*,[1] a rare case of a prosecution of a private pilot under ANO 2000, arts 63 and 64, the defendant had been participating with a microlight aircraft in a flying display at a school fête. On his final departure, he chose a take off run which, once airborne, took him directly towards three tall trees. In banking to avoid the trees, the aircraft stalled and crashed into a crowd of people, killing one of them and injuring several more. The pilot was charged under the Air Navigation Order 1980, arts 45 and 46.[2] Although no detailed particulars were given of the facts on which the charges of recklessness and negligence were brought, it was alleged by the prosecution that the pilot was blameworthy for the following reasons:

- the take off run he selected was unsafe because the trees presented an obstacle and the public were behind them;
- he turned early onto the take off run, diminishing its length;
- he performed a rolling start, diminishing his build up to take off speed; and
- having just cleared the trees, he increased his angle of attack thereby causing a stall.

1 92 Cr App Rep 136, [1991] Crim LR 434, CA.
2 SI 1980/1965, arts 45 and 46. Now enacted as ANO 2000, SI 2000/1562, arts 63 and 64. The wording of these articles is identical.

8.211 The judge directed the jury to evidence that the pilot had been reckless, or at least negligent, in failing to abort the take off. The judge instructed the jury that if they found that the ordinary prudent pilot would have realised there was an obvious and serious risk which was not recognised by the pilot in this case, then recklessness is made out.

8.212 The pilot was convicted by the jury. The Court of Appeal later dismissed the conviction on the grounds that the trial judge had erred in the way he had put the case to the jury. The Court of Appeal commented on the way in which prosecutions such as this should be brought:

'In some cases it would be sufficient for the prosecution to charge an accused person with simple recklessness or negligence, as they did in this case, without supporting those allegations with detailed particulars. For example, in a case of killing by reckless driving, where the defendant has overtaken another vehicle on a blind bend, it is perfectly obvious what facts the prosecution are relying on. The bare allegation of recklessness is sufficient, and it is not necessarily to give particulars of it. But the present case is quite different – it is unusual case, and there may be several different reasons why the aircraft behaved as it did. A number of experts were consulted about this.

In our opinion, it is incumbent on the prosecution, in a case such as this, to particularise the facts upon which they rely in support of their allegations of recklessness and negligence, so that the defence know at the outset what the case is which they have to meet.'[1]

1   92 Cr App Rep 136, [1991] Crim LR 434, CA, per Tucker J.

Conviction of a professional pilot

8.213   There are few instances in the UK of a prosecution of a professional pilot under ANO 2000. The case against Captain Stewart is unreported but went to trial in 1991. The facts are that Captain Stewart was piloting a British Airways 747 from Bahrain to London in November 1989. Coming in to Heathrow in thick fog the Captain mistook the A4 road that runs parallel to the runway for the runway and nearly landed the aircraft on the dual carriageway road. At 75 feet Captain Stewart managed to abort the landing. He narrowly avoided crashing into the Heathrow Penta Hotel and vibrations from the 747 set off car alarms in the hotel car park. At the second attempt he landed safely on the runway.

8.214   Captain Stewart, his co-pilot and the flight engineer were all suspended by British Airways and faced a disciplinary hearing. Captain Stewart resigned before the hearing because he feared the airline intended to dismiss him. The other officers were disciplined and underwent retraining.

8.215   It was found by the AAIB that on approach to London, the visibility in which the aircraft was permitted to operate dropped to its lowest level. Because of the conditions Captain Stewart needed to use the two autopilot systems. When he sought to operate the first some 13 miles from the airport, a red warning light came on and both became disengaged. Heathrow air traffic control also warned that half the supplementary runway approach lighting was out of action.

8.216   Captain Stewart again activated the autopilots, but it was not clear that the systems were fully operational. The view of the BA incident investigation was that at 1,000 feet the autopilot landing should have been abandoned.[1]

1   *Independent* (London), 21 April 1991.

8.217   The aircraft captain was prosecuted under both the Air Navigation (No 2) Order, art 55 and art 56.[1] He was convicted by the jury under art 55 (recklessly endangering the aircraft) based on his decision to continue in the conditions despite the cockpit warnings. The Captain was, however, acquitted under art 56 (recklessly endangering persons or property). Captain Stewart was fined £2,000 and suspended from operation with British Airways. He subsequently committed suicide.

1 SI 1995/1970, arts 55 and 56. Now enacted as ANO 2000, SI 2000/1562, arts 63 and 64. The wording is identical.

8.218 This case has attracted academic criticism in the way it was prosecuted.[1] The primary criticism is based on a failure to understand the policy of the CAA in deciding to prosecute the pilot of this case as opposed to similar or even more serious cases that remained unprosecuted. It is submitted that that the definition of recklessness is derived from areas of law unconnected with the ANO 2000[2] and may not have been used appropriately in this prosecution.[3]

1 See eg M Bennun 'Prosecuting Professional Pilots In The United Kingdom After November Oscar: Reflections on the Law And Policy' (1996) 61 J Air L & Com 331 and the articles cited therein, S Wilkinson 'The November Oscar incident' Pilot, February 1994, at 32; G Cooper 'Safety and the Criminal Law' Aerospace, July 1992, at 14.
2 SI 2000/1562.
3 Bennun, n 1 above, at 360.

Prosecution of an airline

8.219 On 25 July 1996, the CAA achieved a conviction of an airline under the Air Navigation (No 2) Order, art 55,[1] the first time a carrier had been prosecuted by the CAA for recklessly or negligently endangering an aircraft and its passengers.

1 SI 1995/1970, art 55. Now enacted as ANO 2000, SI 2000/1562, art 63.

8.220 The incident arose from the flight of a British Midland 737 which took off from East Midlands Airport bound for Lanzarote. Before the flight, and on commencement of their normal pre-flight checks, the crew noted that the hydraulic power circuit breakers had been left open. The first officer went down onto the apron and asked the despatching engineer why they were not set. The engineer had reviewed the technical log before starting his refuelling and pre-departure checks and had seen that inspections of both engines had been carried out during the previous night. These had been signed off as being completed satisfactorily. The engineer informed the first officer that, so far as he could see, there was no reason for the circuit breakers to be left open, so the first officer returned to the flight deck and closed them.

8.221 After a normal take off, the commander noted that both engine oil gauges were indicating about 15% oil quantity. Both engine oil pressures began decreasing. The commander informed air traffic control that he had engine problems and wished to return to East Midlands Airport. After the oil quantities were indicating zero, the commander declared that he was diverting to Luton. The approach was direct and uneventful. The aircraft touched down and came to stop safely.

8.222 An investigation by the AAIB discovered that each engine should have contained 21 litres of oil. Immediately after the emergency landing, it was found that each engine contained less than 1.5 litres of oil. The cause of the depletion was traced to an oil leak arising out of the failure by a maintenance fitter to replace the engine oil covers after a routine night maintenance check before the flight. This act had been compounded when an engineering supervisor had failed to run the engines after the check, as required by the airline's maintenance procedures. Had the checks been carried out, it would clearly have been discovered that the oil covers were missing.

8.223 The AAIB concluded that factors contributing to the cause of this incident were shortcomings in maintenance and the absence of a system within the airline's procedures to monitor functionally related available manpower against planned workload. Both the fitter and the engineering supervisor were dismissed. More importantly, it was found that it was also the company's failure in that it had not ensured that maintenance procedures were properly carried out. The CAA prosecuted the airline under the Air Navigation (No 2) Order.[1]

1   SI 1995/1970.

8.224   The judge at Luton Crown Court noted that it was only through the vigilance and skill of the pilot and his crew that the dramatic sudden loss of oil pressure was noticed and that aircraft was able to land safely at Luton. Had they not noticed, the engines very shortly would have, if not seized, suffered such dramatic loss of power that the aircraft would have crashed, with a very high probability of killing all 189 persons on board. British Midland was convicted of negligently endangering life and the judge imposed a fine of £150,000 together with costs of £25,000.

8.225   The judge noted that he was imposing a high penalty not only as a punishment for criminal lapses, but also 'to make clear to the industry that any cutting of corners is simply not worth a candle'.[1] The company, for its part, acknowledged that its systems and controls failed to prevent what was a wholly unsatisfactory and inexplicable lapse by a respected engineer.

1   '£150,000 Fine For Airline That Put Passengers At Risk' *The Times*, 26 July 1996; *Financial Times* (London) 26 July 1996.

8.226   An incident in April 1999 concerning Malaysian Airlines System perhaps demonstrates the potential deterrent effect of the CAA's jurisdiction. The carrier landed a B747-400 at London Heathrow Airport with fewer than 4 tonnes of fuel remaining. A minimum of 5 tonnes is set by the CAA to enable aircraft to go around safely in the correct configuration should a landing need to be aborted. The airline denied that it had compromised the safety of passengers or the aircraft. After appearing before the CAA, the airline immediately adopted a new minimum fuel on landing requirement of 6.7 tonnes.[1]

1   Reed Air Transport Intelligence 'MAS Denies Heathrow Low-Fuel Incident', 11 May 1999.

8.227   The prosecution of the professional pilot, Captain Stewart, and of British Midland contributes to the debate on the public policy issues associated with prosecutions of this type. Undoubtedly, the CAA has a primary jurisdiction to sanction pilots in its discretion to revoke, suspend or vary a pilot's licence under ANO 2000.[1] It is likely that this is a discretion that will be exercised primarily before instituting criminal prosecutions.

1   SI 2000/1562, art 22.

8.228   The policy issue in prosecuting professional pilots under ANO 2000, arts 63 and 64[1] is based on the fact that these articles rely on reckless or negligent conduct in order for the criminal offence to be made out. There is no element of direct intent as would be required under the general criminal law. Consequently, there is a strongly held feeling amongst the professional aviation community that prosecutions of this type may hinder rather than promote aviation safety, for the following reasons:

•   Aviation accidents are subject to an established procedure for investigating the circumstances surrounding an accident and determining its cause. The involvement of the police and the Crown Prosecution Service in these investigations may cause aviation professionals not to co-operate to the fullest extent.

- The CAA's jurisdiction with regard to pilots' licences is regarded as a stronger deterrent against reckless and negligent conduct than the threat of criminal proceedings.
- Aviation professionals, and in particular flight crew, have a keenly developed sense of safety procedures, most particularly when they are on board the aircraft in flight and are, therefore, in the same potential danger as their passengers.

1   SI 2000/1562, arts 63 and 64.

8.229   In the US it has been noted that many investigations by the National Transportation Safety Board (NTSB) are being superseded by federal and state prosecutors' offices which are pursuing criminal investigations against companies that might otherwise be guilty of nothing more than negligence.[1]

1   See RM Dunn, D Hazouri and J Rannik 'Criminalization of Negligent Act by Employees of US and Foreign Corporations' (2002) 1 Defense Counsel J 69, at 17.

8.230   The NTSB has supported this view:

'The damage done to aviation safety by prosecutions undertaken where there is no clear intent to commit a crime does not justify the marginal benefit that might result from such a prosecution. This does not mean there is no role for criminal prosecutions in aviation, since such prosecutions continue to be appropriate where there is clear evidence of intent to commit a crime … There are numerous examples of cases where aviation accidents result from criminal intent. Examples include hijacking and terrorism, drunken flying, and theft of an aircraft. Where this intent does not exist, however, the benefits of prosecution are outweighed by the costs.'[1]

1   NTSB Bar Association, Select Committee On Aviation Public Policy 'Aviation Professionals And The Threat Of Criminal Liability – How Do We Maximise Aviation Safety?' (2002) 67 J Air L & Com 875.

Aviation criminal prosecutions in the US

Sabretech

8.231   The paradigm case arose from the crash of a ValuJet DC-9 in the Everglades in 1996. This brought about the first criminal indictment in the US of an aviation organisation for manslaughter.

8.232   On 11 May 1996 ValuJet flight 592 took off from Miami International Airport bound for Atlanta. Meteorological conditions in the Miami area at the time of the take off were good. The aircraft was carrying 110 passengers and crew and over 4,000 lbs of cargo. Six minutes into the flight, the flight crew detected an electrical problem and attempted to return to Miami. Before it could do so, the aircraft crashed in the Everglades 17 miles north-west of the airport. All on board were killed.

8.233   The National Transportation Safety Board ('NTSB') issued its report on 19 August 1997.[1] The NTSB found that ValuJet had sub-contracted the maintenance of its aircraft to a company called Sabretech in order to reduce its own overheads. The

NTSB found that flight 592 caught fire shortly after take off, and that the accident resulted from the fire. The fire started in the cargo compartment. The probable cause of the fire was the activation of one or more oxygen generators carried in the cargo compartment. It was found that Sabretech employees had loaded more than 100 armed oxygen generators into the cargo hold. These had been improperly labelled 'empty'. It was likely that the boxes holding the canisters were upset during taxi or take off and a fire began when at least one of them ignited and set off the others.

1   NTSB/AAR-96/03 (PB96-910404).

8.234   The ill-fated oxygen canisters came from three used jets that Sabretech was renovating on behalf of ValuJet. The canisters, about the size of soft drink cans, provide oxygen to passengers when aircraft cabin pressure drops. These supposedly 'empty' generators were being shipped to ValuJet's stores in Atlanta. As a safety precaution, Sabretech's employees should have fitted small plastic caps on the old canisters to prevent inadvertent activation. The total cost of sufficient caps for all the canisters that were removed was in the region of $9. Instead, the employees concerned merely disconnected the canisters, tied them off and falsely labelled them as 'empty' and consigned them for shipment. The NTSB found that the correct course of action would have been for Sabretech's employees to have taken the canisters to a safe place, intentionally activate them and dispose of the empty cans. In addition, the two Sabretech employees involved also signed work cards that falsely indicated that the shipping caps had been installed on the oxygen canisters.

8.235   In 1999, the Miami County State Attorney announced that 220 counts of murder and manslaughter had been brought against Sabretech, one of each offence for each of the 110 people aboard the flight. In addition, 24 charges were brought against Sabretech and three of Sabretech's employees, Daniel Gonzales, Maintenance Director and Eugene Florence and Mauro Valenzuela, Sabretech mechanics. The wide-ranging charges against the employees were of conspiring to falsify aircraft records, falsifying aircraft records, violating hazardous materials regulations and placing a destructive device on board the aircraft. It was alleged that the maintenance director pressured employees to skip prescribed work steps and then falsely sign documents indicating work had been completed, a practice known in the industry as 'pencil whipping'. It was alleged that the mechanics signed the work cards. If convicted, the employees would face up to 55 years each in a Federal prison and $2.7 million in fines.

8.236   Sabretech faced fines totalling about $6 million. This was the first aviation accident in the US that resulted in criminal charges against a company and its workers. A key factor in the indictment was the understanding that Sabretech had conspired to 'put corporate profits and monetary interests ahead of the safety of the passengers'.[1] A three-week trial took place in December 1999.[2]

1   *Sun-Sentinel,* Broward Metro edn, 15 July 1999, p 1A.
2   *United States v Sabretech Inc,* United States District Court for the Southern District of Florida. DC Docket No 99-00491-CR-JLK.

8.237   At the trial, two of the three employees were acquitted of the charges against them. The third had absconded before the trial. The acquittals were on the basis that there was insufficient evidence of any intention to commit an offence. The jury found Sabretech, however, guilty of eight counts of recklessly causing hazardous materials to be transported, and one count of failing to train employees in handling hazardous materials. Sabretech was fined $2 million and ordered to pay $9 million in compensation to the families of 16 passengers. By this stage, ValuJet's insurers had already paid over $262 million in damages to the victims' families and Sabretech was a bankrupt company.

8.238   Sabretech appealed and in October 2001 the Federal Appeals Court dismissed on technical legal grounds eight of the nine Federal convictions against Sabretech. The remaining conviction was for failing to train employees in hazardous materials. The fines were reduced to $500,000.[1]

1   *United States v Sabretech Inc*, 271 F 3d 1018 US App LEXIS 23595 (11th Cir Fla, 2001).

8.239   On 7 December 2001, the district court in Miami formally dismissed the 110 murder and 110 manslaughter charges against Sabretech, in exchange for a no-contest plea to the one count of unlawfully causing the transportation of hazardous waste. Additionally, the court accepted a $500,000 donation from Sabretech's parent company to be distributed to organisations promoting aviation safety and victim services. The $500,000 donation was split between the National Air Disaster Alliance and Foundation, which promotes aviation safety and advocates for victim's families. The remaining half was provided to the United Way of Miami-Dade for further distribution to victim's services.[1]

1   'Valujet Crash: Case Closed' *The Miami Herald*, 8 December 2001.

8.240   The handling of the criminal procedures following the ValuJet crash is perhaps an extreme illustration of the development of a criminal investigation and prosecution following the discovery of evidence of negligent conduct. One of the drivers of the criminal prosecution was the growing focus on criminal enforcement in the aviation industry in the state of Florida. This followed a public announcement by the US Attorney in Miami that criminal prosecution of aviation-related misconduct would be a top priority of his administration.[1] An extreme view is that companies must be prepared for the likelihood that any and or negligent conduct may become fair game to be investigated as criminal once a criminal investigation is underway.[2] The intensity of the criminal investigation in this case is regarded to have prevented full cooperation by employees of the company, a factor that may have hindered the NTSB accident investigation.[3]

1   See M Raskin 'Criminal Enforcement In The Aviation Industry', paper delivered to the NTSB Symposium on Transportation Safety and the Law, 25–26 April 2000; Dunn, Hazouri and Rannik, **para 1.229 n 1** above, at 17.
2   Dunn, Hazouri and Rannik, **para 1.229 n 1** above, at 17.
3   See *Findings of the United States House of Representatives Subcommittee on Aviation hearing on The Trend Towards Criminalization of Aircraft Accidents*, 27 July 2000.

Statutory basis for prosecutions in the US

8.241   A number of federal and state statutes have been invoked in charges against corporations following accidents.

False statements

8.242   The False Statement Act[1] might be cited to cover false statements made to, for example, investigators of the FAA or NTSB. This statute was invoked against Sabretech employees in respect of the maintenance records.

1   18 USCS § 1001: 'a) Except as otherwise provided in this section, whoever, in any matter
    within the jurisdiction of the executive, legislative, or judicial branch of the Government of
    the United States, knowingly and wilfully – (1) falsifies, conceals, or covers up by any trick,
    scheme, or device a material fact; (2) makes any materially false, fictitious, or fraudulent
    statement or representation; or (3) makes or uses any false writing or document knowing the
    same to contain any materially false, fictitious, or fraudulent statement or entry; shall be fined
    under this title or imprisoned not more than 5 years, or both.'

8.243   In addition, the False Statement Act was relevant in the prosecutions
following the crash of Alaska Airlines Flight 261 at Point Mugu, north of Los Angeles,
on 31 January 2000 with 88 fatalities. Port investigators quickly focused on a lack of
grease on the jackscrew, a tail component that helps move the jet's stabilizer and sets
the angle of flight. The National Transportation Safety Board later cited poor
maintenance as a causal factor.

8.244   Following that finding, the US Attorney's Office in San Francisco reactivated
an investigation 'to review it in light of the final NTSB report'.[1] It is likely that Alaska
Airlines' maintenance records and procedures may now be the subject of a criminal
investigation.[2]

1   'Judge Keeps Boeing In Lawsuit Over Alaska Airlines Crash' The Associated Press State &
    Local Wire, 16 May 2003.
2   '"The NTSB's findings are in keeping with a number of factors that allegedly contributed to
    the fatal Alaska Airlines crash," explained Panish (attorney for claimants), "such as the
    Boeing Company's faulty design and test procedures for its horizontal stabilizer, as well as
    their failure to provide adequate lubrication instructions to Alaska Airlines. The Boeing
    Company's failures, when coupled with Alaska Airlines' poor maintenance of the aircraft in an
    effort to cut costs, were a recipe for disaster. Their negligence was horrific and we will seek full
    vindication on behalf of our clients"': 'Greene, Broillet Responds to NTSB's Dec. 10, 2002,
    Report on Crash of Alaska Airlines Flight 261' Business Wire Inc, 10 December 2002.

Obstruction of justice

8.245   Under 18 USCS § 1505[1] an effort to destroy, alter or falsify records with intent
to obstruct civil investigation can be prosecuted as an obstruction of justice.

1   § 1505. Obstruction Of Proceedings Before Departments, Agencies, And Committees:
    'Whoever, with intent to avoid, evade, prevent, or obstruct compliance, in whole or in
    part, with any civil investigative demand duly and properly made under the Antitrust Civil
    Process Act [15 USCS §§ 1311ff], wilfully withholds, misrepresents, removes from any
    place, conceals, covers up, destroys, mutilates, alters, or by other means falsifies any
    documentary material, answers to written interrogatories, or oral testimony, which is the
    subject of such demand; or attempts to do so or solicits another to do so; or Whoever
    corruptly, or by threats or force, or by any threatening letter or communication influences,
    obstructs, or impedes or endeavors to influence, obstruct, or impede the due and proper
    administration of the law under which any pending proceeding is being had before any
    department or agency of the United States, or the due and proper exercise of the power of
    inquiry under which any inquiry or investigation is being had by either House, or any
    committee of either House or any joint committee of the Congress – Shall be fined under
    this title or imprisoned not more than five years, or both.'

8.246   A Fine Air DC8 cargo aircraft lost control after take off from runway 27R at
Miami International Airport and crashed. The aircraft slid across the road into the
International Airport Centre and burst into flames. There were four fatalities in the
accident. The aircraft had entered an 85° nose-up attitude on take off, stalled and
crashed. Preliminary investigation results showed that more than half the cargo latches

were in an unlocked position. Accordingly, the NTSB concluded that cargo pallets shifted on take off sufficiently to alter the centre of gravity.

8.247 The NTSB concluded that additional causes were a failure of FineAir to exercise operation control over the cargo loading process and a failure of Aeromar (FineAir's subcontractor) to load the aircraft as specified by Fine Air. Contributing to the accident was the failure of the FAA adequately to monitor Fine Air's operational control responsibilities for cargo loading and the failure of the FAA to ensure that known cargo related deficiencies were corrected at FineAir.

8.248 The airline was charged with obstruction of justice and making false statements regarding the weighing of cargo pallets. In March 2000 the company pleaded guilty to two charges including making a false statement concerning maintenance matters and obstructing the government's investigation by destroying, disposing of or altering evidence. The airline was fined over $5 million dollars.[1]

1 NTSB Docket No. DCA 97 MA059

Resource Conservation and Recovery Act[1]

8.249 This governs the transportation, storage, treatment and disposal of hazardous waste products, as well as the making of false statements in the required documents, manifest and labels. This was the basis for a prosecution of American Airlines for improper storage of hazardous waste materials in 1991. American Airlines pleaded guilty and was fined $8 million and ordered to pay $2 million restitution to local authorities.[2]

1 42 USCS §§6901–6987.
2 'South Florida: Visible Bellwether of Growing Focus on Criminal Enforcement', Air Safety Week (1 May 2000).

Destruction of aircraft

8.250 Under US federal law, it is an offence wilfully to damage an aircraft or an aircraft facility or to perform an act of violence against an aircraft or aircraft facility.[1] This statute was intended by the legislature to be used to prosecute alleged terrorists. The statute was invoked, however, against Sabretech.[2] The jury acquitted the company of this offence.

1 18 USCS §32.
2 *United States v Sabretech Inc,* United States District Court for the Southern District of Florida. DC Docket No 99-00491-CR-JLK.

General criminal law

8.251 The general criminal law was also invoked against Sabretech, which was charged with 110 third-degree murder and manslaughter counts, one for each fatality in the Valujet accident.[1]

1 *United States v Sabretech Inc,* United States District Court for the Southern District of Florida. DC Docket No 99-00491-CR-JLK.

Criminal investigations – international

Singapore Airlines (SQ006) at Taipei

8.252   Singapore Airlines flight SQ006 departed Singapore for a flight to Los Angeles via Taipei. The flight left the gate and taxied to the runway for take off. The crew had been cleared for a runway 05L departure because runway 05R was closed for construction work. The Taiwan CAA had issued a NOTAM[1] indicating that the runway 05R was closed for construction. After reaching the end of the taxiway, SQ006 turned onto runway 05R. After a short hold, SQ006 started its take off roll. Weather conditions were poor because of an approaching typhoon. On take off the aircraft hit concrete barriers, excavators and other construction equipment on the runway. The aircraft crashed back unto the runway, breaking up and bursting into flames while sliding down the runway. Of the 159 passengers and 20 crew on board, there were 83 fatalities.[2]

1   'Notice to Airmen', a notice provided to pilots giving up to date information on the condition or change in any aeronautical facility, service, procedure or hazard.
2   www.aviation-safety.net/database/2000/001031-0.htm.

8.253   Although Taiwan is not a member state of ICAO, the Taiwan Aviation Safety Counsel carried out the accident investigation based on the principles of Annex 13 of the Chicago Convention. The final report of the investigation noted the following as probable cause of the accident:

1   The weather conditions were severe, including heavy rain, strong winds and low visibility at the time of the take off.
2   The knowledge of the flight crew as to the taxi route and available runways was deficient, despite the issue of the NOTAM. Accordingly the flight crew lost situational awareness and commenced take off from the wrong runway.

8.254   The Singapore Ministry of Transport did not agree with the accident investigation report and identified alleged deficiencies at the airport in clearly identifying the runway that was out of use.

8.255   After the accident, the flight crew were held in custody in Taipei for nearly two months. They were eventually allowed to return to Singapore after Singapore Airlines and the Singapore government gave assurances that the crew would return to Taiwan if required. Immediately following the release of the accident report, the pilots were subpoenaed by prosecutors for further questioning. It was alleged that the crew could be charged with 'manslaughter caused by negligence'.[1]

1   AP World Stream, 6 May 2002.

8.256   The Singapore Ministry of Transport criticised the ASC report as being incomplete because it 'downplays significant systematic factors which contributed to the accident, such as deficiencies at Chiang Kai Shek Airport, and its non conformance with ICAO standards and recommended practices (SARPs)'.[1]

1   Aviation Week and Space Technology, 6 May 2002.

8.257   In 2002, prosecutors in Taiwan made the decision not to bring manslaughter charges against the Captain and First Officer of SQ006. Authorities in Taiwan initially detained the crew and only permitted them to leave the country after the Singapore government agreed to return them if charges were pursued.

8.258 For more than 18 months, accident investigators attempted to perform their duties with the knowledge that two key participants, whose testimony would be vital to determining probable cause, were facing potential jail sentences over their roles in the tragedy.[1]

1 'Aviation on Trial' Air Transport World, 1 September 2002 2002.

8.259 Two factors that appeared to have persuaded the prosecutors not to bring charges against the SQ006 pilots. First, that the pilots took advertisements in Taiwan newspapers expressing sympathy with those harmed or affected by the accident; and, secondly, the severe weather on the night of the accident may have weakened their case.[1]

1 'Taiwan Drops Pilot Case' (2002) Flight International, 18 June 18.

8.260 Ultimately, the pilots were not charged with any offence under Taiwan law. At the time of writing no other party is facing any charges. The pilots, however, were dismissed by Singapore Airlines.

Mid-air collision over Croatia, 10 September 1976

8.261 A BEA trident took off from Heathrow on 10 September 1976 for a flight to Istanbul. About one-and-a-half hours later, the aircraft approached the ZAG VOR beacon over Croatia. At the same time, and Inex-Adria DC9 was approaching the same VOR from the opposite direction, having taken off from Split for a flight to Cologne. Zagreb air traffic control asked (in Serbo-Croat) the Inex-Adria flight to maintain their present altitude, shortly after which the aircraft collided with the trident. Both aircraft were destroyed with a total of 176 fatalities.

8.262 A primary cause of the accident was found to be improper ATC operation. A contributing factor was the failure of both crews to maintain a proper look out. Following the accident the Zagreb District Court sentenced one of the air traffic controllers to seven years' hard labour for 'criminal negligence and serious acts against the public safety'. Seven other controllers were similarly charged but were acquitted. The jailed controller was subsequently released after two years.

Japan Airlines Flight 706, 8 June 1997

8.263 On 8 June 1997, Japan Airlines flight 706 was descending to Nagoya Airport after a flight from Hong Kong. During the descent it encountered air turbulence and its airspeed increased rapidly during the descent. It is alleged that the captain of the aircraft did not engage the autopilot in his actions to correct the rapid descent. Instead he pulled the control wheel, which in turn caused the nose move sharply up and down repeatedly. As a result, a flight attendant was thrown to the floor and then to the ceiling causing injuries mainly to her head. She died 20 months after the accident. Several other passengers and crew members suffered slight injuries.

8.264 The aircraft captain was charged with criminal negligence in Japan. The prosecution alleged that the captain was aware, through his training, of the special characteristics of a MD11 aircraft, in which manually operating the control wheel would disengage the autopilot and make the aircraft unstable. It was alleged that he applied excessive force to the control wheel, which caused the autopilot to disengage, and resulted in the unorthodox motion of the aircraft. At the time of writing, the conclusion of this trial is unknown

Ansett New Zealand, 9 June 1995

8.265   Flight AN709 approached Palmerston north runway 25 after a flight from Auckland. When the undercarriage was selected down, the right-hand main gear did not extend. The captain continued the descent and the co-pilot carried out the undercarriage alternate extension checklist. The aircraft struck the top of a ridgeline and crashed. There were a total of four fatalities out of the 21 passengers and crew on board.

8.266   The Transport Accident Investigation Commission Report found that the causal factors of the accident could be traced to the Captain's actions and omissions such as not ensuring the aircraft intercepted and maintained the approach profile during the conduct of the non-precision instrument approach, perseverance with the decision to lower the undercarriage without discontinuing the instrument approach, and distraction from the primary task of flying the aircraft safely during the First Officer's endeavours to correct the undercarriage malfunction. The report concluded that the aircraft crashed as a consequence of inadequate crew resource management.[1]

1   TAIC Report No.95-011 (undated).

8.267   The captain was charged with four charges of manslaughter and three charges of injuring passengers. The trial led to international controversy in the aviation community following the prosecution's use of the cockpit voice recorder as evidence. The CVR was used to show that the pilot was aware of the failure of the right hand main undercarriage, and continued with his descent. It took five years of subsidiary legal argument to get the CVR admitted. The captain was acquitted by the jury.[1]

1   For full details of this case and the debate surrounding the use of the CVR, see *New Zealand Air Line Pilots Association Inc v Attorney-General* [1997] 3 NZLR 269; 1997 NZLR LEXIS 562, 16 June 1997.

Liability of the regulator

8.268   There have been several attempts to involve regulators in liability following aviation accidents. It is now established that regulators owe a duty of care only where (i) it is reasonably foreseeable to the regulator that the claimant would suffer harm from the regulator's failure to take care; (ii) there is the necessary relationship of proximity between claimant and the regulator; and (iii) it is just and reasonable in all the circumstances to impose a duty of care on the part of the regulator.[1]

1   See *Philcox v CAA* (1995, unreported), CA.

8.269   Regulators have a duty of care and will fail in this duty of care if they carry out their activities negligently with knowledge that damage will result. The regulators are, however, unlikely to be proximate enough to any accident to be said to be the direct cause of that accident.

8.270   A striking example is provided by the US case of *West v Federal Aviation Administration*.[1] Bishop Airport lies in a deep funnel shaped valley bounded on two sides by mountains. The terrain to the east of the airport begins to rise rapidly at about three-and-a-half miles and to the west of the airport at about eight miles. An FAA procedures specialist designed and approved a special instrument approach and departure procedure for the airport. The procedure was checked according to FAA regulations during a series of daytime flights. Pilots departing from the airport were required to follow the FAA departure procedure. The accident occurred when a charter flight struck the slope of the mountains whilst attempting to depart from the airport. The court found that the probable cause of the accident was a lack of sufficient ground lighting resulting in a visual phenomenon whereby pilots flying on a very black night could be misled into believing that they were closer to the airport than they actually were.

1   830 F 2d 1044 (1987, US App).

8.271   Although FAA employees were aware of the visual phenomenon, no special steps were taken to determine whether there was a problem with the lighting at Bishop Airport or reliance on the two-mile distance requirement on a dark night. The FAA did not make a night flight check of the visual climb aspect of the departure procedure.

8.272   The court held that the FAA had established its procedure according to guidelines as to what is necessary for establishing a safe departure procedure. Whilst the FAA established the procedure, it did not warrant that the procedure would be safe under all conditions. Here, the pilot had the primary responsibility to make sure the aircraft was flown safely. The FAA employees used their judgment in deciding that it was not feasible or necessary to make any more tests on the procedure because the costs of doing the type of tests would greatly outweigh any safety benefits. In this case, the court used various technical legal means in order to exonerate the FAA from liability.[1]

1   830 F 2d 1044 (1987, US App).

Conclusion

The aviation industry has a deeply institutionalised safety culture, the product of a serious commitment to international regulation which was made over 90 years ago. In the UK, aviation safety is the subject of a suite of statutory instruments and regulations, and the role of the CAA as prosecutor as well as regulator brings a high degree of institutionalised regulation to the industry.

8.273   Despite this, fatal accidents have occurred in the UK. As seen from the brief reports in this chapter, the causes of these accidents generally derive from a series or a combination of circumstances, acts and omissions, and seldom from one single identifiable event. Based on the civil law cases arising from aviation accidents, English common law contains highly sophisticated notions of culpability. Aviation accidents have the capacity to, and do, result in multiple fatalities and widespread damage. Yet, no UK aviation operator has been the subject of an indictment for corporate manslaughter following a fatal accident.

8.274   The reasons for this are arguably a combination of the evidentiary complexities of sustaining the prosecution of a corporation, and the high level of mandatory record keeping required by and practised in the industry. Add to this a highly formalistic international accident investigation regime, the primary purpose of which is to promote safety rather than to apportion blame.

8.275 However, serious accidents now attract more attention than before. The immediacy of television coverage brings a wide public close to the aftermath of any accident. Corporations, too, are exposed to public scrutiny as a result of the perceived need for greater transparency in corporate governance. As seen in the context of recent serious rail accidents in the UK, the media tends to fuel the suggestion that the directors and other executives of a corporation involved should be criminally liable. The shift to clamour for the liability of the corporation itself is not a huge one.

8.276 Recent aviation accidents outside of the UK have resulted in criminal proceedings against members of the flight crew, and in some instances pilots have been imprisoned. Again, the move to visiting similar punishments upon directors of corporations in the aviation industry may not be too far away.

CHAPTER 9

Shipping

Jeremy R Farr, Partner, Ince & Co[1]

1   Thanks in particular to Joanne Moody, and also to Brian Boahene and Neil Adams, all of Ince & Co, for their assistance with research and proofreading.

Introduction

9.1   Modern society has some difficulty in accepting the fact that, although a corporate entity and its management may have presided over the deaths at sea of many passengers and crew, they are nonetheless not susceptible to conviction for manslaughter. All the more if an official inquiry into such a tragedy describes the company involved as being 'infected with the disease of sloppiness from top to bottom' and an inquest returns 187 verdicts of unlawful killing. This, however, was the consequence of the capsize of the roll-on, roll-off (ro-ro) ferry *Herald of Free Enterprise* on 6 March 1987, when 193 passengers and crew lost their lives. This modern-day shipping disaster rekindled public demands for legislative changes which would facilitate the prosecution and conviction of corporate entities for manslaughter. It should not, however, be presumed that the shipping industry of the 1980s had a lackadaisical approach to the safety of life at sea or, indeed, to corporate responsibility for ensuring safety at sea and for the actions of the master and crew. As will be shown, these were areas already then well developed by international convention and in English civil law.

9.2   The marriage of commerce and safety in the maritime sphere has never been an entirely easy one. The capsizing of the *Herald of Free Enterprise* is an apposite example. This incident lead to criticism from some that the cause of the disaster was the intense competition amongst ferry operators and a desire to maximise profits.[1] There was, it was argued, a preoccupation with meeting time deadlines rather than ensuring that ships departed in a safe and seaworthy fashion.

1   S Crainer *Zeebrugge: Learning from Disaster* (1987) pp 19–24. In the *Herald of Free Enterprise* the directors of the operating company were quoted as saying that their main concern in running their fleet was in maximising profits for shareholders: see Lloyd's List, 10 April 1991. Crainer argues that at the time of this tragedy safety was not deemed to have offered a competitive edge, but speed of transport was. His view is that investment in safety regimes should not be considered as inconsistent with any desire to produce profits, but should be seen as a strategy to help nurture profits – investment in safety is something which will realise itself in the long term, with benefits in reduced maintenance, insurance premiums and other related costs.

9.3   Until the first part of the nineteenth century, legislatures took the view that those involved in maritime adventures would take the necessary care in relation to safety in order to protect their own financial interests in their ships. However, this rationale became less and less justifiable from the seventeenth century onwards as mechanisms for the transfer of risks developed. Thus, the seventeenth century saw the development of bottomry[1] and the insurance of the maritime adventure as means of sharing risk rather than addressing the underlying issue of making the maritime adventure safer. The nineteenth century saw great technical advances in shipbuilding, driven by the Industrial Revolution. Wooden hulls gave way to iron and then to steel. Sail gave way to the steam engine. These revolutionary developments in technology and in risk transfer were accompanied by a continuing and appalling number of lives lost at sea (for example, 20,000 people died in shipwrecks in the North Sea in the winter of 1820[2]).

1   Bottomry is the name given to a contract whereby the shipowner borrowed money against the security of his ship to carry out a maritime adventure. He would be given a loan and was obliged to repay the lender the value of the loan and interest if the ship arrived safely at its destination. If the ship was lost at sea or did not arrive at its destination, the shipowner did not have an obligation to repay the loan. See further Parks *Law and Practice of Marine Insurance and Average* (1988) vol 1, p 4.
2   *The Courier*, 5 July 1822, quoted in *Le Bureau Veritas 1828–1928, Edition Du Centenaire* (1928) p 10 and cited in P Boisson *Safety at Sea* Bureau (1999).

9.4   The advent of marine insurance in particular removed the rationale of governments for not imposing safety regulations upon the shipping industry. What price safety when a third-party insurer would bear the financial loss, rather than the shipowner? The British government woke up to this fact in 1836 and appointed a Parliamentary Select Committee to examine the causes of the increase in shipwrecks. Its conclusions were devastating, highlighting the facts that ships were badly made and badly outfitted, with drunkenness amongst officers and crew rife and owners relying on insurance to compensate them for their own inadequacies. This led to some minor, but nevertheless important, regulations. These were the precursors to the systematic international regimes which have now been agreed by governments for the purpose of regulating safety and placing the onus upon shipowners to ensure the safety of their maritime adventures. However, the extent to which these regulations are effective depends in large part upon consistent international standards of policing and enforcement.

9.5   Maritime technology continues to develop apace. Ships are more powerful, larger and innovative than the draftsmen of the first merchant shipping Act in 1850[1] could have ever imagined. Regulations of a safety nature, such as for the construction of ships and defining of responsibilities of those involved in the ownership or management of ships, have tended to lag behind technical advances. Technical advance does not necessarily mean 'safer'; it means 'different', and differences require the adequacy of safety systems to be reviewed. The loss of the passenger ship *Titanic* was a classic example of complacency driven by innovation. Indeed, it was the sinking of the *Titanic* in 1912 with the loss of 1,501 lives which led to the first steps being taken to create the sophisticated international regulatory regime for safety which is a feature of modern-day maritime adventures.

1 Mercantile Marine Act 1850 (13 & 14 Vict) Cap XCIII.

9.6   Nowadays the standards of safety against which those responsible for the safety of maritime adventures are to be judged are well defined.

9.7   This chapter will trace the development of measures for ensuring the safety of life at sea, the civil and criminal responsibility of companies and organisations involved in shipping, and the current state of English law with regard to convicting these bodies of manslaughter. It will then consider practical issues as to how a company may best protect itself in the event of an accident involving loss of life.

The origins of corporate responsibility for the safety of maritime adventures

The British approach to safety of life at sea

9.8   The first of what was to become a series of Acts regulating merchant shipping was the Mercantile Marine Act 1850[1] (MMA 1850). This was a ground-breaking Act 'for improving the condition of masters, mates, and seamen, and maintaining discipline, in the merchant service'. It gave the then Board of Trade wide-ranging supervisory powers over merchant shipping and merchant seamen. Its basic aim was to ensure a reasonable standard of safety of life at sea by regulating those on board a ship through a system of certification. So far as matters of shipowner responsibility were concerned, it did no more than provide for the Board of Trade to have power to appoint inspectors to investigate where it had 'reason to apprehend that any serious accident occasioning loss of life or property has been sustained or caused by or has happened on board of any ship, or that any ship has been lost or has received material damage'.[2] Whilst the Act provided for fines or imprisonment (including hard labour) for 'misdemeanours' under it, the only offence for which a shipowner might be convicted in the realm of health and safety related to the amount of living space to be allowed for each seaman and apprentice.[3]

1 13 & 14 Vict Cap XCIII.
2 MMA 1850, s 104.
3 MMA 1850, s 63.

9.9   Having taken up the gauntlet offered to it in 1850, the Board of Trade was quick to formalise its role. The Merchant Shipping Act 1854 (MSA 1854) gave statutory effect to a practice which had commenced in 1846, that of the wreck inquiry.[1] Under MSA 1854 the Board of Trade was given the power to make an application for a formal investigation into the circumstances in which any wreck, or loss of life at sea, or damage to a ship occurred off or near the coasts of the UK. These investigations were of a judicial nature. A detailed study of the structure and procedure of British formal investigations is beyond the scope of this work. However, the philosophy underlying maritime inquiries is of relevance to the responsibility of the shipowner:

> '... it is necessary to remember what are the absolute requisites for these enquiries. In the first place they must be summary, local and inexpensive. If they are not so, they will be oppressive to the parties, they will be impracticable to the Government and they will be ineffectual. It is impossible to keep seamen as witnesses long in port: you must produce your witnesses and take evidence at once, or the thing is at an end. In the second place the Court must be perfectly impartial as between the shipowner and the master on the one side, and the shippers, insurers and passengers on the other. In the third place you must have the enquiry conducted by persons who have judicial habits of enquiries. That is a very great reason for keeping the main content of the enquiry in the hands of Magistrates or persons accustomed to administer justice. There must also be in the Court competent nautical knowledge, and the persons who furnish knowledge must be quite independent of all interests concerned. Thus further (and it is very important to mention this) the object of the enquiry is not so much to punish anyone who may have been in fault as to prevent wrecks in future, whether by punishment of and warning against negligence, or by remedying anything that is wrong by way of navigation.'[2]

1   17 & 18 Vict c 104.
2   Evidence of Sir TH Ferrer, Permanent Secretary to the Board of Trade, before the Select Committee of the House of Commons 1860.

9.10   Further Merchant Shipping Acts followed, gradually increasing the scope of state regulation of the merchant marine. The most important of these was the Merchant Shipping Act 1894 (MSA 1894), which unified and rationalised the statutes which preceded it.[1]

1   57 & 58 Vict c 60.

9.11   In common with its predecessors, MSA 1894 contained few provisions which could be said to punish a shipowner for safety lapses. It did, however, set forth the basis upon which a shipowner could limit its liability for certain civil claims against it where those occurred without its actual fault or privity.

9.12   In the late nineteenth century, developments in company law were also taking place which had a very important impact for companies involved in shipping. The most important of these was the enshrinement of the principle of the corporate veil. Thus, the liability of a company in financial terms was limited to its assets – it was not possible (except in very exceptional circumstances) to pierce the 'corporate veil' and go behind the company to its shareholders for more money if a company's assets were insufficient to fulfil its liabilities.[1] This is a principle recognised in jurisdictions throughout the world and it has been instrumental in the growth of one ship companies.[2]

1   *A Salomon v A Salomon and Co Ltd* [1897] AC 22.
2   The one ship company usually has as its only asset the ship itself. This means that, in the event of a claim against the company, the claimant has limited prospects for recovery, and none at all if the ship is a total loss and is uninsured or the insurance does not cover the loss.

9.13   Many of the provisions in MSA 1894 went through a number of re-enactments in the twentieth century. The most significant of these, in the context of corporate responsibility, was the Merchant Shipping Act 1988 (MSA 1988) which for the first time imposed criminal responsibility upon a shipowner for the unsafe operation of a ship at sea.[1] This was by way of response to the *Herald of Free Enterprise* casualty, a disaster which gave fresh impetus to the need to take further steps to ensure safety of life at sea, not only in the UK, but also on the international stage.

1   The term 'shipowner' includes a demise charterer and a ship manager: see MSA 1988, s 31. Note that the Health and Safety at Work etc Act 1974 (HSWA 1974) has no application to vessels outside Great Britain: see HSWA 1974 s 15(9).

The Herald of Free Enterprise

9.14   On 6 March 1987 the seven-year-old Townsend-owned passenger freight ro-ro ferry, *Herald of Free Enterprise*, under the command of Captain David Lewry, sailed from the inner harbour at Zeebrugge at 7.05 pm bound for Dover. The ship was manned by a crew of 80 and laden with 81 cars, 47 freight vehicles and three other vehicles. There were 459 passengers on board. Some 20 minutes after leaving Zeebrugge Harbour, despite the weather being fine and the sea calm, the ferry rapidly filled with water, listed to port, swung sharply to starboard, and then capsized, settling on a sandbank which allowed it to stay afloat, albeit half submerged in water. 193 people (approximately 40 of whom were crew) were killed, all of them British citizens. Many others were injured.

9.15   The Secretary of State for Transport ordered a formal investigation (pursuant to the powers vested in him by MSA 1970, s 51) which was presided over by the Admiralty Judge, Mr Justice Sheen. The findings of the formal investigation were published on 24 July 1987.[1] It concluded that the *Herald of Free Enterprise* capsized because she went to sea with her inner and outer bow doors open. The central problem was that there was no system to monitor whether the bow doors were closed. For example, there were no warning lights on the bridge indicating that the bow and stern doors were open, and no instructions in place as to what steps could be taken to rectify such safety problems. This lead to various errors by the crew.

1   Department of Transport M/V *Herald of Free Enterprise* Report of the Court no 8074 (1987) (M/V *Herald of Free Enterprise* Report).

9.16   Mark Stanley, the assistant bosun whose job it was to ensure the doors were closed, was found to have been asleep at the time of the incident. He accepted that it was his duty to ensure the doors were closed and that he had failed to carry out this duty. Terry Ayling, the bosun, was also criticised for his failure to close the doors because he underestimated the scope of his duties. The Chief Officer, Leslie Sabel, was negligent when he relieved the Second Officer as Loading Officer of G deck because it then became his duty to ensure that the bow doors were closed, which he failed to do.[1] It was adjudged that when Leslie Sabel left G deck, anticipating that Mr Stanley would be there shortly, there was no one else on the deck.[2] Captain Lewry was criticised for not asking the Chief Officer whether the ship was secure. When an analysis was conducted into the safety system in place on board, it was found to be inherently unsafe.[3] Written instructions requiring the Loading Officer to check that the bow doors were closed were frequently ignored and interpreted as a requirement merely that someone should be in a position to verify that there was a crew member in a position to close the doors. In addition the Senior Master, Captain Kirby, was criticised for assuming that the instruction to ensure that the bow doors were secured had been complied with. Townsend was criticised for a failure to issue adequate instructions to the master and crew, and particularly for the system of negative reporting.

1 M/V *Herald of Free Enterprise* Report, **para 9.15 n 1** above, p 9, para 10.6.
2 M/V *Herald of Free Enterprise* Report, **para 9.15 n 1** above, p 10, para 10.9.
3 Crainer, **para 9.2 n 1** above, pp 46–60, 54.

9.17   The public inquiry also focussed on poor management. In 1986 a meeting of senior members of the ferry's management resolved that it was preferable not to define the roles of Chief Officer and Maintenance Master but to allow them to evolve.[1] This meant that the crew was not entirely sure who had responsibility for certain matters. Indeed Mr Justice Sheen believed that there was a lack of thought given by the management to the structure of the officers' duties.[2] He was particularly critical of the management's standing orders, which made no reference to closing the bow and stern doors and appeared to have led Captain Lewry to assume that his ship was ready for sea since the system of negative reporting meant that he had no report to the contrary.[3] Captain Lewry was also criticised for the practice of leaving port with the bow doors open. It was established that the company was aware that there were problems with regard to the bow doors and the captain of another of its ferries had suggested that warning lights be fitted.[4]

1 M/V *Herald of Free Enterprise* Report, **para 9.15 n 1** above, p 15, para 14.2. This was said to demonstrate 'an inability or unwillingness to give clear orders ... The Board of Directors must accept a heavy responsibility for their lamentable lack of directions. Individually and collectively they lacked a sense of responsibility. This left, what Mr Owen so aptly described as "a vacuum in the centre"'.
2 M/V *Herald of Free Enterprise* Report, **para 9.15 n 1** above, p 11, para 11.2.
3 M/V *Herald of Free Enterprise* Report, **para 9.15 n 1** above, p 12 para 12.3. This negative reporting system was defective in that it required no positive confirmation that the bow doors were closed and that the ferry was ready for sea. The Captain was further criticised for failing to insist on a report that the ferry was all secure: see p 12, para 12.4.
4 M/V *Herald of Free Enterprise* Report, **para 9.15 n 1** above, p 25, para 18.8. Mr Justice Sheen concluded that the company was aware of the problem of the ship sailing with stern or bow doors open, and indeed of the remedy, but had dismissed it.

9.18   The faults of Captain Lewry, Mr Stanley, Mr Sabel, and Townsend at all levels were identified as contributing to the disaster, but the root cause was attributed to the management of the company itself.[1] Mr Justice Sheen found:[2]

'At first sight the faults which led to this disaster were the aforesaid errors of omission on the part of the Master, the Chief Officer and the assistant Bosun, and also the failure by Captain Kirby to issue and enforce clear orders. But a full investigation into the circumstances of the disaster leads inexorably to the conclusion that the underlying or cardinal faults lay higher up in the Company. The Board of Directors did not appreciate their responsibility for the safe management of their ships. They did not apply their minds to the question: What orders should be given for the safety of our ships? The directors did not have any proper comprehension of what their duties were. There appears to have been a lack of thought about the way the Herald ought to have been organised for the Dover/Zeebrugge run. All concerned in management, from the members of the Board of Directors down to the junior superintendents, were guilty of fault in that all must be regarded as sharing responsibility for the failure of management. From top to bottom the body corporate was infected with the disease of sloppiness.'

1 M/V *Herald of Free Enterprise* Report, **para 9.15 n 1** above, p 71.
2 M/V *Herald of Free Enterprise* Report, **para 9.15 n 1** above, para 14.1.

9.19 Mr Justice Sheen drew attention to a Merchant Shipping Notice entitled *'Good Ship Management'* issued by the Department of Transport in July 1986. The advice given in that Notice included the following points:

'The efficient and safe operation of ships requires the exercise of good management both at sea and ashore ... The overall responsibility of the shipping company requires the need for close involvement by management ashore. To this end it is recommended that every company operating ships should designate a person ashore with responsibility for monitoring the technical and safety aspects of the operation of its ships and for providing appropriate shore based backup ... Stress is placed upon the importance of providing the Master with clear instructions to him and his officers. The instructions should include adequate Standing Orders. There should be close co-operation and regular and effective communication in both directions between ship and shore.'[1]

1 Merchant Shipping Notice M1188, July 1986.

9.20 Mr Justice Sheen found that this was very sound advice, but that Townsend's attitude to it was one of 'staggering complacency'.[1]

1 M/V *Herald of Free Enterprise* Report, **para 9.15 n 1** above, p 15, para 14.2.

9.21 Following the public inquiry, an inquest was held which was regarded as unsatisfactory by many press commentators who captured, but also directed, the public mood. First, although the jury in the inquest returned a verdict of unlawful killing in respect of all the victims (except one who died after the disaster), it did not attribute criminal liability to any person.[1] Secondly, the coroner refused to call five directors of the company because they were considered to be too distant from the actual events for their evidence to be considered important. An appeal against the decision was rejected.[2]

1 The Coroners' Rules, SI 1984/552, r 42 provides that the verdict by the jury should not express any opinion on questions of criminal (or civil) liability. This is a matter for the criminal courts.
2 *R v HM Coroner for East Kent, ex p Spooner* (1989) 88 Cr App Rep 10.

9.22 On the basis of the finding of unlawful killing, on 22 June 1989 a summons alleging manslaughter was issued against P & O European Ferries Ltd (which had taken over Townsend) and seven individuals, including directors and some of the crew. P & O sought to have the summons set aside on the basis that it was not a natural person and so could not be convicted of manslaughter.[1] This application was rejected. Reviewing the authorities, Mr Justice Turner considered that 'the identification doctrine' was 'fundamental to the true basis of corporate criminal liability'.[2] He held that prima facie a company could be convicted of manslaughter:

'Suffice it that where a corporation, through the controlling mind of one of its agents, does an act which fulfils the prerequisites of the crime of manslaughter, it is properly indictable for the crime of manslaughter.'[3]

1 *R v P & O European Ferries (Dover) Ltd* (1990) 93 Cr App Rep 72.
2 (1990) 93 Cr App Rep 72 at 84.
3 (1990) 93 Cr App Rep 72 at 82.

9.23   The legal rationale for such liability was not agency but was based upon a finding that acts of senior members of a company can be considered to be those of the company itself, even if those members delegate their duties.[1] Thus, for the company to be found guilty the prosecution had to show that at least one of the individual defendants was reckless in the *Caldwell*[2] sense and that that particular individual represented the company's directing mind and will. Critically, Mr Justice Turner held that criminal liability could not be established by aggregating the acts of individuals.

1   *R v P & O European Ferries (Dover) Ltd* (1990) 93 Cr App Rep 72 at 82. Mr Justice Turner continued (at 83) by saying that the natural persons who are to be treated as being the company are to be established on the basis of its articles and memorandum of association – those persons who have been entrusted with exercise of the company's powers.
2   See also C Wells 'Corporations: Culture, Risk and Criminal Liability' [1993] Crim LR 551 at 551–566. The case is discussed from the perspective of risk assessment.

9.24   There were in addition, some difficulties with the manner of presentation of the prosecution case. Some issues were not dealt with, one of which was whether the known likelihood of a ro-ro capsizing rapidly after water entered the car deck called for special attention in the design of the door and the closing system. Another issue related to whether the risk of the ship capsizing should have been obvious to those responsible for passenger transportation. After hearing the prosecution evidence, Mr Justice Turner concluded that there was no evidence that a prudent marine operator would have found that the risk of the ferry sailing with its bow doors open was 'obvious'. Based upon his decision in relation to the circumstances in which a company could be convicted, the lack of evidence led by the prosecution meant that Mr Justice Turner had to direct the jury to acquit P & O and the defendant directors although the prosecution of Mr Sabel and Mr Stanley continued.[1] The prosecutions of these men were later discontinued on the ground that it was not in the public interest for the prosecutions to proceed solely against them. Captain Lewry's Master's Certificate was however suspended for one year and Mr Sabel's Certificate suspended for two years.

1   *R v P & O European Ferries (Dover) Ltd* (1990) 93 Cr App Rep 72. Whether the prosecution would have succeeded had the prosecution adduced further evidence can only be speculated upon, but the burden of proof to be discharged was so high as to be probably unattainable.

9.25   In short, the prosecutions against the company failed because, on the law as it then was, it could not be established that those directors in charge of the company's senior management were at fault.[1]

1   The court believed that there was insufficient evidence to show that the coroner's ruling that there was no sustainable case of manslaughter against the directors was incorrect: (1989) 88 Cr App Rep 10 at 16. This was because amongst other things, the necessary mens rea could not be proven as against the directors. The company accordingly could not be liable for the crime because of a failure to establish the mens rea and actus reus against those 'who were to be identified as the embodiment of the company itself'.

The internationalisation of safety of life at sea

9.26   Until the advent of the twentieth century safety of life at sea was dealt with in a parochial manner. The British and the French with their great maritime traditions led the way with their own domestic legislation which applied to their own flagged fleets and to merchant shipping within their territorial waters. International codification was not on the agenda and the call for such regulation of the safety of maritime adventures was at best muted. It took a disaster of immense proportions affecting the higher reaches of British and American society with attendant publicity to drive the issue of safety at sea to the forefront of the public conscience, and thus the forefront of governments' agenda worldwide.

The Titanic

9.27   One thousand, five hundred and one souls perished when the *Titanic* failed to live up to its 'unsinkable' billing.

9.28   The *Titanic*, owned by the Oceanic Steam Navigation Company Ltd (known as White Star Line), left Southampton on its maiden voyage on 10 April 1912 calling at Cherbourg, and then proceeding to Queenstown bound for New York. The ship maintained a high speed during the course of its journey and enjoyed clear weather. At 11.40 pm on 14 April 1912 in the North Atlantic Ocean, about 400 miles south of Newfoundland, Canada, the ship hit an iceberg, not detected until it was too late to take evasive action. The collision ripped the ship's starboard side in several places.[1] The ship began to founder and capsized and sank in just under three hours.[2]

1   Report by the Wrecks Commissioner into the Titanic Casualty *Loss of the Steamship 'Titanic'* (1912) p 65 (*Titanic* Report).
2   *Titanic* Report, n 1 above, p 31.

9.29   It was found by the formal investigation into the first major maritime disaster in modern times that it was standard practice for ships on the route employed by the *Titanic* to keep a man posted as a look-out when approaching areas of ice but to maintain their present speed. This practice was attributed to the desire of the public to be transported across the Atlantic Ocean at speed rather than any default or lack of judgment on the part of the shipping company.[1] The practice was routinely followed by other ships and no casualties arose from this. The Report concluded that this practice, although undesirable, was not negligent. Many of the conclusions of the Report absolved the shipowning company from any responsibility, even though the speed at which the ship was travelling shortly before the collision was thought to be excessive.[2]

1   *Titanic* Report, **para 9.28 n 1** above, p 31.
2   *Titanic* Report, **para 9.28 n 1** above, p 64.

9.30   This, however, was the wake-up call that the world needed. Negligent officers and crew can be disciplined, but the possibility cannot be avoided that there will be those at sea who fail to demonstrate requisite skill and care, occasionally with disastrous consequences. Disciplinary proceedings and the withdrawal of licences in punishment merely treat the symptoms, not the root cause of the problem. The question was now asked: how should those with corporate responsibility, such as a shipowner or a shipbuilder, be compelled to apply standards and establish systems more suited to the maritime adventures of the twentieth century and which might reduce the probability of poor seamanship and ameliorate its effects?

The first international conference on safety of life at sea

9.31   In the wake of the loss of the *Titanic*, the British government called an international conference to consider the safety of life at sea. It was held in London in

January 1914 and attended by representatives of Austria, Belgium, Denmark, France, Germany, Italy, The Netherlands, Norway, Russia, Spain, Sweden, the UK and the US. It resulted in the first Convention for the Safety of Life at Sea – the 1914 SOLAS Convention.[1]

1   Convention for the Safety of Life at Sea, signed at London, 20 January 1914.

9.32   The 1914 SOLAS Convention was a watershed. For the first time, it imposed on an international scale a raft of measures, related to the construction of ships and their navigation, designed to secure the safety of life at sea. Of particular importance was the requirement that ocean passenger ships carry lifeboats which could accommodate all people on board the ship, a consequence of it having emerged from the report into the loss of the *Titanic* that there were not enough lifeboats to accommodate all those on board.[1]

1   *Titanic* Report, **para 9.28 n 1** above, pp 62–63.

9.33   Although only ratified by five states (including France, the UK and the US), those nations controlled such a substantial proportion of the world's fleet at that time, that the Convention's application was extensive.

Subsequent international conferences on the safety of life at sea

9.34   London played host to a second international conference on the safety of life at sea in 1929, resulting in the second SOLAS Convention,[1] and the third SOLAS Convention resulted from a third international conference hosted by the UK in 1948.[2]

1   1929 International Convention for the Safety of Life at Sea.
2   1948 International Convention for the Safety of Life at Sea.

9.35   In the same year, another very significant development took place, with the setting up of the Inter-Governmental Maritime Consultative Organisation (IMCO; this was renamed the International Maritime Organisation (IMO) in 1982). The 1960 SOLAS Convention, which entered into force on 26 May 1965, was IMCO's first major achievement.[1] The 1960 amendments represented a major modernisation of the international regime to take account of technical developments.

1   1960 International Convention for the Safety of Life at Sea.

The late twentieth century

Developments in the UK

The Merchant Shipping Acts 1988 and 1995

9.36   MSA 1988, s 31 included for the first time a provision whereby a shipowner could be held to be criminally responsible for the unsafe operation of its ship. This is now re-enacted as MSA 1995, s 100, which states:

'Owner liable for unsafe operation of ship

(1) It shall be the duty of the owner of a ship to which this section applies to take all reasonable steps to secure that the ship is operated in a safe manner.

(2) This section applies to—

(a)   any United Kingdom ship and

(b)   a ship which—

> (i)   is registered under the law of any country outside the United Kingdom, and
>
> (ii) is within United Kingdom waters while proceeding to or from a port in the United Kingdom,

unless the ship would not be so proceeding but for weather conditions or any other unavoidable circumstances.

(3) If the owner of a ship to which this section applies fails to discharge the duty imposed on him by sub-section (1) above, he shall be liable—

(a)   on summary conviction, to a fine not exceeding £50,000;

(b)   on conviction on indictment, to imprisonment for a term not exceeding two years or a fine, or both.

(4) Where any such ship—

(a)   is chartered by demise;[1] or

(b)   is managed, either wholly or in part, by a person other than the owner under the terms of a management agreement within the meaning of section 98[2] any reference to the owner of the ship in sub-section (1) or (3) above shall be construed as including a reference –

> (i)   to the charterer under the charter by demise;
>
> (ii) to any such manager as is referred to in paragraph (b) above; or
>
> (iii) if the ship is both chartered and managed (as mentioned above) to both the charterer and any such manager

and accordingly the reference in subsection (1) above to the taking of all reasonable steps shall, in relation to the owner, the charterer or any such manager, be construed as a reference to the taking of all such steps as it is reasonable for him to take in the circumstances of the case.

(5) No proceedings for an offence under this section shall be instituted—

(a)   in England and Wales, except by or with the consent of the Secretary of State, or the Director of Public Prosecution;

(b)   in Northern Ireland, except by or with the consent of the Secretary of State or the Director of Public Prosecutions for Northern Ireland.'

1   A demise charterer is someone who leases the ship from the shipowner.

2   This subsection seeks to extend liability to those parties which are most closely involved with a ship's management, up-keep and employment. MSA 1988, s 98 states that if any responsibilities of the shipowner have been assumed by another person under either a charterparty or management agreement, then that person will be liable instead of the shipowner.

9.37   In *The Safe Carrier*[1] the provisions of MSA 1988, s 31 were tested when a prosecution was brought against the owners of an offshore standby safety ship. It had set sail on 6 September 1990 from the Tyne bound for Aberdeen, having recently been converted. The chief engineer was very experienced, but he had boarded the ship for the first time only a few hours before she put to sea. Early the next morning, because he was not familiar with the piping arrangements on board, the generators broke down and the engines became flooded with water. The ship was towed back to port. The shipowners were convicted of an offence contrary to s 31, amongst other things, because the company had caused the ship to be operated in an unsafe manner by allowing the chief engineer less than three hours in which to familiarise himself with it before sailing. The minimum time necessary for a chief engineer to familiarise himself with a converted ship was reckoned to be three days. The shipowners appealed from the magistrates' decision to the Divisional Court which upheld their appeal. The Secretary of State then appealed to the House of Lords for reinstatement of the magistrates' decision. The House of Lords accepted that the failure of a shipowner to establish a system for ensuring that a ship did not go to sea before the chief engineer had sufficient time to familiarise himself would constitute a s 31 offence. However, the failure had to be on the part of senior management, ie someone who, by virtue of the company's constitution or otherwise, was entrusted with the exercise of its powers. This being the case, it was not sufficient for there to be merely evidence of fault on the part of persons who were simply employees, such as the chief engineer, or the shipowner's personnel manager. To put the matter another way, the owner of a ship which has been found to be operating in an unsafe manner merely by reason of the negligence of an employee will not be criminally vicariously liable for that negligence under what is now MSA 1995, s 100.[2] In *The Safe Carrier* no evidence had been adduced relating to the culpability of senior management, such that the magistrate had not been in a position to apply his mind to the question of whether the shipowners had failed to establish any system for ensuring that the ship did not go to sea before the chief engineer had sufficient opportunity to familiarise himself with its machinery and equipment. Accordingly, the conviction was overturned.[3]

1 *Seeboard Offshore v Secretary of State for Transport (The Safe Carrier)* [1994] 1 Lloyd's Rep 589.
2 Criminal responsibility for corporations will not extend to such acts unless the person responsible for the negligent act is part of the directing mind of the corporate owner: see *Tesco Supermarkets v Natrass* [1972] AC 153, as applied in *Seeboard Offshore v Secretary of State for Transport (The Safe Carrier)* [1994] 1 Lloyd's Rep 589. For consideration of what might qualify as part of the directing mind of the corporate owner, see *Lennard's Carrying Co v Asiatic Petroleum Co* [1915] AC 705; *The Lady Gwendolen* [1965] 1 Lloyd's Rep 35.
3 The decision in *Seeboard Offshore v Secretary of State for Transport (The Safe Carrier)* [1994] 1 Lloyd's Rep 589 should now be read in light of *Meridian Global Funds v Securities Commission* [1995] 2 AC 500 and in the light of the ISM Code, compliance with (or not) which will be a highly material factor for the success of prosecutions under MSA 1995, s 100.

9.38 It should be noted in addition, in reference to an offence committed by a corporation under MSA 1995, s 277(1) which is proven to have been committed with:

> 'the consent or connivance of, or to have been attributable to any negligent act on the part of, any director, manager, secretary or other similar officer of that body ... [then] he, as well as the body corporate, is guilty of that offence and is liable to be proceeded against and punished accordingly.'

9.39 This adopts the wording used in the HSWA 1974, s 37, thus applying it to vessels outside Great Britain.

9.40 Whilst MSA 1988, s 31 was a legislative response to the *Herald of Free Enterprise* disaster[1] designed to impose criminal responsibility on a shipowner for the unsafe operation of a ship outside Great Britain, it was not intended to be the direct hook upon which to hang criminal responsibility for deaths resulting from maritime tragedies and plainly did nothing to overcome the difficulties of identification and proof which the failed prosecutions of P & O and its directors had brought to the fore. The difficulties inherent in the general law of manslaughter would still prevail. Two further British maritime tragedies demonstrated that this remained an area which needed to be addressed.

1 See **para 9.14**ff above.

The Marchioness

9.41   The 66-year-old pleasure boat *Marchioness* sank in the Thames in the early hours of 20 August 1989 having collided near Southwark Bridge with a dredger/sand carrier named the *Bowbelle*. The ship was carrying a total of 134 passengers and crew, and as a result of the collision 51 of those enjoying themselves at a party lost their lives. The *Bowbelle* was owned by East Coast Aggregates Ltd and managed by South Coast Shipping Ltd. Douglas Henderson, the Master of the *Bowbelle*, was later charged under MSA 1988, s 32 for failing to keep a proper look-out which resulted in the collision with the *Marchioness*. However, after two juries had failed to agree a verdict, the Crown Prosecution Service offered no further evidence and a verdict of not guilty was entered in July 1991.[1]

1   Lloyd's List, 12 April 1995.

9.42   The Marine Accident and Investigations Bureau (MAIB), which had been charged with the formal investigation of the tragedy, reported its conclusions in August 1991. Its report did not identify any one party as being responsible for the incident but blamed the cause of the disaster on the poor look-outs on both ships. It also reserved a great deal of criticism for the Department of Transport (DoT), which, it said, had known of previous collisions on the Thames between large ships and smaller passenger ships and therefore was aware of the visibility problems which the larger ships experienced, but had taken no action.[1] It was also found that the ships' steering positions made it difficult for the crew to have a full view of other traffic.[2] In its defence, DoT contended that the reports of the earlier incidents were made at a time when the regulatory structure did not permit them to be made available to the public.

1   Lloyd's List, 16 August 1991.
2   Department of Transport Environment and the Regions *Marchioness/Bowbelle formal investigation under the Merchant Shipping Act 1995* (2001) p 149, para 15.48.

9.43   In late 1991 Ivor Glogg (whose wife had died on the *Marchioness*) brought private prosecutions for manslaughter against four senior company officials and the managing company of the *Bowbelle*.[1] However, in June 1992 the Chief Stipendiary Magistrate discontinued these proceedings due to lack of evidence.

1   Lloyd's List, 12 April 1995.

9.44   In April 1995 the inquest jury for the *Marchioness* deaths returned a verdict of 'unlawful killing' in respect of the 43 people who died from drowning as a result of the collision (the other victims died afterwards) although this was not attributed to any individual.[1] A number of safety recommendations were also made by the jurors which were passed to the DoT.[2] Among their recommendations was the need for persons to be employed as a look-out to monitor traffic and improve the visibility of ships travelling along the Thames (a necessary measure also highlighted in the MAIB Report[3]). They called for enhanced safety procedures for passenger ships as well (for example, it transpired that there had been no announcements made to passengers on board the *Marchioness* about evacuation procedures[4]).

1   In relation to the *Herald of Free Enterprise* inquest, inquest juries cannot determine any question of criminal liability.
2   Lloyd's List 8 April 1995.
3   See **para 9.42** and n 2 above.
4   Lloyd's List, 23 March 1995.

9.45   Although there had been the MAIB Report into the collision, no contemporaneous public inquiry into the tragedy had been ordered. In October 2000, 11 years after the collision, and due in the great part to the continued lobbying of survivors and relatives and friends of those who had died on board the *Marchioness,* a public inquiry, chaired by Lord Justice Clarke, was finally opened. This inquiry again attributed responsibility for the incident to the poor look-outs on both ships, but the owners and managers of the ships were also criticised for failing to instruct their crews adequately.[1] The Master of the *Bowbelle* received further criticism as it emerged that he was drinking on the day of the incident and had failed to provide for immediate rescue assistance.[2]

1   BBC News article, 23 March 2001.
2   On 3 December 2001 the Maritime and Coastguard Agency ruled that the Master should keep his British Master's certificate: see *The Times,* 4 December 2001.

9.46   The importance of the *Marchioness* tragedy, in this context, was that it also served to highlight the impact of the current state of the law of manslaughter vis-à-vis the possibility of conviction of a corporate entity. As in the *Herald of Free Enterprise,* even though a verdict of unlawful killing was returned at the inquest, no successful prosecutions for manslaughter were brought against either the managing company in charge of the *Bowbelle* or members of any of its senior management. This was because, in terms of criminal liability, no one person had been identified as being responsible for the deaths, due to the lack of evidence necessary to secure convictions.

Lyme Bay

9.47   At about 10 am on 22 March 1993, a group of eight sixth-formers and their teacher set out in kayaks, planning to canoe from Charmouth to Lyme Regis in about two hours, accompanied by two instructors from the St Albans Outdoor Activities Centre. Matters went wrong from the outset. The teacher experienced difficulties and was attended to by one of the instructors. Whilst this occurred the other instructor sought to gather the rest of the group together by linking their canoes into a raft. However, they drifted away from the other instructor and the teacher, and were capsized by a wave. The pupils were wearing lifejackets, but it emerged that they were wrongly instructed not to inflate their lifejackets in the event of kayaks capsizing. Indeed this was said by one expert to be one of the main reasons for their deaths.[1] The teacher and the first instructor, although isolated from the party, remained in their kayaks and were rescued at around 5.30 pm. The rest of the party were rescued between 5.30 pm and 6.40 pm, by which time four pupils had died and the rest of the party was suffering from severe hypothermia and shock.

1   *The Times,* 9 December 1994, p 3.

9.48   OLL Ltd (OLL), which ran the centre, and Peter Kite (the managing director of OLL) were both indicted and successfully prosecuted for manslaughter.[1] Mr Kite was a very hands-on managing director and took all of the decisions in relation to the company. He was therefore identified as OLL's directing mind. It was established that, as the decision-maker, he had routinely failed to employ and train suitably qualified staff (for example, there were no standing criteria for the appointment of potential instructors). There was also the matter of a letter which had been sent to Mr Kite the year before the tragedy, highlighting to him the risks posed by the safety deficiencies at the centre. He was convicted of manslaughter and sentenced to three years in prison.[2] As to OLL, it was found that the trip had been inadequately supervised and organised – there was no emergency equipment and the instructors did not check the weather conditions before they set off. It also emerged that the centre had been slow in contacting the emergency services.[3] The group had been expected back around noon but the emergency services were not called until 3.30 pm. OLL was fined £60,000, which represented its entire assets.

1   *R v OLL Ltd* (1994, unreported); *R v Kite* (1994, unreported).
2   This was reduced to two years on appeal: *R v Kite (Peter Bayliss)* [1996] Cr App Rep (S) 295. Lord Justice Swinton Thomas, noting that Mr Kite was convicted on the basis of negligence and that there had been no criminal intent, believed that the sentence imposed by the trial judge was too severe.
3   (1994) 144 NLJ 1735.

9.49   This maritime tragedy is worthy of note because it was one of the few cases under English law where a *company* has been convicted of manslaughter. The principle, however, is not easily applied to other companies. When trying to bring a successful criminal prosecution for corporate manslaughter, identifying the directing mind in a small company is one thing (there will necessarily be few decision-makers and less need for a complex decision-making structure), but identifying the directing mind in larger corporations, where responsibility for the company's acts will be spread amongst a number of corporate officers or other senior personnel, may be entirely different.

Euromin Ltd

9.50   A further example of the perceived inadequacies and weaknesses of the current law on corporate manslaughter is illustrated by the death of Simon Jones on 24 April 1998 at Shoreham Docks in Sussex.

9.51   Simon Jones was sent by an employment agency to begin work as a casual labourer. On the first day of his employment with Euromin, he was given no formal training from anyone in a position of responsibility. Although another casual labourer had briefed him as to some safety procedures, he himself had received no training for the work he was engaged in. Mr Jones was told to assist in the unloading of bags of cobble-stones from the hold of a Polish vessel, the *Cambrook*. The job involved attaching bags of stone to chains hanging from a grab of a crane. The crane was initially supplied with attachments of a grab bucket and a lifting hook.

9.52   Mr Martell, the managing director of Euromin, had designed a new system for the use of the grab. This involved the addition of two hooks which were welded to the centre columns of the grab. The hooks could then be attached to chains and those chains could be used to lift bags containing cargo such as cobble stones more conveniently. This system meant that the lifting operation was carried out with the grabs open. Workers would have to stand very close to the bucket in order to attach the chains to the bags.

9.53   The system also required the hatchman to direct the crane operator since the crane operator could not see into the hold. The hatchman on the date in question was an untrained Polish seaman. The lever which closed the bucket was found to be very sensitive in its operation and would result in the closing of the bucket within a second. The operator of the crane had not been given any warning about the known sensitivity of the lever. Mr Jones was killed when the lever which closed the bucket was accidentally caught in the clothing of the crane operator, with the grab bucket decapitating Mr Jones.

9.54   The Director of Public Prosecutions (DPP) decided not to bring manslaughter proceedings against Mr Martell or the company because it was thought that there was insufficient evidence to provide a realistic prospect of conviction.[1] Mr Jones' parents sought and obtained a positive judicial review of the DPP's initial failure to bring manslaughter proceedings. After discussions with the DPP it was agreed to proceed with the prosecution of the managing director, Mr Martell, and the company. The trial took place in November 2001. On 29 November 2001 the company and Mr Martell were acquitted of manslaughter charges after trial by jury. The company was found guilty of breaches of health and safety regulations. The reason why the prosecution against both parties failed has been attributed by some to the difficulty in establishing the controlling mind of the company and the difficulty in obtaining a successful prosecution of manslaughter by gross negligence.[2] The quality of the available evidence may, however, have been a more relevant factor.

1   See the review of this decision in *R v Director of Public Prosecution, ex p Jones* All England Official Transcripts CO/3008/99.
2   See the article by M Hickman and Paul W in the *Independent*, 20 November 2001 and the article by G Slapper in *The Times*, 12 December 2001.

International developments

SOLAS

9.55   The 1960 SOLAS was completely revamped in 1974 and the 1974 SOLAS regime, as amended (which entered into force on 25 May 1980) is still the core international regime on issues of maritime safety. In common with its predecessors it sets out minimum standards in relation to all aspects of safety. It contains detailed requirements on, amongst other things, the construction, stability, equipment and operation of ships; fire protection and lifesaving appliances; and radio telephony.

9.56   The SOLAS regime is policed by flag states who are responsible for ensuring compliance of their own ships with its requirements. Additionally, contracting states must exercise a policing function over ships of other contracting states. This takes the form of inspections of ships within the ports or territorial waters of a contracting state where there are clear grounds for believing that the ship or its equipment do not substantially comply with the SOLAS requirements.

9.57   Many of SOLAS' numerous amendments have been precipitated by maritime disasters. For example, the 1981 amendments[1] (which provided for the compulsory introduction of duplicate steering gear control systems in tankers) followed the grounding of the Liberian tanker *Amoco Cadiz* off Porsall in Brittany on 16 March 1978, spilling 223,000 tonnes of crude oil. The accident happened, in part, due to damage to a rudder.

1   Adopted 20 November 1981 and entered into force 1 September 1984.

9.58   The April 1988 amendments,[1] following the capsize and sinking of the *Herald of Free Enterprise*, introduced a series of measures to improve the monitoring of doors and cargo areas and emergency lighting.

1   Adopted 21 April 1988 and entered into force 22 October 1989.

9.59 Some of the amendments in October 1988[1] also resulted from the loss of the *Herald of Free Enterprise*. These included a new requirement that all cargo doors be closed and locked before a ship leaves berth and also included new measures in relation to stability calculations.

1   Adopted 28 October 1988 and entered into force 29 April 1990.

9.60 Further amendments followed, but by far and away the most significant ones for further defining the corporate responsibilities of shipowners and others connected with maritime adventures were the new SOLAS Chapters IX, X and XI which were adopted by IMO in May 1994.

9.61 Chapter IX is dealt with at length at **para 9.63**ff below. Chapter X introduced safety measures for high speed craft, making mandatory the International Code of Safety for High Speed Craft.[1] Chapter XI contains a number of special measures to enhance safety, the most significant of which for present purposes is the regulation which grants authority to port state control officers inspecting foreign flagged ships to check that they comply with operational requirements of SOLAS:

'when there are clear grounds for believing that the master or crew are not familiar with essential shipboard procedures relating to the safety of ships.'[2]

1   Entered into force 1 January 1996. International Code of Safety for High Speed Craft, adopted 20 May 1994.
2   Entered into force 1 January 1996. SOLAS, Chapter XI, reg 4. Chapter XI will be renamed Chapter XI-1 when amendments to it dealing with enhancement of maritime security come into force on 1 July 2004.

9.62 The 'clear grounds' are defined broadly and include matters such as operational shortcomings, cargo operations not being conducted properly, absence of an up-to-date muster list and apparent difficulties of the crew in communicating with each other.

SOLAS Chapter IX – Management for the Safe Operation of the Ships

9.63 Chapter IX is highly significant because, for the first time internationally, a clear benchmark was established against which a corporate entity's criminal responsibility for death at sea could be adjudged. Chapter IX entered into force on 1 July 1998 for all passenger ships, oil/chemical tankers, gas carriers, bulk carriers and cargo high speed craft of 500 gross tonnes and above. It automatically applied to all other cargo ships and mobile drilling units of 500 gross tonnes and above from 1 July 2002. It does not apply to government-operated ships used for non-commercial purposes.[1]

1   SOLAS Chapter IX, regs 2, 3. See Appendix **9.1** at **para A9.1.0** below for the full text of Chapter IX.

9.64 Chapter IX makes mandatory the International Safety Management Code (ISM Code), which was adopted by the IMO in November 1993.[1] Research has suggested that some 80% of accidents at sea are the result of management failures or human error.[2] There is, of course, a significant distinction between the two, for there is no legislating for the master whose negligence or recklessness cannot be laid at the door of management. The main objectives of the ISM Code are to safeguard a master in the proper discharge of his or her responsibilities with regard to maritime safety, prevention of human injury or loss of life, and the protection of the marine environment[3] and to ensure the appropriate organisation of management to enable it to respond to the needs of those on board a ship to achieve and maintain high standards of safety and environmental protection.[4] IMO believes that in relation to such matters it is the commitment, competence, attitudes and motivation of individuals at all levels that determine the end result, but that the cornerstone of good safety management is commitment from the top.[5] Therefore, the ISM Code defines standards which ought to, if properly implemented, reduce the scope for management failure or human error and thereby enhance safety and environmental protection.

1   Resolution A.742(18), Annex, adopted in November 1993. See Appendix 9.1 at **para A9.1.0** for the full text of Resolution A.742(18).
2   H Honka 'Questions on maritime safety and liability, especially in the view of the Estonia Disaster' in Wetterstein and Beijer *Essays in Honour of Hugo Tiberg* p 361; cited in K Sydsjo Norlin 'A Legal Review of the International Safety Management (ISM) Code' (1998) Svenska Sjorattsforeningen Skrifter 72, Swedish Maritime Law Association.
3   Resolution A.741(18), preamble, para 2.
4   Resolution A.741(18), preamble, para 3.
5   Resolution A.741(18), preamble, para 6.

9.65   The ISM Code is expressed in broad terms so that it can have widespread application. It recognises that no two shipowning companies are the same and therefore does not seek to impose a rigid structure, although it is a significant departure from the pre-existing system whereby there were few written instructions on matters which traditionally, and for good reason, formed part of the master's delegated authority in the running of his ship. Rather it sets out the framework for individual shipowners to create their own safety management programmes tailored to their own companies in order to achieve the required international standards of safety and pollution prevention. For the first time, there is put in place a safety management structure which integrates shore-based personnel with those at sea. The ISM Code recognises that different levels of management, whether shore-based or at sea, require varying levels of knowledge and awareness of the items contained within it.[1]

1   Resolution A.741(18) (1993), preamble, para 5.

9.66   In order to achieve the objectives of the ISM Code, a company should have in place safety management objectives which provide for safe practices in ship operation and a safe working environment, which establish safeguards against all identified risks, and which continuously improve safety management skills of personnel ashore and on board ships, including preparing for emergencies related to both safety and environmental protection.[1] The ISM Code does not specify new rules and regulations in relation to safety, but is intended instead to provide for the creation of a safety management system (SMS) which ensures compliance with mandatory rules and regulations, and with any applicable codes, guidelines and standards recommended by IMO, flag administrations, classification societies and maritime industry organisations.[2] The SMS which is required to be developed, implemented and maintained, should:

1   include a safety and environmental protection policy;
2   include instructions and procedures to ensure safe ship operation and protection of the environment in compliance with relevant international and flag state legislation;
3   define the levels of authority and lines of communication between, and amongst, shore-based and shipboard personnel;

4   include a procedure for reporting accidents and non-conformities with the provisions of the ISM Code;

5   include procedures to prepare for and respond to emergency situations; and

6   include procedures for internal audits and management reviews.[3]

1 A bareboat charterer not only leases the ship from the shipowner but also provides and pays for the crew.
2 ISM Code, para 1.2.3.
3 ISM Code, para 1.4.

9.67   The ISM Code is directed at 'the Company', which means the shipowner or any other organisation or person such as a ship manager, or a bareboat charterer,[1] who has assumed the responsibility of operation of the ship from the shipowner and who, on assuming such responsibility, has agreed to take over all the duties and responsibilities imposed by the ISM Code.[2] This is significant given the fact that the vast majority of the world's tonnage is owned by one ship companies, usually with nominee directors and shareholders who have no actual interest, or day-to-day involvement, in a ship's management. Management is instead delegated to management companies and it is often those individuals behind the management companies who are also the true beneficial owners of the ship. The reason for having a one ship owning company with no real assets other than the ship is, self-evidently, to limit the beneficial shipowners' potential financial liability to the value of the ship itself and to provide effective immunity to those beneficial owners whose identities may, thus, never be known. This has a consequence in relation to safety issues in that there can be a temptation amongst some shipowners to do the minimum required to keep a ship at sea – in full knowledge that responsibility for safety lapses resulting in loss of life or injury may never be laid at their door. The clear extension of responsibility for safety management to management companies and to bareboat charterers counters such risk.

1 ISM Code, para 1.2.2.
2 ISM Code, para 1.1.2.

9.68   The company is required to define and document the responsibility, authority and inter-relationship of all personnel who manage, perform and verify work relating to and impacting on safety and pollution prevention.[1] In this regard, to ensure the safe operation of each ship and to provide a link between it and those on board, the company should designate a person or persons ashore having direct access to the highest level of management. The responsibility and authority of the 'designated person' or persons should include monitoring the safety and pollution aspects of the operation of each ship and ensuring that adequate resources and shore-based support are applied as required.[2] The device of the designated person has potentially great significance for identifying the person or persons who can be said to represent the company's directing mind, responsible for safety and, through that person, to hold the company to account for manslaughter. The identification principle, as has been stated earlier, is fundamental vis-à-vis the current law on corporate manslaughter. It is important to note that the proposed changes to the current law (as presently drafted) adopt a very similar philosophy to that of the ISM Code in their watering down of the identification principle to proof of a mere management failure.

1 ISM Code, para 3.2.
2 ISM Code, para 4.

9.69   The increased onus upon the company to create and implement an SMS is not intended to derogate from the master's responsibilities and authority. The company is required to ensure that the SMS operating on board a ship contains a clear statement emphasising that authority. The company must establish in the SMS that the master has the overriding authority and responsibility to make decisions with respect to safety and environmental protection and to request the company's assistance as may be necessary. To this end, the company should clearly define and document the master's responsibility with regard to:

1   implementing the company's safety and environmental protection policy;
2   motivating the crew in the observation of that policy;
3   issuing appropriate orders and instructions in a clear and simple manner;
4   verifying that specified requirements are observed; and
5   reviewing the SMS and reporting its deficiencies to the shore-based management.[1]

1   ISM Code, para 5.

9.70   The ISM Code sets out, for the sake of clarity, certain well-defined obligations of the company. Some of these derive from English case law, in particular those cases concerning a shipowner's ability to limit liability in respect of civil claims under the international limitation of liability regimes (for example, the 1976 International Convention on Limitation of Liability for Maritime Claims), or in relation to issues of seaworthiness in the context of civil claims under charterparties, bills of lading or policies of marine insurance. Thus, the company should ensure that the master is properly qualified for command, fully conversant with its SMS and given the necessary support so that his duties can be safely performed.[1] The company is required to ensure that each ship is manned with qualified, certificated and medically fit seafarers in accordance with national and international requirements.[2] It must establish procedures to ensure that new personnel and personnel transferred to new assignments relating to safety and environmental protection are allowed proper familiarisation with their duties.[3] Instructions which are essential prior to sailing should be identified, documented and provided.[4] The company should also ensure that all personnel involved in the implementation of its SMS have an adequate understanding of relevant rules, regulations, codes and guidelines[5] (and in the context of this, procedures should be established by which personnel receive relevant information on the SMS in a working language or languages understood by them[6] and the company should ensure that they are able to communicate effectively in the execution of their duties related to the SMS[7]). Further, the company should establish and maintain procedures for identifying any training which may be required in support of the SMS and ensure that such training is provided for all personnel concerned.[8]

1   ISM Code, para 6.1.
2   ISM Code, para 6.2.
3   Cf eg the incident involving *The Safe Carrier* referred to at **para 9.37** above.
4   ISM Code, para 6.3.
5   ISM Code, para 6.4.
6   ISM Code, para 6.6.
7   ISM Code, para 6.7.
8   ISM Code, para 6.5.

9.71   The ISM Code also contains functional and procedural requirements relating to the development of plans for shipboard operations, emergency preparedness, reporting and analysis of non-conformities, accidents and hazardous occurrences, and maintenance of the ship and equipment.[1]

1   ISM Code, paras 5, 7–10.

9.72   The company is required to establish and maintain procedures to control all documents and data which are relevant to the SMS. To this end, it should ensure that valid documents are available at all relevant locations, changes to documents are reviewed and approved by authorised personnel, and obsolete documents are promptly removed.[1] This document trail is important in three respects:

1   it ensures that the requirements of the SMS are clearly and easily accessible;
2   it assists those charged with the task of verifying compliance with the ISM Code in undertaking that task; and
3   in this context, it is an important source of evidence in establishing corporate responsibility for death.

1   ISM Code, para 11.

9.73   The company should carry out internal safety audits to verify whether safety and environmental protection activities comply with the SMS.[1] Management personnel responsible for the area involved should take timely corrective action on deficiencies found.[2] The audit requirement is significant for the purpose of establishing the requisite degree of knowledge on the part of individual directors where a corporate entity is prosecuted for manslaughter, in other words, causation.

1   ISM Code, para 12.1.
2   ISM Code, para 12.6.

9.74   A ship's flag state (the Administration) is charged with ensuring that the company complies with the ISM Code[1] (alternatively, the Administration can delegate this task to an independent organisation or the government of the country in which the company has chosen to conduct its business). Every company complying with the requirements of the ISM Code should be issued with a Document of Compliance (DOC), whilst the ship or ships for which it is responsible will be issued with a Safety Management Certificate, when the Administration has verified that the company, and its shipboard management, operate in accordance with the approved SMS.[2] There is also a continuing duty upon the Administration periodically to verify the proper functioning of a ship's SMS.[3] In November 1995, IMO adopted *Guidelines for the Implementation of the ISM Code by Administrations.*[4] These Guidelines are primarily for the benefit of the Administrations tasked with verifying compliance with the ISM Code. As such, the Guidelines are beyond the scope of this work.

1   ISM Code, para 13.2.
2   ISM Code, para 13.4.
3   ISM Code, para 13.5.
4   IMO Resolution A.788(19).

Corporate responsibility for death at sea – current law and practice

9.75   Shipping is a global enterprise and judicial inquiries, courts and legislatures worldwide have had to address the issue of corporate responsibility for deaths which occur in maritime adventures in their territorial waters or on ships registered in their national registries.

9.76   This section is not intended to be an exhaustive account of all those tragedies that have occurred or the manner in which they have been dealt with judicially. What must be recognised at the outset is that some of the worst maritime disasters have taken place in jurisdictions where they have not been reported to the extent of some of the European disasters. For instance, on 20 December 1987, the same year as the *Herald of Free Enterprise*, the *Dona Paz* collided with a coastal motor vessel in the Sibuyan sea near the Philippines.[1] The collision caused raging infernos on both ships, claiming the lives of 4,386 people and destroying both ships. Just 26 people managed to survive. Deficiencies in the ships' communication equipment meant that maritime officials only learned of the collision some eight hours after impact. Similarly, in 1993 the *Neptune*, a Haitian passenger ship, capsized as a result of being severely overcrowded. The ship was licensed to carry 250 people but is thought to have carried in excess of 2,000.[2] A mass movement of passengers from the one side of the ship to the other caused stability problems and lead to the ship sinking, with over 1,700 lives believed to have been lost.

1 N Hook *Maritime Casualties 1963-1996* (2nd edn, 1997) pp 172–174. See further (p 174) the commentary on the greatest loss of life at sea which occurred when 18,000 German refugees died when the ships carrying them were torpedoed by Russian submarines.
2 Hook, n 1 above, p 425.

The English approach

9.77 The general English approach is set out in **chapter 1**. So far as concerns shipping specifically, prosecutions for homicide can be brought before the English court for acts committed on any ship in British territorial waters and on British ships in any waters.[1]

1 Jurisdiction in respect of acts done in England is derived from common law. The common law courts exercised jurisdiction over all persons who committed criminal acts within territorial limits, whether they were British subjects, resident aliens or mere casual and temporary visitors: see *R v Keyn* (1876) 3 ExD 63 at 160. The jurisdiction over British subjects in respect of acts committed abroad is purely statutory and is based on the allegiance of the subject to the sovereign, and on the power of the sovereign, by reason of this allegiance, to pass laws for the regulation of the conduct of subjects wherever they are: see *The Sussex Peerage case* (1844) 11 CL & Fin 85 at 146. Indictable offences committed within the territorial sea of the UK whether by a British subject or a non-British subject or whether committed on, or by means of, a foreign ship are offences within the jurisdiction of the Admiralty and are triable in England: see the Territorial Waters Jurisdiction Act 1878, s 2; the Territorial Sea Act 1987, s 115.

9.78 The test is for gross negligence (the question of whether the negligence was gross and therefore a crime being for a jury to determine). That test is an objective one as to whether a defendant's conduct fell far short of the required standard of care. The meaning of 'gross negligence' has been considered in a civil context in a shipping case. In *The Hellespont Ardent*[1] Mr Justice Mance held that gross negligence is clearly intended to represent something more fundamental than failure to exercise proper skill and/or care constituting negligence. But, as a matter of ordinary language and general impression, the concept of gross negligence is capable of embracing not only conduct undertaken with actual appreciation of the risks involved, but also serious disregard of or indifference to an obvious risk. Comparing the tests for gross negligence in the criminal and civil contexts, Mr Justice Mance found that in the criminal context, in essence a breach of a duty of care will amount to manslaughter if its seriousness in all the circumstances is such that a jury considers that it should be characterised as a crime; whereas in the civil field, it would be regarded as conduct so seriously negligent that the defendant should not be entitled to rely on an exemption clause. He agreed with Lord Mackay in *Adomako*[2] that it was 'necessarily a question of degree, and an attempt to specify that degree more closely is ... likely to achieve only a spurious decision'. Ultimately, the question whether any negligence in the civil context was 'gross' would be very much a matter of degree and judgment.

1 *Red Sea Tankers Ltd v Papachristidis (Henderson, Baarma and Bouckley third parties)* [1997] 2 Lloyd's Rep 547 at 586–587.
2 *R v Adomako* [1995] 1 AC 171.

9.79 Aside from addressing the meaning of 'gross negligence', the *Hellespont Ardent* decision[1] also dealt with the issue of the personal liability of directors. The case concerned a contract between an investment fund and certain other companies which offered services of a technical advisory nature to persons engaged or interested in engaging in the shipping market. The *Hellespont Ardent* was one of four ships purchased by the investment fund with the assistance of these particular technical advisors. The investment proved to be a bad one and the investment fund suffered substantial losses, which it sought to recover from the technical advisors and/or their directors. The defendants were alleged to have been grossly negligent and/or guilty of wilful misconduct in a number of respects, for example, failing to warn of the risks of acquiring *Hellespont Ardent* and in negotiating her purchase without any discount properly reflecting her less than satisfactory condition. It was alleged that the individual directors owed a personal duty of care to the investment fund in respect of their own acts or omissions and that it had relied upon the special expertise which they held themselves out as possessing. The directors sought to rely upon two contractual clauses to exempt them from any tortious liability. Those clauses excluded any liability, save where it resulted from, inter alia, gross negligence. Mr Justice Mance therefore had to determine whether any of the defendants owed a duty of care to the investment fund in contract, tort or otherwise in relation to the acquisition of *Hellespont Ardent* and if so, the nature and scope of such duty or duties; and whether any of the them acted in breach of such a duty.

1 *Red Sea Tankers Ltd v Papachristidis (Henderson, Baarma and Bouckley third parties)* [1997] 2 Lloyd's Rep 547.

9.80 In rejecting the investment fund's claim, Mr Justice Mance held that even if the directors were grossly negligent, there was no basis for treating them personally as having undertaken responsibility in respect of the substantial commercial risks of a financial nature in the success or failure of the relevant transactions.[1] Further, as to the extent to which the knowledge of a director of a company can be attributed to the company itself, in this case much turned on the role of one of the defendants, Mr Anderson. Mr Anderson was managing director of the two technical advisory companies, and also acted as chairman of the board of the investment fund. It was contended that Mr Anderson, acting purely in his capacity as a director of the investment fund, was obliged to bring to its attention any qualification or warning required to be given by the technical advisory companies in relation to the recommendation to purchase the *Hellespont Ardent*. Mr Justice Mance found that such an obligation would, if it existed, clearly undermine the contractual structure and the roles and responsibilities placed on the advisory companies. He held that it was not part of Mr Anderson's role as chairman of the investment fund to undertake any of the functions entrusted to the technical advisory companies or to communicate knowledge of events leading up to a decision by those companies to make an unqualified recommendation to the investment fund. Furthermore, even if Mr Anderson was under a duty to communicate to the investment fund's directors knowledge of factors relevant to the technical advisory companies' recommendation of *Hellespont Ardent*, such knowledge could not be imputed to the investment fund, since Mr

Anderson did not actually communicate it. There was no suggestion that Mr Anderson was the investment fund's directing mind and will for the purposes of attributing his knowledge on that ground. The directing mind and will was the board as a whole, which alone had responsibility for approving or disapproving any recommendation.[2]

1   *Red Sea Tankers Ltd v Papachristidis (Henderson, Baarma and Bouckley third parties)* [1997] 2 Lloyd's Rep 547 at 593.

2   *Meridian Global Funds v Securities Commission* [1995] 2 AC 500, PC, per Lord Hoffmann, reinforces this conclusion, emphasising the common sense underpinning of principles governing attribution of knowledge. The question of whether knowledge of an agent should be attributed to his principal depends upon the context and purpose of the question. In the *Hellespont Ardent*, the context and purpose is a defence to the effect that the investment fund's complaint about the making of an unqualified recommendation without warning must fail because it, through Mr Anderson, was aware of the factors which made the recommendation unsuitable, or of the qualifications and warnings which should have accompanied it. The only persons whose knowledge could sensibly be attributed to the investment fund would be its board as a whole; see at 596–597. On the other hand, for a director to be held to owe a personal duty of care separate to that owed by him on behalf of the company, it will be necessary to show that there was an assumption of personal responsibility on his part to the victim: cf *Williams v Natural Life Health Foods Ltd* [1998] 2 All ER 577. Such personal responsibility will usually only be found if there are some special circumstances since holding a director liable in this context is inconsistent with the principle of limited liability of companies and preservation of the corporate veil. The courts are more likely to find an assumption of personal liability in cases involving physical injury or damage, as opposed to pure economic loss.

Development of the relevant principles in English maritime case law

9.81   In the maritime context, the English courts have been well used to considering issues of negligence and, in turn, corporate responsibility, ie the extent to which directors' acts or omissions are to be identified with, or attributed to, a company. A review of the important case law by way of illustration is useful. Essentially, the cases fall into two broad bands:

1   those involving the right to limit liability for damage; and
2   those involving attempts to recover under marine insurance policies.

Limitation of liability for damage – the issue of actual fault or privity or wilful misconduct

9.82   The entitlement to limit liability for general maritime claims derives from the 1957 Limitation of Liability of Owners of Seagoing Ships Convention and the more modern 1976 International Convention on Limitation of Liability for Maritime Claims (1976 LLMC). The 1976 LLMC was enacted in the UK by MSA 1995, Sch 7. This grants a right to limit liability to several different types of legal person in respect of certain types of damage as long as specific criteria are fulfilled, for example, where the shipowner can establish that the damage was caused without wilful misconduct on its part. Under the 1957 Convention limitation regime, the test was one of actual fault or privity of the shipowner.[1]

1   MSA 1995, Sch 7, art 4. The 1976 LLMC is a general convention – there are specific conventions dealing solely and specifically with particular types of maritime claims, eg oil pollution (the CLC regime) and passenger claims (the Athens regime). These regimes contain similar criteria to those set out in 1976 LLMC which need to be satisfied before the right to limit can be broken. In practice, there is a difference between the tests for breaking limitation in the respective conventions but a discussion of this dichotomy is beyond the scope of this work.

The Marion

9.83 The *Marion* was managed by a company called F.M.S.O. On 14 March 1977 she anchored approximately three miles off shore. A few days later, she attempted to weigh her anchor, but was unable to do so because it had snagged and severely damaged an oil pipeline which ran from the Ekofisk field through Tees Bay to Teeside. The pipeline owners claimed, amongst their remedies, damages exceeding US$25 million. The owners of the *Marion* applied for a decree limiting the amount of their liability in damages in respect of this incident. In so doing, they admitted that the damage was caused partly by the negligence of one of their servants. The reason that the *Marion* came to anchor so close to the pipeline was that Captain Potenza, her Master, was unaware of its existence because he was navigating with the aid of an out-of-date chart. If he had looked at an up-to-date chart of the area, he would have seen the position of the pipeline marked and such a chart was in fact available in the *Marion's* chart room. The sole issue between the parties was whether the *Marion's* owners should be regarded as having established that the incident occurred without their actual fault or privity within the meaning of those words in the then current law which provided inter alia:

> 'The owners of a ship, British or foreign, shall not where ... any of the following occurrences take place without their actual fault or privity... (d) where any loss or damage is caused to any property ... or any rights are infringed through the act or omission of any person (whether on board the ship or not) in the navigation or management of the ship ... or through any other act or omission of any person on board the ship ... be liable in damages beyond the following amounts ... (ii) in respect of such loss damage or infringement as is mentioned in paragraph ... (d) of this sub-section ... an aggregate amount not exceeding the amount equivalent to one thousand gold francs for each ton of their ship's tonnage.'[1]

1   MSA 1894, s 503, as amended by the Merchant Shipping (Liability of Shipowners and Others) Act 1958, s 2(1).

9.84 In the proceedings as to whether the *Marion's* owners were entitled to a decree of limitation, Mr Justice Sheen held that they were. The Court of Appeal overturned this and the House of Lords upheld its decision. By the time the proceedings had reached the House of Lords,[1] certain matters of fact and/or law were common ground. Amongst these were two factors of primary importance for determining whether or not the damage occurred without the shipowner's actual fault and privity. First, since the shipowner had delegated the management and operation of *Marion* wholly to F.M.S.O., the person whose fault would constitute, as a matter of law, the actual fault of the shipowner, was the managing director of F.M.S.O. (a Mr Downard). Secondly, whereas F.M.S.O. employed three other persons in a managerial capacity, no faults of theirs, if they occurred, could constitute, as a matter of law, the actual fault of the shipowner.

1   *Grand Champion Tankers Ltd v Norpipe A/S (The Marion)* [1984] 1 AC 563.

9.85 In giving judgment, Lord Brandon commented upon where the dividing line is to be drawn between the responsibilities of the ship's master for safety of navigation and the responsibility of the shipowning or managing company. These observations are particularly pertinent in relation to the approach the English courts might now adopt to corporate responsibility for manslaughter:

'The question whether, where damage had been done by a ship, such damage occurred without the actual fault of her owners or managers, is primarily one of fact, to be decided by reference to all the circumstances of any particular case. Such question involves, nevertheless, an element of law, in that the answer to it must depend, in part at least, on what approach Courts dealing with contested limitation actions adopt, in relation to safety of navigation, the responsibilities of masters on the one hand and of shipowners or ship managers on the other.

There was a time when Courts dealing with contested limitation actions considered that shipowners or ship managers sufficiently discharged their responsibilities if they appointed a competent master and thereafter left all the questions of safe navigation, including the obtaining at their expense of all necessary charts and other nautical publications, entirely to him. That former approach of Courts has now been out of date for more than twenty years, as appears from the decision of the Court of Appeal in *The England* ...'[1]

1   *Grand Champion Tankers Ltd v Norpipe A/S (The Marion)* [1984] 1 AC 563 at 572, per Lord Brandon.

9.86   Lord Brandon then quoted from the judgment of Sir Gordon Willmer in *The England*:

'... The decision of the House of Lords in the case of *The Norman*, seems to me to have thrown quite a fresh light on the extent of the managerial duties of owners and managers, especially in relation to the supply of navigational information and publications to their vessels. It seems to me that it is no longer permissible for owners or managers to wash their hands so completely of all questions of navigation, or to leave everything to the unassisted discretion of their master.'[1]

1   *Grand Champion Tankers Ltd v Norpipe A/S (The Marion)* [1984] 1 AC 563 at 572; *Rederig Edornn H Groen v The England (Owners) The England* [1973] 1 Lloyd's Rep 373 at 383.

9.87   In the above passage, Sir Gordon Willmer referred back to his own decision in *The Lady Gwendolen* and quoted two sentences from his own judgment:

'... It seems to me that any company which embarks on the business of shipowning must accept the obligation to ensure efficient management of its ships if it is to enjoy the very considerable benefits conferred by the statutory right to limitation.'[1]

1   *Arthur Guinness Son & Co (Dublin) Ltd v Owners of the Motor Vessel Freshfield (The Lady Gwendolen)* [1965] 1 Lloyd's Rep 335 at 346.

9.88   Lord Brandon held that the approach begun in *The Norman*[1] in 1960 and continued in *The Lady Gwendolen*[2] in 1965 and *The England*[3] in 1973 should now be regarded as the correct approach in law to the problem of actual fault of shipowners or ship managers in contested limitation actions. Applying that approach in *The Marion*, he found that there were two actual faults of the shipowners – in Mr Downard's failure to have a proper system of supervision in relation to charts and in his failure to give clear instructions to his subordinates with regard to the matters about which he required to be kept informed.[4]

1   *Northern Fishing Company (Hull) Ltd v Eddom (The Norman)* [1960] 1 Lloyd's Rep 1, HL.
2   *Arthur Guinness Son & Co (Dublin) Ltd v Owners of the Motor Vessel Freshfield (The Lady Gwendolen)* [1965] 1 Lloyd's Rep 335.

3   *Rederig Edornn H Groen v The England (Owners) The England* [1973] 1 Lloyd's Rep 373.
4   *Grand Champion Tankers Ltd v Norpipe A/S (The Marion)* [1984] 1 AC 563 at 572, per Lord Brandon.

The Lady Gwendolen

9.89   In *The Lady Gwendolen*, quoted with approval by Lord Brandon in *The Marion*,[1] the shipowners were the Guinness brewery. They sought a decree of limitation in respect of their liability for damages arising out of a collision between *The Lady Gwendolen* and the motor vessel *Freshfield* in the Mersey in 1961. They admitted liability for the damage, but contended that the collision occurred without their actual fault or privity. Evidence was given at the trial that the Master habitually proceeded at excessive speed in fog and that the collision occurred in consequence of this. At first instance, the court found the shipowners guilty of actual fault and accordingly unable to limit their liability. That decision was upheld on appeal.[2]

1   *Grand Champion Tankers Ltd v Norpipe A/S (The Marion)* [1984] 1 AC 563.
2   *Arthur Guinness Son & Co (Dublin) Ltd v Owners of the Motor Vessel Freshfield (The Lady Gwendolen)* [1965] P 294; [1965] 1 Lloyd's Rep 335.

The Ert Stefanie

9.90   *The Ert Stefanie* is an example of a case where the board of directors of a corporation might not always comprise the whole of the group of people who together constitute its governing mind and will. *The Ert Stephanie* was managed by Sorek Shipping Ltd (Sorek) and Mr Baker, a director of Sorek, ran the technical side of the business which included responsibility for the ship's maintenance. The ship was found in arbitration between shipowners and charterers to have been unseaworthy and unfit for a particular voyage and the arbitrator held that the shipowners were entitled to limit their liability under MSA 1894, s 503 because the breaches occurred without their actual fault or privity. On appeal, Mr Justice Hobhouse held that, in order to consider whether there was actual fault or privity, the position of Sorek, not the actual shipowners, had to be considered. On this basis, he found that the relevant liability of the shipowners did not arise without their actual fault or privity and that they were accordingly not entitled to a decree of limitation of liability. The owners appealed to the Court of Appeal, who dismissed the appeal.[1]

1   *Société Anonyme Des Minerais v Grant Trading Inc (The Ert Stefanie)* [1989] 1 Lloyd's Rep 349.

9.91   On the issue of whether it was the correct approach to consider the knowledge of the management company, rather than the shipowners, Lord Justice Mustill noted that:

> 'While the doctrines of corporate personality call for a ritual nod in the direction of the owners, nobody in practice pays any attention to these one ship companies registered under flags of convenience; and the law takes the same view when questions of limitation are in issue.'[1]

1   *Société Anonyme Des Minerais v Grant Trading Inc (The Ert Stefanie)* [1989] 1 Lloyd's Rep 349 at 350.

9.92   As to identification, or attribution, he held.

'The charterers contend, or have come very close to contending, that, if the fault is laid at the door of a member of the board of directors, it must inevitably involve the actual fault or privity of the company. The point does not arise here, but if it did, I doubt whether I would be prepared to go so far. It seems to me at least theoretically possible for a situation to exist where a particular director had been formally excluded from participation in the company's business and where, if nevertheless he did trespass on that territory, his act in so doing would not be attributed to the company.

Conversely, the owners maintain that, if a particular individual has ultimate control over the policies of the company, only he can be the alter ego of that company. I do not accept this at all. The Articles of Association of Sorek Shipping are not before us, but I have no doubt that they vest the responsibility for the management of the company in the board of directors. The board of directors of a corporation may not always comprise the whole of the group of people who together constitute the governing mind and will of the corporation, for the cases show clearly that the fault of a senior manager below board level may on occasion be included in the group. Nevertheless, it seems to me that any director must necessarily be a member of the group unless formally dis-seized of responsibility in the manner just described.

Thus, I would prefer to steer clear of generalisations about the constituent elements of the "alter ego". Each case must turn on its own facts, and I am not persuaded that the report of decisions to which we have very properly been referred shed any real light on the problems. Looking at the facts here, I really see no scope for controversy. Mr Baker was a director. It was to him that responsibility for operational matters had been devolved ... Mr Baker was the director in charge of the aspects of the company's business which went wrong. He was personally at fault. It seems to me plain that in such circumstances the owners have no right to limit their liability.'[1]

1   *Société Anonyme Des Minerais v Grant Trading Inc (The Ert Stefanie)* [1989] 1 Lloyd's Rep 349 at 351.

Marine insurance – the issue of blind eye knowledge

9.93   The question of privity of the shipowner arises both in relation to an entitlement to limit liability and in relation to recovery under a policy of marine insurance. The Marine Insurance Act 1906, s 39(5) relieves underwriters of responsibility for a claim where, in a time policy (ie a policy of insurance in relation to a ship which is for a period of time, rather than for a particular voyage) the loss occurred because the ship was sent to sea in an unseaworthy state, with the knowledge and concurrence of the assured personally. One of the questions which arose in *The Eurysthenes* was the extent of knowledge required. Lord Denning MR held:

'To disentitle the shipowner, he must, I think, have knowledge not only of the facts constituting the unseaworthiness, but also knowledge that those facts rendered the ship unseaworthy, that is, not reasonably fit to encounter the ordinary perils of the sea and, when I speak of knowledge, I mean not only positive knowledge but also the sort of knowledge expressed in the phrase "turning a blind eye". If a man suspicious of the truth, turns a blind eye to it, and refrains from enquiry – so that he should not know it for certain – then he is to be regarded as knowing the truth. This "turning a blind eye" is far more blameworthy than mere negligence. Negligence in not knowing the truth is not equivalent to knowledge of it.

The knowledge must also be the knowledge of the shipowner personally, or his alter ego, or in the case of a company, its headmen or whoever may be considered their alter ego. It may be inferred from evidence that a reasonably prudent owner in his place would have known the facts and have realised that the ship was not reasonably fit to be sent to sea. But if the shipowner satisfies the Court that he did not know the facts, or did not realise that they rendered the ship unseaworthy, then he ought not be to held privy to it, even though he was negligent in not knowing.'[1]

1 *Compania Maritima San Basilio SA v The Oceanus Mutual Underwriting Association (Bermuda) Ltd (The Eurysthenes)* [1976] 2 Lloyd's Rep 171 at 179, per Lord Denning MR.

9.94 This decision has recently been considered by the House of Lords in the *Star Sea* and a gloss put upon it. Lord Scott held that:

'There must be a suspicion of the relevant unseaworthiness, and a decision not to check. Unless there is a decision not to check, not to obtain confirmation of what is suspected, there will, in my opinion, be no privity, no blind-eye knowledge, however seriously negligent the failure to check may be.'[1]

1 *Manifest Shipping Co Ltd v Uni-Polaris Insurance Co Ltd and La Rénunion Europréene (The Star Sea)* [2001] 2 WLR 170; [1997] 1 Lloyd's Rep 360, [1995] 1 Lloyd's Rep 651.

9.95 It is submitted that a combination of the ISM Code and the development of the common law have the effect of making it far more likely that a large shipping company could be convicted of gross negligence manslaughter today. Of particular relevance is the role of the 'designated person' under the Code; if the attribution principle espoused in *Meridian*[1] is followed, then the knowledge of the designated person may be regarded as that of the company itself. Further, the reporting requirements under the Code are likely to fix more senior management with knowledge of safety deficiencies. The approach of the courts to attributing knowledge in the limitation of liability cases cited above, and to fixing individuals with blind-eye knowledge (although watered down by the House of Lords in the *Star Sea*[2]), also make a conviction more likely. As to whether a jury might regard the negligence as gross, the ISM Code sets a clear benchmark for standards of safety management and it is to be anticipated that death caused by a failure to meet those standards will be punished.

1 *Meridian Global Funds v Securities Commission* [1995] 2 AC 500.
2 *Manifest Shipping Co Ltd v Uni-Polaris Insurance Co Ltd and La Rénunion Europréene (The Star Sea)* [2001] 2 WLR 170; [1997] 1 Lloyd's Rep 360, [1995] 1 Lloyd's Rep 651.

Examples of the international approach

The Haven

9.96 On 14 April 1991 the 18-year-old oil tanker *Haven*, which had just undergone a two-year re-fitting programme costing around US$40 million (where she received the first ever permitted life extension certificate awarded by the American Bureau of Shipping), was anchored just off Genoa's oil terminal. In the course of transferring a cargo of oil, she suffered a series of explosions in the no 2 centre permanent water ballast tank which created a blazing inferno. As a result of the explosions, the ship broke in half and sank. Five people died, including the Master, Chief Officer and the Chief Engineer.

9.97   At the time of the explosion the ship was carrying around 144,000 tonnes of crude oil and the resulting oil pollution damaged the coasts of Monaco, France and Italy.[1] The ship was owned by Venha Maritime Ltd and managed by Troodos Shipping. A Genoa public inquiry team was established to investigate the incident. The inquiry team reported back with its findings and stated that part of the responsibility for the disaster lay with the Master, given that he did not inform the authorities of a fault in the ship's inert gas system. The Chief Officer and the Master were also blamed for transferring cargo contrary to the port regulations, and the Chief Engineer was criticised for permitting the use of a cargo pump which had been reported as faulty.[2] Troodos were also criticised in failing to cease operations when various faults in the ship were found.

1 Lloyd's List, 4 March 1995.
2 Lloyd's List, 14 October 1992.

9.98   The main cause of the explosion was thought to be over-pressurisation when the Chief Officer was transferring cargo from the no 3 port and starboard tanks to the no 1 centre tank or because of a breakage or slippage of an expansion joint passing through the no 2 tank.

9.99   Aside from compensation issues, the Italian prosecutor sought to prosecute the individuals behind the owning company for, amongst other things, the manslaughter of those who died. The first instance court dismissed the manslaughter charges holding that the facts did not point to any crime having been committed.[1] The prosecution had based its case around the theory of a faulty cargo pump brought about by the shipmanagers' failure to maintain it. However, a diving inspection of the ship's wreck had revealed that the cargo pumps in question were still encased in their green paint. If the prosecution case was correct then the pumps in question would have been destroyed by the blast. The evidence suggested that a failure to maintain the pumps was not the cause of the accident, but more likely the over-pressurisation theory concluded by the public inquiry.

1 Lloyd's List, 22 November 1997.

9.100   The Italian state did not pursue a corporate manslaughter prosecution because Italian law did not recognise any such crime. One factor weighing heavily against any such prosecution, however, was that prior to the incident, the ship had undergone a massive re-fit and reconditioning programme.[1] In any case, the report of the court appointed surveyor had pointed towards the Chief Officer's poor supervision of the transfer of cargo, allowing an excessive build-up of pressure.

1 Lloyd's List, 24 November 1997.

9.101   The prosecutor appealed against the dismissal of charges, but in 1997 the Genoa Appeal Court cleared all three men charged of manslaughter, again holding that the facts did not point to any crime having been committed, but indicating that the incident was caused by the Chief Officer's error.[1]

1 It has been suggested that the criminal prosecutions in Italy were brought as a means to try to secure higher compensation payouts from Troodos: see Lloyd's List, 24 November 1997. As has already been stated, in maritime claims it is possible to limit liability for damage, personal injury and death. However, it is possible to break that global limit if amongst other things there has been personal fault or privity on the part of the person claiming the right to limit.

It was thought that successful manslaughter prosecutions against the senior members of Troodos' management would enable claimants in the civil compensation cases to break the right to limit under the 1969 International Convention on Civil Liability for Oil Pollution (CLC), as amended so as to become entitled to higher levels of compensation. For further on the issue of breaking the maximum limit for compensation see C De la Rue and CB Andersen *Shipping and the Environment Law and Practice* (1998) pp 103–107; and P Griggs and R Williams *Limitation of Liability for Maritime Claims* (3rd edn, 1998). For further discussion on this topic see also Lloyd's List, 11 October 2000, p 18.

9.102   This case indicates how difficult it is for prosecutors to succeed with manslaughter charges even against individuals where they have acted within a corporate entity. The legal notion of the 'veil of incorporation' that separates the corporation from its members, directors and employees was strictly adhered to by the Italian court. Under Italian law it is not possible to convict a corporation of any criminal offence, because the corporation in strict legal terms only enjoys a metaphysical existence, and not one annexed to, or shared with its officers. Under of the Constitution of the Italian Republic, art 27 criminal liability is considered a personal concept, in that only a natural person as opposed to a legal person can commit a crime.

9.103   On the facts of the *Haven* case there was no evidence to point to the crime of manslaughter and the issue is raised as to how far senior management can be accountable for employees when such employees commit errors in the performance of their duties. If these errors arise as a result of inadequate training which include the failure to implement and supervise health and safety procedures then the shipowner or manager *may* have a case to answer. But where the error cannot be so attributed, it is difficult for any manslaughter action to be successfully prosecuted against senior management, let alone any corporate manslaughter charge being successfully prosecuted. If a crime is committed by a manager or employee while acting in the course of the company's activities then the individual in question may be pursued in their personal capacity but no prosecution can lie against the company.

The Estonia

9.104   Just before 2.00 am on 28 September 1994 this 14-year-old ro-ro passenger ferry, on a scheduled 217-mile trip from Tallinn to Stockholm, sank after encountering a vicious storm. The official figures seem to vary, but the ship was carrying over 1,000 people and over 900 are thought to have died.[1] The initial inquiry into the incident reported that the high waves generated as a result of the vicious storms led to the visor-style bow door being ripped off the ship which eventually enabled water to pour into the car deck. A three-nation commissioned report (comprising of officials from Sweden, Estonia and Finland) had concluded that deficiencies in the design of the ship's bow visor attachments, its extra speed on the fateful night and poor reactions from the crew in exchanging information prior to the disaster and organising the evacuation of the ship led to its sinking and the mass loss of life.[2] This report concluded that the bow door locks should have been at least five times stronger than those actually used. Further, the locks were said to be badly designed and as such failed to lock effectively, allowing high waves to smash against the visor before finally cracking the inner doors (which also operated as the ship's loading ramp). The bow visor was then ripped off allowing water to enter and flood the car deck. The ship lost stability and capsized in a short space of time sinking just off the coast of Finland.

1   Hook, **para 9.76 n 1** above, p 267.
2   Lloyd's List, 4 December 1997.

9.105   The Master was also criticised for not warning passengers early enough and for failing to send an earlier mayday distress signal. In the end 130 people were rescued; most of those who died were thought to have been trapped in the cabins and a number of people could not make use of the lifesaving equipment – in particular the life rafts could not be employed to their full effect given the ship's huge list.

9.106   The tripartite report tended to shift any blame from the shipowners and managers towards the ship's German builders, Meyer Werft, given that design defects were alleged in the visor locks. Dissatisfied with many of the assumptions in the original report, Meyer Werft commissioned their own report which concluded that the cause of the sinking was the poor maintenance of the ship and its equipment, not faulty design.[1] It was further alleged in that report that when the locks were repaired they were repositioned and the new welds were weaker than those originally installed. The vehicle ramp was also said to be out of alignment and in breach of SOLAS requirements. The ship managers were alleged to have decided not to repair or replace the damaged rubber packings which helped to ensure the internal water-tightness of the visor. As a result the visor is said to have regularly filled with water and the hinges to have become misaligned. It was also suggested that the leaking bow ramp led to the flooding of parts of the car decks. Further it was reported that some of the vehicles on the deck were not properly secured, so that the high speed at which the ship was travelling meant that a 55 ton unsecured truck crashed into the bow ramp forcing it open and allowed a further volume of water into the car deck. The Meyer Werft report also concluded that the visor locks were repaired in an unprofessional fashion and alleged that the ship was unseaworthy when it left Tallinn.[2]

1   BBC News website, www.news.bbc.co.uk, 3 December 1997.
2   Lloyd's List, 4 December 1997.

9.107   The ship's classification society, Bureau Veritas, was also in the spotlight. It allegedly approved the ship for travel when it did not have a watertight bulkhead.[1] The Swedish maritime authorities were also implicated for allegedly approving two surveys on the ship's safety procedure and lifeboats when the initial report into the incident had cast doubt on the efficacy of those safety procedures and access to the lifeboats. It was later revealed that there was a failure by the Swedish maritime authorities to check the ship's bow visor when it had a warning of similar problems with a sister ship, the *Diana II*.[2]

1   Lloyd's List, 17 November 1996.
2   Lloyd's List, 16 September 1996.

9.108   There have also been suggestions in the press that the main cause of the incident was not due to any defects in the bow locks or the lack of maintenance thereof, but rather to a series of small explosions.[1]

1   *Fairplay Daily News*, 19 February 1998.

9.109   Very early on, the prosecution authorities in Sweden announced that no charges would be brought against the parties involved given that there was little evidence to suggest that any of them were guilty of criminal failures.[1] The relatives of those who had died in the tragedy therefore sought to bring actions in France against the Swedish Maritime Authority, Bureau Veritas and Meyer Werft (a compensation package was agreed with survivors and surviving crew members[2]).

1   *Fairplay Daily News*, 19 February 1998.
2   Lloyd's List, 17 October 1996.

Express Samina

9.110 Having hit the Portes Rock, this 34-year-old passenger ship (on a voyage from Piraeus to Paros and several other Greek islands) sank in the Aegean Sea five kilometres off the coast of Paros at 10.30 pm on 26 September 2000.[1] Although the ship was due to retire from service within the following months having reached the legal operating age under Greek law, it had recently undergone a refit to the cost of around £1.5 million, although some commentators have said that it is not clear how much of this sum was spent on upgrading ship safety.[2]

1 *Daily Telegraph*, 28 September 2000, pp 4–5; *Independent*, 28 September 2000, p 2; BBC News article, 27 September 2000.
2 *Sunday Times*, 1 October 2000, p 25.

9.111 At least 80 people, out of the 530 on board, were killed.[1] The Greek government launched an immediate criminal inquiry into the matter. It is thought that on the night of the incident, the Master was feeling unwell and left the bridge to go to his cabin. He left the First Officer in charge.[2] Despite terrible weather conditions (Force 8 gale winds and 12 foot waves) the First Officer then left the ship in the charge of a 22-year-old trainee who had recently graduated from merchant navy school. The trainee called for help when bearing down on the rock, at a speed 50% faster than the ship's usual speed. The First Officer returned to take charge, but too late – the collision with the rock caused a 210-foot gash in the ship's lower starboard side. The Master maintained that he was on his way back to the bridge when the collision with the rock occurred.

1 Lloyd's List, 6 November 2000.
2 BBC News article, 1 October 2000.

9.112 The fact that the ship collided with the 76-foot rock raised suspicion in some quarters, given that the rock is well-known in Greek shipping circles and carries a light visible from seven miles.[1] At some 18 minutes after the collision the first mayday call was made. At that point the ship listed heavily to the right before capsizing in a matter of minutes.

1 See the comments of Andreas Sirigos, a coastguard chief, made in an article in *The Times*, 28 September 2000.

9.113 There were numerous allegations that the evacuation procedures employed by the crew were unorganised.[1] The passengers were not told what to do or where they could find the evacuation equipment. There were also reports of the crew using the lifeboats to escape at the expense of passengers and of several lifeboats being stuck to the deck because the joints had been painted over. In all, over 450 people were rescued due to the efforts of local fishermen, HMS *Liverpool* and HMS *Invincible* and Royal Navy helicopters.

1 *Sunday Times*, 1 October 2000 p 25.

9.114 The Master, First Officer and Third officer were charged with manslaughter.[1] There were also allegations that the ship was unseaworthy, although Mr Katsafados from the Inspectorate Division of the Greek Ministry of Mercantile Marine had inspected the ship shortly before the collision and issued a certificate of seaworthiness. The ship's former First Engineer claimed that he was dismissed five days before the collision, allegedly because of complaints made to the Greek maritime safety officials relating to failures in testing the ship's doors, generators and emergency equipment.

1 Lloyd's List, 7 February 2002. The charges were reduced to misdemeanours on 10 September 2002 by a panel of judges, but a senior prosecutor for the Greek Supreme Court overturned that ruling a few days later. The prosecutor's action also meant that the managing company faces serious criminal charges for the sinking: *Athens News*, 4 October 2002.

9.115 In November 2000 the senior executive at the company which ran the *Express Samina* committed suicide.[1] Mr Sfinias jumped from the sixth floor of his office building landing directly on a car in the street below and was said to have died on impact Some have argued that this act was due to the pressure upon him and the charges of mismanagement levelled against his company. The public prosecutor had also brought a blanket charge of endangering passengers resulting in death against those at the managing company, but further investigation was needed to determine whether any one individual at the company was responsible for this incident and the criminal proceedings in this case continue.

1 *The Times*, 30 November 2000.

9.116 More recently a magistrate's report into the incident has pointed the finger of blame at the crew.[1] A failure to sound the evacuation alarm and the gap of 12 minutes from the collision before the crew started to evacuate people were cited as key failings. Earlier reports suggesting that the evacuation was unorganised were confirmed as the magistrate found that there was a lack of routine emergency procedures which meant that passengers had to fend for themselves. An earlier report into the causes of the sinking released in September 2001 found that the vessel sank because the hatches separating the watertight compartments had been left open as well as the crew's failure to avoid the well-lit rocks.

1 See BBC News report 'Greek Death ferry crew condemned', 22 January 2002.

Particular issues concerning surveyors and classification societies

9.117 Classification societies have been in existence since 1760 when Lloyd's Register became the first of their number. It was followed in 1828 by Bureau Veritas and thereafter by Det Norske Veritas, Germanisher Lloyd and the American Bureau of Shipping (ABS). Nowadays there are some 50 classification societies, the largest of which have formed the International Association of Classification Societies (IACS) whose role is to ensure quality in classification services.

9.118 Classification societies cover some aspects of ship's safety, but not all. They lay down and regularly update standards of safety in relation to hull structures and essential onboard machinery. Standards of safety relating to stability, load lines, safety equipment and radiotelegraphy are dealt with by international convention, notably SOLAS. Most flag states delegate the implementation of the international standards to classification societies because they are, for the most part, uniquely equipped to deal effectively with them throughout the world. Similarly, flag states tend to delegate ensuring compliance with the ISM Code to classification societies.[1] The question therefore arises, where there is a loss in circumstances where the ship has been certified by a classification society, or where the SMS certified is found to be deficient and loss of life, injury or physical damage has resulted, whether this was due to error or omission on the part of the classification society in performing such function.

1 The *Erika* environmental disaster occurred off the coast of Brittany in December 1999. Over 15,000 tonnes of heavy fuel oil cargo leaked into the sea when the ship broke her back, and the

Erika's classification society (RINA) has been subject to immense criticism following the disaster (particularly since the ship was known shortly before the casualty to have been subject to corrosion). As a result of the *Erika*, the EU has drawn up a proposed Directive under which classification societies would have to apply for recognition from the European Commission and from flag states, with attendant demanding criteria – see the *Report from the Commission for the Biarritz European Council on the Communities' Strategy for Safety at Sea*, Brussels, 27 September 2000; COM (2000) 603 Final. In its introductory section it notes that:

> 'Following the Amoco Cadiz disaster in 1978, the Commission has repeatedly drawn the Council's attention to the fact that the conventional forum for international action on safety at sea, the International Maritime Organisation (IMO), has not been adequately effective in tackling the causes of disasters at sea.'

It goes on to set out the proposed short-term measures being examined by the Council and the European Parliament. One of these is an amendment to the existing Directive (Council Directive 94/57/EC) with regard to classification of ships to which the member states delegate a major proportion of their inspection powers, especially as regards the structural quality of ships. Its aim is to centralise and harmonise the approval procedures for classification societies, to impose specific penalties (suspension or withdrawal of approval) on individual classification societies failing to perform their duties and, in general terms, to supervise classification societies' activities. The Report notes that rapid progress has been made regarding this proposal and that there is very broad agreement on its wording within the Council; see Council Directive 94/57/EC of 22 November 1994 on common rules and standards for ship inspection and survey organisation and for the relevant activities of maritime administrators. The Report also notes that the Commission is contemplating the creation of a specific structure which might take the form of a 'European Agency for Maritime Safety', whose purpose would be to support the Commission and the member states' actions in applying and monitoring Community law and in assessing the effectiveness of the tools provided. It would also help in preparing the technical adjustments to Community law. Specifically, it could perform particular main tasks including the assessing and auditing of individual classification societies. The *Prestige's* hull first cracked on 13 November 2002 off Spain's northwest coast, just north of Portugal. It sank amid heavy weather six days later. The initial damage from the spill (in excess of 20,000 tonnes of fuel oil) occurred on Spain's northwest coast, near Vigo, blackening hundreds of beaches and crippling the lucrative fishing industry that provides mussels and clams. The damage later swept around to Spain's northern coast and then hit the French coast. Following sustained criticism, suit has been filed in the US against ABS, the Prestige's classification society, by the Spanish government.

Following the sinking of the *Prestige*, the European Commission reminded member states that the measures taken after the sinking of the *Erika*, in 1999, had to be implemented. It also proposed new measures. The Commission is therefore preparing a set of legislative measures to impose penalties on those responsible for pollution due to negligence, including classification societies. In the case of classification societies, member states will be able to provide for various sanctions ranging from fines to permanent or temporary bans on the pursuit of commercial activities, depending on the seriousness of the offence. See europa.eu.int/comm/transport/themes/maritime/prestige/com_2003_0092_en.pdf.

9.119 The issue of a classification society's culpability first arose under English law in relation to hull claims in the *Morning Watch*.[1] This case concerned the sale of a yacht which had just been surveyed and was subsequently found to be defective by the purchaser. The purchaser sued Lloyd's Register. Mr Justice Phillips held that where a classification society issues a classification certificate, that act might well carry with it express or implied representations as to the condition of the classified ship, but where a third party made representations as to this, that representation amounted to no more than a statement of its classification status and did not constitute any implicit representation by the maker as to the ship's actual condition. In this case, the seller, not Lloyd's Register, had made a representation as to the yacht's classification status. In these circumstances, the representation was a mere statement and did not attract any liability on Lloyd's Register's part. Implicit in this reasoning is the conclusion that if Lloyd's Register had made the representation directly to the buyers then, if negligent, that representation would be actionable by the buyers. Under the *Hedley Byrne* principles[2] the buyers would probably then have recovered their losses from Lloyd's Register even though their loss was purely economic. Mr Justice Phillips, while recognising these principles, failed to find sufficient proximity between Lloyd's Register and the ultimate buyers. He relied on the House of Lords' judgment in *Caparo Industries*.[3] In that case, the House of Lords found that auditors who prepared a report which was read by prospective purchasers of shares owed no duty of care to those prospective purchasers because there was insufficient proximity. Mr Justice Phillips stated:

> 'To accept the general proposition that Lloyd's owes a duty of care to those foreseeably liable to suffer economic loss in consequence of reliance on the negligent classification of a vessel would be to make a substantial further advance to the law of negligence. For this reason I reject that general proposition.'[4]

1   *Mariola Marine Corpn v Lloyd's Register of Shipping* [1990] 1 Lloyd's Rep 547.
2   *Hedley Byrne & Co Ltd v Heller & Partners Ltd* [1961] 3 All ER 891.
3   *Caparo Industries plc v Dickman* [1990] 1 All ER 568.
4   [1990] 1 Lloyd's Rep 547 at 560.

9.120   Although the claim against Lloyd's Register was for pecuniary loss, nevertheless, some of Mr Justice Phillips' general findings as to the circumstances in which a classification society can be responsible for negligence are relevant to cases where physical harm to persons or objects is concerned. So far as concerns the ingredients of a duty of care (reasonable foreseeability, proximity and just and reasonable in all the circumstances to impose a duty of care), he found that it was reasonably foreseeable by Lloyd's Register that a purchaser would be influenced by the results of its special survey when considering whether to buy the yacht. Further, foreseeability that lack of care may result in harm, while enough to give rise to a duty of care when the harm foreseen is physical damage, will not of itself give rise to a duty of care where the harm foreseen is limited to economic loss. Other factors must exist which place the parties in a close relationship before a duty of care will arise. Where a defendant voluntarily assumes responsibility to a claimant, and the claimant relies on that assumption of responsibility, sufficient proximity will often be created. The voluntary assumption of responsibility is not an essential element in creating necessary proximity. Where the relationship between the parties has many, though not all, the incidents of a contract, sufficient proximity may well exist. While foreseeability of reliance will not automatically give rise to a duty of care, foreseeability must play an important part. The primary purpose of the classification system is, as Lloyd's Register's Rules make plain, to enhance the safety of life and property at sea, rather than to protect the economic interests of those involved, in one role or another, in shipping. In so far as negligence in relation to classification is liable to harm economic interests, there is no general ground for distinguishing between the economic interests of the charterer, the mortgagee and the purchaser. All are foreseeably liable to rely upon the classification status of a ship – often to the extent of making the maintenance of classification status a contractual obligation – and all are at risk of being caused economic loss if classification surveys are not carried out with proper skill and care. Mr Justice Phillips went on to find that in the particular circumstances of this case, the facts fell short of those required for defining that the requisite degree of proximity existed.[1]

1   *Mariola Marine Corpn v Lloyd's Register of Shipping* [1990] 1 Lloyd's Rep 547.

9.121   This issue of the liability of classification societies next arose, in relation to cargo claims, in the *Nicholas H.*[1] While on a journey from Chile to Italy cracks were found in the ship's hull. The ship was surveyed by NKK. Temporary repairs were effected, and the classification society then recommended that the ship proceed to its port of discharge in Italy; however en route it sank. The cargo owners attempted to recover their losses from the shipowners and from the classification society. The shipowners were able to limit liability (under the Hague-Visby Rules), so the cargo owners sought to recover the balance of their claim from the classification society.

1   *Marc Rich & Co AG v Bishop Rock Marine Co Ltd, Bethmarine Co Ltd and Nippon Kaiji Kyokai* [1995] 2 Lloyd's Rep 299.

9.122   The High Court found that there was sufficient proximity on which to base a duty of care by the classification society towards the cargo owners. It was helped here by the fact that the classification society surveyor had made specific recommendations to the ship. The Court of Appeal allowed an appeal by the classification society, finding that there was no duty of care owed by it to the cargo owner.[1] It was the shipowner, not the classification society, who was in charge of the cargo and the shipowner was under a non-delegable duty to the cargo owners to use due diligence to make the ship seaworthy before and at the beginning of the voyage. The House of Lords upheld the Court of Appeal's decision by a majority, finding that it would be 'unjust, unfair and unreasonable' to hold the classification society liable in these circumstances.[2]

1   [1994] 1 Lloyd's Rep 492.
2   *Marc Rich & Co AG v Bishop Rock Marine Co Ltd, Bethmarine Co Ltd and Nippon Kaiji Kyokai* [1995] 2 Lloyd's Rep 299 at 316.

9.123   Can a classification society be convicted of gross negligence manslaughter? The issue has never risen for determination, at least in England.[1] These two shipping decisions give some indication of how the English court approaches the issue of duty of care where the losses claimed are economic, but it is submitted that the decisions may have been different had the court been considering death or personal injury. A case in the aviation sphere is illustrative.

1   Although in Greece, the technical director of the Hellenic Register was given a suspended five-year sentence for gross negligence in connection with the sinking of the *Iron Antonis* in the South Atlantic (where 24 lives were lost).

9.124   The Popular Flying Association (PFA), is a voluntary body approved by the Civil Aviation Authority (CAA) to inspect kit-built aircraft and issue certificates of fitness for flight if satisfied that aircraft are fit to fly. An action for negligence was brought by a passenger who was injured following the crash, during its test flight, of a Kitfox aircraft certified by a PFA inspector. The court was asked to deal by way of preliminary issue with the question of whether the PFA and its inspector owed the passenger a duty of care. It was held by Judge Hallgarten QC[1] and the Court of Appeal,[2] on appeal by the PFA, that it did. The Court of Appeal considered the decision of the House of Lords in the *Nicholas H*,[3] finding that it was foreseeable that if the PFA and its inspector granted a certificate of fitness to fly in respect of this aircraft (which had been fitted with an inappropriate gearbox) there was likely to be an accident, and they ought reasonably to have had in contemplation a person travelling as a passenger on the test flight in the aircraft as being so affected when they were directing their minds to the acts or omissions which were called into question. The role of the inspector was not a subsidiary one to that of the PFA. The inspector had an independent and critical role in the granting of a certificate of fitness for flight for this aircraft, without which it could not take off, and he was involved with the inspection of that aircraft throughout. A greater injustice would be done to a person injured in circumstances such as those that arose in this case by not imposing a duty on those responsible for issuing a fitness for flight certificate. The PFA and the inspector had undertaken to discharge a statutory duty for the protection of the public and no injustice was done by imposing such a duty on them in respect of a negligent act. It was right to hold that it was fair, just and reasonable to impose a duty on the PFA and its inspector.

1   *Perrett v Collins* (23 April 1997, unreported).
2   *Perrett v Collins* [1998] 2 Lloyd's Rep 255.
3   *Marc Rich & Co AG v Bishop Rock Marine Co Ltd, Bethmarine Co Ltd and Nippon Kaiji Kyokai* [1995] 2 Lloyd's Rep 299.

9.125   The strong reasoning in this case, allied to the observations in the *Nicholas H*[1] show there must be a real prospect of establishing that classification societies owe a duty in tort in respect of death and personal injuries. On that basis, it can be said that prosecution for corporate manslaughter against classification societies is a real possibility.

1   *Marc Rich & Co AG v Bishop Rock Marine Co Ltd, Bethmarine Co Ltd and Nippon Kaiji Kyokai* [1995] 2 Lloyd's Rep 299.

9.126   In the context of this, it should be noted that in this country, a classification society has been successfully prosecuted for breaches of health and safety legislation. In 1997, Lloyd's Register was fined £500,000 after pleading guilty to a charge under HSWA 1974 in connection with the collapse of a walkway at Ramsgate – the first such occurrence in the society's 240-year history. Fines and costs totalling more than £2.4 million were imposed on Lloyd's Register, the Port of Ramsgate and two Swedish engineering companies in the aftermath of the 1994 Port of Ramsgate ferry walkway disaster. A passenger walkway connected a passenger assembly building to a pontoon. The design of the pin used to connect the walkway was not in keeping with the normal practice of using two fixed surfaces to secure the stability. A single pin was used to hold the seaward end of the bridge and this resulted inevitably in its collapse onto the pontoon below and the deaths of six people. Mr Justice Clarke[1] found that gross errors on the part of the Swedish companies and Lloyd's Register led to the death of six people and injuries to seven others. The design of the walkway made it 'doomed to failure'. He said 'although the risk was foreseeable, no one foresaw it'. It was the duty of Lloyd's Register to check the walkway design to ensure it could cope with its environment and the operational movement of the pontoon. Whoever did this made the same mistake as the engineering company in assuming the walkway would sit on four feet. Lloyd's Register had quality assurance systems, but here the system was inadequate, or those responsible for operating it failed, or both.

1   Lloyd's List, 1 March 1997; see also *The Times*, 18 February 1997.

Particular issues concerning port and harbour authorities

9.127   Duties of a port or harbour authority arise primarily by way of statute.[1] Like all employers, they have a duty to conduct their undertaking in such a way as to ensure, so far as reasonably practicable, that persons not in their employment who may be affected thereby are not exposed to risks to their health and safety.[2] A person having control of premises, or of plant or substance in such premises has a duty to take measures to ensure, as far as is reasonably practicable, that the premises, all means of access and egress, any plant or substance in the premises or provided for use there, is or are safe and without risks to health.[3] Further, every employer shall make a suitable and sufficient assessment of the risks to the health and safety of its employees to which they are exposed whilst they are at work, and the risks to the health and safety of persons not in its employment arising out of, or in connection with, the conduct by it of its undertaking.[4] The authorities are also accountable for the duty to provide a pilotage service and should therefore exercise control over the provision of the service, including the use of pilotage directions, and the recruitment, authorisation, examination, employment status, and training of pilots.[5]

1 See the Pilotage Act 1847 and particular Acts setting up and regulating individual harbour authorities.
2 HSWA 1974, s 3.
3 HSWA 1974, s 4. Eg in 1998 Simon Jones was decapitated by a grab bucket whilst working as a stevedore for a company called Euromin on the docks at Shoreham-on-Sea. Mr Jones was a student taking a year out from his studies at Sussex University. The Director of Public Prosecutions decided that, whilst there had been a breach of the HSWA 1974, there was not sufficient evidence to obtain a conviction for manslaughter. Proceedings were begun in the High Court for judicial review of the DPP's decision not to prosecute and these were successful, the decision not to prosecute being described as 'irrational'. Corporate manslaughter charges against the company failed, see **paras 9.50ff** above.
4 Management of Health and Safety at Work Regulations 1999, SI 1999/3242; cf Port Marine Safety Code, para 1.2.6.
5 See also the Pilotage Act 1987, ss 2–4; cf Port Marine Safety Code, para 2.5.

9.128 Port and harbour authorities typically have an express duty to take such action as they consider necessary, or desirable for, or incidental to, the maintenance, operation, improvement or conservancy of the areas within their jurisdiction.

9.129 There are a number of common law duties. These include, inter alia, a general duty (so long as a port or harbour is open for the public use) to take reasonable care that all who may choose to navigate it may do so without danger to their lives or property. There is also a duty of care against loss caused by the authority's negligence and the obligation to conserve and facilitate the safe use of a port or harbour. Each authority has an obligation to have regard to efficiency, economy and safety of operation in respect of the services and facilities provided.

9.130 Due attention by ports and harbours also now needs to be given to the Port Marine Safety Code, which was published by the government in 2000 and is aimed at promoting best practice in British ports. Although it has no statutory force, it is expressed to be 'not optional – harbour authorities are expected to work to achieve the agreed standard by implementing its requirements'.[1] Like the ISM Code, it does not create new legal duties, rather it summarises the legal duties and powers of port and harbour authorities relating to marine safety. Further, like the ISM Code, it is likely to be regarded as a benchmark against which their activities are measured so far as concerns safety.

1 Port Marine Safety Code, Introduction, para 2. The Code does not apply to the extent that a matter is covered for example by the Docks Regulations 1988, SI 1988/1655 or the Dangerous Substances in Harbour Areas Regulations 1987, SI 1987/37, as amended. Nor does it deal with matters which are regulated by the Health and Safety Executive or by the Maritime and Coastguard Agency.

9.131 The Port Marine Safety Code sets out a summary of the measures that must be taken by authorities to meet the standards required. This includes requirements for the development of policies and procedures and their publication,[1] with the overriding objective of reducing risk as low as reasonably practicable.[2] In common with the ISM Code, the Port Marine Safety Code relies upon the principle that duties and powers in relation to marine operations in ports and harbours should be discharged in accordance with an SMS, and there is an obligation to create such a system. The SMS should cover, amongst other things, the use of port and harbour craft and the provision of moorings and a formal safety assessment should be used to identify the need for, and potential benefits for safety management, of port and harbour craft.[3]

1   Port Marine Safety Code, para 2.1.2.
2   Port Marine Safety Code, para 2.1.12.
3   The authority should ensure that the ships they use are fit for purpose and that crews are appropriately trained and qualified for the tasks they are likely to perform: see the Port Marine Safety Code, para 2.7.1. Further, where tugs are required, the authority is required to develop towage guidelines and incorporate them in the SMS. These guidelines must be based on an objective assessment of safety, not economic considerations: see the Port Marine Safety Code, para 2.7.4.

9.132   The port or harbour authority should make a clear published commitment to the standard of marine safety required to comply with the Port Marine Safety Code, which is the national standard against which the policies, procedures and performance of such authorities may be measured. Executive and operational responsibilities for marine safety must be clearly assigned, and those to whom they are entrusted must be held accountable for their performance. In common with the ISM Code, there must be a 'designated person' who is to be satisfied that the SMS is functioning properly, and with direct access to the board.[1] The function of the designated person is to provide independent assurance to the duty holder that the SMS is working effectively.[2]

1   Port Marine Safety Code, para 5.8.
2   Port Marine Safety Code, paras 2.2.5–2.2.8.

9.133   Every authority is accountable for managing operations within its jurisdiction safely and efficiently. Their boards are accountable for the standards they set, the resources they allocate to safety and for the effectiveness of the systems they choose to adopt. Board members' approaches to safety will be judged by the decisions they make.[1]

1   Port Marine Safety Code, Introduction, p 11.

9.134   The Port Marine Safety Code introduces the concept of 'duty holder', and states that board members are together the duty holder, being jointly and severally responsible for the proper exercise of their authority's legal duties in relation to the standards laid down. Board members may not abdicate their duties on the ground that they do not have particular skills.[1]

1   Port Marine Safety Code, para 5.4.

Prosecuting companies for deaths

9.135   The Health and Safety Executive's (HSE) statutory powers and responsibilities are derived from the HSWA 1974 (principally HSWA 1974, ss 20–23) and associated relevant statutory provisions.[1] The HSE is responsible for enforcing this Act in respect of land-based and offshore work activities, including loading and unloading a ship, and for all the work activities carried out in a drydock. HSE inspectors have, for example, power of entry to all workplaces, including docks and offshore installations, to inspect health and safety conditions and also to investigate accidents to dock workers working in a port or while (onboard) loading or unloading a ship. They can similarly investigate accidents involving a ship's crew. They may issue improvement or prohibition notices, or prosecute those responsible for offences under the HSWA 1974.

1 Eg the Docks Regulations 1988, SI 1988/1655.

9.136 The Marine Accident Investigation Branch (MAIB) was set up in 1979 with responsibility for investigating maritime accidents to determine their circumstances and causes. Its legislative powers are primarily contained in MSA 1995, Pt XI and associated secondary legislation. MAIB inspectors have power to investigate accidents involving or occurring onboard British ships anywhere in the world, and any ships in British territorial waters, but they do not have the power, for instance, to prosecute for unsafe working practices. In practice, they would report serious contraventions to the Maritime and Coastguard Agency (MCA) which has powers of prosecution.

9.137 The MCA was established on 1 April 1998 as an Executive Agency of the Department of the Environment, Transport and Regions. Its main functions are to develop, promote and enforce high standards of marine safety, to minimise loss of life amongst seafarers and coastal users, and to minimise pollution from ships of the sea and coastline. Therefore, in practical terms, the MCA is responsible for enforcing all merchant shipping regulations in respect of occupational health and safety, ship safety, safe navigation and operation (including manning levels and crew competency).[1] The MCA's statutory powers and responsibilities derive primarily from the Coastguard Act 1925, MSA 1995, the Merchant Shipping and Maritime Security Act 1997 and associated secondary legislation. For example, the MCA's surveyors have powers to survey ships flying the British flag under MSA 1995, s 256 and under MSA 1995, s 258 to inspect British ships anywhere in the world and non-British ships in UK ports. MSA 1995, s 259 gives them the power to enter any British ship or any premises in the UK in exercise of their powers. They may detain unsafe ships or issue improvement or prohibition notices in respect of inadequate manning, crew competency and unsafe working practices by the crew, both when at sea and when working under the direction of the master while in a port, even onshore.

1 Merchant shipping health and safety regulations extend to all those working on the ship at sea, and all shipboard activities carried out by the crew under the control of the ship's master.

9.138 As is evident from the above, there is clear potential for an overlap between the jurisdiction of the HSE, MCA and MAIB in relation to the enforcement of safe practices at the waterside and onboard ships. This has been addressed in a *Memorandum of Understanding between the Health and Safety Executive, the Maritime and Coastguard Agency and the Marine Accident Investigation Branch for health and safety enforcement activities etc. at the water margin and offshore* (1999). The Memorandum of Understanding sets out general principles of co-operation. Broadly these are to ensure that there is no duplication of activity, no imposition of conflicting requirements, and clear lines of communication for HSE and MAIB inspectors and MCA surveyors. The MCA is designated as the lead authority for inspection of ships, and MAIB for the investigation of accidents to or on any ship which is used in navigation (their interest is in the seaworthiness of the ship and the safety and competence of the crew). The HSE is designated as the lead authority for enforcement and investigation of occupational accidents (including accidents to workers on ships) resulting from land-based works or undertakings, including, for example, dock work. The responsibilities of a lead authority are to co-ordinate any joint inspection activities, accident investigations etc and to take the lead in setting standards via the agreed liaison procedures. Each organisation is able to call on the expertise of the other as the need arises In relation to the matter of prosecutions (rather than the compliance investigative side of matters), the HSE and MCA are both parties to the Convention Between Prosecuting Authorities which provides for structures for effective co-operation on prosecution matters where two or more prosecuting authorities may have an interest.[1] Note also that although the MCA is not a signatory to the Work-Related Deaths Protocol of March 2003, it has nevertheless indicated its intention to abide by the Protocol's principles.

1   See further the HSE website at www.hse.gov.uk.

Practical considerations: loss of life and corporate survival

9.139   The British government has proposed new legislation, the purpose of which is to reform the law of corporate manslaughter and to facilitate the conviction of corporate entities under whose 'watch' death has occurred. In some industries the latter may be regarded as necessary in order to impose upon senior management a safety culture which is perceived to be lacking despite health and safety legislation. However, recent developments in the regulation of the shipping industry mean that much of what is sought to be achieved by the proposed legislation in the shipping context may already be available to imaginative prosecutors, albeit it may not have been recognised as such and has not yet been used. Accordingly, whilst the proposed legislation will serve to increase awareness in the maritime community of the risks of prosecution and conviction for corporate killing, there is already a real possibility of a conviction succeeding, even against shipping companies with large and complex management structures.

9.140   It is nevertheless likely that the proposed legislation will facilitate convictions, and applied against the backdrop of the ISM Code and the Port Marine Safety Code, it will form a potent weapon against shipping companies who fall short of the safety standards which are nowadays expected by the industry and the general public.

Management failure

9.141   There is no doubt that the ISM Code and the Port Marine Safety Code will be of immense assistance to the prosecution in establishing the evidence required to enable it to discharge the burden upon it of proving these elements in the shipping context:

1   these Codes set the benchmark for standards of safety management in the shipping industry and conduct which falls short of that benchmark will be seized upon by the prosecution and juries alike to secure convictions against shipping companies for corporate killing;
2   compliance with ISM will deliver into the prosecution's hands for critical scrutiny a fully documented SMS; and
3   the SMS necessarily vests responsibility for safety in those who manage a shipping company.

Causation

9.142 It will be sufficient for the management failure to be just one of several causes of the death. How remote can the management failure be? It is conceivable that a shipowner or manager could be convicted of corporate killing where the proximate cause of death was the act or omission of the master if the master was under the influence of alcohol and the management failure was the failure to enforce a dry ship policy. Similarly, the management failure could be in employing an incompetent master without adequate checks into his or her qualifications and experience, a casualty leading to death thereby ensuing. Doubtless in practice some circumspection will be employed on the part of the prosecuting authority as to when it is appropriate to prosecute a remote management failure. However, families of victims may be less circumspect in such circumstances, relying upon the proposed right to bring private prosecutions without needing to obtain permission of the court.

Jurisdiction

9.143 The English court has jurisdiction over its subjects for offences of homicide committed anywhere in the world. The position is different in relation to corporate killing, for which jurisdiction is territorially based. The injury resulting in death must have been sustained, in the maritime context, on a British ship anywhere in the world, or on any ship in British territorial waters. It is important to note that the issue is where the injury resulting in death was sustained, since an injury sustained on board a British ship, or in British territorial waters, will still leave the shipping company open to prosecution even if death occurred after the victim had left the ship. Thus, assuming a management failure, there can be a prosecution for corporate killing where a pilot on board a British ship off, say, Africa is injured in a collision with another ship and dies of his injuries ashore. Similarly, there can be a prosecution of the management company of a Liberian-flagged ship which suffers an explosion in British territorial waters regardless of whether the deaths occur on board the ship or ashore from injuries sustained on board.

9.144 Any company which does business within the jurisdiction of the courts of England and Wales will be susceptible to prosecution under the proposed corporate killing legislation. It does not matter where the company is incorporated. Prosecution of a company incorporated abroad may be pyrrhic since there will often be difficulties in enforcing fines against foreign convicted companies. However, failure to submit to such penalties will restrict any future activities of the company within England and Wales. It will remain to be seen how broadly the courts interpret 'doing business' in England. It is quite conceivable that receiving or paying freight through a bank in England or even chartering or buying/selling ships through a broker in England, will be deemed sufficient. Certainly, the existence of funds in the jurisdiction of the court would overcome any concerns about enforcement against a convicted company. It remains to be seen whether the proposed legislation will extend to Northern Ireland and Scotland.

Investigation and prosecution

9.145   The government considers that there is a good case, in the shipping context, for entrusting the investigation and prosecution of the proposed new offence to the MAIB and the MCA. This would at least have the benefit of ensuring that those taking the decision to prosecute do so from a position of some experience and knowledge of the standards to be expected in the management of safety at sea.

Surviving corporate killing

9.146   The requirement for risk assessments and the development and implementation of safety management systems is now intrinsic to the management of companies in the shipping industry and corporate survival may well depend upon such matters.

9.147   There are two aspects to surviving corporate killing. First, is to have a rigorous, audited and regularly updated safety management system which is in fact implemented. Comment has been made above about the importance of compliance with safety management systems: a good and properly implemented safety management system could be a shield, but one that is poorly set up or not implemented rigorously will be a sword in the hands of a prosecuting authority and in the hands of those who influence opinion. Secondly, experience shows that the response of a company in the immediate aftermath of an accident is of critical importance. Crises arrive suddenly and escalate rapidly. The first 24 hours are usually critical. Action taken during the first 24 hours typically sets the trend of public and market perception. Events rarely conform to a format which can be planned for in detail, but the process of planning – and the practice involved – attunes decision-makers to crises. Those who understand and have thought through crises have a huge advantage if one comes their way. They know what the key issues are, and do not have to work them out under stress.

9.148   How should a company prepare? The following checklist is a guide which needs to be developed to take account of a company's particular needs, profile and market:

* Develop a thorough and effective safety management system in accordance with ISM or the Port Marine Safety Code.
* Ensure that the SMS is implemented rigorously.
* Ensure that there is a complete paper trail evidencing the development and implementation of the SMS.
* Ensure that the SMS is kept constantly under review, is audited regularly, recommendations are acted upon, and that all this is thoroughly documented.
* Ensure that an emergency response plan is drawn up and tested regularly. Use the experience of others who have practical knowledge of handling maritime accidents, such as lawyers and risk managers, to identify issues which need to be planned for and included. Matters which need to addressed include deciding who will be the company spokesman, how to phrase expressions of regret without admitting liability, how the company will handle perhaps thousands of telephone calls within the first few hours, who will co-ordinate the company's response, what role the company's insurers will play in the immediate aftermath of the accident, how evidence will be preserved, where survivors will be taken,

repatriation, hardship payments etc. All these are matters which should be decided before an accident occurs, rather than invented in the heat of a crisis, and should be thoroughly evidenced by documentation.

- Have the SMS and the emergency response plan checked over by lawyers familiar with the potential criminal and civil liabilities which the company, its directors, officers and employees, may incur.
- Above all, do not be complacent.

9.149 In the immediate aftermath of an accident, the emergency response plan must be activated. Practical issues include:

- Follow the emergency response plan. The procedures should have been practised and validated and the company should have faith in them.
- Preserve all documentary and physical evidence for inspection by police, other investigating authorities and for use in civil or criminal proceedings which may follow.
- Appoint experienced lawyers to advise on responses to media and other inquiries and to accompany company personnel at interviews with police or other investigating authorities (if requested by the interviewee), to take statements from the company's personnel, to review the relevant documentary evidence and to retain independent experts to advise on technical issues. It is essential that the company includes in its emergency response team from the outset people who can deal with insurance and legal issues. In certain areas the technical and legal experts are few and other parties involved might also seek to retain the leading firms. Many companies in the shipping industry write their lawyers into their emergency response plans as one of the first organisations to be contacted.
- The collection of evidence is a priority and should not be forgotten in the heat of the moment. Whatever the other parties or the media are alleging, and perhaps because of what they are alleging, an essential part of a company's armoury is knowing, as soon as possible, what really happened. There may well be a flag state or public inquiry and there could well be criminal and civil proceedings. The initial investigation must begin as soon as possible and the collection of oral and written evidence is an essential part of it.
- Whilst memories of the horrors of a disaster may not fade quickly – for many survivors minor details like, for example, the place, type and a time of particular noises, which may help to establish the cause of the accident, can be forgotten quite quickly. If the witnesses have to be evacuated, they will be dispersed and may not be available for interview for some time. It is important that arrangements be made immediately for them to be interviewed. These initial statements should aim at just getting the facts as the witnesses recall them. The physical or mental state of the witnesses may not permit much more than this;
- In the case of some of these witnesses, for example, those who are not employed by the company, this may, for the company, be the last opportunity that it will have of examining them, particularly where, as may be the case, a dispute develops between the company and the other employer.
- It is essential that all relevant documents be identified as a matter of urgency. Crucial files have a habit of going missing for a variety of reasons – sometimes because certain employees are embarrassed by their content; sometimes they are just mislaid. It is best to know the bad news straight away, as well as the good. A file, or even an individual document, will be given a significance which may be disproportionate to its real importance if it is produced at a late stage, possibly in the middle of a public inquiry.

- There will almost certainly be outsiders who will be interested in interviewing the company's witnesses and looking at the company's documents. These will be employees of the government agency which has a statutory duty to look into the disaster and prepare a report, which will almost certainly be made available to any public inquiry. However much of a nuisance they are when the company has many other more pressing things with which to deal, it is important that the company co-operates with them to the best of its ability and deputes someone from within the company to deal with them.

9.150   In the period following the accident, the investigations started in the immediate aftermath will need to be pursued. It will be necessary to interview witnesses in depth. It will also be necessary to interview people within management. Safety procedures, permits to work procedures and handover systems and the way that these are set up and monitored will inevitably come under the spot light in any public inquiry, prosecution or litigation. At this stage, if not earlier, the company should obtain clear guidance from its lawyers as to the extent to which memoranda and reports prepared in the course of the investigation can be privileged from production in legal proceedings or a public inquiry. That will vary depending on the jurisdiction in which such proceedings are brought or inquiry organised.

9.151   Third-party claims: it is easy to think that third-party claims will come later in the day, possibly after a public inquiry or the inquest into the death of those who have died and when the causes of the accident have been considered and possibly even ruled on in public. But that will not always be the case. Where personal injury and loss of life claims are involved the moral pressures imposed on a company to achieve quick settlements will be great. Those pressures will be accompanied by media interest, which is always greater where these types of claim are concerned. However, whatever the moral pressures, the company's insurers may not be interested in negotiating settlements of personal injury or loss of life claims until liability is established. This can lead to adverse media comment, the formation of pressure groups and damage to the company's reputation over and above that directly caused by the accident. A company should therefore consider with its insurers and its advisors whether interim payments should be made, and if so, by whom, without admitting liability.

9.152   Where liability is clear because, for example, there is no other company involved, early settlement of third-party personal injury or death claims is usually advisable, particularly where there is any possibility of civil claims being brought in the US.

9.153   Media coverage tends to fall into four main types: genuine factual reporting and investigative (but not always balanced) journalism; reporting motivated by special interests which are not necessarily directly concerned with the disaster, but which have identified some capital to be gained out of it; coverage initiated by or on behalf of potential claimants; and sensational journalism (for example, all the officers took drugs). The last category can usually be ignored. So far as the first three categories are concerned the temptation is either to ignore them as well or alternatively to try to answer every single allegation. The correct course usually lies somewhere in between. The art is to know which statements have to be responded to and which can simply be left alone. Serious and damaging allegations unanswered, or unhappily worded responses to them, may be referred to in subsequent criminal or civil proceedings or at a public inquiry.

9.154   Charles Dickens wrote that accidents happen in even the best-regulated families. It is as well to remember this and not to think 'it cannot happen to us'. Plan for the unthinkable. The steps which are taken to minimise risk and then to respond to an accident which nevertheless occurs will have a profound effect upon the perception of the courts, an inquiry, the media, the public and the financial markets. History shows that companies in the shipping industry are likely to be in the full glare of media attention after an accident and perceived (by the press) shortcomings (both before and after the accident) will set the scene for prosecutions and for the collapse of the company's shareholder value.

A9.1.0

Appendix 9.1 – SOLAS Chapter IX

Management for the safe operation of ships

A9.1.1   Regulation 1

Definitions

For the purpose of this chapter, unless expressly provided otherwise:

1   *International Safety Management (ISM) Code* means the International Management Code for the Safe Operation of Ships and for Pollution Prevention adopted by the Organisation by resolution A.741(18), as may be amended by the Organisation, provided that such amendments are adopted, brought into force and take effect in accordance with the provisions of article VIII of the present Convention concerning the amendment procedures applicable to the annex other than chapter I.

2   *Company* means the owner of the ship or any other organisation or person such as the manager, or the bareboat charterer, who has assumed the responsibility for operation of the ship from the owner of the ship and who on assuming such responsibility has agreed to take over all the duties and responsibilities imposed by the International Safety Management Code.

3   *Oil tanker* means an oil tanker as defined in regulation II-1/2.12.

4   *Chemical tanker* means a chemical tanker as defined in regulation VII/8.2.

5   *Gas carrier* means a gas carrier as defined in regulation VII/11.2.

6   *Bulk carrier* means a ship which is constructed generally with single deck, top-side tanks and hopper side tanks in cargo spaces, and is intended primarily to carry dry cargo in bulk, and includes such types as ore carriers and combination carriers.

7   *Mobile offshore drilling unit* (MODU) means a vessel capable of engaging in drilling operations for the exploration for or exploration of resources beneath the sea-bed such as liquid or gaseous hydrocarbons, sulphur or salt.

8   *High speed craft* means a craft as defined in regulation X/1.2.

A9.1.2   Regulation 2

Application

1   This chapter applies to ships, regardless of the date of construction, as follows:
   (a) passenger ships including passenger high-speed craft, not later than 1 July 1998;
   (b) oil tankers, chemical tankers, gas carriers, bulk carriers and cargo high-speed craft of 500 gross tonnage and upwards, not later than 1 July 1998; and
   (c) other cargo ships and mobile offshore drilling units of 500 gross tonnage and upwards, not later than 1 July 2002.

2   This chapter does not apply to government-operated ships used for non-commercial purposes.

A9.1.3 Regulation 3

Safety management requirements

1   The company and the ship shall comply with the requirements of the International Safety Management Code.
2   The ship shall be operated by a company holding a Document of Compliance referred to in regulation 4.

A9.1.4 Regulation 4

Certification

1   A Document of Compliance shall be issued to every company which complies with the requirements of the International Safety Management Code. This document shall be issued by the Administration, by an organisation recognised by the Administration, or at the request of the Administration by another Contracting Government.
2   A copy of the Document of Compliance shall be kept on board the ship in order that the master can produce it on request for verification.
3   A Certificate, called a Safety Management Certificate, shall be issued to every ship by the Administration or an organisation recognised by the Administration. The Administration or organisation recognised by it shall, before issuing the Safety Management Certificate, verify that the company and its shipboard management operate in accordance with the approved safety-management system.

A9.1.5 Regulation 5

Maintenance of Conditions

1   The safety-management system shall be maintained in accordance with the provisions of the International Safety Management Code.

A9.1.6 Regulation 6

Verification and control

1   The Administration, another Contracting Government at the request of the Administration or an organisation recognised by the Administration shall periodically verify the proper functioning of the ship's safety-management system.
2   Subject to the provisions of paragraph 3 of this regulation, a ship required to hold a certificate issued pursuant to the provisions of regulation 4.3 shall be subject to control in accordance with the provisions of regulation XI/4. For this purpose such certificate shall be treated as a certificate issued under regulation I/12 or I/13.
3   In cases of change of flag State or company, special transitional arrangements shall be made in accordance with the guidelines developed by the Organisation.

CHAPTER 10

The chemical industry

Dr John Bond C-MIST, Retired Safety Advisor and Auditor, BP Chemicals[1]

Rob Elvin, Partner, Hammonds, Manchester

Mike Shepherd, Partner, Hammonds, Manchester

1 Dr Bond wishes to acknowledge the help and useful comments of his colleagues Brian Mellin and Mehdi Laftavi at C-MIST in developing many of the ideas presented in this chapter.

Introduction

10.1   The use of oil and chemicals has been known from the earliest times of recorded history. The Assyrians[1] used fire-pots of burning pitch as incendiaries in the siege of towns in the ninth century BC, and Pliny refers to a pool on the Euphrates discharging a flammable mud. Pliny also developed and reported on the making of incendiary devices from a mixture of quicklime and a flammable material such as petroleum or sulphur. Gerald of Wales (c 1188) quoted Julius Caesar's reference to the Britons who painted their faces with a 'nitrous ointment' which gave them such a frightening appearance that they unnerved their enemies. On the other side of the world China was developing a mixture of sulphur, graphite and potassium nitrate, subsequently called black powder.

1 JR Partington *A History of Greek Fire and Gunpowder* (1960).

10.2   Apart from warfare, chemicals were also used in earlier times for more peaceful activities. Salt (sodium chloride) was required for food preservation and silica for glass making.

10.3   The modern oil and chemical industries have developed many of the essentials for present-day living, from food preservation to plastic materials, from paper to the electronic chip, from gasoline for cars to methods for converting the sun's energy to electrical power. There is insufficient wool, cotton and linen to clothe the world's population and synthetic fibres have been developed to fill the gap. Many diseases have already been eliminated or controlled by drugs made from a variety of chemicals. Efficient modern transport dependent on the oil industry, together with refrigeration and other methods of food preservation developed by the chemical industry, can make a varied diet available to all.

10.4   With the wide variety of chemicals in use today there are risks in their manufacture and use. These risks are generally well understood by industry but there have been a few well-publicised cases where the risks were not at first appreciated. They include asbestos, cigarette smoke, thalidomide for pregnant mothers and methyl isocyanate used at Bhopal, to name but a few. Industry has learnt from these mistakes but there are accidents in the manufacture of many chemicals which affect employees and the community adjacent to the plant. The disasters at Flixborough in 1974, Piper Alpha in the North Sea in 1988 and at Milford Haven in 1994 are well known in the UK. In the US there have been similar disasters such as those at Pasadena in 1989 and at Decatur in 1974. In Europe there have been disasters at Feyzin in France in 1966, Beek in The Netherlands in 1975, Seveso in Italy in 1976 and Los Alfaques in Spain in 1978. In the rest of the world there have been similar disasters at Mexico City in 1984, Mississauga in Canada in 1987 and Bhopal in India in 1984. Despite many of these disasters the petrochemical industry, with a high risk potential, has a good record for safety in the UK

10.5   The fatal and major injuries rate per 100,000 employees[1] are

Agricultural, hunting, forestry and fishing	221.8
Extractive and utility supply industries	226.9
Manufacturing	201.8
– coke, refined petroleum products and nuclear fuel	191.2
– chemicals, chemical products and man-made fibres	166.7
Construction	392.3
Total service industries	79.6
All industries	**117.7**

1   Health and Safety Commission *Health and Safety Statistics 1999/2000.*

10.6   The good performance of the chemical industry could be the result of:

* Regulations such as the Control of Major Accidents Hazards Regulations 1999.[1]
* Close scrutiny by the Health and Safety Executive.

1   SI 1999/743.

10.7   Or it could be the result of:

* Good management with the prevention of loss at the head of a safety culture.
* The use of management systems to ensure a close control of operations.
* Learning lessons from past accidents.
* The use of risk assessment and the control of particularly hazardous operations by permits to work.
* Measuring performance.
* Auditing and review of operations.

10.8   This performance is the result of good management, as can be seen from Figure 10.1.[1]

Figure 10.1 Safety and profitability: major chemical companies

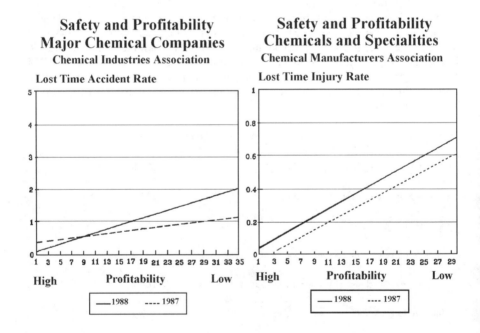

1   J Bond 6th International Symposium 'Loss Prevention and Safety Promotion in the Process Industries', Oslo, Norway, June 1989.

10.9   Oil and chemicals are vital to our standard of living but come at a cost. That cost is safety of the manufacturing process. This section on the petrochemical industry is concerned with the efforts of those employed to manufacture the chemicals in a safe manner.

10.10   Self-regulation by the industry has generally served the community well but there are some areas where this may not be evident. The Health and Safety at Work etc Act 1974 (HSWA 1974) requires reasonable precautions to be taken and the majority of those in the industry comply with this requirement. It is the ones who do not who produce the majority of accidents.

Chemical industry and health and safety

10.11   Health and safety have been important issues in the chemical industry due to the toxicity and flammability characteristics of many chemicals. The containment of these chemicals is therefore an important factor in chemical plant operation. Release of any chemical is avoided by careful and detailed control of all operations.

10.12   The categories of toxicity and their definitions are as follows:

Very Toxic	A substance which if it is inhaled or ingested or it penetrates the skin may involve extremely serious acute or chronic health risks and even death.
Toxic	A substance which if it is inhaled, ingested or it penetrates the skin, may involve serious acute or chronic health risks and even death.
Corrosive	A substance which on contact with living tissues will destroy them.
Irritant	A non-corrosive substance which, through immediate prolonged or repeated contact with the skin or mucous membrane, can cause inflammation.
Carcinogenic	A substance which if it is inhaled, ingested or if it penetrates the skin may induce cancer in man or increase its incidence.
Teratogenic	A substance which if it is inhaled, ingested or it penetrates the skin may involve a risk of subsequent non-hereditable birth defects in offspring.
Mutagenic	A substance which if it is inhaled, ingested or it penetrates the skin may involve a risk of hereditable genetic defects

10.13   Toxic chemicals may be considered under two other categories:

* Acutely toxic, which have an immediate effect on a person; or
* Chronically toxic, which have an effect after prolonged exposure to small quantities.

10.14   The main flammability characteristics of chemicals are:

* Upper and Lower flammable limits in air between which they will ignite.
* The Flashpoint, the temperature above which there is a flammable mixture in air.
* Autoignition temperature, the temperature at which a chemical will ignite in air without a source of ignition.
* Minimum ignition energy, the minimum energy required to ignite a chemical.

10.15   During the 1950s and 1960s chemical plants had increased rapidly in size and at the same time the pressures and temperatures required for their operation also increased.[1] This resulted in many serious fires, explosions and releases of materials from plants. The resultant increase in fatalities is shown in the graph below for one major company.

Figure 10.2 ICI's fatal accident rates, five year moving average, for the period 1960-1982.

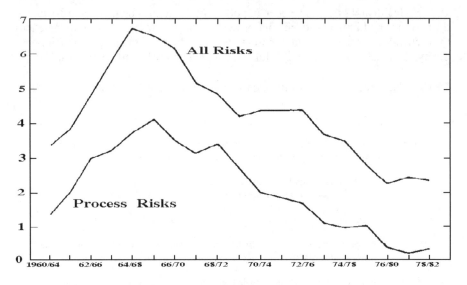

FAR = number of fatalities per 10^8 working hours

1   T Kletz (1999) 77 Trans IChemE, Part B, May, at 109.

10.16   The cost of these incidents escalated to such an extent that much more effort was given to building safer plants. The effort was mainly in the design and operational field and started both in the US and UK. The American Institute of Chemical Engineers and the Institution of Chemical Engineers in the UK spearheaded technical conferences at which ways of preventing accidents in the chemical industry were discussed.

10.17   The increase in fatalities was attributed to the more severe conditions of chemical processing being used and this had expanded both the potential for loss and the financial value of any single loss. The need for a systematic approach to technical safety became a necessity and this led to the concept of loss prevention.

10.18   Prior to this period safety had been treated as a reactive approach to accidents after the event had been examined and when usually only the basic causes found. Loss prevention was a totally different approach which sought the causes of potential accidents and introduced control systems to prevent the undesired event from happening. This proactive approach to safety became the basis of loss prevention, with two principles:

'He who ignores the past is condemned to repeat it.'

'He who anticipates the future can safeguard the present.'

10.19   A major step forward in 1964 was the introduction of Hazard and Operability Studies (HAZOP).[1] The procedure was a systematic methodology for identifying most hazards at the design stage and hence designing out problems before the plant was built.

1   T Kletz 'HAZOP and HAZAN. Identifying and Assessing Process Industry Hazards' (1999) IChemE.

10.20   The Loss Prevention Panel of the Institution of Chemical Engineers was established in 1972. Its objective was to promote the sharing of experiences in order to prevent repetition of a given accident. In 1974 the Information Exchange Scheme was established and in that year the Loss Prevention Bulletin started publication, with reports of accidents that had occurred in the industry. By 1996 an accident database had been developed by the Institution of Chemical Engineers.

10.21   The chemical industry now has extensive management systems to control operations, ensure containment and an auditing system to monitor compliance with the systems established. Safety performance indicators are being introduced to advance the loss prevention process.

Safety in the second part of the twentieth century

10.22   Improvements in safety in the chemical industry came about as a result of voluntary effort by the leading companies. Despite these efforts there were a number of notable incidents.

10.23   The Flixborough accident of June 1974 focused the new Health and Safety Executive (HSE) on the chemical industry which came under the new Control of Industrial Major Accident Hazards Regulations 1984[1] (CIMAH) followed by the Control of Major Accident Hazards Regulations 1999[2] (COMAH). The HSE initially enforced HSWA 1974 in the shore-based industries while the Department of Industry enforced it in the pipeline and offshore industry. After the Piper Alpha incident of July 1988 the responsibility for the offshore industry was transferred to the HSE.

1   SI 1984/1902.
2   SI 1999/743.

10.24   As the twentieth century was ending it became clear that HSWA 1974, which had been in force for 25 years, was an effective regulatory means of controlling industry although the self-regulating nature of the original intent was mainly forgotten. The European Directives, particularly those known as Seveso I[1] and Seveso II,[2] were brought in by regulations under the Act.

1   Council Directive 82/501/EEC, implemented in the UK by the Control of Industrial Major Accidents Hazards Regulations 1984, SI 1984/1902, amended by SI 1990/2325.
2   Council Directive 96/82/EC, implemented in the UK by the Control of Major Accident Hazards Regulations 1999, SI 1999/743.

10.25   Further regulations were brought in although the chemical and oil industries had built up a self-regulating and monitoring culture with extensive auditing systems based mainly on the International Safety Rating System.[1] The Chemical Industries Association in the UK adopted a responsible care programme, originally introduced in Canada, which was extended to the whole of Europe. This was intended to show that the industry took seriously its responsibilities for both safety and the environment.

At the end of the century an independent audit system was established to ensure compliance with the principles of responsible care.

1   FE Bird and GL Germain *Practical Loss Control Leadership* (1985).

10.26   The ideas of loss prevention expanded rapidly in the last part of the twentieth century with particular advances in:

- risk assessment;
- accident investigation;
- auditing of the management system;
- learning lessons from past accidents;
- detailed management systems;
- safety performance indicators; and
- inherent safety.

Safety in the twenty-first century

10.27   The new millennium has introduced fresh approaches to reducing accidents but still within the concept of loss prevention. Further development in the chemical industry of earlier systems, particularly inherent safety and safety performance indicators, will take place. However, the frequency of serious accidents in the chemical industry has raised concern, particularly in five areas:

- Risk assessment is not carried out in all situations.
- Blame for an accident, previously directed to the lowest level in an organisation, is now being levelled at more senior positions. This has resulted from the realisation that there are a number of causes of an accident, not necessarily on the part of the person at the hard end of the accident who might have opened the wrong valve or missed a warning red light.
- Lessons have not been learnt from previous accidents.
- Professional responsibility.
- Company culture.

10.28   These safety areas are discussed in the following sections but the management of risk involved in chemical plant operations is a very large subject that cannot be covered in this book.

The legal framework for health and safety in the chemical industry

Introduction

10.29   As in most areas of health and safety law, there are two principal levels of regulation in the chemical industry. The first of these is EU law and the second is the national law. EU law overrides national law and EU member states cannot introduce valid contradictory legislation. It is important to understand what the key EU laws and national laws are, as non-compliance leaves a company open to potential prosecutions.

10.30   A number of legislative vehicles are available with which to pass EU law and it is important to understand what they are:

1   *Regulations* 'shall have general application' and 'shall be binding in [their] entirety and directly applicable in all Member States'.
2   *Directives* 'shall be binding, as to the result to be achieved, upon each Member State to which it is addressed, but shall leave to the national authorities the choice of form and methods'.
3   *Decisions* 'shall be binding in [their] entirety upon those to whom [they are] addressed'.
4   *Recommendations* and *Opinions* 'shall have no binding force'.

10.31   Regulations are 'directly applicable' in the sense that they become part of a member state's law without the requirement for any implementation. In other words, Parliament need not pass any legislation to bring such a regulation into force. Furthermore, once a piece of EU legislation is transposed into national law, it must be interpreted in accordance with the Directive or Regulation from which it originates.

10.32   EU regulations should not be confused with regulations passed by Parliament which form part of national law.

10.33   However, the main way in which EU law impacts on the chemical industry is through Regulations and Directives, such as the Chemical Agents Directive.[1] Directives must be transposed into national law within the prescribed period. If this does not occur then the Directive may take on the same direct effect features as a Regulation.[2] In addition, once the implementation deadline has expired, an individual can enforce the provisions of a Directive against the government of the member state and so Directives are capable of vertical effect.[3] Directives are not, however, capable of horizontal effect[4] in this way.

1   Council Directive 98/24/EC.
2   Case 41/74 *Van Duyn v Home Office* – it is possible for Directives to be directly effective in this way but it will depend on the facts of each case and the Directive in question. It is to be questioned 'whether the nature, general scheme and wording of the provision in question are capable of having direct effects'.
3   *Francovich v Italy* [1991] ECR I-5357; [1993] CMLR 66.
4   Ie between two individuals.

Key legislation

10.34   We can therefore divide the relevant legislation into two groups:

•   EU Directives and Regulations; and
•   key national statutes and regulations.

10.35   There are many pieces of national legislation, and indeed EU legislation, which impact not only on the chemical industry but more generally on all places of work. The key ones are discussed in the first part of this book.

10.36   Of particular importance are HSWA 1974 and the Management of Health and Safety at Work Regulations 1999.[1] These impose both general and specific duties on employers to maintain a safe place and system of work, in addition to a number of other duties. In this chapter only chemical specific legislation etc is discussed.

1   SI 1999/3242.

Chemical Agents Directive

10.37 The Chemical Agents Directive[1] (CAD) establishes minimum requirements for the protection of workers from risks arising (or likely to arise) out of the presence or use of hazardous chemical agents. Much of CAD follows the well accepted principles previously present in UK legislation, in particular:

* Employers are required to assess the risks to the health and safety of workers from the presence of chemical agents in the workplace.[2]
* Employers must take both general and specific protection and prevention measures to eliminate or reduce the risks to workers' health and safety arising from chemical agents.[3]
* Employers are required to monitor the exposure of workers to chemical agents in certain circumstances[4] and are obliged to place them under health surveillance where such an assessment discloses a risk to their health.[5]
* The Directive imposes a duty on employers to establish arrangements to deal with accidents and incidents, including emergency situations.[6]
* Employers must provide workers with appropriate information and training relating to chemical agents. This information must be updated to take account of changing circumstances.[7]
* The production, manufacture or use at work of certain specified chemical agents or activities involving their use is prohibited.[8]
* Employers are placed under a duty to consult workers or their representatives on, and allow them to participate in, the matters covered by the Directive.[9]

1 Council Directive 98/24/EC.
2 Council Directive 98/24/EC, art 4.
3 Council Directive 98/24/EC, arts 5 and 6.
4 Council Directive 98/24/EC, art 6(4).
5 Council Directive 98/24/EC, art **10.**
6 Council Directive 98/24/EC, art 7.
7 Council Directive 98/24/EC, art 8.
8 Council Directive 98/24/EC, art 9 and Annex III.
9 Council Directive 98/24/EC, art 11. An employer already has general duties under the Health and Safety (Consultation with Employees) Regulations 1996, SI 1996/1513 and the Safety Representatives and Safety Committees Regulations 1977, SI 1977/500 to consult with employees or their representatives and to provide them with information. However, the CAD imposes much more specific requirements than these.

10.38 CAD[1] is implemented in the UK by the Control of Substances Hazardous to Health Regulations 2002.[2]

1 Council Directive 98/24/EC.
2 SI 2002/2677.

Control of Substances Hazardous to Health Regulations 2002[1]

10.39 Each year in Great Britain, approximately 16,000 to 25,000 people become ill as a result of exposure to substances hazardous to health at work. Included in that figure are an estimated 3,000 to 12,000 cancer deaths, the majority of which are related to chemicals (including asbestos).[2] The Control of Substances Hazardous to Health Regulations 2002 (COSHH) aim to protect the health of both workers and others from exposure to hazardous substances during work activities by requiring employers to introduce controls on such exposure.

1 SI 2002/2677.
2 HSE press release E060, 22 April 2003.

10.40   The original version of the COSHH Regulations came into force in October 1989[1] but they have been amended and replaced several times since. The 2002 Regulations[2] implement CAD[3] and are supported by an Approved Code of Practice (ACOP) which gives detailed practical advice on compliance.

1   SI 1988/1657.
2   SI 2002/2677.
3   Council Directive 98/24/EC.

10.41   COSHH[1] imposes a duty on employers to assess the risks to the health of their employees arising from exposure to hazardous substances, and to prevent such exposure. Where this is not reasonably practicable, exposure must be adequately controlled. In some instances employers must monitor employees' exposure to a hazardous substance and place them under health surveillance.

1   SI 2002/2677.

Hazardous substances

10.42   Hazardous substances are those that can harm the health of employees working with them if they are not properly controlled, for example, by using adequate ventilation.[1] As such, they are found in nearly all workplaces within the chemicals industry. For the great majority of commercial chemicals whether a warning label is present or not will indicate whether COSHH[2] is relevant. For example, liquid soap for household use does not contain a warning label, but bleach does, therefore COSHH applies to bleach but not to the liquid soap when used at work.

1   A 'substance hazardous to health' is defined under SI 2002/2677, reg 2, Interpretation.
2   SI 2002/2677.

10.43   The Health Directorate, part of the HSE, summarises that there are eight steps which must be followed in order to comply with COSHH.[1] Employers must:

Step 1	Work out what hazardous substances are used in their workplace and find out the risks to peoples' health from using these substances.
Step 2	Decide what precautions are needed before starting work with hazardous substances.
Step 3	Prevent people from exposure to hazardous substances and where this is not reasonably practicable, control the exposure.
Step 4	Make sure control measures are used and maintained properly and that safety procedures are followed.
Step 5	If required, monitor the exposure of employees to hazardous substances.
Step 6	Carry out health surveillance where an assessment has shown that this is necessary or COSHH imposes specific requirements.
Step 7	If required, prepare plans and procedures to deal with accidents, incidents and emergencies.
Step 8	Make sure employees are properly informed, trained and supervised.

1   SI 2002/2677.

Approaching COSHH[1]

Step 1 – assessing the risks

10.44   The first step is to carry out a risk assessment.[1] This should:

(a)   identify the hazardous substances present in the workplace; and
(b)   consider the risks the substances present to peoples' health.

1   SI 2002/2677.
2   SI 2002/2677, reg 6.

10.45   It is necessary to consider substances that have been supplied to the company, those produced by its work activity and those naturally or incidentally present in the workplace. There must then be an assessment on what risks these substances present to peoples' health.

10.46   This involves making a judgment on how likely it is that a hazardous substance will affect someone's health. The HSE has developed a generic risk assessment guide for supplied substances.[1] Key questions to be considered are:

1   How much of the substance is in use or produced by the work activity and how could people be exposed to it?
2   Who could be exposed to the substance and how often? This involves a consideration of all the groups of people who could come into contact with the substance, ie visitors, members of the public, contractors etc, as well as the company's employees.
3   Is there a possibility of substances being absorbed through the skin or swallowed?
4   Are there risks to employees working at locations other than the main workplace?

1   HSE *COSHH Essentials: Easy Steps to Control Chemicals.*

10.47   The legal responsibility for the assessment under COSHH[1] is on the employer. However, outside parties can be engaged to carry out some or all of the work in preparing the assessment. Employees or their safety representatives must be involved in the preparation of assessments and informed of the results of the assessment.

1   SI 2002/2677.

Step 2 – decide what precautions are needed

10.48   If significant risks are identified companies must decide on the action they need to take to remove or reduce them to acceptable levels. Pre-existing controls may be compared with:

•   *COSHH Essentials: Easy Steps to Control Chemicals Guide.*
•   Occupational Exposure Limits (OELs).
•   Good work practices and standards endorsed for the company's industry sector, for example, the Chemicals Industry Association.

10.49   It is essential for a company to check that its control systems are effective. If risks to health are identified then the company must take action to protect the health of both its employees and others. If the company has five or more employees it must make and keep a record of the main findings of the risk assessment either in writing or in computerised form.[1] This record must be made as soon as practicable after the assessment and contain sufficient information to explain the decisions taken about whether risks are significant and the need for any control measures.[2]

1 SI 2002/2677, reg 6.
2 See the COSHH ACOP which provides information on what the record of the main findings of the assessment should contain.

10.50 The HSE emphasise that an assessment should be a 'living' document which is revised should circumstances change. Assessments must be reviewed when:

- there is reason to suspect that the assessment is no longer valid;
- there has been a significant change in the work carried out; and/or
- the results of monitoring employees' exposure show that the revision is necessary.

Indeed, each assessment should state when the next review is expected to take place.

Step 3 – prevent or control exposure sufficiently

10.51 COSHH[1] imposes a requirement on companies to prevent exposure to substances which are hazardous to health if it is reasonable to do so. As such the company might be expected to use the substance in a safer form, change the process or activity to remove the need for the hazardous substance or replace the substance with a safer alternative.

1 SI 2002/2677.

10.52 Exposure must be adequately controlled if prevention is not reasonably practicable and the measures that are put in place should be both appropriate and consistent with the risk assessment. They may involve:

- use of appropriate work processes;
- control of exposure at source (for example, a ventilation system at source); and
- provision of personal protective equipment.

10.53 As guidance as to what 'adequate control' constitutes, COSHH[1] states that this means reducing exposure to a level that most workers could be exposed to every day at work without any adverse effects on their health.[2]

1 SI 2002/2677.
3 The Health and Safety Commission (HSC) has assigned an Occupational Exposure Limit (OEL) for various commonly used hazardous substances and this may be of use to companies. OELs are divided into two groups – Occupational Exposure Standards (OESs) and Maximum Exposure Levels (MELs).

Step 4 – ensure that control measures are used and maintained

10.54 COSHH, reg 9[1] requires employees to make proper use of control measures and to report defects. It is the duty of the employer to take all reasonable steps to ensure that they do so. The specific duties that COSHH imposes aim to ensure that controls are kept in efficient working order. For example, respiratory protective equipment must be examined and where appropriate tested at suitable intervals. Specific intervals are laid down by COSHH between examinations for local exhaust ventilation equipment. In addition, companies must retain records (or a summary of them) for examinations and tests carried out for at least five years.

1   SI 2002/2677, reg 9.

Step 5   monitoring exposure

10.55   Where a risk assessment concludes that:

1   there could be serious risks to health if control measures failed; or
2   exposure limits might be exceeded; or
3   control measures might not be functioning fully,

an employer must monitor the exposure of employees to hazardous substances in the air that they breathe.

10.56   This need not be done if the employer can show that another method of control is in place adequately to prevent employees' exposure to hazardous substances, for example, an alarm system which activates when hazardous substances are detected.

Step 6 – carrying out appropriate health surveillance

10.57   Health surveillance[1] must be carried out in the following circumstances:

(a)   (i)   Where an employee is exposed to one of the substances listed in COSHH, Sch 6[2] and is engaged in a related process; and
      (ii)   there is a reasonable likelihood that an identifiable disease or adverse health affect will result from that exposure; *or*
(b)   (i)   Where employees are exposed to a substance linked to a particular disease or diverse health affect; and
      (ii)   here is a reasonable likelihood under the condition of work of that disease or affect occurring; and
      (iii) it is possible to detect a disease or health affect.

1   See SI 2002/2677, reg 11.
2   SI 2002/2677, Sch 6.

10.58   Health surveillance could involve examination by a doctor, trained nurse or in some cases a trained supervisor. A basic record ('health record') should be kept of any health surveillance carried out. Health records should be kept for at least 40 years.

Step 7 – preparation of plans and procedures to deal with accidents, incidents and emergencies

10.59   Plans and procedures must be established in workplaces where there is a risk of an accident, incident or emergency involving exposure to a hazardous substance which goes well beyond the risks associated with normal day to day work. The objective is to have a response in place before any such incident takes place. It will involve the preparation of procedures and the setting up of warning and communication systems which can be activated immediately should any such incident occur. Safety drills should be practised at regular intervals.

10.60   Emergency procedures need not be introduced if:

- the quantities of substances hazardous to health that are present in the workplace are such that they present only a slight risk to the health of employees; and
- the measures taken under Step 3 are sufficient to control that risk.

Step 8 – ensuring that employees are properly informed, trained and supervised

10.61   COSHH, reg 12 requires employers to provide their employees with suitable and sufficient information, instruction and training which must include:[1]

(a) the names of substances that the employee could be exposed to, the risks created by such exposure and access to any safety data sheets that apply to those substances;
(b) the significant findings of the risk assessment;
(c) the precautions that should be taken to protect themselves and other employees;
(d) how to use the personal protective equipment provided;
(e) the results of any exposure monitoring and health surveillance (whilst maintaining the anonymity of individual employees); and
(f) the emergency procedures which must be followed.

1   SI 2002/2677, reg 12(2).

10.62   As with many health and safety legal obligations employers need to ensure that they update and adapt the information, instruction and training to take account of significant changes in the nature of work carried out or work methods used. Equally the information provided should be appropriate to the level of risk identified by the assessment and be presented in a way which will be understood by employees.

Control of Major Accident Hazards Regulations 1999[1]

10.63   The main HSE guidance to the Control of Major Accident Hazards Regulations 1999 (COMAH) is contained in the *Guide to the Control of Major Accident Hazards Regulations 1999.*[2] COMAH implements the requirements of the Seveso II Directive[3] which covers the control of major accident hazards involving dangerous substances such as chlorine and explosives.

1   SI 1999/743.
2   L111.
3   Council Directive 96/82/EC.

10.64   The principal aim of COMAH is to prevent and mitigate the effects of those major accidents involving dangerous substances which can cause serious harm to people and the environment. COMAH mainly affects the chemical industry, but also some storage activities, explosives and nuclear sites and other industries, where threshold levels of specified 'dangerous substances' are used.[1]

1   COMAH, SI 1999/743, imposes two categories of duties on operators; 'lower tier' and 'top tier'. The lower tier duties apply to all operators whereas the top tier duties apply only to

certain operators. HSE publication L111 provides guidance on how to ascertain whether an establishment is classified as lower or top tier.

10.65   An incident is a major accident if:

- it results from uncontrolled events[1] (ie unplanned and unexpected) in the course of the operation of an establishment to which COMAH[2] applies;[3]
- it results in a serious danger to people or the environment, whether on or off the site in question: and
- it involves one or more of the dangerous substances identified by COMAH.

1   'Loss of control' is not limited to sudden, unplanned events but also includes expected, planned or permitted discharges.
2   SI 1999/743.
3   'Industrial chemical process' means that premises with no such chemical process do not come within the scope of COMAH solely because dangerous substances are generated during an accident.

10.66   COMAH, reg 2(2)[1] defines an 'operator' as a person who is in control of the operation of an establishment or installation.[2] This can include a company or partnership or arguably a receiver. Where the establishment or installation is to be constructed or operated, the 'operator' is the person who proposes to control its operation. If that person is not known, it will be the person who has commissioned its design and construction.

1   SI 1999/743, reg 2(2).
2   COMAH, SI 1999/743, applies to an 'establishment' where:
- dangerous substances are present; or
- the presence of dangerous substances is anticipated; or
- it is reasonable to believe that they may be generated during the loss of control of an industrial chemical process.
'Establishment' is defined as the whole area under the control of the same person where dangerous substances are present in one or more installations.
A substance is a 'dangerous substance' for the purposes of COMAH if it is:
- specified at the appropriate threshold; or
- falls within a generic category at the appropriate threshold.
The thresholds are split between lower tier and top tier.

10.67   Substances are classified according to the Chemicals (Hazard Information and Packaging for Supply) Regulations 2002, reg 4.[1]

1   SI 2002/1689, reg 4.

Lower tier duties

10.68   Under COMAH, reg 4,[1] every operator has a general duty to take all measures necessary to prevent major accidents and limit their consequences to persons and the environment.

1   SI 1999/743, reg 4.

10.69   COMAH[1] recognises that eliminating a risk entirely will not always be possible. However, prevention measures should aim to reduce risk to as low a level as is reasonably practicable. When considering what is reasonably practicable the balance between cost and benefit as well as what is technically achievable will be considered. Where hazard levels are high, high standards will be required to ensure that risks are sufficiently low. Consequently, operators are expected to demonstrate that they have put in place control measures that are sufficient for the risks identified.

1   SI 1999/743.

10.70   COMAH, reg 5(1)[1] requires every operator to prepare and keep a major accident prevention policy (MAPP) document detailing its policy with respect to the prevention of major accidents.

1   SI 1999/743, reg 5(1).

10.71   The MAPP document needs to be in writing and include sufficient particulars to demonstrate that the operator has established an appropriate safety management system. The principles that must be taken into account are specified in COMAH, Schs 1–4.[1] The MAPP has to be reviewed and updated when required, so that it is kept up to date.[2] Furthermore, it is the operator's duty to implement the policy set out in the MAPP.[3]

1   SI 1999/743, Schs 1–4.
2   SI 1999/743, reg 5(4).
3   SI 1999/743, reg 5(5).

10.72   An establishment should therefore apply the following tests:

1   Does COMAH apply?[1]
2   If so, the MAPP should be drawn up in accordance with COMAH, reg 5.[2]
3   The establishment should then consider the following questions, which appear in the guidance to COMAH:[3]
    • Does the MAPP meet the requirements of COMAH?
    • Will it deliver a high level of protection for people and the environment?
    • Are there management systems in place which achieve the objectives set out in the policy?
    • Are the policy, management systems, risk control systems and workplace precautions kept under review to ensure that they are implemented and that they are relevant?

1   See COMAH, SI 1999/743, reg 3 and SI 1999/743, Sch 1 and check existing and likely inventory of dangerous substances.
2   SI 1999/743, reg 5.
3   As reproduced in (2003) 39 Tolley's Health and Safety Law, April.

Notifications

10.73   COMAH, reg 6[1] contains the notification requirements that must be observed by establishments. Notifications should be in written form.

1   SI 1999/743, reg 6.

10.74   Within a reasonable period of time prior to the start of the operation of an establishment, the operator of the establishment must send the competent authority (CA) a notification containing the information specified in COMAH, Sch 3.[1] The information required includes the address of the establishment concerned and the quantity and physical form of the dangerous substances present.

1   SI 1999/743, Sch 3.

10.75   Once the initial notification has been made, a continuing duty remains to notify the CA in the event of:[1]

- any significant increase in the quantity of dangerous substances previously notified;
- any significant change in the nature or physical form of the substances previously notified, the processes employing them or any other information notified to the CA in respect of the establishment;
- COMAH, reg 7[2] ceasing to apply to the establishment by virtue of a change in the quantity of dangerous substances present there; or
- permanent closure of an existing installation in the establishment.

1   SI 1999/743, reg 6(4).
2   SI 1999/743, reg 7.

Notification of a major accident

10.76   Where a major accident occurs at an establishment, the operator is under a duty to inform the CA of the accident immediately.[1] The CA is then required to conduct a thorough investigation into the accident.

1   SI 1999/743, reg 15(3). NB The duty to notify will be satisfied if the operator notifies a major accident to the HSE pursuant to the requirements of the Reporting of Injuries, Diseases and Dangerous Occurrences Regulations 1995, SI 1995/3163.

Top tier duties

Safety reports

10.77   All operators of top tier establishments must produce a safety report,[1] the key purpose of which is to demonstrate that they have taken all necessary measures to prevent major accidents. In addition, they must show that all steps have been taken to limit the consequences to people and the environment of any such accidents which do occur.

1   SI 1999/743, reg 7.

10.78   The operator is required to submit a safety report to the CA within a reasonable period of time both before construction commences and before start-up.[1] The information that these must contain is specified in COMAH, Sch 4,[2] although any information already contained in the pre-construction report need not be duplicated in the pre-start-up report. In addition, an operator may limit the information a safety report contains if he can show that certain dangerous substances are in a state incapable of creating a major accident hazard.[3]

1   SI 1999/743, reg 7(1) and (5).
2   SI 1999/743, Sch 4.
3   SI 1999/743, reg 7(12).

10.79   Neither the construction of the establishment nor its operation may be begun before the operator has received the CA's conclusions on the report. However, the CA must ensure that these are communicated within a reasonable period of time of receiving the safety report.[1] Should the CA reasonably request further information in writing following its review of the safety report, the operator must provide such information.[2]

1 SI 1999/743, reg 17(1)(a).
2 SI 1999/743, reg 7(13).

10.80 Part, or indeed all, of the information that is required to be included under COMAH, Sch 2[1] can be done so by reference to the content of another notification or report made pursuant to statutory requirements. The information in that notification must be up to date and sufficiently detailed.

1 SI 1999/743, Sch 2.

10.81 It is important for companies to realise that the operator must review the safety report:[1]

* at least every five years;
* whenever such a review is necessary because of new facts or to take account of new technical knowledge about safety matters; and
* whenever the operator makes a change to the safety management system which could have significant repercussions.

1 SI 1999/743, reg 8(1).

10.82 Where a review determines that the report needs revision, the operator must carry that revision out immediately and inform the CA of the details.

10.83 The HSE publication *Preparing Safety Reports*[1] provides practical guidance to operators on the preparation of COMAH[2] safety reports.

1 HS(G)190.
1 SI 1999/743.

Emergency plans

10.84 COMAH imposes a requirement on top tier establishments to draw up a written on-site emergency plan[1] which is sufficient to achieve the following objectives:[2]

1 containing and controlling incidents so as to minimise the effects, and to limit damage to persons, the environment and property;
2 implementing the measures necessary to protect persons and the environment from the effects of major accidents;
3 communicating the necessary information to the public and to the emergency services and authorities concerned in the area; and
4 providing for the restoration and clean-up of the environment following a major accident.

1 SI 1999/743, reg 9(1).
2 SI 1999/743, Sch 5, Pt 1 details the objectives to be attained.

10.85 The information that must be included in this plan is:[1]

* names or positions of persons authorised to set emergency procedures in motion and the person in charge of co-ordinating the on-site mitigatory action;

- name or position of the person with responsibility for liaison with the local authority responsible for preparing the off-site emergency plan;
- for foreseeable conditions or events which could be significant in bringing about a major accident, a description of the action which should be taken to control the conditions or events and to limit their consequences, including a description of the safety equipment and resources available;
- arrangements for limiting the risks to persons on site including how warnings are to be given and the actions persons are expected to take on receipt of a warning;
- arrangements for providing early warning of the incident to the local authority responsible for setting the off-site emergency plan in motion, the type of information which should be contained in an initial warning and the arrangements for the provision of more detailed information as it becomes available;
- arrangements for training staff in the duties they will be expected to perform, and where necessary co-ordinating this with the emergency services; and
- arrangements for providing assistance with off-site mitigatory action.

1   As specified in SI 1999/743, Sch 5, Pt 2.

10.86   An adequate off-site emergency plan must be drawn up by the local authority (LA) for the area where a top tier establishment is located.[1] The same objectives apply to this plan as to the on-site plan[2] and it must also be in writing. COMAH provides a list of required information that plans must contain[3] and an operator must supply all necessary information to the LA to enable the plan to be prepared.[4] In addition, the LA must consult:[5]

- the operator;
- the CA;
- the emergency services;
- each health authority for the area in the vicinity of the establishment; and
- such members of the public as it considers appropriate.

1   SI 1999/743, reg 10(1).
2   SI 1999/743, Sch 5, Part 1.
3   SI 1999/743, Sch 5, Part 3.
4   SI 1999/743, reg 10(3).
5   SI 1999/743, reg 10(6).

10.87   The CA may, in light of a safety report, exempt a LA from the requirement to prepare an off-site emergency plan in respect of an establishment. Any such exemption must be in written form and state the reasons for granting it.[1]

1   SI 1999/743, reg 10(6).

10.88   Once emergency plans have been put in place it is obligatory that these are reviewed, and if necessary revised, at least every three years.[1] COMAH, reg 11(1) specifies certain factors that should be taken into account when carrying out such a review, such as new technical knowledge.

1   SI 1999/743, reg 11.

Local authority charges and powers

10.89   The LA is entitled to charge the operator a fee[1] to cover costs that are reasonably incurred in performing its functions of preparing, reviewing and testing off-site emergency plans.[2] When requesting the fee from the operator the LA must provide a detailed statement of the work carried out and the costs incurred

1   SI 1999/743, reg 13.
2   Under SI 1999/743, regs 10 and 11.

10.90   Where the CA believes that the measures taken by an operator for the prevention and mitigation of major accidents are seriously deficient it must prohibit the operation or bringing into operation[1] of that establishment or installation.[2] The CA also has the discretion to prohibit the operation or bringing into operation of any establishment or installation if the operator has failed to submit any notification, safety report or other information required under COMAH within the required time. The CA must serve a notice on the operator giving reasons for any prohibition and the date when it is to take effect.[3]

1   SI 1999/743, reg 18(1).
2   Or any part of it.
3   SI 1999/743, reg 18(3).

Provision of information to the public

10.91   A final obligation which operators should take into consideration is the duty to supply information to the public within an area without their having to request it. The CA will notify the area to the operator as being one in which people are liable to be affected by a major accident occurring at the establishment.[1]

1   SI 1999/743, Sch 6 specifies the minimum information to be supplied to the public.

Transport and carriage of dangerous chemicals

10.92   The transportation of dangerous chemicals is inherently risky and is governed by Regulations[1] dealing with the carriage of dangerous goods by road or rail. The dual aim of these Regulations is to minimise the risk of spillage etc, as well as making it easier for emergency services to deal with such spillages should they occur. The Regulations are of relevance if a company is going to send, carry or receive dangerous chemicals. To fall within the Regulations chemicals must be classified as 'dangerous goods' under the Approved Carriage List (ACL).[2]

1   In particular, the Carriage of Dangerous Goods (Classification, Packaging and Labelling) and Use of Transportable Pressure Receptacles Regulations 1996, SI 1996/2092, the Carriage of Dangerous Goods by Road Regulations 1996, SI 1996/2095 and the Carriage of Dangerous Goods by Rail Regulations 1996, SI 1996/2089.
2   The current list (1999 edition) is available on CD-ROM from HSE Books.

10.93   If a chemical is not listed by name in the ACL it is necessary to establish its hazardous properties before the appropriate entry can be identified. In order to do this companies should refer to the Carriage of Dangerous Goods (Classification, Packaging and Labelling) and Use of Transportable Pressure Receptacles Regulations 1996, reg 5[1] (CDGCPL2) and the Approved Requirements and Test Methods for the Classification and Packaging of Dangerous Goods for Carriage (ARTM).

1   SI 1996/2092, reg 5, as amended by the Carriage of Dangerous Goods (Amendment) Regulations 1999, SI 1999/303.

10.94   Once the appropriate entry for the chemical has been identified in the ACL a company will also find further items of information which will help it to comply with other regulatory requirements.[1]

1   Eg packaging and labelling requirements.

10.95   It should be remembered that the Regulations apply from the moment that the loading of dangerous goods onto a vehicle begins and continue to apply until all the dangerous goods have been unloaded. Dangerous goods should be packaged suitably and adequately so that they do not escape during handling and carriage. CDGCPL2[1] requires that dangerous goods are packaged according to the packing group established when they were classified. The ARTM details the packaging that should be used for such dangerous goods. Special provisions in the ACL apply to some goods which have special packaging requirements over and above those set out in the ARTM. CDGCPL2, reg 8[2] lays down labelling requirements for dangerous goods which requires consignors to label packages with all necessary information about the goods. Again this information is obtained when the goods are classified.

1   SI 1996/2092.
2   SI 1996/2092, reg 8.

Consignor information

10.96   Once goods have been correctly packaged and labelled and loaded onto a vehicle the consignor must ensure that the person operating that vehicle is provided with all the necessary information about the goods being carried. Consignors have a duty to provide the following information to the operator:[1]

* the shipping name for the goods;
* the class of the goods being carried;
* the UN number;
* the packing group (where appropriate);
* the mass or volume of dangerous goods to be carried;
* the transport category of the goods;[2]
* an authenticated statement confirming that the goods as presented may be carried, are in a fit condition for carriage and are properly labelled;[3]
* the names and address of both the consignor and consignee; and
* any other information to enable the goods to be carried safely.

1   This is not an exhaustive list.
2   Or sufficient information to enable the operator to work this out.
3   If different types of dangerous goods are packed together there must also be a confirmation that such mixed packing is allowed.

10.97   The Carriage of Dangerous Goods by Road Regulations 1996[1] (CDGR) and Carriage of Dangerous Goods by Rail Regulations 1996[2] (CDGRail2), both as amended by the Carriage of Dangerous Goods (Amendment) Regulations 1999,[3] set out further details regarding consignor information.

1   SI 1996/2095.
2   SI 1996/2089.
3   SI 1999/303.

Methods of carrying dangerous goods

10.98 Any company proposing to transport dangerous goods in tanks must check that the goods are suitable by referring to column 7 of the ACL. A tank must be properly designed and constructed and examined and maintained regularly.

10.99 Any vehicle or container used to carry dangerous goods must be suitable for the purpose. The requirements for transportation of dangerous goods by rail are outlined in CDGRail2.[1] Similarly requirements for carriage by road are governed by the CDGR.[2] Two other approved documents should also be considered – the Approved Vehicle Requirements (AVR) and the Approved Tank Requirements (ATR).

1 SI 1996/2089.
2 SI 1996/2095.

Loading, unloading and stowage

10.100 Operators are under a duty to ensure that there is no risk to the health and safety of any person during carriage resulting from the way in which the goods have been loaded, unloaded or stowed. Mixtures of dangerous goods must be loaded with extra care to ensure that they are adequately separated. In some circumstances specific classes of dangerous goods must not be carried together.

Hazard information

10.101 Once packaged dangerous goods other than explosives or radioactive materials go above a specific load threshold, the vehicle in which they are being carried must display plain, reflectorised orange panels at the front and rear. Road tankers carrying dangerous goods must display a plain orange coloured panel on the front, back and both sides of the vehicle. The information that these panels must display is detailed in CDGR, reg 17.[1] The information that needs to be displayed when carrying hazardous goods by rail is specified under CDGRail2, reg 14.[2]

1 SI 1996/2095, reg 17.
2 SI 1996/2089, reg 14.

Equipment requirements

10.102 The operator is under a duty to ensure that certain items of emergency equipment are carried on any road vehicle which is transporting dangerous goods.[1] This equipment includes items such as portable fire extinguishers which enable the driver to take action in an emergency.

1 See CDGR, SI 1996/2095, reg 21 and SI 1996/2095, reg 23.

Safety advisors

10.103 An employer involved in the transport of dangerous goods by road or rail may be required to appoint vocationally qualified safety advisors. This obligation is governed by the Transport of Dangerous Goods (Safety Advisors) Regulations 1999[1] (TDGSA). The Regulations apply to employers who:

1   consign dangerous goods for transport and load the means of transport themselves;
2   are operators of road vehicles/train operators; and
3   load or unload dangerous goods while they are in transit to their final destination.

1   SI 1999/257.

10.104   Employers will be exempt if they only transport, load or unload dangerous goods below the specified thresholds. Furthermore, safety advisors need not be appointed if employers meet all three of the following criteria:

1   its main or secondary activity is not the transport of dangerous goods, ie the transport of dangerous goods is only a minor function of its business;
2   it is only involved in the transport of dangerous goods occasionally (one or two such transport movements per month); and
3   the transport of dangerous goods does not create significant risk to the health and safety of persons or the environment.

10.105   TDGSA, Sch 1[1] provides a number of other specific exemptions. Anybody maybe appointed as a safety advisor provided that they hold a vocational training certificate (VTC) which is valid for both the mode of transport and for the class or type of dangerous goods being transported. The role of the safety advisor is to:

•   provide the employer with advice on all aspects of the transport of dangerous goods;
•   ensure compliance with the legal requirements on the safe transport of dangerous goods (and related health and safety procedures);[2] and
•   ensure that an annual report is prepared detailing the employer's activities relating to the transport of dangerous goods.[3] Reports must be kept for five years and be made available to enforcement agencies on request. The duties of safety advisors are detailed under TDGSA, regs 4, 5 and 6[4] and Sch 2.[5]

1   SI 1999/257, Sch 1.
2   Including the preparation of accident reports.
3   There is no set format for such reports, but they must summarise the result of the safety advisor's monitoring activities and focus on aiding compliance with the legal requirements regarding the transport of dangerous goods.
4   SI 1999/257, regs 4, 5 and 6.
5   SI 1999/257, Sch 2.

10.106   An employer may decide how many safety advisors it needs to appoint.[1] A number of issues must be considered when making this decision, such as how many operating sites the safety advisors will need to cover and whether they will prepare reports and carry out monitoring themselves.[2] Employers may also co-operate with each other to appoint the same safety advisor(s), particularly on sites where more than one employer is involved in the transport, loading or unloading of dangerous goods.

1   TDGSA, SI 1999/257, reg 4.
2   Or delegate this to others.

Drivers

10.107 A driver may need a driver's VTC if he is going to drive any of the following on a road:

- a road tanker containing any dangerous chemicals;
- a vehicle carrying a tank container loaded with any dangerous chemicals;
- a vehicle carrying dangerous chemicals in bulk; or
- a vehicle carrying dangerous chemicals in packages if the vehicle has a maximum permissible weight greater than 3.5 tonnes.

10.108 For the latter of these, drivers need not undertake vocational training courses but they must undertake general training to make them aware of the dangers of the goods being carried.

10.109 The requirements relating to driver training are laid down in the Carriage of Dangerous Goods by Road (Driver Training) Regulations 1996[1] (DTR2). Further exceptions from the requirements, other than those previously mentioned, are listed in DTR2, Schs 1 and 2.[2] Drivers must keep their vocational training certificates with them at all times during a journey.

1 SI 1996/2094.
2 SI 1996/2094, Schs 1 and 2.

10.110 It should be remembered that HSWA 1974 contains general training requirements for everyone at work and will apply to the transport of dangerous goods.

Action to take in the event of an accident or emergency

10.111 Where a vehicle carrying dangerous goods is involved in any sort of accident or incident, drivers must follow the emergency instructions provided and where necessary notify the emergency services by the quickest and safest method. Employers are under a duty to inform the HSE about certain injuries and dangerous incidents arising during the course of work activities.[1] This is also covered under TDGSA, regs 5 and 6.[2] A typical example of a dangerous occurrence related to the transport of dangerous chemicals would be where a road tanker carrying a dangerous chemical overturned and the chemical was released.

1 See the Reporting of Injuries Diseases and Dangerous Occurrences Regulations 1995, SI 1995/3163 (RIDDOR).
2 SI 1999/257, regs 5 and 6.

10.112 In addition there is a separate requirement for dangerous goods safety advisors to ensure that a report is prepared for any accident which either affects the health and safety of any person or causes damage to the environment. The incident must have taken place during the transport of dangerous goods by the employer who has appointed that safety advisor. These reports should be kept for five years and there is no fixed format. Clearly, more serious incidents will require a fuller and more detailed report addressing the causes of the incident, legal implications and any actions necessary to prevent a re-occurrence.

Chemicals (Hazard Information and Packaging for Supply) Regulations 2002[1]

10.113   The Chemicals (Hazard Information and Packaging for Supply) Regulations 2002 (CHIP) requires suppliers of chemicals to classify, package and label dangerous chemicals appropriately and to supply information for their safe use.

1   SI 2002/1689.

10.114   The aim of CHIP[1] is to ensure that people who are supplied with chemicals receive the information that they need to protect themselves, others and the environment. To achieve this aim, CHIP requires suppliers of chemicals to identify their hazards (for example, reactivity, toxicity) and to supply this information together with advice on safe use to the people that they supply the chemicals to. Usually the most suitable means of doing this will be through package labels and safety data sheets.

1   SI 2002/1689.

10.115   Whilst CHIP applies to most chemicals it does not apply to all. It should be remembered that the exceptions[1] generally have regulations of their own.

1   SI 2002/1689, reg 3.

10.116   In a nutshell, CHIP[1] is intended to protect both people and the environment from the harmful effects of dangerous chemicals by ensuring that their users are supplied with adequate information about the dangers. The HSE describes CHIP as the 'foundation of Great Britain's chemical control regime'.[2] In this respect it should be considered together with the regulations previously discussed. Changes to the classification of a chemical may make it subject to the regime under COMAH[3] or could trigger specific work place controls under COSHH.[4] However, it should be remembered that CHIP deals with the packaging or labelling of chemicals, not with deciding if new chemicals on the market are dangerous.

1   SI 2002/1689.
2   see HSE's CHIP homepage at www.hse.gov.uk/CHIP/index.htm.
3   SI 1999/743.
4   SI 2002/2677.

The European angle

10.117   CHIP[1] is based on the following three Directives.

1   SI 2002/1689.

Dangerous Substances Directive[1]

10.118   The Dangerous Substances Directive outlines the hazard classification packaging and labelling requirements for dangerous substances supplied in the EU.

1   Council Directive 67/548/EEC.

Dangerous Preparations Directive[1]

10.119 The Dangerous Preparations Directive specifies the hazard specification and packaging requirements for chemical preparations, ie mixtures or solutions composed of two or more substances.

1 Council Directive 99/45/EEC.

Safety Data Sheet Directive,[1] as amended by Council Directive 93/112/EEC

10.120 The Directive on safety data sheets outlines the EC system for the provisions of specific information relating to dangerous preparations and substances through the use of safety data sheets.

1 Council Directive 91/155/EEC.

Key goals of CHIP

10.121 CHIP[1] applies to the supply of chemicals – this is distinct from controlling dangerous chemicals in the workplace, or their transportation. Supply means for sale, offer for sale, importation, provision of commercial samples or the transfer of chemicals from one person to another.

1 SI 2002/1689.

10.122 CHIP[1] aims to protect people and the environment from the ill effects of chemicals by requiring suppliers to:

1   identify the hazards of the chemicals they supply;
2   give their customers information about the hazards of chemicals; and
3   package the chemicals safely.

1 SI 2002/1689.

Classification

10.123 The fundamental requirement under CHIP is to decide whether a chemical that is being supplied is hazardous. No dangerous substance or dangerous preparation may be supplied unless it has been classified in accordance with CHIP, reg 4.[1] The first step is to decide what kind of hazard the chemical poses and the second, to explain that hazard by assigning a 'risk phrase'.[2] A large number of commonly used substances have already been classified and appear in a list known as the CHIP Approved Supply List (ASL). Where available these classifications are compulsory. Where a substance does not appear in the ASL or if a preparation is being supplied then it must be classified by the supplier.

1 SI 2002/1689, regs 4–7.
2 R-phrase for short.

10.124 For substances the approved classification and labelling guide (ASLG) sets out the general principles of classification and labelling for supply as required by

CHIP.[1] For preparations, either a calculation method or the criteria in the ASLG[2] can be used.

1   SI 2002/1689.
2   For certain hazards.

Provisions of hazard information

10.125   Once the classification of the substance or preparation has been established, customers must be informed about the hazards and how they can use the chemicals safely. Two principal methods by which the regulations ensure this are the requirements for:

*   labelling;[1] and
*   a safety data sheet.[2]

1   SI 2002/1689, reg 8.
2   SI 2002/1689, reg 5. Although a safety data sheet is required where a customer uses the chemical at work, other measures may be sufficient for consumers.

10.126   Labelling is governed by CHIP, reg 8.[1] If a dangerous chemical is supplied in a package that package has to be labelled. Clearly, where chemicals are not supplied in a package but, for example, via a pipeline then labelling is not possible.

1   SI 2002/1689, reg 8.

10.127   The purpose of the label is to inform anyone handling the chemicals about their hazards and to give brief advice on what precautions should be taken. CHIP[1] gives specific instructions as to what has to go on the label and how packages should be labelled.

1   SI 2002/1689.

Safety data sheets

10.128   Safety data sheets (SDSs) are a necessity if a chemical is dangerous and supplied for use at work whether that chemical is in packages or not. SDSs are also required where a chemical is not classified as dangerous yet contains small amounts of a dangerous substance. Whilst CHIP[1] does not provide exact instructions as to what should go into a SDS, it does set a minimum standard which must be attained. In addition it provides headings under which the information should be provided. Quality standards place the responsibility on the supplier to ensure that the information provided is sufficient.[2]

1   SI 2002/1689.
2   Enough to allow the user to decide how to protect people at work and the environment.

10.129   An important point to remember is that whilst provision of an SDS is covered by CHIP,[1] employers' use of SDS to carry out risk assessment and management is covered by workplace control law, for example, COSHH.[2]

1   SI 2002/1689.
2   SI 2002/2677.

Packaging

10.130 The packaging requirements in CHIP are contained in reg 7.[1] The package must be suitable, ie it must:

- be designed and constructed so that the dangerous substance or preparation cannot escape;
- be made from materials which are not susceptible to 'adverse attack' by the contents or liable to form dangerous compounds with the contents; and
- have strong and solid packaging and fastenings throughout to ensure that they will not loosen and will tolerate the normal stresses and strains of handling.

1 SI 2002/1689, reg 7.

10.131 In addition, any replaceable fastening fitted to the package must be designed so that it can be repeatedly re-fastened without the contents of the package escaping.

Consumer protection measures

10.132 CHIP, reg 11[1] sets out certain consumer protection measures relating to the packaging of specified chemicals that are sold to the public. Packaging may not, for example, be of a shape or design that might mislead consumers or arouse the active curiosity of children. The packaging of some dangerous substances sold to the general public must have child-resistant fastenings, to prevent young children from opening the package. In addition, some must have a tactile danger warning to alert blind and partially sighted people that they are handling a dangerous product.

1 SI 2002/1689, reg 11.

Regulation in the chemicals industry and corporate killing

10.133 The regulations that govern the use of chemicals in the workplace and the chemicals industry itself form part of a much wider framework of legislation covering health and safety at work. In many cases, compliance with the industry's specific regulations may help companies to fulfil obligations imposed by regulations applicable to all workplaces, such as the duty to maintain a safe system of work.[1]

1 HSWA 1974, s 2(2)(a).

10.134 The government has made it clear that the offence of corporate killing is to be introduced, and this will be of relevance to those operating in the chemicals sector. It will inevitably increase the need for those operating in the chemicals industry to comply with both industry-specific and the more general workplace regulations and statutory duties.

Looking ahead at the new chemical strategy

10.135 It is widely argued within the EU that the current legislation for chemicals does not provide sufficient protection in relation to the potential impact of chemicals on health and the environment. This led to the European Commission making a commitment in 1998 to assess the operation of the four main legal instruments governing chemicals in the EC.[1] In view of the findings the Council adopted a set of conclusions for a future strategy on chemicals in the EC forming the basis of a White Paper. Due to delays in publication of the consultative document, an eight-week consultation on the draft Regulation was only launched by the European Commission on 7 May 2003. It is thought that a formal proposal from the European Commission will not be put forward until the end of 2003 and therefore legislation is unlikely before 2006.

1   Council Directive 67/548/EEC relating to the classification, packaging and labelling of dangerous substances; Council Directive 76/769/EEC on the marketing and use of certain dangerous substances and preparations; Council Directive 88/379/EEC relating to the classification, packaging and labelling of dangerous preparations; Council Regulation 793/93/EC on evaluation and control of risks of existing substances.

Current system

10.136   At present there are two statutory regimes on chemicals. The current risk assessment system for chemicals, which came into being in 1981, is slow and inefficient. Only about 300 new substances per year have been tested and notified to the authorities before being placed on the market. The second came into force in 1994 to deal with existing substances which were on the EU market before 1981. The second regime placed 140 of the 100,000 existing substances on priority lists for risk assessment and, if necessary, control. Since the implementation of the regime only about a dozen substances have completed the risk assessment process. As a result, there is predominantly only knowledge of the chemical substances placed on the market after 1981 – approximately 2,700 substances, or less than 1% of all chemicals. It is this failure to ascertain information on chemical substances that has prompted the need for the present reforms.

Assessment of chemicals

10.137   The principal objective of assessing the risks of chemicals is to provide a reliable basis for deciding on adequate safety measures when using them, in particular, whether they could cause any adverse effects when used in a certain way. All risk assessments are comprised of two elements. First, a hazard assessment, which is an evaluation of the properties which are intrinsic to the chemical. This identifies any hazardous properties such as sensitising, carcinogenic, toxicity for the aquatic environment and determines the potency of the chemical with respect to the hazardous properties. Secondly, an exposure assessment, which is an estimation of the exposure, which depends on the use of the chemical.

10.138   Detailed knowledge on the properties and exposure arising as a result of a particular use and the disposal is an imperative prerequisite for allowing the safe management of chemicals. Accurate knowledge on the properties of a substance is important as it forms the basis for the classification of a chemical. A number of management provisions set out in specific legislation which protects human health and/or the environment are associated to the classification of chemicals. For example, the labelling of the packaging of chemicals to inform the user about the properties of the chemicals and advice for safe use, a chemical which is classified as carcinogenic, mutagenic or toxic for reproduction currently initiates an examination of restriction measures in the consumer sector and it triggers various safety measures laid down in sector-specific legislation in respect of occupational health, water protection, waste management, prevention of major accident hazards and air pollution

Proposed regulations

10.139 The White Paper proposes that legislation for new and existing chemicals should be merged into one, with all chemicals manufactured at over one tonne being registered. Higher tonnage of manufacture will attract an increasing degree of testing. Chemicals of high concern will have to be positively listed, with manufacturer and use approved prior to marketing. Whilst there is a clear improvement for new substances, the proposal has the potential to be extremely burdensome for all other substances, especially as it is proposed that all testing is completed 11 years from the year that the legislation comes into force. The proposed system will be known as REACH (Registration, Evaluation, Authorisation of CHemicals).

10.140 The three elements of the REACH system to be applied to new and existing substances are:

1 *Registration*
   This requires that a manufacturer or importer notify an authority of the intention to produce or import a substance and to submit information required by the legislation. The required information shall include data on the identity and properties of the substance, the intended uses, estimated human and environmental exposure and any proposed risk management measures. The authority puts this information into an electronic database, assigns a registration number and screens the substances for properties raising particular concern.

2 *Evaluation*
   Authorities will have to carefully examine data provided by the industry and decide on substance-tailored testing programmes on the effects of long term exposure. This shall apply for all substances exceeding a production volume of 100 tonnes (about 15% of all substances). For lower tonnage evaluation shall be carried out if there is concern about the substance.

3 *Authorisation*
   For substances of very high concern (for example, carcinogenic, mutagenic or reprotoxic substances) authorities will have to give specific permission before a substance can be used for a particular purpose. The number of substances estimated to be subject to authorisation is about 5% of registered substances.

10.141 It is proposed that the system will be managed centrally through the establishment of a European Chemicals Agency.

10.142 The main objective of the new chemicals strategy is to protect health and the environment and to stimulate innovation and the competitiveness of the chemical industry. It is intended to anticipate and avoid risks as far as possible, particularly with regard to chemicals that are not degradable and which accumulate in the human body and the environment.

10.143 The chemicals industry will have more responsibility to prove that a substance is harmless and they will be responsible for the testing and risk assessment of chemicals. Eleven years after the legislation comes into force all existing chemicals produced in volumes of more than one tonne per annum, approximately 30,000 substances, will be registered in a central database. The public will be able to find out what they are used for and as a result consumers will be in a position to make an informed choice when deciding which products to buy.

10.144   It has not been established exactly what the enforcement and sanctions will be for the proposed legislation. However, each member state will need to have a system to monitor compliance with the Regulation. It is thought that fines for a company who breaches the Regulations may range up to 10% of the company's global turnover.

Concerns about the proposed legislation

10.145   Clearly the European Commission favours the development of a more effective system which places a greater onus on the chemical industry to make available information on hazards, risks and risk reduction measures for chemicals currently in use to allow dangerous substances to be used safely. The chemical industry has welcomed the need for a new policy and system; however, there are concerns about the impact that the proposed legislation will have on the EU industry. A few of these concerns are outlined below.

Manufacturing industry will suffer

10.146   Virtually all manufactured articles depend on man-made chemicals and therefore the costs of implementing REACH may adversely affect every EU manufacturing industry. This in turn will mean that EU finished products may cost more. Many chemicals may be taken off the market because their turnover is insufficient to bear the costs. However, the proposal for reduced testing requirements for new substances at lower volumes may alleviate a barrier to innovation.

10.147   REACH will not apply to the manufacture and use of chemicals outside the EU. Therefore finished articles imported into the EU will have a cost/performance advantage and the EU will not be able to restrict the import of such articles. The potential consequence of REACH is that it may harm the manufacturing industries within the EU, which in turn will reduce employment and damage the economy. On the other hand, manufacturing operations in areas outside the EU where protection of people and the environment may not be such a high priority will grow.

EU competitiveness will be harmed unnecessarily

10.148   REACH will require information about uses to be put into the public domain. This may threaten companies whose competitive position depends on proprietary and confidential in-house processes particularly proprietary formulation blenders.

A workable system is needed

10.149   There are concerns that the programme is too ambitious and therefore will fail through overloading the industry and regulators. This will have an impact on the industry and also the EU.

Enforcement is essential

10.150   Existing legislation requires that products in the workplace are safe, and it imposes many safeguards to protect the environment. Effective enforcement of this legislation across the EU would have achieved many of the objectives of REACH.

Conclusion

10.151   The White Paper sets out proposals for learning more about all manufactured substances by taking a precautionary approach should anything be found of concern and ensuring that all users of the substance are aware of the hazard and exposure and making information found more widely accessible. The rationale behind the proposals is simply that there must be a system to safeguard society's safety from the use of and exposure to chemicals.

Enforcement trends

General

10.152   Investigation and enforcement of the chemical industry is generally carried out by the Hazardous Installations Directorate (HID), a specialist department of the HSE. This consists of three divisions: Central, Offshore and Land. The Land Division is responsible for the monitoring and regulation of health and safety standards for chemicals and other major hazards, such as gas explosives, pipelines and mines. The land division is also responsible for inspecting relevant sites, the investigation of accidents or incidents, enforcement of health and safety law and assessing safety reports under COMAH[1] obligations.

1   SI 1999/743.

10.153   The Offshore Division of 'HID' monitors the upstream petroleum industry. The Central Division works with the Offshore and Land Divisions by providing support on matters such as policy, technical advice and finance.

Purpose of enforcement

10.154   One purpose of the HSC is to ensure that those with legal obligation take immediate action where there are serious risks and to promote 'sustained compliance with the law'.[1] This is achieved by ensuring those who have failed in their duties under health and safety law are held to account.

1   The HSC's Policy Statement on Enforcement, available at www.hse.gov.uk/pubns/hsc15.pdf.

10.155   All HSC enforcing authorities (including the HID) have four enforcement principles that provide a standard to be expected of them. This helps the body to be accountable for its actions and to ensure fair enforcement of health and safety law.

Proportionality

10.156   Relating enforcement action to the extent of the breach of law. The inspector should take account of how far from the legal requirements and the level of the risk involved.

Targeting

10.157   Enforcement action is concentrated on the more hazardous activities and targeted at those who are in the best position to eliminate or reduce the risk.

Consistency

10.158   This does not necessarily imply that a standard and uniform approach is taken in all cases. The principle refers to the right of those responsible for health and safety to expect similar action in like circumstances and a consistent approach in the advice given. This is often difficult because enforcement action is discretionary, relying on the judgement of the enforcer.

Transparency

10.159   Those who are responsible for health and safety should know what is expected from them. Inspectors need clearly to highlight in their advice what is required by the law and what is simply guidance on best practice. If notices are issued an explanation must be given. It is also intended that duty holders, employees and their representatives know what to expect from the enforcement authority and that they are kept fully informed.

Method of enforcement

10.160   A great deal of the health and safety legislation is concerned with achieving objectives. The best ways to achieve the objectives are outlined in the ACOPs. The ACOPs are not compulsory to follow, if other methods are employed, it must be demonstrated that the objectives achieved meet or exceed the objectives that would have been achieved had the ACOPs been followed. In the pursuit of proportionality, inspectors can vary the ways in which compliance can be achieved. The decision-making process leading up to an enforcement action being taken should be set down in writing and made available to the public.

Improvement and prohibition notices

10.161   An improvement notice contains the opinion of the inspector that the legislation is not being adhered to and advice on the necessary course of action. Such notices can be used as evidence in court proceedings.

10.162   The effect of a prohibition notice is to stop work because its continuance in the opinion of the inspector is likely to cause serious personal injury.

10.163   One piece of legislation proving to be problematic for the chemical industry is COMAH.[1] The majority of improvement and prohibition notices issued for failure to comply with COMAH have been due to the poor standard of MAPP documents, which must conclusively show the health and safety systems are adequate to limit the number and extent of accidents.

1   SI 1999/743.

10.164   The Carriage of Dangerous Goods Regulations have prompted 261 prohibition notices where vehicles containing chemicals were found to be inadequately marked or endangering safety in some other way.

Formal cautions

10.165   In addition to one of the above methods, where a prosecution could be properly brought, a written statement by an inspector detailing the offence that has been committed is tendered.

Prosecutions

10.166   In line with the principle of proportionality, the HID must use its discretion in deciding whether incidents need to be investigated and the investigation resources tend to be focused on the most serious events. The HID may decide to prosecute without using any alternative measures, such as a formal caution.

Health and safety

10.167   The legislation permits the courts to use severe punishment on those who are successfully prosecuted. The courts can impose fines and they also have the power to imprison individuals for some offences, in particular, for failure to comply with improvement and prohibition notices, and in the higher courts, failure to comply with licensing requirements or explosive provisions.

10.168   According to the HSE website[1] there were 42 prosecutions of chemical companies in 2001–02, one of which resulted in an international oil company being fined £1 million due to a major fire at a refinery plant. A look into the HSE database of successful prosecutions reveals that the more hefty fines have been imposed predominantly for failure to control hazardous substances and inadequate risk assessment of employee practices, particularly in relation to the maintenance of machinery.

1   www.hse.gov.uk.

10.169   Examples of prosecutions

10.170   A 1998 prosecution of Exxonmobil Chemical Limited resulted in a £30,000 fine and a heavy bill for costs imposed upon the organic basic chemicals manufacturer when inadequate isolation procedures resulted in 17 tonnes of flammable liquid being released unintentionally.[1]

1   HSE website, enforcement action: www.hse.gov.uk/enforce/index/htm.

10.171   Similarly, Associated Octel Co were fined £80,000 when their Amlwch bromine handling plant was found not to be safe as far as is reasonably practicable. There was potential for significant off site concentrations of bromine.[1]

1   HSE website, enforcement action: www.hse.gov.uk/enforce/index/htm.

10.172   In 1997 a £300,000 fine was imposed on chemicals giant BOC Gases Ltd after an investigation into a fatal explosion during the filling of compressed gas cylinders revealed that there was a lack of adequate risk assessments, unsafe plant, unsafe systems of work and inadequate training and supervision.[1]

1   HSE website, enforcement action: www.hse.gov.uk/enforce/index/htm.

10.173   The lack of adequate risk assessment identified in the BOC prosecution[1] is a common complaint against the chemical industry. The majority of prosecutions follow as a result of accidents in the workplace during machinery maintenance.

1   See **para 10.172** above.

10.174   This is because such incidents attract a larger amount of investigation resources and often expose great risks and breaches of health and safety legislation. The HID is under an obligation to conduct a full site investigation of a work related death in nearly all circumstances. The circumstances of the case may even justify a charge of manslaughter, which the police will be responsible for pursuing.

10.175   The number of incidents where limbs or digits have been severed as a combination of unsafe working practices and insufficient training of employees are high, yet these incidents attract a lower fine upon successful prosecution. Investigations after employee deaths, however, have tended to reveal gross health and safety breaches deserving of the larger fines.

10.176   A plastics company was fined a total of £250,000 after a worker was killed when his head was crushed in a piece of specialist machinery.

The effect of enforcement

10.177   The Chemical Industry Association (CIA) has adopted the Responsible Care programme to encourage improvement in the area of safety, health and environment. The accident statistics gathered by the CIA show a 61% drop in accidents since 1986 and are illustrated in Figure 10.3.

Figure 10.3 Employee accidents per 100,000 hours worked

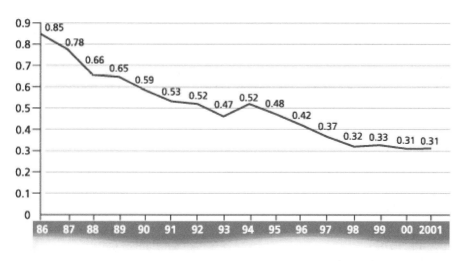

10.178 Other statistics gathered by the CIA indicate that the number of RIDDOR[1] reportable major injuries decreased from 80 in 2000 to 69 in 2001. Thus the number of health and safety incidents in the chemicals industry are on the decline.

1 SI 1995/3163.

10.179 Through the HSC enforcing authorities investigations and enforcement which can result in large fines and imprisonment, it has ensured that companies take the health and safety of their employee's seriously and place it high on a company's agenda. Investigations may be prompted by what an inspector finds on a routine visit, by complaints or a reported incident. However an investigation originates, there is no escaping the fact that a health and safety offence is a criminal offence which can cause a stain on a company's reputation and may also result in an individual being prosecuted.

Risk assessment – analysis and risk minimisation

10.180 The process of risk assessment for significant tasks in the chemical industry is now required by regulation:

- the Management of Health and Safety at Work Regulations 1999;[1]
- the Construction (Design and Management) Regulations 1994;[2] and
- the Control of Substances Hazardous to Health Regulations 2002 (COSHH).[3]

1 SI 1999/3242.
1 SI 1994/3140.
2 SI 2002/2677.

10.181   The process of risk assessment has been described in many papers and booklets but they often lack the practical approach and fail to give a consistent approach to risk assessment that would give reliable figures for the risk. For risk assessment to be successful it has to be carried out:

- Thoroughly and with conviction. It must not be treated as a bureaucratic necessity.
- By experienced and knowledgeable persons with the co-operation and help of those involved in the task.
- With the help of accident databases and journal abstracts.
- Using simple and easy to follow detailed guidelines and procedures incorporated in a management system.

10.182   Experience indicates that all four points are important but the lack of an effective management system for carrying out risk assessment has led to a risk having varying values according to who has carried out the assessment. For example, a hazard may be assessed a high risk by one assessor but might be classified as medium risk by another.

10.183   The main objective of this section is to provide a practical guideline where, regardless of who carries out the risk assessment, the same level of risk will be achieved.

10.184   For an individual task the stages for risk assessment are:

1   Identify the hazards for each task.
2   Assess the risk associated with the hazard and who is harmed.
3   Consider alternative methods of work with a lower risk.
4   Devise suitable control measures for the remaining risks.
5   Reassess the risk to ensure that it is reduced to an acceptable level.
6   Produce a method statement.

10.185   This process requires an experienced person or a team of people with an experienced chairperson to control the operation. In the analysis that is done it is essential that all the reasonable hazards that are identified as possible are recorded and actions noted, even if the team decide the risk is so low that no action is necessary. An accident database is an essential tool for identifying hazards and devising control measures.

Stage 1: identifying the hazard

10.186   This can be carried out in a number of ways:

- Inspection of the work place. Detailed inspection of the work area will always indicate many hazards that will be obvious to the experienced person.
- Use of relevant checklists.
- Experience of the team members who will always be able to draw on similar tasks that they have carried out and possibly lessons that they have learnt.
- Use of accident databases. Hazards can be identified from historical accidents and near misses. They may be unknown to the team members as they have occurred in different companies or countries but the great advantage of the databases is that they will show the lessons learnt by the company and these will be useful in devising control measures.

- Use of statistics. The frequency of certain types of accidents will indicate the likelihood of hazards that may be present.
- Keep up to date with what is going on in the area of your work. This is important as contact with others is a source of information.

10.187 Great care must be used to ensure that the hazard is fully recognised. It is insufficient to say simply that a chemical is the hazard. It must be stated what property of the chemical is the hazard, for example, toxicity, flammability, corrosivity etc.

Stage 2: assess the risk

10.188 Risk is a combination of the event and its probability.

$$Risk = probability\ of\ occurrence \times severity\ of\ harm$$

$$Risk = likelihood\ of\ occurrence \times hazard\ effect$$

10.189 The hazard has been identified in the previous stage but its probability of occurring has to be assessed. Clearly being hit by a meteorite could have a drastic result for a person but recorded history suggests that as only one animal has been known to have been hit the likelihood of such an event causing a fatality to a person is very small and hence the risk is very low. Assessing the probability or likelihood of an event is not easy but the important point has to be its reproducibility. Simple statements as given in Table 10.1 are open to considerable variation in interpretation. Hence there may be considerable variation in the assessment of the risk.

10.190

Table 10.1 Typical table used for establishing probability and occurrence

Rating	Probability of occurrence	Severity of occurrence
1	*An unlikely/unknown occurrence* Very unlikely to occur during the operation/facility or process.	Scratches, minor burns, bruises or abrasions. Minor injury 1 person.
2	*A remotely possible but known occurrence* Unlikely to occur during the life of operation/facility or process.	Minor injury, laceration requiring stitches, secondary degree burns or severe bruises. Minor injuries 2–10 people.
3	*An occasional occurrence* Likely to occur once during the life of operation/facility or process.	Major injury to one person, broken bone, amputation, third degree burns. Major injury 1 person, Minor injuries to >10.
4	*A frequent occurrence* Likely to occur from time to time during the life of the operation/facility or process.	Death or permanent severe disablement of one person. Major injury <5 people.
5	*A highly likely occurrence* Likely to occur repeatedly during the life of the operation/facility or process	Multiple deaths or multiple severe permanent disablement. Major injuries >5 people or fatality

10.191   These are, however, open to considerable variation of interpretation depending on the person carrying   out the risk assessment and even with a group there can be considerable variations. A more definitive interpretation of the rating points is required. Table 10.2 gives a fuller interpretation of the ratings and should lead to less disagreement amongst the team of assessors[1].

1   J Bond 'Linking an Accident Database to Design and Operational Software' (2003) Hazards XVII, The Institution of Chemical Engineers Symposium Series no 149.

10.192

Table 10.2 A more definitive table for establishing probability and occurrence

Rating	Probability of occurrence	Severity of occurrence
1	*An unlikely/unknown occurrence* The risk assessors have not heard of the hazard becoming a reality in either their own company or elsewhere. It has not been reported in any accident database or in a journal.	Potentially would lead to scratches, minor burns, bruises or abrasions. Minor injury 1 person.
2	*A remotely possible but known occurrence* The risk assessors are aware of the hazard occurring in another company but not recently in their own company, i.e. the hazard has not been experienced by the assessors but it is reported in an accident database or in a journal.	Potentially would lead to minor injury, laceration requiring stitches, second degree burns or severe bruises. Minor injuries 2–10 people.
3	*An occasional occurrence* The assessors have seldom experienced such a hazard in their own company but it has occurred at another company and is found in an accident database.	Potentially would lead to major injury to a few persons, broken bone, amputation or third degree burns. Injuries reported in accident database or journal reports. Major injury 1 person, Minor injuries to >10.
4	*A frequent occurrence* The assessors have frequently experienced such a hazard at their place of work and it is reported frequently in accident databases or journals.	Potentially would lead to death or permanent severe disablement of one or more persons. Reported in accident databases or journals with these conditions. Major injury <5 people.
5	*A highly likely occurrence* The assessors recognise that the likelihood of the hazard taking place is very high and that it is very frequently reported in accident databases and journals.	Potentially would lead to severe permanent disablement. Reported in accident databases or journals with these severe conditions. Major injuries >5people or fatality.

10.193

Table 10.3 Table for establishing risk bands

Severity				
5	10	15	20	25
4	8	12	16	20
3	6	9	12	15
2	4	6	8	10
1	2	3	4	5

Probability

Risk bands 12–25	Highly hazardous and highly likely event. In all cases the potential severity is too high to allow the operation to continue. Operation in this risk band must be eliminated, avoided altogether or totally re-planned.
Risk bands 5–10	Within this band severity and probability are high and the work cannot be carried out until risk is reduced to an acceptable level. Mitigating the hazard can be via the provision of written procedures or work instructions, supervising the work, isolation or limiting exposure.
Risk bands 1–4	Within this band it is acceptable to carry out the work but with appropriate personal protective equipment, training, warning signs, barriers etc to mitigate the risks.

Stage 3: consider alternative methods

10.194 Alternative methods of working should be considered which might well eliminate the hazard altogether or at least reduce either the likelihood of the hazard or its severity.
- *Elimination* – the complete removal of the hazard.
- *Substitution* – the replacement for a safer alternative.
- *Isolation/segregation* – isolating the hazard from the worker.
- *Exposure* – the limiting of the exposure to the hazard.
- *Other controls* – additional training etc.

10.195 For example, if painting in a confined space then water-based paints should be sought in place of solvent-based paints.

10.196 If cleaning out a vessel is the task being assessed then an alternative method to a person entering the vessel might be to use a rotating high pressure water jetting machine suspended from the manhole. The hazards involved in confined entry to the vessel would be removed and replaced by a lower risk involved in using the water jetting machine in the vessel.

10.197   Alternative methods considered should be recorded.

Stage 4: devise suitable control measures

10.198   Control measures must be devised for all the remaining hazards to ensure that the risks are as low as reasonably practical. Control measures can include:

- appropriate training;
- protective clothing;
- isolation of equipment;
- removal of chemicals;
- provision of two or more safeguards against the hazard; and
- other systems which prevent the hazard becoming a reality.

10.199   Sources of information for control measures can often be found in an accident database. For example, if one of the hazards considered in the opening up and inspection of a heat exchanger which has been on an olefins duty is the presence of copper acetylide. This can occur if there has been even small traces of acetylene and possibility of copper in some instrumentation pipework. This hazard can be eliminated by the special washing technique found to be effective after such an accident and is detailed in an accident database.

Stage 5: reassess the risk

10.200   Once the control measures have been agreed, reassess the risk to ensure that it is at a suitable low level.

Stage 6: write method statement

10.201   The method statement is a most important document as it states the method you have devised to control the hazards you have identified and assessed the risk. It is the method that you want the work to be carried out so that it is as safe as reasonably practical. Above all the method must be discussed with the operative to ensure that he or she understands fully the method to be adopted for the task.

10.202   The method statement should be retained for audit purposes.

Acceptable and unacceptable risks

10.203   We have to accept that there is a risk in all that we do whether in leisure activities or in our work. They have to be lived with but they can all be reduced to an acceptable level by the process of risk assessment. An acceptable level of risk must always be established.

10.204   The Advisory Committee on Major Hazards states that:

'If assessments indicated with reasonable confidence that in a particular plant a serious accident was unlikely to occur more often than once in 10,000 years ... this might perhaps be regarded as just on the borderline of acceptability, bearing in mind the background of risk faced every day by the general public.'[1]

1 *First Report of the Advisory Committee on Major Hazards* (1976).

10.205 In their regulations for safety evaluation of conceptual oil platform design the Norwegian Petroleum Directorate consider that a fatality risk of 10^{-4} per year (1 fatality in 10,000 years) is acceptable for events which affect personnel outside the immediate vicinity of the accident.

10.206 This does not help in determining what is an acceptable risk if a quantified risk assessment is not being carried out but it does indicate that considerable improvements in our approach to our work and other activities must be made.

10.207 The ALARP principle is often mentioned and requires a risk to be:

As Low As Reasonably Practicable

10.208 Bearing this in mind we must remind ourselves that we have to take all reasonable precautions against foreseeable hazards.

10.209 Risk assessment is an effective way of assessing the risks in any project and should be adopted in all industrial situations, in all service operations as well as in everyday life. There are many incidents that would not have occurred if a risk assessment had been carried out. They include the disasters of Aberfan, Zeebrugge and the BSE incidents.

Inherent safety

10.210 The concept of inherently safer plant has been with us for many years but little approach has been made despite a clear advantage in safety and costs. Safety performance of any plant depends on a number of factors including:

* The quality of the people who design, operate and maintain it.
* The effectiveness of the management and management systems in design, operation, maintenance and accident response.
* The effectiveness of engineered safety systems to control hazards.
* The risk potential of the plant and the process being carried out.

10.211 In practice many of the processes that we carry out require considerable quantities of hazardous materials and these may be involved in runaway reactions. Can we change the process or the equipment to make it inherently safer. The routes have been defined by T Kletz as:[1]

* *Intensification* – reducing the hazardous inventories.
* *Substitution* – substituting hazardous materials with less hazardous ones (but recognising that there could be some trade-offs here between plant safety and the wider product and life cycle issues).

- *Attenuation* – using the hazardous materials or processes in a way that limits their hazard potential, for example, dissolved in a safe solvent, stored at low pressure or temperature.
- *Simplification* – making the plant and process simpler to design, build and operate hence less prone to equipment, control and human failings.

1   T Kletz *Process Plants. A handbook of Inherently Safer Design* (1998).

10.212   Safety is a key factor in design but it has to be balanced against other factors such as economics, practicality, technology, time and markets. Decisions about inherently safer plant have to be considered at each stage of the project and during risk assessment procedures:

- Initial product specification.
- Synthesis route selection.
- Chemical flowsheet development.
- Process conceptual design.

10.213   Ways of considering inherent safety at different stages are:

- Structured brainstorming techniques to identify alternatives prior to flowsheet development.
- More rigid HAZOP-style, techniques to challenge flowsheets and process diagrams.
- Prompt checklists to address aspects of conceptual plant layout.
- Safety indices to measure the degree of inherent safety of a proposed process.
- Product specification:
  – challenge the product need;
  – challenge the means to provide that need; and
  – screen the alternatives.
- Synthesis route selection:
  – use of natural versus recycled versus synthetic materials;
  – use of bio-synthesis or electro synthesis;
  – use of different pressures or temperatures or solvents;
  – use of novel separation techniques;
  – assembly in a different state – solid, liquid or vapour; and
  – use of different solvents or other carrier agents.
- Chemical flowsheet development.
- Process conceptual design:
  – break the process down into its basic unit operations;
  – consider changing each unit operation; and
  – evaluate alternative operations.

10.214   Inherent safety is a concept that must be considered on all occasions.

Lessons learnt by the chemical industry

Introduction

10.215   If hindsight is defined as wisdom after the event, learning lessons from accidents is a process of turning hindsight into foresight. The first part of this process must, of course, be a thorough investigation of the accident. Only when this has been done and the results recorded can a detailed analysis be made to pinpoint those hazards that might recur in a similar operation. Once knowledge of these hazards has been accepted and disseminated it is a straightforward matter to develop protective systems. These control systems may be equipment, instrument or procedure based.

10.216 Four aspects of learning lessons from accidents need stressing:

- The corporate responsibility of an organisation to prevent a recurrence of an event and hence to protect people from injury and equipment and the environment from damage.
- The need for a management system to ensure that all personnel learn the lessons from accidents occurring both within and outside the organisation.
- The professional person's duty to design, operate and maintain equipment and processes to the highest standard that can reasonably be achieved.
- The duty of care of an organisation and professional staff to share information on safety and environmental incidents.

10.217 The tragedy of Aberfan in Wales[1] occurred in October 1966 when a large tip of colliery rubbish slid down a hillside into the town and destroyed the local school. 28 adults and 116 children, mostly between the ages of seven and ten, were killed. There was a history of tip instability in the area and the report stated:

'The stark truth is that the tragedy of Aberfan flowed from the fact that, notwithstanding the lessons of the recent past, not for one fleeting moment did many otherwise conscientious and able men turn their minds to the problem of tip stability.'

1 Sir H E Davies (Chairman) *Report of the Tribunal appointed to inquire into the Disaster at Aberfan on October 21st 1966* (1967).

10.218 In the approach to safety in the twentieth century there has been an emphasis on national and international regulation, and it is noteworthy that current legislation includes a requirement to take into account lessons learnt from previous accidents of a similar kind.

10.219 Organisations in EU countries, for instance, are covered by what is commonly known as the Seveso II Directive.[1] In the UK this Directive is implemented by the COMAH.[2] Section 361 of the Guidance to the Regulations states:

'The SMS [Safety Management System] should describe the arrangements for considering lessons learned from previous incidents and accidents (both within and outside the organisation concerned), from the operating experience of the establishment concerned or similar ones, and from previous safety inspections and audits.'

1 Council Directive 96/82/EC.
2 SI 1999/743.

10.220 The first recommendation in the report[1] on the explosion and fire at the Texaco Refinery at Milford Haven on the 24 July 1994 states:

'Safety management systems should include means of storing, retrieving and reviewing incident information from the history of similar plants.'

1 HSE *The explosion and fire at the Texaco Refinery, Milford Haven, 24 July 1994* (1997).

10.221   The Chemical Industries Association's Responsible Care[1] programme is so convinced that the sharing of accident information will lead to further improvements in their members' safety performance that they have lent their support to the Accident Database[2] initiative. The Guidance Document states:

'Section 6.6.3 Communicating with others.

Organisations should:

Share relevant HS&E (health, safety and environment) knowledge and lessons learnt from incidents to help prevent others from experiencing similar incidents.'

1 Chemical Industries Association *Responsible Care Management System - Guidance* (3rd edn, 1998).
2 The Institution of Chemical Engineers *The Accident Database* (2000).

Areas that can benefit from learning lessons

10.222   Leaving aside its corporate duty of care, a company as a whole will benefit from learning the lessons taught by past accidents, if only from the self-interested motive of avoiding future accidents which can only lead to lost revenue by way of compensation claims, replacement of damaged plant etc. Within the organisation, however, there are individuals who can usefully profit by learning lessons in the areas for which they are responsible. They include the following.

The designer of equipment

10.223   Consider, for example, the design of a distillation column for ethylene oxide.[1] The professionalism of the design engineer would require him or her to consider what accidents had occurred on such equipment. He or she would want to ensure that their design did not have the problems that others had experienced and which had caused fatalities, injuries to people, damage to equipment or discharges to the atmosphere of toxic chemicals. He or she would therefore seek information on such accidents and the causes, and would discover that there had been at least eight explosions involving distillation columns and ethylene oxide and that the lessons learnt were of a similar nature.

1 J Bond 'Linking an Accident Database to Design and Operational Software' (2000) Hazards XVII, The Institution of Chemical Engineers Symposium Series no 149.

10.224   It is clear that all these accidents have a similar cause:

- leak from flange or weld;
- reaction in the insulation with water; and
- auto-oxidation catalysed by rust with heating from an insulation fire.

10.225   If these causes had been recognised and made more widely known after the accidents in the 1950s or 1960s the design engineers would have been able to prevent most of the subsequent explosions in ethylene oxide plants, with a consequent prevention of fatalities, injuries, pollution and loss of profits.

The operator of equipment

10.226 The operator of equipment must be aware of incidents that have happened elsewhere with similar equipment. For example, operators of pipelines must keep themselves aware of incidents involving such equipment, as reported accidents involving equipment associated with pipelines can give valuable details:

10.227 Three incidents involving the failure of trap doors used on pigs and high pressure scrubbers on pipelines are reported.[1] The first occurred in 1971 on an offshore installation, the second in 1988 on a shore-based plant with a fatality and the third in 1991 on an offshore installation with a damage cost of £7 million. In each case the failure of the 'yoke type' closure device on the trap door occurred, resulting in the pressure release of the pig and pipeline. In the 1971 incident the pressure was released from 87.5 bar with the end closure blowing off with hinge and two clamps. In the 1988 incident the pressure had reached 200 bars in a gas scrubber when the closure door was projected across the site approximately 70 metres with other debris scattered over 170 metres away. In the 1991 incident a pig trap door became detached at a pressure of 79.3 bar. The end closure demolished a crane and caused widespread damage to a module structure.

1 The Institution of Chemical Engineers 'Failure of Pig Traps – the importance of learning lessons' (1995) Loss Prevention Bulletin 124.

10.228 The cause of these incidents was attributed to the failure of a nut retaining box. In 1986 an appendix to ASME 8 was issued and these closures would not have met the revised code but all three were designed before the code was promulgated. Nevertheless this type of closure is found in many pig traps, scrubbers, condensate coalescers, large filters etc. It was concluded that if the first '… incident had been made common knowledge, then there is a high probability that the other incidents may not have occurred'.

The manager of a process

10.229 The manager of a process must ensure that all materials brought into a site conform with the specified requirements of the process. Incidents that occur elsewhere in the processing industry must be studied to see if there are any lessons to be learnt. If he or she considers the problem of importing material from another country he or she must take into account the likelihood of a road tanker having the wrong documentation after a ferry crossing.

10.230 Such an incident took place on 3 October 1996 at Avonmouth when a road tanker containing sodium chlorite was offloaded into a tank containing epichlorohydrin. This occurred because the wrong documentation had been picked up after a ferry crossing, resulting in the wrong tanker arriving at the plant. A toxic vapour cloud was released.

10.231 The Chemical Industries Association later found that this was not the first incident of this kind and could easily have been avoided if the previous incidents had been reported and shared.

10.232 The manager must also be aware of all accidents that occur on plants similar to that which he or she is operating.

The maintenance engineer

10.233   The maintenance engineer on a site has to carry out a risk assessment for any significant work. This involves identifying hazards in the work involved and he or she must inform him or herself of hazards they have not already considered, as the following example illustrates:

A piece of chemical plant has been used on olefines duty. It will be necessary to enter the vessel during the coming shutdown and during the risk assessment of the job someone has mentioned the problem of the presence of copper acetylide (an unstable material likely to detonate) in the equipment caused by the use of some copper pipework in the instrumentation. The problem of removing the acetylide before entry is solved when he examines the lessons learnt by other engineers who have experienced the same difficulty with copper acetylide. He is thus able to clean out the equipment with minimum risk.[1]

1   The Institution of Chemical Engineers *The Accident Database* (2000).

The inspector of equipment

10.234   The inspector has to keep abreast of all developments in equipment failures to ensure that his or her inspections will identify any problems. As an example, during the inspection of some pipework the inspection engineer was concerned at the amount of corrosion that had taken place and decided that the section of pipework should be replaced. He was concerned about other pipework that might have underlagging corrosion but could not inspect all of the pipework immediately. To establish which pipework was most likely to be at risk and therefore to be inspected first he examined the records to see if anyone had previously had the same problem. He found an accident where a gasoline pipeline ruptured causing serious injury and fire. The cause was underlagging corrosion and the lessons learnt gave him information on which pipework was most susceptible to this type of corrosion. The inspection engineer was then able to draw up a list of priority inspections.

Those responsible for carrying out a hazard and operability study on a plant

10.235   The leader of a study group given the responsibility of carrying out a HAZOP on a new design has to look at essentially all possible ways the plant can be operated to ensure safety. This involves identifying hazards and the various scenarios that can arise. For example, if a vessel had a submerged pump he or she would have to consider the scenario of having to remove that pump from the vessel for maintenance work. There are no design codes that cover the maintenance of this equipment but the hazard of an open hole in the vessel when the pump is removed is clearly present. Relevant data would show a near-miss, which could have easily been a fatality, when somebody partly fell into an open manhole covered by a piece of thin wood. The lesson learnt was for the provision of a temporary manhole cover of sufficient strength to prevent a person from falling into the vessel. It would therefore be prudent to have a metal cover of at least quarter inch plate attached near to the pump for use when maintenance required it. The HAZOP team has thus used lessons learnt from a near-miss to improve the plant safety.

Those responsible for risk assessments and other safety procedures

10.236 All those responsible for risk assessments and other safety procedures must identify hazards in order to write procedures or control measures to protect those at risk. Some hazards will be known to all experienced person but not all the hazards that others have experienced. The responsible person will consult the records to ensure that all reasonable effort has been made to identify the hazards associated with the job.

10.237

For example, 98% formic acid will decompose at a slow rate, the first order rate constant, K_v, being 13×10^{-10} min^{-1}. This does not tell him that if the product is carried in a marine chemical tanker and transported over an ocean to another continent there is sufficient time for that product to decompose and produce a lethal concentration of carbon monoxide in the tank. This can occur even if the tank is water washed after pumping out, but only full ventilation of the tank will remove the carbon monoxide. Full information of such an accident that occurred on 3 September 1983 is available and the lessons learnt from it can be taken into account.[1]

1 The Institution of Chemical Engineers *The Accident Database* (2000).

10.238 If a material safety data sheet for a product is being prepared the records should be consulted to show what hazards have been experienced with that particular product. In the case of formic acid two accidents involving the release of carbon monoxide will be found.[1] The first, causing fatalities, is given at **para 10.237** above but a second involved the rupture of a glass vessel containing the acid that had been in store for a long period. The person responsible for writing the material safety data sheet would have to consult available accident to find out such information.

1 The Institution of Chemical Engineers *The Accident Database* (2000).

Those responsible for the preparation of emergency plans

10.239 The preparation of emergency plans is required in many cases under COMAH[1] and it is important to plan for the worst scenario that can be reasonably expected. The examination of a report on a possible scenario will assist in determining the emergency services that will be required, the materials, such as foam, that may be required in the event of a fire, the effect on the environment and the remedial efforts that may be necessary.

1 SI 1999/743

Others who can benefit from studying the lessons taught by accidents

10.240 There are others, however, who can profit from lessons of past accidents, and the following points are worth making:

- The emergency services can learn much from the circumstances of actual incidents and hence improve their efficiency. They can learn about the response necessary as well as the materials that they might require.
- Insurance companies can more readily understand the risks associated with production and transport operations if they can see the results in a variety of scenarios of actual accidents. The financial risk is then more readily understood.
- Manufacturers of equipment can improve reliability by knowing the circumstances of a failure in accidents and in some cases improve the design.
- Writers of design standards can take note of relevant accidents to improve the standard.
- Trainers can use case histories to emphasise points to their students. Learning lessons from accidents should be in every engineer's university course to ensure a satisfactory and safe design.

Where lessons can be found

10.241   Accident information should be available within an organisation but recently Trevor Kletz has pointed out in his book *Lessons from Disasters*:[1]

'It might seem to an outsider that industrial accidents occur because we do not know how to prevent them. In fact they occur because we do not use the knowledge that is available. Organisations do not learn from the past or, rather, individuals learn but they leave the organisation, taking their knowledge with them, and the organisation as a whole forgets.'

1   T Kletz *Lessons from Disasters. How organisations have no memory and accidents recur* (1993) p 1.

10.242   While an organisation tries to learn from its own accidents, the loss of experienced staff through early retirement, illness etc often makes this difficult. It is the learning of lessons from accidents occurring *outside* the organisation that presents a greater challenge.

10.243   There are a number of sources of data on accidents from which lessons can be learnt. They are:

- Published reports of serious accidents investigated by a statutory authority either in hardcopy reports or on a website. These are usually of a high quality and much can be learnt from them. They should be incorporated in all accident databases. These reports also report on basic and root causes as well as highlighting the failures in management systems, if any.
- Published reports from conferences and journals devoted to reporting accidents. These are also a good source of information as they contain a full account of the accident and are written by persons having direct knowledge. They may, however, be the company's view and may differ from other reports.
- Organisations' confidential investigation reports. These are good factual reports as they are made for the organisation itself to learn from the accident so as to prevent a recurrence. Most organisations investigate accidents with a thoroughness that establishes most of the causes of an accident including any failures in the management system. However, they are not generally available to professional persons. The Accident Database[1] has been based mainly on these

reports which have been provided to the Institution of Chemical Engineers on a confidential basis and have been abstracted and incorporated in the database, so that all professional persons can learn from the accident.

• Insurance company information. Generally this information has not been found very useful as it does not contain the lessons learnt from the accident. It does, however, help in identifying the frequency of some events.

• Newspaper or journal news reports. These are useful for informing us that an accident has occurred but they are very limited in scope, largely because the information is obtained by journalists who are seeking a human interest story of the injured and who have little training or interest in the details of the accident. They are the basis of many accident databases

1   The Institution of Chemical Engineers *The Accident Database* (2000).

Bretherick's Reactive Chemical Hazards

10.244   There are many lessons to be learnt in the field of chemistry. Early experimenters had to learn the hard way and many a finger or eye was lost as a result of some violent explosion. While chemistry is a science, there are many cases where two or more chemicals do not react in the manner that is normally expected. Additionally there are some by-products from reactions that are not expected. A typical example is the production of a chemical at Seveso in Italy used for the manufacture of an antibacterial compound. In 1976 there was a runaway reaction and discharge to the atmosphere of the product which contained a toxic material, dioxin. This caused serious environmental contamination and a hazard to the public. This incident is used in the EC Directives referred to as Seveso I[1] and Seveso II.[2] The hazard of dioxin formation was well known.

1   Council Directive 52/501/EEC.
2   Council Directive 96/82/EC.

10.245   There are many examples of chemical reaction hazards reported in the literature and it is important that they are recognised before any experimental work is started. Lessons from previous chemical accidents are put together in Bretherick's book.[1] This comprehensive handbook is a standard that should be consulted by every person involved in a new chemical process to ensure that all possibilities of by-products and unusual reactions are considered at an early stage of the project. This handbook is also available in the form of a database on CD that can be searched.

1   *Bretherick's Handbook of Reactive Chemical Hazards* (6th edn, 1999).

The Accident Database of the Institution of Chemical Engineers

10.246   A database has been developed by the Institution of Chemical Engineers[1] to enable industry to learn lessons from accident reports. It has been designed particularly with COMAH[2] in mind to improve the safety, emergency response and environmental performance of the organisation. It is also used in risk assessment, design and other applications and can be combined with other software.[3]

1   The Institution of Chemical Engineers *The Accident Database* (2000).
2   SI 1999/743.
3   J Bond 'Linking an Accident Database to Design and Operational Software' (2003) Hazards XVII, the Institution of Chemical Engineers Symposium Series no 149.

10.247   All accidents and near-misses are keyworded to assist in identifying the hazard or scenario concerned. The following aspects are detailed:

- *Activity*
  The activity that was taking place when the accident happened. This can relate to operation, maintenance, construction etc.

- *Cause*
  The basic cause of the accident and, where reported, the root cause and the failure of the management system involved in the work.

- *Equipment*
  The particular equipment that was involved. These are the normal process equipment names such as distillation column, pump, tank, valve etc.

- *Consequences*
  The consequences of the accident, for example, fatality, injured, explosion, fire etc. In the case of fatalities and injuries the numbers involved are given. The consequences of an accident will allow an organisation to estimate the size of a potential event resulting from a similar accident.

- *Substance*
  The substances (chemical names) involved in the accident.

10.248   The exact nature of an accident that has occurred on a particular process, a particular piece of equipment or with a particular substance can be identified and the lessons learnt established.

10.249   The Accident Database of The Institution of Chemical Engineers obtains its information from those sources listed above. However, it has particular advantages not available in other databases:

- The database receives reports from organisations that have agreed to share their confidential information with others. This includes two large oil companies and a number of chemical companies. These accident reports are not in the public domain and form the basis of the database. All the confidential reports are covered by a management system to protect the confidential nature of the report donated by the organisation.
- There is a free text search facility and a structured keyword system to help the researcher identify a specific type of accident. The keyword system is based on a hierarchy for Activity, Cause, Equipment, Consequence and a separate list of Substances.
- Photographs and diagrams to assist in the understanding of the accident are given.
- Information on the emergency response and environmental damage will be given in future issues.
- The lessons learnt from an accident are an important feature of the database. These are based on the information contained in the original report.
- The database can be used by organisations on their intranet system so that it is readily available to all members. It will be available on the Internet in due course.
- The system is confidential and the database does not report the origin of confidential reports or the town where an event occurred. The company's name and place are only reported when the information is in the public domain.

Other databases

10.250 Other accident databases have been developed by other organisations:
- Major Hazards Incident Data Service (MHIDAS). This database is based on incidents reported in the press and which affect operations only outside a factory. It is produced by AEA Technology for the HSE.
- FACTS. This database is produced by the Prins Maurits Laboratory TNO of The Netherlands and is also based on incidents reported in the press.
- The Process Safety Incident Database produced by the Centre for Chemical Process Safety. This US initiative is only available to those who join and supply information.
- The MARS project of the European Commission is based on information supplied by the member states and is limited to a few major incidents.

10.251 Those reports which base their information on media information lack objectivity and the lessons learnt. However, one problem which applies to all accident databases is the blame culture which forces much of the information to be withheld by companies on advice from their lawyers. This is a short-sighted view as the Comet disasters demonstrated in the 1950s.

10.252 The disasters hit the passengers of the BOAC Comet aircraft in January 1954 with the disintegration in flight of G-ALYP, followed by G-ALYY in April 1954. The investigation involved the pressure testing of a whole aircraft in a water tank. After subjecting the aircraft to simulated pressure fluctuations the main cause of the failure of the aircraft was found to be fatigue cracks at the corner of the windows. This information was released to the whole industry so that aircraft of the future could take advantage of the lessons learnt. The industry and passengers all benefited from this approach. If the information had not been released, many more lives would have been lost before other aircraft manufacturers discovered the problem of fatigue cracks at window corners for themselves.

Journals

10.253 Some journals are specifically devoted to learning lessons from accidents and the systems required to control specific hazards. The Loss Prevention Bulletin, first published in 1974 by The Institution of Chemical Engineers, is one with a long history devoted to learning lessons. The Institution also holds symposia on loss prevention, the most notable of these being the series on HAZARDS.

Management systems

Introduction

10.254 *Successful Health and Safety Management*[1] by the HSE describes in detail the importance of management systems and covers Policy, Organising, Planning and Implementation, Measuring Performance, Reviewing Performance and Auditing operations to identify ways of improving safety.

1   HS(G)65 (1st edn, 1991).

10.255   In the chemical industry establishing detailed management systems is vital for ensuring safe operation and containment of all chemicals. The following systems will often be found:

- Policy statement on subjects such as safety, environment protection etc.
- Preparation of detailed plant operation procedures.
- Permits to work system:
    - clearance certificates;
    - electrical work;
    - hot work certificates;
    - confined entry certificate;
    - excavation certificate;
    - high pressure water jetting certificate;
    - radioactive substance certificate.
- Training system for staff and operators.
- Management of change.
- Learning lessons from accidents.
- Safety audits.
- Occupational health audits.
- Inspection system for all equipment.
- Emergency plans and crisis management.
- Product stewardship.
- Safety cases.

10.256   A systems approach to management is required in the chemical industry:

- To integrate vertically down through a company or organisation a variety of actions covering policies, Directives, safe operating procedures.
- To integrate horizontally across business units to ensure that standards are uniformly met.
- To avoid human, business or financial loss.
- To comply with the law.
- To comply in detail with specific regulations in a uniform manner.

Typical areas requiring management systems

Learning lessons and corporate memory

10.257   A safety management system[1] is necessary to ensure that lessons are learnt from accidents that occur not only within a chemical company but from those that occur in other companies operating the same equipment or process. The management system must cover procedures for learning lessons when developing the concept of the chemical plant, through design, operations, maintenance and inspection to emergency operations and demolition.

1   B Mellin and J Bond 'Learning Lessons from Accidents – The Problems facing an Organisation' (2000) Hazards XV, The Institution of Chemical Engineers Symposium Series no 147.

10.258   Learning the lessons from accidents with chemicals or chemical equipment from within an organisation and from others outside the organisation is a key requirement for achieving continuous improvements in safety. Unless such a commitment is forthcoming, the enhancement of corporate knowledge in the chemical industry will be limited.

10.259 To be effective, health and safety policies need to demonstrate that health and safety is an integral part of business performance and efficiency. The policy statement must reflect a commitment to learn the lessons from accidents and hence produce safer processes, safer designs, safer operations, safer systems of work and a more informed, competent and knowledgeable workforce.

10.260 Corporate memory can be captured and maintained within an establishment but it needs to be augmented by the experience of others, gleaned from an accident database.

10.261 To ensure that this enlarged experience is regularly tapped, a management system has to be devised and used. As with all safety matters, commitment starts at the top, and the management system described above is essential for maintenance of the corporate memory.

Permits to work

10.262 Permits are required to hand over equipment which may be contaminated with chemicals from one set of workers to another. This is necessary to control work between diverse groups of people where formalised systems are essential. They will define the work to be carried out, the safety equipment to be used, the method used for removing any chemical present and give specific permission to carry out certain types of hazardous operations.

10.263 Those permitted to sign the various types of certificates must be clearly specified and it made quite clear that authorisation is limited to only those stated.

10.264 Typical permits are:

- Clearance certificates to carry out work on chemical plant.
- Electrical work.
- Hot work certificate where the work might ignite any flammable material.
- Confined entry certificate into spaces that may contain toxic material.
- Excavation certificates for ground that may have buried electrical cables or pipelines.
- High pressure water jetting certificate.
- Radioactive substance certificate.

Training

10.265 Training is expensive – but the price of not training is far greater! A management system for training is an essential part of the overall system for managing the operation and would cover:

- *Policy for training*
  Induction
  Job-specific knowledge
  Job-specific skills
  Refresher training

- *Identification of training needs*
  Job requirement
  Individual profile
- *Development of programme*
  On-the-job training
  Off-the-job training
  Training competence
- *Testing*
- *Evaluation of the programme*
  Individual performance
  Training methods
  Training content
    – changes in task inventory
    – new equipment
    – new procedure
    – new knowledge required
    – new skills required
- *The supervisor's role*

Management of change

10.266   The modification of a plant may well introduce new hazards and unless these are identified, problems may well be introduced. The famous case of Flixborough was a classical case where a modification was made to an existing plant in order to overcome a production problem. The result was a vapour cloud explosion which killed 28 people, destroyed the plant and damaged many houses surrounding the works.

10.267   A management system for any change is required to control the change so that the authorisation for the change or modification is not given until all possible hazards are considered and the risk assessed. This includes a check against the original design intent.

10.268   What constitutes a change or modification? The basic changes that have to be considered are:
- A change to the plant equipment. This includes:
  – changing the type of equipment, even changing the type of valve used or the supplier of a flexible hose;
  – changing the pipework; and
  – any alteration of the equipment.
- A change in the chemistry of the process. This includes:
  – the order of adding chemicals;
  – changing the temperature or pressure greater than certain values defined in the design intent; and
  – changing the catalyst.
- Alteration to the manning of a plant.

10.269   Any of these changes require a careful consideration of all circumstances to identify any new hazard and the risk established. The change/modification must only be authorised when the risk has been fully examined and reduced to an acceptable level. All documents must be kept with the details of the design.

10.270   A management system to control a change/modification is essential and should be part of the safety manual. Further information on the management of change is given in S G Turner *Pharmaceutical Manufacturing Change Control* (1999).

Inspection system

10.271   Inspection of equipment, both internally and externally, is an essential part of maintaining the integrity of the process. A management system describing and laying down the frequency and conditions for the inspection is necessary to obtain a quality system.

10.272   Inspection of equipment internally and pressure testing is a vital part of ensuring the integrity and hence safety of the equipment. Some of these inspections are a requirement of statutory regulation and some a requirement of company or industry standards. The frequency of internal inspections is determined by:

- statutory requirements;
- the corrosion potential of the chemical involved;
- the risk of release of the chemical involved; and
- company or industry standards.

10.273   A comprehensive list of equipment should be maintained and detailed internal inspection records kept. From the results of the inspection the period to the next inspection can be set unless covered by a statutory inspection requirement. Internal inspections are carried out for:

- Signs of corrosion.
- Defects in welds.
- Defects in metal, for example:
  - cracks from stress corrosion; and
  - cracks from fatigue.
- Defects in internal equipment.

10.274   Internal inspections are carried out on:

- pressure vessels, including boilers;
- reactors;
- heat exchangers;
- furnaces;
- other vessels and tanks;
- pipelines;
- flexible hoses;
- bellows;
- turbines; and
- flame arresters.

10.275   Pressure testing is carried out on:

- pressure vessels including boilers;
- heat exchangers;
- flexible hoses; and
- relief valves and alarm systems.

10.276   External inspection of all equipment is also required to ensure the integrity of equipment. The inspection requirements are primarily for corrosion, damage and wear. All equipment should be covered by a comprehensive record system which details the frequency of inspection and the observations made. The equipment which should be covered includes:

- External corrosion of pipework especially where there has been:
  - moisture penetration of lagging;
  - source of chlorides from lagging, sea water or plant; or
  - containing material above ambient and particularly 60°C to 116°C.
- Support legs of equipment particular those covered in fire protection concrete.
- Explosion relief devices.
- Electrical switchgear and similar equipment.
- Electrical motors for insulation defects.
- Lifting gear, wire ropes and cranes.
- Ladders.
- Pipelines:
  - no building or construction;
  - no subsidence; and
  - Pearson survey.
- Checks on pumps, reciprocating pumps.
- Fire equipment, fire hydrants, sprinklers.
- Tools.

10.277   It is important to ensure the competency of those who are carrying out the inspection system and to see that records are properly kept for all equipment and their state at each inspection. Recommendations from the inspectors should be recorded. Signatures for each inspection and recommendations must be obtained and the reports passed to a senior person in the organisation who can authorise the necessary repair or maintenance work necessary.

10.278   A follow-up procedure for all recommendations should be made to ensure that no recommendation is forgotten.

Emergency plans

10.279   An emergency starts the moment a person discovers something unusual whether it be a fire on the plant, a problem on a ship or a drum at the roadside. The actions that follow the start of the emergency will determine how soon the problem is cleared up or whether it escalates. Emergency instructions local to the event will be activated to deal with the situation and if these are followed then there is a good chance that will be the end of the problem. However, in a number of cases it is not and the local emergency starts to escalate, the problem becomes greater than the local team can manage. It is important at this stage that the company representatives can handle the emergency so that it does not get out of hand.

Crisis management

10.280   Crisis management builds upon the philosophy of emergency management to address the full range of crisis that can strike at all organisational levels of a company and to manage the consequences of those cases. A crisis management programme will apply to those plant emergencies that might create a crisis for the company, as well as the range of other types of potential crises such as financial, legal or communication problems, company image and reputation, natural disasters, product hazards and changes in political or regulatory climate.

10.281 Crisis management is a broader strategic effort, of which the tactical approach of emergency management is an element.

10.282 It is important to recognise that the scale of an incident is not the sole determinant of its potential to develop into a crisis. Other factors could come into play, for example, communications, political environments, recent similar incidents etc.

10.283 Crisis management can generally be defined as those activities undertaken to anticipate or prevent, prepare for, respond to and recover from any incident that has the potential greatly to affect the way a company conducts its business. Rather then being a reactionary process, crisis management encompasses several proactive activities. It is important that the management system is detailed and training carried out to ensure its effectiveness. Dummy runs should also be organised.

Product stewardship

10.284 Product stewardship is the responsible and ethical management of products throughout their life-cycle. It is a management system which seeks to prevent harm to health or the environment at all stages of a product's life (product life-cycle). It is concerned with:

• the production and marketing products that can be used safely; and
• respecting the interests of neighbours and the world community.

10.285 Product stewardship covers all aspects of research, development, manufacture, storage, distribution, applications, foreseeable misuse and disposal.

10.286 It therefore requires commitment from management, employees and all parties involved in the chain of supply from raw material sourcing to the ultimate use and fate.

10.287 The requirements for information which must be available for all products produced include:

• maintain a record of all applicable chemical, physical and biological information and assess all foreseeable risks to health and the environment;
• maintain a database of product material safety data sheets summarising the health, safety and environmental assessments and supporting information;
• ensure periodic review of product information and update as necessary;
• ensure that all involved in product research, manufacture, distribution, business and marketing have access to and understand product health, safety and environmental information;
• ensure that customers are provided with relevant information; and
• ensure that assistance is available in the field sales organisation in communicating and explaining product health, safety and environmental information.

Safety cases

10.288   A safety case has to be prepared under current legislation when certain operations are carried out and when certain quantities of material is stored or used. The safety case is primarily a statement of the management system being used on the site to identify all of the hazards likely to be experienced and to demonstrate the how they are controlled to reduce the risk to acceptable levels.

10.289   The safety case will contain details of:

* design concepts;
* the management system;
* the site organisation;
* the operating and emergency procedures;
* the training programmes;
* etc.

Competent authority

10.290   It is a vital part of each management system or procedure that the authority for all decisions is clearly stated so that there is no ambiguity in any of the management systems. It is vital that the chain of authority through out the company is clear and transparent.

Auditing for safety

Introduction

10.291   A safety audit is a systematic scrutiny of an area of a company's operation by a team of appropriately qualified personnel with the object of minimising loss. Every activity, plant, or installation, including research and site management, should be included. The examination should cover abstract features, such as attitudes and awareness, as well as leadership, condition of plant, operating procedures, emergency plans, personnel protection, maintenance standards, fire protection, housekeeping, accident frequency, training etc.

10.292   An audit sets out to reveal the weaknesses and areas of vulnerability of the system or plant. A formal report is then submitted to management which assesses the hazards with proper regard to economic realities and puts forward recommendations covering the actions necessary to achieve an acceptable standard.

10.293   Safety audits may be used for:

* identification of possible loss-producing situations;
* assessment of potential losses associated with these risks;
* selection of measures to minimise the losses;
* implementation of these measures within the organisation; and
* monitoring of the changes.

Objectives

10.294 It is a recognised part of any good management practice to initiate a system of inspection to check that operations are carried out efficiently, in accordance with company policy and to ensure that complacency has not resulted in a lowering of standards.

10.295 Various yardsticks are available for assessing the efficiency of a safety programme, such as accident frequency and severity rates, financial loss accounting etc. All these methods have one thing in common. They monitor performance after the event when the damage has been done. Moreover, they give little indication of the potential for accidents in a plant or activity. An unsafe condition will not reveal itself in any of the above indices until it has brought about an accident. Auditing seeks to ensure that out assets are effectively safeguarded by drawing attention to unsuspected dangers before an accident takes place.

10.296 Very briefly the objectives can be stated as follows:

- to carry out a systematic critical survey of all potential hazards involving personnel, plant, services and methods;
- to ensure that all operations affecting the health and safety of employees, the public, or the integrity of company property fully meets the requirements laid down in the policy statement for health and safety, fully comply with marketing standards and at least meet local statutory requirements; and
- to report to management any areas of activity which do not meet the standards and to recommend the appropriate remedial action.

Types of safety audits

10.297 Safety audits may be carried out the whole of a safety management system or on individual parts. Typically parts that may be audited are:

- work permit systems;
- modification system;
- vessel inspection system;
- a particular plant;
- construction of a pipeline;
- training system;
- accident reports;
- fire-fighting equipment; and
- contractors.

Scope

10.298 All work areas of a company should be covered by the audit programme. This should include offices, jetties, plants, research, storage areas, loading bays etc as well as management procedures, operating procedures and similar activities. No area of activity need by excluded from a safety audit but clearly priority has to be given to those areas which have the highest potential for loss.

The audit team

10.299   The principle factor in deciding how an audit team is to be organised is the size of the company. Large companies can call on suitable specialists from within their own organisation and should have little difficulty. Smaller companies may feel that they either do not have sufficient experience to make up a team or that their qualified personnel cannot be spared. In this case management should not hesitate to call in outside help.

10.300   While the size of the area to be audited will influence the number of people involved, in general the audit team may consist of one to three people. An experienced person may carry out the audit him or herself or they may have additionally a young engineer who can gain experience from the audit. An audit of a large plant may require a team of three people, sometimes of different disciplines, but very large teams are not recommended.

10.301   The manager or superintendent of the plant or area being audited should be made available for answering questions or provide explanations. He or she should not form part of the audit team.

Frequency of audits

10.302   It is impossible to lay down fixed auditing frequencies since these depend on a number of sometimes conflicting factors. The following criteria will provide guidance to enable a company to establish an auditing programme.

10.303   The factors to be considered are:

*   *Hazard* – what is the potential for accidents? A liquid propane gas plant, for example, would be expected to present a greater hazard than a boiler house.

*   *Environment* – an incident in a plant where toxic or flammable material can be released to the atmosphere will have a greater consequence than the same release in an isolated place.

*   *Importance to company operations* - the plants where an unscheduled shutdown would have a large effect on profitability should receive more frequent attention than those facilities that are less important.

*   *Accident records* – the safety performance as indicated by accident/incident frequency should be taken into account.

10.304   Attention should also be paid to the attitude, experience and qualifications of the manager and senior staff.

10.305   Audits should be in addition to routine visits carried out as part of routine managerial procedures.

Implementation

10.306   Auditing is perhaps an unfortunate word in that it conjures up a picture of some sort of financial investigation. The audit team should therefore make it quite clear to the management of the plant or installation in question that a safety audit is not a disciplinary operation It is a tool to help the local management to create a safer and more profitable place of work. This message must be got across to gain the confidence of the people whose plant is to be audited. Without the co-operation of these people the audit is unlikely to be successful. Informal contact should also be made with individual workers to gain their views on safety. It is a frequent experience that much important information can be obtained by talking to those directly involved. An audit that is confined to discussions with supervisors and management is unlikely to be effective.

10.307   No matter what type of activity is to be covered the whole audit will involve five main elements, three in the report and two in the follow-up procedure:

1   Identification of potential hazards. These may be abstract, such as poor attitudes to safety, or physical such as inadequate fire fighting appliances.
2   Evaluation of the extent and consequences of possible losses due to the above hazards. This may be difficult to assess and too much time should not be spent on it.
3   Recommendations for suitable remedial measures to eliminate or minimise losses which could be caused by the hazard identified. In some cases the recommendation could be to investigate further.
4   Acceptance and subsequent implementation of the recommendations or a written explanation why they will not be implemented.
5   Monitoring the implementation of the recommendations.

10.308   It will be seen that items 1, 2 and 3 are part of the audit team's duties while items 4 and 5 are a management responsibility.

Organisation of an audit

10.309   An important prelude to a safety audit is to study the accident record of the installation together with the plant layout, location and type of operation. This is to obtain a general background to the facility before the audit commences.

10.310   While there are advantages and disadvantages in giving advance warning that a visit is to be made, practical considerations will usually dictate the decision. In general advance notice should be limited.

10.311   The audit itself will start with a discussion with the plant management and the safety representatives or members of the safety committee concerning the administration of safety. While there are a number of detailed questions to be resolved, an important aspect of this part of the inspection is to obtain an idea of the general attitude to safety.

10.312   The interview will be followed by a detailed inspection of the plant area and should include observation of some of the more critical work activities actually being carried out, for example, a road tanker being loaded.

10.313   Finally, the results of the visit and the findings should be reviewed and discussed with the plant management prior to producing the report.

Management control audit

10.314   An audit may also be part of an overall management control system for safety, for pollution control or for quality assurance. In this case a regular audit may be carried out of various aspects of the safety system by different people each time to ensure overall control of the risk management system.

Auditing contractors

10.315   Contractors are always audited to establish:

- the quality of the product or service given;
- their productivity and efficiency; and
- loss prevention aspects of their work.

10.316   Typically this type of audit is carried out on:

- those providing an engineering service;
- those concerned with transporting the company's products by road, rail or sea; and
- other services.

10.317   It is important to establish a relationship with the contractor so that they are aware of the standards required by the company.

Safety management auditing

10.318   More extensive and detailed auditing systems have been developed which measures the performance of management in a number of areas relating to safety, occupational health and pollution control. An example is given below using the International Safety Rating System for safety and occupational health.

10.319   Typical areas for which such processes are required include:

- management, leadership;
- information and documentation;
- design and construction chemical plant;
- risk assessment/management;
- training/competence;
- operations/maintenance;
- management of change;
- contractors and suppliers;
- accident investigation/analysis;
- emergency preparedness;
- products and customers;
- community relations; and
- evaluation and improvement.

10.320   Twenty elements are audited in addition to a physical inspection of the site. The elements are audited using a series of questions to ascertain what is actually done. It is not based solely on what procedures are in place but tries to audit what is actually done by the management. It encourages a new management philosophy of prevention rather than reaction to events.

10.321 This system of auditing has many advantages:

* it identifies the weak points in the system adopted;
* it shows where limited resources should be used to improve safety; and
* it shows the performance of the site against a high standard.

10.322 It is not intended as an audit to blame people for any shortcomings. It recognises that all personnel wish to see an improvement in safety and therefore the system may be used to achieve this objective.

10.323 It may appear to be somewhat lengthy and associated with a lot of paperwork but I would assure you that it is very efficient in its operation and does create a new approach to loss prevention. It is very motivating to people to achieve a better safety performance and for the first time shows management where the weak points are. Knowing this management can use scarce resources in an efficient manner.

10.324 The emphasis is on the importance of measuring the preventative approach of management in the field of loss prevention. In financial management you do not wait for an embezzlement to occur before you carry out a balance.

Professional responsibility in the chemical industry

General duty of care

10.325 Every person employed in the chemical industry is covered by HSWA 1974 and has a duty of care under HSWA 1974, s 7:

'It shall be the duty of every employee while at work—
(a) to take reasonable care for the health and safety of himself and other persons who may be affected by his acts or omissions at work, and
(b) as regards any duty or requirement imposed on his employer or any other person by or under any of the relevant statutory provisions, to co-operate with him so far as is necessary to enable that duty or requirement to be performed or complied with.'

10.326 The professionally qualified person not only has this duty of care under HSWA 1974 but also has duties laid down by virtue of membership of their professional body. These professional bodies encourage professional development and usually have a recording system to ensure that the development covers safety matters. They also provide safety information and it could be argued that a professionally qualified person should be a member of their professional body in order to obtain this information to carry out their duty of care. It can also be said that an organisation should provide for continuous professional development, if only to receive the safety information necessary for him or her to carry out their work.

The Engineering Council

10.327 A Royal Charter established the Engineering Council in 1981 and one objective was:

> '… to advance education in, and to promote the science and practice of engineering (including relevant technology) for the public benefit and thereby to promote industry and commerce …'

10.328 The Engineering Council seeks to achieve this objective by a number of aims including:

- increasing awareness of the essential and beneficial part engineering plays in all aspects of modern life;
- spreading best engineering practice to improve the efficiency and competitiveness of business; and
- advancing engineering knowledge through education and training.

10.329 These aims are achieved in a number of ways, including:

- stressing the need for a proper balance between efficiency, public safety and the needs of the environment when carrying out engineering activities.

10.330 Chartered engineers, incorporated engineers and engineering technicians registered with the Engineering Council undertake a duty to the community under the Code and Rules of Conduct, rule 1:

> 'A registrant shall at all times and in all aspects:
> (a) take all reasonable care to avoid creating any danger of death, injury or ill-health to any person or of damage to property by any act or omission whilst carrying out his/her work, save to the extent that the creation of such danger is lawfully authorised;
> (b) take all reasonable care to protect the working and living environments of himself/herself and others and to ensure the efficient use of materials and resources;
> (c) conduct himself/herself so as to safeguard the public interest in matters of safety and health and in a manner consistent with the dignity and reputation of the engineering profession; and
> (d) notwithstanding the provisions of any of the Rules or Codes of professional Practice, comply with all laws and regulations applicable to his/her professional work.'

10.331 In the Notes for Guidance it is stated:

> 'The important feature of this Rule (viz 1(d) [see **para 10.330** above]) is that more is demanded of the registrant than bare compliance with existing law. Full compliance is required, not only in the letter but also in the spirit. Ambiguities or loopholes in the law, regulations, etc, must not be exploited in an effort to reduce costs if engineering judgement shows that safety or the environment would be jeopardised as a result. In safety and environmental matters the statutory requirements should be regarded as no more than minima. Even when these requirements have been satisfied, the Council still looks to the registrant

to take such further measures as his or her engineering judgement shows to be necessary for securing public safety and preservation of the environment, in accordance with Rule 1.'

10.332 *Guidelines on Risk Issues*[1] published by the Engineering Council, in section 6, Communications, states:

'Engineers should pay particular attention to effective feedback on incidents and 'near misses', so that lessons can be learned.'

1 The Engineering Council *Guidelines on Risk Issues* (1993).

The Institution of Chemical Engineers

10.333 The Institution of Chemical Engineers was founded in 1922 and incorporated by Royal Charter in 1957. Section 12 ii) (b) of the By-laws[1] states:

'Every Corporate Member shall at all times so order his conduct as to uphold the dignity and reputation of his profession and safeguard the public interest in matters of safety, health and otherwise. He shall exercise his professional skill and judgement to the best of his ability and discharge his professional responsibilities with integrity.'

1 Institution of Chemical Engineers *Royal Charter, By-laws, Rules of Professional Conduct and Disciplinary Regulations* (1999).

10.334 The Rules of Professional Conduct[1] states in section 4:

'A member shall take all reasonable care in his work to minimise the risk of death, injury, or ill-health to any person, or of damage to property. In his work, a member shall respect all laws and statutory regulations applicable to the design, operation and maintenance of chemical and processing plant. In addition a member shall have due regard for the need to protect working and living environments, and the need to ensure efficient use of natural raw materials and resources.'

1 Institution of Chemical Engineers *Royal Charter, By-laws, Rules of Professional Conduct and Disciplinary Regulations* (1999).

10.335 More recently on the 20 September 2001 at the Sixth World Congress of Chemical Engineering the 20 organisations representing chemical engineers worldwide signed up to The Melbourne Communiqué.[1] In the field of safety this statement makes the following points:

'… We are committed to the highest standards of personal and product safety.

… We will practice our profession according to its high ethical standards.

… We acknowledge both our professional responsibilities and the need to work with others as we strive to meet the challenges facing the world in the Twenty-First Century.'

1 The Institution of Chemical Engineers *The Melbourne Communiqué*, 27 September 2001.

The Royal Society of Chemistry

10.336   In the Code of Conduct and Guidance on Professional Practice[1] and the section on The Chemist and Society it is stated:

'As members of the Society, chemists have social responsibilities arising from their fundamental duty to serve the public interest, particularly in the fields of health, safety and the environment.
    Chemists have a duty to identify the hazards and assess the risks of scientific and technological activities and processes. They must strive for the highest standards of care in their own workplace and take an active interest in safety throughout the organisation. They have a right to protest about malpractice, while maintaining a sense of proportion, and they can expect the support of the Society if their efforts are unavailing.'

1   Royal Society of Chemistry *Code of Conduct and Guidance on professional Practice* (1999).

The professional person in the chemical industry

10.337   Every person has a duty of care towards others under HSWA 1974 but the professionally qualified engineer or scientist has an additional duty as a result of belonging to his or her professional organisation. This additional duty results from the training they have received to identify the risks involved in their sphere of work. There is a general requirement to achieve a risk as low as reasonably practical (ALARP).

10.338   The ALARP principle is an important concept that requires a professional person:

*   To balance the cost involved against the benefit to be achieved.
*   To consider other ways of carrying out the work which lowers the risk but which is also practical.
*   To identify not only those hazards that a professional might reasonably be expected to know but also those that can be established by consulting:
    –   other persons;
    –   books;
    –   databases; and
    –   other sources.

10.339   The professional must use all resources he or she considers appropriate in order to reduce the risks to him or herself, to others at his or her place of work and to the public at large. If these resources are withheld or not available then this must be drawn to the attention of his or her manager.

Technical integrity and competence

10.340   Technical integrity has been defined:[1]

'Technical integrity is concerned with the development of the design such that it is carried out by well trained personnel, who have been assessed competent, in accordance with recognised, sound practices and procedures and such that there is adequate provision by way of reviews and audits, to ensure the design intent is unimpaired in any way that could cause undue risk or harm to people or damage to the environment.'

1   EA Bale and DW Edwards 'Technical Integrity – An Engineer's View' (2000) 78 Trans IChemE Part B, September.

10.341   The question of competence is also mentioned in this reference[1] from the Australian Institute of Engineers:

'The ability to perform the activities within the occupation or function to the standard expected in employment.'

1   EA Bale and DW Edwards 'Technical Integrity – An Engineer's View' (2000) 78 Trans IChemE Part B, September.

10.342   All engineering and managerial staff in a company must display these attributes of integrity and competence. This approach must also be established in the contractors employed for certain activities.

Company culture

10.343   The prime concerns of an organisation are:

*   to produce a quality product or service that satisfies the customer;
*   to operate efficiently so that there is an adequate return on the capital involved; and
*   to provide a safe system of work that minimises the impact on the environment.

10.344   The emphasis on each of these concerns will be dependent upon various factors including the potential to cause harm. The amount of time, money and effort spent on these primary areas of concern has to be judged by the management. The operations in the chemical industry by their nature require a high level of money and effort to maintain a satisfactory level of safety and environmental protection. The successful organisation is the one that gets the blend of these correct. Organisations have to remember that as a result of their operations:

*   at risk are the employees, the community and the customers; and
*   the audience is the authorities, the pressure groups, the media, other companies and the trades unions.

10.345   The clear responsibility for all this lies with the management of the organisation and the chief operating executive as the head of the management team. Safety, occupational health and environmental issues have, in the past, been based on reacting to events but the more modern concept of loss prevention is concerned with preventing the loss of people or their services, of equipment or of material. It incorporates safety, occupational health and environmental issues and is concerned with preventing the unwanted event from happening. Loss prevention is thus a proactive approach to accident prevention and must be part of the policy of the organisation.

10.346   An organisation will reflect its culture in its:

- commitment to the customer, the employee and the community by the senior management team;
- commitment to the importance of human factors, covering the job, the individual and the organisation;
- commitment to measuring the performance of individuals against standards; and
- commitment to sharing accident information to prevent a recurrence.

Responsible care in the chemical industry

10.347   Responsible care is a voluntary commitment to a continuous programme for all aspects of health, safety and environmental (HS&E) improvements. The programme is agreed with the International Council of Chemical Associations (ICCA). In the UK the Chemical Industries Association has adopted this programme.[1] The Responsible Care Guiding Principles are:

'Members of the Chemical Industries Association are committed to managing their activities so that they present an acceptable high level of protection for the health and safety of employees, customers, the public and the environment.

The following Guiding Principles form the basis of the commitment:

- Companies should ensure that their health, safety and environmental policy reflects the commitment and is clearly seen to be an integral part of their overall business policy.
- Companies should ensure that management, employees at all levels and those in contractual relationships with the Company are aware of their commitment and are involved in the achievement of their policy objectives.
- All Company activities and operations must be conducted in accordance with relevant statutory obligations. In addition, Companies should operate to the best practices of the industry and in accordance with Government and Association guidance.

In particular, Companies should:

- Assess the actual and potential impact of their activities and products on the health and safety of employees, customers, the public and the environment.
- Where appropriate, work closely with public and statutory bodies in the development and implementation of measures designed to achieve an acceptable high level of health, safety and environmental protection.
- Make available to employees, customers, the public and statutory bodies, relevant information about activities that affect health, safety and the environment.

Members of the Association recognise that these Principles and activities should continue to be kept under regular review.'

1   Chemical Industries Association *Responsible Care Management System – Guidance* (3rd edn, 1988).

10.348   The responsible care programme requires:

- Leadership and commitment – strong and effective leadership is essential to ensure that high standards are maintained and performance targets are achieved.

Leadership should demonstrate their commitment to all employees and stakeholders in a highly visible way.
- Managers and leaders at all levels in the organisation should ensure that the effectiveness of the management system is maintained.
- Under current HS&E legislation, employers have legal obligations to provide safe and healthy working conditions and carry out operations in such a way that prevents harm to the environment.

10.349   The Guidance Document states:

'Section 6.6.3 Communicating with others.

Organisations should:

Share relevant HS&E knowledge and lessons learnt from incidents to help prevent others from experiencing similar incidents.'

The Nigel Turnbull Report and the chemical industry

10.350   The *Turnbull Report*[1] states in Principle D.2 of the Code:

'The board should maintain a sound system of internal control to safeguard shareholders' investment and the company's assets.'

1   N Turnbull *The Internal Control: Guidance for Directors on the Combined Code* (the *Turnbull Report*) (1999).

10.351   A working party on internal control chaired by Nigel Turnbull examined Principle D.2 and the associated provisions and produced a report.[1] The following sections of this report refer to the management of risk and are particularly relevant to the chemical industry:

'10. A company's system of internal control has a key role in the management of risks that are significant to the fulfilment of its business objectives. A sound system of internal control contributes to safeguarding the shareholders' investment and the company's assets ...

It is the role of management to implement board policies on risk and control. In fulfilling its responsibilities, management should identify and evaluate the risks faced by the company for consideration by the board and design, operate and monitor a suitable system of internal control which implements the policies adopted by the board ...

19. All employees have some responsibility for internal control as part of their accountability for achieving objectives. They, collectively, should have the necessary knowledge, skills, information and authority to establish, operate and monitor the system of internal control. This will require an understanding of the company, its objectives, the industries and markets in which it operates, and the risks it faces ...

When reviewing reports during the year, the board should:

Consider what are the significant risks and assess how they have been identified, evaluated and managed; etc.'

1   N Turnbull *The Internal Control: Guidance for Directors on the Combined Code* (the *Turnbull Report*) (1999).

What the boardroom must deal with

10.352   The HSE has reported:[1]

> 'The cost to employers of personal injury work accidents and work related ill
> health is estimated to be around £1.5 billion a year (in 1990 prices) about £900
> million for injuries and £600 million for illness. In addition, the cost caused by
> avoidable non-injury accidental events is estimated to be between £2.9 billion
> and £7.7 billion a year. The cost of these non-injury accidental loss events
> should be added to the costs of personal injury accidents and work-related ill
> health since the same or similar underlying management failures are responsible
> for non-injury accidental events and personal injury accidents; the outcome
> severity of a management failure is largely a matter of chance. The total cost to
> employers can on this basis be estimated to be between £4 billion and over £9
> billion a year (including insurance). To put this cost into context, it is equivalent
> to around 5% to 10% of all industrial companies' gross trading profits, and
> averages between £170 and £360 per person employed.'

1   HSE *The costs to the British economy of work accidents and work-related ill health* (1994).

10.353   Clearly the experience of all industrial bodies indicates that safety is worth
a lot of money and that profits can be increased appreciably by preventing accidents.
The emphasis has to be on using a variety of loss prevention approaches and not just
those that are the minimum needed to comply with the regulations.

10.354   To help others avoid losses the industry as a whole and its professional
engineers and scientists must be prepared to share the lessons learnt. The sharing of
lessons learnt from accidents are an essential part of loss prevention. Identifying
hazards is the starting point.

Conclusions

10.355   While management systems and auditing of chemical plants are well
established it is important that these are maintained at all times. Other important areas
that must be established and recognised are learning lessons from other accidents
and recognising the responsibilities of engineers and scientists.

Learning lessons

10.356   The globalisation of industry calls for a greater emphasis on learning lessons
from accidents if the increased number of manufacturing plants around the world is to
avoid their own disasters. Learning the hard way, as a colloquial English saying has it;
means learning from ones own bad experience. An easier and less costly way for industry
is, of course, to learn from the experience of others. Organisations in newly developed
countries, for instance, can take advantage of the combined experience of nations that
have been industrialised for a longer period of time. To adapt a well-known saying:

> 'A wise organisation learns from its own experience but a wiser organisation
> learns from the experience of others.'

10.357 Growing public unease over safety and environmental matters will inevitably lead to more litigation, whether in the civil or the criminal courts. It seems probable that in the twenty-first century defendants will have to show that they have learnt and put into practice the lessons taught by previous accidents not only within their own organisation but also outside it. Given modern communications and the electronic storage and retrieval of accident data, ignorance will no longer be acceptable as a mitigating factor. A rigorous management system to incorporate the learning of lessons at all levels in an organisation should therefore be a priority in this century's approach to safety and environmental protection.

The professional person

10.358 Professionals in the chemical industry, as in other industries, have a duty of care in all their work, and as members of a professional organisation they have additional responsibilities under its Charter and Rules. Moreover, by virtue of their training and experience, they have a greater knowledge of processes, equipment, substances etc and must use this knowledge to foster a culture of safety at all levels.

10.359 As the twenty-first century advances and the pace of technological innovation quickens, it can be expected that fresh hazards will present themselves. There will consequently be a greater onus on the professional to keep abreast of new developments in his or her sphere of expertise and to investigate the safety implications of them.

CHAPTER 11

Oil and gas

David Leckie[1] Maclay Murray & Spens

1   Thanks to Graeme Anthony, Dr Tony Cox and Judith Tocher for their review and to Claire Andrew, Simon Bennett, Simone Girson, and Keith Miskelly for their research and assistance.

11.1

'North Sea oil is, and has been, of fundamental significance to the UK economy. It generates wealth to the Exchequer, profit to the oil companies, and employment for many thousands of people. However, it must be said that oil production is a frontier industry. Its employees work in extreme conditions, often in circumstances of great danger, and in a market that is both volatile and highly competitive. There must be no possibility at any time of profit being put before the welfare of those in the industry who create the profit. Those brave men and women who work offshore are entitled to the highest possible standards of safety and to the full guarantee of the state that it will police those standards, enforce them rigorously and prosecute any who break them.'[1]

1   Mr Tony Blair MP, 203 HC Official Report (6th series) col 677, 10 February 1992.

Introduction

11.2   Mainstream exploration for oil and gas in the UK commenced in 1965.[1] The industry was pioneering, dynamic and promised great rewards. It also faced enormous technical, operational and safety challenges. The hazards which are inherent in such exploration activity soon led to disaster. In December 1965, the *Sea Gem* jack-up barge sank in the southern North Sea, with the loss of 13 lives. The resulting public inquiry[2] noted that there was no legislation in place to enforce a licensee's[3] safety duties and led to the enactment of the Mineral Workings (Offshore Installations) Act 1971.

1   The first commercial discovery was made in 1918 in Nottinghamshire. However, the first offshore gas field was discovered in the Sole Field in 1965 and the first oil was discovered in the Arbroath Field in 1967. Wytch Farm in Dorset was the first major onshore oil field discovery in 1973.
2   *Report of the Inquiry into the Causes of the Accident to the Drilling Rig Sea Gem* (Cmnd 3409, 1967). See **para 11.40** below.
3   A licensee is a company licensed by the Government to explore and produce oil and gas in UK waters.

11.3   Despite these changes and the enactment of the Health and Safety at Work etc Act 1974 (HSWA 1974), there was relatively little industry-specific safety legislation in the UK until the publication of the Cullen Report,[1] following the tragic loss of 167 lives in the Piper Alpha disaster in 1988.[2] Although this remains the worst offshore disaster in oil and gas history, no criminal prosecution was ever instigated by the Scottish authorities. However, the disaster led to a public inquiry, chaired by Lord Cullen, which itself made history at the time by becoming the longest ever public inquiry of its kind, lasting 180 days. Legal history was also made by the length of the ensuing civil litigation, which finally concluded in the House of Lords in 2002.[3]

1   The Hon Lord Cullen *The Public Inquiry into the Piper Alpha Disaster* (the Cullen Report) (Cmnd 1310, 1990). See **para 11.59** below.
2   See **para 11.48** below.
3   *Caledonia North Sea Ltd v London Bridge Engineering Ltd* [2002] UKHL 4, (2002) 1 All ER (Comm) 321; see also the English case of *E E Caledonia Ltd v Orbit Valve Co* (1994) 1 WLR 1515.

11.4   The result of the Cullen Report was a fundamental and radical overhaul of the safety regime in the industry. Billions of pounds have been spent by the industry in implementing all of Lord Cullen's 106 recommendations and in making other changes to the safety regime, in an attempt to ensure that a disaster on the scale of Piper Alpha will not happen again..[1] The Cullen Report also led directly to the enactment of a range of detailed industry-specific regulations which set up a new and rigorous safety regime.

1   Cullen Report, **para 11.3 n 1** above. The AUPEC survey, *Evaluation of the Offshore Safety Legislation Regime* (EOSLR) (1999), estimates that for the period 1988–98 total 'Cullen costs' were between £2.24 and £2.43 billion: see www aupec.com.

11.5   Criminal liability for health and safety failures in the industry can arise as follows:

*   HSWA 1974 – general duties under ss 2–7;
*   individual directors, managers and officers – HSWA 1974, s 37;
*   offshore safety regulations, such as the Offshore Installations (Safety Case) Regulations 1992[1] (SCR), the Offshore Installations and Pipeline Works (Management and Administration) Regulations 1995[2] (MAR), the Offshore Installations (Prevention of Fire and Explosion, and Emergency Response) Regulations 1995[3] (PFEER) and the Offshore Installations and Wells (Design and Construction, etc) Regulations 1996 (DCR);[4]

- other regulations such as the Management of Health and Safety at Work Regulations 1999[5] (MHSWR), the Control of Major Accident Hazards Regulations 1999[6] (COMAH) and the Provision and Use of Work Equipment Regulations 1998[7] (PUWER);[8]
- common law – manslaughter and culpable homicide (Scotland);[9] and
- corporate killing proposals (presently for England and Wales only);

1   SI 1992/2855.
2   SI 1995/738.
3   SI 1995/743.
4   SI 1996/913.
5   SI 1999/3242.
6   SI 1999/743.
7   SI 1998/2306.
8   See **appendix A.11.1** for a list of relevant legislation.
9   See **para 11.208** below.

11.6   As a major hazard industry, liability for health and safety failure is of fundamental significance to all companies and individuals who are involved in the oil and gas industry. This chapter considers the existing legislative, enforcement and safety regimes in the industry. In the context of the corporate killing proposals, the existing safety regime will be central to any consideration of what amounts to a 'management failure' and what constitutes falling 'far below what could reasonably be expected'.

11.7   As oil and gas activity is UK-wide, with a significant concentration in Scotland, this chapter will consider the issue of corporate liability from the overall UK perspective. The differences between the jurisdictions of England and Wales and Scotland and Northern Ireland are dealt with specifically in para **11.34** below. The diverse nature of the oil and gas industry clearly means that reference should be made to the chapters of this book on construction (**chapter 5**), aviation (**chapter 8**), shipping (**chapter 9**), environment (**chapter 14**) and chemicals (**chapter 10**). In particular, many of the regulations which affect both upstream and downstream activity, such as COMAH,[1] CHIP,[2] COSHH[3] and the Environmental Protection Act 1990, are covered in other chapters. This chapter will accordingly focus mainly on the offshore regime.

1   SI 1999/743.
2   Chemicals (Hazard Information and Packaging for Supply) Regulations 2002, SI 2002/1689.
3   Control of Substances Hazardous to Health Regulations 2002, SI 2002/2677.

Industry overview

Industry hazards

11.8   With its offshore installations, standby boats, helicopters, seismic vessels, divers, pipelines and refineries, the oil and gas industry faces a wide range of significant hazards. The offshore environment is particularly hazardous, with a unique combination of features which distinguish it from any other working environment. These include:

- a complex infrastructure, much of which is ageing – offshore installations, drilling rigs, Floating Production Storage and Offload Vessels (FPSO), pipelines etc;
- the risk of hydrocarbon release and the extreme volatility of such hydrocarbons and other substances used by the industry, such as chemicals, explosives and radioactive sources;
- the risk of well blowout and other catastrophic well risks;

- human error, stress and other behavioural safety factors, contributed to by the pressurised working and living conditions which personnel on board an installation can experience;
- the fragmented nature of the personnel on board, including employees of operators, contractors, sub-contractors, self-employed contractors and consultants, visitors and other third parties;
- the environmental hazards of the North Sea – its depth, temperature and weather systems make it one of the most hostile working environments in the world;
- the rapid escalation of emergency situations and the dangers of evacuation to life boats and helicopters in such emergencies; and
- the isolation from mainland emergency services.

11.9 This operating environment has led the offshore operators' association, UKOOA, to describe the industry as 'a major hazard industry … which has to manage incidents with potentially high consequences but low probability of occurrence' and to state that, 'underpinning commitment to safety is knowledge that the possibility of an incident offshore can never be totally eliminated'.[1]

1   See www.oilandgas.org.uk/issues/piperalpha/v0000864.htm.

11.10   Recent tragedies, such as the helicopter crash in 2002,[1] in which 11 operator and contractor personnel died in the Southern North Sea, the double fatality on the Shell Brent Bravo platform in September 2003,[2] and numerous other incidents involving major injuries, hydrocarbon releases and other dangerous occurrences provide explicit evidence of the hazards faced by the offshore sector. The continuing need for improvement is underlined by Health and Safety Executive (HSE) statistics and the fact that the Offshore Division of the HSE issued 49 improvement notices and seven prohibition notices during 2002–03.[3] As Minister for Work, Des Browne, has recently stated:

'The North Sea and other offshore areas remain hazardous places to work and safety must remain the top priority. The structure of the industry, patterns of employment and expectations of society are all changing, and legislation needs to change too.'[4]

1   16 July 2002 – see www.news.bbc.co.uk/1/hi/england/2232812.stm.
2   See HSE Press Release on 25 September 2003 – www.hse.gov.uk.
3   Provisional figures from HSE Offshore Division database, available at www.hse.gov.uk. See para 11.149 below.
4   HSE Press Release 27 November 2003 – see www.hse.gov.uk.

11.11   However, it is not only the offshore sector of the industry which is hazardous.. In December 1999, a gas explosion at a house in Larkhall caused the deaths of a family of four who were asleep inside. This is alleged to have been caused by the corrosion of a ductile iron pipe. Following a lengthy investigation, Transco were prosecuted in Scotland for culpable homicide and breaches of HSWA 1974.[1] In April 2001, a leak of liquefied petroleum gas caused a massive blast at the Conoco refinery[2] in North Lincolnshire. Although there were no fatalities, there was significant potential for a large-scale disaster. Two separate serious incidents within days of each other at the BP refinery at Grangemouth in June 2001 resulted in a total fine of £1 million.[3] Although no one was killed or seriously injured, the fine was a record for such incidents and reflects the gravity with which the courts treat the issue of potentiality.

1   The culpable homicide prosecution failed, following a successful plea to the relevancy of the charge – *HMA v Transco* (3 June 2003) – see www.scotcourts.gov.uk. However, the trial in respect of the remaining HSWA 1974 charge will take place in 2004: see **para 11.210** below.

2   *The Times*, 17 April 2001.
3   Falkirk Sheriff Court, 18 January 2002; HSB 306, p 2. See **para 11.182** below.

11.12   Although the UK oil and gas industry is in many respects more stringently regulated than any other industry in the UK and has one of the most sophisticated safety regimes in the world, these recent events demonstrate that quality, health, safety and environmental (QHSE) issues must remain a top priority for the industry from board level down.

Economic overview

11.13   The North Sea holds Western Europe's largest oil and natural gas reserves and is one of the world's key non-OPEC producing regions. With some 251 offshore oil and gas fields, both offshore and onshore,[1] 11,472 kilometres of offshore oil and gas pipelines,[2] and nine major oil refineries,[3] the scale of the UK oil and gas industry is enormous

1   213 offshore and 51 onshore: see www.og.dti.gov.uk for a list of fields.
2   See www.og.dti.gov.uk for a list of pipelines.
3   The refineries are operated by Esso, BP (two), Petrolpus, Shell, TotalFinaElf (two), Conoco Phillips and Texaco and have a distillation capacity of around 88 million tones per annum – www.og.dti.gov.uk/downstream/refining/index.htm.

11.14   The UK is the world's fourth largest gas producer and tenth largest oil producer.[1] In 2000, the industry produced 126 million tonnes of crude oil and 115 billion cubic meters of gas which translated into government revenue of £2.6 billion.[2] The projections are that 102 million tonnes of crude oil and 105 billion cubic meters of gas will be produced in 2003.[3] It is estimated that the Treasury has received a total of £190 billion in North Sea taxes since the mid-1960s.[4] The economic importance of the industry can also be seen from the estimated 270,000 jobs which are directly and indirectly supported by the industry in some 6,000 companies. The sheer scale of the industry is evident from the massive offshore installations, which cost millions of pounds to construct, and the huge refineries in places such as Grangemouth, Milford Haven and Humberside.

1   UKOOA 2002 Economic Report.
2   All figures for the year 2000, from the Oil and Gas Inspectorate of the DTI.
3   All figures for the year 2002, from the Oil and Gas Inspectorate of the DTI.
4   UKOOA 2002 Economic Report.

Other North Sea producers

11.15   Norway and the UK are by a wide margin the largest producers of North Sea oil. The UK is the EU's only significant energy exporter and is also one of the world's largest energy consumers. Norway discovered its oil reserves at exactly the same time as the UK and the two countries share a similar geology and scale of industry. However, the way in which each industry developed differed greatly.

11.16   The UK government wanted to extract oil as quickly as possible in order to break the control over production by OPEC. North Sea oil is extremely costly to extract because of its depth and the inhospitable environment. As a result, Britain became heavily reliant on funding from the US. The construction of the North Sea platforms and pipelines accounted for 20% of British industrial investment for over a decade. However, US financial input secured 54% of the North Sea fields for their own companies. This international influence continues today, with many of the operators in the North Sea owned by US parent companies.

11.17 By contrast, the Norwegian industry was, from the outset, state-controlled in order to develop an indigenous Norwegian oil sector. Trade unions were powerful and exacting health and safety standards were maintained. The pace of development was also controlled. It is no coincidence that it was the Norwegian model which the Cullen Report[1] turned to in the wake of the Piper Alpha disaster.

1 See para 11.3 n 1 above.

11.18 Unlike North Sea oil production, exploitation of natural gas in the region is on the increase and most of continental Europe is now connected directly or indirectly to North Sea gas sources as energy demands in Europe grow. The Netherlands remains Europe's largest net gas exporter while the UK has become a minor net exporter as production has grown over recent years.

Future activity

11.19 As far as future activity is concerned, the Oil and Gas Directorate of the DTI has ambitious visions for securing improvements to the UK's competitiveness on the international market, including a 50% increase in the value of industry-related exports by 2005, additional revenue of £1 billion from new businesses, a sustained investment level of £3 billion per year, a production level of 3 million barrels of oil equivalent per day in 2010, 100 000 more jobs than would otherwise have been created by 2010 and prolonged self-sufficiency in oil and gas for the UK.[1] The proposals for expansion are mainly controlled by PILOT,[2] which aims to increase the current UK share of world oil and gas market from 4% to 6% by 2005. It is estimated that oil industry UK expenditure in exploration, development and operations in 2003 will be around £8 billion.[3]

1 DTI Development of UK Oil and Gas Resources (2001) p 2.
2 'Phase 2 of the Oil and Gas Industry Task Force'.
3 UKOOA 2002 Economic Report.

11.20 The Secretary of State for Trade and Industry gave rise for further optimism in the oil industry with another new field coming on stream having a life expectancy of approximately 23 years.[1] The project is expected to produce up to 5% of the UK's gas, creating 260 jobs in Scotland and a further 400 in support services. The government has also announced a £2.4 million plan to speed up approvals for oil and gas developments in future by allowing applications to be processed automatically. In 2003, a further seven projects were approved by the DTI, including four offshore gas fields.[2]

1 Elgin Franklin, developed by TotalFinaElf: see DTI press release, 25 September 2001.
2 Carrack, Nuggets N4, Rose and Rhum.

The changing North Sea environment

11.21 The contracting environment in the North Sea has changed dramatically in the past decade. As the North Sea oilfields have matured and become less profitable, the traditional contracting structure of operator to principal contractor to sub-contractor has been replaced by concepts such as 'integrated project management' whereby contractors become project managers and in some cases share in the risk/ reward of a project by way of payment from production and other creative payment schemes.

11.22   At the same time, a number of major oil and gas companies have sold the rights to their assets to smaller companies, who in turn try to develop 'brown fields'. These are old fields which have already been in production in the past and which are re-stimulated using the latest technological developments to produce further hydrocarbon. Such fields tend to be high cost and low margin.

11.23   In addition, in order to encourage smaller independent companies to invest in the North Sea, the government has launched a new 'Promote' licence – this offers the licensee the opportunity to assess and promote the prospectivity of the licensed acreage for an initial two-year period without the stringent financial, technical and environmental entry checks to be passed for a traditional licence. The success of this initiative can be seen from the 21st Offshore Licensing Round, which closed in May 2003. Licences have been offered to 62 companies, with a record 27 new entrants. Of the 88 licences awarded, 53 are 'Promote' licences.[1]

1   See www.og.dti.gov.uk.

11.24   These changes may raise a number of important QHSE issues. The resources of the smaller independent companies are considerably more limited than the major oil companies, which have always aimed to achieve safety standards which go beyond the minimum legal requirements. Driven by low-cost 'workover' operations of brown fields, it is possible that QHSE issues will not be given the prominence or resources enjoyed in the past. The risk/reward nature of the new contracting environment may exacerbate this. The blurring of the traditional distinction between operators, owners, contractors and subcontractors and the complexity of the contracting structures used may lead to uncertainty about who the 'duty holder' is. This is particularly important in the context of the definitions of duty holder under PFEER,[1] MAR[2] and DCR[3] (see **para 11.89** below).

1   SI 1995/743.
2   SI 1995/738.
3   SI 1996/913.

11.25   Although it is not possible to 'contract out' of criminal liability for health and safety, the way in which health and safety risks, responsibilities and liabilities are contractually apportioned is of considerable relevance and significance to the prosecuting authorities when deciding which companies in the contractual chain should be prosecuted and which should be called as Crown witnesses. In practice, the line to be drawn is a very fine one and there is considerable inconsistency in the way prosecuting authorities interpret and apply their enforcement policies across the UK. What is certain is that clear and unambiguous contractual documentation which precisely defines the respective health and safety duties and responsibilities in the contractual chain will be carefully considered by the prosecuting authorities and will have a material impact on the enforcement decision. Accordingly, in the new contracting environment, all QHSE issues require meticulous consideration by all parties in the contractual chain.

Profit versus safety

11.26   The oil and gas industry is highly profitable. BP, which currently produces three million barrels of oil a day, has reported profits for the second quarter of 2003 of £1.95 billion, representing a 42% rise. This was achieved despite oil production being down 5%. Shell's profits for the same period increased by 51%, and Exxon Mobil announced a threefold jump in profits to £4.4 billion.[1] Although the war in Iraq was responsible for some of these increases, the industry nevertheless reaps substantial rewards from its activities.

1   See www.news.bbc.co.uk.

11.27   There is always a potential conflict between profit and safety. A comprehensive survey of the oil industry carried out for the HSE by AUPEC[1] confirmed that such a potential conflict is an issue which is recognised by most of the companies surveyed. In the context of health and safety prosecutions in the industry, profitability and the sophistication of a defendant's safety management systems are important legal considerations for a number of reasons:

1   Evaluation of the Offshore Safety Legislative Regime (EOSLR) (1999): see **para 11.4** below.

11.28   Oil and gas is a major hazard industry which has both a complex legislative safety regime and very high industry standards. Such standards ensure compliance not only with the minimum requirements of UK law but, in many instances, go well beyond such requirements. It is a defence to a charge under the general duties of HSWA 1974 and under many of the regulations to show that a defendant did everything 'reasonably practicable' to prevent the commission of an offence. Under HSWA 1974, s 40, where a defendant seeks to rely on this defence the onus of proof is on the defendant to establish, on a balance of probabilities, that such reasonably practicable steps were taken. In making such a computation, a court will take into account a number of factors, including the costs involved in taking the necessary steps to avert the breach, industry standards and the industry safety regime.

11.29   Under the proposed new corporate killing law,[1] the financial position of a defendant is likely to become an important factor when considering the question of 'management failure' and 'falling far below what could reasonably be expected'. Again this issue can only be determined by having regard to industry standards and a cost-benefit analysis.

1   A draft Bill is expected in 2004.

11.30   In the sentencing guideline case of *R v F Howe and Son (Engineers) Ltd*,[1] a breach of health and safety legislation to save costs or maximise profits significantly aggravates an offence:

'Financial profit can often be made at the expense of proper action to protect employees and the public. Cost-cutting is a crucial tool in achieving a competitive edge. A deliberate breach of the health and safety legislation with a view to profit seriously aggravates the offence'.[2]

1   [1999] 2 All ER 249.
2   [1999] 2 All ER 249 at 254, per Scott Baker J.

11.31   In addition, a court will take the profitability of a defendant company into account when assessing the level of fine, as evidenced by the BP fine of £1 million which was imposed at Falkirk Sheriff Court on 18 January 2002.[1]

1   See **para 11.182** below.

International standards

11.32   The safety challenges faced by the oil and gas industry are global in nature and it is often the case that international standards which go beyond the minimum requirements of UK law are applied by the industry to UK operations. As mentioned above, one of the factors which a court will give considerable weight to in determining the question of reasonable practicability is the question of industry standards. As the oil and gas industry is international in nature, it is often international standards which will be considered by way of expert evidence in court proceedings. In addition, if there is evidence that a defendant has experienced a similar incident in another country, or been made aware of a particular hazard, this could provide strong evidence to rebut the reasonable practicability defence and could seriously aggravate an offence.

11.33   There are many examples of international incidents which could be relevant to procedures, risk assessments and safety management systems (SMS) in the UK. On 15 March 2001, the P-36 platform, which was the world's largest oil platform, operated by state-owned Petrobras, was lost off the coast of Rio de Janeiro, Brazil. In a series of explosions, 11 men died and the rig sank five days later causing what has been described as 'the world's worst disaster to date in terms of financial loss and potential ecological damage from oil producing rigs'.[1] The cause of this incident is still being investigated.

1   See www.chipcenter.com.

11.34   Other recent international incidents include a blast at an operational gas turbine in Russia which killed three personnel; two fatalities in Brazil caused by a toxic gas leak on a platform; a fire in 1999 which killed four workers at Tosco's Avon refinery in California; and in 1998 an ESSO oil refinery explosion in Australia which killed two people, seriously injured eight and resulted in the entire state of Victoria having no electricity for two weeks. A pending class action is estimated to be worth over $1 billion.

11.35   International standards are further promoted by a number of organisations, including the following.

International Association of Oil and Gas Producers

11.36   In 1994, as part of an effort to improve the overall management of HSE issues, guidelines were issued by the International Association of Oil and Gas Producers (OGP) entitled *Guidelines for the development and application of health, safety and environmental management systems*. These internationally respected standards describe the main elements needed to develop, implement and maintain a management system in these areas. OGP also produces safety statistics which give some insight into international safety standards.[1]

1   See www.ogp.org.uk/pubs/345.pdf.

North Sea Offshore Authorities Forum

11.37 The North Sea Offshore Authorities Forum (NSOAF) was set up by the European governmental agencies responsible for regulating offshore oil and gas industry health and safety. It includes not only the five producing North Sea coastal states, Denmark, Germany, The Netherlands, Norway and the UK, but also countries with oil and gas interests in adjacent waters (including Eire, the Isle of Man, France, Belgium, Sweden and the Faroe Islands).

11.38 The aim of NSOAF is to ensure the health, safety and welfare of offshore workers by providing a forum to discuss technical and legislative developments in member states, disseminate topical information and address strategic regional issues. Member states are represented by the national authorities who supervise the industry's compliance with health and safety legislation.

Legislative regime

Background

11.39 When exploration and production activity began in the North Sea, the main legislation governing the industry was the Petroleum (Production) Act 1934. The Continental Shelf Act 1964 created some provision for the health and safety of persons employed by the oil and gas companies offshore by way of model clauses required in licenses. However, there was no provision for the enforcement of licensees' obligations.

Mineral Workings (Offshore Installations) Act 1971

11.40 This legislation gave effect to the recommendations arising from the Inquiry into the Sea Gem disaster.[1]

1 *Report of the Inquiry into the Causes of the Accident to the Drilling Rig Sea Gem* (Cmnd 3409, 1967).

11.41 The Sea Gem was an offshore self-elevating jack-up barge located approximately 43 miles east of the mouth of the river Humber. The barge collapsed and sank, resulting in the deaths of 13 of the 32 men on board. This resulted in a public inquiry, called for by the Minister of Power. The Report of the Inquiry concluded that structural failure of 'tie bars on the port side jacks was the most probable prime cause of the collapse'[1] which involved widespread disintegration of the whole structure.

1 *Report of the Inquiry into the Causes of the Accident to the Drilling Rig Sea Gem* (Cmnd 3409, 1967) p 26.

11.42 The Report also noted that: 'the only sanction for ensuring the proper operation of the safety procedures was the revocation of the licence. There were no penal sanctions which can be invoked by anyone in this regard.'[1] The Inquiry recommended that a code similar to those in other countries, such as the US, for regulating the industry be established, supported by 'credible sanctions'.

1 *Report of the Inquiry into the Causes of the Accident to the Drilling Rig Sea Gem* (Cmnd 3409, 1967) p 2.

Offshore installation manager

11.43   In addition to creating penal sanctions, the Mineral Workings (Offshore Installations) Act 1971 established the role of the offshore installation manager (OIM). The OIM today remains the single most important decision-maker onboard an installation, with general authority for all matters concerning the installation and in particular for any health and safety issues. An OIM has specific responsibility for the platform throughout any emergency, including ultimately whether a platform should be abandoned.

HSWA 1974

11.44   Around the same time, the recommendations of the Robens Committee on Safety and Health at Work[1] were put into place and HSWA 1974 was enacted. This was followed by the Petroleum and Submarine Pipe-lines Act 1975. HSWA 1974 remains the main piece of legislation under which oil and gas companies are prosecuted for health and safety failures.

1   The Robens Report (Cmnd 5034, 1972).

Jurisdiction

11.45   The continental shelf underlying the North Sea is divided into six national sectors, adjoining the UK, Belgium, Denmark, Germany, The Netherlands, and Norway. Apart from Belgium, all actively exploit the offshore hydrocarbon resources. HSWA 1974 extends to the UK continental shelf (UKCS), which consists of those areas of the sea bed and subsoil beyond the 12-mile territorial sea over which the UK exercises sovereign rights of exploration and exploitation of natural resources. The designated areas are made by orders under the provisions of the Continental Shelf Act 1964. The most recently designated part of the UKCS is between the Faroe Islands and Shetland Islands.[1]

1   The Continental Shelf (Designation of Areas) Order 1999, SI 1999/2031.

11.46   The Petroleum Act 1998 provides that any act or omission constituting an offence under UK law which takes place on, under or above an offshore installation in UK waters or within 500 metres of such an installation (the safety zone) shall be treated as taking place in the UK. The Health and Safety at Work etc Act 1974 (Application Outside Great Britain) Order 2001[1] extends the offshore application of HSWA 1974 to the use and operation of all buildings within the 12-mile territorial sea (including wind and wave power generators) and to diving work carried out in order to examine the sea bed after an installation has been removed. The definition of 'offshore installation' has been amended to include all supplementary units which provide power and other support activities to installations.

1   SI 2001/2127.

The Burgoyne Committee[1]

11.47   The Burgoyne Committee on Offshore Safety reported to Parliament in 1980. The report recognised that the disparate collection of regulations and enforcement agencies in place at the time represented a danger to safety. It recommended a goal setting approach to North Sea safety and that a single government agency should be in charge of policing it. Little was done to implement the recommendations and it regrettably took a disaster on the scale of Piper Alpha to finally implement the necessary legislative changes.

1 *Offshore Safety* (Cmnd 7866, 1980).

Piper Alpha

11.48   The current legislative and safety regime in the North Sea is dominated by the catastrophic events at the Piper Alpha installation on the night of 6 July 1988. The safety failures which led to the world's worst oil and gas disaster send a chilling reminder that safety must remain a fundamental priority for everyone in the industry.

11.49   Of the 226 personnel on board the installation 165 died, along with two of the crew of a rescue vessel. This was 'the most serious industrial accident in Britain in over 50 years and … the most serious to occur anywhere in the history of offshore development'.[1] Until the terrorist attacks on the Twin Towers on 11 September 2001 in New York, Piper Alpha was also the most expensive man-made disaster with over $3 billion paid out in insurance claims.

1 180 HC Official Report (6th series) col 331, 12 November 1990.

11.50   Piper Alpha was operated by Occidental Petroleum (Caledonia) Ltd on behalf of a consortium to which the platform was worth a reported £3.5 million per day. At its peak, Piper Alpha accounted for 10% of the UK's North Sea oil production.

11.51   Occidental had narrowly escaped a disaster in 1984 which required a mass evacuation of the platform and in 1987 it experienced a fatal incident. The Cullen Report[1] made it clear that the company had failed to learn from these mistakes.

1 See **para 11.3 n 1** above.

11.52   The deflagration explosion which initiated the eventual disaster occurred at approximately 10.00 pm on the production platform and was followed immediately by a large oil pool fire at the west end of one of the quarters modules and a fireball on the west face. The location and nature of the source of ignition are still unknown.[1] However, the conclusion reached by the Inquiry, on a balance of probabilities, was that the leakage of condensate was 'from a blind flange assembly … which was not leak-tight' and which was attributable to work on the overhaul of a particular site being left incomplete overnight, following the handover of shifts.

1 Cullen Report, **para 11.3 n 1** above, p 68, para 5.103.

11.53   The fires spread extremely rapidly extending downwards to the lower levels and engulfing the upper parts of the north end of the platform in dense black smoke. The extent of the fires is attributed partly to the rupture of pipelines caused by projectiles in turn themselves caused by the disintegration of a firewall which was due to the initial explosion. The breached firewall allowed the fires to extend to other levels.[1] A series of smaller explosions followed.

1 Cullen Report, **para 11.3 n 1** above, p 132, para 7.17.

11.54   At 10.20 pm, a second major explosion occurred as the gas riser from Tartan ruptured, by which time only 22 personnel had left the platform. 'The effects of the explosion were felt on vessels several hundred yards away.'[1] At this point several men jumped into the sea, due to the intensification of the heat generated by the high pressure gas fire. This rupture is attributed to the high temperatures created by a pool fire beneath the riser.[2]

1   Cullen Report, **para 11.3 n 1** above, p 4, para 4 7
2   Cullen Report, **para 11.3 n 1** above, p 134, para 7.24. 'The rupture of the riser would have been delayed by fireproofing for a substantial period, perhaps 1–3 hours, and by a cooling deluge system': p 134, para 7.24(iii).

11.55   Another massive explosion occurred at approximately 10.50 pm by which stage only about 39 personnel had left the platform. This further explosion is attributed to the rupture of the MCP-01 gas riser and appears to have started the structural collapse of the platform at the 68-feet level. Major explosions continued with debris projected 800 metres from the platform, forcing more personnel on board to jump at each stage of the deterioration.

11.56   The amount of crude oil which fuelled the initial fire must have come partly from the main oil line (MOL) or by reason of a fracture of MOL itself. The MOL at Piper Alpha was also fuelled by Claymore and Tartan. The Inquiry investigated the responses of the neighbouring installations, finding those responses to have been inadequately slow and that 'Claymore continued the production of oil until about 23.10 hours' effecting a controlled shutdown, as opposed to an emergency shutdown which would have taken immediate effect.[1] Similarly, the OIM on Tartan did not effect shutdown until 10.25 pm, although this failure is attributed in part to the freezing of the telemetry system.[2] The Inquiry concluded that there was 'no physical reason why' the shutdowns of the oil supplies could not have been done earlier at Claymore and Tartan as part of a controlled shutdown – this would have caused an almost immediate reduction in the flow of oil which was fuelling the fire in the centre of the platform, 'probably' delaying the rupture of the Tartan riser.[3]

1   Cullen Report, **para 11.3 n 1** above, p 138, para 7.35.
2   Cullen Report, **para 11.3 n 1** above, p 141, para 7.41.
3   Cullen Report, **para 11.3 n 1** above, p 143 at para 7.47.

11.57   The actions of the OIM, as the person 'who was primarily responsible for the taking of decisions for the safety of those on board the installation' were strongly criticised by Lord Cullen who concluded that, 'in my view the death toll of those who died in the accommodation was substantially greater than it would have been' if the initiative had been taken of moving as many personnel as possible down to sea level and away from the accommodation block.[1]

1   Cullen Report, **para 11.3 n 1** above, p 163, para 8.35.

11.58   The fires were not extinguished fully until 2.02 am on 7 July. Approximately 66% of the deaths were principally occasioned by inhalation of smoke or gas, the other main causes having been drowning, physical injury or burns, while in many cases the cause of death was not ascertained. In the opinion of the medical expert, many of the physical injuries were sustained on impact with water after the descent from the platform. Many of the bodies were not found until November 1988, four months after the tragedy, while 30 bodies remain missing today.[1]

1   Cullen Report, **para 11.3 n 1** above, p 163, para 8.35.

Recommendations of the Cullen Report

11.59   Lord Cullen was appointed on 13 July 1988 to chair a public inquiry to establish the circumstances of the accident on Piper Alpha and its cause. The report was published in November 1990.[1] Lord Cullen made 106 recommendations, all of which were accepted by the industry, which led to a complete restructuring of the offshore safety regime. Responsibility for their implementation was apportioned between the HSE, the operators, Standby Ship Owners Association and finally the industry as a whole. Three main recommendations are generally singled out as the most significant:

*   the requirement that every offshore installation should conduct a formal safety assessment thereby identifying and quantifying potential risk factors and this evaluation should be submitted to the HSE or approval (the safety case);
*   the existing prescriptive legislation was found to be inadequate and was to be replaced by 'goal-setting' regulations, whereby standards would be raised; and
*   the responsibility for health and safety offshore should pass from the Department of Energy to the HSE.

1   Cullen Report, **para 11.3 n 1** above.

11.60   The Inquiry identified the need for a formal safety assessment (FSA) whereby potential risks are identified and assessed 'over the whole life cycle of a project, from the initial feasibility study through the concept design study and the detail design study to construction and commissioning, then to operation, and finally to decommissioning and abandonment'.[1] This FSA was thus identified as an 'essential element in a modern safety regime for major hazard installations'[2] with a crucial role to play in assuring safety offshore, and a legitimate expectation of both the workforce and of the public. It was decided that the FSA should take the form of a safety case which has become one of the legislative legacies of the Inquiry, in the form of the Offshore Installations (Safety Case) Regulations 1992.[3]

1   Cullen Report, **para 11.3 n 1** above, p 275 at para 17.3.
2   Cullen Report, **para 11.3 n 1** above, p 281, para 17.33.
3   SI 1992/2885.

11.61   This conclusion took into account the onshore Control of Industrial Major Accident Hazards Regulations 1984[1] (CIMAH), since superseded by COMAH,[2] which already required a written report on the safety of an onshore installation. The recommendations were also modelled on a similar longstanding offshore safety regime in operation in Norway since 1976. Lord Cullen concluded that:

'An installation needs to be self sufficient in providing protection for personnel.'[3]

and

'The offshore safety case, should be a demonstration that the hazards of the installation have been identified and assessed, and are under control and that the exposure of personnel to these hazards has been minimised.'[4]

1   SI 1984/1902.
2   SI 1999/743.
2   Cullen Report, **para 11.3 n 1** above, p 282, para 17.38.
3   Cullen Report, **para 11.3 n 1** above, p 282, para 17.37.

11.62   Crucially, risk management 'should include as a central feature a demonstration that the threat from ... hazards to the arrangements for refuge, evacuation and escape of personnel in the event of an emergency, is under control'.[1]

1   Cullen Report, **para 11.3 n 1** above, p 282, para 17.37.

11.63   The safety case was deemed to be required by mobile and fixed, new and existing installations, and it should be 'part of a continuing dialogue between the operator and the regulatory body' as opposed to a one-off exercise, and kept up to date, noting any material differences in circumstances which should arise.[1]

1   Cullen Report, **para 11.3 n 1** above, p 283, para 17.46.

GOAL SETTING

11.64   The Cullen Report[1] concluded that the principal offshore regulations should take the form of requiring that stated objectives should be met, ie *goal setting*, rather than prescribing what detailed measures should be taken. Four broad categories of regulations were proposed: construction; plant and equipment; fire and explosion protection; and evacuation, escape and rescue.

1   Cullen Report, **para 11.3 n 1** above.

REGULATORY BODY

11.65   Lord Cullen observed that there were significant flaws in the way in which safety was managed by Occidental and that senior management were all too easily satisfied that safety was being maintained.[1] The former regime of inspection was found to have concentrated too much on hardware and not enough on management systems.

1   Cullen Report, **para 11.3 n 1** above.

11.66   A single regulatory body for offshore safety was to be set up, and the responsibility for ensuring compliance with the proposed legislation was recommended to shift from the Department of Energy to the HSE. At the time of Piper Alpha there were 217 installations in the North Sea which had to share the attentions of just eight professional full-time field inspectors employed by the Department of Energy. Those inspectors were accused by Lord Cullen of being 'inadequately trained, guided and led' and their investigations were 'superficial to the point of being of little use'. Nine of the 46 jobs in the safety section were vacant and only 40% of fatal and serious accidents were investigated. As a result of the Cullen Report,[1] the HSE took over responsibility for health and safety in the oil and gas sector in 1991.

1   See **para 11.3 n 1** above.

Offshore regulatory regime

The safety case

11.67   'It is ... clear to me that the offshore safety regime has fallen significantly behind the onshore regime in a number of respects in which thinking on safety matters has advanced over the last 10 years. The respect which is most relevant ... is the concept of the Safety Case ... The evidence has shown that the industry consists of a relatively small number of companies running high technology operations where there is a strong need for a systematic approach to the management of safety.'[1]

1 Cullen Report, **para 11.3 n 1** above, pp 370–371.

11.68 The Cullen Report noted the importance of 'systematic scrutiny' of remote but potential risk and the need for a comprehensive system of safety assessment – 'work related injuries are usually attributable to a failure of risk management systems, exacerbated by individual carelessness'.[1] Recommendation 1 of the Cullen Report provided that:

- operators should be required to submit a safety case to the regulatory body in respect of each of its installations;
- safety cases should demonstrate that the safety management system of the company and installation are adequate to ensure that the design and operation of the installation and its equipment are safe;
- potential major hazards of the installation and the risks to personnel are identified and controlled; and
- adequate provision is made in the event of a major emergency for a temporary safe refuge and safe evacuation, escape and rescue.

1 Cullen Report, **para 11.3 n 1** above, p 275, para 17.2.

Offshore Installations (Safety Case) Regulations 1992[1]

11.69 The Offshore Installations (Safety Case) Regulations 1992 (SCR) implement the central recommendations of the Framework Directive[2] and of the Cullen Report.[3] The SCR are complemented and supported by MAR,[4] PFEER[5] and DCR.[6] The SCR should be read in conjunction with HSE Guidance.[7] The current safety case regime is currently under review and the HSE intend to enter a formal consultation period in 2004. As Minister for Work, Des Brown, recently stated:

'Although the safety case regime is still effective, research shows that the main benefits from its introduction were achieved in the early years. The regime needs to be updated to meet the circumstances of a mature oil and gas province and new challenges to offshore health and safety.'

Ageing infrastructure, maintenance management, staff reductions and new players entering the UKCS were cited as examples of such challenges.[8]

1 SI 1992/2885.
2 Council Directive 89/391/EEC.
3 See **para 11.3 n 1** above.
4 SI 1995/738.
5 SI 1995/743.
6 SI 1996/913
7 HSE L30 *A Guide to the Offshore Installations (Safety Case) Regulations 1992* (SCR).
8 See HSE Press Release 27 November 2003 – www.hse.gov.uk.

11.70 Safety cases are required for:

- all fixed and mobile installations operating or to be operated in British waters and in UK-designated areas of the Continental Shelf;

- new fixed installations which are to be established offshore – operators are required to submit a safety case at the design stage;
- mobile installations – a safety case must be submitted before the installation is moved; and
- decommissioning – a safety case must be prepared before the commencement of the decommissioning.

11.71   For *fixed installations* the relevant officer is the *operator*, defined as, 'the person appointed by a concession owner to execute any function of organising or supervising any operation to be carried out by such installation or, where no such person has been appointed, the concession owner'.[1] For *mobile installations*, it is the *owner* who defined as, 'the person who *controls the operation* of the installation'.[2]

1   SI 1992/2885, reg 2.
2   SI 1992/2885, reg 2.

11.72   For new fixed installations, operators must submit the safety case at the design stage. For fixed installations, the safety case must be submitted at least six months before commencing operations. The operator must ensure that the installation is not operated unless the safety case has been accepted by the HSE. HSE acceptance is required for all safety cases except for the design of new fixed installations. 'Acceptance' is a written notification to the duty holder.

11.73   There are three broad categories of information required for a safety case:

- the *facility description* – general information about the personnel on board, activities, interaction with other installations etc;
- the *safety management system* – the system by which safety is to be achieved and maintained in the design, construction and operation of the facility; and
- the *formal safety assessment* – detailed information about the nature, likelihood and potential impact of hazards and the means to prevent such or to mitigate their effect should they occur.

11.74   The Schedules to SCR[1] should be considered alongside SCR, reg 8[2] and the HSE Guidance. Regulation 8 stipulates that the safety case should include:

'sufficient particulars to demonstrate that—
(a) his management system is adequate to ensure that the relevant statutory provisions will (in respect of matters within his control) be complied with in relation to the installation and any activity on or in connection with it:
(b) he has established adequate arrangements for audit and for the making of reports thereof;
(c) all hazards with the potential to cause a major accident have been identified; and
(d) risks have been evaluated and measures have been, or will be, taken to reduce the risks to persons affected by those hazards to the lowest level that is reasonably practicable.'

1   SI 1992/2885, Schs 1–9.
2   SI 1992/2885, reg 8.

11.75   Sufficient information is required to demonstrate to the HSE that reasoned arguments have led to appropriate judgements as regards risk analysis and that there is an effective SMS in place. The Guidance states that: 'The evaluation of risk should involve both a qualitative and a quantitative approach.' Risks should be assessed in an integrated manner so that they may be reduced to 'the lowest level that is reasonably practicable'.

11.76 The Guidance notes that the format of the presentation of the safety case is a matter for the duty holder; however, the following suggestion is made:

1 an executive summary covering the main features of the case;
2 factual information about the installation, its environment and activities;
3 the main demonstrations and analyses required under the Regulations; and
4 remedial measures – an account of any measures proposed in the light of the risk assessments and analyses referred to and timescales for their implementation.

11.77 A failure to follow the procedures and arrangements of a safety case is a criminal offence. However, it is a defence if it can be established that in the circumstances it was not in the best interests of the health and safety of persons to follow the procedures or arrangements concerned and there was not sufficient time to revise the safety case, or where the commission of the offence was due to a contravention by another person who had a duty to co-operate and the accused had taken all reasonable precautions and exercised all due diligence to ensure that the procedures or arrangements were followed.

Revision of safety cases

11.78 The safety case should be a 'living document' which reflects the reality of the situation on the installation: 'The operator who has prepared the Safety Case must revise its contents as often as may be appropriate, but nothing ... shall require the revision to be sent to the Executive.'[1] The Guidance states that even minor changes should be assessed and logged. A formal revision may be required under SCR, reg 9(2)[2] where changes merit the reappraisal of the risk control arrangements. The Guidance gives examples of such changes. However, this is ultimately a matter for the judgment of the duty holder. Suggested circumstances when a revision would be required include:

• modifications or repairs to structure which may have a negative impact on safety;
• introduction of new activities on the installation;
• changes of operator or ownership involving changes in the management system;
• following an accident or 'near miss' or as a result of an audit; and
• where there have been major advances in technology.

1 SI 1992/2885, reg 9.
2 SI 1992/2885, reg 9(2).

11.79 In any event, a revised safety case must be submitted to the HSE every three years, calculated from the HSE's acceptance of the original safety case or subsequent revision. The submission must be received by the HSE at least three months before the three-year period expires.

11.80 The operator or owner must inform the HSE of an address in Great Britain when it submits the safety case. A copy of the safety case, and any revisions thereof, must be kept at this address and on the installation concerned. Any audit reports must also be kept at that address along with written statements in response to the audit any action taken.

Health and Safety (Fees) (Amendment) Regulations 1999[1]

11.81   The Health and Safety (Fees) (Amendment) Regulations 1999.[2] make provision for the HSE to charge fees for carrying out safety case assessment work and inspections to ensure compliance with the provisions of SCR.[3] An offshore charging review group was set up to discuss terms of reference, guides on charging, potential improvements to systems of work, with representatives from the HSE, British Rig Owners Association, CBI, IADC, IMCA, OCA and UKOOA.

1   SI 1999/2597.
2   Guidance is contained in an HSE booklet 'Charging for Offshore Activities – A Guide' (3rd edn, 2002).
3   SI 1992/2885.

11.82   In respect of offshore installations, a fee is payable to the HSE for the performance by the HSE of any function which relates to the enforcement of any statutory provisions against the operator/owner or against a contractor in relation to work carried out by him on or in connection with the installation. Costs in respect of legal proceedings are excluded.

11.83   As regards offshore installations, charges will be made for

*   *Assessing*:
    –   design safety cases submitted by operators of fixed installations;
    –   safety cases for fixed and mobile installations;
    –   revisions of safety cases;
    –   three-yearly revisions of safety cases;
    –   safety cases for combined operations;
    –   safety cases for abandonment of fixed installations; and
    –   whether to grant an exemption under SCR, reg 17.[1]
*   *Inspection* to assess compliance with SCR.[1]
*   Carrying out formal *enforcement activities*, including preparation and serving of improvement or prohibition notices.
*   *Investigation* of incidents.

1   SI 1992/2885, reg 17.
2   SI 1992/2885.

11.84   The fee is to be paid by the owner or operator who prepared the safety case pursuant to the SCR.[1] The HSE fees will be charged on an 'actuals' basis at an hourly rate of £155 per hour.[2] The full costs of the time spent by the HSE inspectors is recovered. It was estimated that the total revenue which this would bring the HSE would be £40 million in the first three years. The total compliance costs for the first year of operation were estimated at £11.9 million.

1   SI 1992/2885.
2   As at 1 April 2003.

As Low as Reasonably Practicable

11.85   The As Low as Reasonably Practicable (ALARP) principle is one which is not only central to the evaluation of safety cases, but also to the entire offshore safety regime. According to the HSE: 'ALARP involves an assessment of the *risk* to be avoided, of the *sacrifice* (in money, time and trouble) involved in taking measures to avoid that risk, and a *comparison* of the two. This process can involve varying degrees of rigour which will depend on the nature of the hazard, the extent of the risk and the control measures to be adopted. The more systematic the approach, the more rigorous and more transparent it is to the regulator and other interested parties. However, duty-holders (and the regulator) should not be overburdened if such rigour is not warranted. The greater the initial level of risk under consideration, the greater the degree of rigour HSE requires of the arguments purporting to show that those risks have been reduced ALARP.'[1]

1   HSE *Policy and guidance on reducing risks as low as reasonably practicable in design*, available at www.hse.gov.uk/dst/alarp3.htm.

11.86   The following HSE documents provide guidance as to how this term is to be interpreted:

1   Principles and guidelines to assist HSE in its judgements that duty holders have reduced risks as low as reasonably practicable, available at www.hse.gov.uk/dst/alarp1.htm.
2   *Assessing compliance with the law in individual cases and the use of good practice*, available at www.hse.gov.uk/dst/alarp2.htm.
3   *Policy and guidance on reducing risks as low as reasonably practicable in design*, available at www.hse.gov.uk/dst/alarp3.htm.
4   *Reducing Risks, Protecting People, HSE's decision making process* (R2P2), available at www.hse.gov.uk/dst/r2p2.pdf
5   SPC/Permissioning/ 09 HID's approach to ALARP decisions.
6   *Guidance on ALARP for Offshore Division Inspectors* (SPC 38).

Evaluation of safety cases

11.87   In June 2003, the HSE published *Fire Explosion and Risk Assessment Topic Guidance*. This sets out the minimum standard which should be achieved to comply with the assessment principles and provides more detailed guidance on aspects relevant to fire, explosion and risk assessment. It expands upon and complements the following documents:

- *Assessment Principles of Offshore Safety Cases*[1] (APOSC).
- SCR[2] Guidance.
- *Guidelines for Fire and Explosion Hazard Management*.[3]
- ALARP 'trilogy'.[4]
- Offshore Division's ALARP Guidance (SPC 38).
- R2P2.[5]

1   HS(G)181.
2   SI 1992/2885.
3   GFEHM UKOOA (1995).
4   See points 1, 2 and 3 at **para 11.86** above.
5   HSE (2001).

11.88   The Guidance covers hazard identification, quantified risk assessment (QRA), risk evaluation and risk reduction, risk management (concerning the measures in place to eliminate, prevent, detect, control and mitigate major fire and explosion hazards, and their associated performance standards) and emergency arrangements.

Offshore duty holders

11.89   In the offshore health and safety regime, the question of who the 'duty holder' is under MAR,[1] PFEER[2] and DCR[3] is a question of fundamental importance. The AUPEC survey of the UK oil and gas industry identified this question as one of the most difficult questions within the legislative regime.[4] The government's paper 'Revitalising Health and Safety'[5] also notes that fewer than 18% of respondents were sure of their contractual health and safety position. One of the main problems is that at the time when the offshore regulations were drafted, the contracting environment in the North Sea was very different to the modern day contractual structures.

1   SI 1995/738.
2   SI 1995/743.
3   SI 1996/913.
4   AUPEC Survey – *Evaluation of the Offshore Safety Legislative Regime (EOSLR)* (1999).
5   June 2000.

11.90   MAR,[1] PFEER[2] and DCR[3] must be read in conjunction with the HSE Guidance to MAR, two Guidances for DCR and the PFEER ACOP. There are a number of variances between some of the definitions in the MAR, PFEER and DCR regulations and the precise wording of each regulation should be specifically considered. A summary of the position is as follows:

1   SI 1995/738.
2   SI 1995/743.
3   SI 1996/913.

Fixed installations

11.91   A fixed installation is an offshore installation, other than a mobile installation. A list of offshore installations can be found in the Guidance to MAR. Floating production platforms are fixed installations. However, the term 'floating production platform' is not defined in the Regulations.[1]

1   SI 1995/738, SI 1995/743 and SI 1996/913.

11.92   The duty holder is the operator. The operator is either the concession owner or the person appointed by the concession owner to execute any function of organising or supervising any operation to be carried out on the installation.

11.93   The words 'appointed' and 'any' are very important. If a concession owner fails to appoint a duty holder for a fixed installation, then the concession holder will be the duty holder under MAR,[1] PFEER[2] and DCR.[3] 'Appoint' is not defined, but can be done either by inserting it in the contract or by a letter of appointment.

1   SI 1995/738.
2   SI 1995/743.
3   SI 1996/913.

Mobile installations

11.94   A mobile installation is an offshore installation (other than a floating production platform) which can be moved from place to place without major dismantling or modification, whether or not it has its own motive power. The duty holder is the owner. The owner is the person who controls the operation of the installation.

11.95 A Mobile Offshore Drilling Unit (MODU) falls within this definition. The word 'control' is again very significant but is not defined. It will be a question of fact and degree as to who exactly controls the installation's operations. In some situations, this could be the operator.

Wells (DCR[1])

11.96 The duty holder is the well-operator, which is defined as either the concession holder or the person appointed by the concession holder to execute the function of organising and supervising all operations to be carried out by means of such well.

1   SI 1996/913.

MAR,[1] PFEER[2] and DCR[3]

11.97 Together with the SCR,[4] these Regulations form the cornerstone of the offshore legislative regime. The Regulations impose both civil and criminal liability upon duty holders and consist of a mix of absolute duties and qualified duties, with the reasonable practicability defence applicable to some of the regulations but not others.

1   SI 1995/738.
2   SI 1995/743.
3   SI 1996/913.
4   SI 1992/2885.

MAR[1]

11.98 MAR makes provision for:

- the notification to the HSE in writing of the date of an installation's intended entry into or departure from relevant waters and any change of duty holder or owner;
- ensuring that the installation is at all times under the charge of a competent person appointed by the duty holder (installation manager) to manage on his behalf the installation and the persons on it that the installation manager is provided with appropriate resources to be able to carry out effectively his functions and duties and that the identity of the installation manager is known to or readily ascertainable by every person on the installation;
- the need for co-operation among duty holders;
- the keeping of a record of the persons who are on or working from the installation;
- the provision of a permit to work system, where, as a result of the kind of work which may be done or the circumstances in which work may be done, it is necessary for the health or safety of persons to do so;
- comprehensible written instructions on procedures to be observed on the offshore installation and to be brought to the attention of every person who is to do anything to which such procedure relates;
- keeping of records of personnel on board;

- effective communication between the installation and the shore, vessels, aircraft and other installations;
- arrangements for helideck operations on the installation to ensure, so far as is reasonably practicable, that helideck operations, including the landing and take-off of helicopters, are without risks to health and safety;
- the collection and keeping of meteorological and oceanographic information and such information relating to the motions of the installation as is necessary for securing, so far as is reasonably practicable, the safe operation of the installation and the safety of persons on or near it; and
- the provision of health surveillance as is appropriate to the health and safety risks incurred in the work.

1   SI 1995/738; HSE Guidance L70.

PFEER[1]

11.99   PFEER provides that the duty holder must take appropriate measures with a view to protecting persons on the installation from fire and explosion and securing effective emergency response. The duty holder must carry out an assessment, record it and thereafter repeat it as often as may be appropriate. This consists of identification of the various events which could give rise to a major accident involving fire or explosion or the need for evacuation, escape or rescue to avoid or minimise a major accident; evaluation of the likelihood and consequences of such events; establishment of appropriate standards of performance to be attained; providing measures for ensuring effective evacuation, escape, recovery and rescue to avoid or minimise a major accident; and otherwise protecting persons from a major accident involving fire or explosion.

1   SI 1995/743, ACOP and Guidance L65.

11.100   In addition PFEER[1] makes detailed provision for:

- preparation for emergencies;
- equipment for helicopter emergencies;
- the preparation and revision of an emergency response plan;
- prevention of fire and explosion; and
- detection of incidents and other matters such as communication, control of emergencies, mitigation of fire and explosion, muster areas, arrangements for evacuation, means of escape, arrangements for recovery and rescue, suitability of personal protective equipment for use in an emergency and suitability and condition of plant.

1   SI 1995/743.

DCR[1]

11.101   DCR is essentially divided into two parts, as reflected in the Guidance: (1) integrity, workplace environment and other miscellaneous matters; and (2) specific well aspects.

1   SI 1996/913, Guidance L84 and L85.

11.102   DCR[1] provides that the duty holder shall ensure that an installation at all times possesses such integrity as is reasonably practicable. The duty holder shall ensure that installations are designed and built so that, so far as is reasonably practicable:

1   it can withstand such forces acting on it as are reasonably foreseeable;
2   its layout and configuration, including those of its plant, will not prejudice its integrity;
3   fabrication, transportation, construction, commissioning, operation, modification, maintenance and repair of the installation may proceed without prejudicing its integrity;
4   it may be decommissioned and dismantled safely; and
5   in the event of reasonably foreseeable damage to the installation it will retain sufficient integrity to enable action to be taken to safeguard the health and safety of persons on or near it.

1   SI 1996/913.

11.103   The duty holder must also ensure that suitable arrangements are in place for maintaining the integrity of the installation, including suitable arrangements for:

1   periodic assessment of its integrity; and
2   the carrying out of remedial work in the event of damage or deterioration which may prejudice its integrity.

11.104   The HSE must be informed in writing within ten days after the appearance of evidence of a significant threat to the integrity of an installation, identifying such threat and specifying any action taken or to be taken to avert it.

HELICOPTERS

11.105   The duty holder must ensure that every helicopter landing area forming part of an installation is large enough, and has sufficient clear approach and departure paths, to enable any helicopter intended to use the landing area to land and take off safely.

11.106   MAR, Sch 1[1] sets out detailed additional requirements in relation to the organisation of an installation, accommodation, room temperature, lighting, traffic routes and other matters.

1   SI 1995/738, Sch 1.

WELLS

11.107   The main provisions are as follows:

•   The well-operator must ensure that a well is designed, modified, commissioned, constructed, equipped, operated, maintained, suspended and abandoned so that, so far as is reasonably practicable, there can be no unplanned escape of fluids from the well; and risks to the health and safety of persons from it or anything in it, or in strata to which it is connected, are as low as is reasonably practicable. In order to comply with this duty an assessment must be made, before the design of a well is commenced, of the hazards in the geological strata and formations. All such matters shall, so far as is reasonably practicable, be kept under review and modifications must be made to both design and procedures if there is any change.

- Wells must also be designed and constructed so that, so far as is reasonably practicable, they can be suspended or abandoned safely and there can be no unplanned escape of fluids from the well or the reservoir after such suspension or abandonment.
- Before any well operations are commenced, the well-operator must ensure that suitable well control equipment is provided for use during such operations to protect against blowouts.
- The well-operator must send to the HSE, at such intervals as may be agreed or, failing agreement, at intervals of one week, a report setting out various information concerning the operation of the well.
- Every person who is, or is to be concerned (in whatever capacity) in an operation in relation to a well (including the drilling of a well) shall co-operate with the well-operator so far as is necessary to enable him to discharge his duties under DCR.[1]
- No drilling, well intervention or workover operations can be carried out on a well unless the persons carrying out the operation have received such information, instruction and training, and are being so supervised, that the risk to health and safety from such operation is reduced to the lowest level that is reasonably practicable.
- It is a defence to a charge under DCR for a defendant to prove that the commission of the offence was due to the act or default of another person (not being one of his or her employees) and that he took all reasonable precautions, and exercised all due diligence, to avoid the commission of the offence.

1   SI 1996/913.

Reporting of Injuries, Diseases and Dangerous Occurrences Regulations 1995[1]

11.108   As evidenced by the case of *R v BG Exploration and Production Ltd*,[2] a failure to comply with RIDDOR is a criminal offence in itself and can seriously aggravate any other breaches. The HSE has launched a new enforcement initiative to ensure that RIDDOR is complied with in the offshore environment. HSE inspectors will routinely ask owners and operators what systems they have to determine the reportability of injuries, particularly those involving contractor's employees. A confidential hotline has been set up for offshore workers if they have information about accidents which they believe have not been reported. The RIDDOR 'Offshore' leaflet has also been revised[3] and an operations notice has been sent to offshore companies.

1   SI 1995/3163.
1   (10 February 2000, unreported), Kingston-upon-Hull Crown Court. See **para 11.163** above.
3   HSE 33 (rev 1).

Safety representatives on offshore installations[1]

11.109   Personnel on board offshore installations are entitled to elect safety representatives to deal with health and safety on the installation. Once a representative has been elected, the duty holder must establish a safety committee. The regulations contain detailed provisions regarding the procedures which must be followed to elect safety representatives and establish a safety committee. The OIM can choose how the safety committees are run and organised with regards to elections and the establishment of constituencies.

1   The Offshore Installations (Safety Representatives and Safety Committees) Regulations 1989, SI 1989/971, as amended, and Guidance L110.

11.110   Duty holders must ensure that both safety representatives and safety committees have the necessary facilities to perform their functions. They must also consult safety representatives on all matters concerning the health and safety of the workforce, including consultation on the preparation of a safety case and introduction of any measure or new technology which might affect the health and safety of the workforce. They must also provide training and relevant information and documentation relating to the occupational health and safety of the workforce.

11.111   The safety representatives can inspect any part of the offshore installation, investigate potential hazards, dangerous occurrences and complaints by the workforce, and make representations to the OIM on these matters. The representative is also entitled to attend meetings on health and safety measures and inform employees about health and safety.

11.112   The OIM must chair the safety committee which must meet at least once every three months. The main role of the committee is to encourage and maintain health and safety standards with the mutual assistance of the management and the workforce. It may also take into account and recommend issues such as health and safety measures, the system of constituencies, the training of safety representatives, health and safety matters raised by members and the causes of accidents and job related illness.

11.113   It is a criminal offence for a duty holder, OIM or other employer to fail to comply with the provisions of the Offshore Installations (Safety Representatives and Safety Committees) Regulations 1989.[1]

1   SI 1989/971, as amended.

WorkingTime (Amendment) Regulations 2003[1]

11.114   The amendment to the Working Time Directive[2] (WTD) was adopted by the European Parliament and Council as Council Directive 2000/34/EC. The WTD now covers the previously excluded sectors, including offshore workers.

1   SI 2003/1684.
2   Council Directive 93/104/EC.

11.115   As a result, the Working Time (Amendment) Regulations 2003[1] came into force on 1 August 2003. Offshore workers must not now work more than 2,304 hours a year. UKOOA has confirmed that the UK oil and gas industry complies with the new regulations, as a typical work pattern of two weeks offshore and two weeks' leave means that most offshore workers work in the region of 2,000 hours per annum. The Regulations recognise the unique working conditions in the North Sea and accordingly allow companies to calculate working time by averaging the maximum 48-hour week over a 52-week period, as opposed to the usual 17-week period.

1   SI 2003/1684.

11.116   It is a criminal offence to fail to comply with the Working Time (Amendment) Regulations 2003.[1] As human error is often a factor in oil and gas health and safety failures, the importance of complying with these Regulations must not be underestimated.

1   SI 2003/1684.

Petroleum operations notices (PONs), operations notices and safety notices

11.117   These outline in more detail the requirements of licensees to fulfil their obligations under the legal framework of Acts and Regulations whilst undertaking exploration, appraisal and development programmes on their licenses. See Appendix 11.3 at **para A11.3.0** below for a list of relevant notices.

Evaluation of the offshore safety legislative regime

11.118   It is the policy of the HSE to undertake formal evaluations of any major new legislation where there may be a substantial change in practice for industry. The development of the safety case regime was such a major project that the HSE conducted several evaluations of the impact of the SCR.[1] In 1995 an interim evaluation was conducted by AUPEC to evaluate their impact on the operation of management.[2] In 1999 the same organisation conducted a comprehensive follow-up report, the results of which provide a valuable insight into the operational successes and failures of the new legislative regime.[3]

1   SI 1992/2885.
2   The AUPEC Survey *Interim Evaluation of the effectiveness of the Offshore Installation (Safety Case) Regulations 1992 (SCR)* (1999). The report was conducted on behalf of the HSE by AUPEC in conjunction with specialists from the University of Aberdeen.
3   AUPEC Report *Evaluation of the Offshore Safety Legislative Regime (EOSLR)* (the AUPEC Report) (1999).

11.119   A sample was taken of the views and experiences of management and personnel from 28 duty holding companies. The results were 'broadly positive with both senior managers and workers reporting tangible safety benefits from the introduction of the Safety Case Regime'.[1] The majority of respondents believed that the objectives for the regulatory regime set out in the Cullen Report[2] had been largely met, with no perceived gaps, that the pace of reform was appropriate, and that the regime was capable of dealing with likely future challenges.[3] The post-Cullen regime was regarded as far reaching and radical – resulting in a sea change in philosophy.

1   AUPEC Report, p 6, **para 11.4 n 1** above.
2   See para **11.3 n 1** above.
3   AUPEC Report, p 5, para **11.4 n 1** above.

11.120   The framework currently in place was regarded by the companies surveyed as 'among the best in the world' with the SCR[1] forming the 'centrepiece of the offshore safety legislative regime'.[2] The key effects of the legislation were broadly, 'heightened awareness of risks throughout the industry, a more structured decision-making process, targeting of risk reduction efforts, Safety Management System improvements and an improved safety culture'.[3]

1 SI 1992/2885.
2 AUPEC Report, p 6, para **11.4 n 1** above.
3 AUPEC Report, p 11, para **11.4 n 1** above.

11.121   Many respondents indicated uncertainty regarding the MAR[1] definition of duty holder and felt that the HSE had difficulty in identifying the duty holder in complex interrelationship between contractors and operators. The complexity of the duty holder structure highlighted the importance of regular interface meetings between client/duty holder. DCR[2] was regarded generally as complex and with the Guidance lacking clarity. PFEER[3] was found to have produced a 'more structured and rigorous' approach to risk assessments and mitigation programmes, providing 'scope for more systematic approaches to maintenance and inspection.' A need to clarify PFEER, reg 17,[4] 'prospects of good recovery', was also identified.

1 SI 1995/738.
2 SI 1996/913.
3 SI 1995/743.
4 SI 1995/743, reg 17.

11.122   The involvement of the entire workforce in safety management was identified by the Cullen Report[1] as crucial. Yet AUPEC concluded that 'while much had been achieved in enhancing communication on safety issues – including those relating to the installation Safety Case and Safety Management Systems – there was evidence that achievements in encouraging active workforce participation in safety were more modest'.[2]

1 See para **11.3 n 4** above.
2 AUPEC Report, p 9, para **11.4 n 1** above.

11.123   The most frequently raised issue concerning the industry-regulator relationship was the perceived inconsistency in HSE's enforcement and assessment actions. Many respondents stated that inspection enforcement and assessment decisions varied from one inspector to another, between different geographical parts of the HSE, and between HSE topic specialists and field inspectors'.[1] Many respondents were of the view that the HSE should take a more proactive role.

1 AUPEC Report, p 9, para **11.4 n 1** above.

Enforcement regime

Hazardous Installations Directorate[1]

11.124   The Hazardous Installations Directorate (HID) is a directorate of the HSE which is responsible for the health and safety regulation of the majority of hazardous industries in UK. HID results from the amalgamation of the Offshore Safety Division, HM Mines Inspectorate and the Chemical and Hazardous Installations Division and is made up of the Central, Land and Offshore Divisions.

1 See www.hse.gov.uk/hid

11.125   The aim of HID is to 'improve the health and safety of people by being an independent, expert, effective and a fair regulator of the offshore and onshore oil and gas industries, diving at work, the chemical and explosives industries and the mining industry', which can be achieved 'by ensuring the industries they regulate are properly controlled, by ensuring compliance with the law and promoting improvement in standards'. HID's priority programmes include reducing musculoskeletal disorders arising from 'manual handling' operations, reducing slips, trips, falls from height and road tankers and reducing stress in the natural gas supply industry.[1]

1   HID *Strategic Plan 2001–2004.*

11.126   HID has the responsibility for ensuring health and safety compliance in around 9,000 companies. The HSE plan is to improve the focus of its campaigns to look at improving compliance in specific hazardous sectors. Amongst these is the Offshore programme which aims to achieve a 15% reduction in accidents and dangerous occurrences involving lifting operations and mechanical handling, with a three-year programme aimed at work related lifting operations offshore and raising awareness of risks and control measures.

Offshore Division

11.127   The Offshore Division's aim is to ensure that risks to people who work in the oil and gas extraction and diving industries are properly controlled.[1] The Offshore Division's work includes visiting, auditing and inspecting offshore installations, enforcing diving legislation, investigating accidents, assessing safety cases, providing technical information and statistical intelligence as well as providing advice and guidance on operational and technical matters with the aim of reducing the release of hydrocarbons.

1   See www.hse.gov.uk/hid/noframes/osd.htm.

Land Division

11.128   The Land Division has operational responsibility within HSE for, among other matters, gas supply and network integrity issues and also for pipeline safety, including technical support, guidance and advice both onshore and offshore.

Field Operations Directorate

11.129   The Field Operations Directorate (FOD) is the largest operational inspectorate in the HSE[1] and is concerned with reducing risks, providing advice, assisting in compliance with the law, inspecting workplaces, investigating accidents and taking action where necessary.

1   See www.hse.gov.uk/fod/fodhome.htm.

11.130   From an oil and gas perspective, the relevance of FOD is that it is responsible for construction, general manufacturing, engineering, and domestic gas safety. The Central Specialist Division provides technical advice across the HSE on many health hazards, particularly chemicals (including notification of new substances), pesticides and biocides, noise and vibration.

11.131   FOD's priority issues include falls from height, workplace transport, musculoskeletal troubles, stress, construction, agriculture, health services and slips and trips. In addition to this FOD plans to investigate all fatal injuries and 95% of RIDDOR[1] incidents; follow up at least 90% of complaints; and continue to expand its safety awareness programme.[2]

1   SI 1995/3163.
2   FOD *2003/2004 FOD Work Plan Activity Tables.*

Offshore Industry Advisory Committee[1]

11.132   The Offshore Industry Advisory Committee (OIAC) is one of a number of groups set up by the Health and Safety Commission (HSC). It advises the HSC on the protection of people at work from hazards in the workplace within the oil industry and such activities. The Committee was reconstituted in April 2000 and now has more of an influence on the offshore oil and gas industry. The key issues are technical safety such as the foundations of installations, human factor issues, risk management, occupational health, competence, workforce interface and communication on health and safety issues.

1   www.hse.gov.uk/aboutus/hsc/iacs/oiac/.

Oil and Gas Directorate of the DTI[1]

11.133   The overall objective of the Oil and Gas Directorate of the DTI is to:

'Maximise the economic benefit to the UK of its oil and gas resources, taking into account the environmental impact of hydrocarbon development and the need to ensure secure, diverse sustainable supplies of energy at competitive prices.'[2]

1   See www.og.dti.gov.uk.
2   DTI *Development of UK Oil and Gas Resources* (2001) p 2.

11.134   The development of UK oil and gas resources is monitored by the Directorate which is also involved in licensing exploration. The Directorate also supports the upstream and downstream oil and gas industry and is also a part of the DTI's Energy Command.

Other enforcement bodies

11.135   There are other enforcement bodies which regulate certain aspects of health and safety in the oil and gas industry. These are dealt with in other chapters and include the Civil Aviation Authority, the Maritime and Coastguard Agency, local authorities, the Environment Agency and the Scottish Environment Protection Agency.

Industry organisations

UK Offshore Operators Association[1]

11.136   Members of the UK Offshore Operators Association (UKOOA) are companies licensed by the government to explore and produce oil and gas in UK waters. The role of UKOOA is to boost links with government and the public. The prime objectives are safety, energy and environment policy, operations and technical issues, industrial relations, fiscal and economic affairs in the industry and gas issues including the UK upstream and downstream industry.

1   www.ukooa.org.uk.

11.137   UKOOA monitors operational issues which impact upon safety in the industry. UKOOA played an important part in the Cullen Inquiry Part II[1] on preventative measures for the future and the Health and Safety Committee Practice Sharing Team continues to promote the sharing of safety information and good practice.

1   See **para 11.3 n 1** above.

International Association of Drilling Contractors[1]

11.138   Created in 1940, the International Association of Drilling Contractors (IADC) represents the worldwide oil and gas drilling industry. The aim of the IADC is to promote and preserve the environment and to progress drilling technology. Membership of the Association is open to companies involved in oil and gas exploration and production, well servicing, oilfield manufacturing and other rig site services, although the majority of members are companies who own or provide drilling rigs.

1   www.iadc.org.uk.

11.139   A number of committees form the IADC including the Health, Safety and Environment Committee, which distributes all the best practices to the IADC membership and works to improve the performance of the industry in matters with regards to occupational safety and health and environmental affairs. The main task of the Committees is to ensure a forum of exchanging safety information and health and regulatory issues. The IADC also monitors the findings of the IADC Accident Statistics Program and make suggestions for revision as needed to the board of Directors. The IADC has developed *IADC North West European HSE Case Guidelines for MODUs*[1] primarily to support IADC members in preparing HSE safety cases that would enable mobile offshore drilling units (MODUs) to move between different sectors of the North Sea without necessitating revision of the HSE safety case.

1   IADC (2002).

International Marine Contractors Association[1]

11.140   The International Marine Contractors Association (IMCA) is the international trade association representing offshore diving, marine and underwater engineering companies. IMCA issues guidance notes and Codes of Practice relating to quality, health, safety, and environmental and technical standards. IMCA is also involved in offshore safety information which it distributes to its members. It also facilitates members' input in the 'Step Change in Safety' initiative. IMCA's Safety, Environment & Legislation Core Committee promotes the sharing of experience and helps to avoid duplication of effort in issues concerned with legislation.

1 www.imca-int.com.

Offshore Contractors Association[1]

11.141   Founded in 1995, the Offshore Contractors Association (OCA) is an industry body which represents oil and gas contractors and suppliers. It aims to ensure a voice on industry matters in order to promote health and safety issues and to encourage special courses to train personnel.

1 www.oca-online.co.uk.

PILOT

11.142   PILOT[1] is the successor to the Oil and Gas Industry Task Force (OGITF) which was created in 1998 in recognition of the challenges faced by the industry as a result of the dramatic fall in oil prices, the prospect of reduced world demand and the maturing of the UKCS.

1 www.pilottaskforce.co.uk.

11.143   The PILOT concept aims to unite the senior management of operators, contractors, suppliers, unions and relevant government Departments, thereby working to address the need to reduce the cost base of activity in the UKCS. It also aims 'to create a climate for the UKCS to retain its position as a pre-eminent active centre of oil and gas exploration and development and production and to keep the UK contracting and supplies industry at the leading edge in terms of overall competitiveness'.

11.144   PILOT's strategy is to achieve the following outcomes by the year 2010:

* 3 mmboe/d production beyond 2010;
* £3 billion per annum Industry investment;
* Prolonged self-sufficiency in oil and gas;
* Up to 100,000 more jobs (than there would otherwise have been);
* 50% increase in exports (by 2005);
* £1 billion per annum additional revenue for new business; and
* to make the UK the safest place to work in the worldwide oil and gas industry

Step Change[1]

11.145   Launched in September 1997, 'Step Change in Safety' was an initiative by industry leaders, including organisations such as UKOOA, IADC and OCA, to promote a step change in safety culture and to enhance co-operation between companies working in the UKCS. A commitment was made to:

- improve the sharing of safety information and good practice across the whole industry through the involvement of trade unions, employees, service companies, regulators and representative bodies;
- establish leadership safety performance contracts; and
- deliver a 50% improvement in the industry's safety performance in three years.

1 See http://step.steel-sci.org.

11.146 Since its launch in 1997, Step Change has seen an enormous increase in cross industry co-operation through active participation in numerous forums, networks and workgroups. This has contributed to a significant improvement in the safety performance of the industry.

The Energy Institue[1]

11.147 The Energy Institute was created in 2003, following the merger of the Petroleum Institute and the Institute of Energy. The purpose of the Energy Institute is to promote the safe and environmentally responsible use of energy in all its forms and applications.

1 www.petroleum.co.uk.

Others

11.148 Other industry bodies include the Northern Offshore Federation, the Well Services Contractors Association, the Scottish Enterprise Energy Group, the UK Onshore Operators Group and the UK Petroleum Industry Association.

HSE safety statistics

11.149 Following the launch of the government's *Revitalising Health and Safety* initiative in June 2000 , the offshore industry announced a strategy for responding to the '*Revitalising*' targets by agreeing its own specific targets. These are:

- to achieve a continuous, year-on-year improvement trend in safety, culminating in a 50% reduction in the fatal and major injury rate by 2010;
- to reduce the number of working days lost per 100,000 workers by 30% by 2010; and
- to achieve half the improvement under each target by 2004.

Hydrocarbon release statistics

11.150 The Cullen Report[1] identified the release of hydrocarbons as particularly alarming in all cases due to their extreme flammability.[2] As a result, detailed provisions are contained in PFEER[3] concerning the appropriate measures which duty holders must take to prevent fire and explosion, including preventing uncontrolled releases of flammable or explosive substances, preventing unwanted or unnecessary accumulation of combustible, flammable or explosive substances and preventing the ignition of such substances.[4]

1   See **para 11.3 n 1** above.
2   Hydrocarbon is a term used mainly in a catch-all sense for oil, gas and condensate which are the main hydrocarbon fuels found upon installations.
3   SI 1995/743.
4   SI 1995/743, reg 9, ACOP and Guidance L65.

11.151   The HSE has been monitoring hydrocarbon releases for a number of years because they are a very simple indicator of trends in major accident potential. A campaign was announced by the HSE in December 2000 to reduce major and significant releases by 50% by the end of 2003–004.[1] In the first two years of the campaign, up to the end of March 2002, major and significant releases fell by 21.6%, whilst the number of releases in the major category alone fell by 66%.[2] The breakdown by installation type shows that fixed installations were responsible for 2,229 of the 2,312 reported cases, or 96.4%, from October 1992 to March 2002.[3] By contrast only 3.6% were reported from mobile drilling and accommodation installations.

1   Taf Powell, head of OSD quoted in HSE press release E244;00, 19 December 2000: www.hse.gov.uk.
2   HSE press release 'Safety watchdog targets offshore hydrocarbon leaks', 28 November 2002.
3   HSE *Offshore Hydrocarbon Release Statistics 2002.*

11.152   Releases are notified to the HSE on a voluntary basis. However, the HSE warned operators that from 1 April 2001 it would start to investigate every hydrocarbon release in the UK offshore sector. Previously it had only investigated the major releases. Clearly the importance of hydrocarbon releases is the risk of their ignition and consequential injuries and damage to installations. According to the HSE, 148 ignitions (6.2% of all releases) have been reported since 1992. To date there have been no ignited major releases, however, 7.3% of all ignitions involved significant releases'.[1]

1   HSE *Offshore Hydrocarbon Release Statistics 2002.*

11.153   The fact that 55% of the releases are caused by 'hard' equipment issues, such as pipework, flanges, instrumentation corrosion and erosion and 45% of the releases are caused by 'soft' people issues which require a focus on training, competencies, procedures and behavioural culture, demonstrates the difficulties which the industry faces to eradicate the problem.

11.154

Hydrocarbon releases notified to the HSE from 1 October 1992 to 31 March 2003[1]

	1992 –93	1993 –94	1994 –95	1995 –96	1996 –97	1997 –98	1998 –99	1999 –2000	2000 –01	2001 –02	2002 –03
Major	12	24	20	20	19	13	15	12	8	4	6
Significant	50	151	194	134	129	139	134	127	117	109	79
Minor	19	96	111	58	78	66	85	95	145	128	N/A
Total	**81**	**271**	**325**	**212**	**226**	**218**	**234**	**234**	**270**	**241**	**N/A**

1   2003 – 'provisional' statistics – see HSE Press release 3 September 2003 – www.hse.gov.uk.

Severity classification[1] definitions

SIGNIFICANT MAJOR

11.155 'Potential to quickly impact outwith the local area, for example, affect the Temporary Refuge (TR), escape routes, escalate to other areas of the installation, causing serious injury or fatalities.' A major leak, if ignited, would be likely to cause a 'major accident', ie it would be of a size capable of causing multiple casualties or rapid escalation affecting TR, escape routes etc.

1   HSR 2002 002 *Offshore Hydrocarbon Releases – Statistics 2002* (2002), available at www.hse.gov.uk/hid/osd/hsr2002/section6.htm.

SIGNIFICANT

11.156 'Potential to cause serious injury or fatality to personnel within the local area and to escalate within the local area, for example, by causing structural escalation, secondary leaks or damage to safety systems.' A significant leak, if ignited, might have the potential to cause an event severe enough to be viewed as a 'major accident' or be of a size leading to significant escalation within the immediate area or module.

MINOR

11.157 'Potential to cause serious injury to personnel in the immediate vicinity, but no potential to escalate or cause multiple fatalities.' A minor leak, even if ignited, would not be expected to result in a multiple fatality event or significant escalation, but could cause serious injuries or a fatality local to the leak site or within that module only.

HSE offshore hydrocarbon releases go online

11.158 The HSE launched the online version of the offshore hydrocarbon releases (HCR) system on 14 July 2003. The HCR system contains detailed voluntary information on offshore hydrocarbon release incidents supplementary to that provided under RIDDOR.[1]

1   SI 1995/3163.

11.159 The HCR system was created in response to recommendation 39 of the Cullen Report.[1] This required that such a database be set up by the HSE for and on behalf of the industry, and that industry access be given to the data. UKOOA has supported the enhancement of this HSE database and the use of the Internet to help both the industry and regulator in speeding up the reporting and analysis of hydrocarbon releases. This collaboration represents a milestone in the overall joint industry/HSE campaign to further improve the safety of offshore installations.

1   See **para 11.3 n 1** above.

11.160 Offshore releases of hydrocarbons are currently reported to the Offshore Division as dangerous occurrences under RIDDOR[1] which applied offshore from 1 April 1996. The HCR system contains detailed voluntary information on offshore hydrocarbon release incidents supplementary to that provided under RIDDOR (and offshore legislation prior to 1996) and the database contains data dating from 1 October 1992.

1 SI 1995/3163.

11.161   Since 1994, the HSE has produced offshore hydrocarbon release statistics reports annually, derived from the HCR database.[1] The HSE is working closely with industry to examine the problem areas to try to reduce further the number of releases. The HCR statistics are also being used to measure performance against the stated aim of reducing the number of major and significant releases to 50% of the 2000 baseline figure of 139 by 2003.

1 The latest version is available at www.hse.gov.uk/hid/osd/hsr2002/index.htm.

Recent cases

11.162   There have been a number of recent cases which demonstrate the seriousness with which the courts treat hydrocarbon releases.

R v BG Exploration and Production Ltd[1]

11.163   BG pleaded guilty to breaches of HSWA 1974, PFEER[2] and RIDDOR[3] and was fined £300,000, with costs of £198,596, following a release of natural gas from an offshore gas platform. A large volume of gas leaked accidentally through a pipework joint which had been isolated for maintenance work. There was no ignition or explosion but the lives of 15 employees on the central platform were put at risk. Investigations by the HSE concluded that there had been management shortcomings in the way the joint was installed, how the leak was tested and how the incident was managed after the escape of gas. In addition, BG failed to notify the HSE in accordance with RIDDOR.

1 (10 February 2000), Kingston-upon-Hull Crown Court; HSB 286 (March 2000) p 3.
2 SI 1995/743.
3 SI 1995/3163.

11.164   BG pleaded guilty to six health and safety offences, for failing to:

- ensure the safety of its employees (of HSWA 1974, s 2(1));
- prevent the exposure of people other than its employees to risks to their safety (HSWA 1974, s 3(1));
- prepare and revise an emergency response plan covering the organisation, arrangements and procedures which are to have effect in an emergency (PFEER, reg 8(1)[1]);
- take appropriate action to prevent fire and explosion, including preventing the uncontrolled release of flammable or explosive substances (PFEER, reg 9(1)[2]);
- take appropriate measure to protect persons on an installation during an emergency from the effects of fire and explosion (PFEER, reg 13[3]); and
- notify the enforcing authority of a dangerous occurrence (RIDDOR, reg 3(1)[4]; RIDDOR, Sch 2, Pt V[5] lists as a dangerous occurrence any unintentional release of petroleum hydrocarbon on, or from, an offshore installation which results in action to limit the consequences of a potential fire or explosion which results in action to limit the consequences of a potential fire or explosion or has potential to cause death or major injury to any person).

1   SI 1995/743, reg 8(1).
2   SI 1995/743, reg 9(1).
3   SI 1995/743, reg 13.
4   SI 1995/3163, reg 3(1).
5   SI 1995/3163, Sch 2, Pt V.

R v AMOCO (UK) EXPLORATION CO[1]

11.165   On 12 October 2001 Amoco (UK) Exploration Company pleaded guilty to a contravention of HSWA 1974, s 3 and were fined £140,000 plus costs, following a release of gas from a 30-foot sphere (pig) launcher on the Leman 27a installation on 9 December 1998. The release was caused by the failure of an 'o' ring between the hub flange faces of the sphere launcher. The failure of the 'o' ring was caused by the methods used to clean corrosion around the door. The automatic safety systems ensured the safe shutdown of operations and no one was injured.

1   (12 October 2001), Norwich Crown Court; HSB 303 (November 2001) p 6.

R v TRANSCO[1]

11.166   Transco, at that time the gas distribution wing of British Gas, was fined £120,000 with £39,545 costs for failing to have a safe system of work which led to a gas explosion on 23 April 1997 injuring ten workers. Due to the neglect of basic safety standards, gas escaped from pipes being repaired by the company. Failure to deal adequately with the leak, exacerbated by the presence of an electro-fusion generator in the area, allowed the leak to ignite and an explosion caused severe burns to those employees present. The defendant pleaded guilty to two charges under HSWA 1974, s 2 and 3 for failing to protect the health and safety of employees and non-employees.

1   (20 February 1999), Warrington Crown Court; HSB 277, (1 April 1991) p 1.

R v BG STORAGE LTD[1]

11.167   BG Storage was fined £50,000 and ordered to pay costs amounting to £38,000 for failing to comply with a prohibition notice on its Rough 47/3B installation. Following a plea of guilty, the magistrates declined jurisdiction and the case was committed to Hull Crown Court for sentence on 26 April 2001. The fine was one of the highest ever imposed for a breach of a prohibition notice. The breach concerned pressure relief valves which in the opinion of HSE's Offshore Division inspectors posed a risk of serious personal injury to employees. A prohibition notice was issued which stopped on the use of the pressure relief valves until the company either adopted the five measures laid down in the schedule to the notice or demonstrated that it had in place an equally safe alternative. The company undertook the type of maintenance work specified in the notice but did not fulfil its other terms and were therefore in breach of the notice.

1   (26 April 2001), Kingston-upon-Hull Crown Court; HSB 299 (June 2001) p 3.

R v BP OPERATING CO LTD[1]

11.168   Following an uncontrolled gas release on an offshore gas platform, BP pleaded guilty to two breaches of HSWA 1974 and were fined a total of £50,000 and ordered to pay costs of £33,000 at Derby Crown Court on 22 August 2003. The incident arose while a contractor was refitting a pressure safety valve. The release occurred when the worker placed his foot on the unsecured handle of an isolation valve, causing it to open.

1 (22 August 2003), Kingston-upon-Hull Crown Court; HSB 322, p 3.

R v Paul Timson[1]

11.169 Paul Timson, a valve manufacturer, was jailed for 15 months after forging valve safety certificates for oil and gas platforms. Timson pleaded guilty to:

- 19 charges of forging safety certificates for ball valves;
- one charge under the Theft Act 1968 of using forged business documents for financial gain; and
- three charges under HSWA 1974 of supplying unsafe valves.

1 (12 September 2003), Derby Crown Court; HSB 323, p 1.

11.170 Prosecuting counsel told the court that Timson's actions could have resulted in a significant hydrocarbon release which could have 'set off a catastrophic chain of events as seen on Piper Alpha'. He was sentenced to 15 months' imprisonment, concurrent on each of the forgery charges. There was no separate penalty for the health and safety charges. All offences happened when he was working for Nixon Industrial valves and VSL Valves Products Ltd, between March 1997 and June 1998. As a result of Mr Timson's activities, the HSE had to issue a safety alert in May 1999.

Provisional HSE Offshore Statistics Bulletin for 2002–03[1]

11.171

- No fatalities – compared to three in 2001–02.
- Fifty-eight major injuries – a 7% increase on 2001–02.
- The combined fatal and major injury rate increased to 260.5 per 100,000 workers compared with 245.6 in 2001–02.
- One hundred and twenty-three over-three-day injuries, a 31% drop on 2001–02.
- Six hundred and thirty-six dangerous occurrences which is 25 fewer than during 2000–01 – a 4% decrease.

1 HSA Press Release, 3 September 2003 – www.hse.gov.uk.

Fatal injuries in 2001–02

11.172 During 2001–02 three fatal injuries were reported and details of these were as follows.

11.173 July 2001: on the drill floor of a jack-up mobile offshore drilling unit. A roughneck was assisting in running sand screens downhole. Whilst he was placing the stab-in guide onto the stand-up in the rotary, his head was pushed into the guide by the topdrive when it descended. On 10 April 2003, Global Santa Fe Drilling Company (North Sea) Ltd appeared at Aberdeen Sheriff Court accused of causing the death by failing to take reasonable precautions to ensure the health and safety of its employees. The company, which denies the charges, is alleged to have failed to provide a safe system of work and failed to ensure that adequate information, training and supervision was provided for its employees.

11.174   November 2001: in one of the columns of a semi-submersible offshore drilling unit. During a routine maintenance operation to replace the hoist rope of a personnel elevator/lift, the deceased fell with the cage to the bottom of the shaft.

11.175   March 2002: on the deck of a semi-submersible offshore drilling unit. The deceased, a banksman/slinger, became trapped between lifting baskets during attendant vessel offloading operations.

11.176   The main cause of fatal and major injuries was being struck by moving objects, which accounted for 31%, with fracture as the most likely harm caused.

11.177

Number of fatalities of offshore workers compared with total fatalities in all other industries – 1993–94 to 2002–03[1]

	1993 –94	1994 –95	1995 –96	1996 –97	1997 –98	1998 –99	1999 –2000	2000 –01	2001 –02	2002 –03
Offshore	1	1	5	2	3	1	2	3	3	N/A
Other	296	272	258	287	274	253	220	292	251	226

1   www.hse.gov.uk – see HSE Press Release 3 September 2003. It should be noted that the offshore statistics only relate to fatalities which come within the authority of the HSE – in practical terms this means that accidents such as the helicopter crash which killed 11 personnel in 2002 (see **para 11.10** above) are not included, as that particular accident is a matter for the Civil Aviation Authority.

11.178

Three-year rolling average of number of injuries (P) April 1992– March 2002[1]

	1992 –95	1993 –96	1994 –97	1995 –98	1996 –99	1997 –2000	1998 –2001	1999 –2002 (P)
Combined fatalities and major injuries	91	76	62	65	66	69	62	56
Over-3-day	365	321	296	314	279	243	205	181

1   www.hse.gov.uk.

11.179

Summary of injury rates per 100,000 workers (P)April 1993–March 2002[1]

	1993 –94	1994 –95	1995 –96	1996 –97	1997 –98	1998 –99	1999 –2000	2000 –01 (P)	2001 –02 (P)
Fatalities	2.9	3.7	17.2	7.4	13.0	3.9	10.5	12.9	12
Major	254.4	250.0	231.0	163.9	321.7	290.2	273.7	227.2	237
Combined fatalities and major injuries	257.3	253.7	248.3	171.3	334.8	294.1	284.2	249	240
Over-3-day	1102.3	878.7	1199.9	1124.6	1256.2	960.8	1015.8	758.7	741.2

1 www.hse.gov.uk.

Sentencing

11.180 The sentencing guidelines and procedures set out in the Court of Appeal decisions of *R v F Howe and Son (Engineers) Ltd*[1] and *R v Friskies Petcare UK Ltd*[2] should be followed in all health and safety cases and will undoubtedly be applied to corporate killing cases. Neither decision is binding on the Scottish courts, although they are persuasive.

1 [1999] 2 All ER 249.
2 [2000] Cr App R (S) 401.

11.181 Although the guideline case of *Howe*[1] sets out the mitigating and aggravating features to be taken into account, it does not in any way set any tariffs for such offences and, to that extent, it is wholly unhelpful. The oil and gas cases listed below are set out in order of the size of fine and cover the whole of the UK. They give some indication of the level of fines which a court might consider for a similar conviction under HSWA 1974 or the regulations or under the proposed new law of corporate killing. Whilst the facts in each case are different, nevertheless the cases demonstrate that there is a wide disparity in levels of sentencing for oil and gas health and safety cases, which is further highlighted by the significant differences in fine levels between Scotland and England. These cases also demonstrate how the rule in Scotland that parties in criminal proceedings cannot apply for their costs makes a significant difference in health and safety cases. Details of further cases can be found in the enforcement section of the HSE website.[2]

1 *R v F Howe and Son (Engineers) Ltd* [1999] 2 All ER 249.
2 See www.hse.gov.uk.

HMA v BP Grangemouth Oil Refinery Ltd and BP Chemicals Ltd[1]

11.182 BP were fined a total of £1million for breaches of the HSWA 1974, following two incidents at BP's Grangemouth refinery in June 2000. The fines were imposed at Falkirk Sheriff Court on 18 January 2002, following a plea of guilty. The first incident, for which a fine of £250,000 was imposed, occurred when a steam pipe ruptured and one passer-by was injured. Three days later, there was a fire in a catalytic converter. The fine of £750,000 for the second incident was a record for such a case. The Sheriff found that there had been a 'gross dereliction of duties' and that it had been a matter of chance that there were no serious injuries or deaths. The important development which this sentence demonstrates is an increasing tendency by both the HSE and the courts to focus on the potential of an incident to escalate, as opposed to what actually did occur. An HSE major investigation report into these incidents was published on 18 August 2003.[2]

1   (18 January 2002), Falkirk Sheriff Court; HSB 306, p 2.
2   www.hse.gov.uk.

HMA v British Petroleum[1]

11.183   Two accidents at Grangemouth involved a fire on 13 March 1987 and a fire and an explosion on 22 of March 1987 which killed two workers and seriously injured another two. The first arose from a failure to ensure that a section of the flare system was effectively drained of gases and hydrocarbon maintenance when work on a valve was started and resulted in a fine of £250,000 for breaches of HSWA 1974. The second stemmed from the escape of high pressure flammable gas from a high pressure to a low pressure separator vessel and led to a fine of £500,000 for beaches of HSWA 1974. The HSE found that more extensive monitoring and supervision of work would have prevented this accident.

1   HSB 149, p 5.

R v Amec and BJ Process and Pipeline Services[1]

11.184   Two engineering companies were fined a total of £450,000 when three pipefitters were killed in an explosion on an offshore gas platform in 1995. The men were all employed by AMEC Process and Energy Ltd in the construction of an offshore gas platform at Wallsend, Tyne and Wear. Tests on pipework were being carried out by a contractor, Nowsco Ltd (now BJ Process and Pipeline Services Ltd) and the AMEC pipefitters were repairing leaks. They believed one of the pipes to be depressurised but in fact it still contained gas at test pressure, which was released as they undid a clamp. One man was killed instantly and the other two died a few hours later in hospital.

1   (18 November 1997), Newcastle Crown Court.

11.185   The Crown Court heard that Nowsco's safe system of work was faulty because the points in the pipework from which pressurised gas could be released were not identified before the tests were made. Because of the complexity of the task which had been compounded by the simultaneous testing, the system broke down. AMEC's first breach was the failure to maintain its permit-to-work system. No checks by AMEC were made to ensure that the pipework had been depressurised before issuing new permits for each test. AMEC also allowed several repairs to go ahead covered by only one permit which made it more difficult to ascertain whether or not all of the pipes had been depressurised. The companies also relied on verbal exchanges to assure that depressurisation had taken place.

11.186   Both companies pleaded guilty to breaches of HSWA 1974, ss 2(1) and 3(1). AMEC was fined a total of £150,000, with £8,750 costs and BJ Process and Pipeline Services Ltd was fined a total of £300,000, with £8,750 costs·

R v British Oxygen Co[1]

11.187   Following a plea of guilty, British Oxygen Co was fined £300,000 (with costs of £58,000) under HSWA 1974 following a fatality after an explosion during the filling of compressed gas cylinders with special gases. The explosion killed one employee, injured another and caused extensive site damage. Investigation revealed lack of adequate risk assessment, unsafe plant, unsafe system of work, and inadequate training and supervision.

1   (2 August 1999, unreported – case number TI9990421), Kingston-upon-Hull Crown Court.

R v Gulf Oil and Texaco[1]

11.188   Texaco and Gulf Oil pleaded guilty to four charges under HSWA 1974, ss 2(1) and 3(1). The case concerned an explosion caused by a process failure and led to parts of the Milford Haven refinery being shut down. During the course of the incident, about 20 tonnes of flammable vapour were released which became ignited and caused the explosion. Damage was even caused in Milford Haven town two miles away. The HSE claimed that over a four-hour period, the cause and seriousness of the problem was not addressed and that a number of preventative systems had failed. The total fines were £200,000 (£100,000 per company) with costs of £143,700.

1   (22 November 1997), Swansea Crown Court; HSB 253, p 3.

HMA v Odeco Drilling (UK) Ltd & Arco British (Ocean Odyssey)[1]

11.189   This case was the first health and safety prosecution of a company in the offshore industry in the High Court of Justiciary in Scotland. The case concerned a fatality on board the Ocean Odyssey. Following a plea of guilty to charges under HSWA 1974, Odeco was fined a total of £250,000 while Arco was fined £50,000.

1   High Court of Justiciary, August 1993 – HSE case numbers F20000 231 and F 200000 234 – www.hse.gov.uk.

HMA v MacGregor Energy Services Ltd and Global Marine UK Ltd[1]

11.190   Two workers, employees of MacGregor Energy Services, were killed in a fire following a blast inside the leg of Global Marine's Glomar Arctic IV while it was berthed in Dundee in July 1998. The men, a welder and a plater, were caught in the explosion as leaking propane ignited in a confined space while the rig was undergoing repairs. Charges under HSWA 1974, s 2(1) were brought and the companies were fined a total of £100,000 (£50,000 each) at Dundee Sheriff Court for failing to take the necessary precautions which might have prevented the tragedy. MacGregor Energy Services had failed to make sure that standard safety procedures had been carried out by their supervisors. The court was also told that Global Marine had failed to issue a current permit to work for the type of work being carried out because of the time pressures involved in getting the rig ready for going offshore.

1 Dundee Sheriff Court, 19 July 1999 – HSE case numbers F200000 231 and F200000234 – www.hse.gov.uk.

HMA v Santa Fe Drilling Co (North Sea) Ltd[1]

11.191   At Aberdeen Sheriff Court on 19 November 2001, Santa Fe were fined £60,000 after a worker was winched into a 12-inch hole and crushed to death. The incident occurred on the Magellan rig, 120 miles east of Aberdeen, on 9 October 2000. The deceased died from multiple asphyxia injuries when he was pulled waist-first into the hole. The winch operator had failed to hear shouts to stop. Santa Fe admitted failing to ensure that a proper risk assessment and hazard identification had been carried out. Sheriff Annella Cowan said that Santa Fe was guilty of a 'glaring failure' but, taking into account the efforts made to improve safety, stated that the fine of £60,000 was appropriate.

1 Aberdeen Sheriff Court, 19 November 2001; *The Herald*, 20 November 2001.

11.192   At the subsequent fatal accident inquiry in May 2003, Sheriff McLernan criticised the 'staggering' list of safety failures that led to the death in this case. The Sheriff indicated that unless changes in practices were made, there was a real risk of another serious accident.[1]

1 *Express*, 20 May 2003.

PF (Aberdeen) v Diamond Offshore Drilling UK Ltd[1]

11.193   Somewhat surprisingly, this case was prosecuted on a summary complaint (maximum fine of £20,000) and arose as a result of an offshore fatality on the Ocean Nomad semi-submersible in January 2001 which was operating in Shell UK's Curlew Field. The accident occurred when a dropped length of casing which was being moved by crane from pipe deck to catwalk fell and crushed the deceased. The lifting slings on the casing joint were single wrapped instead of double wrapped. Diamond Offshore were fined £12,500 under HSWA 1974, s 2(1).

1 Aberdeen Sheriff Court, 5 March 2001. HSE case number 049 – www.hse.gov.uk. Diamond Offshore Drilling were also fined £75,000 at Aberdeen Sheriff Court for a fatality which occurred on 18 May 2000 – HSE case number 050.

HMA v Robb[1]

11.194   In August 1990, in the first prosecution of an offshore worker for culpable homicide, the accused was unanimously acquitted of culpable homicide but was found guilty of the alternative charge of failing to comply with duties under the Continental Shelf Act 1964, s 32(3) (not to do anything likely to endanger the safety of health of persons on the installation or to render unsafe any equipment used by or near it).

1 High Court of Justiciary, Aberdeen, 16 August 1990.

11.195   The incident involved drilling operations on a semi-submersible installation to extract and store a riser. Mr Robb was in charge of the operation on the drill floor as

Assistant Rig Superintendent and Pusher. As the riser was extracted, the accused failed to ensure that the riser was adequately supported, that it was placed in a horizontal position and that the lifting equipment had been detached from the riser thus resulting in the dangerous instability of the riser. The riser became detached, striking the deceased and propelling him from the drill floor onto a ramp and pipe deck wherein he sustained fatal injuries. The accused was fined £1,500.

Civil claims

11.196 It is not the purpose of this chapter to deal with civil liability. However, clearly this is a major issue for companies in the oil and gas industry and it is therefore appropriate to briefly mention a few cases. As previously indicated, the civil liabilities arising from the Piper Alpha disaster took a record 14 years to resolve (see **para 11.48** above).

11.197 The case of *Staves v Gulf Oil and Texaco*[1] followed upon the criminal prosecution mentioned at **para 11.188** above in respect of which the companies were fined £200,000. The case concerned the civil claims of three employees for severe post-traumatic stress disorder (PTSD) following the explosion at the oil refinery which was so forceful that it blew them off their feet. The explosion was caused by a gas leak which removed the armoured doors and roof from the room in which two of the men were working. The high state of alert and anxiety which followed overwhelmed the workers whose mental health deteriorated subsequently.

1 Swansea County Court, 25 November 1999, HSE 285, p 5.

11.198 The victims subsequently developed a phobia about returning to the scene, suffering flashbacks. Texaco had had all three men examined by a psychiatrist who diagnosed severe PTSD, after which they were given ill-health retirement from work. However, once the men lodged their compensation claims, backed by the Transport and General Workers Union, Texaco contested the claims. The quality of the psychiatric evidence offered by Texaco was severely criticised by the judge in the case as 'cavalier' and 'defective' and awards of £340,000, £289,000 and £210,000 were made, reflecting the men's permanent unfitness for work.

11.199 Many of the regulations affecting the oil and gas industry impose strict liability, as can be seen from the case of *MacMillan v Wimpey Offshore Construction*.[1] In that case, a rigger on an offshore installation sought damages from his employers for personal injury suffered when his head was battered against a metal rubbish skip by the foreman. The Scottish Appeal Court decided that the responsibility placed on the employer by the Offshore Installations (Operational Safety, Health and Welfare) Regulations 1976, regulation 32[2] was an absolute one, imposing a direct duty on employers to guarantee compliance from employees as well as creating vicarious liability for the default of an employee. Thus the employer was bound to ensure that his employees observe the Regulations even when they are not engaged in work or are acting outside the scope of their employment.

1 1990 SLT 5800, OH.
2 SI 1976/1019.

Scotland

11.200   The majority of offshore oil and gas activity is carried out in Scotland, within the jurisdiction of the Scottish courts, as is a considerable amount of downstream activity. The extent of the activity in Scotland can be seen from the fact that it is estimated that the oil and gas sector supports some116,000 'oil-related' jobs in Scotland, some 6% of the Scottish workforce.

11.201   From a legal perspective, Scotland is in a unique position. The statutory framework of HSWA 1974 and related Regulations applies to Scotland. Following devolution, the provisions of the Scotland Act 1998 ensure not only that the main provisions of HSWA 1974 are reserved to Westminster[1] but also that the ownership, exploration for and exploitation of deposits of oil and natural gas are also reserved.[2] However, the prosecution of criminal offences under Scots law is a matter for the Scottish Executive and is not reserved to Westminster.

1   Scotland Act 1998, Sch 5H.2.
2   Scotland Act 1998, Sch 5D.2.

11.202   There are a number of important differences between Scots and English law in respect of the court structure, the common law and in relation to the rules of criminal evidence and procedure.[1] These differences have a significant impact upon the way in which health and safety prosecutions are investigated, prosecuted and defended.

1   Criminal Procedure (Scotland) Act 1995.

The Scottish court structure

11.203   In Scotland, health and safety prosecutions are brought either in the Sheriff Court or in the High Court of Justiciary. If the case is brought in the Sheriff Court, this can either be on solemn or summary procedure. If the case is solemn, it will be on indictment and tried by a Sheriff and jury. If on a summary complaint, the case will be tried by a Sheriff sitting without a jury. If the case is tried in the High Court of Justiciary it will be on indictment and tried by a judge and jury. The High Court of Justiciary also sits as the ultimate criminal appellate court in respect of appeals against conviction and sentence.[1] There is no right of appeal to the House of Lords, although there is a limited right of appeal to the Privy Council in respect of 'devolution issues', which can include any human rights appeal points.

1   See eg *Crummock (Scotland) Ltd v HMA* 2000 SLT 677. This concerned the question of delay and human rights in bringing a health and safety prosecution.

11.204   The maximum criminal penalties at present in the Sheriff Court, summary procedure, are £5,000 for breaches of the regulations, £20,000 for breaches of the general duties under HSWA 1974 and £20,000 or six months' imprisonment or both for failure to comply with an improvement or prohibition notice or court remedy order.

11.205   In the Sheriff Court under solemn procedure or in the High Court, unlimited fines can be imposed for breaches of the regulations and general duties, unlimited fines or two years' imprisonment or both for failure to comply with an improvement or prohibition notice, court remedy order, for contravening licence requirements or provisions relating to explosives.

Conduct of prosecutions

11.206 In Scotland, it is the Procurator Fiscal Service and not the HSE which prosecutes criminal cases. This is a department of the Scottish Executive which provides Scotland's public prosecution and deaths investigation service. Headed by the Lord Advocate, the Procurator Fiscal Service is divided into regions for each of the six Sheriffdoms. All health and safety prosecutions in Scotland are conducted by the Regional Procurator Fiscal. The HSE will generally send a report to the Fiscal who will then consider the report, in conjunction with the Crown Office. The Fiscal has sole discretion in deciding:

* whether to instigate proceedings;
* who to prosecute and under what charges;
* in which court to bring the prosecution and whether under solemn or summary procedure; and
* the content and degree of specification in the complaint/indictment.

11.207 The Sheriffdom of Grampian Highlands and Islands is unique, as the Aberdeen office is the only Procurator Fiscal's Office in Scotland which has a Depute who is dedicated to health and safety prosecutions in the offshore oil and gas industry, including oil pollution, maritime incidents and emergency planning. This post was created in response to the Cullen Report[1] and reflects the seriousness with which such breaches are treated by the Crown. In the past few years, Aberdeen Sheriff Court has seen a significant increase in the number of health and safety prosecutions being brought against the oil and gas industry.

1 See **para 11.3 n 1** above.

Culpable homicide

11.208 The Scottish common law offence of culpable homicide is broadly similar to the English common law offence of manslaughter. Prior to the recent case of *HMA v Transco*[1] there had never been a prosecution of a company in Scotland for culpable homicide. There had previously been one prosecution of an individual for culpable homicide; a toolpusher who was tried and acquitted in 1990.[2] Instead, the Crown generally prosecuted fatalities under HSWA 1974 and relevant regulations and often prosecuted such cases under summary procedure. The 1990 *Ocean Odyssey*[3] prosecution was the first High Court case to be instigated against a company under HSWA 1974.

1 *HMA v Transco* (3 June 2003 www.scotcourts.gov.uk).
2 *HMA v Robb* (August 1990, unreported), Aberdeen; see **para 11.194** above.
3 *HMA v Odeco Drilling (UK) Ltd & Arco British (Ocean Odyssey)* (August 1993 unreported), High Court of Justiciary; see **para 11.189** above.

11.209 This contrasts markedly with the position in England where prosecutions for manslaughter against both corporations and individuals have not only been attempted but have succeeded and sentences of imprisonment have been imposed on directors and other officers and managers. The police are referring more and more work related manslaughter cases to the Crown Prosecution Service (CPS) and the recent decision of the CPS to prosecute Balfour Beattie and Railtrack for manslaughter and offences under HSWA 1974, together with 12 directors and other individuals, provides further evidence of the determination of the Crown to pursue manslaughter cases.

HMA v Transco

11.210   The case of *HMA v Transco*[1] made legal history in 2002 by becoming the first prosecution of a corporation for culpable homicide in Scotland. The case followed the tragic death of a family of four when an allegedly corroded ductile iron pipe caused an explosion in their home. The Crown indicted Transco for culpable homicide, with a charge under HSWA 1974 in the alternative, and alleged that Transco had shown a complete and utter disregard for the safety of the public through the actions of a number of Transco engineering and other management committees. This was an attempt by the Crown to establish guilt by a principle of aggregation.

1   *HMA v Transco* (3 June 2003 www.scotcourts.gov.uk).

11.211   Transco took a plea to the relevancy of the charge, arguing that the charge failed, inter alia, to identify the directing mind of Transco. English common law authorities were relied upon in support of this argument. On 3 June 2003, the Appeal Court ruled that the charge of culpable homicide was irrelevant. In his written judgment, Lord Osborne stated:

> 'It appears to me that the clear rules concerning these matters, developed in England and now accepted in Scots Law, demand that the person who is possessed of the guilty mind must occupy such a position in the control of the company that they are capable of being characterised as its directing mind and will, in relation to the subject matter of the action in question, be responsible to no superior in the company and charged with that responsibility himself, before the rules can operate.'[2]

This decision has effectively brought the common law of Scotland in respect of corporate culpable homicide into line with that of the English law of corporate manslaughter. The trial in respect of the remaining charge under HSWA 1974 will take place in 2004.

1   *HMA v Transco* (3 June 2003, unreported), High Court of Justiciary, available at www.scotcourts.gov.uk, at para 23.

Corporate killing

11.212   The corporate killing proposals currently do not apply to Scotland. The Scottish Executive has been asked whether it intends to bring forward legislation on corporate homicide. In a written answer on 29 May 2001, Jim Wallace, Justice Minister, replied that while legislation to introduce such a new offence would be a matter within the competence of the new Scottish Parliament, he went on to say that 'any such legislation is likely to have implications for matters which are reserved, such as health and safety and Crown immunity'. In any event, it was his opinion that 'the three offences proposed for England and Wales are adequately covered by the Scottish common law offence of culpable homicide'. In his opinion, 'a complementary approach to the prosecution of companies for corporate homicide throughout the UK would be desirable'

11.213 Following the collapse of the Transco prosecution for culpable homicide, the case for a reform of the law is now compelling and the Scottish Executive will almost certainly follow the English corporate killing proposals. The Scottish Appeal Court judges made their position clear in the *Transco* case:

> 'If, however, Parliament considers that a corporate body, in circumstances such as the present, should be subjected, not only to potentially unlimited financial penalties, but also to the opprobrium attaching to a conviction for culpable homicide, then it must legislate.'[1]

1   *HMA v Transco* (3 June 2003, www.scotcourts.gov.uk) at para 25.

Evidence and procedure

11.214 Although the statutory framework is identical, there are many significant differences in the rules of evidence and procedure which have a material impact on health and safety prosecutions.

Form of indictment

11.215 Following the cases of *Carmichael v Marks and Spencer*[1] and *HMA v Heeremac*,[2] an accused is entitled to fair notice of the essential features of the Crown's case and accordingly the Crown must provide detailed specification of the facts alleged in the body of the indictment or complaint. As a result, complaints and indictments in Scotland are significantly longer than their English equivalents. For example, the Transco indictment was ten pages long. The Crown will also generally prosecute under the general duties of HSWA 1974 and roll into the narrative of the charge any specific breaches of regulations, such as the MHSWR.[3] This differs from the English approach, where it is commonplace for breaches to be charged under both HSWA 1974 and regulations.

1   1996 SLT 1167.
2   1999 SLT 492.
3   SI 1999/3242.

Disclosure

11.216 Once the prosecution has commenced, the disclosure rules in Scotland are vastly different. None of the provisions of the Criminal Procedure and Investigations Act 1996 apply in Scotland and accordingly there is no right to primary or secondary disclosure, nor do the defence need to provide a defence statement. The Crown is under no obligation to provide an accused with copies of the Crown statements, copies of the productions which the Crown will be relying upon or any schedule of unused material which is not relied upon.[1]

1   Criminal Procedure (Scotland) Act 1995, ss 66 and 67.

Access to witnesses

11.217   Although in Scotland the defence are not entitled to copies of the Crown statements, they are, however, entitled to be given the names and addresses of all Crown witnesses and to take 'precognitions' from the witnesses. If a witness refuses to co-operate, the precognition can be taken under oath by a Sheriff. A precognition is not a statement and a witness cannot be cross-examined on the content of a precognition, unless it was taken under oath.

Corroboration

11.218   Although the burden and standard of proof are the same as in England,[1] the rule of corroboration, which has long been abolished in England, is still a part of the rules of Scottish criminal evidence. Under this rule, in order to prove its case, the Crown must produce evidence from more than one source. In health and safety prosecutions this is usually not difficult.

1   The burden of proof is on the Crown, subject to HSWA 1974, s 40, and the standard of proof is proof 'beyond reasonable doubt'.

Jury

11.219   Defendants in England have the fundamental and inalienable right to elect trial by jury for offences which are triable either way (as health and safety cases are). As Lord Devlin famously stated, 'trial by jury is the lamp which shows that freedom lives'.[1] However, an accused in Scotland has no right to elect trial by jury. It is entirely a matter for the Procurator Fiscal whether the case is sufficiently serious or complex to merit a jury trial. A Scottish jury consists of 15 jurors and a simple 8:7 majority is sufficient for a conviction. This means that in order to secure a conviction in Scotland the Crown need only convince 53% of the jury of guilt, as opposed to 83% in England (10:2, following a majority direction). In addition, a Scottish jury can return three verdicts: guilty, not guilty and not proven. A note proven verdict amounts to an acquittal.

1   Lord Devlin *Trial by Jury* (1956) p 146.

Sentencing

11.220   If convicted of a health and safety offence in Scotland, the sentence is likely to be lower than an equivalent offence in England, not because the maximum sentences are lower but simply because Scottish judges generally impose lower sentences. The sentencing guidelines set out in *R v F Howe and Son (Engineers) Ltd*[1] and *R v Friskies Petcare Ltd*,[2] though persuasive, are not binding on Scottish courts and are rarely referred to.

1   [1999] 2 All ER 249.
2   [2000] Cr App R (S) 401.

Costs

11.221   There are no awards of costs to either party in criminal cases in Scotland. In England, costs are generally awarded to the party which prevails and it is often the case that prosecution costs can be higher that the fine itself.

Fatal accident inquiries

11.222   The system of coroner's inquests does not apply in Scotland. A fatal incident occurring in Scotland may result in a fatal accident inquiry (FAI). This statutory public inquiry is undertaken by a Sheriff and is governed by the Fatal Accidents and Sudden Deaths Inquiry (Scotland) Act 1976 and the Fatal Accidents and Sudden Deaths Inquiry Procedure (Scotland) Rules 1977.

11.223   An FAI is mandatory if 'it appears that the death has resulted from an accident occurring in Scotland while the person who has died was in the course of his employment'. The Lord Advocate has ultimate discretion over whether or not the FAI proceeds and one will not be required 'in a case where criminal proceedings have been concluded against any person in respect of the death or any accident from which the death resulted and that the Lord Advocate is satisfied that the circumstances of the death have been sufficiently established in the course of such proceedings'. On a plea of guilty, it is often the case that the circumstances of the death are not sufficiently established.

11.224   The Fatal Accidents and Sudden Deaths Inquiry (Scotland) Act 1976 also applies to deaths which are not due to natural causes and the FAI has a broad remit to determine all circumstances relevant to the death or accident. The Sheriff's determinations on these matters are not admissible in evidence at any proceedings which arise out of the accident or death. The examination of a witness at an FAI is not a bar to criminal proceedings being taken against him or her. However, in both the Piper Alpha and Ocean Odyssey inquiries, a limited form of immunity was given by the Crown to witnesses who gave evidence.

Northern Ireland

11.225   Petroleum exploration licensing in Northern Ireland is the responsibility of the Department of Enterprise, under the provisions of the Petroleum (Production) Act (Northern Ireland) 1964, the first licences were issued in 1965. Since then, 19 exploration licences have been issued and the 'potential for a sizeable discovery is good'.[1]

1   British Geological Survey website, www.bgs.ac.uk, 26 September 2001.

11.226   The Health and Safety Executive for Northern Ireland (HSENI) was established on 1 April 1999. HSENI oversees safety measures in the oil and gas industry with the assistance of the Field Operations Chemicals Group. It is concerned with ensuring safety within the industry including, the storage and distribution of energy including natural gas, liquefied petroleum gases (LPG) and petroleum products and the implementation of the Control of Major Accidents Hazards Regulations (Northern Ireland) 2000.

11.227   Until 1997, Northern Ireland did not have a public natural gas supply. The construction of a pipeline between Scotland and Northern Ireland was completed in 1996. The onshore line has been extended to serve wider industrial, commercial and domestic markets and this extension is still continuing. British Gas committed a total investment of over £450 million to its Northern Ireland gas project, supplemented by some £80 million from the EU. The government is keen to develop further this expansion of the natural gas industry in Northern Ireland.

HSENI: health and safety at work legislation

11.228   The basic framework of Northern Ireland health and safety legislation is very similar to that of Great Britain. In 1999–2000, 13 sets of Regulations concerning health and safety at work were marked by the HSENI, such as the Lifting Operations and Lifting Equipment Regulations (Northern Ireland) 1999, the Provision and Use of Work Equipment Regulations (Northern Ireland) 1999, the Control of Major Accident Hazards Regulations (Northern Ireland) 2000, the Transport of Dangerous Goods (Safety Advisers) Regulations (Northern Ireland) 2000 and the Control of Substances Hazardous to Health Regulations (Northern Ireland) 2000. The HSENI administers to the Health and Safety at Work (Northern Ireland) Order 1978 and the Offshore and Pipelines, Safety (Northern Ireland) Order 1992.

Conclusions

11.229   From a health and safety perspective, the UK oil and gas industry is one of the most stringently regulated in the world and the applicable legislative regime is both complex and far reaching. Since the Piper Alpha disaster and the recommendations of the Cullen Report, the industry has taken enormous steps to improve every aspect of safety in both upstream and downstream operations. The safety management systems which have been set up are comprehensive and sophisticated. Industry initiatives, such as Step Change, encourage an ever-evolving culture of safety and help to facilitate co-operation and sharing of safety information among those who play a part in the industry. The result, as evidenced by HSE statistics, is that there has been a significant reduction in the number of hydrocarbon releases and other dangerous occurrences over the past ten years.

11.230   However, oil and gas remains one of the UK's most inherently dangerous industries and the risk of a fatality or a catastrophic event can never be eliminated. Recent tragedies involving the loss of life clearly demonstrates that there can be no room for complacency and the industry must continue to ensure that health and safety issues are given the highest priority and prominence. Ongoing issues such as the ageing infrastructure, maintenance management, staff reductions and new players entering the UKCS mean that the entire safety regime must be continually assessed and modified where appropriate.

11.231   Both under the existing legislative regime and under the proposed new corporate killing law, the issue of management failure, and how far short of industry standards such a failure falls, is of central importance when considering culpability for health and safety failures. Safety management systems, safety cases, risk assessments, method statements, QHSE procedures, and all other systems, procedures and documentation which impact upon safety must be comprehensively implemented and kept under constant review in order to ensure a safe environment for all those working in or affected by the industry. Driven from board level down, safety must remain a top priority for everyone in the oil and gas industry.

A11.1.0
Appendix 11.1 – Relevant legislation[1]

A11.1.1

Statutes
Coast Protection Act 1949
Continental Shelf Act 1964
Fire Precautions Act 1971
Mineral Working (Offshore Installations) Act 1971
Prevention of Oil Pollution Act 1971
Health and Safety at Work Act 1974
Environmental Protection Act 1990
Offshore Safety Act 1992
Radioactive Substances Act 1993
Petroleum Act 1998
Pollution Prevention and Control Act 1999

A11.1.2

Industry-specific statutory instruments
Offshore Installations (Inspectors and Casualties) Regulations 1973, SI 1973/1842
Offshore Installations (Construction and Survey) Regulations 1974, SI 1974/289
Offshore Installations (Operational Safety, Health and Welfare) Regulations 1976, SI 1976/1019
Offshore Installations (Safety Representatives and Safety Committees) Regulations 1989, SI 1989/971
Offshore Installations and Pipeline Works (First-Aid) Regulations 1989, SI 1989/1671
Offshore Installations (Safety Case) Regulations 1992, SI 1992/2885
Health and Safety at Work etc Act 1974 (Application outside Great Britain) Order 1995, SI 1995/263
Offshore Installations and Pipe-line Works (Management and Administration) Regulations 1995, SI 1995/738
Offshore Installations (Prevention of Fire and Explosion, and Emergency Response) Regulations 1995, SI 1995/743
Offshore Installations and Wells (Design and Construction, etc) Regulations 1996, SI 1996/913
Pipelines Safety Regulations 1996, SI 1996/825
Offshore Installations (Safety Zones) Order 1997, SI 1997/608
Offshore Installations (Safety Zones) (No 2) Order 1997, SI 1997/1224
Offshore Electricity and Noise Regulations 1997, SI 1997/1993
Diving at Work Regulations 1997, SI 1997/2776
Petroleum (Current Model Clauses) Order 1999, SI 1999/160
Offshore Petroleum Production and Pipe-Lines (Assessment of Environmental Effects) Regulations 1999, SI 1999/360
Offshore Installations (Safety Zones) Order 1999, SI 1999/547
Health and Safety (Fees) Regulations 1999, SI 1999/645
Offshore Installations (Safety Zones) (No 2) Order 1999, SI 1999/1150

Petroleum Pipe-Lines Regulations 1999
Offshore Petroleum Activities (Conservation of Habitats) Regulations 2001, SI 2001/
1754
Working Time (Amendment) Regulations 2003, SI 2003/1684

A11.1.3

Some other applicable statutory instruments

Safety Representatives and Safety Committee Regulations 1977, SI 1977/500
Health and Safety (First-Aid) Regulations 1981, SI 1981/917
Control of Asbestos at Work Regulations 1987, SI 1987/2115
Electricity at Work Regulations 1989, SI 1989/635
Noise at Work Regulations 1989, SI 1989/1790
Management of Health and Safety at Work Regulations 1992, SI 1992/2051
Health and Safety (Display Screen Equipment) Regulations 1992, SI 1992/2792
Manual Handling Operations Regulations 1992, SI 1992/2793
Personal Protective Equipment at Work Regulations 1992, SI 1992/2966
Workplace (Health, Safety and Welfare) Regulations 1992, SI 1992/3004
Supply of Machinery (Safety) Regulations 1992, SI 1992/3073
Notification of New Substances Regulations 1993, SI 1993/3050
Waste Management Licensing Regulations 1994, SI 1994/1056
Construction (Design and Management) Regulations 1994, SI 1994/3140
Chemicals (Hazard Information and Packaging for Supply) Regulations 1994,
SI 1994/3247
Reporting of Injuries, Diseases and Dangerous Occurrences Regulations 1995,
SI 1995/3163
Health and Safety (Safety Signs and Signals) Regulations 1996, SI 1996/341
Health and Safety (Consultation with Employees) Regulations 1996, SI 1996/1513
Construction (Health, Safety and Welfare) Regulations 1996, SI 1996/1592
Confined Spaces Regulations 1997, SI 1997/1713
Fire Precautions (Workplace) Regulations 1997, SI 1997/1840
Control of Lead at Work Regulations 1998, SI 1998/543
Working Time Regulations 1998, SI 1998/1833
Provision and Use of Work Equipment Regulations 1998, SI 1998/2306
Lifting Operations and Lifting Equipment Regulations 1998, SI 1998/2307
Chemicals (Hazard Information and Packaging for Supply) (Amendment) Regulations
1999, SI 1999/197
Transport of Dangerous Goods (Safety Advisers) Regulations 1999, SI 1999/257
Carriage of Dangerous Goods (Amendment) Regulations 1999, SI 1999/303
Control of Substances Hazardous to Health Regulations 1999, SI 1999/437
Control of Major Accident Hazards Regulations 1999, SI 1999/743
Anti-Pollution Works Regulations 1999, SI 1999/1006
Pressure Equipment Regulations 1999, SI 1999/2001

1 This list is indicative only and should not be regarded as exhaustive.

A11.2.0

Appendix 11.2 – HSE oil and gas publications[1]

A11.2.1

HSE publications

Guidance on the safe use and operation of lifting equipment offshore
Guidance on multi-skilling in the petroleum industry
Guidance on permit-to-work systems in the petroleum industry
Play your part: How offshore workers can help improve health and safety
Offshore health and safety law leaflets
A brief guide on COSHH for the offshore oil and gas industry
Dealing with offshore emergencies
Well handled
Assessment principles for offshore safety cases
A guide to the Offshore Installations (Safety Case) Regulations 1992
Prevention of fire and explosion and emergency response on offshore installations
A guide to the Offshore Installations and Pipeline Works (Management and Administration) Regulations 1995
A guide to the Borehole Sites and Operations Regulations 1995
A guide to the Pipeline Safety Regulations 1996
A guide to the well aspects of amendments of the Offshore Installations and Wells (Design and Construction etc) Regulations 1996
A guide to the integrity, workplace environment and miscellaneous aspects of the Offshore Installations and Wells (Design and Construction etc) Regulations 1996
Management of occupational health risks in the offshore oil and gas industry
The safe isolation of plant and equipment
A guide to the Offshore Installations (Safety Representatives and Safety Committees) Regulations 1989
Health care and first aid on offshore installations and pipeline works (first aid) regulations 1989 approved code of practice and guidance
Safety representatives and safety committees on offshore installations
Safety zones around oil and gas installations in waters around the UK
How offshore helicopter travel is regulated
How HSE assesses offshore safety cases
Health and safety leadership for offshore industry
Rash decision offshore
Lifeboat on-load release gear
To cop it all
Regulating health and safety in the UK offshore oil and gas fields

1 See HSE Books, www.hse.gov.uk.

Oil and gas 421

A11.2.2

HSE free leaflets – offshore
Organisational change and major accident hazards – Chemical Information Sheet No
    CHIS7
How HSE assesses offshore safety cases
How offshore helicopter travel is regulated
Leadership for the Offshore Industry
Play your part: How you can help improve health and safety offshore
Safety representatives and safety committees on offshore installations
Safety zones around offshore oil and gas installations in waters around the UK
Regulating health and safety in the UK offshore and gas fields

A11.3.0
Appendix 11.3 – PONs, operations notices and safety notices

A11.3.1

PONs[1]

PON 1 Oil and Pollution
PON 2 Loss or dumping of synthetic materials or other refuse at sea
PON 3 Damage to submarine telecommunications cables and plant
PON 4 Application for consent to drill exploration, appraisal, and development wells
PON 5 Application to abandon or temporarily abandon a well
PON 6 Measurement of petroleum
PON 7 Reporting of petroleum production
PON 8 Application to complete and/or workover a well
PON 9 Record and sample requirements for surveys and wells
PON 10 Buoys
PON 11 Report on incidents during well operations
PON 12 Department of Trade and Industry well numbering system
PON 13 Applications for consent to drill or re-enter HP/HT exploration and appraisal wells
PON 14 Notification of seismic surveys
PON 15 Assessment of environmental effects
PON 16 Assessment of environmental effects

1 Last updated May 1996.

A11.3.2

Safety notices

No	Title	Issue date
10/80	Guidance on procedures for the transfer of personnel by basket	Apr 01
1/94	Mobile installations and vessels: movement of helidecks	Jan 02
3/95	Interactions between utility system connections	Jan 02
7/95	Electrical switchboards – Safe working practices	Jan 02
1/96	Testing of TEMPSC release gear	Jan 02
2/96	Proof testing of dual channel control systems	Jan 02
3/96	Swing check valves – potential problems	Jan 02
4/96	Working time	Jan 02
5/96	Falling ice from installation structures – potential hazards	Jan 02

No	Title	Issue date
2/98	Single fall crane swivel block castings	May 98
4/98	Sprag clutches used on crane boom hoist systems	Nov 98
2/99	Container loading and emptying	Mar 99
3/99	Steel socket failures	Sep 99
4/99	Offshore helideck design and operation	Sep 99
5/99	Single joint elevators	Dec 99
1/00	Food hygiene and incidents involving sewerage leaks	Mar 00
2/00	Bolting of flanged joints for pressurised systems	Jul 00
3/00	Installation and maintenance of steamer ovens in offshore galleys	Dec 00
1/01	Disposal of tri-ethylene glycol soaked installation	Sep 01
2/01	Jack-up (self-elevating) installations: Floating damage stability survivability criterion	Sep 01
1/02	Thorough examination of offshore passenger lifts	Jan 02
2/02	Balanced bellows pressure relief valves – problems arising form modification of the bonnet vent	May 02
3/02	The risks posed by exposure to inerting gases in the open air	Apr 02
4/02	Jack-up (self-elevating) installations: Rack phase difference	Aug 02
5/02	The thorough examination and inspection of offshore cranes	Sep 02
1/03	Ageing semi-submersible installations	May 03

A11.3.3

Operations notices

No	Title	Issue date
3	Liaison with other bodies	Jan 02
4	Radioactive Substances Act 1993	Jan 02
6	Reporting of offshore installation movements	Jun 02
9	Exclusions and exemptions from offshore safety legislation	Jan 02
11	Reporting of safety zone infringements	Jan 02
14	Guidance on Coast Protection Act – consent to locate and the marking of offshore installations	Jan 02
22	Complaints relating to safety issues on offshore installations	May 02
27	Status of technical guidance on design, construction and certification	Jan 02
30	Arrangements for reporting under RIDDOR 95	May 02

No	Title	Issue date
33	Safety case submissions	Jan 02
34	Ionising Radiations Regulations 1999: Notification of offshore site radiography work	Sep 01
37	Offshore Installations and Wells (Design and Construction, etc) Regulations 1996	
	Arrangements for reporting danger to an installation	Jan 02
39	Offshore Installations and Pipeline Works (Management and Administration) Regulations 1995 Guidance on identification of offshore installations	Jan 02
42	Offshore development areas	Jan 02
47	Offshore helidecks – advice to industry	Dec 99
51	Revised Approved Code of Practice and Guidance on health care and first aid offshore	Apr 01
52	Health and Safety at Work etc Act 1974 (Application outside Great Britain) Order 2001 (SI 2001/2127)	Sep 01
54	Establishment of Safety Zones for Sub-Sea Installations	Jan 02
55	Suitable Secondary Roles for Offshore Medics	Mar 02
56	Offshore First Aid and Medic Training and Examinations	Mar 02
57	Offshore Installations and Pipeline Works (Management and Administration) Regulations 1995 (MAR) – As amended by the Offshore Safety (Miscellaneous Amendments) Regulations 2002 (SI 2002/2175)	Oct 02
58	Dangerous Substances and Explosive Atmospheres Regulations 1996	Jan 03
59	The Equipment and Protective Systems Intended for Use in Potentially Explosive Atmospheres Regulations 1996	Jan 03
60	Reporting cases of disease under the Reporting of Injuries, Diseases and Dangerous Occurrences Regulations 1995 (RIDDOR)	Apr 03
61	Management of collision risk – Radio communication between offshore installations, their standby vessels and merchant ships	Apr 03
62	Goals for the provision of accommodation on offshore installations	Apr 03

A11.4.0

Appendix A11.4 – Glossary of terms

Glossary of terms

ACOP	Approved Code of Practice
ALARP	As Low as Reasonably Possible
APOSC	Assessment Principles of Offshore Safety Cases
AUPEC	Aberdeen University Petroleum and Economic Consultancy
CBI	Confederation of British Industry
CHIP	Chemicals (Hazard Information & Packaging for Supply) Regulations 2002, SI 2002/1689
CIMAH	Control of Industrial Major Accident Hazards Regulations 1984, SI 1984/1902
COMAH	Control of Major Accident Hazard Regulations 1999, SI 1997/743
COSHH	Control of Substances Hazardous to Health Regulations 2002, SI 2002/2677
CPS	Crown Prosecution Service
Cullen Costs	Costs incurred attributable to the recommendations of the Cullen Report (1990)
DCR	Offshore Installations (Design and Construction) Regulations 1996, SI 1996/913
DTI	Department of Trade and Industry
FAI	Fatal Accident Inquiry
FAR	Fatal Accident Rate
FOD	Field Operations Directorate
FPSO	Floating Production Storage and Offload Vessel
FSA	Formal Safety Assessment
HCR	Hydrocarbon Releases
HID	Hazardous Installations Directorate
HSB	Health and Safety Bulletin (published by LexisNexis)
HSC	Health and Safety Commission
HSE	Health and Safety Executive
HSENI	Heath & Safety Executive for Northern Ireland
HSWA 1974	Health and Safety at Work etc Act 1974
IADC	International Association of Drilling Contractors
IMCA	International Marine Contractors Association
IR	Individual Risk
LPG	Liquefied Petroleum Gas
MAR	Offshore Installations (Management and Administration) Regulations SI 1995/738

MOL	Main Oil Line
MHSWR	Management of Health and Safety at Work Regulations 1999, SI 1999/3242
MODU	Mobile Offshore Drilling Units
NSOAF	North Sea Offshore Authorities Forum
OCA	Offshore Contractors Association
OGP –	International Association of Oil And Gas Producers
OIM	Offshore Installation Manager
OPEC	Organisation of Petroleum Exporting Countries
OSD	Offshore Safety Division
PFEER	Offshore Installations (Prevention of Fire and Explosion, and Emergency Response) Regulations 1995, SI 1995/743
PILOT	Phase 2 of Oil and Gas Industry Task Force
PON	Petroleum Operations Directive
PTSD	Post Traumatic Stress Disorder
QHSE	Quality, Health , Safety and Environmental
QRA	Quantified Risk Analysis
RIDDOR	Reporting of Injuries, Diseases and Dangerous Occurrence Regulations 1995, SI 1995/3163
SCR	Offshore Installations (Safety Case) Regulations 1992, SI 1992/2885
SMS	Safety Management System
TR	Temporary Refuge
UKCS	UK Continental Shelf
UKOOA	UK Offshore Operators Association
WTD	Working Time Directive

CHAPTER 12

Healthcare

Kiran Bhogal (with contribution on the management of health and safety risks from Andrew Stokes)

The National Health Service

12.1   Since its inception on 5 July 1948 the National Health Service (NHS) has undergone change unlike any other organisation in the UK and, as one of the largest organisations in Europe, is a major employer. From the very start the NHS has had responsibility for a huge workforce and budget and despite having been in existence for just over 55 years still faces challenges in organising and managing the demands and expectations of patients and staff.

12.2   The 1989 government White Paper *Working for Patients* set plans for the most significant change in the NHS and was passed into law as the National Health Service and Community Care Act 1990. Health authorities were allocated budgets and were able to purchase services from, amongst others, NHS Trusts. The first wave of NHS Trusts came into being on 1 April 1991. By 1995 all health care was provided by NHS Trusts. Over the same period many general practitioners (GPs) were given budgets so that they could buy services from NHS Trusts under a scheme known as GP Fund Holding. Not all GPs joined the scheme however and their budgets remained under the control of health authorities which bought health care from NHS Trusts.

12.3   With the NHS Plan (the government's plan for investment and reform) in July 2000 came even more changes for the NHS and with 'Shifting the Balance of Power' in July 2001 the plans for the creation of Primary Care Trusts (PCTs), the abolition of Health Authorities and creation of Strategic Health Authorities (StHAs), the abolition of NHS Executive regional offices and creation of four new Regional Directors of Health and Social Care.

12.4   Primary and secondary care are now provided and procured in the main by primary care practitioners (for example, GP's, dentists etc) and NHS Trusts and each have responsibility for ensuring the provision of quality care. For such large organisations then, it is not surprising that the opportunity for errors (whether innocent or reckless) are great and whilst up until now the NHS has been protected somewhat from successful criminal prosecutions because of the difficulties in establishing a direct causal link between any act or omission and a death, it remains to be seen whether this will be so in light of the Health and Social Care (Community Health and Standards) Bill 2003, s 133 (Offences by bodies corporate).

12.5   Regardless of the flux in the law, no organisation should be complacent at a time when the emphasis is to deliver a more patient-centred service. The NHS has to be aware of the potential for it, as an organisation, and those considered to be at the helm of the organisation (the Board), to be called upon to account for the delivery of services, especially when it involves adverse incidents such as the death of patients. This is not, however, the only time that the NHS can be called upon to account for its actions, as any significant failure to plan or respond to an incident or emergency could lead to breaches in the law and civil and/or criminal charges.

Civil or criminal?

12.6   Over the last few years, however, there have been a number of instances where doctors in particular have faced criminal charges and there is no reason to expect that such charges will not also be brought against other healthcare professionals such as nurses.

12.7   So far, claims have been brought by patients who have sustained injury during the course of medical treatment and in the main these patients are looking for compensation for injuries and losses sustained. Claims are pursued through the civil courts and in order for the claim to succeed, the claimant will need, on a balance of probabilities, to show that the NHS organisation in question owed him or her a duty of care, that there was a breach of that duty of care and that as a consequence of that breach, he or she has suffered loss and damage. If the claimant is successful, damages will be recoverable and the level of the award will depend on the particular circumstances of each individual case.

12.8   A member of the public (who must show a relationship of proximity) or an employee can bring a claim. With the public, however, becoming increasingly aware of their rights and with organisations such as the NHS becoming more accountable for their own actions as well as those of their employees, it is not surprising to see the public looking for more than is available in the civil courts, particularly where an act on the part of an employee results in the death of a patient.

12.9   The law as it currently stands allows for criminal charges to be brought against an individual where that individual's actions have resulted in death, even where the death or personal injury was not intended. If it can be shown that there was no intention to kill, the offence is one of manslaughter, and if it can be shown that there was an intention to kill, the offence will be one of murder. It will be for the Crown Prosecution Service (CPS) to initiate proceedings through the Criminal Court and to decide whether or not the individual should be prosecuted and to determine the charges to be brought. The CPS must be satisfied that the evidence it has before it is sufficiently strong to result in a conviction, and also be satisfied that it is in the interest of the public for the prosecution to proceed.

The existing law

12.10   The law as it currently stands recognises two offences: corporate manslaughter and involuntary manslaughter.

12.11   Where an organisation, through the controlling mind of one of its agents,[1] does an act which fulfils the requirement of the crime of manslaughter the charge of corporate manslaughter may follow and it is only if the individual is found guilty of gross negligence that the organisation can be convicted.

1   A person employed to act on behalf of another or any person who represents him or herself to have authority to act as an agent.

12.12   Where, on the other hand, a death occurs as a result of some act (usually negligent act) where there was no intention to cause serious harm or death, the offence of involuntary manslaughter may follow.

12.13   Despite attempts to bring prosecutions of manslaughter (corporate or involuntary) against organisations, including the NHS, there has been little success. The reason is that in practice it has proved difficult to satisfy the criteria set. For corporate manslaughter it is necessary to identify one person (and it must be one person) who is the 'controlling mind' of the corporation who is guilty of gross negligence which has unlawfully caused the death (or deaths), otherwise known as the identification doctrine.

12.14   Up until the 1990s it was rare for charges of manslaughter to be brought against doctors. We know of the 1925 case of Dr Bateman,[1] who was convicted of manslaughter after an obstetric patient died, but on appeal, pardoned. Between 1970 and 1989 statistics show that four doctors were charged with manslaughter; between 1990 and 1999, 17; and in 2000, six. Between 1970 and 1999, ten of those charged were convicted but three verdicts set aside on appeal.[2] There has been much debate on what constitutes 'gross negligence'. In the case of *Bateman*, the Court of Appeal considered that the threshold was that the negligence was so gross, that is showed a disregard for the life and safety of others as to amount to a crime, and deserved punishment.

1   *R v Bateman* (1925) Cr App R 8.
2   (2002) 3 European Health Law Newsletter, September.

12.15   The reality is that where death does occur at the hands of an individual, the death is not necessarily as a consequence of any 'disregard' on the part of, in the case of the NHS, a healthcare professional, but may be due to a complete breakdown in systems within the organisation. Where 'systems failures' are shown to be the cause of the death it will be very difficult to a successful prosecution, as was demonstrated in the following case.

12.16 In 1999, a 12-year-old boy with T cell non-Hodgkin's lymphoma was admitted to a general paediatric ward instead of a paediatric oncology ward because the paediatric oncology ward was full. His lumbar puncture procedure had been postponed until the evening as he had had a biscuit and it was not therefore possible to undertake the procedure during the day. Consequently, the procedure was to be undertaken by a registrar in paediatric anaesthesia who had never given intrathecal cytotoxic treatment before, although he had discussed the procedure by telephone with his haematological colleague. Unaware that vincristine should not be taken into theatre, a nurse provided the paediatric anaesthetist with two syringes, one of which contained vincristine and bore a label indicating that the drug was for intravenous use only. Without reading the label, the paediatric anaesthetist administered the drug intrathecally, subsequent to which the boy died some days later. The doctors were formally cleared of manslaughter charges after the CPS were unable to offer any evidence of gross negligence on the part of the doctors and the evidence showed that significant system failures within the hospital administration were significant factor's in the boy's death.[1]

1 *Daily Telegraph*, 6 January 1999; Report of an expert group learning from adverse incidents in the NHS, chaired by the Chief Medical Officer *An organisation with a memory* (2000).

12.17 Whilst the systems within an organisation may make it difficult successfully to bring prosecutions against individuals, it is worth noting that there have been successful prosecutions brought.

12.18 In the case of *R v Adomako*,[1] a case involving an anaesthetist, anaesthesia was commenced at about 9.45 am. The patient was paralysed by injection of a drug and an endotracheal tube (ET tube) was inserted to enable the patient to breathe by mechanical means. At about 11.05 am a disconnection occurred at the ET tube connection. The supply of oxygen to the patient ceased and this led to a cardiac arrest at about 11.14 am. During this period the anaesthetist failed to notice or remedy the disconnection. The first he became aware that something was amiss was when an alarm sounded on the Dinamap machine, which monitors the patient's blood pressure. On the evidence it appeared that some four-and-a-half minutes would have elapsed between the disconnection and the sounding of the alarm. On hearing the alarm, the anaesthetist checked the equipment and administered atropine to raise the patient's pulse but at no stage before the cardiac arrest, did he check the integrity of the ET tube connections. The disconnection itself was not discovered until after resuscitation had been commenced.

1 [1995] 1 AC 171.

12.19 The prosecution's case was that the anaesthetist was guilty of gross negligence for the failure to notice or respond appropriately to what were, obvious signs of a disconnection.[1] The prosecution also alleged that the anaesthetist had failed to notice at various stages during the period, after the disconnection and before the arrest either occurred or became inevitable, that the patient's chest was not moving and the dials on the mechanical ventilating machine were not operating. It was accepted that the anaesthetist has been negligent, but the question then arose as to whether his actions constituted a crime.

1 *R v Adomako* [1995] 1 AC 171.

12.20   The jury felt they did and a conviction for manslaughter and a six-month imprisonment sentence imposed, suspended for 12 months. On appeal by the anaesthetist on the question of the true legal basis of involuntary manslaughter involving a breach of duty the House of Lords held, dismissing the appeal, that in such cases the ordinary principles of the law of negligence applied to ascertain whether the defendant had been in breach of a duty of care towards the victim; that on the establishment of such breach of duty the next question to ask was whether it caused the death of the victim, and if so, whether it should be characterised as 'gross negligence' and therefore a crime.[1] It was up to the jury to decide, whether having regard to the risk of death involved, the conduct was so bad in all the circumstances as to amount to a criminal act or omission. They clearly did.

1   *R v Adomako* [1995] 1 AC 171.

12.21   In 1982, charges for manslaughter were brought, successfully, against a locum anaesthetist. The 55-year-old patient in this instance died during general anaesthesia after a fine bore 'microlaryngeal' tube was connected directly to an oxygen cylinder and not a ventilator. Within a few minutes, the lady in question had received over 1,000 litres of oxygen and had inflated to 'resemble a Michelin man of the tyre advertisements'. The supervising locum anaesthetist was convicted of manslaughter and sentenced to six months in prison, suspended for 18 months.[1]

1   'Anaesthetist convicted of manslaughter' *Guardian*, July 1990.

12.22   A general practitioner was sentenced to 12 months in prison, suspended for 12 months after he pleaded guilty to manslaughter following the death of a nine-year-old boy who remained unconscious and suffered irreversible brain following a circumcision, at which time diamorphine was administered as a sedative. The general practitioner admitted to using 'excessive amounts of … drugs, and it was accepted that they were wholly inappropriate as sedatives'.[1]

1   'Doctor admits killing' *Guardian*, March 1995.

12.23   Following the death of a 41-year-old woman, another general practitioner was convicted and sentenced to 12 months' imprisonment, suspended for two years.[1] The general practitioner in this instance had been charged with administering an amount of drug (pethidine) which amounted to gross negligence. The patient in question had been seen by the GP for severe migraine. Whilst prochlorperazine and diazepam had stopped her vomiting they had not relieved her pain. At the suggestion of the patient's husband (a consultant surgeon) the GP sought to administer pethidine. As the pharmacy had no pethidine, the GP obtained an ampoule of diamorphine containing 100 mg and administered the whole dose intramuscularly. Whilst the dosage was reasonable for pethidine, it was ten times too high for diamorphine.

1   *Daily Telegraph*, 28 November 1998.

12.24   In September 2003, a doctor who mistakenly ordered the wrong chemotherapy drug to be injected into a cancer patient's spine pleaded guilty to manslaughter at Nottingham Crown Court and was subsequently sentenced to eight months' imprisonment for manslaughter and a further ten months' for five, unrelated, assault charges. Nine months of the total 18-month prison sentence was suspended.[1] The patient, a teenager, had been diagnosed with leukaemia at the age of 16 but was in remission at the time of the incident. The doctor, who was only three days into his first specialist registrar appointment, supervised the injection, which was given by a junior doctor who was also new to the ward. The prosecution submitted that it was the specialist registrar's job to check the route of administration and the syringe, and had he done so he would have realised that the drug was to be injected into a vein. The prosecution also submitted that his conduct fell far below that which could be expected of a competent doctor in his field and that the doctor had failed in a number of respects which were absolutely basic and that these failures led to the Wayne Jowett's death.

1   (2003) BMJ, 27 September.

12.25   It is of note that an independent report[1] into the circumstances leading up to the death of the teenager criticised procedures at the hospital in Nottingham and highlighted design faults in syringes. The report concluded that the Wayne Jowett died as a result of a 'complex amalgam of human organisational, technical and social interactions' at the hospital where he received the injection. Furthermore that 'the safety culture surrounding Ward E17's patient chemotherapy supply and administration system [did] not appear to be all that it should'. It was said that the inquiry undertaken identified 'classic systems failures'.

1   *External Inquiry into the adverse incident that occurred at Queen's Medical Centre, Nottingham,* 4 January 2001 by Professor Brian Toft.

12.26   Previous to this, , four doctors were prosecuted for manslaughter over the same error but not convicted and whilst two doctors at Peterborough General Hospital were convicted in 1991, their convictions were overturned on appeal. As the Nottinghamshire coroner, Dr Nigel Chapman said at the conclusion of the inquest into the death of Wayne Jowett: 'We can put a man on the moon, but why can't we find a safe method to prevent these deaths?'[1]

1   (2003) BMJ, 27 September.

12.27   The custodial sentence imposed has left many doctors worried. Mr Nizam Mamode of the British Medical Association said: 'Mistakes happen all the time in every walk of life. I think a lot of doctors will be concerned that if they now do make an error they may be facing criminal charges and possibly even jail.'[1] Dr Edwin Borman of the British Medical Association in the same article said: 'There have been previous cases of this particular error and it is very disturbing that an individual doctor has been found culpable when in reality it is a failure of multiple parts of the system.' He added: 'Doctors have become increasingly worried about our increasingly litigious society and the effects of that are now being seen.' It is important in this instance to remember though that the doctor was not 'found culpable' but rather changed his not guilty plea to a guilty plea.

1   BBC News, 23 September 2003.

12.28   For each successful prosecution however, there are just as many unsuccessful prosecutions. On 1 March 2000, Graham Reeves (aged 69) died five weeks after his healthy kidney was taken out instead of the diseased one. The operation was overseen by a consultant urologist and undertaken by a consultant surgeon. The prosecution submitted that negligence on the part of each fell so far below the standard of care to be expected of competent surgeons that that the negligence must be regarded as gross negligence. They also submitted that the kidney operation played a significant part in causing Mr Reeves' death, five weeks later. However, as the CPS could not prove that any act or omission by either surgeon was more than a minimal cause, both surgeons were acquitted on the direction of the judge.

12.29 In 1991, during a lumbar puncture being undertaken by two junior doctors in Peterborough, one of the doctors passed two syringes to the other. The doctor to whom the syringe was passed injected the drugs without checking what was in the syringes. Attempts were made, once the error had been noticed to reverse the procedure but during these attempts, the brain stem was punctured and the 16-year-old patient subsequently died. The two junior doctors were convicted of manslaughter but their convictions later overturned on appeal. The convictions were in fact quashed on the ground that the trial judge had failed to direct the jury that they were to decide whether the doctors were guilty not of 'recklessness', but of 'gross negligence'.[1]

1 *R v Prentice* [1994] Queen's Bench Law Reports, CA.

12.30 The NHS is a complex organisation of individuals working within structures either designed by itself or imposed by regulatory bodies. How is one then to identify who the sole 'controlling mind' in in the organnisation is? Is it to be the chief executive in his role as the accounting officer or will it be the Board which has the management role? Is it right also that an individual should not be held accountable for an organisation's failure to ensure patient safety and minimise risk? After all doctors do not (in the main) go out to intentionally harm their patients. They are but human beings who will make mistakes. In many settings mistakes are made on paper without fatal consequences; in the medical world the very opposite is true. As the registrar said in Wayne Jowett's case, when interviewed by the police: 'I know it's a lame excuse, but I am a human being'.

The proposed law

12.31 It is intended that the new offence of corporate killing should extend to all corporations irrespective of the legal means by which they are incorporated, for example, limited companies, statutory corporation etc. The Law Commission has also considered whether the proposed offence should apply to partnerships, Trusts (such as hospital trusts and charities) and other unincorporated bodies. Whilst arguable that their liability for fatal accidents should be the same, the Law Commission concluded that it would be inappropriate for such a recommendation to be made 'at the present time'. The Law Commission in its paper *Legislating the Criminal Code Involuntary Manslaughter* went on to state that:[1]

> '... Under the existing law the individuals who comprise an unincorporated body may be criminally liable for manslaughter, as for any other offence; and, by contrast with the law relating to corporations, the question of attributing the conduct of individuals to the body itself does not arise. In this respect the law will be unaffected by the replacement of manslaughter with the offences in the draft Bill[2] of reckless killing and killing by gross carelessness.'

1 Law Commission *Legislating the criminal code: involuntary manslaughter. Item 11 of the sixth programme of law reform: criminal law* (Law Com no 237, 1996) p 117 para 8.54.

12.32 The Home Office, when it published its consultation paper setting out the government's proposals for the reform of the law on involuntary manslaughter,[1] simply reiterated the Law Commission's views and stated that if the Law Commission's proposals were accepted, it would not alter the present position of such organisations. It also indicated that management failure '... should not cover very minor acts or omissions ... but rather, substantial and operating causes including diffuse negligence

of health and safety requirements which are endemic in the organisation ...'
Furthermore, that '... the proposed new law requires nothing more of organisations
than compliance with existing health and safety regulation'.

1   Home Office *Reforming the law of involuntary manslaughter – the government's proposals* (2000).

The effect of the proposed reforms

12.33   It would appear that the government intends to make all undertakings
responsible for their actions regardless of the contrary views of the Law Commission
and the Home Office. This would include all corporations, unincorporated bodies (for
example, partnerships, hospital trusts, schools, charities, trade unions) and any foreign
company doing business in Great Britain.

12.34   If enacted, the recommendations will have a serious impact on the NHS and
its employees. The potential for healthcare professionals to face criminal charges will
increase significantly and the NHS as an organisation, will need to be even more
vigilant of its activities than it is now.

12.35   There is a view that the health service should not be exempt from the proposed
offence of corporate killing. That in terms of public accountability and justice it is
right that the NHS should be covered on the basis that the penalties will not be that
different to the present, of an unlimited fine. The main difference will of course be the
adverse publicity that the NHS would face and the stigma attached to being found
guilty of corporate killing rather than of an offence under the Health and Safety at
Work etc Act 1974.

12.36   The NHS is there to prevent and treat disease. Death is something that is part
and parcel of the business it operates. Healthcare professionals are working in a high-
risk environment and are on a daily basis undertaking procedures which may result in
death. Many, despite being aware of the risk of death associated with any procedure,
have to undertake the procedure in order to prevent further deterioration and in some
instances, death. Death will, and can, occur even in the best of hands and despite all
precautions being taken.

12.37   Science and technology, which underpins the services that are provided by
the NHS, are themselves inherently full of risks which are passed on for use in hospitals
and general surgeries. How is one to safeguard those who work in an environment
such as the NHS from unjustified prosecutions when outcomes do not meet a patient's,
sometimes unrealistic, expectation?

12.38   But the provision and delivery of services is not the only area where the NHS
is likely to face challenges. The Law Commission's paper[1] states that there will be
management failure if the way the corporation manages or organises its activities is
such, that it fails to ensure the health and safety of persons employed in or affected
by those activities.

1   Law Commission *Legislating the criminal code: involuntary manslaughter. Item 11 of the
sixth programme of law reform: criminal law* (Law Com no 237, 1996).

12.39   The government's proposals and reforms intend to make it easier for
prosecutions to be brought successfully against organisations such as the NHS. It

will surely be easier to get a conviction against NHS Trusts and PCTs where systems failures are the cause of an incident on the basis that the management (chief executive and/or Board) failed to manage and organise its activities to ensure the health and safety of persons employed in or affected by its activities. Remember that whilst it will be necessary for the organisation's conduct to fall far below that which could reasonably be expected, it is not necessary to show that the risk was obvious or that the organisation was capable of appreciating the risk, nor will it be necessary to show that the incident was caused by an act or omission on the part of an individual.

12.40 Are accounting officers such as chief executives of Trusts therefore going to be held responsible for each and every failing for the organisation that they are responsible for on the basis that their conduct (in terms of the management and organisational skills) fell far below what could reasonably be expected? Are accounting officers to be considered to be on notice of the potential for criminal charges to be brought because they have received repeated complaints of defective equipment etc and how in such instances, are they to protect themselves and their organisations against criminal charges? Remember that the NHS is a non-profit-making organisation working with finite resources and offers such treatment as it reasonably can, having regard to the various, sometimes conflicting, demands on its resources.

12.41 There is a shortage of doctors and nurses. Those that are working within the NHS carry, at times, excessive workloads and sometimes work in excess of the hours they should be working. As a consequence, the likelihood of clinical errors occurring increases. If a patient were to die as a consequence of a clinical error in such a setting, is the organisation and the individual to be held accountable under the proposed laws for corporate killing and killing by gross carelessness respectively? Will the defence, if such charges are brought, not unnecessarily divert resources which are so badly needed for the provision of healthcare in the first instance?

Prevention?

12.42 It remains to be seen whether the proposal to extend the new reforms to all undertakings will be accepted. Even if the proposal is rejected, it is incumbent on NHS organisations to ensure that they are operating systems which promote the safety and well-being of all those who are affected by the services they provide.

12.43 And how are they to do that? Education and supervision that is proper, up to date and appropriate to the service in question is a start. It is clear from the cases that have been discussed in this chapter, that education and a knowledge of the dosages and uses of drugs could reduce the incidence of mistakes. Often tasks which are familiar are performed automatically and without thought. One may, in such circumstances, put in place safeguards and checks to reduce the incidence of mistakes. Whilst the conviction of doctors may satisfy the general public, it may not necessarily prevent the errors from recurring. Mandatory induction courses for new members of staff would also be an invaluable tool with the use of case studies to highlight problematical areas, especially where doctors have been recruited from abroad to deal with staff shortages. It is inevitable that these doctors will not be familiar with the policies and procedures in place or be familiar with local working practices. Are NHS organisations confident that new members of staff are being briefed adequately before being let loose?

12.44   Doctors' working hours are another area where improvements can be made. Doctors often state that they are working long hours and under pressure. It is not surprising therefore that errors in judgement occur. Even the slightest lapse in concentration can result in a mistake with potentially devastating effects for not only the patient and the family, but the healthcare professional as well. Human error is inevitable and therefore steps should be taken to minimise its consequences.

12.45   One way of doing so is to ensure that systems are in place to encourage the reporting of all incidents. The evaluation of 'near misses' has got to be the most fundamental and important of all. There are very few instances where one can learn and improve systems, policies and procedures without the consequences. Each NHS organisation must be committed to learning from its adverse incidents. Proactive risk management is an essential. More often than not, the root cause of an adverse incident lies in the management and organisational aspects which underpin the delivery of services and in such instances, it would be wrong to attribute blame to an individual.

12.46   Patrick Butler in an article in the *Guardian* on 6 June 2002 said that: 'Services must be safer. There must be better monitoring of poor performing clinicians and hospitals; unsafe working practices must be rooted out and good practice more widely disseminated, and staff must undergo regular skills checks to ensure they are competent to treat patients.' Furthermore that 'the inquiry into children's services at Bristol Royal Infirmary ... reported in July 2001, has re-emphasised the need to tackle what is identified as the lax approach to clinical safety in the NHS, secrecy surrounding the performance of doctors, and slack NHS performance monitoring'.

12.47   In 2001, a consultant surgeon pleaded not guilty to the manslaughter of a 16-year-old in September 1998, at a hospital near Truro, Cornwall. The teenager, who had acute myeloid leukaemia, was added to the consultant surgeon's operating list at short notice, after attempts by the teenager's own consultant to insert a Hickman line had failed. As a consequence of adding the teenager's name to an already full list, the consultant surgeon had approximately 40 minutes in which to operate on him. Two theatre nurses told the court that they were shocked by the consultant surgeon's behaviour during the operation, his language and the manner in which the patient was handled. The prosecution submitted that whilst the consultant surgeon was accepted to be a competent and respected vascular surgeon, on this 'rare if not unique occasion', shortness of time together with things going wrong and the normal tension and stress of the operating theatre caused him to lose his temper and act in a way that eventually became dangerous.[1]

1   (2001) BMJ, 15 December.

12.48   The environment in which doctors work and the pressures to which they are subjected have to be one of the most stressful. Yet it is not known if those managing these doctors and those with responsibility for delivering quality care are aware of this. It must be said that it is not just the doctors and other healthcare professionals who are under stress and pressure: management may and will equally be pressured to meet target waiting lists and reduce waiting times.

12.49   There is a need therefore for a systematic approach to the delivery of services. Management needs to ensure that its systems are transparent and known to staff and healthcare professionals need to truly understand the organisation they are working in, and to maintain and update their knowledge and skills regularly.

Clinical and corporate governance

12.50 Risk management through clinical and corporate governance has been at the forefront of the NHS agenda for some years now.

12.51 Clinical governance has been defined as: 'A framework through which NHS organisations are accountable for continuously improving the quality of their services and safeguarding high standards of care by creating an environment in which excellence in clinical care can flourish.'[1]

1 HSC 1999/065 *Clinical Governance: Quality in the new NHS* (1999).

12.52 *Building a Safer NHS for Patients*[1] set out the government's plans for promoting patient safety. A new mandatory national reporting scheme for adverse healthcare events and 'near misses' in the NHS was set up so as to impress upon the NHS the need to learn from, and in turn prevent similar adverse incidents in the future. The National Patient Safety Agency (NPSA) was established to implement and operate the scheme with one core purpose: to improve patient safety by reducing the risk of harm either through human error or service failures.

1 Department of Health (2001).

12.53 The intention is to cut out ad hoc investigations undertaken by individual organisations and Trusts and to manage investigation through the Department of Health or the Commission for Health Improvement (CHI). The Secretary of State does, however, retain, pursuant to his statutory powers, the ability to order a public inquiry where a service failure results in serious harm to a large number of patients, where there is serious national concern or where there is a major issue of ethics or policy raised.

12.54 Intrinsic to the effective management of clinical risk is the need to incorporate messages received through the complaints procedure (which is currently under review) and to act on staff concerns (who will be protected by legislation dealing with whistleblowing). As a minimum, NHS Trusts and PCTs are expected to have undertaken baseline assessments of capability and capacity for the implementation of clinical governance and reporting on clinical governance arrangements within their Annual Reports.[1]

1 HSC 1999/065 *Clinical Governance: Quality in the new NHS* (1999).

12.55 Hand-in-hand with clinical governance is corporate governance. The system by which an organisation is controlled and is directed at the most senior levels with a view to meeting its objectives and the necessary standards of accountability and probity. The NHS verifies the effectiveness of its aims and objectives through what has been termed 'controls assurance'.

12.56 Controls assurance underpins the duty of quality and is defined as a 'process designed to provide evidence that NHS bodies are doing their reasonable best to manage themselves so as to meet their objectives and protect patients, staff, the public and other stakeholders against risks of all kinds'.[1]

1 HSC 1999/123, issued 21 May 1999.

12.57 Guidance on the governance framework for PCTs[1] has been made available as has guidance on governance for Care Trusts. It is clear that managers in the NHS are to be held responsible for ensuring that the care provided is proper and of a standard to be expected in the NHS. However, they cannot do this in isolation nor should they be expected to. It is imperative that those working within the NHS alert managers to deficiencies in services so that positive steps can be taken to eradicate such deficiencies in so far as is possible.

1   *Corporate Governance Framework for PCTs* (4th edn, 2002).

12.58   There is obligation on medical practitioners to report any concerns they have in relation to colleagues, and on nursing staff to ensure that any concerns they have are passed onto senior nurses. The role of management and staff and other bodies concerned with quality of patient care is pivotal in ensuring the adequacy of systems and patient care. Not only can issues and repeat trends be identified through the adverse incident reporting system but also through other performance management indicators such as clinical audit and appraisals.

12.59   In order for there to be effective risk management there is a need for clear lines of responsibility and accountability and a comprehensive programme of quality improvement, for example, clinical audit, implementation of clinical standards and guidelines, training and education of personnel and introduction of policies aimed at managing risk all designed to identify and remedy poor performance. There is a need also for clinical strategic direction by Trust Boards and it is the absence of these factors that lead to an under performance in healthcare organisations and leave organisations open to possible corporate and personal liability.

Clinical Negligence Scheme for Trusts

12.60   The Clinical Negligence Scheme for Trusts (CNST) is a voluntary pooling arrangement administered by the National Health Service Litigation Authority (NHSLA). Although concerned primarily with the management of risk within the context of clinical negligence claims in civil courts, the NHSLA has addressed the question of risk management and set standards and procedures which NHS Trusts are required to meet. These provide not only useful guidance for NHS bodies in controlling their risk exposure but provide guidance also on useful preventative measures.

Whose responsibility?

12.61   The primary responsibility for improving performance rests with the individual Trusts and PCTs.[1] Given the complex make up of the NHS, it is important to have an understanding of the way the NHS is structured so as to understand where the actual liabilities will lie in the event that the proposed reforms are extended to include NHS bodies which in the main would be NHS Trusts and PCTs.

1   *Raising Standards: Improving Performance in the NHS* (2003).

12.62   It is important from the outset to remember that the NHS is not just the Secretary of State or the Department of Health. The Secretary of State acts through the Department of Health and its function is to improve the health and well-being of the population. It is there to secure management and accountability of the overall healthcare system in the UK and is involved in developing policy and regulating and inspecting NHS bodies through parallel bodies such as the Commission for Health Improvement and, if need be, to intervene in the running of the NHS at any level.

12.63 Strategic Health Authorities are in fact the link between the Department of Health and the NHS and in effect manage NHS bodies. PCTs, NHS Trusts and Care Trusts are accountable to the Strategic Health Authorities, who are accountable to the Directors of Health and Social Care, who are accountable to the Department of Health, who in turn i are accountable to the Secretary of State.

12.64 The *Code of Conduct for NHS Managers Directions 2002* requires managers to 'use resources available … in an effective, efficient and timely manner having proper regard to the best interests of the public and patients' and ensure that '… NHS staff are provided with a safe working environment'. Chief executives and directors of Trusts as part of their duties are already considered to be personally accountable for achieving high quality of patient care. The Health Act 1999, s 18 states that it is the duty of each Health Authority, Primary Care Trust and NHS Trust to put and keep in place arrangements for the purpose of monitoring and improving the quality of health care which it provides to individuals.

12.65 Yet by the very nature of the complex organisation that the NHS is, the chief executive, directors and managers are required by necessity to delegate functions and rely on others to ensure that they meet the objectives which they have been set. This is where in practice the difficulty arises when bodies such as the police and the HSE are considering whether or not to bring a prosecution.

12.66 Under the present law, remember, before an organisation can be faced with a charge for corporate manslaughter it is necessary to identify one person who is said to be the 'controlling mind' of the organisation and for that one person also to be guilty of gross negligent manslaughter.

12.67 However, the constitution of the NHS makes it virtually impossible for such a person to be identified. With the proposed reforms it will of course no longer be necessary to identify such a controlling mind. All that will be required to be shown is that there was a management failure and that that failure amounted to conduct far below that which could reasonably be expected in the circumstances, albeit a grossly careless failure . Suddenly a door that seemed quite tightly shut is open wide.

12.68 Will 'management' which must mean at least meant the chief executive and other members of the Board, be likely to be hauled over the coals just because they did not manage or organise the activities of the Trust for which they are responsible in such a way as to ensure the health and safety of persons employed in or affected by those activities? And what of the individuals themselves, the doctors and healthcare professionals, who will still be able to be prosecuted for gross negligence manslaughter?

Management in the event of an adverse incident resulting in death

12.69 NHS organisations are open to prosecution as the law currently stands for corporate manslaughter, as are individuals for involuntary manslaughter. In the event of an adverse incident it is essential that the organisation is able to deal with the incident as quickly and efficiently as possible and to ensure that the incident is managed and reported to a designated officerwithin the organisation in accordance with its internal protocols.

12.70   The incident ought to be graded according to its seriousness and the impact on the patient, their family and the individuals concerned. Evidence should be gathered and preserved (for example medical records, defective equipment etc). An investigation should be undertaken to understand the events and circumstances leading up to the incident and a root cause analysis undertaken. In certain cases, as where the incident results in the death of the patient, the NHS organisation will need to notify the Department of Health and other stakeholders of the incident so that they can undertake their own inquires.

12.71   Where obvious errors have been made consideration should be given to early admissions with approval from those stakeholders who will ultimately be responsible financially for any civil claims (such as the NHSLA). Organisations should be open and keep those individuals affected by the incident informed and up to date. There may be occasions where the mistake made is such that the NHS organisation itself would wish to take disciplinary action against the individual healthcare professional and it is imperative that if this is the case, the individual be notified of any such disciplinary action at the earliest opportunity and if necessary, steps be taken in order to ensure patient safety, to relieve the individual of his or her duties until such time as the investigation into the incident is complete and an informed decision can be made as to that individual's future employment.

12.72   Staff should be interviewed, site inspections undertaken and policies and procedures reviewed. It is inevitable that an adverse incident will become public knowledge and with this in mind, consideration should be given at an early stage to press statements and media handling. Where an incident is likely to have a impact on other patients, consideration should be given to setting up a 24-hour helpline so that patients can be provided with information and be reassured.

12.73   Once an investigation is complete and a final report is to hand, it is important that the organisation study the report to understand the root cause of the incident and to determine what lessons can be learnt so as to prevent a similar occurrence in the future. This may necessitate a change in systems, policies, procedures and/or working practices.

Health and safety issues

12.74   The Health and Safety Executive (HSE) is the authority that enforces health and safety law in the UK in relation to health services and other authorities. Whilst it is the police who would lead any investigation into a major incident involving the NHS and decide whether or not to bring charges against the organisation or an individual, the HSE will be involved in the investigations with a view to determining the root cause of the incident.

12.75   The law relating to health and safety issues has been considered in some depth elsewhere in this book. It is still proper, however, that we consider how the law applies in practice to NHS bodies and for that matter private bodies also providing healthcare.

12.76 The majority of deaths that occur at work are a consequence not of any particular act or omission on the part of an individual but due to omissions on the part of the employer in ensuring a safe working environment. Where a death at work occurs there is a need to investigate the accident to determine what went wrong and to try and prevent similar accidents in the future.

12.77 The responsibility for minimising the risks that employees are exposed to in the workplace rests with those at Board level.[1] Given the high-risk environment in which NHS personnel operate, one does need to ask just how far those responsible for managing and organising the NHS' activities are likely to be held accountable should the proposed reforms become law.

1 Directors' Responsibilities for health and safety - Health and Safety Commision and Internal Control – Guidance for Directors on the Combined Code (the Turnbull report) September 1999.

12.78 The Combined Code on corporate governance[1] requires the board of directors of a company to maintain a sound system of internal controls to safeguard shareholder's investment and the company's assets and to conduct a review of the effectiveness of the company's system of internal controls at least annually and report to shareholders on this review in the annual report. To assist those charged with implementing the corporate governance principles embodied in the Combined Code, in 1999 the Turnbull Report[2] was published and this places responsibility for internal controls firmly on the directors (both executive and non executive). By making the board responsible for review of internal audits, *Turnbull* forces all directors to become aware of, and accountable for all areas of risk, not just those relevant to their particular area of responsibility.

1 *Combined Code Principles of Good Governance and Code of Best Practice* (2000).
2 *Internal Control – Guidance for Directors on the Combined Code* (1999).

12.79 These principles are not that different to those that the NHS is subject to through the clinical and corporate governance agendas. NHS organisations should be re visiting their health and safety policies and their safety management practices as a matter of course as part of the government's health and safety agenda.

12.80 On 20 May 2003 the Home Secretary, David Blunkett, said: 'There is great public concern at the criminal law's lack of success in convicting companies of manslaughter where a death has occurred due to gross negligence by the organisation as a whole. The law needs to be clear and effective in order to secure public confidence and must bite properly on large corporations whose failure to set or maintain standards causes a death. It is not targeted at conscientious companies that take their health and safety responsibilities seriously.'[1]

1 BBC News: 'Corporate killing law planned' 20 May 2003.

Management of health and safety risks

12.81 In the same way as any other employer, health authorities and trusts are required to manage their business to minimise the health and safety risks to their employees and those affected by their undertakings. If they fail to do so, they risk prosecution for health and safety offences, and also for corporate manslaughter in the case of work related deaths.

12.82   Similarly, individuals within their organisations may be exposed to prosecution as employees under the Health and Safety at Work etc Act 1974, s 7 for failing to take reasonable care for health and safety or as directors, managers or officers under the Health and Safety at Work etc Act 1974, s 37, if an offence by the organisation is committed with their consent, connivance, or attributable to their neglect. Additionally, the chief executive and board as 'controlling minds' risk gross negligence manslaughter prosecutions where there has been a death, although that risk is presently low, given the problems under the current law of securing convictions against large body corporates.

12.83   It is necessary for health authorities and trusts' clinical and corporate governance and control assurance systems to encompass the management of health and safety risks to their employees, contractors, visitors and patients. Indeed, clinical and health and safety risks should not be viewed in isolation; there can be an overlap between clinical and health and safety risks that emphasises the need for authorities and trusts to co-ordinate their management and assessment of these risks. An example of this type of overlap would be the need to assess the risk of self-harm to mentally disordered patients having regard to the health and safety risk of falling from unsecured high-level windows.

12.84   The role and responsibilities of health authority and trust boards to ensure that the management of health and safety risks are addressed are entirely analogous to those of directors in the private sector (see **chapter 1**) and include the risk assessment responsibilities of the Management of the Health and Safety at Work Regulations 1999[1] (see **chapter 1**).

1   SI 1999/3242.

12.85   Health authorities and trusts will be required to manage a variety of risks, some general associated with any business and some specific to their industries. By way of example, general risks will include those relating to the control of contractors and those associated with sharing their sites with organisations contracted to supply services, such as catering and laundry services and also managing the risks of vehicular and pedestrian traffic on site. The HSE's imposition of an improvement notice on West Dorset Hospital NHS Trust for it to carry out risk assessments and improve its standards relating to the management of stress in the Trust in 2003 demonstrates the importance of health authorities' and trusts' compliance with risks common to modern business .

12.86   There are also many specific risks relevant to the health sector that require priority management, some of which have been the subject of HSE guidance, such as manual handling risks associated with risk groups such as ambulance personnel and nursing staff,[1] slips and trips[2] and violence and aggression to staff.[3]

1   HSC 03/98 *Manual Handling in the Health Services* (1998).
2   HSE Information sheet '"Slips and trips" in the Health Services' (2003).
3   HSC Health Services Advisory Committee 'Violence and aggression to staff in Health Services, guidance on assessment and management' (1997).

12.87   In particular compliance with the Provision and Use of Work Equipment Regulations 1998[1] (PUWER) in relation to medical devices and other work equipment, the Personal Protective Equipment at Work Regulations 1992[2] (PPE) and the Control of Substances Hazardous to Health Regulations 1999[3] (COSHH) are priority areas in the NHS. For example, in the case of *Dudmore v Swansea and Morrison NHS Trust*,[4] the Trust was found liable to an employee for a latex allergy from latex gloves under its absolute duty under the COSHH Regulations. The HSE has issued a number of information sheets by way of guidance to health service providers on the safe use of particular equipment and handling of drugs to comply with the COSHH Regulations.[5]

1   SI 1998/2306.
2   SI 1992/2966.
3   1999/437.
4   (2002).
5   HSE information sheets 09/99 'Safe use of pneumatic air tube transport systems for pathology specimens' (1999); 09/03 'Safe handling of cytotoxic drugs (2003).

12.88   Failure to manage these issues can risk exposure to health and safety prosecutions. Many of these risks will not be life-threatening but failures to manage, for instance, legionnaires' risks and risks from failures of infection control and from blood borne viruses, for instance, through needle stick injuries, could well lead to deaths and exposure to corporate manslaughter.

Conclusion

12.89   The challenges that face NHS organisations if the proposed laws are enacted cannot be underestimated. It is essential therefore that these organisations understand and start to plan now, if they are not to be caught out. It is essential also that the accountable officers have a real understanding of how the proposed laws will affect them not only individually but as an organisation as a whole through the clinical, corporate and health and safety agendas. Social attitudes have changed and the public is all the more eager to ensure that those responsible for failures are held accountable. The rise in prosecutions for medical manslaughter reflects this change in attitude. NHS organisations should therefore as a matter of priority, be ensuring that risk management is incorporated effectively into all activities of the organisation and reviews of systems be undertaken now to ensure they are safe and effective. The focus has to be in preventing charges being brought rather than to reacting to them.

1   A Norfolk 'Doctor admits fatal blunder over cancer boy' *The Times*, 23 September 2003, p 7.

CHAPTER 13

Waste management

Paul Rice, Lawrence Graham Solicitors, London

Introduction

13.1 As evidenced by the preceding chapters the twin disciplines of environment and health and safety (EHS) law are amongst the most heavily regulated areas under both national and European legislation. As a specific subset of environmental law, the law and policy on waste and waste management is a particularly complex area which presents a challenge to all involved in the waste management chain. It is relevant to waste producers, carriers, reprocessors, waste collection and disposal authorities and all involved in the waste disposal industry, not to mention the general public.

13.2 The industry is currently faced not only with rapidly increasing volumes of waste production[1] but also demands resulting from EU legislation for increases in recycling and recovery of waste as well as diversion from landfill,[2] together with an ever-increasing penal regime for waste offences.

1 The foreword to a Cabinet Office report on the UK's Waste Strategy predicts that the volume of household waste alone will double by the year 2020. This will cost UK plc an incredible £3.2 billion per annum to dispose/treat.
2 Landfill of Waste Directive, Council Directive 99/31/EC.

13.3 In recent years fines for waste related offences have increased dramatically while the courts have also indicated a greater willingness to award both fines and custodial sentences to directors and officers of offending companies in addition to exercising powers in relation to the disqualification of directors and confiscation of vehicles.

13.4 This chapter looks at the corporate liability aspects of the following:

- the general regulatory framework for waste management in the UK;
- licensing of waste management activities;
- unlicensed and unlawful deposits of waste;
- the 'fit and proper person' test
- the statutory 'duty of care';
- transfrontier movements of waste; and
- asbestos waste.

13.5 However, as a foreword it should be noted that the concept of and the application of director and officer (D/O) responsibility for EHS offences has been gaining ground at a considerable rate throughout the 1990s. Indeed we now have government reports and Codes of Practice[1] dealing specifically with the issue as well as the more generic (but related) proposals in relation to corporate manslaughter.

1 Eg ICA *Internal Control' Guidance for Directors on the Combined Code* (the Turnbull Report) (1999); Health and Safety Commission *Revitalising Health and Safety* (2000); and Health and Safety Executive *Guidance on Boardroom Responsibility: Directors Responsibilities* (2001).

13.6 However, the prosecution of individual directors for EHS offences is not new. The two key statutes in this area, the Environmental Protection Act 1990 and the Health and Safety at Work etc Act 1974, both provide for corporate as well as individual criminal D/O liability where it can be shown that the company committed the offence with the '… consent, connivance or neglect …' of an individual officer or senior manager. It has already been mentioned above that this requires knowledge and a failure to address risks or complete disregard or recklessness in failing to turn one's mind to potential EHS risks within the company's operations.

13.7 Moreover, the prosecution policies of both the Environment Agency and the Health and Safety Executive (HSE) have specific references to dealing with D/O liability and the HSE has gone as far as establishing protocols with the police to assist in investigations where there are fatalities.

13.8 Directors have been prosecuted and received fines and in some instances custodial offences and arguments that the company itself has not been prosecuted for the offence have been ignored[1] by the court.

1 Unreported case taken by the author on behalf of a director of a clinical waste management company being charged with clinical waste management offences. The company itself was in liquidation and the stipendiary magistrate did not entertain arguments based on *Dickson v Wright* (1992) 94 Cr App Rep 7 that it must first be shown that the company must also have been prosecuted and convicted. In this instance the director was fined but decided not to appeal.

The waste regulatory framework

13.9 Before the introduction of the modern age of waste regulation in the UK under the Environmental Protection Act 1990, Pt II (EPA 1990), the deposit or disposal of waste was regulated through 'waste disposal' licences pursuant to the Control of Pollution Act 1974 (COPA 1974).

13.10   Even in 1974 the maximum penalty for waste related offences under COPA 1974 was an unlimited fine and/or a prison term of up to five years,[1] although the range of possible offences was rather limited. However, EPA 1990, Pt II established a much more comprehensive system of waste management licensing which introduced new offences and also required applicants for waste management licences to prove their competence, both financial and technical, to hold a licence.

1   COPA 1974, s 3(3).

13.11   EPA 1990 also established:

- a statutory duty of care[1] on all persons who produce, transport, handle, store, treat or dispose of waste to take all appropriate measures to ensure that it does not cause harm; and
- the outsourcing of local authority waste management functions to local authority waste disposal companies[2] (LAWDCs) which in turn led to new regulatory provisions in relation to the collection, disposal and treatment of controlled waste.

1   EPA 1990, s 34 and Environmental Protection (Duty of Care) Regulations 1991, SI 1991/2839.
2   EPA 1990, s 34.

13.12   EPA 1990 is still the main source of regulatory powers in the UK albeit that it has been supplemented by changes introduced by the Environment Act 1995 and more latterly the Pollution Prevention and Control Act 1999 (amongst others) which are detailed in **chapter 14**, Environment.

13.13   It was the Environment Act 1995 that established the Environment Agency as the primary regulatory authority for waste licensing. This was formerly the preserve of Local Authority Waste Regulation Authorities (WRAs).

Waste management licensing

13.14   Following the introduction of legislation to implement the provisions of the Integrated Pollution Prevention and Control Directive[1] (IPPC) waste management licensing is somewhat in a state of flux. The EPA 1990 licensing regime will, however, continue to apply to certain waste management operations while the new IPPC requirements will be applied to major new waste facilities, including all landfills and incinerators and certain disposal and recovery facilities depending on volumes of waste handled.

1   Council Directive 96/61/EC. See **chapter 14**, Environment.

13.15   Procedures for the application for IPPC[1] permits and the regulatory and the corporate liability provisions on which the new regime rests are also dealt with in **chapter 14**. This section deals with the current procedures and jurisprudence which still persist under the EPA 1990 system of waste management licensing and will no doubt also continue to apply to waste management law in the future whether regulated under EPA 1990 or IPPC.

1   Council Directive 96/61/EC.

The requirement for a licence

13.16 Almost all corporate liability for waste arises either out of a failure to have or act in accordance with a waste management licence (EPA 1990, s 33) or to observe the statutory duty of care (EPA 1990, s 34).

13.17 All operations where waste is stored, transported or finally disposed of must be done pursuant to and in accordance with a waste management licence issued by the Environment Agency. EPA 1990, ss 33 and 34 detail various offences in relation to the unauthorised handling and disposal of wastes.

13.18 EPA 1990, s 33 requires that a person shall not:

'(a) deposit controlled waste,[1] or knowingly cause or knowingly permit controlled waste to be deposited in or on any land unless a waste management licence authorising the deposit is in force and the deposit is in accordance with the licence;

(b) treat, keep, or dispose of controlled waste, or knowingly cause or knowingly permit controlled waste to be treated, kept or disposed of—
(i)   in or on any land, or
(ii) by means of any mobile plant,
except under and in accordance with a waste management licence;

(c) treat, keep or dispose of controlled waste in a manner likely to cause pollution of the environment or harm to human health.'

1   'Controlled Waste' is rather vaguely defined in EPA 1990, s 75 as including '… household, industrial and commercial waste or any such waste'.

13.19 The procedures for obtaining a waste management licence which are broadly similar to the IPPC Directive[1] application procedure are referred to below along with the consequences of failure to comply.

1   Council Directive 96/61/EC.

13.20 However, the Schedules to the Waste Management Licensing Regulations 1994[1] detail exemptions from the requirement to hold a licence for certain permitted activities. The long list of exempt activities include operations which have little or no environmental impact or, those that result in environmental improvement, for example, temporary storage pending final disposal, storage of demolition materials pending reuse in the ultimate construction or development on the site where they arose and activities relating to the recovery and reuse of wastes.

1   SI 1994/1056.

13.21 Even where an exemption is available it must first be applied for and registered with the Environment Agency. In order to rely on an exemption as a defence it must be notified to and registered by the Environment Agency.

Unauthorised disposal and handling of waste

The offences

13.22 Unless special waste is involved, offences under EPA 1990,s 33 will be liable:

'(a) on summary conviction to imprisonment for a term not exceeding six months
    or a fine not exceeding £20,000 or both; and

(b) on conviction on indictment, to imprisonment for a term not exceeding two
    years or a fine or both.'[1]

1 EPA 1990, s 33(8).

13.23 The penalties increase substantially where special waste has been handled
or disposed of without a licence. Special waste is defined in the Special Waste
Regulations 1996[1] (SWR) and is essentially controlled waste which because of its
hazardous properties is subject to additional and more onerous regulatory controls. A
person who commits an offence under EPA 1990, s 33 in relation to special waste will
be liable on summary conviction to a maximum prison sentence of six months and/or
a fine of up to £20,000 and upon conviction in the Crown Court to a prison term of up
to five years and/or an unlimited fine.

1 SI 1996/972.

13.24 In an attempt to deal with the growing problem of the fly tipping of waste at
unlicensed sites EPA 1990, s 33(5) places the onus on the owner or manager of vehicles
used to transport controlled waste to ensure that their employees, and those to whom
they might lend their vehicles, do not fly tip waste. It provides that the person who
controls or who is in a position to control the use of the vehicle is to be treated as
'knowingly causing the deposit' whether or not he or she has given any instructions
for this to be done. The main rationale would seem to be to attempt to redress the
common claim by companies that they cannot be responsible for the unlawful and
unauthorised use of their vehicles by employees.

13.25 In *Environment Agency v Melland*[1] the court held that ownership of a vehicle
was sufficient to establish evidence of control or of a position to control the use of a
vehicle for the purposes of an EPA 1990, s 33(5) offence. In this instance the prosecution
was not required to show that the owner was aware of its use to prove that an offence
has been committed. So, it would seem that businesses need also to monitor or have
written policies in place relating to the use of vehicles by employees and/or other
third parties.

1 (2002) QED 11/04/02.

13.26 There are, however, some important defences to EPA 1990, s 33 proceedings.
These are set out below.

Defences

13.27 EPA 1990, s 33(7) sets out the three statutory defences available to companies
or individuals charged with s 33 offences:

* exercise of all reasonable precautions and due diligence to avoid commission of
   an offence;
* acting under the instructions of an employer and the defendant did not know or
   have reason to suspect that he or she was committing an offence; or
* that the act alleged to constitute the contravention was done in an emergency in
   order to avoid danger to the public and that, as soon as reasonably practicable
   thereafter, full details were given to the local Environment Agency offices.

13.28 These defences will clearly be relevant to the potential liability of companies where management structure necessitates the delegation of responsibilities. Most commonly invoked is the reasonable precautions/due diligence defence. Companies that can show that they had adequate management systems in place may be able to prove a defence. Co-operation at the early stages of any investigation by the Environment Agency is recommended where one seeks to rely on such a defence.

13.29 A single case not only shows the extent to which the courts are willing to award quite harsh custodial sentences but also gives an indication as to the extensive powers of the Environment Agency to investigate and bring proceedings in relation to waste defences. In the 1997 case of *R v Hertfordshire County Council, ex p Green Environmental Industries*[1] the director of Green Environmental Industries was sentenced to 18 months' imprisonment in relation to the unauthorised disposal of clinical waste as well as a further nine months' in relation to fraudulent activity.

1   [1998] ENV LR 153.

13.30 At the hearing in St Albans Crown Court Mr Moynihan pleaded guilty to two offences of disposing of controlled waste on two sites in Hertfordshire without a waste management licence contrary to EPA 1990, s 33. He was sentenced to ten months' imprisonment for the first offence and 18 months' for the second, to run concurrently. The offences came to light after complaints from local residents. Officers of the then local authority's Waste Regulation Authority visited one of the sites and found a number of trailers as well as various other containers and vehicles containing clinical waste collected from local hospitals. The director of the company then undertook to ensure that the waste was removed to a clinical waste incinerator for final disposal. However, it transpired that the waste was simply moved to another site and, upon further investigation, that neither Green Environmental Industries Limited nor Mr Moynihan, were registered as waste carriers or held a valid waste management licence for any of their operating premises. At other premises also used by the company and again following complaints the Local Waste Regulation Authority also found some 61,000 bags of clinical waste and 30,000 bins of sharps (syringes, needles, blades etc).

13.31 Other company directors have also been imprisoned. Most recently in October 2002, Mr John Bruce, a director of Ivory Plant Hire Limited, was convicted at Worcester Crown Court of various unauthorised depositing offences in relation to the disposal of contaminated soils.[1] Mr Bruce was sentenced to 12 months' imprisonment after he pleaded guilty to various offences in relation to arranging the unlawful tipping of contaminated waste on land which did not have a waste management licence. He was also disqualified from acting as a company director for ten years. Separately, a fellow director of the company was sentenced to 120 hours of community service and was likewise disqualified from acting as a director for five years and ordered to pay a contribution to costs of £20,000.

1   Ends Report, October 2002, No 333.

13.32 However, the highest jail term for an operator of an unlicensed waste management business came in July 1998 when a former farmer, Mr John Hawksworth, was prosecuted for running an illegal landfill operation at his premises near Sheffield.[1] He was sentenced to 21 months' imprisonment. Mr Hawksworth had a long history of waste related offences but continued accepting waste onto his site and ignored an Environment Agency waste removal notice served pursuant to EPA 1990, s 59 requiring him to remove the waste on his land.[2] Thereafter, rather than prosecuting for failure to comply with the notice the Environment Agency mounted a surveillance operation at the property and was able to give evidence that up to 7,000 tons of industrial waste had been deposited at the site over a period of two years which had raised the land by a height of eight metres. Mr Hawksworth pleaded guilty to 19 charges of depositing, keeping and burning waste on unlicensed land, contrary to EPA 1990, s 33. In addition, various firms which delivered waste to the site have since been prosecuted. Mr Hawksworth's illegal landfill has led to convictions of individuals, companies and at least one other director.

1   Ends Report, July 1998, No 282.
2   EPA 1990, s 59 empowers authorities to serve land clearance notices in relation to unlawfully deposited waste. It is an offence to fail to comply with a s 59 notice and in certain circumstances the Environment Agency may carry out the clearance itself and seek to recover its costs from the persons served with the notice.

The waste management licence

13.33   So, the key way to avoid liability is to ensure your operations and those to whom you entrust your waste are appropriately licensed. Applications for waste management licences are made in writing to the local Environment Agency office in the area where the site is to be situated. A fee is payable and is calculated pursuant to the agency charging scheme; both application and subsistence fees are revised annually.

13.34   Applications for licences should be determined within four months (or such longer time as may be agreed between the parties) but experience shows that even the best prepared applications have taken in excess of 12 months until final determination. It is likely that IPPC Directive[1] applications will in time follow a similar protracted application procedure.

1   Council Directive 96/61/EC.

13.35   At the end of this four-month period (if not extended) the application (if not granted) is deemed to be refused and the applicant has a right of appeal. Similarly, where applications are refused or granted subject to onerous conditions the applicants may appeal to the Secretary of State. The appeals office is situated within the Planning Inspectorate.[1]

1   Temple Quay House, 2 The Square, Bristol BS1 6PN.

13.36   Applications are only granted where planning permission or an established use certificate is already in place. From a corporate liability and management perspective it is vital to appreciate that applications for waste management licences *must* be rejected where the applicant is not a 'fit and proper person'[1] or where there is a danger to public health, the environment or the amenities of the locality.

1   See **para 13.43** below.

Licence conditions

13.37   Where granted, licences will be subject to continued compliance with a number of conditions designed to protect the environment, public health and local amenity.

Conditions will cover such issues as hours of operation, volumes of waste permitted on site, security, lighting, odour, vermin, fires etc as well as the aftercare and/or clearance or closure of the site.

13.38 It is an offence to fail to comply with licence conditions. In February 2003 a Kent-based waste management company was fined a total of £52,500 in relation to various EPA 1990, s 33 offences including the handling of waste outside of the permitted operating hours as set down in the company's waste management licence.[1] In obtaining the evidence the Environment Agency began video surveillance of the company following complaints from neighbouring businesses. The relevant director refused to co-operate with the Environment Agency despite an earlier court appearance in which the company was fined £6,000 for failure to comply with other conditions in the licence in relation to the suppression of dust at the site.

1 Ends Report, February 2003, No 337.

13.39 Separately, one of the UK's leading waste management businesses was prosecuted on five separate occasions in the 12 months to February 2003 in relation to various EPA 1990, s 33 offences. The latest related to failure to comply with licence conditions relating to gas-controlled systems at its Arden Quarry landfill in Derbyshire.[1] On this occasion the company was fined a total of £12,000.

1 Ends Report, February 2003, No 337.

Transfer and surrender of a licence

13.40 Waste management licences can only be transferred with the agreement of the Environment Agency after a joint application by the transferor and transferee. The Agency will want to satisfy itself that the transferee is also a fit and proper person.

13.41 EPA 1990 provides that a licence can only be terminated if revoked by the Environment Agency or, after application by the holder, the Agency agrees to accept the surrender. The Agency will only agree to a surrender where it is satisfied that the site does not present a risk to human health or the environment. Upon acceptance of surrender it will issue a certificate of completion which will determine the licence holder's obligations under the licence.

13.42 In certain instances liquidators of companies holding waste management licences have been able to determine licences by way of disclaimer or dissolution of the company. The area where waste management regulation meets insolvency law has given rise to an interesting line of cases dealing with the ability of liquidators to disclaim waste management licences and the continuing ability of the Environment Agency to enforce the provisions of an operating licence after the dissolution of, or in the course of the liquidation of, a company. Whilst at least three High Court judgments can be said to have favoured environmental protection over the 'interest of creditors in the speedy winding up of a company' the situation was reversed by the Court of Appeal and to date, no further points have been taken on the issue. However, Mr Justice Neuberger, noted in *Re Mineral Resources Ltd* ('Stout')[1] that:

'... the inter-relationship between liquidator and Environmental Protection remains in its infancy.'

With the increasing obligations on waste management professionals to make financial provision as part of the licensing procedures (See **para 13.43** below) as well as the continuing competitive market and the constant threat of business failure it is very possible that this point will be revisited.[2]

1 Also called *Environment Agency v Stout* [1999] 1 All ER 746.
2 See also *Wilmott Trading* cases [1999] LS Gaz R 29; and *Celtic Extraction Ltd* (14 July 1999, unreported), Ch D.

Fit and proper person test

13.43   In order to hold a waste management licence the applicant must prove that he or she is a 'fit and proper person'. To satisfy, and continue to satisfy, the test, the applicant or licence holder must be able to show that he or she:

•   has committed no relevant offences (waste related or environmental offences);
•   is technically competent to manage the activities; and
•   has arranged sufficient financial provision to ensure compliance with the terms and conditions of the licence.

13.44   Although transitional provisions were available for older and experienced waste management professionals, technical competence is ordinarily required to be shown through training and subsequent certification by the Waste Management Industry Training and Advisory Board (WAMITAB) and the award of a Certificate of Technical Competence.

13.45   There is no single route of ensuring financial provision and in general the Environment Agency will accept performance bonds, money held in escrow accounts and insurance policies.

13.46   The requirement that an applicant or licence holder have committed no relevant offences will be extremely important to the continued management or operation of companies. In the event that the company commits an EPA 1990, s 33 or 34 duty of care offence it will be open to the Agency to withdraw its licence on the basis that it is no longer a fit and proper person.

13.47   In February 2003 the Environment Agency issued two consultation papers proposing significant changes to the 'fit and proper person' test.[1] The consultation papers acknowledged that little use has been made of powers to refuse or revoke licences or suspend registrations. The Agency revoked only 11 registrations and refused a further 11 applications between 1996 and 2002.[2]

1 Environment Agency 'New approaches to the relevant convictions test' and 'New approaches to financial provision' 7 February 2003.
2 ENDS Report 335 (December 2002) p 19.

13.48   The Consultation proposes that offenders will now to be asked to draw up a 'post-conviction' plan explaining how they will conduct their operations in future in order to ensure compliance with legislation as well as licence conditions. The new rules will apply to businesses which have a series of relevant convictions and to group companies where the Environment Agency will take into account convictions committed by sister or associated organisations. The post-conviction plans will be required to be placed on the public register. The impact of negative PR has already been mentioned above and failure to comply with the company's own proposals for improvement will not only add to the penalties and related losses arising from a conviction but also cause increased embarrassment to relevant companies. In the event of failure to follow a post-conviction plan it is likely that the Agency will now be more inclined to refuse or revoke licences and licence applications.

Duty of care

EPA 1990, s 34

13.49 The statutory duty of care was introduced by EPA 1990, s 34. It applies to all persons in the waste management chain and requires all persons involved in the 'cradle to grave' handling of waste (ie from producers to final disposers) to take all reasonable and appropriate measures to ensure that:

- Waste is only kept, treated, deposited or disposed of in accordance with a waste management licence or other authorisation. This will require that the original producer or holder of the waste checks that all subsequent holders of the waste within the chain are duly authorised and that the waste has been disposed of correctly. Technically, transfer to a waste contractor will not relieve a waste producer of his duty.
- Waste does not escape from the control of the holder. This requires that the waste is stored or packaged properly, for example, in drums or secure containers if the waste is a liquid or that lorries are covered to prevent waste becoming windborne.
- Waste is only transferred to authorised persons such as registered waste carriers or licensed disposal operations permitted to accept that type of waste. As above, this can extend to checking authorisations including confirming that they are still valid before waste is transferred either to the carriers or waste management companies involved at all stages right up to final disposal.
- All transfers/movements of the waste are accompanied by an adequate written description (the 'waste transfer note') which will allow waste to be identified and subsequently handled correctly.

13.50 These statutory provisions are supplemented by the Environmental Protection (Duty of Care) Regulations 1991[1] and a statutory Code of Practice which was re-released by the Department of the Environment in March 1996.

1 SI 1991/2839.

Duty of care offences

13.51 Failure to comply with the duty of care as set out in EPA 1990, s 34 and the Environmental Protection (Duty of Care) Regulations 1991[1] are amongst the most commonly prosecuted of environmental offences. Moreover, while it is not an offence to fail to follow the Code of Practice this can be taken into account by the court when considering any failure to comply with the s 34 duty itself and the penalty to be imposed. The Code of Practice is an extremely useful document, with advice on waste labelling, secure storage and transport as well as completion of the appropriate waste tracking documents.

1 SI 1991/2839.

Waste transfer notes

13.52   The requirement in EPA 1990 for an adequate description of the waste has been extended in the supporting Environmental Protection (Duty of Care) Regulations 1991[1] to require that a waste transfer note ('WTN') accompanies each movement of waste, with copies being retained for future inspection. The WTN itself has no definitive form but must record as a minimum the type and quantity of the waste including the type of container, details of the transferor and transferee as well as the time and place of transfer. WTNs must be retained for at least two years.

1   SI 1991/2839.

13.53   While special wastes are also subject to the duty of care they must comply with a different transfer note system which also requires pre-notification of movements to the Environment Agency; the special waste consignment note.

Duty of care cases

13.54   Duty of care offences are punishable with a fine of up to £5,000 in the magistrates' court. This rises to an unlimited fine if prosecuted upon indictment in the Crown Court.

13.55   In the case of *R v Newcastle City Council and Contract Heat & Power*[1] both the Council and the incinerator operator, Contract Heat & Power, were prosecuted in relation to the deposit of some 2,000 tons of incinerator fly ash between 1994 and 1999. In 1999, an allotment owner discovered that the Council had disposed of mixtures of ash across various allotments throughout Newcastle. After the ash was tested it was found to contain dangerously high levels of dioxins, potentially fatal carcinogens. In September 2000 the Environment Agency announced that it was to charge the Council and the incinerator operators with various waste offences. In January 2002 they were fined a total of £35,000 plus £35,000 costs. It was noted at sentencing that the Council had already spent over £500,000 on remedial works. Both the Council and Contract Heat & Power were charged with offences including failure to ensure that waste transfer notes were completed and retained for inspection as required by the EPA 1990,s 34 duty of care. Although the defendants were, in this instance, awarded relatively modest fines the case has had a huge impact on how incinerator wastes are now dealt with throughout the country. Not only has the case resulted in negative PR consequences for the Council and the company but also for the incinerator and waste to energy industries. It is now up to the industries to attempt to look to other methods of treating and/or disposing of their ultimate waste materials.

1   (2002, unreported), ENDS report 324.

Transfrontier shipment of waste

13.56   When waste crosses national borders, international, EU and national regulations will apply. In the UK this will be of primary concern to movements of waste for recovery/recycling in other countries only. The UK Management Plan on Imports and Exports of Waste prohibits all exports of waste for disposal.

13.57   Regulatory requirements are based on the 1989 Basel Convention on the Control of Transboundary Movements of Hazardous Wastes and their Disposal. The Convention was the basis for the 1993 EU Regulation on Transfrontier Shipments of Waste.[1] Like the Basel provisions the EU rules established a classification of wastes comprising Green List, Amber List and Red List materials based on their perceived environmental risk, with greater controls on the more hazardous Red List wastes. It also introduced a system of requiring prior authorisation for movements of wastes from the competent authorities in each member state.

1   Council Regulation 259/93/EC.

13.58   Both the 1989 Convention and the EU rules are implemented in the UK by the Transfrontier Shipment of Waste Regulations 1994[1] and the 'UK's Management Plan for the Export and Import of Waste'.[2]

1   SI 1994/1137.
2   Department of the Environment (1996).

13.59   The regulatory requirements for waste movements will depend on the categories of waste involved and can include the prior agreement and consent of the country of dispatch as well as the country of destination, bills of lading and tracking documents and a form of financial surety, bond or guarantee.

13.60   The Environment Agency is the competent authority for transfrontier movements of waste in the UK. As well as checking consent applications, financial security provisions and shipment documents prior to granting approval to movements the Agency will also prosecute breaches of the Regulations.

Producer responsibility

Generally

13.61   The Environment Act 1995 introduced the concept that a producer bears responsibility for the environmental consequences of its product. These new provisions were to facilitate implementation of the EU Packaging and Packaging Waste Directive[1] but went much wider by permitting the Secretary of State power to introduce regulations governing '... such products or materials, as may be prescribed'.

1   Council Directive 94/62/EC.

13.62   At present regulations have been issued introducing a regulatory scheme in respect of packaging and packaging waste only. In due course, government will be introducing statutory schemes to give effect to the Directives on End of Life Vehicles[1] ('ELVs') and the proposals on Waste Electrical and Electronic Equipment[2] ('WEEE'). Thereafter, we can expect proposals on batteries and accumulators with other products such as newspapers and magazines to follow.

1   Council Directive 2000/53/EC.
2   COM (2000) 347

Packaging waste

13.63   The Producer Responsibility Obligations (Packaging Waste) Regulations 1997[1] implement (in part) the provisions of the 1994 EC Directive on Packaging and Packaging Waste.[2] In short, they impose obligations on producers of both packaging and packaging waste to recover and recycle percentages of the waste packaging for which they are responsible (ie the packaging they make or in which they place their products). As such, the EC obligations on the UK are a shared obligation, spread across members of the packaging chain from producers of actual packaging through to manufacturers of products which use packaging as well as retailers.

1   SI 1997/648.
2   Council Directive 94/62/EC.

13.64   In order not to impact unduly on small businesses the UK scheme only applies to those packaging waste producers who have an annual turnover of above £2 million and who handle more than 50 tonnes of packaging a year.

13.65   All obligated businesses must either register with the Environment Agency and be allocated an annual recovery and recycling target or join a registered compliance scheme. If obligated, it is an offence to fail to register with the Agency or a scheme.

13.66   In April 2002 three units of the Lear Manufacturing Group were fined £96,000 for numerous waste packaging offences.[1] The fine is by far the largest ever recorded for packaging waste prosecution and is in stark contrast to the derisory fines handed out in the early days of packaging waste prosecutions. Investigations into the Lear Corporation showed that one of the subsidiaries had registered in the early days of the scheme but that it failed to do so in subsequent years. Other companies within the Group had also failed to register and take reasonable steps to recover and recycle packaging.

1   Ends Report, April 2002, No 327.

13.67   The Group received huge relative fines in this instance which by far exceed the previous record fine of £25,000 handed down in 2001 to the Snack Factory.[1] While the average fine is less than £5,000 the Regulations provide that proceedings brought on indictment before the Crown Court can be subject to a maximum penalty of an unlimited fine.

1   Ends Report, September 2001, No 320.

Registered compliance schemes

13.68   A compliance scheme is a body registered with the Environment Agency, SEPA or the EHS to enrol members for whose recovery and recycling obligations the scheme will then be responsible. The scheme will source the recovery/recycling capacity, contract with those facilities undertaking the recovery/recycling and provide the regulators with evidence of compliance on behalf of all its members.

13.69   Accredited recovery/recycling processes issue packaging waste recovery notes (PRNs) in relation to the packaging wastes they reprocess. Where packaging waste is exported for recovery the exporter is entitled to issue packaging waste export recovery notes (PERNs). Both PRNs and PERNs are accepted as evidence of compliance with recovery and recycling obligations by the Environment Agency.

ELVs

13.70 The provisions of the EU Directive on End of Life Vehicles[1] (ELV) came into force in October 2000. The ELV Directive requires member states to take measures to:

- ensure that ELVs can only be scrapped ('treated') by authorised dismantlers or shredders, who must meet high environmental treatment standards;
- require economic operators (this term includes manufacturers, dismantlers and shredders among others) to establish adequate systems for the collection of ELVs from the outset;
- ensure that last-owners must be able to return vehicles to these systems from January 2007;
- require vehicle manufacturers or importers to pay 'all or a significant part' of the costs of take back and treatment from January 2007;
- set rising re-use, recycling and recovery targets which must be met by January 2006 and 2015; and
- restrict the use of heavy metals in new vehicles from July 2003.

1 Council Directive 2000/53/EC.

13.71 Amongst the options being considered for the implementation scheme in the UK is a permitting system for vehicle recycling facilities which will then provide vehicle manufacturers with appropriate evidence of compliance for vehicles recovered and recycled on their behalf. The detail of a UK scheme remains to be finalised.

WEEE

13.72 In June 2000 the European Commission adopted proposals for a Directive on Waste Electrical and Electronic Equipment[1] (WEEE) and a Directive on the Restriction On Use of Certain Hazardous Substances in electrical and electronic equipment[2] (ROHS). The Directives are designed to tackle the fast increasing waste stream of electrical and electronic equipment by increasing recycling and limiting the total quantity of waste going to final disposal.

1 Directive 2002/96/EC.
2 Directive 2002/95/EC

13.73 Producers will be responsible for WEEE take-back schemes. It is hoped that this will encourage environmental improvements in the design of electrical and electronic equipment. As with the ELV Directive[1] consumers will be able to return their equipment free of charge.

1 Council Directive 2000/53/EC.

13.74 In order to prevent the generation of hazardous waste the proposed ROHS Directive[1] on the restriction of the use of certain hazardous substances requires the substitution of various heavy metals and brominated flame-retardants in new electrical and electronic equipment from 1 January 2008 onwards.

1 Directive 2002/95/EC

13.75   The Department for Trade and Industry issued a joint discussion paper[1] on both sets of proposals and already the Industry Council for Electronic Equipment Recycling (ICER) has set up an independently audited voluntary accreditation scheme for WEEE recyclers and refurbishers. The accreditation service being offered by ICER is open to all firms involved in WEEE recycling including those operating in mechanical processing, chemical processing, plastics processing and dismantling.

1   'Discussion paper of 28 March 2003 by UK Government, Scottish Executive, Welsh Assembly and Northern Ireland Administration on the 'Implementation of [WEEE and RoHS Directives]' published by DTI

Asbestos waste

13.76   The continued use of asbestos has been severely restricted in the UK as a result of prohibitions on use of certain types of asbestos and controls over the condition and maintenance of asbestos in a workplace. These restrictions are to be supplemented in May 2004 by the implementation of Regulation 4 of the Control of Asbestos and Work Regulations 2002[1] (CAWR 2002) which will require 'persons in charge of premises' to inspect their premises for the existence of asbestos and thereafter to draw up a maintenance plan. The plan is required to be notified to all employees as well as contractors who may be working within the premises. In relation to asbestos waste these must be disposed of under the Special Waste Regulations 1996[2] and all asbestos from labour must be carried out by a licensed asbestos contractor. In September 1998 the directors of a Birmingham-based company which employed roofing contractors behind a major asbestos dumping incident in Birmingham in 1997 were convicted and sentenced to nine months' imprisonment.[3] Bags of various types of asbestos were dumped at various locations including a school and supermarket car park around Birmingham. The asbestos came from the Rollco Rivet & Screw Company's factory in Aston, Birmingham. The company employed a roofing contractor to remove and dispose of the existing asbestos roof. The employed contractor then employed a sub-contractor to do the work and had various skips in which to dump the waste asbestos containing materials. The sub-contractor, however, hired a van to dump excess materials at various locations around the city. He was subsequently sentenced to nine months' imprisonment while the company was fined £40,000 with £30,000 costs for failure to protect the health of its employees. Two directors were also fined £6,000 and £4,000 respectively for health and safety offences.

1   SI 2003/2675.
2   SI 1996/972.
3   Ends Report, September 1998, No 284.

13.77   The new duty to manage introduced by CAWR 2002 will impose requirements on employers, landlords, tenants, licensees and managing agents in relation to the identification of asbestos in buildings and the preparation and dissemination of a management plan. Although it will be a criminal offence to fail to carry out the survey it is likely that insurers will require surveys to be completed before buildings and/or employers cover is reissued. Moreover, failure to undertake the survey will also provide powerful evidence in any claims for loss or death following exposure by employees or visitors. It is therefore likely to be insisted upon by all subsequent tenants, licensees of purchasers of property where asbestos or asbestos containing materials are likely to be present.

1   SI 2002/2675.

CHAPTER 14

Environmental liability

Caroline May, Partner, Head of Safety, Health and Envoronment Group, Hertfordsire

Introduction

14.1   As has been discussed elsewhere environmental regulation is increasing. Many laws applicable in the UK arise as a direct result of European Directives. There is increasing pressure upon enforcement standards to minimise emissions to the environment.

14.2   In the UK, the Environmental Protection Act 1990 (EPA 1990) introduced, for the first time, an integrated approach to environmental protection with separate regulatory regimes governing emissions to air, land and water. Each of these areas is addressed in this chapter. These form the basic framework for environmental legislation in the UK. However, there are other related areas of regulation which overlap with public health issues and for these reasons this chapter will also address statutory nuisance, asbestos, legionnaires' disease and genetically modified organisms which have both environmental and health and safety implications. Waste, is of course addressed in a separate chapter. The interrelationship between environmental and health and safety issues is highlighted by the contents list of this chapter, recognising that what is discharged into the environment also has implications for human health and other life forms. The law has evolved from the basic concept of recovery of damages for harm to property, through the torts of nuisance and negligence, to a criminal regulatory regime. Many companies are surprised to find that if they are in breach of environmental and health and safety permits then the enforcement remedy is a criminal one, which can involve them in appearing before the criminal courts. This can often be an unpleasant surprise for senior management who are otherwise unfamiliar with such circumstances. Potential for individual responsibilities (as discussed elsewhere in this chapter) also impresses upon directors and other senior officers the importance of demonstrably discharging their environmental and health and safety obligations to minimise those risks. An individual or a company with a criminal record will find that its operations will come under increasing scrutiny, not only by its employees and shareholders but also its financiers, analysts, competitors and potential merger partners. Clearly, the risks are to be minimised or avoided at all costs.

14.3 In this chapter, we examine some key environmental and public health related areas which are the subject of specific regulation and specific criminal penalty. Topics covered in this chapter are not intended to be exhaustive but to highlight the principal areas of likely concern.

Water pollution

Introduction

14.4 Water pollution incidents are costly to companies. Licences may be revoked, penalties imposed, clean-up, investigation and legal costs will be incurred (all of these directly affecting the company's profit and loss accounts). Further cost considerations include the damage done to a company's image, brand and public relations by press coverage of water pollution incidents and the Environment Agency's (EA) policy to 'name and shame' offenders.

14.5 In terms of criminal liability the EA's Enforcement Policy (the 'Policy')[1] contains a mandate not only to prosecute companies but also individuals where they can be shown to have turned a 'blind eye' to the circumstances which caused the offence.

1   In force from 1 November 1998.

Brief legislative history

14.6 The first recorded law prohibiting water pollution dates from 1388. However, modern water pollution legislation derives from the six Consolidation Acts.[1] Of particular importance to this chapter are the Water Resources Act 1991 (WRA 1991) which contains in Part III the main water pollution offences and the Water Industry Act 1991 which regulates the new privatised water industry.

1   Namely the Water Resources Act 1991; the Water Industries Act 1991; the Land Drainage Act 1991; and as defined by the Water Consolidation (Consequential Provisions) Act 1991.

The Regulator

14.7 As part of the drive for privatisation of national industry in the 1980s, the Water Act 1989 was passed to transfer the water supply and wastewater treatment functions of the regional water authorities into the private sector.

14.8   The EA is today the main water regulator and was created by the Environment Act 1995. The EA was given the former functions of the National Rivers Authority in relation to water.

14.9   The EA's broad remit is to protect the environment and to do so it was granted the power to investigate water pollution incidents and institute legal proceedings.

Criminal liabilities

Regulatory offences

14.10   The principal offences relating to water pollution are contained in WRA 1991, s 85 which makes it a criminal offence:

'… to cause or knowingly permit any poisonous, noxious or polluting matter or any solid waste to enter any controlled waters.'

TO CAUSE OR KNOWINGLY PERMIT

14.11   The leading authority on 'to cause' for water pollution cases is the House of Lords decision in the *Alphacell* case.[1] In this case a paper manufacturing company had a settling tank on the bank of a river. The tank was controlled by two pumps which prevented it from overflowing into the river. Despite regular inspections, the tank had become blocked with leaves within 45 minutes causing the contents of the tank to pour into the river. Alphacell was convicted of causing pollution and appealed on the basis that the company had no knowledge of the pollution nor had it acted negligently.

1   *Alphacell v WoodWard* [1972] AC 824.

14.12   The House of Lords held that there was no need to show intent on the part of the offender, and that 'to cause' had a common sense meaning which did not require knowledge of the offender's action or inaction. It was enough to show that the tank was the company's tank, and under its control, and that the overflow of the contents of the tank had caused the pollution.[1]

1   *Alphacell v WoodWard* [1972] AC 824.

14.13   To 'knowingly permit' involves a failure to act to prevent pollution accompanied by knowledge. However, knowledge can be either implied or express.

THE TRIGGER FOR PROSECUTION

14.14   A prosecution can be brought when polluting, noxious or poisonous matter or solid waste or trade or sewerage effluent[1] enters controlled waters. 'Polluting, noxious or poisonous matter' is not defined by statute but the courts have interpreted it as substances that are likely to harm the environment.

1   It is a defence to discharge in accordance with a discharge consent: WRA 1991, s 88.

14.15   Controlled waters, are defined as groundwater, inland waters, coastal waters and territorial waters.[1]

1   WRA 1991, s 221.

EA ENFORCEMENT POLICY

14.16   At the core of the Policy are four governing principles: proportionality, consistency, transparency and targeted enforcement action. What is proportional depends on the balance between the risks taken, the harm caused to the environment and the cost of bringing a prosecution. Consistency means that the EA should be taking a similar approach in similar circumstances. Transparency is translated into a need to inform those whom are regulated what is expected of them. Whilst targeted action means targeting prosecution of those activities which give rise to the most serious effects on the environment.

14.17   In all cases the EA will not prosecute until it is satisfied that there is sufficient admissible and reliable evidence to bring a prosecution, there is a realistic prospect of securing a conviction and it is not against the public interest to bring a prosecution. The EA will look at factors such as the seriousness of the offence; the foreseeability of the harm; the intention of the offender, and the offender's action/inaction following the incident etc.

14.18   The EA has published Guidelines[1] to accompany the Policy. These clarify the enforcement policy and confirm that prosecution will commonly result following an incident which has had a major impact on the environment. For incidents with a significant impact a caution will normally follow and for incidents which cause minor impact a warning will normally be issued.

1   *Guidance for the Enforcement and Protection Policy* (2001).

14.19   The Policy encourages the EA to prosecute senior company officers individually if they believe that the company officers have turned a 'blind eye' to the circumstances which caused the pollution incident. The senior company officers will be charged with the same office as the company.[1]

1   WRA 1991, s 157.

PENALTIES

14.20   Water pollution offences are criminal offences and can be tried by the magistrates' court or the Crown Court.

14.21   If the case goes to the magistrates' court, the offender can be liable to a fine not exceeding £20,000 or to a maximum of three months' imprisonment or to both. For each day the offence is said to have continued to occur a further maximum of £20,000 fine per day can be imposed. At the Crown Court the maximum penalties include an unlimited fine and/or a term of imprisonment not exceeding two years.

14.22   It is unusual for custodial sentences to be imposed by the courts. However, directors, managers, company secretaries and other officers of a company can be prosecuted individually if the company is found to have committed a water pollution offence with their consent, connivance or neglect.[1] With today's best practice requiring companies to report on who and how environmental management decisions are taken from site to board level, a paper trail is being left behind which may in future allow more prosecutions to be brought against individual company officers. Disqualification of directors is also possible following a conviction.[2]

1 WRA 1991, s 217(1).
2 Company Directors Disqualification Act 1986, s 2.

14.23   There is increasing pressure for larger fines to be levied but this is often a fraction of the true cost. When the *Sea Empress*[1] tanker was grounded at the entrance to the Milford Haven port due to the negligent navigation of the pilot causing 72,000 tonnes of crude oil to be released the Milford Haven Port Authority was fined £4 million pounds (reduced on appeal to £750,000). The clean-up operation was estimated at £60 million. Average fines for water offences amount to £20,000.

1 *EA v Milford Haven Port Authority (The Sea Empress)* [1999] 1 Lloyds Rep 673.

RELATIONSHIP WITH CONTAMINATED LAND

14.24   Water pollution and contaminated land can be directly linked. The enforcing authority may choose to prosecute under WRA 1991 or EPA 1990. Contaminated land is dealt with elsewhere in this chapter but here it is sufficient to point out that under the contaminated land regime the enforcing authority can serve a remediation notice specifying exactly what work is to be done and the degree of remediation to be carried out, potentially increasing the offender's clean up costs.

Contaminated land

Introduction

14.25   EPA 1990, Pt IIA first introduced the regulatory regime for dealing with contaminated land. A proposal for public registers of contaminated land (under EPA 1990, s 143) was shelved amid fears of its potential impact upon an already depressed property market. Following further lengthy consultation the Environment Act 1995, s 57 inserted more detailed proposals of the current regime which did not come into force in England and Wales until 1 April 2000.[1] The details of the scheme are set out in the Contaminated Land (England) Regulations 2000[2] and further augmented by a DETR circular.[2]

1 SI 2000/340.
2 SI 2000/227.
3 DETR circular 02/2000.

14.26   The contaminated land regime is commonly referred to as 'Part IIA'[1] and introduces a complex scheme of strict and retrospective liability for the remediation of contaminated land. This raises the prospect that innocent owners or occupiers of land may find themselves liable to criminal fines and penalties (and/or civil damages) for contamination liabilities pre-dating their period of ownership or occupation of the land. This is a landmark piece of legislation in environmental law and has far reaching consequences.

1 EPA 1990, Pt IIA.

Definitions

14.27   The provisions of EPA 1990, Pt IIA envisage a sequence of steps starting with the identification of contaminated land, following a process of consultation which leads to voluntary or mandatory remediation of the land. The statutory definition of contaminated land is as follows:

> 'Contaminated Land is any land which appears to the Local Authority in whose area it is situated to be in such condition, by reason of substances in, on or under the land that—
> (a) significant harm is being caused or there is a significant possibility of such harm being caused; or
> (b) pollution of controlled waters is being, or is likely to be caused; ...'[1]

1   EPA 1990, s 78A(2).

14.28   EPA 1990, Pt IIA therefore places responsibility upon local authorities to apply the statutory definition to sites within their area to see whether they meet the definition provided in EPA 1990. The definition itself relies upon the concept of 'harm' which is difficult to define and capable of subjective judgment. The following definition is offered by way of assistance:

> '"Harm" means harm to the health of living organisms or other interference with the ecological systems of which they form part and, in the case of man, includes harm to his property.'[1]

1   EPA 1990, s 78A(4).

14.29   While the statutory guidance in the DETR circular[1] provides some assistance as to how these concepts are to be dealt with it still poses problems for the local authority in determining what harm is to be regarded as significant and at what level to apply any de minimis concept with regard to pollution of controlled waters.

1   DETR circular 02/2000.

Pollution linkages

14.30   The local authority must consider and identify the pollution linkages which it considers may exist on the land which are sufficient to render it capable of classification as contaminated. In this, the local authority seeks to identify a source, pathway and receptor along which the contamination can travel. It is not necessary to have an offsite receptor; onsite contamination is still sufficient to trigger liability.

Appropriate persons

14.31   If the local authority is satisfied that such linkages exist and that the site does meet the definition under EPA 1990 it must identify and notify all potentially 'appropriate persons' giving full details of each and every pollution linkage and why it considers that each appropriate person may be liable for some or all of them. If a site is badly contaminated it may be further notified as a special site in which case it will pass to the EA who will become the appropriate regulator.

14.32   EPA 1990 offers the following definition of the 'appropriate person':

'A person who has caused or knowingly permitted any substance ("substance A") to be in, on or under any land shall also be taken for the purposes of this section to have caused or knowingly permitted there to be in, on or under that land any substance which is there as a result of the chemical reaction or biological process affecting substance A.'

1   EPA 1990, s 78F(9).

14.33   Appropriate persons fall into two potential liability categories. The greatest liability category known as 'Class A' identifies as appropriate persons those who have caused or knowingly permitted the contamination to have occurred (ie the polluter pays principle). The unusual aspect of the regime is that there is a secondary class of appropriate person, known as 'Class B' – this can be an innocent owner or occupier of the land who may not have even known of the contamination, still less done anything to contribute to it.

14.34   EPA 1990, Pt IIA envisages that having identified a site as potentially contaminated the local authority will then seek to establish the number and identity of appropriate persons (either Class A or Class B) and notify them of the identified pollution linkages. There should then follow a consultation period (the Guidance[1] suggests three months but is not definitive) during which time the parties are intended to agree upon an appropriate programme of remediation for the land and the local authority in consultation with them and following the Guidance will seek to apportion liability for those remediation works so identified.

1   DETR circular 02/2000.

14.35   The Guidance sets out a system of complex rules for apportioning liability between Class A and Class B appropriate persons.[1] Class A appropriate persons will rank in priority. If a Class A is identified a Class B will not be pursued. If more than one Class A appropriate person is found liable then responsibility for remediation costs etc shall be apportioned between the group of Class A persons according to their perceived culpability (to be determined by the regulator). If Class A polluters cannot be found or identified then liability will rest with Class B appropriate persons irrespective of fault. Here, the Guidance suggests that liability should be apportioned between Class B appropriate persons according to their period of ownership or occupation of the land in question. This poses the greatest potential liabilities for innocent occupiers or owners of sites with latent or previously unidentified pollution. They can then find themselves identified as appropriate persons and become involved in a lengthy consultation process which ends with a substantive costs bill for remediation.

1   EPA 1990, s 78F(2).

Enforcement

14.36   EPA 1990, Pt IIA envisages an entirely voluntary system of consultation with clean up standards imposed on a suitable for current use basis. However, Pt IIA also provides for mandatory controls in circumstances where appropriate persons do not co operate or volunteer to meet remediation costs. Part IIA provides in those circumstances that the regulator may use enforcement powers similar to those discussed elsewhere in this chapter relating to statutory nuisance. It provides that the regulator has a duty in circumstances where it has followed the regime set out under Pt IIA to serve on each appropriate person a remediation notice specifying what the person is to do by way of remediation and the periods within which he or she is required to do each of the specified things.[1]

1   EPA 1990, s 78E(1).

14.37   Further details are given in the detailed statutory guidance of the form and content of such a notice and of what may be reasonably required. The duty to serve a notice is one that may be enforced by judicial review proceedings. It is not a matter for the general discretion of the regulator. Remediation notices will be placed on a public register and therefore available for public consultation. If satisfied, an authority may serve more than one remediation notice upon more than one appropriate person as circumstances dictate and may also serve consecutive notices where phased remediation of the land is appropriate.

Offences

14.38   EPA 1990, s 78M(1) provides that a person served with a remediation notice who fails, without reasonable excuse, to comply with any of its requirements shall be guilty of a criminal offence. It is open to the regulator to commence a prosecution in the magistrates' court (the Guidance only envisages summary conviction – EPA 1990, s 78M(3)) and must be brought within six months of the time when the offence was deemed to be committed.[1] As a remediation notice must stipulate a date for compliance then it is obvious that the six-month period will run from the deadline in the notice.

1   Magistrates' Courts Act 1980, s 127.

14.39   In the event of a successful prosecution the potential maximum penalty would be level 5 on the standard scale, (ie a maximum of £5,000 for individuals and £20,000 where the notice relates to industrial, trade or business premises) with the potential for continuing daily fines of a further tenth of the maximum sum for each day the offence continues. The Secretary of State can order an increase in the upper limit of the penalty for business premises. It should also be noted that a company so prosecuted will have a criminal conviction which will remain on the record.[1]

1   NB the Rehabilitation of Offenders Act 1974 does not apply to companies.

14.40   The question of whether to prosecute (unlike whether to serve a notice) is a discretionary matter for the regulator who will usually have regard to their own local strategy (in the case of a local authority) or published prosecution policy (in the case of the EA or the Scottish Environmental Protection Agency (SEPA)). However, in most cases where a notice has been disregarded prosecution will follow. Once a matter is before the magistrates' court the usual evidential rules will apply.[1]

1   The proceedings will be governed by the Magistrates' Courts Act 1980.

Civil remedies

14.41 Alternatively, if the regulatory authority feels that criminal proceedings under EPA 1990, s 78M(1) would be an ineffectual remedy then they may commence proceedings in the civil courts (High Court in England and Wales and a court of competent jurisdiction in Scotland) for the purposes of securing compliance with the remediation notice by means of a mandatory injunction (a specific implement in Scotland). This would secure compliance with the remediation notice where as criminal prosecution would only effect a criminal penalty for non-compliance.

Appeals

14.42 EPA 1990, s 78L provides a 21-day period in which to appeal against a remediation notice. Appeals against notices served by local authorities will go to the magistrates' court in England and Wales or in Scotland to the Sheriff by way of summary application. Appeals against notices served by the EA or SEPA will go to the Secretary of State or Scottish ministers. While appeals to the magistrates' court follows the tradition of statutory nuisance (and other similar legislation) the Guidance provides only scant detail of the rules which should govern appeals although the grounds of appeal are set out in the Contaminated Land (England) Regulations 2000, reg 7.[1] These provide no less than 19 separate grounds of appeal. Again, concerns have been expressed about the complexity (and lack of particularity) of the appeals procedure and of the difficulties for the lower criminal courts in having to deal with such technical and specialist legislation.

1 SI 2000/227, reg 7.

14.43 Appeals to the Secretary of State are even less adequately specified. It appears that the Secretary of State may, in practice, pass such appeals to the Planning Inspectorate for determination. This complexity and lack of uniformity has hastened calls for an appropriate environmental court or tribunal (perhaps upon similar lines to the Planning Inspectorate) as an appropriate forum in which such appeals and prosecutions could be heard. As yet, there is no indication that such proposals are likely to be implemented in the short to medium term. Clearly, there is also scope for alternative dispute resolution particularly with regard to the question of the appeal procedure.

14.44 There is also the possibility to challenge a remediation notice by way of judicial review, proceeding on the basis that the regulator has acted outside the grounds of his or her authority (ie his or her actions were ultra vires) or that there has been some procedural defect or failure to take relevant considerations into account. An applicant may seek judicial review in the High Court in order to quash the notice. However, leave to seek judicial review is only given in the most extreme of circumstances and is a very limited remedy which is used sparingly by the courts and only for the clearest examples of error. Although EPA 1990, Pt IIA does not specifically exclude judicial review the fact that there is an appeal procedure under the regime may, of itself, preclude the grant of leave to appeal.

Conclusion

14.45   EPA 1990, Pt IIA is an extremely complex and technical piece of legislation which relies heavily upon the wording of statutory guidance for its implementation. As this is a relatively new piece of legislation precedent has not yet been established and there has been few challenges through the court system. However, as the regime 'beds in' it is inevitable that appeals, challenges and prosecutions will emerge which may assist in further defining the scope of the legislation. It is clear, however, that the concepts of criminalising liability for contamination of land or water have been firmly established and that in the case of the contaminated land principles of strict (ie no fault liability) can be applied retrospectively. At June 2003 58 sites in England and Wales had been identified as contaminated, with 14 special sites.

Air emissions – IPPC/PPC

Introduction

14.46   Air pollution legislation remains focused on reducing the adverse human effects of air pollutants, although during the 1980s acid raid and ecosystem damage were a principal concern. The levels of air pollutants measured today can still give rise to significant health impacts.

14.47   The regulatory framework for air pollution consists of the following:

*   Local authorities have control over the management of air quality through the identification of Air Quality Management Areas under the Local Authority Air Pollution Control system[1] (LAAPC), they also regulate the less polluting industrial processes under the Integrated Pollution Control system[2] (IPC) and the permitting system of the Integrated Pollution and Prevention Control (IPPC) system.[3] The EA regulates air emissions from the more polluting processes under the IPC and IPPC. The controls set over emissions from industrial processes include the use of the 'best available techniques' for the process.
*   The common law of nuisance enables a claim for damages where emissions unreasonably interfere with the enjoyment of private rights or property. Common law nuisance is outside the scope of this chapter. Further discussion of statutory nuisance can be seen elsewhere in this chapter but the ability to take action under the statutory nuisance provisions is restricted where other statutory controls apply.

1   Under EPA 1990, Pt IV.
2   Under EPA 1990, Pt I.
3   IPPC is implemented into UK law by the Pollution Prevention and Control Act 1999 (PPC) in accordance with the Integrated Pollution Prevention and Control Directive, Council Directive 96/61/EC.

IPC and IPPC

14.48   Industrial emissions from an installation or mobile plant carrying on prescribed activities are regulated by the EA in England and Wales and local authorities under IPC. This is progressively being replaced the Pollution Prevention and Control Act 1999, which implements IPPC and is largely based on the IPC.

14.49 Whilst the provisions of EPA 1990, Pt I dealing with IPC will gradually become less important as the IPPC system is brought in there are many practical procedural similarities between the two systems. The relevance of IPC will remain but diminish during the transitional period hence the focus of this chapter will be on the IPPC because no new IPC permits will be issued.

14.50 The IPPC Directive[1] lays down a framework requiring member states to issue operating permits for certain installations carrying on industrial activities. This is being introduced throughout the EU and over 17,000 companies in the UK alone will be affected. IPPC is in essence about applying an integrated approach to managing environmental impacts related to certain industrial activities. It is designed to prevent, reduce and minimise pollution at source.

1 Council Directive 96/61/EC.

14.51 The UK introduced IPPC through the Pollution Prevention and Control (England and Wales) Regulations 2000[1] (PPC(EW)R). Similar regulations have been created to implement IPPC in Scotland, Northern Ireland and offshore oil and gas industries.

1 SI 2000/1973.

14.52 IPPC replaces the existing systems IPC, LAAPC and waste management licensing. However, the system of IPPC goes further than just measuring and regulating emissions to air (and also to land and water) but also other environmental issues such as noise and vibration, energy efficiently, waste minimisation, environmental accidents and site protection. The integrated impact of the whole authorised process is assessed.

Controlled activities

14.53 PPC(EW)R, Sch 1[1] lists the controlled activities and is divided into six Chapters of industrial activity including the energy industry; the chemicals industry; the production and processing of metals; the minerals industry; waste management and a generic category referred to as 'other activities'. Each Chapter is further divided into more specific definitions of particular groups or activities and then these are further divided into categories A and B for the purposes of allocation to a regulatory agency. In summary Part A installations are larger and feature more significant polluting processes to be controlled by the EA. Part B installations are smaller and feature less significant polluting capacity and are controlled by the relevant local authority.

1 SI 2000/1973, Sch 1.

14.54 Pollution prevention and control (PPC) permits have been required for all new installations and existing installations undergoing a substantial change since 31 October 1999. Existing IPC permits will continue to be in force until IPPC permits are phased in on a sectorial basis up to October 2007.[1]

1 The timeframes for obtaining PPC permits are shown in PPC(EW)R, SI 2000/1973, Sch 3.

14.55 In order to achieve a high level of protection for the environment the wider implications of operating an installation or plant must be taken into account when the regulators set the permit conditions. These conditions are based upon the use of the best available techniques (BAT),[1] which balances the cost to the operator against the benefits to the environment. The concept of BAT is broadly similar to the best available techniques not entailing excessive costs (BATNEEC)[2] used under IPC; however, there are some practical differences. BATNEEC included not only technical means and the technology pollution abatement but also the number, qualifications, training and supervision of persons employed in the process in addition to the design, construction, layout and maintenance of the buildings. BAT includes both the technology used and the way in which the installation is designed, built, maintained and decommissioned.

1 BAT is defined in the Pollution Prevention and Control (England and Wales) Regulations 2000, SI 2000/1973, reg 3 and explored in more detail reg 3(b).
2 BATNEEC is defined in EPA 1990, s 7(2).

Best available techniques

14.56 Emission limits and operating conditions are based on BAT taking into account the technical characteristics of the installation, its geographic location and local environmental conditions. Measures beyond BAT may also be required to achieve environmental quality standards. It is important that a company explores BAT comprehensively to ensure that their process is operated in accordance with BAT and in turn the PPC regime.

14.57 'Best' means, in relation to techniques, the most effective in achieving a high general level of protection of the environment as a whole.

14.58 'Available techniques' means those techniques which have been developed to a scale which allows implementation in the relevant industrial sector under economically and technically viable conditions, taking into consideration the costs and advantages, whether or not the techniques are used or produced inside the UK, as long as they are reasonably accessible to the operator.

14.59 'Techniques' includes both the technology used and the way in which the installation is designed, built, maintained, operated and decommissioned.

14.60 The determination of BAT is aided by referring to BAT reference documents, which describe levels of environmental performance which can be achieved through the use of BAT.

Authorisations

IPC

14.61 EPA 1990, s 6 provides a specific prohibition on any person carrying on a prescribed process, after the prescribed date, except by virtue of an authorisation granted by the local authority or the EA and in accordance with the conditions of that authorisation.

14.62 The enforcing authority has the responsibility to either grant the authorisation on the application made or refuse it. The enforcing authority will not grant an application if it considers that the applicant will be unable to comply with the conditions, which would be attached to the authorisation.

PPC

14.63 With effect from the dates set out in PPC(EW)R, Sch 3,[1] no person shall operate an installation or mobile plant except under a permit granted by the appropriate regulator and in accordance with the conditions imposed.

1 SI 2000/1973, Sch 3.

Enforcement

14.64 There is a division of responsibility between the local authorities which control the less polluting processes and the EA which has responsibility for the processes which give rise to more significant pollution. The administrative split is also reflected in the scope of control.

IPC

14.65 Under EPA 1990, ss 10 and 11 an enforcing authority may vary an authorisation at any time. Under EPA 1990, s 12 the enforcing authority is able to revoke an authorisation. By virtue of EPA 1990, s 13 an enforcing authority can serve an enforcement notice for the contravention of any condition of an authorisation or the authority's anticipation that contravention is likely. In addition under EPA 1990, s 14 the enforcing authority may serve a prohibition notice where it is believed an authorised process involves an imminent risk of serious pollution of the environment.

PPC

14.66 The regulating authority has a variety of powers to combat the breaches of permits, similar to the IPC enforcement. These powers include the ability to serve enforcement notices (PPC(EW)R, reg 24[1]), revoke a permit (PPC(EW)R, reg 21[2]) and to vary the conditions of a permit (PPC(EW)R, reg 17[3]).

1 SI 2000/1973, reg 24.
2 SI 2000/1973, reg 21.
3 SI 2000/1973, reg 17.

Offences

14.67 The controls employed by the regulating authority are continuing in the sense that to operate a prescribed process without the authorisation, or in breach of the conditions of any authorisation is a criminal offence under both IPC and PPC. An offence may be committed, for example, by non-compliance with an authorisation.

IPC

14.68 Under EPA 1990, s 23 a person is guilty of an offence if a person:

- fails to comply with the requirements of EPA 1990, s 6 (authorisation);
- fails to give notice to transfer the authorisation under EPA 1990, s 9;
- fails to comply with an enforcement notice;
- fails without reasonable excuse to comply with a notice under EPA 1990, s 19 requiring information;
- makes a false or misleading statement;
- intentionally make a false entry in any record required to be kept under a condition of an authorisation; or
- forges or uses an authorisation with the intent to deceive.

14.69   An offence will be committed under the Environment Act 1995, s 110 if a person does the following:

- intentionally obstructs an inspector in the exercise or performance of his or her duties;
- without reasonable excuse fails to comply with any requirement under the Environment Act 1995, s 108 (powers of entry), fails or refuses to provide facilities or assistance or information or to permit any inspection or prevents any other person from answering questions which might be raised by the inspector in the course of the exercise of his or her powers under the Environment Act 1995, s 108; or
- falsely pretends to be an inspector.

PPC

14.70   The PPC(EW)R provide an extensive list of offences to the IPPC system under PPC(EW)R, reg 32.[1] The offences include:

- contravention of PPC(EW)R, reg 9,[2] operation of an installation prescribed for control without a permit;
- contravention of the terms and conditions of a permit;
- failure to comply with PPC(EW)R, reg 16[3] the proposed change in operation of an installation;
- failure to comply with the requirements of an enforcement notice, a suspension notice or a closure notice;
- failure, without reasonable excuse, to comply with the requirement of providing information imposed by a notice under PPC(EW)R, reg 28;[4]
- making a false or misleading statement;
- intentionally making a false entry in any record required to be kept under the condition of a permit;
- with intent to deceive, to forge or use a document issued or authorised to be issued under a condition of a permit; or
- failure to comply with an order of the court under PPC(EW)R, reg 35[5] for the offence to be remedied.

1   SI 2000/1973, reg 32.
2   SI 2000/1973, reg 9.
3   SI 2000/1973, reg 16.
4   SI 2000/1973, reg 28.
3   SI 2000/1973, reg 35.

Penalties

14.71 All offences for both IPC and PPC are triable either way (ie in the magistrates' court or the Crown Court) with the more serious offences having a maximum fine of £20,000 in the magistrates' court. In the Crown Court all offences are subject to a maximum term of imprisonment of two years and/or an unlimited fine. In any trial the onus of proof for PPC falls upon the operator to show that there was no better available technique which could be employed for that particular installation.

14.72 In addition to sentencing the defendant for breaching the permit or failing to comply with an enforcement or suspension notice, PPC(EW)R, reg 35[1] and EPA 1990, s 26 provide that the court can order that the effects of the offence are to be remedied. Therefore, relevant clean up costs and compensation will be borne by the defendant.

1 SI 2000/1973, reg 35.

14.73 The regulating authority may also take direct action and arrange for reasonable steps to be taken towards remedying any harm caused as a consequence and recover the costs of taking such steps from the person who committed the breach.

14.74 PPC(EW)R, reg 32[1] and EPA 1990, s 157 includes the provision that where an offence committed by a body corporate is proved to have been committed with the consent or connivance of or attributable to any neglect on the part of any director, manager, secretary or similar officer, he or she and the body corporate shall be guilty of an offence and liable to be proceeded against and punished accordingly. A similar provision applies where the affairs of a body corporate are managed by its members. Proceedings for an offence are also possible where the commission of an offence by one person is owing to the act or default of some other person irrespective of whether or not proceedings are taken against the first mentioned person.

1 SI 2000/1973, reg 32.

Statutory nuisance

Introduction

14.75 The concept of statutory nuisance provides the basis of public health protection against a range of environmental threats and provides indirect protection for the environment. This includes emissions to air dust, vibration, odour or noise pollution. There are many ways in which the tort of statutory nuisance can lead to abatement of environmental concerns. The primary purpose of the statutory nuisance provisions is to provide a prompt local remedy to prevent the nuisance recurring

14.76 Statutory nuisance provides a basis for requiring the abatement, non-recurrence or prohibition of certain activities or states of affairs, deemed to be a nuisance or prejudicial to health. The local authority through their environmental health officer is the regulatory authority.

14.77 EPA 1990, s 79 contains a list of statutory nuisances, which are consolidated by EPA 1990, Pt III in 1990. EPA 1990 provides that certain activities of states or affairs which will amount to a statutory nuisance if 'prejudicial to health or a nuisance'. They are as follows:

- State of premises.
- Smoke emitted from premises.
- Fumes or gases emitted from premises.
- Dust, steam, smell or other effluvia from industrial, trade or business premises.
- Accumulation or deposits.
- Animals kept in such a place or manner.
- Noise emitted from premises.
- Other matters declared by any enactment.

The basis of statutory nuisance.

14.78   Nuisance is not defined in EPA 1990 and is a common law concept. An actionable nuisance at common law arises where the use or enjoyment of land, or some right over or in connection with land, is interfered with by the action of another and as a result an owner or occupier of the land may sue for an injunction or damages.

14.79   The notion prejudicial to health is defined in EPA 1990, s 79(7) as matters 'injurious, or likely to cause injury to health'. In *Coventry City Council v Cartwright*,[1] the Council owned a vacant site within a residential area on which people dumped inert rubbish. It was held in the Divisional Court that such accumulations or deposits were prejudicial to health if they were likely to cause a threat of disease or attract vermin but not if, as in this case, they were inert matter that could cause physical injury only to people who walked on it.

1   [1975] 1 WLR 845.

14.80   This raises the problem of particularly vulnerable groups suffering adverse effects. It was seen in a noise nuisance case *Heath v Brighton Corpn*[1] where the claimant failed in his action in respect of noise from a generator as it was established that he had hypersensitive hearing. It was held that the test for determining whether a statutory nuisance existed was an objective one and should be judged according to the standards of an average man. The courts should not have regard to abnormal sensitiveness of particular occupiers. This was demonstrated again in *Cunningham v Birmingham City Council*[2] where claims that a property was hazardous to an autistic child failed, since the property was not a statutory nuisance for an ordinary child.

1   (1908) 98 LT 718.
2   [1998] Env LR 1.

Regulation of statutory nuisance

14.81   Local authorities have a duty to inspect their areas from time to time in order to control statutory nuisances. More cases are prompted by public complaint however. An environmental health officer may visit the premises to make an objective decision as to whether or not the state of the premises or anything on those premises amounts to a nuisance. When considering the common law definition of nuisance, it is up to the environmental health officer to balance the various factors used when deciding on whether or not a common law nuisance exists. The most important of these factors are:

1   the nature and location of the nuisance;
2   the time and duration of the nuisance; and

3   the utility of the activity concerned.

14.82   EPA 1990, s 80(1) provides that for a local authority to act, the statutory nuisance must exist or be likely to occur or recur. The local authority must be satisfied only on the balance of probabilities that the statutory nuisance exists and in the case of anticipated nuisances, there must be evidence that the forthcoming activity is likely to give rise to a statutory nuisance.

Person responsible

14.83   The enforcement of a statutory nuisance is normally against the person responsible which is defined in EPA 1990, s 79(7) as being 'the person to whose act, default or sufferance of the nuisance is attributable'. This is a very wide definition and can include a local authority or a landlord who has allowed a tenant to carry on offensive activities, and can also include those who failed to abate nuisances which arise naturally, for example, occupiers of land where tree roots cause damage. In addition it can include a tenant who was denied access to a landlord who wished to carry out works to abate a nuisance. The courts will look to see whether there has been some failure to meet acceptable standard, for example, sound insulation standards at the time of construction.

14.84   If there are any difficulties in locating the person responsible for the statutory nuisance, EPA 1990, s 80(2) states that the definition of the person responsible can be extended to include the owner or occupier of the premises in question.

Enforcement scheme

The abatement notice regime

14.85   Where the local authority is satisfied that a statutory nuisance exists or is likely to occur or recur, it shall serve an abatement notice.

14.86   The recipient of a notice may appeal to the magistrates' court within 21 days. Under certain circumstances lodging an appeal may provide a stay in the application of the notice but otherwise failing to comply with the abatement notice is a criminal offence. Once an abatement notice has been served, a party normally has 21 days in which to appeal to the magistrates' court. This may be preferable to challenging the notice upon prosecution, because of the grounds available under the Statutory Nuisance (Appeals) Regulations 1995.[1] These are:

* the abatement notice is not justified under EPA 1990, s 80;
* substantive error in the notice or procedure error in its service;
* the requirements of the notice are unreasonable or that the period of compliance is unreasonable and that the local authority refuses to accept alternative arrangements; and
* best practicable means was used to counteract the effects of a nuisance from business/trade premises.

1   SI 1995/2644.

14.87   In general, an appeal will have the advantage of suspending the operation of the notice. However, when the nuisance is prejudicial to human health, or where the timescales demands immediate action, the local authority can insist that the notice is not superseded. In making this decision, the local authority should weigh costs of compliance against burdens falling on the public.

14.88   An individual may also bring a private action in the magistrates' court to issue an abatement notice. Such a notice so issued would have the same consequences as a notice issued by the environmental health officer.

Contents of notices

14.89   EPA 1990, s 80(3) provides the rights of appeal.[1] In general, the notice must clearly and precisely identify the nuisance complained of, and provide information as to what is required to avoid recurrence or indeed occurrence.

1   EPA 1990, s 60; Statutory Nuisance (Appeals) Regulations 1990, SI 1990/2276, 1 January 1991.

14.90   To what extent the notice can give directions in relation to day to day business operations is arguable. A prohibition may be sufficient as in *McGillibay v Stephenson*[1] in which there was a requirement to desist from using premises for keeping pigs. The Divisional Court held that this was a good notice as a statement of steps which might be taken would in these circumstances be surplus to requirements.

1   [1950] 1 All ER 924.

14.91   In some situations the person responsible may have the freedom to abate the nuisance in a manner of their choice. However, they may need to know precisely what will satisfy the local authority. A great deal would depend on the content including the type of nuisance, the technical competence of the person responsible and the possible means of abatement. It must be borne in mind that in general it may not be reasonable to demand a complete cessation of an activity[1] and that the contravention of the notice will constitute a criminal offence under EPA 1990, s 80(4), and therefore the courts may demand that the local authority specifies the plan of work needed to alleviate the statutory nuisance.

1   *R v Falmer and Truro Port Authority, ex p SW Water* [2000] 3 All ER 306.

Service of the notice

14.92   Notices should be served on the person responsible for the nuisance under EPA 1990, s 79(7) as defined at **para 14.83** above.

Consequences of non-compliance

14.93   A company can be guilty of breaching a notice and hence can commit a criminal offence as can an officer of the company under EPA 1990, s 157. EPA 1990, s 157(2) provides that where the affairs of the corporation are managed by its members then a member fulfilling a managerial function shall be liable where it can be proved that the officer was a decision-maker in the company and he was at least partly responsible for the breach

14.94 A company in the hands of administrators may be prosecuted but the requirements of the Insolvency Act 1986, s 11 will apply, so the consent of the company's administrator must be given or leave obtained from the court.[1]

1 *Re Rhondda Waste Disposal Co Ltd* [2001] Ch 57. The leave of the High Court is required for the prosecution to be commenced or continued in the magistrates' court.

14.95 Failure to comply with a notice without reasonable excuse is an offence under EPA 1990, s 80(4). Nuisance arising on industrial or business premises carries a maximum penalty of £20,000 in accordance with EPA 1990, s 80(6).

14.96 Fines for non-business offenders is £5,000 maximum penalty plus £500 for each day the offence continues after conviction. In addition to these sanctions, the magistrates have a discretion to award compensation, but only up to a maximum of £5,000.

Defences

14.97 The usual defences on a matter of fact and/or law may apply, but there are certain specific defences written into legislation. The first of these is 'best practicable means' by reference to efforts used to prevent or counteract the effects of the statutory nuisance under EPA 1990, s 80(7) and (8). The burden of proof rests on the defendant.

14.98 Certain elements of best practicable means are offered in EPA 1990, s 79(9) but this stops short of a full definition. For example, 'practicable' is defined as meaning reasonably practicable, having regard, amongst other things, to local conditions and circumstances, the current state of technical knowledge and the financial implications. The 'means' to be employed include design, installation, maintenance, manner and periods of operation of plant and machinery, as well as the design, construction, and maintenance of buildings and structures. It is not necessary to show that the means employed brought the nuisance to an end, but it is probably enough if they were adequate to prevent or to counteract the effects of the nuisance.

14.99 As this is a statutory defence the burden of proving the best practicable means defence lies on the defendant. The defence is available only where the nuisance arises on industrial, trade or business premises and is due to the state of the premises being prejudicial to health or a nuisance. This may be due to dust, steam, smell or other effluvia or due to noise, accumulations, deposits or animals being kept in such a place or manner as to be prejudicial to health or a nuisance. Smoke being emitted from premises (unless emitted from a chimney) and fumes or gases emitted from premises and nuisances under other statutes, do not carry a best practicable means defence.

14.100 The other defence available is 'reasonable excuse' under EPA 1990, s 80(4) which provides that a person who is served with an abatement notice, 'without reasonable excuse' fails to comply with any requirement will be guilty of an offence. The defendant who wishes to rely on such a defence must discharge the evidential burden by specifying the excuse and the prosecutor must prove that the excuse is not a reasonable one beyond all reasonable doubt.

Asbestos

14.101   Asbestos is the biggest cause of work related death in the UK. Although the use of asbestos is now banned, the number of deaths is expected to rise due to the 1 million non-domestic premises in which asbestos remains present. The widespread use of the material before the link was made between exposure to asbestos and various diseases has led to the creation of new legal duties, enacted in the Control of Asbestos at Work Regulations 2002[1] (CAWR).

1   SI 2002/2675.

14.102   Research in the form of the Peto Report[1] suggests that exposure to one single fibre of asbestos can be enough to cause various fatal illnesses such as asbestosis and mesothelioma. Symptoms can often occur more than 15 to 40 years after exposure took place. The House of Lords in 2002[2] decided that for reasons of public policy, families of the victims of those illnesses should not be denied a legal remedy at civil law purely because it could not be established the exact exposure event which caused the affected person to contract the disease.

1   HSE *Continuing Increase in Mesothelioma Mortality in Britain* (the Peto Report) (1995).
2   *Fairchild v Glenhaven Funeral Services Ltd* (2002) 3 ALL ER 305.

14.103   Most enforcement action against companies for asbestos to date has followed the exposure of routine repair or maintenance workers carrying out drilling or removal work and in the process, disturbing asbestos without realising the contents of the material. In the Court of Appeal, the leading case of *R v Brintons Ltd*[1] stated that the level of financial penalty imposed on a company for asbestos exposure offences should be large enough to send out a message to the shareholders to 'sit up and take notice' of the presence of asbestos in premises.

1   LTL 22/6/99, CA.

14.104   There is no specific duty on the company to remove asbestos but, from May 2004, employers are under a new 'duty to manage' the risks posed by asbestos. The CAWR[1] already contain detailed requirements regulating work known to involve asbestos. The duty to manage seeks to make sure that workers are not unintentionally exposed to asbestos and to ensure they are aware of the possibility of disturbing the material and releasing potentially 'fatal fibres'.

1   SI 2002/2675.

14.105   The duty to manage applies to all persons with contractual obligations for the maintenance or repair of non-domestic premises or any means of access or egress to and from those premises. Where no such obligation exists in a contract, that duty is imposed on all persons with any control over the premises or access from or egress to and from it. Potentially this includes owners of buildings, some tenants and could include managing agents.

14.106   The costs of compliance with the duty are determined by the extent of each duty holder's obligations. In practice, owners and landlords of buildings will need to negotiate with all the other parties involved and may agree to undertake works and recharge the costs to the tenants in accordance with the service charge provisions in the lease.

14.107   Architects, surveyors, contractors and construction and maintenance companies may also be subject to a duty to co-operate with the primary duty holder if they have information about the presence or otherwise of asbestos in a building. If such persons fail to pass on relevant information and workers are exposed, those third parties can be expected to be prosecuted as well as the primary duty holder.

14.108   The duty to manage makes the failure to comply with CAWR[1] requirements a criminal offence. The duty holders must conduct a suitable and sufficient assessment of whether asbestos is (or might be) present in premises and if so, must ascertain where the material is located and its condition. The assessment needs to be reviewed and a written management plan devised to set out how the risk is to be controlled. If asbestos is in a good condition and encapsulated it can often be left in situ.

1   SI 2002/2675.

14.109   The condition of the asbestos must be monitored and, crucially, the duty to manage includes a requirement that anyone liable to disturb it is told of its location and the content of the material.

14.110   It will invariably be a practical requirement to ensure that a full survey of premises is undertaken. By November 2004 such surveys will need to be conducted by accredited surveyors. There are three levels of survey which can be undertaken and the Health and Safety Executive (HSE) will look to investigate those businesses who have not obtained information on the risks from their own building in the event that any individuals are exposed. Businesses can create some measure of protection by assuming that material does contain asbestos until they are shown strong evidence to the contrary. However, this would subject them to the detailed requirement of such work set out elsewhere in the CAWR.[1]

1   SI 2002/2675.

14.111   Experts in the property industry believe that the CAWR[1] may lead to the creation of a 'dual' market between those premises with asbestos issues and those without.

1   SI 2002/2675.

14.112   Insurance premiums have increased several-fold since links between exposure to asbestos were made to various diseases. Companies with interests in mobile phone masts, electricity pylons and genetically modified foods may want to consider future potential liability as scientific knowledge evolves.

Legionnaires' disease

14.113   As with asbestos, the legal duties on businesses to control legionnaires' disease are extensive, and preventative measures often overlooked due to ignorance of the risks or lack of awareness of the potential sources of the legionella bacteria.

14.114   The number of reported cases has increased since the year 2000, to 222 in 2002, of which 202 were fatal. It is often difficult for the HSE or local authority to identify the source of the outbreak, and for those affected to realise that they have contracted the illness. Statistics on a possible 'safe limit' of inhalation of the bacteria are very hard to come by and the characteristics of the person exposed will determine the extent of their illness.

14.115   Businesses are under a duty to notify their local authority of any high-risk devices such as cooling towers and evaporative condensers, and to control the risk from legionella bacteria from their premises. Outbreaks have occurred from boilers, air conditioning units and even staff showers. The most at-risk areas are leisure centres, gyms, swimming pools, hospitals, universities, schools and industrial premises, where old pipework or water storage facilities create temperatures and conditions where the bacteria thrive. Where refurbishment is undertaken particular care is needed where water droplets remain stagnant while a system is not in use. The leading case of *R v Board of Trustees of the Science Museum*[1] established that the failure to maintain an air conditioning unit so as to create a risk of inhaling the bacterium is enough to establish liability, even where no one actually does inhale or sustain injury from the bacteria. Where such risks are identified they must be eliminated or, where that is not possible, minimised as far as possible.

1   [1993] 3 All ER 853.

14.116   Whenever an employer becomes aware of a case of legionella related illness, they are under a duty to notify pursuant to the Reporting of Injuries, Diseases and Dangerous Occurrences Regulations 1995 (RIDDOR).

1   SI 1995/3163.

14.117   Employers are subject to the requirements of the Management of Health and Safety at Work Regulations 1999, reg 3[1] to undertake a suitable and sufficient risk assessment of the specific risks of legionella, and to monitor the condition of water and to conduct regular testing.

1   SI 1999/3242, reg 3.

14.118   Hotels in Europe where legionella is found need to be aware of a Decision of the European Parliament and Council in June 2003. Endorsement was given to a plan to publish European-wide details of all premises where incidents occur on a 'travel website' to inform customers of any potential health risks in their journey. Several hotels have already been 'named and shamed'.

14.119   Companies providing services in relation to water treatment, cleaning, disinfection and risk assessment have to comply with the Code of Conduct for Water Treatment Service Providers established jointly by the British Association of Chemical Specialists and the Water Management Society in 1999, when dealing with these issues.

14.120   Aside from the Notification of Cooling Towers and Evaporative Condensers Regulations 1992[1] employers are also under general duties to protect health and safety. Guidance on how to comply is contained in an Approved Code of Practice issued by the Health and Safety Commission.[2]

1   SI 1992/2225.
2   L8 (1995).

14.121   Manufacturers and suppliers of products for use in air conditioners and water systems must ensure that their equipment is effective and without risks to health. A further duty exists to notify the duty holder of any deficiencies identified in the employer's plant or safety systems

14.122   As with asbestos, legionella is still a risk, which often remains unidentified and unknown. Enforcement will follow for exposure where the cause can be established, and prohibition notices can be expected whenever statutory monitoring is not maintained, or control systems do not appear to be adequate.

Offences

14.123   Offences for breach of any health and safety requirements can be dealt with in the magistrates' court. Those duties imposed under regulations carry a maximum penalty of £5,000 each. If the conduct of the company constitutes a breach of the duty owed to employees, or affects members of the public under the Health and Safety at Work Act etc 1974, s 2 or 3 the maximum fine is £20,000.

14.124   Many cases are transferred to the Crown Court, where the penalties are unlimited, irrespective of whether the obligation arises by statute or regulations.

14.125   Individual directors or senior managers can be held personally liable where offences under the Health and Safety at Work Act etc 1974 are committed by the company and they consented to, connive with or were neglectful as to the commission of offences. Those convicted can face the same penalties as their companies.

Genetically modified organisms

14.126   Genetically modified organisms (GMOs) are micro-organisms, plants and animals, which have had their genetic substance altered by artificial means, a technique known as genetic modification.

Regulation of GMOs

14.127   GMOs are regulated at international, EU and UK level. In the EU the regulation of GMOs is founded upon the following principles:

1   Environmental legislation should provide preventative measures, which help to preserve the environment. The purpose of GMO regulation, therefore, is to prevent damage to the environment, which may arise from the release of GMOs.
2   Genetic modification should proceed providing there are no adverse risks to the health of the community and no harm to the environment. This precautionary 'step-by-step' principle[1] endorses a presumption against the release of GMOs into the environment where the exact effect of their release is not known.

1   As referred to in the Deliberate Release Directive, Council Directive 2001/18/EC, recital 8.

14.128   Based upon these principles, a legal framework has emerged in the EU, which provides that activities involving GMOs can only take place with the explicit consent of the regulatory authorities. The UK government has implemented the following legislation to implement this strategy.

EPA 1990, Pt VI

14.129   EPA 1990 provides that persons who import, acquire, release or market GMOs are under a duty to carry out risk assessments and notify the relevant authorities of their intention to undertake such activities.[1] This obligation is more onerous in the context of the release and marketing of GMOs, such that explicit consent must be obtained before these activities are embarked upon.[2]

1   EPA 1990, s 108(1).
2   EPA 1990, s 111(1), as amended by the Genetically Modified Organisms (Deliberate Release) Regulations 2002, SI 2002/2443.

14.130   It is an offence to do anything in contravention of the provisions of EPA 1990.[1] Unless an offender can prove that he or she took reasonable precautions and exercised due care to avoid committing the offence,[2] they will be liable to a fine or imprisonment, or both.[3] The maximum penalties are £20,000 and six months' imprisonment in the magistrates' courts and an unlimited fine and two years' imprisonment in the Crown Court.

1   EPA 1990, s 118(1).
2   EPA 1990, s 118(2).
3   EPA 1990, s 118(3).

14.131   The court also has the power to order that the offender remedies the cause of the offence within specified period of time, as an alternative or in addition to the imposition of a penalty.[1]

1   EPA 1990, s 120(1).

14.132   Where an offence causes harm to the environment, EPA 1990 provides the Secretary of State for the Environment with authority to arrange for that harm to be remedied where possible, the cost of which is recoverable from the offender.[1]

1   EPA 1990, s 121(1).

Genetically Modified Organisms (Deliberate Release) Regulations 2002[1]

14.133   The Genetically Modified Organisms (Deliberate Release) Regulations 2002 (GMO(DR)R) control the marketing and deliberate release of GMOs into the environment by imposing a obligation to obtain prior consent from the regulatory authorities to undertake such activities. If the consent is granted it will contain a number of conditions, which must be complied with. For example:

1   environmental risk assessments must be undertaken, which examine indirect and long-term effects of the release and/or marketing;
2   post-market monitoring must be administered to highlight any unanticipated effects of any GMO that is released;
3   public consultation must be undertaken before the regulatory authorities can make decisions on applications for consent;
4   all GMOs, which are released commercially, must be labelled and traceable throughout the production and supply process; and
5   consents must be reassessed after a specified time (maximum ten years).

1   SI 2002/2443. The Regulations implement Council Directive 2001/18/EC.

14.134   The obligation to procure consent for GMO activities arises from EPA 1990.[1] Consequently, failure to comply with the GMO(DR)R[2] constitutes an offence under EPA 1990 to which the penalties noted above will apply.[3] To date, there have been few prosecutions.

1   EPA 1990, s 111(1).
2   SI 2002/2443.
3   Under EPA 1990, s 118(1).

The Genetically Modified Organisms (Contained Use) Regulations 2000[1]

14.135   The Genetically Modified Organisms (Contained Use) Regulations 2000[2] (GMO(CU)R) control GMO activities, which are carried out in containment (such as in laboratories) for the purpose of minimising the risk to humans and the environment of exposure to GMOs. These regulations provide that any activity involving GMOs is prohibited unless preliminary measures are taken, such as:

1   a risk assessment (having due regard to human health and the environment);
2   the establishment of a Genetic Modification Safety Committee to advise of risk; and
3   notification to the appropriate authorities of the nature of the activities and the location where they will be carried out.

1   SI 2000/2831, as amended by the Genetically Modified Organisms (Contained Use) (Amendment) Regulations 2002, SI 2002/63.
2   SI 2000/2831 implements Council Directive 90/219/ECC.

14.136   Failure to comply with the provisions of the GMO(CU)R[1] may lead to prosecution by the HSE under the Health and Safety at Work etc Act 1974.

1   SI 2000/2831. A breach of the GMO(CU)R is an offence under the Health and Safety at Work etc Act 1974, s 33(1)(c).

14.137   Where an offence has been committed, the HSE may take enforcement action against the offender, which could result in a financial penalty from the courts. In a Scottish case, *McFadyen v University of Edinburgh*,[1] a routine inspection of the defendant's premises revealed that the defendant had contravened the GMO(CU)R[2] by failing to carry out risk assessments for all of the GMO activities it was undertaking.[3] The defendant pleaded guilty to the charges and was fined a total of £3,500.

1   (1999) GWD 7-344.
2   SI 2000/2831.
3   SI 2000/2831, reg 7.

Liability – the current regime

14.138   The legislation regulating GMOs seeks to control the activities of those involved in the contained use, release and marketing of GMOs, and focuses primarily upon penalising offenders for breaches of the law. It does not, however, provide an effective mechanism for obtaining compensation for harm caused to humans and/or the environment by GMOs, nor does it make provision for remediation of the environment. Civil remedies would need to be pursued using the torts of negligence and nuisance.

14.139 At international level, the Lugano Convention provides an opportunity to recover compensation for environmental damage, which results from 'dangerous activities' (deemed to include GMOs). The fundamental hindrance is that the UK has declined to sign up to the Convention and thus its provisions do not have any effect in the UK.

The future

14.140 In 2000 the European Commission published its proposal for the introduction of a GMO liability regime,[1] to establish a public law regime for the prevention and restoration of damage to the environment caused by GMOs. However, the adoption of any such measures is likely to take several years and if implemented in its proposed form is unlikely to allow individuals and public interest groups to claim against those who cause environmental damage.

1   European Commission Draft Directive of the European Parliament and of the Council on environmental liability with regard to the prevention and restoration of environmental damage COM (2002) 17: 2002/0021: C151E/06.

CHAPTER 15

Corporate manslaughter: an international perspective

Victoria Howes, Lecturer in Law, European Law Research Centre, University of Salford

Frank B Wright,[1] *Professor of Law and Director, European Law Research Centre, University of Salford*

1   The authors gratefully acknowledge the assistance of Andrew Groszmann and Kim Tinline, of the European Law Research Centre, University of Salford for their work on initial drafts and the compilation of materials for this chapter.

Introduction

15.1   The issue of corporate criminal liability has been a concern not only in the UK, but also in other jurisdictions worldwide. Death resulting from accidents at work, and which have been caused by the failure of corporations to ensure safe working conditions and practices, is the subject of increased scrutiny by legislators. The world's worst industrial accidents have led to the imposition of more stringent controls over workplace activities. These include the Seveso disaster, when, in 1976, an explosion occurred in a TCP reactor of the ICMESA chemical plant on the outskirts of Meda, a small town about 20 km north of Milan, Italy. A toxic cloud containing TCDD[1] then widely believed to be one of the most toxic man-made chemicals was accidentally released into the atmosphere. Toxic materials were released over an area of 2.8 square km. Four per cent of the domestic animals living in the contaminated zones died spontaneously and the remaining 77,716 animals were slaughtered as a protective measure to protect the food chain. Some 736 people were exposed to relatively high doses of TCDD.[2] A much worse accident took place at the Union Carbide chemical plant at Bhopal, India in December 1984. In the early hours of 3 December 1984, gas leaked from a tank of methyl isocyanate (MIC) at a plant in Bhopal, India, owned and operated by Union Carbide India Limited (UCIL). The state government of Madhya Pradesh reported that approximately 3,800 persons died, 40 persons experienced permanent total disability and 2,680 persons experienced permanent partial disability. The US-based corporation was able to transfer proceedings from the US courts to India, where a final settlement was reached with the Indian government for $470 million.[3] The world's most serious nuclear power accident took place in Chernobyl, Ukraine, on 26 April 1986. Thirty people were killed immediately, and as a result of the high radiation levels in the surrounding 20-mile radius, 135,00 people had to be evacuated. There was a prolonged release to the atmosphere of large quantities of radioactive substances. Activity transported by the multiple plumes from Chernobyl was measured not only in Northern and in Southern Europe, but also in Canada, Japan and the US. Only the Southern hemisphere remained free of contamination.[4] Fortunately, the list of major accidents in the twentieth century and the first part of this century remains short, at least on this scale, although there is little room for complacency. Globally, each year 2,000,000 women and men die as a result of occupational accidents and work related diseases.

1   2,3,7,8-tetrachlorodibenzo-*p*-dioxin.
2   L Conti *Visto da Seveso* (1977); F Pocchiari, V Silano and G Zapponi 'The Seveso accident and its aftermath' in P Kleindorfer and H Kunreuther (eds) *Insuring and Managing Hazardous Risks: From Seveso to Bhopal and Beyond* (1987) pp 60-78.
3   P Shrivastava, *Bhopal: Anatomy of a Crisis*, (1992) Chapman Pub; T Jones, *Corporate Killing: Bhopals Will Happen*, (1988) London: Free Association Books; K Fortun, *Advocacy after Bhopal: Environmentalism, Disaster, New Global Orders*, (2001); and *Re Union Carbide Corpn Gas Plant Disaster at Bhopal, India in December* 1984 809 F 2d 195 (2nd cir, 1987). Cf 11 September 2001 where around 3,000 people were killed in the hijacked airline attacks on the World Trade Centre and Pentagon and in the air crash in rural Pennsylvania. On 9 September 2003, US district judge Alvin Hellerstein ruled that the hijacking of commercial jets was a foreseeable risk that the airline industry should have guarded against. So far there have been 2,275 claims: *Guardian*, 9 September 2003).
4   Chernobyl Nuclear Disaster, www.chernobyl.co.uk.

15.2   Breaches of health and safety regulations usually result in administrative or regulatory sanctions imposed by the health and safety authorities of the country concerned. They may also be relied on in civil claims as evidence of negligence. When regulatory offences result in fatal accidents, the question of criminal responsibility then needs to be addressed.

15.3   The approaches that have been adopted by various countries as to whether to criminalise the corporate behaviour for death at work, and thus to impose criminal liability on corporations for the offence of manslaughter, are quite different. In general, a corporation is in the same position in relation to criminal liability as a natural person and may be convicted for criminal offences including those requiring mens rea. There are, however, some crimes which a corporation is incapable of committing, for example, reckless driving. Nor can a corporation be found guilty of a crime for which imprisonment is the only punishment, for example, murder. The question of whether the corporation can be guilty of manslaughter is a complex one.

15.4   A natural person will be guilty of gross negligent manslaughter if his or her recklessness or negligence was the substantial cause of death. The liability of a natural person has been well established in criminal laws of all jurisdictions and is not at issue. Giving corporations total immunity would take away the means of effectively controlling corporate conduct. There is an assumption, perhaps counter to the Kantian notion of treating persons as an end not a means, that criminal responsibility, or the threat of prosecution, has a deterrent effect in the context of strict liability regulatory offences, and a punitive effect in relation to offences where culpability is an aggravating factor. Whilst criminal liability can lie with directors and officers, it can be further be argued that this simply enables the corporation to delegate and so avoid responsibility, which some would argue properly lies with the corporation itself as an entity greater than the sum of its staff and assets. It is often difficult to identify the individuals responsible for criminal acts. Further, it is argued that the corporate culture can create actions which are not attributable to the criminal intent of any particular individual but which only reflect the collective whole, such as a company wide neglect of proper health and safety precautions. This is the source of the notion of collective responsibility. Running counter to this is the common perspective that corporations themselves are not truly actors in the criminal sphere and in essence a legal conception without any physical personal manifestation beyond their employees.

15.5 In this chapter we will examine the position of criminal laws in relation to corporate liability for the crime of manslaughter. First, we will consider the position in common law countries, such as the US, Canada and Australia. Secondly, we will look at some European countries, such as France, Italy, The Netherlands, Germany, Finland, Sweden, Norway and Denmark. Ultimately, we will analyse the position of the development of the law of corporate manslaughter from international and European perspective.

The US

Introduction

15.6 Corporate liability for manslaughter in the US is governed by State law. Companies in the US are, on a regular if not frequent basis, prosecuted by state and county district attorneys, and investigated by state government bodies in relation to fatalities. This relies on the state penal codes, founded if not still governed by the principle of vicarious liability, respondeat superior, as it is still referred to. However, these by no means reflect the rate of violations of health and safety regulations nor the rate of fatalities.

15.7 On the federal level the Model Penal Code and sentencing guidelines reinforce the regime created at common law. It also remains the case that the civil law is the popular remedy for corporate wrongdoing. More positive, preventive penalties are already available alongside the traditional armoury of the District Attorney, and recourse to them is growing, albeit that there remains scepticism as to their effectiveness.

At common law

15.8 Vicarious civil liability is well established in the civil context. Criminal vicarious responsibility was recognised first, perhaps, at the federal tier in *United States v Von Schaik*.[1] This concerned steamship operators who had failed to provide properly functioning life preservers contrary to the statutory provisions. The company and its directors were prosecuted and both were held liable, the latter for aiding and abetting the commission of the corporation's offence. The court took a pragmatic view of the legislation which only stipulated the punishment of imprisonment. The court considered that the social utility of allowing the prosecution would outweigh the oversight to legislate for this eventually. The seminal decision, following *Van Schaik*, came in 1909 in the context of the interpretation of the regulatory Elkins Act 1903 in relation to rebates to preferred customers. The Elkins Act 1903, s 1 stipulated that the acts of a carrier's officers, agents and employees could be attributable to the carrier.

The Supreme Court upheld the natural reading of the section, rejecting arguments that a companies' liability would be unconstitutional.[2]

1   *United States v Von Schaik* (1904, CC NY) 134 F 592.
2   *New York Central and Hudson River Railroad Company v United States* (1909) 212 US 481.

15.9   There are essentially three requisite elements to vicarious liability:

1   The commission of a criminal act with the requisite intent by an employee such as an officer or director.
2   Within the scope of the employee's authority.
3   Intended to benefit the employer.

15.10   In strict liability offences, it need simply be proved that the relevant act was committed to establish liability. However, the company may be able to establish a defence of due diligence.

15.11   It is the individual states that have jurisdiction in relation to manslaughter and its prosecution. Definitions of homicide vary between states, particularly in relation to the categorisation of negligence or gross negligence when the outcome is a fatality. Some courts at the level of the state were more reluctant to extend vicarious liability beyond regulatory offences to cover manslaughter and this approach was not immediately universally adopted, creating inconsistency and uncertainty. For example, in New York the court adopted a restrictive reading of the homicide legislation and found that a company could not be held liable for manslaughter.[1] In Kentucky and New Jersey the courts adopted a different approach, holding that the there was no good reason why a company could not be found guilty.[2] Despite the fact that a number of state Penal Codes still define manslaughter as a human killing another human, it is now universally accepted that if the requisite culpability can be shown, a corporation itself can be convicted. We will return to this shortly.

1   *People v Rochester Railway & Light Co* (1908) 195 NY 102, 88 NE 22.
2   *Commonwealth v Illinois Central Railway Co* (1913) 152 Ky 320, 153 SW 459; *State v Leigh Valley R Co* (1917) 90 NJL 103 A.

15.12   In relation to crimes where intention is necessary, the second major hurdle after establishing the criminal act is to prove the guilty mind (mens rea). Some corporations today have large boards of directors consisting of executive and non-executive directors, numerous officers and some have a workforce which goes into six figures. When a fatality occurs it may exceptionally be possible to attribute the blame to a single ordinary employee. However, it may be that senior supervisory personnel are truly at fault. The courts have also recognised the culpability of directors and officers. Three possibilities for establishing corporate liability present themselves:

1   attributing the intention of an individual to the company;[1]
2   accepting 'wilful blindness' as culpable intent, where one or more corporate agents have reason to suspect that a crime may have been committed, but refrain from investigating the matter further;[2] and
3   adopting a concept of collective knowledge.[3]

1   J Gobert and M Punch *Rethinking Corporate Crime* Butterworths (2003) chapters 2 and 3; *Commonwealth of Pennsylvania v Penn Valley Resorts Inc* 343 Pa Super 387, 494 A 2d 1139.
2   *Continental Banking Co v US* 281 F 2d 137 (6th Cir, 1960); *Stere Tank Lines Inc v United States* 330 F2d 719 (5th Cir, 1963); *United States v Mapelli* 971 F 2d 284 (9th Cir, 1992).
3   *United States v Bank of England* 821 F 2d 844 (1st Cir, 1987).

15.13 The latter are the more conceptually difficult. However, the court has favoured these over the first. Consequently, there is no need to identify an individual who had the requisite intention in US law.[1] For example, in *US v Time-DC Inc*, the corporation was successfully prosecuted under an International Chamber of Commerce regulation which forbade lorry drivers from driving when ill. One employee knew that the driver concerned in the case had telephoned to say that he could not work but had then, when learning of the company's absentee policy, which required a doctor's note, changed his mind. It was held that the corporation could be found to have 'knowingly and willingly violated the regulation'. The court summarised the principle as follows:

> '… knowledge acquired by employees within the scope of their employment is imputed to the corporation. In consequence, a corporation cannot plead innocence by asserting that the information obtained by several employees was not acquired by any one individual employee who then should have comprehended its full report. Rather, the corporation is considered to have acquired the collective knowledge of its employees and is held responsible for their failure to act accordingly.'

1 *US v American Stevedores Inc* (1962).

15.14 It could be said that the corporation has few means to control the intentions of its employees, but in the era of information and communication management, this may no longer be the case.

15.15 The company may be prosecuted even if individual employees actually responsible for the act are not convicted. We will return to prosecution of corporate employees, directors and officers briefly below.

15.16 If the corporation is to be held liable, it must be clear that the crime was not a personal aberration of the employee acting on his or her own. It must in some way fall within the employee's scope of employment. This turns largely on the law of agency and actual or apparent authority.[1] However, corporations have been found liable even for acts which they expressly forbade their employees from carrying out, provided those remain in some way within the course of employment.[2] The variety of employees whose have acts have been considered attributable to the company include directors, officers, managers, white and blue-collar workers and independent contractors where the latter have been sought in an attempt to contract out of criminal responsibility.[3]

1 *United States v American Radiator and Standard Sanitary Corpn* 433 F 2d 174 (3rd Cir, 1970).
2 *United States and Twentieth Century Fox Film Corpn* 882 F 2d 656 (2nd Cir, 1989); *United States v Hilton Hotels Corpn* 467 F 2d 1000 (9th Cir, 1972).
3 *United States v Parfait Powder Co* 163 F 2d 1008 (7th Cir, 1947).

15.17 Further, whilst the act must in some way have been in order to benefit the company, it need not be exclusively for its benefit. If the agent is acting in violation of the fiduciary duty owed to the corporation, in order to gain personal profit, for example, the corporation will not be liable.[1] The court has gone so far as to say that vicarious liability existed even where the corporation did not in the event benefit, where the employee had the intention of benefiting the company.[2] The *Federal Guidance on the Prosecution of Business Organizations*[3] referred to *Automated Medical Laboratories*[4] in which the court stated:

> '[B]enefit is not a "touchstone of criminal corporate liability; benefit at best is an evidential, not an operative, fact." Thus, whether the agent's actions ultimately

redounded to the benefit of the corporation is far less significant than whether the agent acted with the intent to benefit the corporation. The basic purpose of requiring that an agent have acted with the intent to benefit the corporation, however, is to insulate the corporation from criminal liability for actions of its agents which be inimical to the interests of the corporation or which may have been undertaken solely to advance the interests of that agent or of a party other than the corporation.'

1   *Standard Oil Co of Texas v US* (1962).
2   *United States v Carter* 311 F 2d 934 (6th Cir); *Old Monastery co v United States* 147 F 2d 905 (4th Cir).
3   20 January 2003, available at www.usdoj.gov/dag/ctft/corporate_guidelines.htm.
4   *Automated Medical Laboratories* 770 F 2d at 407.

15.18   A company may also be held vicariously liable for the actions of its subsidiaries. This reaches back beyond takeovers. A new parent company may be prosecuted for the acts of the subsidiary which took place prior to the acquisition, extending overseas if necessary.[1] The most famous failure in this context is the Union Carbide litigation referred to at **para 15.1** above.

1   Gobert and Punch, **para 15.12 n 1** above, chapter 5.

Federal and state law

15.19   The only remaining federal statute in the context of manslaughter is the Occupational Safety and Health Act[1] which penalises wilful or repeated failure on the part of employers to fulfil their duties and meet the stipulated standards made under the federal provisions.[2] Section 3 of the Act defines person as 'one or more individuals, partnerships, associations corporations, business trusts, legal representatives, or any organized group of persons'.

1   29 USC 666(e).
2   29 USC 654, 655.

15.20   The US Department of Justice Guidance cites the only case addressing the issue of 'wilfulness' for the purposes of finding a criminal violation under the Act, *United v Dye Construction*[1] as authority that the government need not prove that the employer entertained a specific intent to harm the employee or that the employer's actions involved moral turpitude, rather the court approved the following jury direction:

'The failure to comply with a safety standard under the Occupational Safety Health Act is wilful if done knowingly and purposely by an employee who, having free will or choice", either intentionally disregards the standard or is plainly indifferent to its requirement. An omission or failure to act is wilful if done voluntarily and intentionally.'

1   510 F 2d 78, available at www.usdoj.gov/usao.

15.21   Indifference can in fact be sufficient to show 'wilfulness' for the purposes of the statutory offence.[1]

1   *Georgia Electric Co v Marshall* 576 F 2d, *FX Messina Construction Co v OSHRC* 522 F 2d.

15.22   The state legislatures have been influenced by the Model Penal Code produced by the American Law Institute in 1962. The codification of homicide in chapter 2 of the Code includes corporate manslaughter and offers a more systematic approach to the imposition of criminal liability. Section 2.07 of the Code limits the scope of liability as compared with vicarious liability. Section 2.07 states:

'A corporation may be convicted of an offence if …
(c) The commission of the offence was authorised, requested, commanded, performed or recklessly tolerated by the board of directors or by a high managerial agent acting on behalf of the corporation within the scope of his office or employment.'

New York, California, Kentucky, Pennsylvania and Texas compared

15.23 These states represent a broad spectrum of demography, geography, political climate and industry.

15.24 The New York Penal Code closely follows the Model Penal Code. It defines person generally as meaning 'a human being and where appropriate, a public or private corporation, an unincorporated association, a partnership, a government, or a governmental instrumentality'.[1] Homicide is defined generally as 'conduct which causes the death of a person …'[2] The New York Code includes criminally negligent homicide (albeit as a class E felony).[3] Culpability is defined in s **15.05** of the Code:

'"Intentionally'. A person acts intentionally with respect to a result or to conduct described by a statute defining an offence when his conscious objective is to cause such result or to engage in such conduct.

"Knowingly'. A person acts knowingly with respect to conduct or to circumstances described by a statute defining an offence when he is aware that his conduct is of such nature or that such circumstances exist.

"Recklessly". A person acts recklessly with respect to a result or to a circumstance described by a statute defining an offence when he is aware of and consciously disregards a substantial and unjustifiable risk that such result will occur or that such circumstances exist. The risk must be of such nature and degree that disregard thereof constitutes a gross deviation from the standard of conduct that a reasonable person would observe in the situation …

"Criminal negligence". A person acts with criminal negligence with respect to a result or to a circumstance described by a statute defining an offence when he fails to perceive substantial and unjustifiable risk that such result will occur or that such circumstance exists. The risk must be of such nature and degree that the failure to perceive it constitutes a gross deviation from the standard of care that a reasonable person would observe in the situation.'

1 New York Penal Code, s 10.7.
2 New York Penal Code, s 125.00.
3 New York Penal Code, s 125.10.

15.25 Things have clearly moved on since the *People v Rochester Railway & Light Co,*[1] discussed at **para 15.11** above. Even prior to the present New York Penal Code, the state had come to accept the role of corporate criminal liability. In *The*

People of the State of New York v Ebasco Services Inc[2] the defendant corporation was charged with negligent homicide when two workmen lost their lives when the cofferdam they were working on collapsed and flooded. The defendant corporation initiated a motion to dismiss the indictment against them relying on the statutory definition of 'person' at the time person, 'a human being who has been born and alive'. Louis Wallace J rejected the contention which he reasoned: 'flies in the face of the statute which equates "person" with human being only in regard to the victim of the homicide ... The reference to human being is of limited application.'

1   (1908) 195 NY 102, 88 NE 22.
2   (1974) 77 Misc 2d 784, 354 NYS 2d 807.

15.26   In California, the Penal Code simply states '"person" includes a corporation as well as a natural person'.[1] Murder is defined as 'the unlawful killing of a human being ... with malice aforethought'.[2] Manslaughter is defined as 'the unlawful killing of a human being without malice'.[3] The Code departs widely from the Model Penal Code and sets out its own provision for corporate manslaughter.

1   California Penal Code, s 7.
2   California Penal Code, s 187.
3   California Penal Code, s 192.

15.27   A potential difficulty would seem to arise from the California Penal Code, s 193 which provides only for imprisonment as a sanction for manslaughter. This was litigated in *Granite Construction Co v The Superior Court of Fresno County*.[1] The court circumvented the problem by turning its attention to s 672 of the Code, which provided an alternative source of punishing corporations for criminal offences, a catchall fine system enacted in 1872.

1   (1983) 149 Cal App 3d 465.

15.28   The Kentucky Criminal Code follows the Model Penal Code definition of persons.[1] However Ch 507 of the Code which addresses homicide states: 'A person is guilty of criminal homicide when he causes the death of another human being under circumstances which constitute murder, manslaughter in the first degree, manslaughter in the second degree, or reckless homicide.'[2]

1   Kentucky Criminal Code, s 500.080(12).
2   Kentucky Criminal Code, s 507.010.

15.29   In *Commonwealth v Illinois Central Railway Co*,[1] although the courts held that the legislature could enact legislation creating an offence of corporate manslaughter, it had not done so in Kentucky. The strict definition of killing by one human being by another human being, as the legislation was then, was adhered to. A subsequent attempt to rely on the decision was rejected in *Commonwealth of Kentucky v Fortner LP Gas Company Inc*[2] in which two schoolchildren were run over by a truck belonging to the corporation whilst getting off the school bus when the truck's brakes failed. Gant J held that *Illinois Central Railway* was no longer applicable given statutory developments and the age of the case.

1   (1913) 152 Ky 320, 153 SW 459.
2   610 SW 2d 941.

15.30   In the Pennsylvania Penal Code, 'person' is undefined. However, s 307 of the Code is dedicated to the liability of organisations and 'related persons'. It states explicitly that:

'(a) Corporations generally – A corporation may be convicted of the commission of an offence if

1. the offence is a summary offence or the offence is defined by a statute other than this in which a legislative purpose to impose liability on corporations plainly appears and the conduct is performed by an agent of the corporation acting on behalf of the corporation within the scope of his office or employment, except that if the law defining the offence designates the agents for whose conduct the corporation is accountable or the circumstance under which it is accountable, such provisions shall apply;
2. the offence consists of an omission to discharge a specific duty of affirmative performance imposed on corporations by law; or
3. the commission of the offence was authorized, requested, commanded, performed or recklessly tolerated by the board of directors or by a high managerial agent acting on behalf of the corporation within the scope of his office or employment.'

15.31 The Pennsylvania Penal Code goes on to include unincorporated associations. Homicide is defined in accord with the Model Penal Code except that negligent homicide is defined as involuntary manslaughter[1] as it is considered a misdemeanour of the first degree.

1 Pennsylvania Civil Code, s 2504.

15.32 In *Commonwealth of Pennsylvania v McIlwain School Bus Lines Inc*[1] a corporation was found guilty of vehicular manslaughter, despite the fact that the legislature had 'inadvertently' failed to provide a suitable punishment for the offender.

1 (1980) 283 Pa Super 350, 443 A 2d 1157.

15.33 In *Commonwealth of Pennsylvania v Schomaker*[1] the court held that the provisions of the Penal Code, s 307(a)(3) dealing with corporate criminal liability applied to all offences in the Code.

1 (1981) 293 Pa Super 78, 437 A 2d 999.

15.34 In *Commonwealth of Pennsylvania v Penn Valley Reports Inc*[1] a corporation was convicted, inter alia, of involuntary manslaughter following the death of an underage drinker in a road traffic accident. It was alleged that the President of the defendant corporation had knowingly served drink to an underage patron at a college students' dinner held at his resort. He was further accused of failing to require proof of the patron's age and of serving him alcohol whilst he was visibly intoxicated, all of which were contrary to state law. The court held that this pointed to the fact that he had acted in a 'reckless or grossly negligent manner'. The court could have relied on the Penal Code, s 307 and *Commonwealth v Schomaker*[2]. Instead, it held that the question was simply one of agency and did not rely in any way on the company condoning the officer's actions. The company was a person for the purposes of the homicide offence and convicted accordingly.

1 343 Pa Super 387, 494 A 2d 1139.
1 *Commonwealth of Pennsylvania v Schomaker* (1981) 293 Pa Super 78, 437 A 2d 999. See **para 15.33** above.

15.35 The Texas Penal Code defines person as 'an individual, corporation or association'.[1] Manslaughter is defined as 'recklessly causing the death of an individual'.[2]

1   Texas Penal Code, s 1.07(38).
2   Texas Penal Code, s 19.04.

15.36   In *Vaughan and Sons Inc v The State of Texas*[1] the defendant corporation
was alleged to have caused the death of two individuals in a car crash. The corporation
claimed that the court had erred in finding that a corporation could be guilty of
criminal homicide under the provisions of the Texas Penal Code, particularly s 19.07
(governing homicide). The case reached the Court of Criminal Appeals after the Court
of Appeal held in favour of the corporation.

1   (1987) 737 SW 2d 805.

15.37   The court looked at the definition of 'persons', the provision in the Texas
Penal Code, s 7.22 that corporations could be convicted of any criminal offence set
out in the Code and s 12.51 dealing with the punishment of corporations and permitting
the imposition of fines in those cases where imprisonment is the sole sentence provided
for the offence.[1] The court consequently took the view that logic dictated that a
corporation could commit the offence of homicide and the corporation was convicted
accordingly.

1   *Vaughan and Sons Inc v The State of Texas* (1987) 737 SW 2d 805.

Prosecution and sentencing

15.38   The criminal justice system in the US pays little attention to corporate
manslaughter.[1] Investigation is carried out at the state level by health and safety
officers under the Department of Labour (for example, in New York State) or the
equivalent state department. Undoubtedly the police will be called, but there are not
specialist sections of the police force designated to dealing with corporate
manslaughter.

1   Eg D Neubauer *America's Courts and the Criminal Justice System* (1988) chapter 2.

15.39   The federal body responsible is the Occupational Safety and Health Authority
(OSHA). State departments of OSHA have established local Fatality Assessment and
Evaluation Control Evaluation (FACE) schemes. These report on fatalities, inspecting
the scene of the incident and preparing a report. They do not address the issue of
liability. The reports set out means of avoiding future incidents. However, a
corporation's co-operation may affect sentencing and possibly liability in relation to
a prosecution. Departments of Health in conjunction with Departments of Labour
also produce statistics in relation to fatalities.[1] This work is picked up at the state
level by bodies such as the Centers for Disease Control and Prevention (CDC) and
National Institute of Occupational Safety and Health (NIOSH) through its National
Occupational Research Agenda (NORA).[2] These are of some assistance in evaluating
the impact of corporate criminal litigation.

1   See eg www.health.state.ny.us/nysdoh/environ/cfoi/contents.htm.
2   See www2.cdc.gov/NORA/NaddinfoTrauma.html.

15.40   Public interest groups also play an important role in investigating and reporting
workplace fatalities.[1]

1   Eg Corporate Crime Reporter, available at www.corporatecrimereporter.com.

15.41   Whilst civil prosecutions may be brought by individuals or by local regulatory bodies, criminal prosecutions are only brought by District Attorneys. They are assisted by the federal Justice Department's *Guidance on the Prosecution of Corporations and Business Organizations.*[1] This sets out the general principle that:

> 'Corporations should not be treated leniently because of their artificial nature nor should they be subject to harsher treatment. Vigorous enforcement of the criminal laws against corporate wrongdoers, where appropriate results in great benefits for law enforcement and the public … Indicting corporations for wrongdoing enables the government to address and be a force for positive change of corporate culture, alter corporate behaviour, and prevent, discover and punish white collar crime.'

1   Available at www.usdoj.gov/dag/cftf/corporate_guidance.htm.

15.42   The Guidance lists nine factors to be considered in deciding whether to prosecute. These focus around the seriousness, pervasiveness of the act, any history of similar conduct, voluntary disclosure, co-operation, collateral consequences of the act, remedial action and the adequacy of alternatives such as prosecution of individual employees, civil or regulatory enforcement actions. The Guidance goes into some depth on each of these. It also discusses plea agreements with companies.

15.43   Corporations are extended civil rights in relation to prosecutions For instance, in *Boyd v United States*[1] the court upheld the Fifth Amendment preventing any individual's being 'compelled in any criminal case to be a witness against himself' in favour of a corporation. This led to the enactment of numerous regulatory statutes with criminal sanctions attached such as the Elkins Act 1903, the Sherman Act 1890 and the Interstate Commerce Act 1887. Subsequently the Supreme Court refused to extend these rights to artificial persons and other 'collective entities'.[2] They have also been restrictively interpreted in relation to individuals in the corporate context.[3]

1   16 US 616 (1886).
2   *Bellis v United States* 417 US 85 (1974); *Wilson v United States* 221 US 361 (1911).
3   *Hale v Henkel* 201 US 43 (1906).

15.44   Federal Guidelines also exist in relation to sentencing corporations.[1] The Guidelines provide for restitution for victims, without prejudice to civil claims. They also recommend alternative sanctions such as remedial orders and community service.

1   Available at www.ussc.gov/2002guid/CHAP8.htm.

15.45   The primary sanction for corporate liability remains a fine. Part C of the Guidance sets out the method for calculating the appropriate fine. The base fine is determined to be the greater of:

- a specified amount beginning (at level 6) at $5,000 to reflect the seriousness of the offence;
- the pecuniary gain to the organisation; or
- the pecuniary loss from the offence.

15.46   The court then multiplies this base fine by a multiplier representing the culpability of the offender. The product yields a recommended fine range. The court finally selects an appropriate fine from the recommended range. Factors include high-level involvement in or tolerance of criminal activity, prior history of corporate offending, violation of a judicial order or injunction, and obstruction of justice. Mitigating factors include self-reporting, co-operation and acceptance of responsibility. The Guidelines also set out provisions for corporate probation. The ultimate sanction is a fine amounting to the total assets of the company where the purpose of the company itself is criminal.

15.47 The courts have been creative in their use of sentencing powers. In *United States v Missouri Valley Construction Co*[1] the court ordered the convicted corporation to endow a chair of ethics at the state university. This touches on the border with the growing field of social responsibility law and practice.

1   741 F 2d 1542 (8th Cir).

15.48 Emphasis in both the Sentencing and Prosecution Guidelines is placed on corporate compliance programs. Consultancy can provide this commercially and large corporations are unlikely to overlook the advantages of having a program in place. The court's general approach has been to attempt to prevent incidents occurring and to achieve remediation first and foremost, reducing fines where this has been assured.[1] However, this has of course not manifested itself to the same degree in relation to corporate manslaughter. Having in place a corporate compliance program may support a defence that the corporation was not liable to begin with. This applies particularly in relation to strict liability, regulatory offences with criminal sanctions. Here there is often a due diligence defence which a company with some foresight should be able to take advantage of.

1   Eg *Logan County Farm Enterprises Inc* OSHRC Docket no 78-4535.

15.49 The concept of vicarious liability and corporate manslaughter under the relevant state statutes does not exclude liability of individual employees, directors and officers. The guidelines on prosecution and sentencing explicitly recognise this. Under the 'responsible corporate officer' doctrine, a corporate official who holds a position of 'responsibility and authority' within a company can be held criminally liable for not exercising the 'highest standard of foresight and vigilance' to prevent a crime from occurring in the sphere of the company's operations for which the officer had responsibility.[1]

1   *United States v Park* 421 US 658 (1975), following *United States v Dotterweich* 320 US 277 (1943).

15.50 Under the Occupational Health and Safety Act 1970, for the purposes of criminal enforcement only, an individual who is a corporate officer or director may be an 'employer' within the meaning of the Act and consequently found personally guilty of the offences set out in the Act.[1] This is particularly the case where the officer's role in running the company is so pervasive that it is in effect a sole proprietorship.[2]

1   *United States v Doig* 950 F 2d 411.
2   *United States v Cusack* 806 F Supp 47 (DNJ, 1992).

15.51 Whilst directors and officers cannot be charged as aiders and abettors under the Occupational Health and Safety Act 1970, they regularly, if infrequently, are in relation to other offences, and corporate manslaughter is very much the type of offence that individual directors and officers are likely to be investigated at least in relation to.

15.52   In *Sabine Consol Inc v State*[1] a reporting supervisor was successfully charged with the offence of criminally negligent homicide when trench walls collapsed [2]

1   (1974) 806 SW 2d 553 (Tex Crim App, 1991).
2   See also *People v Pymm* 563 NE 2d 1,3 (NY, 1990); *Chicago Magnet Wire Corporation* 534 NE 2d 963, *People v Hegedus* 443 NW 2d 127, 128 (Mich 1989); *Cornellier* 425 NW 2d at 22.

Conclusion

15.53   The dangers of corporate compliance programs and individual programs as well as corporate crime in general is that this can induce a minimal standard from corporates and undermine their willingness to invest more in safety if they can protect themselves through delegating responsibility to officers or to consultants providing compliance programs.[1]

1   W Laufer 'Corporate Liability, Risk Shifting and the Paradox of Compliance' (1999) Vand LR 1344.

15.54   The Census of Fatal Occupational Injuries has year on year suggested a decrease in the level of workplace fatalities,[1] not including victims of 11 September 2001. There is very wide variation between states. The media regularly reports incidents of corporate killing and the like.[2] Non-governmental groups monitor workplace fatalities and provide information about the worst 100 corporations and reports of fatalities.[3] In the words of Robert Weismman, there is a relative academic Siberia in the field of statistics regarding corporate manslaughter.[4]

1   Bureau of Labour Statistics *Census of Fatal Occupational Injuries*, available at www.bls.gov/news.release/cfoi.nr0.htm.
2   Eg 'Criminal charges can hit bottom line' Delware Online New Journal, 28 June 2003.
3   Eg Corporate Crime Reporter, available at www.corporatecrimereporteer.com.
4   R Weissman, editor of Multinational Monitor, letter to Corporate Crime Reporter, December 1998.

15.55   The 1990s saw global actors concerned about human rights shift their attention from abuses committed by governments to close scrutiny of the activities of business enterprises, particularly multinational corporations.[1] In the light of Enron, World.com and the relative weakness of regulatory bodies in the field, corporate criminal prosecutions are unlikely to reduce. There remains much work to be done in assessing their effectiveness. None of the available statistics show a break down in the numbers of civil or criminal prosecutions. It is impossible without an in depth study to assess the impact on the level of workplace fatalities. The cost of criminal sanctions, whether financial or otherwise, can be enormous and cannot be justified on the basis of unconsidered assumptions which seem to underpin the present law.[2]

1   (2001) 111 Yale LJ 443.
2   V Khanna *A Political Theory of Corporate Crime Legislation* (2003).

Australia

Introduction

15.56   Australia has a common law legal tradition similar to that of the UK. Australia, like the US and Canada,[1] has a federal structure and so demonstrates some similarities with North America also. Under the Australian Constitution federal, state and territory courts may exercise the judicial power of the Commonwealth of Australia. The development of the law of manslaughter has also followed a similar path to that in the UK, but the Australian Criminal Code Act 1995 is adventurous in providing perhaps the most detailed requirements globally relating to corporate organisational liability.

1   Australia and Canada are realms of Queen Elizabeth II and are members of the Commonwealth.

15.57   Some important manslaughter cases were taken in the early 1990s, including the prosecution of Civil and Civic Pty Ltd,[1] construction contractors, in 1992. In this case the prosecution was dropped following an agreement by the company to plead guilty to a series of lesser charges under the Occupational Health and Safety Act 1985. In 1994, another construction company pleaded guilty to manslaughter charges following the death of one of its employees.[2]

1   *R v Civil and Civic Pty Ltd* (15 December 1992, unreported), CC of Victoria (Crossley J).
2   *The Queen v Denbo Pty Ltd and Timothy Ian Nadenbousch* (1994) 6 VIR 157. In this case, a truck driver with a small two-person business died when the brakes of his truck failed. The director of the company, who operated the business, knew that the brakes were faulty. He was convicted and fined A$10,000. The company was convicted and fined A$120,000.

15.58   In a further case the failure to follow a 'hot work permit' procedure while repair work was being carried out on a tank with an oxyacetylene torch resulted in an explosion which killed one employee and seriously injured two others. Manslaughter charges against senior individuals were withdrawn before committal and Hampel J directed that there should be an acquittal against the corporation for manslaughter because the allegedly culpable individuals were not the 'guiding mind'. There were two individuals (the plant manager and safety co-ordinator and the plant engineer) who bore some responsibility for the accident but the actions of neither amounted to criminal negligence.[1]

1   *The Queen v AC Hatrick Chemicals Pty Ltd, Robert Arthur Hill and Tyronne Alexander de Silva* (8 December 1995, unreported), Supreme Court of Victoria (Criminal Division).

Federal law

15.59   After applying the concept of vicarious liability until 1995, the law took a different direction when the Australian legislature changed the criminal code to base corporate criminal liability on a test of the 'corporate culture. However, the 1995 Criminal Code Act (Cth) only has application at the federal level and manslaughter is not a federal offence. It is for the states and Territories to adopt similar provisions in their Criminal Codes or (in the case of common law states) other criminal legislation. The Act applies the general principles of criminal responsibility to corporations. For offences of intention, knowledge or recklessness the 'fault element must be attributed to a body corporate that expressly, tacitly or impliedly authorized or permitted the commission of the offence'.[1] Such authorisation or permission can be shown in one of three ways.

1   Department of Justice *Federal Principles of Prosecution of Corporations* (1999).

15.60   The first restates the rule in *Tesco v Nattrass*.[1] The requisite state of mind here is gross negligence which may be proved by showing:

'that the act which caused the death was done by the accused consciously and voluntarily, without any intention of causing death or causing grievous bodily harm, but in circumstances which involved falling short of the standard of care which a reasonable person would have exercised and which involved such a high degree of risk that death or grievous bodily harm would follow that the doing of the act merited criminal punishment.'[2]

1 *Tesco Supermarkets Ltd v Nattrass* [1972] AC 153. The concept of 'directing mind or will' was approved by the High Court of Australia in *Hamilton v Whitehead* (1988) 82 ALR 626.
2 *Nydam v R* [1977] VR 430 at 435.

15.61 Thus, under the doctrine of identification, for a corporation to be held liable for manslaughter under Australian law, the prosecution must show that a 'directing mind' committed the negligent act or omission, and possessed the requisite state of mind as set out in *Nydam*.[1]

1 *Nydam v R* [1977] VR 430 at 435.

15.62 The second extends the group to include 'high managerial agents, ie directors and senior managers. The third path marks a fundamental departure from traditional lines. The idea of 'corporate culture' is specifically given legislative recognition. Where the corporation's attitude, policy rule, course of conduct or practice leads to non-compliance the company will be responsible. Alan Rose, the President of the Australian Law Reform Commission, described the proposals as follows:

'This approach quite clearly seeks to address the significant criticisms of the 1972 Tesco decision,[1] which restricted corporate criminal liability to the conduct or fault of high-level managers or a delegate with full discretion to act independently of in-house instructions, an approach ironically appropriate to the small and medium-sized business, with which large national and multi-national corporation [sic] have almost nothing in common.'[2]

1 *Tesco Supermarkets Ltd v Nattrass* [1972] AC 153. The concept of 'directing mind or will' was approved by the High Court of Australia in *Hamilton v Whitehead* (1988) 82 ALR 626.
2 A Rose, Australian Law Reform Commission (1995).

15.63 Australian Criminal Code Act 1995, s 12 makes it clear that these provisions are applicable to corporations as well as individuals. It begins by attributing the physical conduct of an agent, employee or officer to the corporation. The fault requirement will be proved if the corporation 'expressly, tacitly or impliedly authorized or permitted the commission of the offence'.[1] Authorisation and permission may be demonstrated by:

'(a) proving that the body corporate's board of directors, intentionally, knowingly or recklessly carried out the relevant conduct, or expressly, tacitly or impliedly authorized or permitted the commission of the offence; or

(b) proving that a high managerial agent of the body corporate intentionally, knowingly or recklessly engaged in the relevant conduct, or expressly, tacitly or impliedly authorized or permitted the commission of the offence; or

(c) proving that a corporate culture existed within the body corporate that directed, encouraged, tolerated or led to non-compliance with the relevant provision; or

(d) proving that the body corporate failed to create and maintain a corporate culture that requires compliance with the relevant provision.'[2]

1 Australian Criminal Code Act 1995, s 12.3.
2 Australian Criminal Code Act 1995, s 12.3(2)

15.64   These provisions are qualified by the Australian Criminal Code Act 1995, s 12.3.4 which states that the factors relevant to the application of para 2(c) or (d) include:

(a)   whether authority to commit an offence of the same or a similar character had been given by a high managerial agent of the body corporate; and
(b)   whether the employee, agent or officer of the body corporate who committed the offence believed on reasonable grounds, or entertained a reasonable expectation, that a high managerial agent of the body corporate would have authorised or permitted the commission of the offence.

15.65   Thus even if a junior employee was not specifically authorised to commit the crime it will be sufficient if he or she had a 'reasonable expectation' that he or she would have been permitted to engage in the crime by a director or senior manager who would be seen as a 'high managerial agent' for these purposes. A corporation would thus be liable when key actors lacked mens rea. Negligence would be sufficient. The question would be whether the corporation took appropriate precautions to minimise the risk of the crime. For as Coffee explains[1] '…the corporation would not be strictly liable (as it is in the United States) for the agent's misconduct, but it could have liability for negligent or non-knowing conduct by the agent (whereas it might not have such liability in the United States)'. In relation to the latter, a defence of due diligence exists, if the 'body corporate [can prove] that it exercised due diligence to prevent the conduct, or the authorization or permission'.

1   Professor JC Coffee 'Corporate Criminal Liability: An Introduction and Comparative Survey', in A Eser, G Heine and B Hubert (eds), *Criminal Responsibility of Legal and Collective Entities*, International Colloquium, May 1998.

15.66   Furthermore, corporations may be prosecuted for offences where the only available punishment is imprisonment, although in these circumstances the custodial sentence would be replaced by a fine, as permitted by the provisions of the Crimes Act 1914, s 48. Other innovative measures under consideration include new forms of reparation and restitution (including community service and remedial orders); new forms of fines (including fines based on turnover, or in the form of divestment of equity); probation and other types of surveillance; novel forms of disqualification from certain commercial activity; receivership and ultimately the winding–up of the corporation itself.[1]

1   US Sentencing Commission *Federal Sentencing Guideline Manual* (1 November 2000); SS Simpson and CS Kopher 'Deterring Corporate Crime' (1992) 30(3) Criminology 347; J Braithwaite and B Fisse 'On the Plausibility of Corporate Crime Control' in G Geis, RR Meier and LM Salinger (eds) *White Collar Crime: Classic and Contemporary Views* (3rd edn, 1995); M Punch 'Suite Violence: Why Managers Murder and Corporations Kill (2000) 33 Crime, Law and Social Change 243; and K Polk, F Haines and S Perrone 'Work Death in Victoria, 1987– 1990: An Overview' (1995) 28 Australian and New Zealand J Criminology 178 at 187.

State law

15.67   Much effort is now being made by activists, legislators, social reformers and trades unionists, to institute changes at state level. Bills have been presented in Victoria, Queensland, New South Wales and the Australian Capital Territory.

15.68   Professor Brent Fisse, a leading figure in this movement,[1] has argued as follows:

'A corporation should be subject to liability for an offence where two basic conditions are met:

1. the external elements of the offence have been committed by a person for whose conduct the corporate defendant is vicariously liable; and
2. the corporation has been at fault in one or other of the following ways:
    (a) by having a policy that expressly or impliedly authorizes or permits the commission of the offence or an offence of the same type;
    (b) by failing to take reasonable precautions or to exercise due precautions to prevent the commission of the offence or an offence of the same type;
    (c) by having a policy of failing to comply with a reactive duty to take preventive measures in response to having committed the external elements of the offence; or
    (d) by failing to take reasonable precautions or to exercise due diligence to comply with a reactive duty to take preventive measures in response to having committed the external elements of the offence.'

1   See further B Fisse and J Braithwaite J *Corporations, Crime and Accountability* (1994) Cambridge University Press.

Victoria

15.69   In November 2001, the Bracks government introduced the Crimes (Workplace Deaths & Serious Injuries) Bill in the Victorian Parliament.[1] Union leaders have hailed the initiative as ground-breaking and long overdue, and hundreds of union delegates rallied outside the Victorian Parliament House in support of the Bill. Under this proposed legislation, if an employer fails to provide a safe place of work, a corporation could be fined up to A$600,000 (increased from A$250,000) and an individual up to A$120,000 (increased from A$50,000) and serve a maximum of 12 months' imprisonment. Where an employer has obstructed health and safety inspectors, discriminated against employees for health and safety activities or failed to comply with prohibition notices issued by Worksafe then the maximum fine would be A$750,000 for a corporation and A$150,000 for individuals.

1   According to a report in *The Australian* 30 April 2002, p 9, the Beattie government in Queensland is drafting legislation to introduce a new crime of 'dangerous industrial conduct', with penalties of up to seven years' imprisonment and fines of A$500,000 for criminally negligent managers. The ACT has an amendment to its Crimes Act currently being debated, WA has a draft paper on work safety laws, and NSW has recently overhauled its health and safety laws but has not pursued the notion of corporate killing offences. See 'Legislative Attempts to Imprison those prosecuted for Criminal Manslaughter in the Workplace' (2002) 9(3) Murdoch University Electronic Journal of Law.

15.70   Under the Bill, a court was empowered to look at the conduct of the corporation as a whole, rather than just the conduct of one person who was the 'directing mind and will' of the corporation. Aggregation of conduct would have been permitted. If the combined conduct had amounted to gross negligence, the corporation would have been adjudged to be guilty. Fines totalling A$5 million for a death and A$2 million for a serious injury were liable to be imposed. A court could also have ordered a company to publicise its wrongdoing.

15.71   The Bill also allowed for the prosecution of company senior officers where they had knowledge of a high risk to their workers' safety and had been in a position to prevent death and serious injury. Maximum penalties for senior officers convicted of these offences were set at a fine of A$180,000 or five years' imprisonment where a death has occurred and an A$120,000 fine or two years' imprisonment where a serious injury had occurred.

15.72   The Bill was rejected in the Upper House in May 2002, following sustained pressure from the Australian Industry Group and the Victorian Employers Chamber of Commerce. The feeling was that there was an insufficient requirement for a causal nexus between the prescribed conduct and serious injury or death. However, following elections in November 2002 control of the Upper House is now with the Bracks government. The Bill may be re-introduced but with less severe penalties.

15.73   Following this setback Professor Glasbeek said:

'I would suggest we go as far as charging the shareholders of grossly negligent companies. Just as you would charge someone who benefited from the criminal behaviour of a thief receiving stolen goods.'[1]

1   See www.hazards.org/deadlybusines/deadlybusiness.pdf.

Queensland

15.74   In Queensland the state government sought to introduce a new offence of dangerous industrial conduct in the Queensland Criminal Code. This proposed offence was similar in concept to that of 'dangerous driving' causing death or grievous bodily harm. It was proposed that both individuals and corporations would be liable for the offence, with a maximum penalty of a fine of 6,700 penalty units (A$502,500) or seven years' imprisonment. It was felt that the high number of fatalities[1] was a concern and that hitherto the penalties imposed in Queensland for cases where industrial negligence and breaches of legislation result in death or serious injury were inadequate. Directors were being fined relatively small sums. Moreover, there were a number of important examples where cases had not been taken against corporations although a prosecution for manslaughter would prima facie have been appropriate, this is a serious omission since individuals are readily prosecuted. One reason for this was the inherent individualism of the criminal law.[2]

1   Between 60 and 100 persons die in workplace accidents per year in Queensland. See Division of Workplace Health and Safety, Department of Employment, Training and Industrial Relations and Qstats, Queensland Treasury. Discussion Paper, Dangerous Industrial Conduct – Queensland Government, Department of Justice and Attorney General 2001.
2   B Fisse and J Braithwaite 'The Allocation of Responsibility for Corporate Crime: Individualism, Collectivism and Accountability' (1988) 11 Syd LR 468.

15.75   It was proposed that there would be a new offence so that a person would be liable for the offence of 'dangerous industrial conduct' where they behave dangerously in the workplace (that is, in a way that is unlawful or falls far below what would reasonably be expected), resulting in death or grievous bodily harm.

15.76   Apart from individual liability, it was proposed that a 'corporation' and its 'management' would be criminally liable for intentional, reckless or negligent behaviour that results in death or injury to persons affected by the activities of the corporation (that is, employees and members of the public) where:

1   the behaviour was dangerous, in that it was unlawful or otherwise fell far
    below what would reasonably be expected (within the current definition of
    criminal negligence);[1]
2   the behaviour was that of an officer, agent or employee of the corporation
    acting within the actual or apparent scope of their employment or within their
    actual or apparent authority; and
3   where the behaviour was intentional or reckless, the behaviour was to be
    attributed to the corporation if it expressly, tacitly or impliedly authorised or
    permitted the behaviour.

1   *R v Bateman* [1925] All ER Rep 45.

15.77   Such authorisation or permission would have been established by proving
that:

* the corporation's board of directors intentionally or recklessly carried out the
  relevant behaviour, or expressly, tacitly or impliedly authorised or permitted the
  behaviour;
* a high managerial agent of the corporation intentionally or recklessly engaged
  in the relevant behaviour or expressly, tacitly or impliedly authorised or
  permitted the behaviour, unless the corporation could prove that it had
  exercised due diligence to prevent the behaviour, or the authorisation or
  permission;
* a corporate culture existed within the corporation that directed, encouraged,
  tolerated or led to the behaviour;
* the corporation failed to create and maintain a corporate culture that required
  the prevention of the behaviour.

15.78   The proposal also provided that where the behaviour was negligent, the
conduct of any number of the corporation's employees, agents or officers might
be aggregated. Negligence would have been evidenced by the fact that the
behaviour would be substantially attributable to inadequate corporate
management, control or supervision of the behaviour of one or more of its
employees, agents or officers; or failure to provide adequate systems for conveying
relevant information to relevant persons in the corporation.

15.79   In December 2002, however, the government admitted that any plans for
this legislation had been shelved for the immediate future.

Australian Capital Territory

15.80   Ministers in the Australian Capital Territory are also keen to legislate in
this area. The Crimes (Industrial Manslaughter) Bill 2002, which amends the Crimes
Act 1900 provides for improved protection of the health and safety of workers by
establishing a new offence of industrial manslaughter. Under this provision
employers and 'senior officers' would be liable for industrial manslaughter with
maximum penalties of fines of up to A$250,000 (natural persons) or A$1,250,000
(corporations) or 25 years' imprisonment, or both. Ms Katy Gallagher, the Industrial
Relations Minister for the Australian Capital Territory is pressing for the passage
of this legislation in 2003.

New South Wales

15.81   Finally, in April 2003 in the New South Wales Legislative Council Dr Chesterfield Evans introduced the Crimes Amendment (Corporate Manslaughter) Bill. It provides for custodial sentences for gross negligence causing death. A corporation can be fined up to $5 million and a senior officer up to $180,000 or be sent to prison for five years. The Bill also allows for crimes to be reported on TV, in daily newspapers and in annual reports, and for offenders to perform community service. The government of New South Wales do not appear to support this move, however.

Canada

Introduction

15.82   As in the UK, the US and Australia, corporations can be found guilty of criminal offences in Canada. The Canadian Criminal Code defines a 'person' to include 'public bodies, bodies corporate, societies, [and] companies'.[1] Most corporate wrongdoing is not prohibited by the Criminal Code, but by various regulatory statutes, including occupational health and safety legislation.[2] Thus, the issue of corporate responsibility for workplace health and safety, including work related deaths, is largely dealt with in provincial level health and safety statutes rather than in the federal Criminal Code. It is however, well established that corporations can be convicted of 'true' crimes requiring a culpable mental state.[3] The Criminal Code contains a specific offence of criminal negligence causing death.[4] Although corporations are capable of committing such an offence through the identification doctrine, they have not historically been charged with so doing in Canada, largely because of the difficulties associated with attributing the fault of a senior officer to the company. As with many other jurisdictions, the issue in Canada has been extensively reviewed and government proposals to reform the law on the criminal liability of corporations, directors and operators has recently been introduced in Parliament.

1   Criminal Code of Canada, RSC 1985, c C-46, s 2. Many of the offences under the Criminal Code, however, are not capable of being committed by a corporation. Those mens rea crimes under the Code which are, at least in theory, capable of corporate commission, including corporate manslaughter, have not traditionally been brought against corporations.
2   P Puri 'Sentencing the Criminal Corporation' (2001) 39(2&3) Osgoode Hall Law Journal at 611.
3   See eg *R v Fane Robinson Ltd* [1941] 2 WWR 235.
4   Criminal Code of Canada, RSC 1985, c C-46, s 220.

The application of criminal law to corporations in Canada: general principles

15.83   For mens rea crimes the basis for corporate liability is not presently found in any codified form, but has been developed through the common law on a case-by-case basis. Corporate criminal liability in Canada is currently based on the theory that corporations are only capable of acting through the intentions of human beings. As with the UK this remains one of the most central and difficult issues in imposing corporate liability for manslaughter. The doctrine of vicarious liability was rejected by the Supreme Court of Canada in preference of the identification doctrine in the leading case of *Canadian Dredge & Dock Co v The Queen*.[1] Several corporations and their senior officers were convicted of conspiracy to defraud after bid-rigging for dredging contracts for the government. In the judgment, the court expressed its opinion that under the theory of vicarious liability, the 'net is flung too widely': '[c]orporations are punished in instances where there is neither moral turpitude nor negligence.'[2] However, recognising that limiting the number of individuals that may be identified as the directing mind of the company had a correlated effect on the application of the criminal law the court adopted a somewhat broader interpretation of the identification theory expressed in *Nattrass*.[3] Using the example of the Canadian transport industry, where the organisation of the corporation can be geographically diffuse, necessitating the delegation of responsibility for management decisions, the court indicated that a narrow interpretation of the identification doctrine did not suit the realities of life in Canada. In so doing, the court held that there may be more than one directing mind in that the 'identity doctrine merges the board of directors, the managing director, the superintendent, the manager, or anyone else who is delegated the governing executive of the corporation, and the conduct of the merged authorities is thereby attributed to the corporation'.[4]

1 [1985] 1 SCR 662.
2 [1985] 1 SCR 662 at para 47.
3 *Tesco Stores Ltd v Nattrass* [1972] AC 153.
4 [1985] 1 SCR 662 at para 50.

15.84 As noted above the application of the identification doctrine presently occurs on a case-by-case basis. Ferguson[1] argues that the doctrine is in 'a state of flux in Canada' following two more recent decisions. In *The Rhone v Peter AB Widener*,[2] the lead of four tugs pulling a barge, was travelling too fast and made a crucial turn too quickly causing the barge to go out of control and collide with a nearby ship. Amongst other issues, the court considered whether the captain of the lead tug was the directing mind of the company. However, despite the fact that he was towmaster of the flotilla with the ability to give direct orders to the other vessels and his employers exercised very little control over him, he was held not to be the directing mind of the company. The court held that: '[t]he key factor which distinguishes directing minds from normal employees is the capacity to exercise decision-making authority on matters of corporate policy, rather than merely to give effect to such policy on an operational basis.'[3] Similarly, in the criminal case of *R v Safety-Kleen Canada Inc*[4] an employee who was the sole representative of the company in a very large geographical area was not held to be the directing mind of the company because did not have any managerial or supervisory function. Both these cases take a rather more restrictive interpretation of the identification doctrine that in previous cases which have followed the *Dredge Dock*[5] decision.

1 G Ferguson 'Corruption and Corporate Criminal Liability', paper presented at the Seminar on New Global and Canadian Standards on Corruption and Bribery in Foreign Business Transactions, Vancouver, 4–5 February 1999, available at www.transparency.ca/Vancouver/FergusonG.pdf (11 September 2003).
2 [1993] 1 SCR 497.
3 [1993] 1 SCR 497 at para 42.
4 (1997) 114 CCC (3d) 214.
5 *Dredge & Dock Co v The Queen* [1985] 1 SCR 662.

15.85 Therefore, in Canada the position is somewhat more akin to the UK than the US. The Canadian court was unprepared to accept vicarious liability for the fault of all employees for crimes requiring intent in the US, but considered the interpretation of the identification doctrine expressed in *Nattrass*[1] somewhat too restrictive, and has therefore extended the list of persons which may constitute the directing mind of the corporation to suit the realities of life in Canada, with the effect that there may be more than one and it may be located at a lower level in the corporation that in the UK. In 1989, the Canadian Law Reform Commission suggested that the problems outlined above with reference to the identification doctrine could be circumvented through the addition of aggregation to the formula for attribution for negligence offences; however, reforms along these lines were never made.[2]

1   *Tesco Stores Ltd v Nattrass* [1972] AC 153.
2   See eg Report of the Law Reform Commission of Canada *Recodifying Criminal Law* (1989).

15.86   In common with the UK and Australia, the Canadian approach to identification theory has been criticised as being simultaneously too narrow and too broad and simplistic.[1] On the one hand, only the highest managerial level employees with decision-making authority can trigger corporate liability, although in practice decision-making on matters of company policy can be delegated to lower level managers. On the other hand, the identification theory may operate to attribute the actions of certain individuals automatically to the company, even though their actions are in fact wholly independent of the company and for their own benefit or gain.

1   *Legislating the Criminal Code: Involuntary manslaughter* (Law Com no 237, 1996). Canadian government 'Response to the Fifteenth Report of the Standing Committee on Justice and Human Rights: Corporate Liability' (November 2002).

The law on corporate liability for health and safety offences and deaths in the workplace

15.87   Currently responsibility for health and safety of employees falls under provincial and federal labour laws rather than the Criminal Code. The Canada Labour Code and provincial labour statutes impose a general duty on employers to ensure the safety and health of their employees and provides detail on safety regimes and inspection procedures. The Canada Labour Code applies to employees who work under federal jurisdiction, which accounts for approximately 10% of the Canadian workforce.[1] In most statutes, breach of these regimes is usually a punishable offence. For example, the Canada Labour Code provides that the wilful breach of health and safety standards in knowledge that serious injury or death is likely is a criminal offence.[2] Actual proof of injury or harm is not necessary. Maximum financial penalties range from $100,000 to $1,000,000. However, unlike mens rea offences, the penalties actually imposed are much lighter. Similarly, the Occupational Health and Safety Act 1990 of Ontario provides that every person who contravenes or fails to comply with the Act is guilty of an offence, and further that corporations convicted of such an offence may be fined up to a maximum of $500,000.[3] The basic elements of the provincial health and safety laws are similar across all 13 provinces. However, there are variances in the detailed provisions and in the way the laws are enforced.

1   The Constitution of Canada did not specify which jurisdiction had responsibility for health and safety matters. This was resolved in 1925 when the Judicial Committee of the Privy Council ruled that health and safety matters are primarily a responsibility of the provinces.
2   Canada Labour Code, RS 1985 c L-2, s 148.
3   RSO 1990, s 66(2).

15.88   The law on corporate criminal liability in general, as well as more specifically in relation to death by gross negligence, came under more intense scrutiny following the Westray mining disaster in 1992 when 26 miners lost their lives in an explosion at the mine in Nova Scotia. The report of the inquiry conducted in 1997 into the disaster stated that the deaths were caused by corporate mismanagement which had created unsafe working conditions.[1] Despite evidence of gross negligence in the mine, crown prosecutors had to stay charges against the company because they could not get a conviction under the current Criminal Code. In 1993, the government responded to a study by a subcommittee of the House of Commons Standing Committee on Justice and the Solicitor General by tabling a White Paper *Proposals to amend the Criminal Code (general principles)* in the form of a draft Bill which contained provisions on corporate liability.

1 Justice KP Richard *The Westray Story: A Predictable Path to Disaster* (the Westray Inquiry Report) (1997).

15.89   The Westray Inquiry report recommended that the government 'institute a study of the accountability of corporate executives and directors for the wrongful or negligent acts of the corporation and should introduce in the Parliament of Canada such amendments to legislation as are necessary to ensure that corporate executives and directors are properly held accountable for workplace safety'.[1] The Inquiry prompted the introduction of Private Member's Bills to the House of Commons, calling for corporate accountability and amendments to the Criminal Code.[2] On 26 February 2001, Bill C-284 was reintroduced to the House of Commons by Bev Dejarlais, seeking to add a new Pt XIII.I to the Criminal Code on offences by corporations, directors and officers.[3] The Bill called for corporate liability for offences of members of staff where the corporation management knew or should have known of the act or omission or condoned or was wilfully blind to it. It sought to shift the burden of proof to the corporation to show that that act or omission is not tolerated or condoned. The act would not need to be committed by the same person who committed or authorised it. Criminal liability would also be established for directors or managers who knew or should have known of the offence. Finally the Bill sought to create a new offence for corporations who failed to provide a safe working environment for employees, and for directors and officers who knew or should have known of the unsafe conditions but failed to report them.

1 Westray Inquiry Report, **para 15.88 n 1** above, recommendation 73.
2 Bill C-468 *An act to amend the Criminal Code (offences by corporations, directors and officers)*, received its first reading in the House of Commons on 5 February 1999. Bill C-468, First Session, 36th Parliament, 1999-98-97.
3 Bill C-284 *An act to amend the Criminal Code (offences by corporations, directors and officers)*, First Session, 37th Parliament, 49-50 Elizabeth II, 2001.

15.90   The Bill was referred to the House of Commons Standing Committee on Justice and Human Rights. In its report delivered in March 2002, the Committee concluded that legislative change was required to make it a crime for corporate managers and directors knowingly to put their employees in danger.[1] The government issued its response to the Committee report in November 2002. The 'first line of defence against death and injury in the workplace is workplace safety and health regulation'. It acknowledged that criminal law can provide an additional level of deterrence but that the criminal law should be reserved for the most serious offences. However, there is clearly an underlying desire not to interfere with the provincial regulatory role in relation to health and safety. It also acknowledged the deficiencies that existed in the present system which prevented the successful operation of the criminal law in this area. The 'requirement that one individual be liable before liability can be ascribed to a corporation was seen as providing a measure of impunity to large corporations while exposing smaller corporations to conviction'. The government expressed preference for changes to the general rules regarding corporate responsibility to the creation of specific offences like the British corporate killing model. The Australian corporate culture model was also felt to require too radical a departure from established general principles. In short, however, it agreed with the Committee's conclusion that legislative amendment was necessary.

1 Department of Justice 'Corporate Criminal Liability; Discussion Paper' (March 2002). Available at www.canada.justice.gc.ca/en/dept/pub/ccl_rpm/discussion/index.html (September 2003).

15.91 As a result, the government presented to the House of Commons Bill C-45, An Act to amend the Criminal Code (criminal liability of organizations). The proposed government Bill amends the Criminal Code to establish rules for attributing to organisations, criminal liability for the acts of their representatives; establish a legal duty for all persons directing work to take reasonable steps to ensure the safety of workers and the public; set out factors for the courts to consider when sentencing an organisation; and provide optional conditions of probation that a court may impose. Section 1 of the Bill inserts 'an organization' into the definition under the Criminal Code, s 2. 'Organization' means (a) a public body, body corporate, society, company, firm, partnership, trade union or municipality, or (b) an association of persons that (i) is created for a common purpose, (ii) has an operational structure and (iii) holds itself out to the public as an association of purpose. The proposed law is broader than the British proposals on corporate manslaughter from the outset as the definition of organisation is wider than corporate bodies.

15.92 Under the proposed amendments to the Criminal Code, 'everyone who undertakes, or has authority, to direct how another person does work or performs a task is under a legal duty to take reasonable steps to prevent bodily harm to that person, or any other person, arising from that work or task'. For less serious offences, corporations may be fined up to $100,000 and individuals may be sentenced to a maximum of six months' imprisonment. For more serious offences, there is no maximum prescribed limit to fines that may be imposed. These penalties are in addition to those existing under occupational health and safety legislation.[1]

1 At time of writing the Bill has had its first reading before the House of Commons and requires to be read twice more in the House of Commons before going before the Senate.

15.93 Thus Canada has decided not to focus legislative reform on the specific issue of corporate liability for manslaughter, but has instead has focused on reforming the law in two broader areas: first, being the issue of corporate criminal liability in general and, secondly, introducing a general duty for all persons directing work to take reasonable steps to ensure the safety of workers and the public. It is probably this last measure which represents the most significant departure from earlier Bill C-284. There is also a distinct element of the principle of aggregation as corporations may be liable when the actions of those with authority and other employees demonstrate criminal negligence.

15.94 The Canadian Bar Association has expressed concern that the Bill imposes liability on an 'ought to have known' or 'after-the-fact' standard. It is argued that this is unacceptable given that the legislation is criminal as opposed to regulatory and will result in severe penalties and stigma.[1] In addition, the Canadian Bar Association has argued that there is inadequate guidance as to what the use of terminology such as 'allowed the development of a common culture or attitude' actually means. An undesirable side-effect of the breadth and vagueness of the legislation is that it may deter qualified people from becoming directors of corporations or lead to the resignation of experienced directors if concerned about the imposition of criminal consequences based on an external assessment of what they should have known.

1 Canadian Bar Association, letter to the House of Commons Standing Committee on Justice and Human Rights, 17 May 2002, available at www.cba.org/CBA/News/2002_Releases/2002-05-23_corporate.asp (11 September 2003).

Enforcement and sentencing issues

15.95 Several Canadian cases offer general guidance on sentencing of corporations.[1] Recent guidance on the issue of sentencing corporations for health and safety offences is provided in the case of *R v General Scrap Iron & Metals Ltd.*[2] The employer appealed against fine of $100,000 plus 15% victim surcharge out of a total maximum allowable fine of $150,000 for conviction of failure to ensure the health and safety of an employee after an employee in his scrap metal plant was killed whilst sorting metal. On the basis that the employer had been found grossly negligent, the accident had been preventable and the employer had previous knowledge of the risk but chose to ignore it, Watson J refused to overturn the sentence. He held that the trial judge had reached a reasonable conclusion as to sentence, notwithstanding that the fine was close to the maximum for first offenders and upheld the paramount importance of deterrence in such cases. He did consider, however, that there are some notable distinctions with regards the sentencing of individuals compared with the sentencing of corporations. In that light he suggested that three issues be taken into account when sentencing corporate offender: first, the conduct, circumstances and consequences of the offence; secondly, the objectives of the relevant regulation in the context of legitimate corporate functioning in the relevant areas; and, thirdly, the participation, attitude and character of the offender in the larger context of corporations engaged in the relevant industry in a process which identifies the aggravating and mitigating factors so as to allow rational comparison between cases,[3] in a similar manner to that set out by the English Court of Appeal in the case of *R v F Howe & Son (Engineers) Ltd.*[4] It is intended that such a principled approach to sentencing of corporate offenders would offer clearer guidance to corporate behaviour and refute allegations about the arbitrariness of sanctions for such offences.[5]

1 See eg *R v United Keno Hill Mines Ltd* (1980) 10 CELR 43; *R v Hoffman La-Roche Ltd (No 2)* (1980) 56 CCC (2d) 563; *R v New Brunswick Electric Power Commission* 10 CELR (NS) 184; *R v Ford Motor Co of Canada Ltd* (1979) 49 CCC (2d) 1; *R v K Mart Canada Ltd* (1982) 66 CCC (2d) 329.
2 [2003] 5 WWR 99.
3 [2003] 5 WWR 99 at [35].
4 [1999] 2 Cr App R (S) 37.
5 [1999] 2 All ER 249.

15.96 The proposed government Bill C-45 also sets out guidance to the court in sentencing organisations. The Bill requires that courts take into account any advantage realised by the organisation as a result of the offence; the degree of planning involved in carrying out the offence and its duration and complexity; the impact of the sentence on the organisations economic viability; the cost to the public authorities of the investigation and prosecution of the offence; any regulatory penalty that was imposed; previous convictions for similar offences; any restitution the company is ordered to make; and any measures that the organisation has taken to reduce the likelihood of committing the offence. Further, the Bill also sets out a list of optional conditions of probation that a court may impose on an organisation. These include, the requirement to make restitution to any person for any loss or damage they suffered as a result of the offence; to establish policies, standards and procedures to reduce the likelihood of the organisation re-offending, including a requirement to communicate those policies to its representatives and to report back to the court on their implementation; and to comply with any other reasonable conditions that the court considers desirable to prevent the organisation from re-offending or to remedy the harm caused by the offence. This feature of the Bill represents quite an innovative use of sanctions for organisations, particularly because management time which is tied up in criminal proceedings is typically one of the most expensive aspects of criminal liability for organisations. In theory therefore, extensive use by Canadian courts of the condition of probation that organisations to report back to the court periodically, for example, may increase the deterrent impact of the law in this area. At the same time it may help to ensure that commitments to improvements within an organisation are actually implemented instead of rhetoric.

Conclusion

15.97   The issue of corporate criminal liability and responsibility for health and safety have been exhaustively reviewed in Canada over a substantial period of time. Careful attention has been paid to the experiences of other common law jurisdictions in this developing area of the law. It seems generally to have been accepted that the restrictive interpretation of the identification doctrine as expressed in recent case law is unacceptable as the sole basis of corporate liability. In the latest reforms, the Canadian government appears to have steered clear of temptation to introduce new specific offences relating to corporate liability for work related deaths, but has proposed more general reforms that the circle of liability be extended to those who exercise delegated authority. There also seems to be a greater interest in the issue of appropriate sentencing of corporations in Canada, given that the range of sanctions is invariably considered to be far more narrow for corporations than for individual offenders. In this respect, the proposed legislative amendments show some originality in the possible use of probation as a sanction on corporate offenders.

Europe

The European approach in general

15.98   In 1988 the Council of Europe made a Recommendation[1] to member states concerning the liability of enterprises, with legal personality, for offences caused in the exercise of their activities. Although it was not competent to legislate in the area of criminal law, the Council suggested the development and introduction of a system of administrative sanctions and monetary penalties for legal entities. It recommended that member states should adopt legislation which would hold corporations criminally liable, but it also clearly expressed the difficulties that could occur in arriving at a proper solution:

> 'The difficulty, due to the often complex management structure in an enterprise, of identifying the individuals responsible for the commission of an offence ...
>   The difficulty, rooted in the legal traditions of many European states, of rendering enterprises which are corporate bodies criminally liable ...

The difficulty to capture the reality of the decision-making in large modern corporations companies' and to determine 'what the company has done wrong to merit being subjected to criminal prosecution'.[2]

These difficulties find their roots in the legal traditions of the [Council of Europe] Member States. Most of their criminal laws are based on two major principles: "a person is responsible for his own acts', and 'corporations cannot make any wrong".'

1   Committee of Ministers, Council of Europe, Recommendation on Liability of Enterprises Having Legal Personality for Offences Committed in the Exercise of their Activities, Recommendation no R(88) 18, October 1988.
2   Council Recommendation R(88) 18, n 1 above.

15.99   In spite of these problems, the willingness to impose corporate liability for the specific offence of manslaughter brought about changes in the law in some member states.

France

Introduction

15.100   France has a centralised government, although its 22 regions, 95 departments, and 36,000 municipalities, enjoy a certain amount of autonomy. The French legal system is governed by the principal of unity of the civil and criminal justice system, which means that the same court can hear both criminal and civil cases.

15.101   Under both the Penal Law and the Penal Procedure, offences may be classified according to their respective seriousness: crimes, misdemeanours, and violations.[1] There are distinctions between completed and attempted acts for crimes and misdemeanours, but not for violations. The punishment for crimes and misdemeanours can result in up to 20 years' imprisonment. Crimes are also classified into crimes against the person, crimes against property and crimes against public security.[2]

1   New Penal Code, art 111-1.
2   J Borricand, 'France', *Report prepared for The World Factbook of Criminal Justice Systems under Bureau of Justice Statistics* grant no 90-BJ-CX-0002 from the Bureau of Justice Statistics to the State University of New York at Albany (1993). The project director for the World Factbook of Criminal Justice was Graeme R. Newman. Available at http://www.ojp.usdoj.gov/bjs/abstract/wfcj.htm.

15.102   'Corporate liability' is a relatively new provision in French criminal law. The former Criminal Code stated that only individuals could be held liable for criminal offences such as manslaughter if they caused death. There was no criminal legislation which governed liability for legal entities. The Penal Code was entirely reformed in 1992. Since then,[1] the French New Penal Code provides that all legal personalities may be held criminally liable. Legal persons can be liable for most of the offences provided by the Penal Code.

1   The New Penal Code came into force in 1994.

Law on corporate criminal liability

15.103   The French Penal Code, art 121-1 provides that no person may be held criminally liable except for his or her own conduct. The principle of criminal liability of legal persons has been introduced in the Penal Code by virtue of art 121-2,[1] which states that juridical persons, with the exception of the state, are criminally liable for the offences committed on their account by their organs or representatives, according to the distinctions set out in arts 121-4 and 121-7 and in the cases provided for by statute or regulations. Article 121-4 provides that the perpetrator of an offence is the person who commits the criminally prohibited act; and attempts to commit a felony or, in cases provided for by statute, a misdemeanour. Article 121-7 provides that the accomplice to a felony or a misdemeanour is the person who knowingly, by aiding and abetting, facilitates its preparation or commission and that any person who, by means of a gift, promise, threat, order, or an abuse of authority or powers, provokes the commission of an offence or gives instructions to commit it, is also an accomplice.

1   Act no 2000-647 of 10 July, art 8, OJ of 11 July 2000.

15.104   The Penal Code, art 121-3 enables the courts to charge corporations for the offence of manslaughter. It specifically refers to art 221-6 which expressly provides[1] that manslaughter is a criminal offence. These sections act as the general legal basis. These are not specific to manslaughter in the course of work. In 2000, the New Criminal Code, art 121-3 was amended: then, the legislator introduced sub-art 4, enabling courts to charge individuals for injuries that were due to a failure to comply with an obligation of due diligence or safety. Although, this subsection only governs individuals' criminal liability, it has affected the legal regime of corporate liability, extending its scope, and so from that point, directors and heads of corporations are more likely to be held responsible for such criminal offences.

1   This element is a very important, given that French law is based on the idea of *legalite des delits et des peines,* which means that 'no one may be punished for a felony or for a misdemeanour whose ingredients are not defined by law…'and 'no one may be punished a penalty which is not provided for by the law…' (Article 111-3 of the French Penal Code).

15.105   The law does not require that there be 'fault' for corporations to be held liable for such crimes, in other words the law imposes strict liability. The following conditions must be met to hold a corporation criminally liable: first, the act must be qualified as a criminal offence in law; the offence must have been committed by either a member or a representative of the corporation and the person must have acted in the name of the corporation.

15.106   The criminal liability of legal persons does not exclude natural persons who are perpetrators or accomplices to the same act, subject to the provisions of the Penal Code, art 121-3. Public bodies may also be held liable for criminal manslaughter.

15.107   The French model is based on the concept of 'the directing mind', and the Penal Code, art 121-2 is restricted by the requirement that each crime needs to mention specifically that a corporation can be punished. The application of corporate criminal liability is confined to a limited number of crimes.[1] Moreover, corporations can only be held liable under the French Penal Code when one of the legal representatives or organs of the corporations has positively acted. On the other hand, the violation of supervisory duties is considered to be sufficient to warrant proceedings on the basis of corporate criminal liability.[2]

1   See G Stessens 'Corporate Criminal Liability: A Comparative Perspective' (1994) 43 ICLQ at 496–497.

2 M Wagner 'Corporate Criminal Liability: National and International Responses', background paper for the International Society for the Reform of Criminal Law 13th International Conference, Commercial and Financial Fraud: A Comparative Perspective, Malta, 8–12 July 1999.

15.108 Sanctions under the new provisions include fines, the closure of the company and probation. Corporate fines may be up to three times higher than those imposed on a natural person.[1]

1 See Wells, **para 15.13 n 1** above.

Italy

Introduction

15.109 The system of justice in Italy is divided into the following areas: ordinary civil and criminal, administrative, accounting, military and taxation. Jurisdiction over administrative matters is exercised by Tribunali Amministravi Regionali (TAR). All criminal laws are contained within the Penal Code and other statutes and are applied throughout the whole country. The different parts of the criminal justice system are part of a state system which operates through districts and other minor territorial jurisdictions. Although each district has the power to make laws, providing they do not conflict with the Constitution, only the state has jurisdiction over substantive and procedural penal legal matters.

15.110 The Italian legal system is based on written laws made by Parliament. Criminal law defines criminal behaviour and sanctions. The basic principles of 'no penalty without a law' (nulla poena sine lege) and 'no crime without a law' (nullum crimen sine lege) are stated in the Penal Code, art 1 and in the Constitution, art 25. The Italian Penal Code that is currently in force, as amended (the so-called Rocco Code, named after the then Minister of Justice) dates back to 1930.

15.111 All criminal offences (reati) are divided by the Penal Code (Codice Penale) into two broad categories: delitti, which are serious criminal offences and contravvenzioni, which are less serious offences. The two categories are also used to classify special law statutes. The distinction between crimes classified as delitti and contravvenzioni is based on the seriousness of the crime and on the severity of punishment. Although both categories of crime are punishable by imprisonment and/ or fine, the sentences for delitti are more severe than those for the contravvenzioni. For delitti crimes, penalties may be imposed of up to 24 years' imprisonment, and as much as 30 years' or life imprisonment in special cases. For contravvenzioni crimes, the penalty imposed may be up to three years' imprisonment. Normally, sentences for contravvenzioni crimes are served in different types of prison facilities than those used for delitti. Fines vary considerably and can amount to US$500,000, for example, for serious drug offences (Penal Code, arts 22, 23 and 25).

15.112 The Penal Code generally classifies each crime under a specific heading including crimes against public safety (delitti contro l'incolumita pubblica – poisoning of food or water, drugs, arson, provoking a railway or air disaster etc), crimes against the person/violent crimes (delitti contro la persona – murder, assault, non-ransom kidnapping, defamation).[1]

1 P Marongiu, 'Italy', *Report prepared for The World Factbook of Criminal Justice Systems under Bureau of Justice Statistics* grant no 90-BJ-CX-0002 from the Bureau of Justice Statistics

514 Chapter 15

to the State University of New York at Albany (1993). The project director for the World Factbook of Criminal Justice was Graeme R. Newman. Available at http://www.ojp.usdoj.gov/ bjs/abstract/wfcj.htm.

15.113 Corporate criminal liability was not recognised in Italian law until very recently. In the Italian system, criminal responsibility was limited exclusively to natural persons. Legal persons could not be subjected to any type of sanction, including even administrative ones.[1]

1 See Draft Law 689 of 1981.

15.114 This provision has been increasingly criticised by major legal scholars. Since the beginning of the 1970s the meaning, usefulness and legitimacy of the maxim societas delinquere non potest has been questioned. In particular, it was stressed that the most serious economic crimes had been committed as a result of precise and conscious corporate policies. Therefore, the fact that these corporations were exempt from any form of sanction presented a high risk for society. It was for this reason that some legal experts proposed the introduction of provisions that would deal with legal entities as 'actively and directly involved' individuals. They emphasised the fact that the elimination of the maxim societas delinquere non potest was not in opposition to the principle of culpability in the Constitution, art 27, para 1.[1]

1 A Manna and E Infante *ITALY, Criminal Justice Systems in Europe and North America* Helsinki (Finland) : HEUNI, the European Institute for Crime Prevention and Control affiliated with the United Nations, 2000, (series; national criminal justice profile series), available at http://www.heuni.fi/uploads/3muutxlfl.pdf

15.115 A new statute, 'Decreto Legislativo'[1], was enacted in 2001 to rectify a problem created by the Italian Constitution which provided that 'criminal responsibility could only be imposed on individuals'[2] that meant that only a natural person could be charged for a criminal offence. The statute was designed to ensure that companies would be regarded as legal persons at law, and could be held criminally liable for offences committed in their names. The adoption of the Italian statute was designed to enforce European Conventions and Protocols[3]in Italian law.

1 Italian Constitution, art 27.
2 DLgs (Legislative Decree) of June 8, 2001 n. 231. Published in Gazzetta Ufficiale n 140 of 19 June 2001. A 'Decreto Legislativo' (often shortened as 'D Lgs') is a complex statute passed by the government after a 'Legge' has instructed it to do so (see the Constitution, art 76).
3 These texts recommended that legal personalities be liable for a range of offences.

The law on corporate liability for health and safety offences and deaths in the workplace

15.116 The new statute[1] classified offences committed by corporations as administrative ones. However this may be misleading.

'... Companies will be liable for criminal offences and not just administrative misdemeanours, the fact that case will be heard in the criminal courts rather than administrative tribunals, and the fact that criminal rather than administrative procedures will be in force, all suggest that the contemplated liability is more criminal than administrative in nature. Significantly, under Article 8 of the statute, a company can be held responsible even if it is not possible to identify or convict the human perpetrator of the offence.'[2]

1 DLgs (Legislative Decree) of 8 June 2001 n 231 (Decreto Legislativo).

2 J Gobert and E Mugnai 'Coping with Corporate Criminality: Some Lessons from Italy' [2002] Crim LR 619 at 624.

15.117 According to Italian law corporate liability arises in two ways. First, when the crime is committed by the head of the corporation, the director, or manager. The decreto legislativo provides that a legal personality can be criminally liable for a lethal injury caused either by its director,[1] or a subsidiary.[2] Art. 5 of the Decreto Legislativo 231/2001 distinguishes between acts that are committed by the heads of the corporation, its directors, or managers (art 5(1)(a)) and those that are committed by its subordinate staff (art 5(1)(b)). Article 5(1)(b) creates a liability which can be imposed on a corporations for the acts of those who do not constitute the directing mind of the corporation. This provision establishes a regime of vicarious liability. Article 5 requires proof that the offence either was 'an expression of corporate policy', or that it was the result of 'structural negligence within the corporation'.[3] Furthermore, art 5(2) requires that the offence should be committed 'in the interest and for the benefit of the corporation'.

1 Art 5(1)(b), D.Lgs, 231/2001.
2 Art 5(1)(a), D.Lgs, 231/2001.
3 Gobert and Mugnai, **para 15.116 n 1** above, at 625.

15.118 The second situation is one in which corporate liability arises 'which is based on the negligence of a corporate body in not considering that the offence which has been committed might have occurred, and in not having in place a mechanism to avert its commission'.[1] A company can be held criminally liable for manslaughter if death was caused by a management failure of the corporation. This provision allows the company to be held responsible even when it is not possible to determine which person committed the offence.

1 Gobert and Mugnai, **para 15.116 n 1** above, at 625.

15.119 Articles 6 and 7 of the DLgs 231/2001 provide for the defence of due diligence. Article 6 sets out the defence which is to be used by those who are in control of the corporation. Article 7 creates the defence which might be used by subordinates. The defence of due diligence allows the corporation to show that an appropriate control system was in place. This will discharge the onus of proof on the accused; it then falls on the prosecution to rebut the defence and to prove that the system was either 'inadequate or ineffective to prevent offences of the kind that occurred'.[1]

1 Gobert and Mugnai, **para 15.116 n 1** above, at 628.

15.120 The introduction of criminal liability is a major change in Italian criminal law. The statute, however, is restricted as to its applicability. It applies solely to profit making organisations, whether or not they are incorporated, and it does not apply to public bodies. Non-profit-making organisations are seen as 'acting for the benefit of the State and its citizens' and thus should not be prosecuted.

The Netherlands

Introduction

15.121 The Kingdom of The Netherlands is a constitutional and hereditary monarchy. The Netherlands is divided into 12 provinces and 672 municipalities. Each province has an elected representative body known as the Provincial Assembly. Central legislative power is vested in the Crown and Parliament, comprising two chambers (States-General). The first or upper chamber (Erste Kamer) is elected by the Provincial Council; the second or lower chamber (Tweede Kamer) is elected under a system of direct universal suffrage and proportional representation. Both the Second Chamber and the Crown may propose legislation; the First Chamber may only approve or reject legislation without amendment.

15.122   The principal laws which guide the criminal justice system in The Netherlands are the Constitution, the Criminal or Penal Code, the Code of Criminal Procedure and Special Acts. All prohibited acts are classified either as crimes or felonies (misdrijven), infractions or transgressions (overtredingen). The legislature determines whether an offence constitutes a crime or an infraction.[1] Generally, serious offences involving physical harm are classified as crimes or felonies (murder, intentional homicide, theft combined with violence etc). The classification of an offence determines the level of the court that will try the case at first instance. In general, transgressions are tried in cantonal courts and crimes are tried in district courts.[2]

1   P Tak *Criminal Justice Systems in Europe: The Netherlands*, HEUNI (European   Institute for Crime Prevention and Control, affiliated with the United Nations Deventer: Kluwer Law and Taxation Publishers, 1993
2   W Hoyng and F Schlingmann 'The Netherlands' in M Sheridan and J Cameron (eds) *EC Legal Systems: An Introductory Guide* (London: Butterworths, 1992), pp 1–42.

15.123   The Netherlands was one of the first European countries to establish criminal liability for legal persons, including liability for manslaughter. This was established in two steps. First, in 1951 law-makers decided that corporate bodies could 'commit' an offence. However, at that time, legal persons could only be held liable for offences committed against public welfare. Secondly, in 1976, the Dutch Criminal Code was amended, so that it now provides that both natural persons and corporations can be held liable for a wide range of offences, including battery and involuntary manslaughter.[1]

1   Dutch Criminal Code, art 51.

The law on corporate criminal liability

15.124   The Dutch Criminal Code, art 51 states that 'offences can be committed by natural persons and corporations'. The explanatory memorandum to this article provides a list of offences that might be committed by a corporation and manslaughter is included. A corporation can be thus both charged and sentenced.[1]

1   Dutch Criminal Code, art 51.

15.125   Under Dutch law, criminal liability can be imposed on any legal person, including corporations. For instance, in the case of *Ijzerdaad*, both the Courts of Appeal[1] and the Supreme Court held that an export firm was criminally liable, although it was unincorporated and owned by a sole proprietor.

1   Hoge Raad, 23 February 1954, NJ 378.

15.126   Public bodies can also be held criminally liable under the Dutch criminal law. A good illustration of this can be seen in the case *Rechtbank Leeuwarden*.[1] Here, the governing body of a hospital was charged 'with grossly negligently failing to ensure properly that old, redundant anaesthetic equipment was removed from the hospital or made unusable'.[2] The equipment had not been properly maintained since it was not listed in the hospital's itinerary, and the hospital had failed to ensure that the replacement of old equipment was properly carried out. This equipment therefore, was still used in an operation. In this particular instance the technicians, who acted without proper supervision, connected the tubes wrongly. This last act of negligence caused the death of a patient. On 23 December 1987, the Dutch courts convicted the hospital's governing body of negligent homicide. This was the first case in The Netherlands where manslaughter charges were successfully brought against a corporation.

1   Hospital Case, Rechtbank Leeuwarden, 23 December 23 1987, partially reported at NJ 1988, 981.
2   S Field and N Jörg 'Corporate Liability and Manslaughter: Should We Be Going Dutch?' [1991] Crim LR 156 at 157.

15.127   According to Dutch law corporations can be held liable irrespective of who committed the offence, whether they are mere employees or heads of corporations with the power of control. The law is not based on principle of identification. There is a suggestion that corporate criminal liability is based on two main principles of 'power' and 'acceptance'.[1] This is a twofold test. The court must first determine whether the company had the power to determine whether the employee carried out the reprehensible act. If the answer is positive, the court must then try to establish whether the corporation usually 'accepts' such acts.

1   See S Field and N Jörg, **para 15.126 n 2** above, in citing the *Kabeljauw Case*, Hoge Raad, 1 July 1981, NJ 1982, 80 and the *IJzerdraad Case*, Hoge Raad, 23 February 1954, N.J. 1954, 378.

15.128   Stewart Field and Nico Jörg stated that '"acceptance" involves making a judgement on the corporate monitoring of risks or illegal behaviour and "power" is a judgement on the corporate response to those risks'.[1] These principles are largely concerned with the organisation and management of the company. A company, however, is able to escape liability if it can prove that there was nothing it could have done to eliminate the risks and the unfortunate consequences were beyond its powers.

1   Field and Jörg, **para 15.126 n 2** above, at 157.

15.129   A proper application of the principle of 'power and acceptance' leads to corporations being liable for corporate manslaughter if the company has not acted in accordance with the expected standards of health and safety. As a result, although no one might be directly at fault, the company may be convicted of manslaughter, because of the general failure of the corporation to take proper steps to ensure an adequate system of health and safety at work.

15.130   The Dutch approach is important in that it concentrates on corporate behaviour and recognises corporate fault rather than individual fault. The arguments considered in the paper by Field and Jörg were referred to in a report published by the Accident Prevention Unit of the Health and Safety Executive in 1989 which stated:

'The report notes that in organisations where safety is not considered paramount individuals may be unwilling to follow good safety procedures for fear of being criticized or even disciplined. Furthermore, where priorities are confused, safety is likely to come into conflict with commercial pressures. Thus even individual acts of negligence are often identifiable as a product of collective responses.'[1]

1   Field and Jörg, **para 15.126 n 2** above.

15.131   Dutch law recognises that because the corporations' pressure can shape the behaviour of an individual, who acts in accordance with corporate policies and structure, the corporation should be considered as a collective entity rather than as a group of individuals who might be identified.

Germany

Introduction

15.132   The legal system in Germany is guided by federal laws which are created by the Bundestag or Lower House of the German Parliament and approved by the Upper House (Bundesrat). Federal laws apply nationwide. Those specifically applicable to the criminal justice system are the Criminal Code (Strafgesetzbuch, StGB)[1] and the Code of Criminal Procedure (Strafprozeßordnung, StPO). Among other laws which concern the criminal justice system are the Gesetz ber Ordnungswidrigkeiten (OWiG) or laws governing administrative or regulatory offences.

1   The Criminal Code was promulgated on 13 November 1998 (Federal Law Gazette I, pp 945, 3322).

15.133   Federal laws establish a framework for the 16 individual states or Länder.[1] The states have their own constitution and create their own special laws. The Penal Code (StGB), and the Code of Criminal Procedure (StPO), are federal Codes, which have national application. The administration of the criminal justice system (police, courts and correctional institutions) are matters left for the individual states.

1   P Wilkitzki 'Comments on Developments in Germany' in A Eser, G Heine and B Huber (eds) *Criminal Responsibility of Legal and Collective Entities* (1998).

15.134   As with other European countries criminal offences in German law can be categorised as Verbrechen, crimes or felonies, and Vergehen, misdemeanours. Less serious offences have, through a lengthy reform process, either been decriminalized, upgraded into misdemeanours, or reclassified as Ordnungswidrigkeiten, regulatory or administrative offences. Verbrechen comprise serious offences involving severe injury or extensive property damage or loss (for instance, homicide, rape, robbery, arson) which is punishable by a minimum prison sentence of up to one year, whereas Vergehen are offences such as simple assault, theft, vandalism, and are punishable by sentences of less than one year or a fine.[1]

1   AA Aronowitz *Germany, Report prepared for The World Factbook of Criminal Justice Systems under Bureau of Justice Statistics* grant no 90-BJ-CX-0002 (1993), available at www.ojp.usdoj.gov/bjs/abstract/wfcj.htm

15.135   There is no principle of 'corporate liability' under German criminal law, as it does not currently provide for criminal liability for legal persons or associations of persons. 'Corporate manslaughter', for example, was not mentioned in the ruling on the ICE-disaster at Eschede, a rail accident where 101 people were killed in 1998. Although three persons were to some extent blameworthy, the court dismissed the case for formal reasons. An appeal against this decision to the Constitutional Court (Bundesverfassungsgericht) was unsuccessful.

15.136   According to German criminal law criminal penalties may only be imposed on natural persons.[1] Instead of the imposition of criminal liability on legal persons, the German legal system provides for a mechanism of liability on legal persons under laws governing administrative or regulatory offences. As a consequence, only non-criminal fines can be imposed as penalties on corporations. Furthermore, measures of confiscation and forfeiture can be ordered against legal persons, where this is necessary for the purpose of confiscating the financial advantage gained as a result of the offence.[2]

1 G Fieberg, 'National Developments in Germany: An Overview' in Eser, Heine and Huber (eds), **para 15.133 n 1** above, p 83.
2 B Shloer and O Filipenko 'Criminal liability of legal persons Criminal Codes examples (within the context of the corruption offences): European states experience', Ukrainian-European Policy and Legal Advice Centre, project funded by European Union implemented by GTZ-IRZ-PLEY Consortium.

Law on corporate criminal liability

15.137 In Germany, liability on corporations may be imposed by state authorities only for administrative infractions such as health and safety offences. In most cases a breach of health and safety regulations, such as the breach of duty of care or the violation of administrative orders, can give rise to administrative sanctions. Administrative offences are governed by the Code of Criminal Procedure (StPO) and the Ordnungswidrigkeitengesetz (OWiG). The German law of Ordnungswidrigkeiten (administrative penalties) empowers administrative authorities, generally the Labour Inspectorate, as well as criminal courts to impose administrative fines (Geldbußen) on both natural persons and companies.[1] The key provision for the sanctioning of corporations is OWiG, s 30,[2] which calls for the imposition of fines on corporate entities. The class of natural persons, whose acts may make the corporation liable, is very limited.[3] In general, liability is restricted to instances in which the company's legal representatives or directors have acted improperly or failed to supervise their employees properly. So far, German policy towards corporate liability is very restrictive compared with that of other European countries. In Germany, penalties imposed on corporations may, at most, be regarded as 'quasi-criminal' sanctions.[4]

1 R Hefendehl 'Corporate Criminal Liability: Model Penal Code Section 2.07 and the Development in Western Legal Systems' (2000) 4 Buffalo Crim LR 283.
2 Several translations for this law exist, among them are Regulatory Offences Act and Law of Administrative Sanctions.
3 See OwiG, s 30.
4 Hefendehl, n 1 above.

15.138 There has been much debate in legal circles about whether such penalties should be considered criminal sanctions or administrative penalties. Today, they are not perceived as criminal sanctions either by the public or by defendants, even when imposed by a criminal court, and are viewed in a similar way to that of regulatory offences in the UK.[1]

1 Wagner, **para 15.107** n 2 above.

15.139 Criminal sanctions can be imposed on natural persons. Those who are found guilty of causing accidents through fault may be liable to be charged with general criminal offences, such as negligent manslaughter under the Criminal Code, s 222, or bodily injury by negligence under s 230, or dangerous construction under s 323 [1] (Strafgesetzbuch, StGB). Criminal negligence requires proof of personal breach of a duty on the part of the employer and foreseeability of the consequences of this breach.

1 The terms Criminal Code and Penal Code are adopted from translation of existing literature. However, there is no substantial difference in meaning between the two terms.

Enforcement

15.140   The enforcement of health and safety law in Germany is the task of two bodies, the Labour Inspectorate and the Insurance Associations. Compliance with health and safety law in Germany at the state level is monitored by the Labour Inspectorates (Gewerbeaufsicht). The Labour Inspectorates are overseen by and are answerable to elected political representatives of the Länder. Each Land is compelled to set up a Labour Inspectorate under the Industry Act, s 139b (Gewerbeordnung) and is free to decide both the organisation and the functions of its Labour Inspectorate although the fundamental principles governing the activities of the Inspectorates are similar throughout Germany. Their responsibilities include the observance of technical, medical and social regulations intended to ensure acceptable standards of health and safety at work. The Labour Inspectorates also have responsibility to monitor employers who put the health and safety of the general public at risk as a consequence of the work activities they are undertaking.

15.141   In addition to the state system, there is a further system for worker protection administered by the Employers' Liability Insurance Associations (Berufsgenossenschaften, BG). The 35 German BG or institutions for statutory accident insurance and prevention represent different branches of trade and industry. Every company is required by law to be a member of one of these Associations who are the providers of statutory accident insurance and have as their main aims the prevention of industrial accidents and occupational diseases, and the compensation, rehabilitation and promotion of vocational retraining for person injured at work.[1] The BG insure employees against the consequences of occupational accidents, accidents on the way to and from work and occupational diseases. Because the employer has a statutory obligation to insure its employees against accidents with one of the BGs, it will not be held liable for the personal injury of its employees injured by accident at work unless it has caused such injury intentionally.

1   See European Commission *Labour Inspection (Health and Safety) in the European Union, A Short Guide* (1999).

15.142   Both the Labour Inspectorate and the Insurance Associations have similar powers at their disposal, but the technical inspectors of the Insurance Associations are regarded as more of an advisory body whilst the labour inspectors of the Länder are often referred to as the 'police', because they can ultimately shut down production. The Labour Inspectorates may issue admonitions, warnings, inspection reports, orders and prosecutions. Orders have a legally binding effect and in case of non-compliance can be enforced by an action for specific performance under the Administrative Procedure Acts of the Länder. Orders issued by the technical inspectors of the Insurance Associations are generally based on the State Insurance Act, s 712 (*Reichsversicherungsordnung*) and are also legally binding. Non-compliance with these orders can lead to administrative action resulting in sanctions.

15.143   The Accident Insurance Associations are also empowered to impose administrative sanctions on the employer or employee for breaches of an accident prevention regulation intentionally or negligently[1] or committal of an administrative offence under the State Insurance Act, s 710. However, as with their British counterparts in the Health and Safety Executive, both organisations are encouraged to advise the employers before prosecuting.[2] There has been an attempt to co-ordinate the activities of both enforcing bodies in Germany.[3] In practice, however, they tend to work independently of each other.

1 State Insurance Act, s 710 (*Reichsversicherungsordnung*, RVO) of 19 July 1911.
2 K Koch and N Salter 'The Health and Safety System in the Federal Republic of Germany' (1999) 30(1) Industrial Relations Journal 61 at 67.
3 See R Wank, 'Germany' in R Baldwin and T Daintith (eds) *Harmonization and Hazard: Regulating Health and Safety in the European Workplace* (1992) pp 49–75 at p 68.

15.144 In cases of death at work an investigation is carried out by the police, who are empowered, in this respect, by the Code of Criminal Procedure, s 163. The results of the investigation are sent to the prosecutor's office. In urgent cases, however, the case can be sent directly to the court. The sentences, which are imposed by the court, are mainly fines and imprisonment. Fines range from 2 to 10,000 Euros depending on the offender's income. Imprisonment can range from six months to 15 years (StGB, ss 38, 39). Life imprisonment is imposed for murder and may be imposed for manslaughter. Cases of negligent manslaughter are dealt with by the State Attorney. Crimes of manslaughter carry a mandatory sentence of imprisonment.1 Only a natural person can be found guilty of manslaughter.

1 AA Alexis *Germany, Report prepared for The World Factbook of Criminal Justice Systems under Bureau of Justice Statistics*, grant no 90-BJ-CX-0002 (1993), available at www.ojp.usdoj/ gov/bjs/abstract/wfcj.htm#G.

15.145 The German legislature has established a working group in early 1998, which was given the task to review and improve the current situation by strengthening the role of criminal law with regard to corporate entities.[1] Discussions have now started in Germany as to whether it would be wise to introduce and codify a crime of corporate manslaughter and thereby follow the example and overall development seen in other jurisdictions. Traditionally there has been an aversion to the attribution such crimes to companies. So far, this view is still reflected by the courts. During the current economic crises new developments are likely to be kept on hold.

1 Wagner, **para 15.107 n 2** above.

Finland

Introduction

15.146 Finland is a republic with a strongly centralised government. The country is divided into 12 provinces, which in turn are divided into 248 police districts, each of which generally comprises one or two municipalities. The criminal law is contained in the Criminal Code 1889 and separate statutes such as the Young Offenders Act 1939, the Narcotics Act 1972, the Traffic Act 1981 and the Conditional Sentences Act 1918. The law on criminal procedure is contained in the Code of Judicial Procedure 1734. Both the Criminal Code and the Code of Judicial Procedure have undergone several amendments since their enactment.

15.147 In Finland, there are no general distinctions or categories of crime. Rather, 'offence' distinctions are based on the expected punishment for the offence, or the 'penal latitude' defined by law.

15.148 Up to 1996 according to Finnish criminal law only a natural person could be held liable for the commission of a criminal offence. There were sanctions that could be imposed on corporations and the like, the most important of which were probably sanctions for damages caused by crimes committed in their operation. These sanctions, however, did not carry substantial criminal weight, rather they were considered as regulatory or administrative matters. The opportunities to develop a range of sanctions that could be imposed on crimes committed by the activities of 'artificial' persons without imposing direct criminal liability on them were, however, considered to be very limited.[1]

1   J Muhonen 'The proposed legislation for criminal liability of enterprises in Finland' (1995) 6 ICCLR 1 at 3–5.

15.149   Since then, however, the situation has changed. According to the current Finnish Penal Code[1] a corporation may be held to be criminally liable for any criminal offence defined by Finnish criminal law.[2] According to the Penal Code a corporation may be sentenced to a corporate fine, if an offender has been an accomplice to an offence or allowed the commission of the offence or if the care and diligence necessary for the prevention of the offence has not been observed. A corporate fine may be imposed even if the offender cannot be identified.[3] The offender is the person who acted on behalf or for the benefit of the corporation, and belongs to its management or is in a service or employment relationship with it or has acted on assignment by a representative of the corporation.[4]

1   626/1996.
2   Penal Code, 626/1996, Ch 1 Scope of application of the criminal law of Finland.
3   Penal Code, Ch 9, s 2.
4   Penal Code, Ch 9, s 3.

Law on corporate criminal liability

15.150   Death at work is usually a result of the failure to comply and follow health and safety requirements. The Act which governs protection of employees at workplace against health and safety risks and hazards is the Labour Protection Act (Occupational Safety and Health Act) 299/1958 which was amended by several Acts including no 223/90. The employer is in charge of all occupational safety and health matters at the workplace.[1] Since there is no provision in Finnish health and safety law for proceedings to be taken against a corporation, a prosecution may only be taken against an individual or individuals within a company.

1   See the Labour Protection Act, 299/58, s 9(2).

15.151   Corporations, however, can be criminally liable under the Finnish Penal Code, Ch 9.[1] The principle, however, is still focused on a natural person committing the criminal offence in question. The criminal liability of legal persons is therefore structured around liability for the actions of the natural persons within a corporation, which is similar to the identification principle which currently governs English law on corporate manslaughter. The general prerequisite for liability is that of the management of the corporation which has itself committed the crime or served as an accomplice thereto, the management has allowed a crime to be committed, or the required diligence and caution have not been observed in the operation of the enterprise.[2]

1   743/1995.
2   Penal Code, 743/1995, Ch 9, s 2(1) Prerequisites for liability.

15.152   The offence has to be committed as part of the operation of the corporation. The offence has to be committed on its behalf or for its benefit. The relationship between cause and effect regarding the lack of diligence and the crime is also required.[1]

1 Penal Code, s 3 Connection between offender and corporation.

15.153 There is, however, another prerequisite for corporate criminal liability, which is that a corporate fine may be imposed even if the offender cannot be identified. However, no corporate fine will be imposed for a complainant offence, which has not been reported by a complainant with a view to having charges brought, unless there can be shown to be a very important public interest in bringing charges.[1] In other words, a fine can also be imposed on a corporation when no individual can be identified from within the corporation or when criminal proceedings cannot be brought against this individual for one reason or another. What is required is the identification of 'organisational fault'. No burden of proof is placed on the organisation but the prosecutor must show the prerequisites for a crime according to established principles.[2] English law does not currently provide for this type of liability.

1 Penal Code, s 2(2) Prerequisites for liability.
2 Muhonen, **para 148 n 1** above, at 3–5.

Enforcement

15.154 In general, in cases of wilful intent or negligence and normally following an accident, an inspector may draw up a report for the public prosecutor who will initiate an investigation by the police, will have the necessary powers to ensure that compliance is achieved and sanction the employer for breach of health and safety provisions. Any prosecution which follows may lead to an offender being fined or sent to prison.

15.155 An employer who infringes the Labour Protection Act will be punished by a fine, or, depending on the circumstances, by imprisonment for a term of not more than six months, unless heavier penalties are prescribed by law.[1] If because of the negligence of an official, the provisions of the Labour Protection Act relating to work that he or she directs or supervises are not observed, the official in question will also be punished by a fine or, depending on the circumstances, by imprisonment for a term of not more than six months.[2] Any representative of the employer will be similarly sanctioned whenever his or her act or omission is to be considered as the fault of the representative and a violation of his or her duties. When the case is heard, the duties and powers of the representative are taken into consideration, as well as their competence and their share, in general, in the origin and continuation of the infringement.[3]

1 Labour Protection Act, s 49(1).
2 Labour Protection Act, s 49(3).
3 Labour Protection Act, s 49(4).

15.156 When sentencing a corporation and where a corporate fine is being considered under the provisions of the Finnish Penal Code, the court takes into account the nature and extent of the corporate neglect and the participation of the management in the offence; the status of the offender as a member of the organs of the corporation; the seriousness of the offence committed in the operations of the corporation and the extent of the criminal activity; the other consequences of the offence to the corporation; the measures by the corporation to prevent new offences, to prevent or remedy the effects of the offence or to further the investigation of the neglect or offence; and where a member of the management of the corporation is sentenced to a punishment, the size of the corporation and the share of the corporation held by the offender, as well as the personal liability of the offender for the commitments of the corporation.[1] The corporate fine ranges between minimum of FIM 5,000 and maximum of FIM 5,000,000.

1   Finnish Penal Code, Ch 9, s 4.

15.157   The amount of the corporate fine is determined in accordance with the nature and extent of the neglect and the participation of the management, as referred to in the Penal Code, Ch 9, s 2, and the financial standing of the corporation. When evaluating the significance of the neglect and the participation of the management, the court must take into account the nature and seriousness of the offence; the status of the offender as a member of the organs of the corporation; whether the violation of the obligations of the corporation manifests heedlessness of the law or the orders of the authorities; as well as the bases for sentencing provided elsewhere in law. When evaluating the financial standing of the corporation, the court must take into account the size of the corporation and its solvency, as well as the earnings and the other essential indicators of the financial standing of the corporation

15.158   The public prosecutor may waive the bringing of charges against a corporation, if the corporate neglect or participation of the management are of minor significance, or if only minor damage or danger has been caused by the offence committed in the operations of the corporation and the corporation has voluntarily taken the necessary measures to prevent new offences.

15.159   The bringing of charges may be waived also if the member of the management of the corporation has already been sentenced to a punishment and it is to be anticipated that the corporation for this reason will not be sentenced to a corporate fine.[1]

1   Penal Code, Ch 9, s 7.

15.160   If a corporation is at the same time to be sentenced for two or more offences, multiple fines may be imposed, except for two offences, one of which was committed after a corporate fine had already been imposed. If charges are brought against a corporation which has been previously sentenced to a corporate fine, for an offence committed before the said sentence was passed, a joint corporate fine will not be imposed, but the prior corporate fine will be taken into account during sentencing.[1]

1   Penal Code, Ch 9, s 8.

Sweden

Introduction

15.161   Swedish law, draws on Germanic, Roman, and Anglo-American law, and is neither codified to the same extent as France and other countries influenced by the Napoleonic Code, nor as dependent on judicial practice and precedents as in the UK Australia, Canada or the US. Legislative and judicial institutions include the Swedish Parliament (Riksdag), the Supreme Court, the Supreme Administrative Court, the Labour Court, Commissions of Inquiry, the Law Council, District Courts and Courts of Appeal, the Chief Public Prosecutor, the Bar Association, and ombudsmen who oversee the application of laws with particular attention to abuses of authority

15.162   Much of Swedish criminal law is based on legislation, while case law plays a smaller, albeit, an important role. The first Penal Code in Sweden came into force in 1734. This Penal Code was replaced in 1864.[1] The current Swedish Penal Code was adopted in 1962 and entered into force on1 January 1965. It governs the provisions for most of the acts that constitute crimes in Sweden. The provisions on other crimes are to be found in special legislation. It also contains general provisions on all crimes, the sanctions for crimes and the applicability of Swedish law.

1   OOH Wilkstrom and L Dolmen *Sweden, Report prepared for The World Factbook of Criminal Justice Systems under Bureau of Justice Statistics*, grant no 90-BJ-CX-0002 (1993), available at www.ojp.usdoj/gov/bjs/abstract/wfcj.htm#G.

15.163   The Swedish Penal Code does not differentiate between crimes and infractions. The classification of crime in the official crime statistics is based on the definitions of crimes given in the Penal Code. However, the main groups of crimes are divided into subcategories. These divisions are not systematic but are guided by general principles. The subdivisions have developed over a long period and have been determined from a pragmatic point of view.[1]

1   Swedish Penal Code 1962, as amended in 1999, English translation by Norman Bishop, Ds 1999:36.

15.164   A corporation cannot be held liable for a criminal offence, such as manslaughter under Swedish criminal law. Liability for death at work may only be imposed on natural persons under the Swedish Penal Code.

Law on corporate criminal liability

15.165   The corporation may be held liable for administrative offences, such as the infringement of health and safety provisions in the workplace. These offences are defined in Swedish work environment legislation, for example, where employers fail to take the necessary precautions to prevent their employees from being exposed to health hazards or accident risks.[1] However, there is no concept of 'corporate criminal liability' under the Swedish Penal Code.

1   Work Environment Act 1977 no 1160 of 1977, Ch 3, s 2, as amended by Act no 585 of 2002.

15.166   The Swedish Work Environment Act 1977, as amended, and its subordinate legislation sets out those situations where the liability will arise and provides various sanctions such as penalties, fines and sometimes imprisonment. Liability arises when a person intentionally or negligently fails to comply with an injunction or a prohibition notice issued by the Labour Inspectorate. These provisions are similar to the liability which arises under the UK's Health and Safety at Work Act 1974 for non-compliance with the requirement or prohibition imposed by an improvement notice or a prohibition notice issued by the Health and Safety Executive.[1]

1   See the Health and Safety at Work Act 1974, s 33.

15.167   In contrast with British legislation, the Work Environment Act 1977 does not create an offence or impose liability for contravening the main duty to take all necessary measures to safeguard employees from ill health or injury imposed on the employer. Rather the Swedish Act penalises the defendant for non-compliance with well-defined and prescribed provisions.[1]

1   V Howes and FB Wright *Health and Safety Law and Environmental Law in Sweden* report prepared for TXU plc (1999).

15.168   In cases where the infringement of health and safety provisions results in an accident from which a death results, or there are serious injuries or others are endangered, a natural person will be held criminally liable under the Penal Code (Ds 1999:36).[1] The relevant sections are contained in Pt 2 of the Code. Section 7 provides that a person who through carelessness causes the death of another shall be sentenced for *causing another's death* to imprisonment for up to two years or, if the crime is petty, to a fine. If the crime is gross, a term of imprisonment will be imposed of between six months and six years. Section 8 states that a person who through carelessness causes another to suffer bodily injury or illness not of a petty nature, shall be sentenced for *causing bodily injury or illness* to a fine or imprisonment for up to six months. If the crime is gross, a term of imprisonment for up to four years will be imposed. Section 9 provides that a person who through gross carelessness exposes another to mortal danger or danger of severe bodily injury or serious illness, shall be sentenced for *creating danger to another* to a fine or for a term of imprisonment for up to two years. And finally, the Penal Code, s 10 states that where a crime is referred to in the Penal Code, ss 7–9 has been committed by a person with intent or by carelessly neglecting his duty under the Work Environment Act 1977[2] to prevent sickness or accidents, the punishment will be for an *environmental offence* and as provided for in the said provisions.

1   Ds 1999:36. The Swedish Penal Code, as amended, was adopted in 1962 and entered into force in 1965.
2   Law 1977:1160.

15.169   By way of summary, according to Swedish law, only natural persons can commit crimes. However, a corporate fine can be imposed on a company owner for a crime committed in the exercise of business activities at the instance of a public prosecutor if the crime has entailed gross disregard for the special obligations associated with the business activities or is otherwise of a serious kind, and the owner of the company has not done what could reasonably be required of him or her to ensure the prevention of the crime. These provisions, however, will not apply if the crime was directed against the owner or if it would otherwise be manifestly unreasonable to impose a corporate fine.[1]

1   Ds 1999:36, Ch 36, s 7 (Law 1986:1007)

15.170   The company owner may also be vicariously liable for the crime committed by a person working in the company even if that person does not have a leading position. The conditions are that the crime has signified a serious disregard of the special responsibilities which are connected with the business or any other way is by a serious kind and that the company owner has not taken reasonable measures to prevent it.

15.171   A corporate fine, in this instance, consists of not less than ten thousand Swedish crowns and not more than three million Swedish crowns.[1] In determining the amount of a corporate fine, special consideration is given to the nature and extent of the crime and to its relation to the business activity.[2]

1   Ds 1999:36, Ch 36, s 8 (Law 1986:118).
2   Ds 1999:36, Ch 36, s 9 (Law 1986:118).

Enforcement

15.172   Enforcement of the Swedish Work Environment laws and prevention of so-called health and safety 'crimes' is the task of the National Board of Occupational Safety and Health (Arbetarskyddsstyrelsen), which is the central administrative authority, similar in its constitution and remit to the Health and Safety Commission in the UK, and the Labour Inspectorate which is accountable to the National Board.[1] The Labour Inspectorate and the National Board of Occupational Safety and Health have wide-ranging powers to order or prohibit certain measures; including the employment of persons under 18 years; the prescription of penalties for non-compliance with their rules; the making of rules for access to premises and the summoning of the police for assistance. Inspectors are also empowered to visit a workplace at any time; to question both employers and employees about matters connected with occupational safety and health and working conditions; to take photographs and measurements, to take samples of substances and products for analysis. The Labour Inspectorate may issue inspection notices if deficiencies need to be rectified, injunctions (for example, to improve the machinery guarding) and prohibitions (for example, to prohibit the use of a particular machine). The Labour Inspectorate is also empowered to set contingent fines.[2] In general, the powers of the Swedish Labour Inspectorate is very similar to those of the Health and Safety Executive under the Health and Safety at Work etc Act 1974, s 20 in the UK.

1   The Swedish National Safety and Health Administration *European Co-operation*, available at www.arbsky.se/europe.htm.
2   Howes and Wright, **para 15.167 n 1** above.

15.173   The Swedish Work Environment Act 1977, as amended, and its subordinate legislation provide for various sanctions including penalties, fines and, in some circumstances, imprisonment. If penalties which become payable by the corporation for non-compliance and which are not regarded as criminal sanctions, but rather as administrative ones, have not been instituted, a natural person representing the employer, including directors of the companies, may be required to pay a fine or to serve a term of imprisonment of up to one year for deliberate or negligent infringements of the Act or subordinate legislation.

15.174   In cases of death at work an investigation will be carried out by Sweden's Public Prosecution Office and this may be result in a natural person being charged with manslaughter under the Swedish Penal Code. A prosecution may be taken against an employer where there is evidence of criminal negligence. Proceedings will be instigated by the Crown Prosecutor following an investigation by the police. The Labour Inspectorate may be asked to give technical support during this investigation. Breaches of certain legal requirements will automatically be referred to the Prosecutor, for example, if pressure vessels have not been tested, or where there has been the employment of minors in certain work or the use of certain chemicals without a permit.[1]

1   Senior Labour Inspectors Committee, European Commission *Labour Inspection (Health and Safety) in the European Union, A Short Guide* (1999).

15.175   The sanctions, ie fines and imprisonment of up to six years, provided by the Swedish Penal Code, can only be levied against physical persons, such as directors or managers of the company. It is not surprising, therefore, that in complex cases, with large corporations when it is difficult to define a person who is responsible for the crime, that the prosecution may ultimately be fruitless. A good example of this is a recent case where more than 50 patient deaths worldwide were caused by the dialyser filters manufactured by Baxter's plant in Ronneby, Sweden.[1]

1   See www.fdanews.com/pub/ddl/29_2/deviceapprovals/2144-1.html (11 January 2002).

Norway

Introduction

15.176   Norway is a unified state in which governmental power is divided between the judiciary, executive and legislative branches, each of which is mutually independent. The executive branch is made up of the King and members of the Cabinet. Legislative power is vested in the national parliament (Stortinget). Although the parliament is unicameral, it is divided into two chambers (the Lagting and Odelsting) for the purpose of passing legislation. Both chambers must approve a bill before it can be passed.

15.177   For administrative and political purposes, the country is divided into 19 counties (fylker) and approximately 450 municipalities (kommuner). The Norwegian system is similar to the legal systems of the other Nordic countries, particularly those of Denmark and Sweden. Similarly to these countries Norwegian courts do not attach the same weight to judicial precedents as the members of the judiciary in common law countries.

15.178   Criminal law is mostly to be found in the Penal Code, which groups criminal offences into felonies (forbrytelser) and misdemeanours (forseelser). Felonies are, with some exceptions, offences which carry a maximum penalty exceeding three months' imprisonment. The majority of felonies are defined and listed in the Penal Code, Pt 2 and include murder and manslaughter. Misdemeanours are generally minor offences carrying a maximum penalty of three months' imprisonment. Examples of these types of offences are to be found in the Penal Code, Pt 3.[1]

1   See www.straffet.com/eng/legalclass.htm.

15.179   The first comprehensive Penal Code was enacted in 1842. This was replaced by the General Civil Penal Code of 22 May 1902, which is still in force, although it has undergone several amendments.[1] The concept of criminal liability for legal persons as opposed to natural persons was introduced to the General Civil Penal Code[2] in 1991 by including Ch 3a.

1   See L Bygrave *Norway, Report prepared for The World Factbook of Criminal Justice Systems under Bureau of Justice Statistics*, grant no 90-BJ-CX-0002 (1993), available at www.ojp.usdoj/gov/bjs/abstract/wfcj.htm#G.
2   Act no 10 of 22 May 1902, as subsequently amended, most recently by Act no 50 of 1 July 1994.

15.180   The principles, which govern the corporate criminal liability in Norway, are very similar to those set out in the Finnish Penal Code. Under the Norwegian Penal Code, s 48(a) and (b), a legal person can be held responsible for the contravention of any penal provision of the Code. However, it is discretionary whether the legal personality should be prosecuted or not. Where criminal charges are brought against legal persons fines are invariably imposed. Legal persons can also be held liable for acts committed by a natural person abroad; however, this depends on whether or not Norway has jurisdiction over the criminal acts of the natural person.[1]

1   Shloer and Filipenko, **para 15.136 n 2** above.

Law on corporate criminal liability

15.181   In the context of a workplace, the main legislative provisions, which govern health and safety protection at work, are set out in Act no 4 of 4 February 1977 relating to Worker Protection and the Working Environment. By virtue of this Act a natural person can be held liable for the commission of a health and safety offence. The Act defines an employer as any natural person who has engaged employees to perform work in his service.[1] Section 85 concerns the liability of company owners, employers and their representatives. It states that any proprietor of an establishment, employer or person managing an establishment in the employer's stead who wilfully or negligently commits a breach of the provisions or orders contained in or issued by virtue of this Act shall be liable to a fine, imprisonment for up to three months, or both.

1   Worker Protection and Working Environment Act, s 4.

15.182   In the event of particularly aggravating circumstances the penalty may be up to two years' imprisonment. When determining whether such circumstances exist, particular importance is attached as to whether the offence involved or could have involved a serious hazard to life or health, and whether it was committed or allowed to continue notwithstanding orders or requests from public authorities, decisions adopted by the working environment committee, or notwithstanding demands or requests from safety representatives or from safety and health personnel. In the event of infringements that involved or could have involved a serious hazard to life or health, any proprietor of an establishment, employer, or person managing an establishment in the employer's stead will be liable to penalty under the Worker Protection and Working Environment Act, s 85, unless the person concerned has acted in a fully satisfactory manner according to his or her duties under this Act.

15.183   Employees can also be held liable under the Worker Protection and Working Environment Act, s 86. An employee who negligently infringes the provisions or orders contained in or issued pursuant to this Act may be liable to a fine. Those found to be contributorily negligent will be subject to the same penalty. If the infringement is committed wilfully or through gross negligence, the penalty may be a fine, up to three months' imprisonment or both. In the event of particularly aggravating circumstances imprisonment for up to one year may be imposed. When determining whether such circumstances exist, particular importance is attached to whether the offence was contrary to special directives relating to work or safety and whether the employee understood or should have understood that the offence could have seriously endangered the life and health of others.[1]

1   Worker Protection and Working Environment Act, s 86.

15.184   With regard to corporate criminal liability it is stated in the Worker Protection and Working Environment Act, s 87, that the criminal liability of corporations is regulated by the provisions of the General Civil Penal Code, ss 48(a) and 48(b).

15.185   A corporation may be liable if a natural person who has acted on its behalf has contravened a provision of the Norway Penal Code, similarly to the English principle of the identification of a directing mind of the corporation. The liability on the corporation also applies even where no individual person is punishable for the contravention. The meaning of the corporation includes a company, society or other association, one-man enterprise, foundation, estate or public activity.[1]

1   Norway Penal Code, s 48(a).

15.186   The penalty imposed on corporation is a fine. The corporation may also by a judgment be deprived of the right to carry on business or may be prohibited from carrying it on in certain forms. The Norway Penal Code, s 29 states that when it is so required in the public interest, any person who is found guilty of a criminal act may be sentenced to loss of any public office that the offender has by the criminal act shown himself to be unfit for or unworthy of, and loss for a specific period not exceeding five years or forever of the right to hold office or to carry out any activity or occupation that the offender has by the criminal act shown himself to be unfit for or might conceivably misuse, or for which a high degree of public confidence is required.[1]

1   Norway Penal Code, s 29.

15.187   There are also special provisions in the Norway Penal Code concerning offences against public safety.[1] In particular, any person who causes any fire, collapse, explosion, flood, maritime damage, railway accident or aircraft accident which may easily result in loss of human life or extensive destruction of another person's property, or who is an accessory thereto, will be liable to imprisonment for a term of not less than two years and not more than 21 years, but not less than five years if as a result of the felony any person dies or is seriously injured in body or health.[2] A person who tries to hinder the prevention or combating of any such accident will be liable to imprisonment for a term of not less than one year.[3] A person will be liable to imprisonment for a term not exceeding six years who brings about any such danger by omitting to perform any special duty incumbent on him or her, by unlawfully destroying, removing or damaging any object or guiding signal, by giving or setting a false signal, by placing any obstruction in a seaway, by interfering with the safe operation of a ship, railway, aircraft or any installations or constructions on the continental shelf, or by being accessory to any such conduct. If any such accident is caused, imprisonment for a term not exceeding 12 years will be imposed. An attempt shall be liable to the same penalty as a completed felony. If a person has committed any of the above-mentioned acts without being aware of the danger or negligently, he or she will be liable to fines or imprisonment for a term not exceeding one year. If any such fire, collapse, explosion, flood, maritime damage, railway accident or aircraft accident is caused by negligence, the offender will be liable to fines or imprisonment for a term not exceeding three years.

1   Norway Penal Code, Ch 14.
2   Norway Penal Code, s 148.
3   Norway Penal Code, s 149.

Enforcement

15.188   The Norwegian Labour Inspection Authority is a governmental agency under the Ministry of Labour and Government Administration, which has administrative, supervisory and information responsibilities in connection with the Worker Protection and Working Environment Act. In dealing with enterprises that do not comply with the requirements of this Act, the Labour Inspection Authority may respond with orders to correct the situation within a given time limit,[1] coercive fines when the order is not complied with,[2] shutdown of operations, which may be done with immediate effect if the life and health of its employees are in imminent danger, or it may be imposed when corporations fail to comply with orders given. The Agency may report corporations to the police for serious breaches of the Act. A serious violation can result in fines, or, in the worst case, imprisonment.[3]

1 Worker Protection and Working Environment Act, s 77.
2 Worker Protection and Working Environment Act, s 78.
3 See www.arbeidstilsynet.no/om/engelsk.html.

15.189 Criminal acts committed by the corporations are subject to public prosecution and are governed by the Norway Penal Code. In deciding whether a penalty shall be imposed on an enterprise pursuant to s 48(a), and in assessing the penalty in relation to the corporation, particular consideration are paid to the preventive effect of the penalty, the seriousness of the offence, whether the corporation could by guidelines, instruction, training, control or other measures have prevented the offence, whether the offence has been committed in order to promote the interests of the corporation, whether the corporation has had or could have obtained any advantage by the offence, the corporation's economic capacity, whether other sanctions have as a consequence of the offence been imposed on the corporation or on any person who has acted on its behalf, including whether a penalty has been imposed on any individual person.[1]

1 Norway Penal Code, s 48(b).

Denmark

Introduction

15.190 The criminal law in Denmark naturally has very much in common with Norway due to their geographical positions and common history. In general, the influence on the development of the criminal judicial system in Denmark has largely been Germanic compared, for example, with Sweden where the French tradition has prevailed.

15.191 Criminal offences are defined either in a special part of the Criminal Code or in separate statutes. The general conditions for imposing criminal penalties can be found in the general part of the Criminal Code, which also apply to separate statutes. The sanctions described in the general part of the Criminal Code are the same whether the criminal offence consists of a violation of the Criminal Code or of separate statutes.

15.192 The substantive Danish criminal law is monistic, meaning that violations of the law have never been divided into categories like felony/misdemeanour, crime/delicts or the like. It does not mean, however, that major offences are treated in the same manner as petty offences in all respects.[1]

1 L Rawn *Denmark, Report prepared for The World Factbook of Criminal Justice Systems under Bureau of Justice Statistics*, grant no 90-BJ-CX-0002 (1993), available at www.ojp.usdoj/gov/bjs/abstract/wfcj.htm#G.

15.193 There are three main types of punishment: ordinary imprisonment, lenient imprisonment and fines/day fines. In addition, in special cases, dangerous offenders may be sentenced to indeterminate periods of preventive detention. Terms of imprisonment may be meted out with determinate sentences from 30 days to 16 years or life and lenient imprisonment from seven days to six months. Terms of imprisonment may be imposed in the form of suspended or non-suspended sentences. Since 1982 the rules governing probation and suspended sentences formed the basis of an experiment with community service orders, and from 1992 the scheme was made permanent.[1]

1   Rawn, **para 15.192 n 1** above.

15.194   Criminal law is to be found in the Danish Criminal Code of 1930, which has been amended on several occasions. The Danish Criminal Code is the primary, though by no means the exclusive, criminal law source. Case law plays an important role. By omitting the detailed description of offences, the Criminal Code 1930 allows the use of 'law by similarity', which provides wide scope for a judicial discretion.

15.195   Under Danish criminal law a corporation can be held criminally liable and legal mechanisms to impose criminal liability on corporations and other legal persons have been established in the Danish Criminal Code.[1]

1   Hefendehl, **para 15.137 n 1** above.

Law on corporate criminal liability

15.196   The law relating to health and safety at work provides for the liability of employers and employees. The legal basis for activities to promote safety, health and welfare at work is set out in the Work Environment Act 1975. The Work Environment Act 1975 places the overall responsibility for safety on management and supervisors. Although the Act provides for penalties which might be imposed on individual employees, it has become common practice to prosecute and fine both employees and employers for disregarding safety, even where the employees themselves are largely responsible.[1] The Work Environment Act 1975 does not, however, provide liability for corporate crimes such as manslaughter.

1   See www.eiro.eurofound.eu.int/1997/04/feature/DK9704107F.html.

15.197   Criminal liability of legal entities is set out in the Danish Criminal Code[1] and defined in Ch 5 of that Code. It states that a legal entity may be sanctioned with fine if such is provided by the law or respectively adopted procedures.[2] The provisions concerning criminal liability of the legal entities are applicable to any entity, including joint stock companies, co-operative societies, partnerships, associations, foundations, estate compounds, municipalities and public administration authorities, unless expressly specified otherwise.[3] These provisions may also apply to privately owned enterprises.

1   Direction no 648 of 12 August 1997, as amended by Act no 403 of 26 June 1998, Act no 473 of 1 July 1998 and Act no 141 of 17 March 1999.
2   Danish Criminal Code, s 25.
3   Danish Criminal Code, s 26.

15.198   The scope of criminal liability of a legal entity depends on the criminal act perpetrated by one or more persons connected to the legal entity in question, and is similar to the identification doctrine in English law. The Criminal Code is silent as to liability for organisational fault when no one can be identified for the commission of the offence. Government and municipal bodies may be liable to be criminally sanctioned only where the acts perpetrated were within the scope of the performance of their respective functional responsibilities as compared with functional responsibilities of natural persons or legal entities.[1]

1   Danish Criminal Code, s 27.

Enforcement

15.199   The enforcement of health and safety law under the Work Environment Act 1975 is carried out under the auspices of the Ministry of Labour, but on the day-to-day level it is administered by the Labour Inspectorate. Its responsibilities include providing guidance in health and safety matters to the employers' associations, trade unions and public authorities and, not least, ensuring enforcement of the Act through, for example, the inspection of individual workplaces. On completion of such an inspection its inspectors may give instructions requiring certain measures to be taken to improve safety, or issue a prohibition notice banning the continued use of highly dangerous procedures, machinery, substances and materials etc.[1]

1   See EMIRE, Denmark, Arbejdsmiljo, Work Environment, at www.eurofound.eu.int/emire/ DENMARK/WORKENVIRONMENT-DN.html.

15.200   Additionally the Labour Inspectorate is empowered to penalise companies which do not comply with the working environment rules. As regards clear violations of the substantive rules of the Work Environment Act 1975, the Labour Inspectorate has the power to issue administrative fines. In cases of extreme danger, the Labour Inspectorate may also order that the work to be suspended.[1]

1   See *Actors in the Field of Safety and Health at Work*, at www.am.dk/english/publications/ fact_sheets/Actors.

15.201   When death at work occurs the case is investigated by the police and the offender is prosecuted by the Director of Public Prosecutions. The structure of prosecutions in Denmark is hierarchical. The political responsibility rests with the Minister of Justice, but in practice the Director of Public Prosecutions enjoys a high degree of independence. The Director of Public Prosecutions exercises instructive powers towards the lower prosecution instances and conducts criminal cases before the Supreme Court. Otherwise, serious criminal cases are handled by district public prosecutors and less serious cases by the chief constables.[1]

1   Rawn, **para 15.192 n 1** above.

15.202   The penalties are described in the general part of the Criminal Code. They are: fines, lenient prison (seven to 30 days); prison (one month to 16 years or imprisonment for life); and community service orders. Prison sentences and fines may be conditionally suspended. The maximum penalty is imprisonment for a lifetime which is prescribed for murder and manslaughter. Each statute in the special part of the Criminal Code sets out the kind of penalty applicable for the crime and the upper range of its duration. This gives the court the opportunity to choose the actual penalty freely within the ranges. As in other jurisdictions sentencing in Denmark is ultimately determined by the court.

Conclusions

15.203   Criminal liability of corporations has been high on the legal agenda for three decades, when corporations began to play a significant role in social and economic life.[1] In general, the law on corporate criminal liability seems to have developed along three main lines: the doctrine of identification (of the directing mind of a corporation), or direct liability; vicarious liability; and, finally, the fault of the corporation as one collective body.

1   See eg LH Leigh *The Criminal Liability of Corporations* (1977).

15.204   There has been strong opposition to the imposition of corporate liability in different legal systems. The leading legal opponent was the continental system, which had forcefully rejected this principle over many decades and was unsupportive of the imposition of such general liability, maintaining that the appropriate point of principle on this issue is that of societas delinquene non-potest.[1]

1   E Lederman 'Models for Imposing Corporate Criminal Liability: From Adaptation and Imitation Toward Aggregation and the Search for Self-Identity' (2000) 4(1) Buffalo Crim LR 641.

15.205   The situation has, however, changed largely because of the new socio, political and economic realities. Legal entities have acquired great power and control in almost all spheres of industry and commerce. Corporations have their own 'minds', and the capacity to make important decisions and to commit crimes. Policy and law-makers began to recognise that changes in law were needed to reflect the reality. As a result of this, the approach to corporate criminal liability worldwide has undergone significant transformation.

15.206   The law of the US is based on a model of vicarious liability. This law, which renders corporations criminally liable, originated in the law of torts. It has been established for some time in that jurisdiction that corporations can be criminally liable for acts committed by individuals on their behalf. Even at the beginning of the twentieth century, some US courts began to expand the concept of corporate criminal liability to include mens rea offences,[1] a move which was confirmed by the US Supreme Court in *New York Central & Hudson River Railroad Company v United States*.[2] This confirmation came after Congress had passed the Elkins Act 1903, which stated that the acts and omissions of an officer acting within the scope of his employment were considered to be those of the corporation, thus promulgating the concept of vicarious liability.[3] Several decades later, in 1983, the 4th Circuit Court stated that 'a corporation may be held criminally responsible for antitrust violations committed by its employees if they were acting within the scope of their authority, or apparent authority, and for the benefit of the corporation, even if ... such acts were against corporate policy'.[4] According to the doctrine developed by the US law, a corporation is liable for the criminal offences of its employee if the employee commits the crime both within the scope of his or her employment and with the intention of benefiting the corporation. The courts of the US have now added a third condition that 'the criminal acts were authorised, tolerated, or ratified by corporate management',[5] thereby making the doctrine of vicarious liability similar to the doctrine of direct liability.[6] There are only two situations now in which corporate criminal liability cannot be imposed: when crimes cannot be punished by fines – since fines are the principle means for punishing a corporation – and when the crime, by its nature cannot be committed by a corporation (for example, rape).[7]

1   Wagner, **para 15.107 n 2** above.
2   212 US 481 (1909).
3   See Stessens, **para 15.107 n 1** above, at 496–497.
4   *United States v Basic Construction Co* 711 F 2d 570 at 573 (4th Cir, CA, 1983).
5   See B Lowell 'Vicarious Criminal Liability of Corporations for the Acts of Their Employees and Agents' (1995) 41 Loyola LR 279.
6   Lederamn, **para 15.204 n 1** above.
7   See Hefendehl, **para 15.137 n 1** above, at 290.

15.207   Both Australia and Canada are Commonwealth countries and, unsurprisingly, their positions in relation to corporate manslaughter are similar to those of the UK. In some respects, however, because they are federal governments with a common law system they also share the approach adopted by the US.

15.208   The development of the law of manslaughter in Australia has followed a similar path to that in the UK, although their legislatures are more progressive on this matter. The current Australian law on corporate manslaughter is based on two models of liability: vicarious liability and the doctrine of identification. Recently steps have been taken towards the introduction of the notion of organisational blameworthiness as the means for establishing corporate guilt, namely the Australian Criminal Code Act, 1995 (Cth), and the Crimes (Workplace Deaths & Serious Injuries) Bill.[1] The Australian Criminal Code Act 1995 provides for detailed requirements relating to corporate organizational liability. The Criminal Code, s 12.1(1) makes it clear that the Code applies to corporations as well as individuals. The Code provides that the 'fault element must be attributed to a body corporate that expressly, tacitly or impliedly authorised or permitted the commission of the offence',[2] which can be shown by proving 'that a corporate culture existed within the body corporate that directed, encouraged, tolerated or led to non-compliance with the relevant provision, or proving that the body corporate failed to create and maintain a corporate culture that required compliance with the relevant provision'.[3]

1   A Coles 'Corporate Killers : A "Republican" Alternative to Corporate Manslaughter Prosecution', paper submitted for the Research Unit, Faculty of Law, the Australian National University, October 1998.
2   Australian Criminal Code Act 1995 (Cth), s 12.3(1).
3   Australian Criminal Code Act 1995 (Cth), s 12.3(2)(c)–(d).

15.209   As with the UK and Australia there are two main models which give rise to corporate criminal liability in Canada, vicarious liability and the doctrine of identification. Its case law has very much developed in line with English decisions. The form of the identification doctrine, however, has been modified from that adopted by the English courts and is referred to as the delegation theory. Under this theory: 'The identity doctrine merges the board of directors, the managing director, the superintendent, the manager or anyone else delegated by the board of directors to whom is delegated the governing executive authority of the corporation, and the conduct of any of the merged entities is thereby attributed to the corporation.'[1] The importance of this approach is that it recognises that a corporation may have more than one 'directing mind'.[2] This delegation theory has, however, its limits.[3] Iacobucci J held in *Rhõne (The) v Peter AB Widener (The)*:[4]

> 'The key factor which distinguishes directing minds from normal employees is the capacity to exercise decision-making authority on matters of corporate policy , rather than merely to give effect such policy on an operational basis, whether at head office or across the sea.'

1   A-M Boisvert 'Corporate Criminal Liability: A Discussion Paper' (August, 1999), available at www.ulcc.ca/en/criminal/index.cfm?sec.
2   Boisvet, n 1 above.
3   See *Rhõne (The) v Peter AB Widener (The)* [1993] 1 SCR 497.
4   [1993] 1 SCR 497.

15.210   This shows that although a person in the company could be delegated to carry out many responsibilities, it could well be that their position was not such as to allow them to formulate corporate policies and thus they could not represent the directing mind of the company. In order to determine the directing mind of the company the courts will seek the person who had direct control over the corporate activity in which the criminal act was committed.

15.211   Some European countries have also recently undergone significant changes in the law on corporate criminal liability. In 1988, the Council of Europe recommended to member states that they should endorse and approach allowing the imposition of criminal liability on legal bodies.[1] The Dutch courts started to adopt this direction in the mid-1970s in anticipation of the Council of Europe Recommendation.[2] The provision regarding the criminal liability of corporation can be found in the Dutch Criminal Code, art 51, which states that offences can be committed by both human beings and corporations. The Dutch approach is very far-reaching in that that it recognises that corporations act as collectives and thus they could be held liable even if no particular individual was identifiable for a crime, but rather the corporations were in fault in failing to adopt adequate safety systems which resulted in death.

1   Committee of Ministers, Council of Europe, Recommendation on Liability of Enterprises Having Legal Personality for Offences Committed in the Exercise of their Activities, Recommendation no R(88) 18, October 1988.
2   See Field and Jörg, **para 15.126 n 2** above.

15.212   France, on the other hand, changed its criminal law on this issue following the recommendation, and in the early 1990s erased the prohibition against rendering corporation (personnes morales) criminally liable from its Penal Code.[1] As a result strict liability offences were enforced vicariously against corporations. The reformed Penal Code states that legal entities may be liable if the offence provision specifically declares that they should be and if an employee of officer is shown to have acted on the corporation's behalf. The actions of 'rogue' employees would not be imputed to the corporate entity.[2]

1   See Lederamn, **para 15.204 n 1** above.
2   Wells, **para 15.13 n 1** above.

15.213   In Germany the imposition of criminal liability on legal bodies was 'unthinkable' until very recently.[1] Much attention was focused on the question of whether corporations should be held responsible under the civil or public law. There is still no legal provision in Germany which allows corporations to be held criminally liable. Corporations can only be liable for administrative offences (Ordnungswidrigkeiten). Roland Hefendehl has observed:

> 'Administrative remedies, which consist primarily of the imposition of fines, do not aim to establish personal responsibility or guilt but to provide preventive – as well as repressive – means for controlling and regulating risks emerging from economic processes and decisions. The focus does not lie on the personal but on the instrumental aspect of a particular wrongdoing. Thus, the difference between the law of administrative offences and the criminal law is not merely quantitative. If civil courts or economic control boards were limited to imposing future-oriented sanctions but could not sanction past acts, civil courts and economic control boards could not effectively control businesses. The purpose of administrative penalties is to fill in this gap.'[2]

1   Wells, **para 15.13 n 1** above.
2   Hefendehl, **para 15.137 n 1** above.

15.214   In Italy a new statute was enacted in 2001 to deal with the problem created by Italian Constitution which did not allow imposing criminal liability on legal persons. The statute classified criminal offences as administrative ones, which was misleading since in practice and procedurally there were considered as criminal. There are two models of corporate criminal liability created by the Italian statute: where the offence is committed by the head of the corporation, ie direct liability, and where a corporate body was negligent in not considering and not averting the risk of the possibility of the offence, failure of the corporation. The imposition of criminal liability on corporations is a key development in the Italian law, since formerly it refused to accept this type liability alongside countries such as Germany.

15.215   In Finland corporations can be criminally liable under the Finnish Penal Code, Ch 9. This criminal liability is based on two main prerequisites:[2] the doctrine of identification and the organisational failure of the corporation. The general prerequisite for liability is that the management of the corporation has itself committed the crime or served as an accomplice thereto, the management has allowed a crime to be committed, or the diligence and caution required have not been observed in the operation of the enterprise. Another prerequisite for corporate criminal liability is that a corporate fine may be imposed even if the offender cannot be identified or otherwise is not punished, which means that the offence was committed because of the failure of the corporation to adopt adequate safety systems in place. This approach is similar to the ones adopted in Italy and Holland.

1   Finnish Penal Code, 743/1995.
2   Finnish Penal Code, Ch 9, s 2(1) Prerequisites for liability.

15.216   In Sweden a corporation cannot be held liable for a criminal offence, such as manslaughter. Liability for death at work may only be imposed on natural persons under the Swedish Penal Code. In this regard, corporations can be penalised for administrative offences and sanctioned respectively.

15.217   In Denmark criminal liability of legal entities is governed by the Danish Criminal Code[1] and defined in Ch 5 of the Code. The criminal liability of a legal entity in Denmark is based on the identification principle. The criminal act must be committed on behalf of a legal entity by one or more persons tied with the legal entity in question. The Code is silent as to the liability for the organisational fault when no one can be identified for the commission of the offence.

1   Direction no 648 of 12 August 1997, as amended by Act no 403 of 26 June 1998, Act no 473 of 1 July 1998 and Act no 141 of 17 March 1999.

15.218   The principles, which govern the corporate criminal liability in Norway, are very similar to those set out in the Finnish Penal Code. Under the Norwegian Penal Code, s 48(a) and (b) a legal person can be held responsible for contravention of any penal provision of the Code. The models which govern corporate liability include the identification principle and the organisational fault of a corporation. A corporation may be liable if a natural person who has acted on its behalf has contravened a provision of the Norwegian Penal Code, and it also applies where no individual person is punishable for the offence in question.

15.219   We can thus see that all the above jurisdictions have adopted different approaches when dealing with the question of corporate liability for industrial manslaughter. Many have based liability on the models of direct liability and vicarious liability. Others, for example, Holland and Finland, have extended the scope of liability and allowed the possibility of holding corporations liable for the managerial fault without identifying any particular individual responsible for the crime. The practice shows that this model works and perhaps deserves a closer look by legal policy-makers in other countries, including the UK.

Index

544   *Index*